Contents *Wilsons*

D0981333

Abruzzo: Abruzzi	**Lazio:** Lazio	**Sicilia:** Sicily
Basilicata: Basilicata	**Liguria:** Liguria	**Toscana:** Tuscany
Calabria: Calabria	**Lombardia:** Lombardy	**Trentino-Alto Adige:**
Campania: Campania	**Marche:** Marches	Trentino-Alto
Emilia-Romagna:	**Molise:** Molise	Adige
Emilia-Romagna	**Piemonte:** Piedmont	**Umbria:** Umbria
Friuli Venezia Giulia:	**Puglia:** Puglia	**Valle d'Aosta:** Valle d'Aosta
Friuli-Venezia Giulia	**Sardegna:** Sardinia	**Veneto:** Veneto

Principal sights

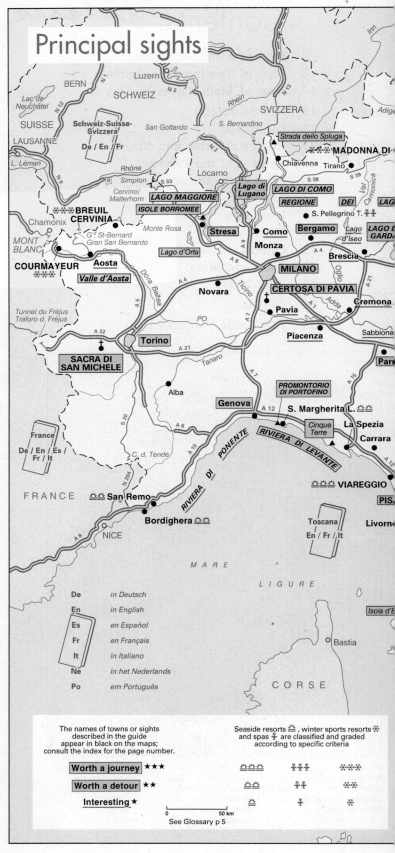

De	in Deutsch
En	in English
Es	en Español
Fr	en Français
It	in Italiano
Ne	in het Nederlands
Po	em Português

The names of towns or sights described in the guide appear in black on the maps; consult the index for the page number.

Seaside resorts ☆, winter sports resorts ✳ and spas ♨ are classified and graded according to specific criteria

Worth a journey ★★★	☆☆☆	♨♨♨	✳✳✳
Worth a detour ★★	☆☆	♨♨	✳✳
Interesting ★	☆	♨	✳

0   50 km
See Glossary p 5

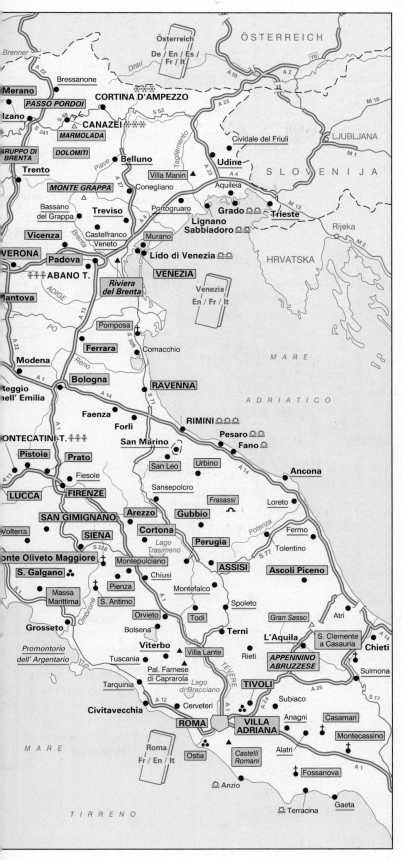

Brenner
Österreich
De / En / Es / Fr / It
ÖSTERREICH

Merano
Bressanone
PASSO PORDOI
Izano
CANAZEI ✶✶✶
MARMOLADA
DOLOMITI
GRUPPO DI BRENTA
Trento
MONTE GRAPPA
Belluno
Cividale del Friuli
LJUBLJANA
Villa Manin
Udine
SLOVENIJA
Coneglione
Aquileia
Bassano del Grappa
Treviso
Portogruaro
Grado ♨♨
Trieste
Vicenza
Castelfranco Veneto
Lignano Sabbiadoro ♨♨
Rijeka
VERONA
Padova
Murano
HRVATSKA
ABANO T.
Lido di Venezia ♨♨
Mantova
VENEZIA
Riviera del Brenta
Venezia En / Fr / It
Pomposa
Ferrara
Comacchio
MARE
Modena
Bologna
RAVENNA
ADRIATICO
Reggio nell' Emilia
Faenza
Forlì
RIMINI ✶✶✶
Pistoia
Prato
San Marino
Pesaro ♨♨
Fano ♨
MONTECATINI-T. ♨♨♨
Fiesole
San Leo
Urbino
Ancona
LUCCA
FIRENZE
Sansepolcro
SAN GIMIGNANO
Arezzo
Gubbio
Frasassi
Loreto
Volterra
SIENA
Cortona
Perugia
Fermo
onte Oliveto Maggiore
Montepulciano
Lago Trasimeno
ASSISI
Tolentino
S. Galgano ∴
Chiusi
Ascoli Piceno
Massa Marittima
Pienza
Montefalco
S. Antimo
Orvieto
Todi
Spoleto
Gran Sasso
Atri
Grosseto
Bolsena
Terni
L'Aquila
S. Clemente a Casauria
Chieti
Promontorio dell' Argentario
Viterbo
Villa Lante
Rieti
APPENNINO ABRUZZESE
Sulmona
Tuscania
Pal. Farnese di Caprarola
Lago di Bracciano
TIVOLI
Tarquinia
Subiaco
Civitavecchia
Cerveteri
Anagni
Casamari
ROMA
VILLA ADRIANA
Montecassino
Alatri
Roma Fr / En / It
Ostia
Castelli Romani
Fossanova
MARE
Anzio
Gaeta
TIRRENO
Terracina

3

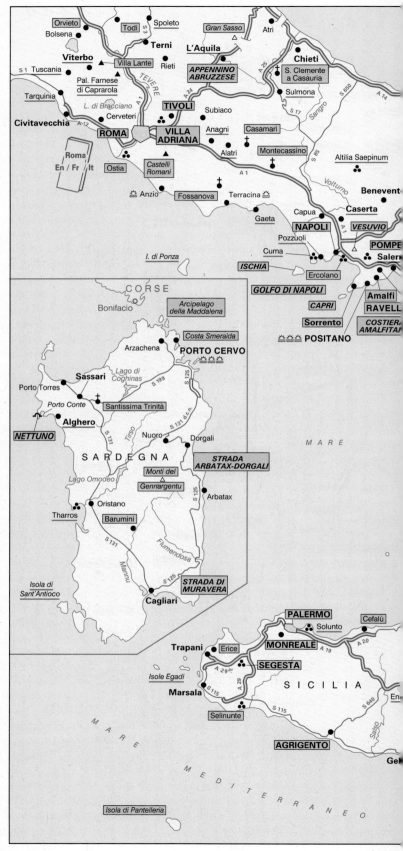

Orvieto
Todi
Spoleto
Gran Sasso
Atri
Bolsena
Terni
L'Aquila
Chieti
Viterbo
Villa Lante
Rieti
S. Clemente a Casauria
APPENNINO ABRUZZESE
Tuscania
S 1
Sulmona
Pal. Farnese di Caprarola
S 24
TEVERE
Tarquinia
L. di Bracciano
A 25
A 14
TIVOLI
S 17
Sangro
Subiaco
Civitavecchia
A-12
Cerveteri
ROMA
VILLA ADRIANA
Anagni
Casamari
S 85
Altilia Saepinum
Roma En / Fr / It
Alatri
Montecassino
Ostia
Castelli Romani
A 1
Volturno
Benevent
Anzio
Fossanova
Terracina
Caserta
Gaeta
Capua
NAPOLI
VESUVIO
A 1
Pozzùoli
POMPE
Cuma
Saler
I. di Ponza
ISCHIA
Ercolano
GOLFO DI NAPOLI
Amalfi
CORSE
Arcipelago della Maddalena
CAPRI
RAVELL
Bonifacio
Sorrento
COSTIER AMALFITAN
POSITANO
Costa Smeraida
PORTO CERVO
Arzachena
Sassari
Lago di Coghinas
S 189
S 125
Porto Torres
Porto Conte
Santissima Trinità
Alghero
Tirso
S 131 d.c.n.
NETTUNO
Nuoro
Dorgali
MARE
SARDEGNA
STRADA ARBATAX-DORGALI
Lago Omodeo
Monti del Gennargentu
S 125
Arbatax
Oristano
Tharros
Barumini
S 131
Flumendosa
Mannu
Isola di Sant'Antioco
S 125
STRADA DI MURAVERA
Cagliari
PALERMO
Cefalù
Solunto
A 20
MONREALE
A 19
Trapani
Erice
SEGESTA
A 29 dir
Isole Egadi
SICILIA
Marsala
S 115
A 29
S 640
En
S 115
Selinunte
MARE
AGRIGENTO
Ge
MEDITERRANEO
Isola di Pantelleria

4

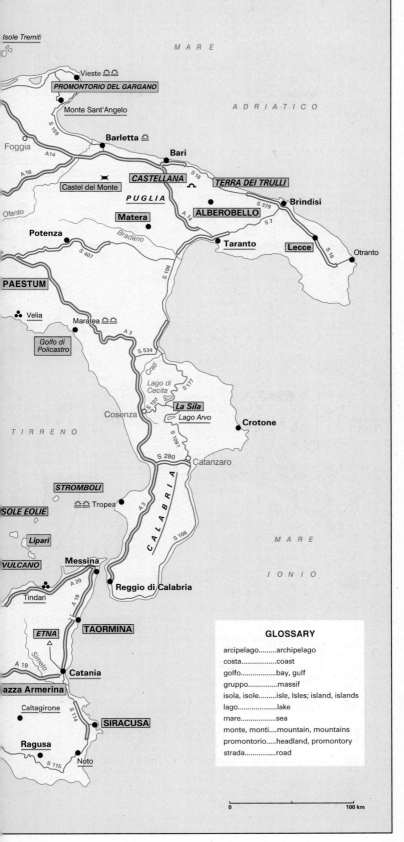

Isole Tremiti

MARE

Vieste

PROMONTORIO DEL GARGANO

Monte Sant'Angelo

ADRIATICO

S 159

Foggia

A14

Barletta

Bari

A 16

CASTELLANA

S 16

Castel del Monte

TERRA DEI TRULLI

Ofanto

PUGLIA

ALBEROBELLO

S 379

Brindisi

Matera

A 14

S 7

Potenza

Bradano

Taranto

Lecce

S 16

Otranto

S 407

S 106

PAESTUM

Velia

Maratea

A 3

Golfo di
Policastro

S 534

Crati

Lago di
Cecita

S 177

S 107

La Sila

Cosenza

Lago Arvo

Crotone

TIRRENO

S 109

S 280

Catanzaro

STROMBOLI

C A L A B R I A

Tropea

A 3

SOLE EOLIE

S 106

MARE

Lipari

VULCANO

I O N I O

Messina

A 20

Reggio di Calabria

A 18

Tindari

ETNA

TAORMINA

△

A 19

Simeto

Catania

azza Armerina

Caltagirone

S 114

SIRACUSA

Ragusa

S 115

Noto

GLOSSARY

arcipelago.........archipelago
costa.................coast
golfo.................bay, gulf
gruppo...............massif
isola, isole.........isle, Isles; island, islands
lago...................lake
mare.................sea
monte, monti....mountain, mountains
promontorio.....headland, promontory
strada...............road

0   100 km

Touring programmes

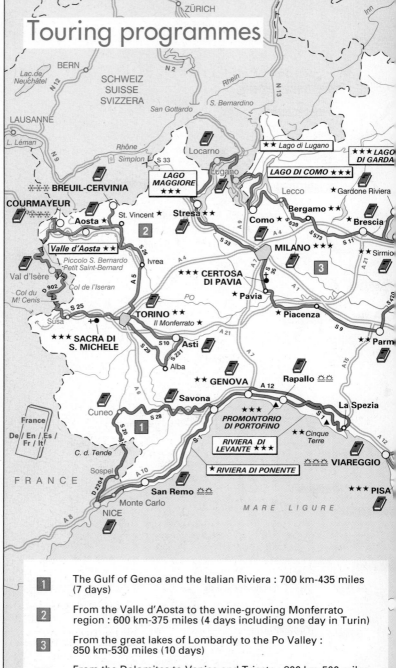

1. The Gulf of Genoa and the Italian Riviera : 700 km-435 miles (7 days)

2. From the Valle d'Aosta to the wine-growing Monferrato region : 600 km-375 miles (4 days including one day in Turin)

3. From the great lakes of Lombardy to the Po Valley : 850 km-530 miles (10 days)

4. From the Dolomites to Venice and Trieste : 800 km-500 miles (10 days including 2 in Venice)

5. From the rich cities of the plain to the lagoons of the Adriatic : 600 km-375 miles (10 days including 2 in Venice)

6. Art, nature and spirituality in Tuscany and Umbria : 750 km-465 miles (15 days including 2 in Florence)

7. From the heart of Umbria to the Adriatic : 850 km-530 miles (8 days)

8. From Rome and its region to the Abruzzi : 1 000 km-620 miles (8 days including 3 in Rome)

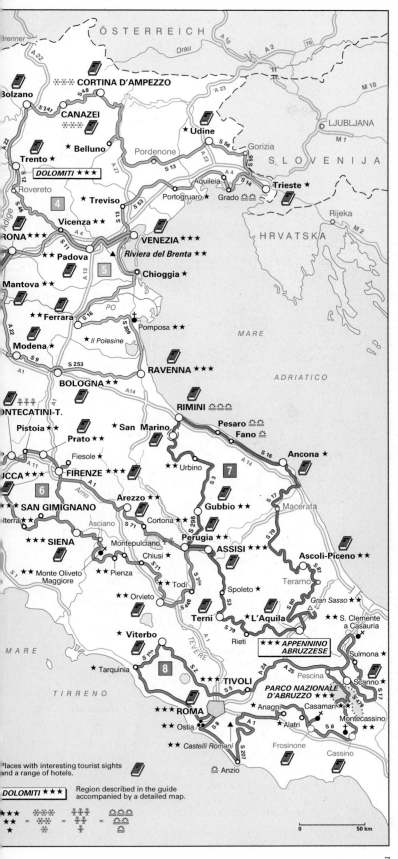

ÖSTERREICH

Drau

★★★ CORTINA D'AMPEZZO

S 48

Bolzano

S 241

CANAZEI
★★★

Trento ★   ★ Belluno

Rovereto

DOLOMITI ★★★

★ Udine

Pordenone

S 56

Gorizia

S L O V E N I J A

Aquileia

Portogruaro ★   Grado ☖☖

Trieste ★

LJUBLJANA

★ Treviso

RONA ★★★   Vicenza ★★

★★ Padova

VENEZIA ★★★

▲ Riviera del Brenta ★★

Rijeka

HRVATSKA

Mantova ★★

★★ Ferrara

★ Il Polesine

Modena ★

PO

Chioggia ★

Pomposa ★★

MARE

BOLOGNA ★★

RAVENNA ★★★

ADRIATICO

ONTECATINI-T.

Pistoia ★★

Prato ★★

Fiesole ★

UCCA ★★★   FIRENZE ★★★

★ San Marino ★

RIMINI ☖☖☖

Pesaro ☖☖
Fano ☖

★ Urbino

Ancona ★

★★ SAN GIMIGNANO

Iterra ★★

Arezzo ★★

Cortona ★

Gubbio ★★

Macerata

Asciano

★★★ SIENA

Montepulciano ★

Perugia ★★

ASSISI ★★★

Ascoli-Piceno ★★

S 1   ★★ Monte Oliveto
Maggiore

Chiusi ★

★★ Pienza

★ Todi

Spoleto ★

Teramo

Gran Sasso ★★

★★ Orvieto

Terni ★

L'Aquila ★

★★ S. Clemente
a Casauria

★ Viterbo

Rieti ★

★★★ APPENNINO
ABRUZZESE

Sulmona ★

MARE

★ Tarquinia

TEVERE

★★★ TIVOLI

Pescina

Scanno ★

TIRRENO

PARCO NAZIONALE
D'ABRUZZO ★★★

★★★ ROMA

★ Anagni

Casamari ★★

★★ Ostia

★ Alatri

Montecassino
★★

★★ Castelli Romani

Frosinone

Cassino

☖ Anzio

Places with interesting tourist sights
and a range of hotels.

DOLOMITI ★★★   Region described in the guide
accompanied by a detailed map.

★★★   ❋❋❋   ‡‡‡   ☖☖☖
★★ = ❋❋ = ‡‡ = ☖☖
★   ❋   ‡   ☖

0   50 km

7

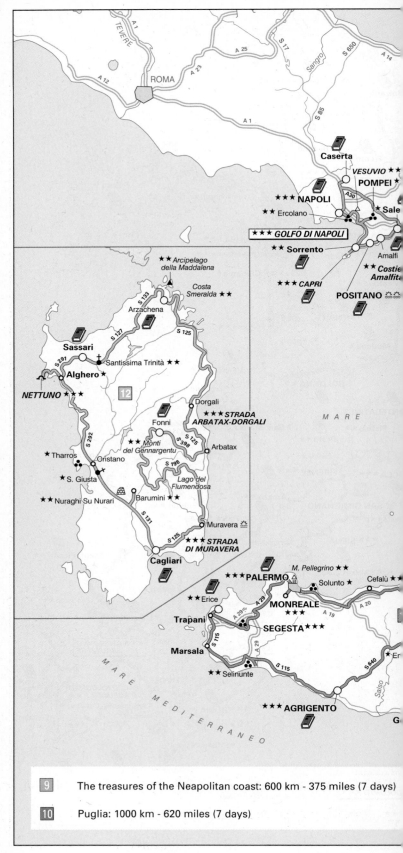

TEVERE

ROMA

Caserta

VESUVIO ★★
POMPEI ★

★★★ NAPOLI

★★ Ercolano

Sale

★★★ GOLFO DI NAPOLI

★★ Sorrento

Amalfi

★★ Costie
Amalfit

★★★ CAPRI

POSITANO

★★ Arcipelago
della Maddalena

Costa
Smeralda ★★

Arzachena

S 133

S 127

S 125

Sassari

S 291

Santissima Trinità ★★

Alghero ★

NETTUNO ★★★

S 292

12

Dorgali

★★★ STRADA
ARBATAX-DORGALI

Fonni

S 125
S 398

★★ Monti
del Gennargentu

Arbatax

★ Tharros

Oristano

S 196

Lago del
Flumendosa

★ S. Giusta

★★ Nuraghi Su Nurari

Barumini ★★

S 131

Muravera

S 125

★★★ STRADA
DI MURAVERA

Cagliari

MARE

★★★ PALERMO

M. Pellegrino ★★

Solunto ★

Cefalù ★★

A 20

★★ Erice

MONREALE
★★★

A 19

Trapani

A 29

SEGESTA ★★★

S 115

Marsala

A 29

Er

S 640

★★ Selinunte

S 115

MARE

MEDITERRANEO

★★★ AGRIGENTO

G

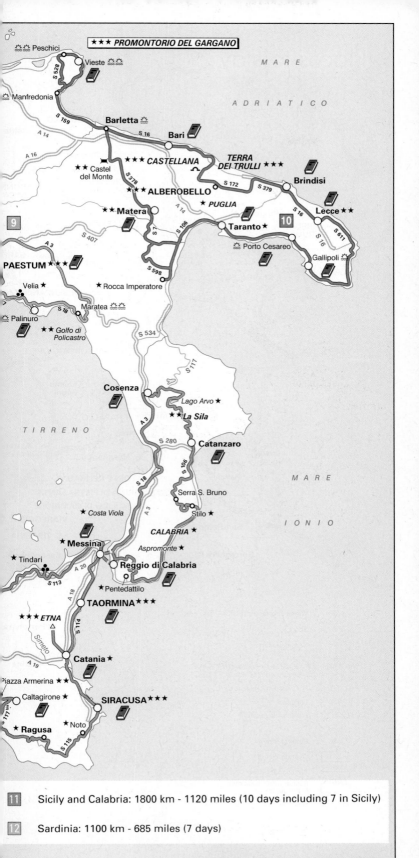

★★★ PROMONTORIO DEL GARGANO

MARE

ADRIATICO

☆☆ Peschici

Vieste ☆☆

Manfredonia ☆

S 528

S 159

A 14

A 16

Barletta ☆

S 16

Bari

★★★ CASTELLANA

TERRA DEI TRULLI ★★★

Brindisi

★★ Castel del Monte

S 378

★★★ ALBEROBELLO

S 172

S 379

Lecce ★★

★ PUGLIA

A 14

★★ Matera

S 7

S 106

Taranto ★

S 16

Porto Cesareo ☆

S 611

Gallipoli ☆

9

S 407

S 598

10

PAESTUM ★★★

A 3

Velia ★

★ Rocca Imperatore

S 18

Maratea ☆☆

Palinuro ☆

★★ Golfo di Policastro

S 534

Cosenza

S 117

Lago Arvo ★

★★ La Sila

TIRRENO

A 3

S 280

Catanzaro

S 18

S 106

Serra S. Bruno

★ Costa Viola

A 3

Stilo ★

Messina ★

CALABRIA ★

Aspromonte ★

MARE

IONIO

★ Tindari

S 113

A 20

Reggio di Calabria

A 18

★ Pentedattilo

★★★ ETNA

TAORMINA ★★★

S 114

Simeto

A 19

Catania ★

Piazza Armerina ★★

Caltagirone ★

SIRACUSA ★★★

S 117 bis

★ Ragusa

★ Noto

S 115

---

11   Sicily and Calabria: 1800 km - 1120 miles (10 days including 7 in Sicily)

12   Sardinia: 1100 km - 685 miles (7 days)

Places to stay

BASEL · N 3
Liechtenstein
Luzern · N 2
BERN · N 1
Inn
SCHWEIZ
SUISSE
SVIZZERA
Rhein
*** **BORMIO**
*** **LIVIGNO** Solda
Madesimo Stelvio
** S. Caterina-V.
Lac de
Neuchâtel
LAUSANNE
Rhône · 9
Crodo ‡
*** Ponte di Legno
Chiesa in
Valmalenco
MADONN
DI C.
L. Léman · N 9
LAGHI
Val
Grande
Lugano
S 38 Aprica
Foppolo
‡ Bognanco
BREUIL
CERVINIA
* Macugnaga
VERBANIA-P.
BELLAGIO
Lovere
‡‡
BOARIO T
Alagna
Valsesia
STRESA
BAVENO
S. Pellegrino
Terme ‡‡
● Selvino *
Iseo
GARD
COURMAYEUR
Gressoney
ST. VINCENT
Como
Sarnico
SIRMIONE
A 9
A 8
** la Thuile
Cogne **
Gran Paradiso
Dora Baltea
A 4
Ticino
MILANO
Adda
DESENZANO LAG
Oglio
A 5
PO
A 7
A 1
A 21
A 32
Bardonecchia
Sauze d'Oulx
TORINO
A 21
Tanaro
‡‡‡ **SALSOMAGGIORE T.**
SESTRIERE
***
Salice Terme ‡‡
Parma
Acqui Terme
‡‡
A 7
‡‡ **Tabiano**
Bagni
A 15
LA RIVIERA
A 12
RAPALLO ⌂⌂
‡ Bagni di Vinadio
Terme
di Lurisia
A 6
A 10
GENOVA
S. Margherita L. ⌂⌂
Marina
di Mass
Terme di Valdieri
Limone Piemonte
**
⌂⌂ **FORTE DEI MARMI**
A 12
⌂⌂ **MARINA DI PIETRASANTA**
FRANCE
S 204
⌂⌂ **LIDO DI CAMAIORE**
⌂⌂⌂ **VIAREGGIO**
ALASSIO
San Remo ⌂⌂
⌂ **TIRRENIA**
N 204
A 8
NICE
Bordighera ⌂⌂
⌂ **Castiglioncello**

MARE *LIGURE*

Isola
d'Elb
⌂ **Portoferra**

⌂⌂ **Marciana**
Marina
Bastia

Legend

● Winter sports resort
● Spa
● Seaside resort

These resorts are classified according to
the range of activities they offer :

*** , ** , * For winter sports resorts
‡‡‡ , ‡‡ , ‡ For spas
⌂⌂⌂ , ⌂⌂ , ⌂ For seaside resorts

● Cultural centre
▢ Overnight stop
─ Traditional resort
LAGHI Region with a local map
in the guide
⬭ National park

0 ____ 50 km

CORSE

Ajaccio

Bonifacio

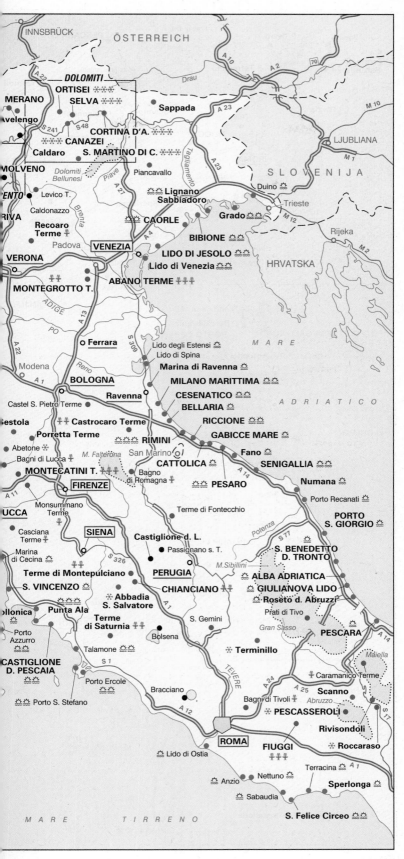

INNSBRÜCK
ÖSTERREICH
A 10
A 2
70
Drau

DOLOMITI
MERANO
ORTISEI ✳✳✳
SELVA ✳✳✳
Sappada
A 23
M 10
Avelengo
S 241
S 48
CORTINA D'A. ✳✳✳
LJUBLIANA
M 1
✳✳✳ CANAZEI
Caldaro
S. MARTINO DI C. ✳✳✳
S L O V E N I J A
MOLVENO
Dolomiti
Bellunesi
Piancavallo
Duino ♨
M 1
ENTO
Levico T.
Piave
♨♨ Lignano
Sabbiadoro
Trieste
RIVA
Caldonazzo
Brenta
A 21
Tagliamento
♨♨ CAORLE
Grado ♨♨
Rijeka
M 2
Recoaro
Terme ♨
Padova
BIBIONE ♨♨
M 12
HRVATSKA
VERONA
VENEZIA
A 4
LIDO DI JESOLO ♨♨
Lido di Venezia ♨♨
♨♨ ABANO TERME ♨♨♨
MONTEGROTTO T.
ADIGE
A 13

PO
Ferrara
S 309
Lido degli Estensi ♨
Lido di Spina
M A R E
A 22
Modena
Reno
Marina di Ravenna ♨
A 1
BOLOGNA
Ravenna
MILANO MARITTIMA ♨♨
A D R I A T I C O
Castel S. Pietro Terme
CESENATICO ♨♨
BELLARIA ♨
Sestola
♨♨ Castrocaro Terme
RICCIONE ♨♨
Porretta Terme
RIMINI
GABICCE MARE ♨
Abetone ✳
M. Falterona
San Marino
Fano ♨
Bagni di Lucca ♨
CATTOLICA ♨
A 14
SENIGALLIA ♨♨
MONTECATINI T. ♨♨♨
Bagno
di Romagna ♨
♨♨ PESARO
Numana ♨
FIRENZE
A 11
Porto Recanati ♨
LUCCA
Monsummano
Terme
Terme di Fontecchio
PORTO
S. GIORGIO ♨
Casciana
Terme ♨
SIENA
Potenza
S 77
Marina
di Cecina ♨
Castiglione d. L.
♨
S. BENEDETTO
D. TRONTO
S 326
Passignano s. T.
M.Sibillini
Terme di Montepulciano
PERUGIA
♨♨ ALBA ADRIATICA
S. VINCENZO ♨
CHIANCIANO ♨♨
♨♨ GIULIANOVA LIDO
✳ Abbadia
S. Salvatore
A 1
♨ Roseto d. Abruzzi
ollonica
Punta Ala
Terme
di Saturnia ♨♨
S. Gemini
Prati di Tivo
Gran Sasso
♨♨♨
Porto
Azzurro
♨♨
Bolsena
PESCARA
A 14
CASTIGLIONE
D. PESCAIA
♨♨
Talamone ♨♨
S 1
✳ Terminillo
Maiella
Porto Ercole
Bracciano
♨ Caramanico Terme
♨♨ Porto S. Stefano
A 12
A 24
A 25
Scanno
TEVERE
Bagni di Tivoli ♨
Abruzzo
S 17
✳ PESCASSEROLI
ROMA
FIUGGI
♨♨♨
Rivisondoli
Lido di Ostia ♨
✳ Roccaraso
Terracina ♨
A 1
Anzio ♨
Nettuno ♨
Sperlonga ♨
Sabaudia ♨
S. Felice Circeo ♨♨
M A R E
T I R R E N O

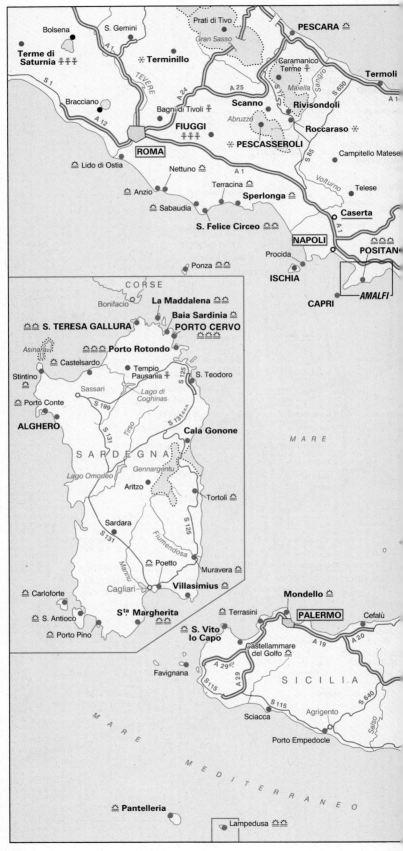

Bolsena

S. Gemini

Prati di Tivo

PESCARA ⚓

Gran Sasso

Terme di Saturnia ♨♨♨

☼ **Terminillo**

Caramanico Terme ♨

Maiella

Termoli

Bracciano

Bagni di Tivoli ♨

Scanno

Rivisondoli

Roccaraso ☼

Abruzzo

FIUGGI ♨♨♨

☼ **PESCASSEROLI**

Campitello Matese

ROMA

⚓ Lido di Ostia

Nettuno ⚓

Terracina ⚓

Sperlonga ⚓

Telese

Anzio ♨

⚓ Sabaudia

S. Felice Circeo ⚓⚓

Caserta

NAPOLI

♨♨♨

POSITAN

Procida

⚓ Ponza ⚓⚓

ISCHIA

AMALFI

AMALFI

CORSE

La Maddalena ⚓⚓

CAPRI

Bonifacio

Baia Sardinia ⚓

⚓⚓ **S. TERESA GALLURA**

PORTO CERVO

♨♨♨

Asinara

⚓⚓⚓ **Porto Rotondo**

⚓ Castelsardo

Tempio Pausania ♨

S. Teodoro

Stintino ⚓

Sassari

Lago di Coghinas

⚓ Porto Conte

ALGHERO

Cala Gonone

MARE

S A R D E G N A

Lago Omodeo

Gennargentu

Aritzo

Tortoli ⚓

Sardara

⚓ Carloforte

Muravera ⚓

⚓ Poetto

Cagliari

Villasimius ⚓

Mondello ⚓

⚓ S. Antioco

Sta. Margherita

⚓⚓

⚓ Terrasini

PALERMO

Cefalù

⚓ Porto Pino

⚓ **S. Vito lo Capo**

Castellammare del Golfo ⚓

Favignana

S I C I L I A

Sciacca

Agrigento

Porto Empedocle

MARE

MEDITERRANEO

⚓ **Pantelleria**

Lampedusa ⚓⚓

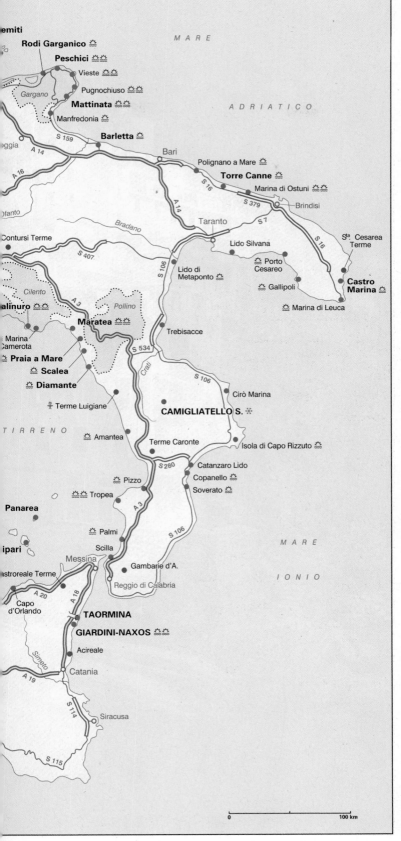

emiti
Rodi Garganico ♨
Peschici ♨♨
Vieste ♨♨
Pugnochiuso ♨♨
Gargano
Mattinata ♨♨
Manfredonia ♨
S 159
Barletta ♨
ggia
A 14
A 16
Bari
Polignano a Mare ♨
Torre Canne ♨
Marina di Ostuni ♨♨
ofanto
Bradano
Taranto
Brindisi
S 379
S 16
S 7
Contursi Terme
Lido Silvana
S 407
Sª Cesarea
Terme
S 15
Lido di
Metaponto ♨
♨ Porto
Cesareo
S 106
**Castro
Marina** ♨
Cilento
A 3
Pollino
♨ Gallipoli
alinuro ♨♨
Maratea ♨♨
Trebisacce
♨ Marina di Leuca
Marina
Camerota
♨ **Praia a Mare**
S 534
Crati
♨ **Scalea**
♨ **Diamante**
S 106
Cirò Marina
⊹ Terme Luigiane
CAMIGLIATELLO S. ❄
TIRRENO
♨ Amantea
Terme Caronte
♨ Isola di Capo Rizzuto ♨
S 280
Catanzaro Lido
♨ Pizzo
Copanello ♨
Soverato ♨
♨♨ Tropea
Panarea
A 3
♨ Palmi
S 106
ipari
Scilla
MARE
Messina
astroreale Terme
Gambarie d'A.
IONIO
Reggio di Calabria
A 20
A 18
Capo
d'Orlando
TAORMINA
GIARDINI-NAXOS ♨♨
Acireale
Simeto
A 19
Catania
S 114
Siracusa
S 115
MARE
ADRIATICO

0   100 km

Riomaggiore

Introduction

Landscape

The boot of Italy which stretches 1 300km – 808 miles from north to south, juts into the Mediterranean between Greece and Spain. This peninsula enjoys an extraordinary variety of climate and topography.

Italy's rugged relief rises from great swathes of plain which cover barely one quarter of its total area of 301 262km² – 139 087sq miles. Its coastline (almost 7 500km – 4 660 miles long) is washed by the waters of four inner seas: the Ligurian, Tyrrhenian, Ionian and Adriatic.

The **Alps**, which were created as the earth's crust folded in the Tertiary Era, form a gigantic barrier with northern Europe and are a formidable source of hydro-electric power. Several transalpine passes and tunnels link Italy with France and northern Europe. On the southern side of the Alps between the fertile Po valley and the foothills there are several lakes of glacial origin.

The **Apennines**, a range of limestone hills formed by a more recent Tertiary geological movement, extend from Genoa down into Sicily, dividing the country into two zones which have been subjected to different influences and have for long remained independent of one another. The peaks of this limestone chain are generally lower than those of the Alps. The Corno Grande at 2 912m – 9 560ft is the highest mountain of the chain's tallest massif, the Gran Sasso. The section between Naples

and Sicily is subject to tectonic plate movements resulting in earthquakes, restless volcanoes and marked changes in sea level. Such activity in turn has altered the relief of this southern part of the peninsula. The distribution of vegetation and crops follows quite closely the subdivision of the peninsula into natural regions *(map p 3)*.

By the end of 1991 the population of Italy had reached 56 757 236, making it the fifth most densely populated country in Europe after the Benelux countries, the United Kingdom and the Federal Republic of Germany. Towns are more numerous in northern and central Italy and over 54% of the population is concentrated in substantial urban conurbations of 20 000 or more.

REGIONS

Valle d'Aosta – This great deep furrow between the highest mountains in Europe is watered by the Dora Baltea River, whose tributaries run along picturesque lateral valleys: the Valtournenche, Val di Gressoney, Val d'Ayas, Val Grisenche.

Aosta, well situated in the centre of the valley, is the capital of this region and has enjoyed a degree of administrative autonomy since 1947. In addition to the pastoral activities of the mountain people and the iron mines at Cogne, the valley's economy depends primarily on tourism which has developed as a result of the Great St Bernard and Mont Blanc tunnels.

From Pont-St-Martin to Courmayeur the local population – essentially mountain people and shepherds – remain attached to their traditions and have retained their French family names. Many still speak French and other varied dialects.

Courmayeur : Valle d'Aosta

Piedmont – Piedmont, at the foot of the mountain range, consists mainly of the extensive Po Plain. Between the Alps and the Apennines this fertile area is intersected by long rows of poplars as grassland alternates with fields planted with cereals and rice. Three-fifths of the Italian rice production is concentrated in the districts of Vercelli and Novara. Southeast of Turin the gently-rolling chalk hills of the **Monferrato** bear the well-known Asti vines and produce the Gorgonzola cheese. Numerous hydro-electric power stations supply electricity to local industry: textile factories in Biella and the metal, engineering and chemical works in Turin. **Turin**, on the Po, is a dynamic town famous for its fashion houses and cars.

Lombardy – Lombardy is the busiest region in Italy located in the green Po plain between the Ticino and the Mincio, which together with the Adda supply Lakes Maggiore, Como and Garda. To the north the great lake valleys give access to the Alpine passes. Lombardy, with the mulberry bushes of the **Brianza** district, takes first place in the production of silk. The permanent grazing and grasslands are used by modern dairy farming and processing industries. In the **Lomellina** district, large areas are given over to rice growing.

The many towns, scattered throughout the countryside, were important banking and trading centres in medieval and Renaissance times and spread the name of the Lombards all over Europe. Today Como is the centre of the silk industry, Brescia steel, chemical and engineering industries, Bergamo textile and engineering works, Mantua petrochemicals and plastics, Cremona agriculture and Pavia the seat of an important university.

Portofino

It is Milan, the economic capital of Italy, that has the highest density of population and businesses. This town with its modern architecture and numerous commercial enterprises and cultural institutions has an outer ring of industrial suburbs which are the home base of textile, oil, chemical, steel and food industries.

Veneto (Venetia) – This comprises mainly the vast alluvial Po Plain and its tributaries which are overlooked in the north by the Venetian Pre-Alps, and further north again in the **Cadore** district by the western massifs of the Dolomites. It is an agricultural region growing wheat, maize, mulberry bushes, olives, fruit trees and vines. The industrial sector includes oil refineries, smelting works and chemical plants which are concentrated in the vicinity of Venice at Mestre-Marghera, as well as a large production of hydro-electric energy in the valleys of the Pre-Alps. The latter supplies the textile industry.

The landscape is punctuated by two small volcanic groups, the Berici Mountains south of Vicenza and the **Euganean Hills** near Padua. The slopes of these blackish heights support vines and peach orchards, and there are several hot springs.

In the **Po delta** (Polesina) and that of the Adige lie improverished, grandiose and desolate areas, subject to flooding. Following reclamation certain areas are farmed on an industrial scale for wheat and sugar beet. The coastline takes the form of lagoons *(lido)* separated from the sea by spits of sand pierced by gaps *(porti)*. **Venice**, whose industrial sector is continually growing, is built on piles in one of these lagoons.

Trentino-Alto Adige – This is one of five Italian regions to enjoy a special autonomous statute and the people are partly of Germanic culture and German-speaking. The area includes the Adige and Isarco valleys and the surrounding mountains. The Adige Valley, at the southern exit from the Brenner Pass, has always been easy of access and much used by traffic. Though deep, it opens out towards the sunny south and is very fertile. Cereals are grown on the flatter areas of the valley bottom, with vines and fruit trees on the lower slopes and pastures above. Avelengo in the vicinity of Merano is well known for its breed of horses. **Bolzano** and **Trento**, where there is some industrial development, are the regional markets. The highly-eroded limestone massif of the **Dolomites** extends across the Veneto and Trentino-Alto Adige.

Friuli-Venezia Giulia – This region prolongs the Veneto to the east and it forms the Italian boundary with Austria and Slovenia. The area enjoys a large degree of autonomy in administrative and cultural affairs. In the north is the schistous massif of the **Carnic Alps** with its forests of conifers and alpine pastures. Friuli-Venezia Giulia is an important silkworm breeding and spinning area. Udine is one of the busiest towns. By way of the **Trieste** Riviera you will reach this town which was once the busy port of Austria and now trades with the Far East. Trieste is still subject to a special statute.

Emilia-Romagna – The plain skirting the Apennines derives its name from the Via Emilia, a straight Roman road that crosses it from Piacenza to Rimini. South and east of Bologna the district is known as **Romagna**. Its soil, which is intensively cultivated, is among the best in Italy for wheat and beet. The monotonous landscape consists of extensive fields intersected at regular intervals by rows of mulberries and vines clinging to tall poles, and of maples or elms. Other vines grow on the slopes of the Apennines.

The towns are strung out along the Via Emilia: the most important, **Bologna**, famous for its very old university, is today a communications and industrial (steel, engineering and food) centre and a market for wheat and pigs.

The region to the east of Ferrara through which runs the Po river is devoted to rice growing. To the south is an area of great lagoons, **Valli di Comacchio**, where fishermen catch eels. **Ravenna**, which has been somewhat revitalised by its port and its oil refinery, was once the capital of the Western Roman Empire, and the chief town of Romagna before the creation of Emilia-Romagna, with Bologna as the regional capital.

Liguria – Liguria, furrowed by deep, narrow valleys at right angles to the coast, had a maritime civilisation before the Roman era. The steep slopes of the inner valleys are dotted with poor hilltop villages, watching over groves of chestnut or olive trees and cultivated terraces. The rocky, indented coastline has few fish to offer but has enjoyed heavy coastal traffic since the time of the Ligurians, facilitated by many small deep-water ports. The Roman Empire gave its present appearance to the country, with olive groves and vineyards, now complemented by vegetables, fruit (melons and peaches) and flowers grown on an industrial scale.

The **Riviera di Ponente** (Western Riviera) west of Genoa, is sunnier and more sheltered than the **Riviera di Levante** (Eastern Riviera), but the latter has a more luxuriant vegetation. The chief towns are Imperia, Savona and **Genoa** (shipyards, steel production, oil terminal and thermal power station) and La Spezia (naval base, commercial port, thermal power station and arms manufacture).

Tuscany – The harmony of the beautiful Tuscan landscape of low-lying hill with graceful curves affording wide views and planted with olive groves, vineyards and cypress trees bathed in the soft, golden light, reflects the great artistic sense and sophistication of the Tuscan people.

The region has a variety of soils. The Tuscan Archipelago, with the mountainous **Island of Elba** and its rich iron-bearing deposits, faces a shore which is sometimes rocky (south of Leghorn), sometimes flat and sandy as in the area around Viareggio, known as **Versilia**. To the north of the Arno the **Apuan Alps** are quarried for marble (Carrara).

Sienese landscape

In the heart of Tuscany lies the fertile and beautiful **Arno Basin**, an ideal setting for **Florence**. Vines and silvery olives alternate with fields of wheat, tobacco and maize. Peppers, pumpkins and the famous Lucca beans grow among the mulberries. The old farms, with their distinctive grand architectural style, often stand alone on hill tops.

Southern Tuscany is a land of hills, soft and vine-clad in the **Chianti** district south of Florence, quiet and pastoral near Siena, dry and desolate round Monte Oliveto Maggiore, and massive and mysterious in the **Colli Metalliferi** (metal-bearing hills) south of Volterra. Bordering Lazio, **Maremma**, with its melancholy beauty, was once a marshy district haunted by bandits and shepherds. Much of the area has now been reclaimed.

Umbria – The land of St Francis is a country of hills, valleys and river basins, where the poplars raise their rustling heads to limpid skies. This is the green Umbria of the Clitumnus Valley **(Valle del Clitunno)**, whose pastures were famous in ancient times. Umbria has two lakes, **Trasimeno** and Piediluco, and many rivers, including the Tiber. Medieval cities which succeeded Etruscan settlements overlook ravines and valleys: grim Gubbio, haughty **Perugia**, the capital of Umbria, Assisi, Spoleto and Spello. Others stand in the centre of a plain, such as Foligno and Terni, the metallurgical centre.

Marches – So called because they were formerly frontier provinces of the Frankish Empire and papal domains, the Marches form a much sub-divided area between San Marino and Ascoli Piceno, where the parallel spurs of the Apennines run down into the Adriatic, forming a series of deep, narrow valleys. There is, however, a flat and rectangular coastal belt dotted with beaches and canal-ports. The inhabitants of the Marches have a reputation for friendliness, piety and diligence. Apart from the capital, Ancona, a busy port, most of the old towns are built on commanding sites; Urbino (centre of the arts) and Loreto (church) are noteworthy.

Lazio (Latium) – Lying between the Tyrrhenian Sea and the Apennines, from Tuscan Maremma to Gaeta, Latium, the cradle of Roman civilisation, borders a sandy coast whose ancient ports, such as Ostia at the mouth of the Tiber, have silted up. Civitavecchia today is the only modern port on the coastline. In the centre of Lazio, **Rome**, the Italian capital and seat of the Catholic Church, is mainly a residential city attracting civil servants, churchmen and tourists alike. To the east and north, volcanic hills, with lonely lakes in their craters, overlook the famous **Roman Campagna**, beloved by the writers and painters who have often described its great, desolate expanses, dotted with ancient ruins. Today these waste lands *(latifundia)*, formerly hotbeds of malaria, have regained a degree of activity: the drainage of the Pontine Marches, near Latina, was a spectacular achievement. Cassino is the most important industrial centre. A flourishing industrial zone has developed around the atomic centre at Latina.

To the south is the distinctive **Ciociaria**. This area takes its name from the shoes *(ciocie)*, which are part of the traditional costume. They have thick soles and thongs wound round the calf of the leg. It is a mainly agricultural area with strong folklore traditions.

Abruzzi – Under its harsh climate, this is the part of the Apennines which most suggests a country of high mountains, grand and wild, with its **Gran Sasso** and **Maiella Massifs**. The Upper Sangro Valley is now a nature reserve. In basins sheltered from the wind are vineyards, almond and olive groves, whose products are sent to the market town of Avezzano. Near the latter is the great drained marsh which is now given over to beet growing. The area has acquired an industrial sector with the development of the Chieti-Pescara zone and other areas such as Vasto (glass making), Sulmona (car factories) and L'Aquila (steel works).

Molise – Molise, with its capital, **Campobasso**, extends south of the Abruzzi, with which it has several common features: a mountainous relief, dark valleys and wild forests which are still haunted by wolves. The region is bordered to the west by the Maiella. Agriculture forms the basis of the local economy and the main crops are wheat, oats, maize, potatoes and vines (dried raisins).

Campania – Campania forms a fertile crescent around the Bay of Naples. Hemp, tobacco and cereals alternate with olive groves and vineyards. **Naples** is the port for a region which is developing its industrial sector (food industries, steel works, oil refineries and engineering works). As for the **Bay of Naples**, its charm and its mystery stirred the imagination of the ancients and it was here that they located the entrance to the Underworld. The characteristic silhouette of **Vesuvius** dominates the landscape. Although the coast has lost much of its charm owing to building developments, the **Sorrento Peninsula** and the **Island of Capri** are two notable beauty spots.

Puglia (Apulia), Basilicata and Calabria – These three regions cover the foot of the Italian "boot". Puglia, on the east side, facing the Adriatic, has many assets. Cereals are grown in the plain between Foggia and Manfredonia and in the plains of Bari, Taranto, Lecce and Brindisi. Vines flourish almost everywhere and are associated with olives (the Apulian production of olive oil represents 10% of the world total) and almonds on the coast. The elevation of the **Gargano Promontory**, otherwise known as the "boot's spur", is distinctive. The country to the south of Bari has an almost Oriental aspect, with strange dwellings, known as *trulli*, and customs.

Bari, the capital of Puglia, is a busy port, which still enjoys numerous trading links with the Middle East. Along with Taranto and Brindisi it is one of the three main industrial centres in the region. Basilicata or **Lucania**, and Calabria, comprise very different types of country; the rocky corniche from the Gulf of Policastro to Reggio; the grim, grand mountains of the **Sila Massif** with its extensive mountain pastures and wide horizons; and at the southern extremity of the peninsula between two inner seas, lies the **Aspromonte Massif** clad with pine, beech and chestnut forests.

Sardinia and Sicily – *See SARDINIA and SICILY at the end of the Guide.*

Historical Table and Notes

Roman History

BC	**From the Origins to the Empire** (753-27 BC)
753	Foundation of Rome by Romulus according to legend. (In fact it was born of the union of Latin and Sabine villages in the 8C.)
7C-6C	Royal Dynasty of the Tarquins. Power is divided between the king, the senate, representing the great patrician families, and the *comitia*, representing the rich families.
509	Establishment of the Republic: the king's powers are conferred on two consuls, elected for one year.
451-449	Law of the XII Tables, instituting equality between patricians and plebeians.
390	The Gauls invade Italy and take Rome but are expelled by Camillus.
281-272	War against Pyrrhus, King of Epirus; submission of the southern part of the peninsula to Rome.
264-241	First Punic War: Carthage abandons Sicily to the Romans.
218-201	Second Punic War. Hannibal crosses the Alps and defeats the Romans at Lake Trasimeno. Hannibal routs the Romans at Cannae and halts at Capua *(see CAPUA)*. In 210 Scipio carries war into Spain, and in 204 he lands in Africa. Hannibal is recalled to Carthage. Scipio defeats Hannibal at Zama in 202.
146	Macedonia and Greece become Roman provinces. Capture and destruction of Carthage.
133	Occupation of all Spain and end of the Mediterranean campaigns.
133-121	Failure of the policy of the Gracchi, who promoted popular agrarian laws.
118	The Romans in Gaul.
112-105	War against Jugurtha, King of Numidia (now Algeria).
102-101	Marius, vanquisher of Jugurtha, stops invasions of Cimbri and Teutons.
88-79	Sulla, the rival of Marius, triumphs over Mithridates and establishes his dictatorship in Rome.
70	Pompey and Crassus, appointed Consuls, become masters of Rome.
63	Plot of Catiline against the Senate exposed by Cicero.
60	The first Triumvirate: Pompey, Crassus, Julius Caesar. Rivalry of the three rulers.
59	Julius Caesar as Consul.
58-51	The Gallic War (52: Surrender of Vercingetorix at Alesia).
49	Caesar crosses the Rubicon and drives Pompey out of Rome.
49-45	Caesar defeats Pompey and his partisans in Spain, Greece and Egypt. He writes his history of the Gallic War.
early 44	Caesar is appointed Dictator for life.
March 15	Caesar is assassinated by Brutus, his adopted son, among others.
43	The second Triumvirate: Octavius (nephew and heir of Caesar), Anthony, Lepidus.
41-30	Struggle between Octavius and Anthony. Defeat (at Actium) and suicide of Anthony.
	The Early Empire (27 BC to AD 284)
27	Octavius, sole master of the Empire, receives the title of Augustus Caesar and plenary powers.
AD	
14	Death of Augustus.
14-37	Reign of Tiberius.
54-68	Reign of Nero, who causes the death of Britannicus, his mother Agrippina and his wives Octavia and Poppaea, and initiates violent persecution of the Christians.
68	End of the Julio-Claudian dynasty: Augustus, Tiberius, Caligula, Claudius, Nero.
69-96	Flavian dynasty: Vespasian, Titus, Domitian.

96-192	The Century of the Antonines, marked by the successful reigns of Nerva, Trajan, Hadrian, Antoninus and Marcus Aurelius, who consolidated the Empire.
193-275	Severus dynasty: Septimius Severus, Caracalla, Heliogabalus, Alexander Severus, Decius, Valerian, Aurelian.
235-268	Military anarchy; a troubled period. The legions make and break emperors.
270-275	Aurelius re-establishes the unity of the Empire.

GIRAUDON

The Later Empire (AD 284-476)

284-305	Reign of Diocletian. Institution of Tetrarchy or 4-man government.
303	Persecution of the Christians: reign of Diocletian known as "the age of martyrs".

Hadrian (Musée du Louvre, Paris)

306-337	Reign of Constantine. By the Edict of Milan (313) Constantine decrees religious freedom. Constantinople becomes the new capital.
379-395	Reign of Theodosius the Great, the Christian Emperor, who establishes Christianity as the state religion. At his death the Empire is divided between his two sons, Arcadius (Eastern Empire) and Honorius (Western Empire) who settled at Ravenna.
5C	The Roman Empire is repeatedly attacked by the Barbarians: in 410, Alaric, King of the Visigoths, captures Rome. Capture and sack of Rome in 455 by the Vandals under Genseric.
476	Deposition by Odoacer of the Emperor Romulus Augustus ends the Western Empire.

From the Roman Empire to the Germanic Holy Roman Empire

493	Odoacer is driven out by the Ostrogoths under Theodoric.
535-553	Reconquest of Italy by the Eastern Roman Emperor Justinian (527-565).
568	Lombard invasion by King Alboin.
752	Threatened by the Lombards, the Pope appeals to Pepin the Short, King of the Franks.
774	Pepin's son, Charlemagne (Charles the Great), becomes King of the Lombards.
800	Charlemagne is proclaimed Emperor by Pope Leo III.
9C	The break-up of the Carolingian Empire causes complete anarchy and the formation of many rival states in Italy.
951	Intervention in Italy of Otto I, King of Saxony, who becomes King of the Lombards.
962	Otto I, now crowned Emperor, founds the Holy Roman Empire.

The Quarrel of the Church and the Empire

11C	Progressive establishment of the Normans in Sicily and southern Italy.
1076	Quarrel between Pope Gregory VII and the Emperor Henry IV about Investitures.
1077	Humbling of the Emperor before the Pope at Canossa *(see REGGIO NELL'EMILIA)*.
1155	Frederick Barbarossa crowned Emperor. Resumption of the struggle between the Empire and the Papacy, with the **Ghibellines** supporting the Emperor and the **Guelphs** supporting the Pope.
1167	Creation of the **Lombard League**. An association of Lombard cities with Guelph tendencies to counter the Emperor.
1176	Reconciliation between Frederick Barbarossa and Pope Alexander III.
1216	Triumph of the Papacy on the death of Pope Innocent III.
1227-1250	A new phase in the struggle between the Empire (Frederick II) and the Papacy (Gregory IX). New triumph of the Papacy.

French Influence and Decline of Imperial Power

13C	Peak of economic prosperity of the Communes.
1252	The Florentine florin, a silver coin from 1182, is minted in gold and is a popular currency in international trade.
1265	Charles of Anjou, brother of St Louis, crowned King of Sicily.
1282	Sicilian Vespers: massacre of French settlers in Sicily.
1302	The Anjou Dynasty establishes itself in Naples.
1303	Attack of Anagni, instigated by King Philip of France, on Pope Boniface VIII.
1309-1377	The popes established at Avignon, France. The Avignon popes included Clement V to Gregory XI who took the papacy back to Rome at the instigation of St Catherine of Siena.
1328	Failure of the intervention in Italy by the Emperor Ludwig of Bavaria. This is the first sign of the slow erosion of the German Emperors' will to exercise political and economic power over the territories of the old Roman empire.
1378-1418	The Great Schism of the West (anti-popes in Pisa and Avignon) is brought to an end by the Council of Constance (1414-18).
1402	Last German intervention in Italy (emperor defeated by Lombard militia).
1442	Alfonso V, King of Aragon, becomes King of the Two Sicilies.
1453	Constantinople, capital of the Christian Eastern territories, falls to the Turks.
1492	Death of Lorenzo de' Medici, the Magnificent. Christopher Columbus discovers America.
1494	Intervention of King Charles VIII of France for Ludovico II Moro.

Florin

Economic and Cultural Golden Age (15C, early 16C)

The centre and the north of the country were transformed by the dynamism of the bourgeois class, while the south kept its feudal structures based on land ownership. The economic importance of Italy derived from the large-scale production of consumer goods (cloth, leather, glass, ceramics, arms etc) as well as from trade and wide-ranging banking activities. Merchants and bankers who had settled in countries throughout Europe spread the influence of the Italian civilisation, which flourished at the courts of the Italian rulers. There was great rivalry regarding the patronage of artists and the commissioning of splendid palaces among enlightened patrons of the arts such as the Medici of Florence, the Sforza of Milan, the Montefeltro of Urbino, the Este of Ferrara, the Gonzaga of Mantua and the Popes in Rome (Julius II, Leo X).

Decline set in as trade shifted towards the Atlantic with grave consequences for the maritime republics which had prospered during the Middle Ages. Genoa soon faced ruin, Pisa was taken over by its age-old rival Florence, and Venice was in serious trouble as the Turks advanced westwards. In addition, although Italy had great economic potential, it fell once again under foreign domination because of the failure to achieve the unity of the country.

From the 16C to the Napoleonic era

16C	France and Spain engage in a struggle for the supremacy of Europe.
1515-1526	François I, victor at Marignano but vanquished at Pavia, is forced to give up the Italian heritage.
1527	Capture and sack of Rome by the troops of the Constable of Bourbon, in the service of Charles V.
1559	Treaty of Cateau-Cambrésis: Spanish domination over Naples and the district of Milan, Sicily and Sardinia until the early 18C.
17C	Savoy becomes the most powerful state in northern Italy.
1713	Victor-Amadeus II of Savoy acquires Sicily and the title of King. The Duke of Savoy is compelled to exchange Sicily for Sardinia in 1720.
1796	Napoleon's campaign in Lombardy. Creation of the Cispadan Republic.
1797	Battle of Rivoli. Treaty of Campo-Formio. Creation of the Cisalpine and Ligurian Republics.
1798-1799	Proclamation of the Roman and Parthenopaean (Naples) Republics.

1805	Napoleon transforms the Italian Republic into a Kingdom, assumes the iron crown of the Lombard Kings and confers the vice-royalty on his stepson, Eugène de Beauharnais.
1808	Rome is occupied by French troops. Murat becomes King of Naples.
1809	The Papal States are attached to the French Empire. Pius VII is taken to France as a prisoner (1812).
1814	Collapse of the Napoleonic regime. Pius VII returns to Rome.

Towards Italian Unity (1815-1870)

1815	Congress of Vienna. Hegemony of Austria.
1815-1832	The "Carbonari" patriots oppose the Austrian occupation but their revolts are crushed.
1831	Founding of the Young Italy movement by Mazzini. Growth of national feeling against Austria: the **Risorgimento.**
1834-1837	Revolts at Genoa and in the Kingdom of the Two Sicilies.
1848	First War of Independence against Austria, led by the King of Sardinia, ruler of Piedmont. Italian successes followed by a violent Austrian counter-attack.
1849-1852	Accession of Victor Emmanuel II. Cavour's government reorganises the State of Piedmont.
1854	Participation of Piedmont, with Britain and France, in the Crimean War.
1856	Paris Congress. Cavour officially raises the question of Italian unity.
1858	Meeting of Cavour and Napoleon III at Plombières. Alliance between France and Piedmont.
1859	Second War of Independence against Austria led by Piedmont with France as ally. Franco-Piedmontese victories of Magenta and Solferino and Villafranca Armistice. Piedmont obtains Lombardy and France, Savoy and the County of Nice.
1860	Bologna, Parma, Modena and Tuscany unite with Piedmont. Expedition of Garibaldi and the Thousand to Sicily and Naples. Union of the South.
1861	Proclamation of the Kingdom of Italy with Turin as its capital. Death of Cavour.
1865-1870	Florence becomes the capital of the Kingdom of Italy.
1866	Austria at war with Prussia and Italy. Venetia united to Italy.
1867	Garibaldi, marching on Rome, is defeated at Mentana.
1870	On 20 September, the Italian troops occupy Rome. It is proclaimed the capital of Italy in 1871. Italian unity is complete.

UNIFICATION OF ITALY

Although Machiavelli had already dreamed of a united Italy in the 16C, it was not until after the French Revolution that the question of uniting the various regions under the same political regime was seriously contemplated. The Risorgimento provided the initial impetus which resulted in the uprisings of 1848 against Austrian rule and their defeat at Novara (1849). The problem of Italian unity was brought to the forefront of European affairs with the accession of **Victor Emmanuel II** and the skilful campaigning of his minister **Camillo Cavour**, an ardent advocate of Italian liberty. Napoleon III allied himself with the Piedmontese in order

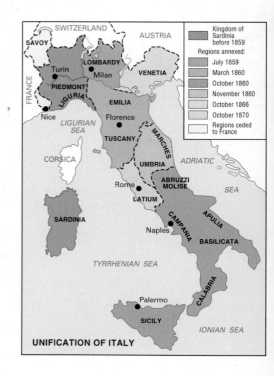

UNIFICATION OF ITALY

to oppose the Austrians. After the combined Franco-Piedmontese victories of 1859 and the disillusionment caused by the Treaty of Villafranca when Savoy was surrendered to France, several regions of central Italy planned a concerted revolt and united with Piedmont. **Garibaldi** liberated Sicily and southern Italy from the domination of the Bourbons. On 17 March 1861 the inauguration of the Kingdom of Italy was proclaimed with Turin as the capital and Victor Emmanuel as King. Five more years had to pass before the war of independence with the Prussians as allies led to the annexation of Veneto, and more than ten before Italian troops captured Rome in 1870, thus achieving the unification of Italy.

From 1870 to the Present Day

1882	Italy, Germany and Austria sign the Triple Alliance.
1885	The Italians gain a footing in Eritrea and on the Somali Coast.
1900	Assassination of King Umberto I by an anarchist. Accession of Victor Emmanuel III.
1904-1906	Rapprochement of Italy with Britain and France.
1915	Italy enters the First World War on 24 May on the side of the Allies in their struggle against Austria-Hungary.
1918	The Battle of Vittorio Veneto marks the end of the First World War for Italy (4 November).
1919	Treaty of St Germain: Istria and the Trentino are attached to Italy.
1921	Social disturbances fomented by Mussolini's Fascist Party.
1922-1926	The March on Rome. Mussolini becomes Prime Minister, then *Duce* (Leader).
1929	Lateran Treaty concluded between the Italian Government and the Papacy.
1936	Italian occupation of Ethiopia. Rapprochement with Germany. Rome-Berlin Axis formed.
1940	Italy enters the Second World War against Britain and France.
1943	10 July: The Allies land in Sicily. 25 July: Overthrow and arrest of Mussolini. 8 September: Armistice. Much of the country is occupied by German troops. 12 September: Mussolini is freed by the Germans and sets up the Italian Socialist Republic in the north of the country with Salò as its capital.
1944-1945	The Allies slowly reconquer Italy. The country is liberated (25 April 1945) and the war ends. Mussolini is arrested while trying to flee into Switzerland, is tried and shot.
May 1946	Abdication of Victor Emmanuel III and accession of Umberto II.
June 1946	Proclamation of the Republic after a referendum.
1947	Treaty of Paris: Italy loses its colonies as well as Albania, Istria, Dalmatia and the Dodecanese. Frontier redefined to the benefit of France.
1948	1 January: The new Constitution comes into effect.
1954	Trieste is attached to Italy.
March 1957	Treaty of Rome instituting the European Economic Community (now the European Union): Italy is one of the six founding members.
1968	Uprisings against the socio-economic system: *Autunno caldo* (literally, hot autumn).
1970-1980	Riots and terrorism as a result of political unrest.
1970	Institution of the regional system.
1978	Aldo Moro, former Council President, assassinated.
1992	Operation to fight economic and political corruption in Italy commences. Two judges, Giovanni Falcone and Paolo Borsellino, are assassinated in Sicily.
1994	Beginning of the Second Republic.

Rome and the Papacy

Capital of Christendom – Vatican City is a Free State ruled by the pope. Although in terms of the priesthood the pope has the same powers as a bishop, in the hierarchy he is the head of the Roman Catholic Church. The Vatican Council of 1870 laid down the principle of papal infallibility in matters of dogma. The pontiff is the symbol of the spiritual influence of the Roman Catholic Church throughout the world. The pope is elected by the Sacred College of Cardinals who meet in conclave in the Sistine Chapel. A majority of two-thirds plus one is required. As the Christian community grew, the pope assumed a growing political role in parallel with his functions as Head of the Church. Thus the history of the papacy reflects the relationship between Church and State.

Birth of the Church and Origin of the Papacy – Christianity was born in the Levant with the preaching of Jesus and spread to the west through the apostles and their disciples. By the end of the 1C the early Church was made up of small communities led by bishops who were Christ's representatives. From the end of the 2C the Bishop of Rome, the capital of the Empire, claimed primacy over the other bishops. Gradually the term Pope (Low Latin *Papa*: Father) ceased to be used in relation to all bishops and was reserved exclusively for the Bishop of Rome.

Growth of the Church – At first regarded as a harmless cult, Christianity was soon subjected to persecution under Nero and Domitian as well as under Decius, Valerian, Diocletian and Maximian. However, these events failed to check the spread of the new religion, and the Church stood out as the only great moral force able to withstand the fall of the weakened and divided Empire. In 313, the Emperor Constantine granted religious freedom to Christians by the **Edict of Milan**. Pagan cults were tolerated and later banned. When Christianity was recognised as the state religion in 382 it became the surest prop of imperial power and when Rome reeled under the repeated assaults of the Barbarians, it remained the last bulwark of civilisation.

Papal Authority – The authority of the pope and the ascendancy of the Church grew all the stronger over the next centuries, in particular owing to the strong personality of **Gregory the Great** (590-604). In the 8C, when faced with the occupation of the imperial territories by the Lombards, the then pope appealed to Pepin the Short, King of the Franks, thus initiating an era of alliances with the Carolingian dynasty culminating in two important events. By the Donation of **Quiersy-sur-Oise** (AD 756) the King of the Franks gave an undertaking to return all occupied territories to Pope Stephen II and not to the Byzantine emperor. This donation is the origin of the Papal States and of the pope's temporal power. The second event was the coronation of Charlemagne as Emperor of the West in the year AD 800. In the period of anarchy which followed the fall of the Carolingian Empire at the end of the 9C, the papacy lapsed into great laxity; its prestige was restored under the strong leadership of **Gregory VII** (1073-85). The decrees of this great reformer led to the Quarrel of the Investitures, a long drawn-out conflict between the pope and the emperor. The papacy emerged weakened from the Captivity of Avignon (1309-77) and after its return to Rome had to face a still more serious crisis with the **Great Schism of the West** (1378-1417), as a succession of antipopes elected by the Sacred College ruled in Avignon. From 1520 onwards, the Reformation started by Martin Luther posed a new threat to Church authority which was countered by the Council of Trent *(see TRENTO)*. The Church emerged stronger after each religious crisis. In the 18C it met the challenge from the philosophical movement, and after the fall of Napoleon (1814) the pope returned to Rome.

GIRAUDON

Pope Paul III (Alessandro Farnese) with his nephews by Titian (Capodimonte, Naples)

The "Roman Question" – As the spiritual head of the Church and temporal sovereign, the pope in the 19C was involved in the problem of Italian unity. Unity brought about by the House of Piedmont-Sardinia could be achieved only if the pope renounced all temporal power. When the troops of Victor Emmanuel II occupied Rome in 1870, the pope was a virtual prisoner in the Vatican. The problem was solved by the **Lateran Treaty** of 1929 signed between the Holy See and Mussolini. From then on the people enjoyed sovereignty over the Papal State (Vatican City, the four major basilicas, the catacombs, the Roman Curia, several colleges and Castel Gandolfo). The authority of the Church was recognised in the fields of education and marriage. On this basis, in 1947, the Constitution defined the relations between the Church and the State. The Lateran Treaty was modified further in 1984.

Bernini's baldaquin, Basilica di San Pietro, Roma

Ancient Civilisations

Since 2000 BC and throughout antiquity, Italy, the meeting-place of races, has seen the Etruscan, Greek and Latin civilisations flourish on her soil. Two thousand years later, Western civilisation is still impregnated with them. Greeks, Etruscans and Romans were preceded by two peoples who came from the north: the Ligurians, who also occupied southern Gaul and the Iberian Peninsula, and the Italics or Italiots, who settled in Umbria and Latium and from whom the Latins sprang. The former transmitted their fair hair and blue eyes to some of the present inhabitants of Liguria. The latter built acropolises of which the gigantic foundations still exist in some places, as for instance at Alatri.

THE GREEKS

Cities and Men – The shores of Sicily and southern Italy held a sort of fascination for the ancient Greeks, who regarded them as the limits of the inhabited earth. Many scenes of Greek mythology are set there: the Phlegrean Fields, near Naples, hid the entrance to the Kingdom of Hades; Zeus routed the Titans, with the help of Hercules, on Etna, where the Cyclops lived and Hephaestus, the God of Fire, had his forges; Kore, the daughter of Demeter, was kidnapped by Hades, who had emerged from the River Tartara near Enna. In the *Odyssey*, Homer (9C BC) relates the adventures of Ulysses (Odysseus) after the siege of Troy, sailing between Scylla and Charybdis in the Straits of

Akragas: Agrigento
Caere: Cerveteri
Clusium: Chiusi
Faesulae: Fiesole

Felsina: Bologna
Poseidonia: Paestum
Selinus: Selinunte
Tuder: Todi

Velitrae: Velletri
Veii: Veio
Volsinii: Bolsena
Zancle: Messina

Messina and resisting the temptations of the Sirens in the Gulf of Sorrento. Pindar (5C BC) describes these mysterious shores, to which Virgil (1C BC) also refers in the *Aeneid*. After the Phoenicians had settled at Carthage and set up trading posts, the Greeks founded a large number of colonies on the coasts of Sicily and southern Italy (8C BC), known as **Magna Graecia**. It included Ionian, Achaean and Dorian colonies, named after the Greek peoples who had colonised them. The social unit was the "city". One of them, Crotone, was governed by a school of philosophers, the Pythagoreans. The 6C and 5C BC marked the zenith of Greek civilisation in Italy, corresponding to the period of Pericles in Athens. Greek seaborne trade was so successful that Syracuse soon rivalled Athens. Syracuse and Taranto were the two main centres of this refined civilisation. Philosophers, scientists and writers settled in Sicily. Aeschylus lived at Gela. Theocritus defined the rules of bucolic poetry and Archimedes was murdered by a Roman soldier in Syracuse.

But rivalry between these many and varied cities led to warfare, which, with Carthaginian raids, led to decline, culminating in the Roman conquest at the end of the 3C BC.

Art in Magna Graecia – The 6C and 5C BC were marked by the building of the temples of Paestum, Selinus and Agrigento. The vigorous design of these magnificent examples of Doric architecture contrasts with the delicate grace of the Ionic order.

At the end of the 5C BC the Doric style was still used for the beautiful temple at Segesta, while in Greece itself the Ionic style was at its height and the Corinthian style was just making its appearance. Decline began in the 4C BC, after the

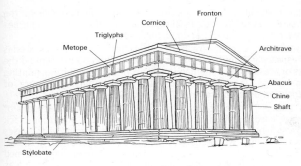
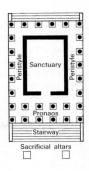

An ancient temple

Peloponnesian War between Sparta and Athens, which impoverished the Greek world. This was the beginning of the so-called **Hellenistic** period, when sculpture gained preeminence over architecture.

The museums of Naples, Paestum, Reggio di Calabria, Taranto, Palermo and Syracuse illustrate the development of sculpture, from the archaic low reliefs of the metopes of Paestum or Selinus and the monumental telamones (male figures used as pillars) of Agrigento to the delightful statuettes of the decadent period modelled at Taranto in the 3C BC. Innumerable statues of youths, Apollo and Aphrodite also issued from the sculptors' studios. They were all more or less copied from Phidias, Praxiteles, Sco-pas or Lysippus, but their harmony of form and proportion remained admirable.

THE ETRUSCANS

While the Greeks were disseminating their civilisation throughout the south of the peninsula and Sicily, the Etruscans were building up in central Italy, from the 8C BC onwards, a powerful empire whose growth was checked only by that of Rome (3C BC).

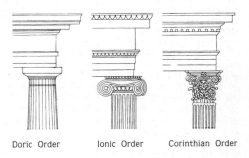

Doric Order   Ionic Order   Corinthian Order

They are a little-known people whose alphabet along with certain tombstone inscriptions have now been deciphered. Some authorities think they were natives of these parts; others, following the example of Herodotus, say they came from Lydia in Asia Minor. The Etruscans at first occupied the area between the Arno and the Tiber *(see map)* but later spread into Campania and the Po Plain. They reached their zenith in the 6C BC. **Etruria** then comprised a federation of 12 city-states known as *lucumonies*, among which are named Veii, Bolsena, Tarquinia, Volterra, Perugia etc. Having grown rich by working iron (Island of Elba), copper and silver mines and by trading in the western Mediterranean, the Etruscans, who were artisans and technicians, had a civilisation derived from a mixture of savagery and refinement. In religion their gods were the same as those of the Greeks. They believed in life after death and in divination, and they studied the entrails of animals (for haruspices) and the flight of birds (for auspices), a form of superstition which the Romans adopted and developed. Their towns, built on elevated sites with walls of huge stones, show an advanced sense of town planning. Near them are vast burial grounds with underground chambers or hypogea filled with utensils and adorned with mural paintings revealing their customs.

Etruscan Art – Etruscan art is primitive in character, though strongly influenced by the Orient and especially by Greece from the 5C BC onwards. It has a marked individuality sustained by realism and expressive movement. Etruscan art was discovered in the 18C, but was regarded as an offshoot of Greek art. The discovery in the 19C of masterpieces like the Apollo and Hermes of Veii and the systematic study of artefacts in the 20C have given this vigorous and refined art the place it deserved.

Sculpture – Since architectural specimens are lacking, sculpture appears to us as the artists' favourite medium. The great period is the 6C BC, when large groups of statuary adorned the pediments of temples: the famous Apollo of Veii (in the Villa Giulia museum in Rome) of obvious Greek influence, belongs to this period. Some portrait busts are more original in their striking realism, intensity of expression and stylised features: their large prominent eyes and enigmatic smiles are characteristic of the Etruscan style. The same applies to the famous groups of semi-recumbent figures on the sarcophagi, many of which are portraits. The sense of movement is shown mainly in sculptures of fantastic animals (such as the Chimera from Arezzo in the Archeological Museum of Florence) and in figurines representing warriors fighting, women at their toilet etc.

Painting – The only surviving specimens are in the burial chambers of the cemeteries (Cerveteri, Veii and especially Tarquinia), where they were supposed to remind the dead of the pleasures of life: banquets, games and plays, music and dancing, hunting etc. The delicate paintings, in colour laid on flat, show amazing powers of observation. They form an excellent record of Etruscan life.

Pottery and goldsmiths' work – Even more than artists, the Etruscans were artisans of genius. In pottery they used the little known **bucchero** technique, producing black earthenware with figures in relief. Initially decorated with motifs in *pointillé*, the vases developed more elaborate shapes with a more complicated ornamentation. In the 5C BC they modelled beautiful burial urns, *canopae*, in animal or human shape adorned with geometric designs. Greek pottery continued to be popular in Etruria where it was faithfully copied. In the domain of goldsmiths' work, both men and women wore heavy often solid gold ornaments of remarkable workmanship, showing the skill of Etruscan goldsmiths particularly in the filigrane and granulation techniques. Engraved mirrors, cists (cylindrical vessels which usually served as marriage coffers), scent-burners and bronze candelabra of great decorative elegance also show the artisans' skill.

THE ROMANS

For about 12 centuries, from the foundation of Rome in the 8C BC to the end of the Western Empire in AD 476, a civilisation, from which Western Europe emerged, reigned in Italy. Royal Rome (753-509 BC) was followed by the Republic (509-27 BC) and then the Empire (27 BC). The Roman eagle then spread its wings from Britain to the Persian Gulf and from Africa to Germany. Decline set in during the Later Empire (AD 284-476) in civil wars and with Barbarian invasions.

Political and Social Life – At the time of the kings, the political organisation of Rome comprised two bodies, the Senate and the *Comitia*, composed of patricians. These were a privileged class who kept idle but devoted hangers-on. The plebeians had no access to public affairs. At the bottom of the scale, the slaves formed the under-privileged section of the population, but they could be freed by their masters. Under the Republic, power was given to two consuls, elected for one year and assisted by quaestors in charge of public finance and the criminal police, together with censors of public morals, aediles in charge of the municipal police, and judicial praetors. The Senate had a consultative role and sanctioned laws. Ten Tribunes of the People watched over the rights of the masses. Consuls or praetors administered the provinces.

Generally speaking, the Empire kept the administrative structure of the Republic, but the powers of the consuls were taken by an emperor *(Imperator)* who was commander-in-chief of the army; he appointed the Senate, and had the right to make peace or war. Under the Later Empire the power of the emperors became absolute. Outside the State, society was divided into clans *(gentes)*, or groups of people descended from a common ancestor, and families, each under a *pater familias* who wielded absolute authority.

Religion – Religion played a part in public or private life. As regards **domestic cults**, a small oratory called the *lararium* enshrined the household gods, Lares and Penates, before whom a sacred flame burned always. The souls of the dead were also venerated. **Public worship** took place in buildings copied from the Etruscan or Greek temples *(see sketch above)*. Sometimes they were circular in form, as in the case of temples dedicated to Vesta.

With the exception of Janus, the chief gods were derived from the 12 (if Pluto god of the Underworld is omitted) Greek gods of Olympus.

A Roman Town

Planning – Roman towns often have a military origin: when the land placed under their control was shared out, the legionaries and veterans who had stayed in the camps were joined by the civil population. Towns which had been surrounded with walls during troubled periods were divided, whenever possible, into four quarters by two main streets, the *decumanus* and the *cardo*, intersecting at right angles and ending in gateways. Other streets parallel to these two gave the town a grid plan.

Streets – The streets were edged with footpaths, sometimes 50cm-18in high, and lined with porticoes to shelter pedestrians. The roadway, paved with large flagstones laid diagonally, was crossed at intervals by stepping-stones laid at the same level as the pavements but between which horses and cart-wheels could pass.

A Roman house – Excavations at Herculaneum, Pompeii and especially Ostia have uncovered Roman houses of various types: the small bourgeois house, a dwelling of several storeys, shops open to the street and finally large, luxurious patrician mansions. These last had a modest external appearance owing to their bare walls and few windows. But the interiors, adorned with mosaics, statues, paintings and marbles and sometimes including private baths and a fish pond, revealed the riches of their owners. A vestibule overlooked by the porter's lodge led to the *atrium*.

The **atrium** ① was a large rectangular court open, in the middle, to the sky. A basin called the *impluvium,* under the open section, caught rainwater. The rooms *(cubiculae)* opened off the atrium, which was the only part of the house to which strangers were usually admitted. At the far end was the **tablinum** ② or study and reception room of the head of the family. Money and

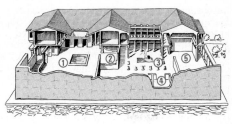

A Roman house

books were kept there. The atrium and adjoining rooms formed the basic house of the poorer citizen. High officials, rich colonials and prosperous tradesmen often added a second house, of the more refined Greek type, joined onto the *tablinum.* The **peristyle** ③, a court surrounded by a portico in the centre of the part of the house reserved for the family, was generally made into a garden with basins lined with mosaics, fountains and statues. The living quarters opened on to it. The bedrooms were simple sleeping-chambers, containing a stone platform built against the wall or a movable bed. There were mattresses, cushions and blankets but no sheets. The dining-room or **triclinium** ④ takes its name from the three inclined platforms which served as couches for the guests, who, adopting a custom that originated in Greece, would eat whilst reclining, stretched out on cushions and leaning on one elbow. In the centre was a table at which the slaves busied themselves. Lastly, there was the great hall or **œcus** ⑤ which was sometimes embellished with a colonnade. The outbuildings included the kitchen with a sink and drain, a built-in stove and oven; baths, which were like the public baths on a smaller scale, and the slaves' quarters, attics, stables etc. The latrines with drains were either in a corner of the kitchen or in some other recess.

The forum – The forum was a large square, often surrounded by a portico. Originally it was a market, usually at the crossing of the two main streets, but it became the centre of the public and commercial life of Roman towns. Men came to read public notices, listen to political speakers, stroll and talk. The women did their shopping, either in shops around the square or from hawkers and artisans who set up their stalls under the porticos. Slave markets were held on certain days. Government offices surrounded the forum. These included the *curia* or headquarters of local government; the voting hall for elections; the public tribune from which candidates for office harangued the crowd; the Temple of Money or exchange *(argentaria)*; the municipal treasury; the public granaries; the Temple of Justice or law courts; the prison and one or more temples.

The tombs – Roman cemeteries were placed along the roads, at some distance from the towns. The most famous in Italy is that on the Via Appia Antica, south of Rome. Directly after death the body of the deceased was exposed on a funeral couch surrounded with candlesticks and wreaths of flowers. Then it was buried or burnt by the family. The deceased was provided with objects for use in the after-life: clothes, arms and tools for men, toys for children, and jewellery and toilet articles for women.

Buildings

Great builders – The art of building was highly developed by the Romans. The speed with which they erected their buildings was due less to the number of workmen employed than to the special training of workers, the building methods and the use of lifting devices such as levers, winches and tackle to move heavy material into place. The Roman vault is semicircular in shape. At the end of the Empire, brick was used in preference to stone. The Roman architectural orders were derived from the Greek orders *(see ANCIENT CIVILISATIONS: The Greeks)*, from which they are distinguished by certain details. Roman Doric, the simplest and strongest, is found in the ground floors of buildings. The Corinthian order was the most popular one with the Romans.

Temples – Rome liberally adopted gods from all the mythologies. The emperors, when raised to divine status, were themselves objects of worship. The Roman temple consists of a closed chamber, the *cella* (sanctuary) containing the image of the god, and an open vestibule *(pronaos)*. The building is surrounded, partly or completely, by a colonnade or peristyle.

Triumphal arches – In Rome these commemorated the "triumphs" of generals or conquering emperors. The low reliefs on the arches recorded their feats of arms. In the provinces, such as Aosta, Benevento and Ancona, there are municipal arches commemorating the founding of a city or erected in honour of some member of the Imperial family.

The baths – The Roman baths, which were public and free, were not only baths but also physical fitness centres, casinos, clubs, recreation centres, libraries, lecture halls and meeting-places, which explains the amount of time people spent there.

Decoration in these great buildings was lavish: mosaic ornaments, coloured marble facings, columns and statues. The bather followed a medically approved circuit. From the gymnasium *(palestra)* he entered a lukewarm room *(tepidarium)* to prepare for the high temperature of the hot room *(caldarium)* and the steam-room. Then came the hot cleaning-bath, the tepid transition-bath and the cold plunge *(frigidarium)* to tone up the skin. To heat air and water a number of underground furnaces *(hypocausts)* were used. The hot air was circulated to heat the rooms from below and from the sides.

The amphitheatre – This typically Roman structure, several storeys high, encircles the usually oval arena and was destined to seat the spectators. Posts were fixed to the upper part of the wall to carry a huge adjustable awning, the **velum**, which sheltered the spectators from the sun and rain. Inside, enclosing the arena, a wall protected the spectators in the front rows from the wild animals in the ring. Three circular galleries forming promenades, various staircases and corridors enabled all the spectators to reach their seats quickly without crowding and without any mingling of the classes.

Always very popular, the performances were announced in advance by painted posters, giving the names of the performers and details of the programme which included fighting of three kinds: between animals, between gladiators and animals, and between gladiators. In principle, a duel between gladiators had always to end in the death of one of the opponents. The public could ask for a gladiator's life to be spared and the President of the Games would indicate a reprieve by turning up his thumb. The victorious gladiator received a sum of money if he was a professional, or he was freed if he was a slave or a prisoner.

Other performances included chariot races, naval battles *(naumachia)*, Olympic games or impressive boxing contests, when the opponents wore copper gloves.

The theatre – Theatres had rows of seats, usually ending in colonnades, a central area or **orchestra** occupied by distinguished spectators or used for acting, and a raised **stage**. The actors performed in front of a wall which was the finest part of the building: its decoration included several tiers of columns, niches containing statues, marble facings and mosaics. The perfect acoustics were generally due to a combination of subtle architectural features. The scenery was either fixed or mobile and there was an ingenious array of machinery either in the wings or below stage. The chief function of the theatre was the performance of comedies and tragedies; however, Roman theatres were also used for competitions, lottery draws and the distribution of bread or money.

Until 100 BC all actors wore wigs of different shapes and colours according to the nature of the character they represented. After that date they adopted pasteboard masks and again each character had a distinctive mask. Tragic actors, to make themselves more impressive, wore buskins or sandals with thick cork soles.

Art

To appreciate fully Italian art in all its diversity and richness from the 12C to the late 18C, it is necessary to keep in mind the illustrious historical context. The rightful heir of the Greek, Etruscan and Roman civilisations, Italian art has adopted from each period some of the most essential principles and characteristics. Italy, with its vast geographical area from the Alps in the north down to Sicily, has always been open to diverse foreign influences. Following the fall of the Western Roman Empire, it was Byzantium that held sway and greatly influenced the northern Adriatic shores for several centuries. A succession of invading peoples followed, namely the Ostrogoths, Lombards, Franks, Arabs and Normans, and each left their imprint on the conquered territory.

The extraordinarily malleable Italian character absorbed the various foreign influences and one after another the cities of Florence, Siena, Verona, Ferrara, Milan, Rome, Venice, Naples and Genoa became the cradle of a flourishing artistic movement. As early as the 12C, in spite of the regional diversities, Italian artists were already beginning to show certain common characteristics. This phenomenon gathered momentum right up to the Renaissance. Initially it was a common taste for harmony and solidity of form as well as an innate sense of space. Both as an idealist and a mystic, the Italian has always worshipped beauty: the Italian landscapes were his source of inspiration where the clearly defined outlines are softened by the effect of the colours and the play of shimmering light.

The Italians rejected the importance accorded to realism which was so popular with northern schools, and tempered the excessive emphasis placed on decoration by Oriental artists. Slowly the Italian artist evolved a representational technique which reflected his emotions. A preoccupation with idealisation is evident in the emphasis given to femininity whether it be profane or religious in inspiration.

In spite of this scholarly and well-mastered image, Italian art is a strong popular and social force. A good example of this is the medieval square, the famous **piazza**, containing the main public buildings in the Roman forum: the church, baptistery, town hall or the princely seat. Law courts, a hospital or a fountain were sometimes added. This was the venue for local markets and meetings. Often designed like stage scenery and embellished with ornamentation, the piazza is also the place for business, political decision-making and other important events. History can be interpreted by studying how certain elements were reused, ornamental motifs copied and styles mingled or superimposed. This is where the artist who also aspires to be architect, sculptor and painter can best exercise his talents where it may be admired by all.

These excellent town planners, however, retained harmony with nature and the Italian countryside. From Roman times on they embellished the countryside with sumptuous **villas**, splendid terraced gardens with basins, fountains and springs, all landscaped with skill to create shade and please the eye. Follies invited the passer-by to rest, meditate or simply enjoy the beauty of nature. Thus the Italian architects and landscape gardeners, often indifferent to the solemn grandeur of French classicism, have created a great many places where man has established a harmonious relationship with nature: from Hadrian's Villa near Rome to the flower-bedecked terraces of the Borromean Islands, including the Oriental charm of the Villa Rufolo in Ravello, the elegant buildings of the Florentine countryside, the fantastic Mannerist creations of Rome, Tivoli or Bomarzo adorned with grottoes and statues, and finally the delightful mansions of the Brenta Riviera; all the work of Palladio.

BYZANTIUM

When Constantine transferred the seat of the Empire to Constantinople in the 4C AD, Rome began to decline and ancient Byzantium became the centre of a brilliant civilisation. While much of Italy was subjected to invasions, such as those by the **Lombards** in the north – extensive remains have survived: in particular, Lombard vestiges in Cividale del Friuli – Byzantine art flourished in Ravenna. After Honorious, who with his sister Galla Placidia fixed the capital of the Empire at Ravenna, and Theodoric, King of the Ostrogoths, who favoured the Greco-Latin civilisation and died there, this town came under Byzantine rule in the reign of Justinian (527-565 AD) and his wife Theodora. The Byzantine Emperors ruled the region of Ravenna and Venezia Giulia only until the 8C, but they held sway in Sicily and part of southern Italy until the 11C. Byzantine art was born of the Christian art of the catacombs and early basilicas and the Greek Oriental style, with its rich decoration. The capital of Byzantine art in Italy was Ravenna, whose tradition was carried on by Venice, Rome, Sicily and even Lombardy until the early 13C. The Byzantine artists had a sense of sanctity which appears in their works, with their air of grandeur and mystery.

Architecture and sculpture – The palaces have vanished but religious buildings remain. They are built in brick, with domes, on the basilical plan inspired by the Roman basilica, or on a circular plan for mausoleums or baptistries. The sober exteriors of these buildings give no hint of the splendour of the mosaic-decorated interiors. The low reliefs on the sides of sarcophagi, chancel parcloses, ambos and pulpits, assume an essentially decorative character: symbolic and stylised figures, animals facing front to front etc.

Mosaics – Byzantine artists excelled in this sumptuous art form. Mosaics consisted of *tesserae*, or fragments of hard stone, glazed and irregularly cut to catch the light. They covered oven-vaults, walls and cupolas, their gold high-lights sparkling in the mysterious semi-darkness. Enigmatic, grandiose figures stood out against midnight blue backgrounds and landscapes with trees, plants and animals. The most famous mosaics are those of Ravenna (5C-6C). However, the Byzantine style still prevailed in the 11C-12C at St Mark's in Venice and in Sicily (Cefalù, Palermo, Monreale), and up to the 13C in Rome.

MIDDLE AGES – ROMANESQUE AND GOTHIC (11C-14C)

As elsewhere in Europe, cathedrals were built all over Italy, but here the Italian predilection for harmony and the Roman tradition of monumental ensembles meant that architecture did not reach the sublime heights of the great achievements of religious art in France.

Lombard Style   Pisan Style   Florentine Style   Sicilian-Norman Style

Romanesque Period – Romanesque architecture in Italy received constant contributions from the Orient and, in the 12C especially, was influenced by France, notably by Normandy and Provence.
The most flourishing school was that of Lombardy, whose master masons, the **maestri comacini**, created the **Lombard style** which spread all over north and central Italy. They built vaulted churches decorated with bands and arcades, detached campaniles, carved façades and porches supported by lions (Como, Milan, Pavia, Verona etc). In the **Pisan style**, architecture showed a strong Lombard influence, while the decorative work borrowed more from Oriental art. This style included tiers of arcades with a multitude of small columns on the façades, tall blind arcades on the side walls and east end, and decorative marble incrustations. The highly original **Florentine-Romanesque style** did not spread beyond the city. It is characterised by simple lines inspired by antique art and by the decoration of façades with white and green marble used alternately.
In Latium and as far as Campania in the 12C-13C, the **Cosmati**, a Roman guild of mosaic and marble workers, held sway. They specialised in assembling fragments of multicoloured marble (pavings, episcopal thrones, ambos or pulpits and candelabra) and the incrustation of columns and friezes in the cloisters with enamel mosaics.
Finally, in southern Italy and Sicily, Lombard, Saracen and Norman influences mingled, the first two exercising their effect chiefly on decoration and the last on the building plan. The combined result was the **Sicilian-Norman style** *(see SICILY)*.
Sculpture was closely linked with architecture, which was essentially religious and decorative.

Romanesque   Gothic   Renaissance   Classical   Baroque
Venetian Palaces

Gothic Period – As far as architecture was concerned it was the Cistercians who systematically introduced the Gothic idiom into Italy in the 13C, starting at the Abbey of Fossanova *(see Abbazia di FOSSANOVA)*; the Franciscans (at Assisi) and the Dominicans (at Florence) soon followed their example. In the same period the Angevin architects imported by the Anjou Dynasty, which reigned at Naples, spread the use of arched vaulting and façades flanked by turrets in part of southern Italy.

Duomo, Siena

Arnolfo di Cambio, the architect and sculptor, was influenced by both these traditions. He worked mainly in Florence and Rome.

In the 14C the Cathedral of Genoa and the huge unfinished Duomo at Siena were derived from Burgundian art, but in the 15C the great Church of St Petronius at Bologna and the gigantic and florid Milan Cathedral marked the end of a style for which the Italians never showed much enthusiasm.

There was more originality in civil architecture of the Gothic period. Numerous prosperous towns chose to show their civic pride by embellishing their city centres with municipal palaces and loggias. In Venice *(see above)* the ornate Gothic style relieved bare façades with window openings and loggias. Venetian Gothic was to persist until the late 15C.

The **Pisano** family from Pisa gave a decisive impetus to the art of **sculpture** by combining their continued use of ancient traditions (Nicola) and their vigorously expressive realism (Giovanni). These masters influenced the Sienese **Tino di Camaino** and the Florentines **Andrea Orcagna** and **Arnolfo di Cambio** with their new iconography and ambitious projects for pulpits and funerary monuments, all of which exhibited the new humanism.

The painted Crucifixes in relief which appeared in the 12C were the first specimens of Italian painting. Gradually the hieratic tradition inherited from Byzantine art lost its extreme rigidity. In the 13C a Roman, **Pietro Cavallini**, executed frescoes and mosaics with a greater breadth of style reminiscent of antique art. His Florentine contemporary, **Cimabue** (1240-1302) adorned the Upper Basilica of Assisi with frescoes displaying a new sense of pathos. This new approach influenced **Giotto** (1266-1337) who revolutionised painting by introducing naturalism into his works: movement, depth and atmosphere were indicated or suggested, and emotion came to light in the frescoes at Assisi, Padua and Florence.

In Siena at the same time **Duccio**'s (born c1260) work still showed a strong Byzantine influence. He founded the Siena school which continued to employ a graceful linear technique and show a pronounced taste for the decorative use of colour. Some of the most delicate exponents of this school were **Simone Martini** and the brothers, **Pietro** and **Ambrogio Lorenzetti**. A famous school of miniaturists was founded at Rimini.

The leaders of the Florentine Trecento period (14C) were **Andrea Orcagna** and **Andrea di Bonaiuto**, known also as **Andrea da Firenze**. Their mystical and realistic style became known as **International Gothic**, which is characterised by harmonies of line and colour as well as a great refinement in the decorative elements. Several artists of the Marches, Umbria, Lombardy and Piedmont, such as **Allegretto Nuzi** and **Gentile da Fabriano**, worked in this style, as did the Veronese, Stefano da Zevio and **Pisanello** (15C) a portraitist, animal painter and distinguished medallist *(see VERONA)*, as well as the Piedmontese Giacomo Jaquerio.

ITALIAN RENAISSANCE PAINTERS

(13 C)

| SIENESE SCHOOL | SCHOOL OF ROME | FLORENTINE SCHOOL |

Pietro Cavallini

Jacopo Torriti ■   ■ Cimabue

DUCCIO ■

GIOTTO ■

TRECENTO (14 C)

Ambrogio Lorenzetti ■

Simone Martini ■

Pietro Lorenzetti ■

Lippo Memmi ■

Traini ■   **Andrea Orcagna** ■

Taddeo Gaddi

Bernardo Daddi ■

Mino del Pellicciaio ■

| UMBRIAN SCHOOL |

| ASSISI |

Giovanni da Milano

Antonio Veneziano ■

Giottino ■

Agnolo Gaddi

Andrea da Firenze ■ →

Bartolo di Fredi ■
Paolo di Giovanni ■

Andrea Vanni ■

Allegretto Nuzi
(International Gothic) ■

Ottaviano Nelli ■

Spinello Aretino ■

N. di Pietro Gerini ■

Taddeo di Bartolo ■

Gentile da Fabriano ■

Lorenzo Monaco ■

Masolino ■

Donatello
(Sculptor) ■   **MASACCIO**

QUATTROCENTO (15 C)

Domenico di Bartolo ■

FRA ANGELICO ■

Neri di Bicci ■

Sassetta ■

| PERUGIA |

Giovanni Boccati ■

Andrea del Castagno ■

Domenico Veneziano ■

Fra Filippo Lippi ■

Lorenzo Vecchietta ■

Matteo da Gualdo ■

Giovanni di Paolo ■

Sano di Pietro ■

Piero della Francesca ■

Paolo Uccello ■
Antonio Pollaiolo ■

Pesellino ■

Baldovinetti ■

Benedetto Bonfigli ■

Niccolò da Foligno ■

Benozzo Gozzoli ■

Piero Pollaiolo

Cosimo Rosselli ■

Matteo di Giovanni ■

Fiorenzo di Lorenzo ■

Melozzo da Forlì ■

Verrocchio ■

D. Ghirlandaio ■

Francesco di Giorgio Martini ■

Giovanni Santi ■

Pinturicchio ■

Signorelli ■

BOTTICELLI ■

Lorenzo di Credi ■

Filippino Lippi ■

Piero di Cosimo ■

Benvenuto di Giovanni ■

Lo Spagna ■

Perugino ■

Palmezzano ■

LEONARDO DA VINCI ■

Fra Bartolomeo ■

CINQUECENTO (16 C)

Baldassarre Peruzzi ■

RAPHAEL ■

Perino del Vaga ■

Solario ■

Boltraffio ■

Andrea del Sarto ■

MICHELANGELO ■

Sodoma ■
(School of Milan)

Giovanni da Udine ■

Giulio Romano ■

Il Primaticcio ■

| SCHOOL OF MILAN |

Rosso Fiorentino ■

Pontormo ■

Beccafumi ■

Sodoma ■   ■ Bernardino Luini

Gaudenzio Ferrari ■

Bronzino ■

| FONTAINEBLEAU SCHOOL |

QUATTROCENTO (15C)

The early Renaissance was characterised by an abiding passion for antiquity and distant lands, the well-organised city-states governed by a noble or princely patron, a new vision of man's place at the centre of the universe, and a large number of artists, scholars and poets. The Medici city of Florence united all these conditions and it was an appropriate birthplace for this cultural movement, designated much later as the Renaissance.

Architecture – **Filippo Brunelleschi** (1377-1446) revealed himself as a great innovator in the art of building. Drawing on antique sources he advocated a purity and elegance of line. Among his disciples were **Michelozzo** (1396-1472) **Leon Battista Alberti**, Antonio and Bernardo Rossellino, Giuliano and Benedetto da Maiano, as were Francesco di Giorgio Martini in Siena and Luciano Laurana at Urbino.

Sculpture – In the design of the doorways of the Baptistery at Florence, **Lorenzo Ghiberti** (1378-1455) shook off the Gothic tradition, still followed by the Sienese **Jacopo della Quercia**, who like Brunelleschi was eliminated from the competition.

The most powerful sculptor of the period was undoubtedly **Donatello** (1386-1466) who, although a Florentine, worked throughout Italy. His contemporary **Luca della Robbia** (1400-82) specialised in coloured and glazed terracotta works, while Agostino di Duccio, Desiderio da Settignano and Mino da Fiesole continued in the Donatello tradition. At the end of the Quattrocento, **Verrocchio** (1435-88) showed remarkable power in the famous statue of Colleoni at Venice. The most remarkable sculptor

Annunciation
by Donatello, Firenze

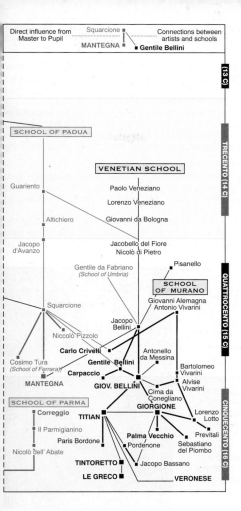

Legend:
Direct influence from Master to Pupil | Squarcione — Connections between artists and schools
MANTEGNA ■ ■ Gentile Bellini

(13 C)

TRECENTO (14 C)

SCHOOL OF PADUA

VENETIAN SCHOOL

Guariento

Paolo Veneziano
Lorenzo Veneziano

Altichiero

Giovanni da Bologna

Jacopo d'Avanzo

Jacobello del Fiore
Nicolò di Pietro

Gentile da Fabriano
(School of Umbria)

Pisanello

QUATTROCENTO (15 C)

SCHOOL OF MURANO

Squarcione

Giovanni Alemagna
Antonio Vivarini

Jacopo Bellini

Niccolò Pizzolo

Carlo Crivelli

Antonello da Messina

Cosimo Tura
(School of Ferrara)

Gentile Bellini

Bartolomeo Vivarini

Carpaccio

MANTEGNA

GIOV. BELLINI

Alvise Vivarini

Cima da Conegliano

SCHOOL OF PARMA

GIORGIONE

CINQUECENTO (16 C)

Correggio

Lorenzo Lotto

Il Parmigianino

TITIAN

Palma Vecchio

Previtali

Paris Bordone

Pordenone

Sebastiano del Piombo

Nicolò dell' Abate

TINTORETTO ■

Jacopo Bassano

LE GRECO ■

VERONESE

---

outside Florence was the Dalmatian, **Francesco Laurana**, a sculptural portraitist of the greatest sensibility.

Painting – With **Masaccio** (1401-28), a new era opened for Italian art. He was the first to insist, in the Carmine frescoes in Florence *(see FIRENZE)*, on an illusion of perspective and the notion of space. **Paolo Uccello** (1397-1475) made clever use of foreshortening in his admirable battle scenes. At the same time the Dominican friar, **Fra Angelico** (1387-1435), who remained very attached to Gothic tradition, was attracted to the new theories of the Renaissance.

His successors such as **Domenico Veneziano** and **Fra Filippo Lippi** (1406-69) developed his technique while retaining his delicacy of detail. **Benozzo Gozzoli** (1420-97) also recalls Angelico but adapts his style to the portrayal of brilliant festivities, always purely secular.

No one has produced better than **Sandro Botticelli** (1444-1510), a pupil of Filippo Lippi, that miraculous purity of line which gives a graceful and almost unreal fragility to the figures and a deep sense of mystery to his allegorical scenes. Baldovinetti (1423-57) adopted Botticelli's manner while **Andrea del Castagno** (1423-57) emphasised modelling and monumental qualities *(see FIRENZE)*. **Domenico Ghirlandaio** (1449-94) on the other hand had a particularly good gift for narrative painting.

The work of **Piero della Francesca** (c1415-92) from Sansepolcro is a supreme example of Tuscan Renaissance art displaying faultless harmony and sure draughtsmanship *(see AREZZO)*. He influenced other artists such as Melozzo da Forlì.

At the Gonzaga court in Mantua, **Mantegna** (1431-1506) painted scenes full of grandeur and rigour. In Ferrara **Cosimo Tura** with his realism inherited from northern painters, created his troublingly strange but original compositions.

The first Venetian painters to emerge from the Byzantine style were the **Vivarini**. It was however the **Bellini** family *(see VENEZIA)* which gave Venetian painting its outstanding characteristic of luminosity. **Carpaccio** *(see VENEZIA)* and the elegant but somewhat precious artist, **Carlo Crivelli**, with his minutely detailed drawings and refined colours, are both chroniclers.

CINQUECENTO (16C)

The 16C saw the development of human sensibility which had already marked the previous century. Artists were attracted more and more by antiquity, mythology and the discovery of man.

The artistic centre of the Renaissance moved from Florence to Rome where the popes rivalled one another to embellish palaces and churches. The artist became more independent and acquired a certain prestige.

By the end of the century, the canons of Renaissance art were already being exported and put into practice elsewhere in Europe, notably at Fontainebleau and in the Low Countries.

Architecture – It was in the course of this century that the style of the Florentine palace was formed. The imposing rustication and elaborate cornices were replaced by a less massive appearance with a strong classical influence.

Bramante (1444-1514) invented the "rhythmic façade". He worked at Milan then Urbino before conceiving the original central plan of St Peter's in Rome. **Vignola** (1507-73) also worked in Rome and **Palladio** (1508-80) did much in Vicenza *(see VICENZA).* In his important works on architecture he advocated the Classicism of ancient art and was himself responsible for many churches, palaces and luxury villas in Venetia.

Sculpture – **Michelangelo** (1475-1564) did most of his life's work in either Florence or Rome and was the most outstanding character of the century owing to his creative, idealist and even troubled genius which found its expression in such works as David, Moses or the groups of slaves for the tomb of Julius II.
His contemporaries paled beside him: neither the elegant and refined **Benvenuto Cellini** (1500-71), a skilled goldsmith and able sculptor known for his Perseus now in Florence, nor the powerful sculptor **Giambologna** or **Giovanni Bologna** (1529-1608) of Flemish origin and author of numerous group sculptures, bore comparison with the master Michelangelo.

Painting – The 16C is an important period for painting with numerous outstanding artists producing works in the new humanist vein in several centres throughout Italy (Rome at first, then Venice, Mantua and finally Parma) and France.
The century began with exceptional but complementary masters. The fascinating **Leonardo da Vinci** (1452-1519) was the archetype of the enquiring mind of the new humanists. He is famous in painting for his *sfumato* (literally mist), a sort of impalpable, luminous veil which created an impression of distance between persons and things. After having worked in Florence and Milan he went to France at the behest of that Renaissance prince, François I. **Raphael** (1483-1520) was not only a prodigious portraitist and painter of gently drawn madonnas, but also a highly inventive decorator with an exceptional mastery of composition which was given free rein in the Stanze of the Vatican. **Michelangelo** (1475-1564), the last of the three great men, although he was really a sculptor, took on the formidable task of decorating the ceiling of the Sistine Chapel where his skill with relief and his power are triumphant. His powerful figures are the origins of Roman Mannerism.
In addition there was **Andrea del Sarto** and the portraitist **Bronzino** at Florence, **Sodoma** at Siena, **Correggio** at Parma, **Bernardino Luini** at Milan etc. The 16C Venetian school produced many great colourists. **Giorgione** had a wonderful sense of landscape and atmosphere. **Titian** (c1490-1576), a disciple of Bellini, was as a youth influenced by Giorgione and imbued with his skill for

Lady with a Veil by Raphael
(Palazzo Pitti, Firenze)

both mythological and religious compositions. He was also a fine portraitist and was commissioned by numerous Italian princes and European sovereigns. His work is the high point in Venetian painting. **Tintoretto** (1518-94) added a tormented violence to the luminosity of his predecessors, and ably exploited this in his dramatic religious compositions. He had a strong influence on his amiable pupil, the Cretan, Theotocopoulos, known as **El Greco**, who finally took refuge in Toledo. **Veronese** (1528-88) was first and foremost a decorator in love with luxury and sumptuous schemes who delighted in crowd scenes with grandiose architectural backgrounds. As for the very endearing **Jacopo Bassano** (1518-92), he handled rustic and nocturnal scenes with a freedom of touch and composition.

MANNERISM (16C-17C)

The art of the Counter-Reformation, with its continued use of Renaissance canon often in an exaggerated or mannered way, marked the transition between Renaissance and baroque. If Mannerism was widely adopted throughout Europe it was countered in Italy by the opposition of the Roman Catholic Church, which following the Council of Trent proposed the purging of religious art. The Counter-Reformation movement was characterised in the domain of architecture by the Church of Gesù in Rome, an austere work by Vignola. The numerous fountains and gardens where the natural and artificial were found side by side are also expressions of the Mannerist taste for festivities and frivolities.
The art of the period shows a certain elongation of the figures, unusual attitudes and rather violent light, factors which would seem to translate a certain anxiety and impatience in the artists of the time. The main exponents include **Beccafumi**, **Pontormo** (1494-1556), **Rosso Fiorentino** (1494-1540), **Parmigianino** *(see PARMA)*, Giulio Romano, Niccolò dell'Abbate, and the Zuccaro brothers.

BAROQUE (17C-18C)

Painting – In reaction against Mannerism, a group of Bolognese artists founded the Academy of the Eclectic (Incamminati), under the leadership of the **Carracci** family (Annibale, the most original, Lodovico and Agostino). They tried to codify beauty in large, careful but rather cold compositions which paved the way for baroque art. Their Bolognese followers, Guido, Albano and Guercino, continued in this manner with rather more vigour. However it was the work of **Caravaggio** (1573-1610) which revolutionised several centuries of Italian idealism. His intense and often cruel realism drew its inspiration from everyday life in Rome. His unusual use of contrasting light gave a dramatic visual impact to his work. He was widely imitated both in Italy and in France and was without doubt the most influential artist in 17C Europe.

The characteristics of baroque art and architecture are effects of movement, inverted perspectives, *trompe-l'œil*, and scrolls. Often painting and architecture were associated, giving sumptuous interior decoration schemes such as Andrea Pozzo's work in Sant'Ignazio in Rome. Rome was the main centre of this movement but other exponents worked in Florence **(Luca Giordano)**, Venice **(Tiepolo)** and Naples (Giordano again, **Mattia Preti** and **Ribera)**.

During the 18C, Venetian painting became more serene with **Pietro Longhi, Canaletto** and **Francesco Guardi**.

Architecture and sculpture – The Gesù Church built in 1568 in Rome became the prototype of baroque churches. Under the sway of the **Jesuits** architecture and sculpture gained an ornate and theatrical quality with architects such as **Carlo Maderno**, who designed the façade of St Peter's (1614) in Rome; **Borromini**, a tormented spirit, who built the elliptical Church of St Charles by the Four Fountains in Rome; and especially **Bernini** (1598-1680), the most creative of them all, who designed the colonnades of St Peter's Square, the unusual baldachin and the tombs inside the basilica as well as many sculptures and fountains.

In Piedmont baroque architecture evolved in an interesting way with Guarini and **Juvara**. This was also the case in Apulia (especially in Lecce) and in Sicily where buildings were decorated with great fantasy and ornateness under the influence of the Spanish Plataresque style.

MODERN ART

In the late 18C and early 19C the vogue for all things Classical spread throughout Italy and all over Europe. The Italian neo-classical style is exemplified by the sculptor **Antonio Canova** (1757-1822) whose statue of Pauline Borghese, now in Rome, displays purity of line and rather cold elegance. The 19C makes a clean break with the creative richness of previous centuries.

In the field of architecture, Alessandro Antonelli (1798-1888) adopted the neo-classical idiom for the curious buildings which he designed for Milan and his native town, Novara.

As regards painting, the **Macchiaioli** group, founded in 1855, started a revolt against academism, which was to last about 20 years. The group, who were also known as the "spotters" and were the precursors of the Impressionist school, often worked outdoors, used colour and simple lines and drew inspiration from nature. The main exponents of this movement were **Giovanni Fattori** (1825-1908), Silvestro Lega and Telemaco Signorini (1835-1901). The last named travelled widely in Britain and was known for his street scenes of Edinburgh and London. Three artists worked with the Impressionists in Paris: the society painters De Nittis and Boldoni, and Zandomenighi who benefited most from his stay in the French capital. At

Brawl in the Galleria by Boccioni (Pinacoteca di Brera, Milano)

Alinari/GIRAUDON

39

the end of the 19C **Segantini**, the leader of the divisionist school, ensured the transition into the 20C. The 20C began in an explosive manner with the sensational and anti-aesthetic style of the **Futurists**, who under the leadership of the poet Marinetti, the movement's theorist, proclaimed their belief in the age of speed, crowds and machinery. They attempt to render the dynamism of the modern world often by fragmented forms similar to the cubist style but with a marked difference in the strong and vibrant colour combinations. The members of this avant-garde movement were: Boccioni, Balla, Severini, **Carrà** (who later joined the surrealists) and the architect Sant'Elia. **Giorgio de Chirico** created metaphysical painting, **Modigliani** outlined all his figures, while Giorgio Morandi painted still-lifes of everyday objects on a table which are conducive to meditation.

Contemporary sculptors include Arturo Martini who paved the way for dramatic simplicity and a return to archaic art; his followers were Marino Marini who adopted a less passionate but angular style and **Giacomo Manzù** who showed deeper feeling. There are many famous names in architecture: Pier Luigi Nervi, a pioneer in the use of reinforced concrete, and Gio Ponti who embraced rationalism. Finally the interior designers Carlo Scarpa and Gae Aulenti are renowned on the international scene.

Literature

Birth and splendour of Italian literature – The Italian language acquired a literary form in the 13C. At Assisi **St Francis** (1182-1226) wrote his *Canticle of the Creatures* in the vernacular instead of the traditional Latin, so that the people could read the word of God. The 13C also gave rise to the **Sicilian School** which, at the court of Frederick II, developed a language of love inspired by traditional ballads from Provence. The most famous of the 13C schools of poetry was, however, the **dolce stile nuovo**: followers included Guinezzelli and Cavalcanti. The term was appropriated by **Dante Alighieri** (1265-1321) indicating the lyrical quality of the poetry which would sing of spiritual love in verse. It was with this new tool that he wrote one of the most powerful masterpieces of Italian literature: the *Divine Comedy* is the account of a lively, enquiring and impassioned visitor to *Inferno, Purgatorio* and *Paradiso*. It is also an epic account of the Christianised Western world and the height of spiritual knowledge of the period. During the 14C **Petrarch** (1304-1375), the precursor of humanism and the greatest Italian lyrical poet *(see PADOVA)*, and his friend **Boccaccio** (1313-1375), the astonishing storyteller who seems almost modern at times *(see SAN GIMIGNANO: Certaldo)*, continued in the tradition of Dante. Each enriched the Italian language in his own way.

Petrarch in the Sonnets of the *Canzoniere* brought a fluidity and depth of psychological interrogation inspired by his love for Laura, while Boccaccio in his *Decameron* added a liveliness of narration and accuracy of description to the 100 tales of chivalry.

Humanism and Renaissance – Florentine humanism reinterpreted the ancient heritage and invented a scholarly poetry in which the tension of the words and images reflected the aspiration of the soul to attain an ideal. **Politian, Lorenzo de' Medici** (1449-1492) and especially **Michelangelo** were exponents of the Neo-Platonic notion of ideal poetry. However the Florentine Renaissance also favoured the development of other quite different lines of thought: scientific with Leonardo da Vinci, theorist with Leon Battista Alberti, philosophical with Marsile Fincin and encyclopaedic with the fascinating personality of Pico della Mirandola. Later Giorgio Vasari *(see FIRENZE)* became the first-ever art historian.

In the 16C writers and poets perfected the Italian language to a height of refinement and elegance rarely attained, and all this in the service of princes whom they counselled or entertained. The most famous was **Machiavelli** (1469-1527) *(see Index)*, the statesman and political theorist whose name now symbolises cunning and duplicity. In his work entitled **The Prince** he defined with clarity and intelligence the processes which control the society of man, and the moral and political consequences of these relationships.

At the court in Ferrara, Boiardo (1441-94) fused the epic and courtly genres in the poem celebrating chivalry, *Orlando Inamorato (Roland in love)*. **Ariosto** (1475-1533) and **Tasso** (1544-95) provided an element of intellectual brilliance. The former wrote *Orlando Furioso (Roland the Mad)*, an epic poem in episodes which enjoyed an extraordinary vogue, and Tasso, his successor at court in this genre, published his *Jerusalem Delivered (Gerusalemme Liberata)*.

At Urbino, Baldassare Castiglione (1478-1529) was the author of one of the great works of the period *The Courtier (Il cortegiano)* which was read throughout Europe. In Venice, Aretino (1492-1556) sketched the implacable portrait of his contemporaries *(Letters)* while in Padua, Ruzzante (1502-42) favoured realism in the local dialect.

The Counter-Reformation and the Baroque period – After the discovery of America in 1492, an event which affected the Mediterranean economy adversely, and the death of Lorenzo de' Medici, the 17C to the early 18C marked a period of decadence for Italian literature. The exception was **Galileo** (1564-1642), a scientist, who demonstrated that while divine laws are presented as allegories in the Bible, the laws of mathematics ruling the physical world could not be dismissed. He was implacably opposed by the Church in an attempt to reassert its influence under the onslaught of the Reformation. The fear of the Inquisition hampered original thought and favoured the development of Baroque poetical concepts in a quest for fantasy.

The Age of Enlightenment and Romanticism – The early 18C was marked by Arcadia, a literary academy which preached "good taste" inspired by the purity of classical bucolic poetry, in opposition to the "bad taste" of the Baroque period. The philosopher **Giambattista Vico** (1668-1744) elaborated the theory of the ebb and flow of history based on three stages (sense, imagination and reason). The dramatist **Metastasio** (1698-1783) was also a leading figure of the period whose exiting yet well-thought out vision advanced scientific and philosophical thought. In Venice, the 18C was dominated by the dramatist **Carlo Goldoni** (1707-93), known as the Italian Molière, who peopled his plays in an amusing, alert and subtle manner with the stock characters and situations of the *Commedia dell'Arte (see BERGAMO)*, an art form which was then highly popular in Venice.

From the end of the 18C writers began to express a new national spirit consciousness which developed until the upheaval of the Risorgimento). **Giuseppe Parini** (1729-99), a didactic writer, and **Vittorio Alfieri** (1749-1803) who became known for his tragedies on the themes of liberty and opposition to tyranny, were the precursors of the violent and tormented **Ugo Foscolo** (1778-1827) whose patriotic pride is given full vent in *Of the Sepulchres.* In his later works Foscolo adopted the literary genre of Richardson, Rousseau, Goethe and Gray.

It was **Giacomo Leopardi** (1798-1837) who in some of the finest poems of his verse collection *Canzoni* expresses with a certain lucidity and lyrical purity the growing gulf between the old faith and a fear of the unknown future. He was the main exponent of Italian romanticism and of the theory of historical pessimism based on the contrast between a happy natural state and Reason (or civilisation) which brings unhappiness. This was followed by cosmic pessimism which posits the condemnation of Nature and unhappiness as an intrinsic human condition.

The Milanese author, **Alessandro Manzoni** (1785-1873), wrote one of the most important novels of 19C Italian literature, *The Betrothed (I promessi sposi)*, a grandiose epic of ordinary folk based on the notion of providence in human existence.

Realism and Decadence – The Sicilian **Giovanni Verga** (1840-1922) assured the transition between the 19C and 20C with his novels. He was one of the most important members of the Italian realist *(verismo)* school of novelists which took its inspiration from the French naturalist movement. In his extravagant fiction series entitled *Vinti* he presents his pessimistic vision of the world and his compassion for the disinherited.

In the field of lyrical poetry in the second half of the 19C **Giosuè Carducci** (1835-1907), a Nobel prize winner, drew inspiration from Classical poetry. He was a melancholy figure who criticised the sentimentality of the romantic movement. **Grabriele d'Annunzio** (1863-1938) adopted a refined and precious style to express his sensual love of language. The complex and anxious voice of the poet **Giovanni Pascoli** (1855-1912) filled the early years of the century. His nostalgic poetry recalls the age of innocence and a sense of wonder.

Modern and contemporary authors – In the early 20C, magazines devoted to political, cultural, moral and literary themes were published. Giuseppe Prezzolini (1882-1982) and Giovanni Papini (1881-1956) were among the contributors.

Futurism, which influenced other forms of artistic expression, was the most important of the contemporary literary movements. Tommaso Marinetti, the leader and theoretician of the movement, exalted the attractions of speed, war and feverish insomnia" in his *Manifesto* (1909).

In line with the European sensibility expressed by Musil, Kafka, Proust and Joyce, Italian letters favoured the theme of discovery which was influenced by studies on repression and the unconscious in the early years of psychoanalysis. In *Zeno's Conscience*, **Italo Svevo** (1861-1928) examines the alienation of the main protagonist as past and present unfold in a long internal monologue. The Sicilian dramatist **Luigi Pirandello** (1867-1936) also analyses man's tragic solitude and the way in which the identity of the individual is eclipsed by the perceptions of the different persons with whom he associates. The only escape is madness.

The evocative and intense verses of **Giuseppe Ungaretti** (1888-1970) represent a significant departure from D'Annunzio's idiom. The poetry of **Eugenio Montale** (1896-1981) relates the anguish which afflicts human nature.

The **Hermetic Movement** was influenced by both Ungaretti and Montale (1896-1981): man achieves a precarious balance between the real world which is in disarray and his dreams of happiness. **Salvatore Quasimodo** (1901-68) was its leading figure; his translations of Greek and Latin classical literature and of Shakespeare were very successful.

After the Second World War, **Neo-Realism** – which was ideally suited to the cinema with its popular appeal – gave a graphic account of the life and misery of the working class, of peasants and street children.

The recurring themes in the works of **Cesare Pavese** (1908-1950) are the loneliness and difficulty of existing, described with anguish in his diary which was published posthumously with the title *This Business of Living*.

During recent decades the Italian novel has shown a strong vitality with such diverse personalities as Pratolini *(A Tale of Poor Lovers)*, Guido Piovene *(Pietà contro pietà)*, Ignazio Silone *(Fontarama)*, Mario Soldati *(A cena col commendatore)*, Carlo Levi *(Christ stopped at Eboli)* and Elsa Morante *(Arthur's Island)*.

Alberto Moravia

In recent years, a handful of Italian authors have achieved international fame: **Alberto Moravia** (1907-1990) is regarded as a significant narrator of contemporary Italy identifying the importance of such issues as sex and money. His book, *The Time of Indifference*, recounts the decline and forbearance of a bourgeois Roman family. **Pier Paolo Pasolini** (1922-1975) provoked and contested the received ideas of his time, contrasting Marxist ideology with Christian and peasant values. Another well-known neo-realist author was **Italo Calvino** (1923-1985) who wrote short stories tinged with subtle irony.

Leonardo Sciascia (1921-1989) concentrated on revealing some of the ills of Italian society, such as the Mafia. He wrote essays, detective stories, historical memoirs and romantic surveys.

Dino Buzzati (1906-72), an original figure, was a poet, writer, illustrator and journalist. His penchant for fantasy and surrealism is tinged with scepticism and is reminiscent of Kafka and Poe.

Music

Italy has played a significant role in the evolution of music with the invention of the musical scale and the development of the violin. It is the birthplace of Vivaldi who inspired Bach and in the late 19C Verdi created operatic works to celebrate the Risorgimento.

Great composers and musical composition – As early as the end of the 10C, a Benedictine monk, **Guido Monaco** of Arezzo, invented the scale naming the notes with the initial syllables of the first lines of John the Baptist's hymn *(1)*.

In the 16C, the golden age of vocal polyphony which was then very popular was marked by **Giovanni Pierluigi da Palestrina**, a prolific composer of essentially religious music (105 masses). During that period, Andrea Gabrielli (c1510-86) and his nephew Giovanni who were the organists at St Mark's in Venice were masters of sacred and secular polyphonic music. The latter composed the first violin sonatas.

Instrumental music from the Baroque period to the 18C – It was only in the 17C and 18C that a proper musical school (for operatic as well as instrumental works) was born in Italy which was characterised by charm and freshness of inspiration and melodic talent. The old and new musical forms evolved with the expressive and stylistic innovations of **Frescobaldi** (1583-1643) for the organ and harpsichord, **Corelli** (1653-1713) for the violin – the great Cremona violin-makers perfected the art of instrument-making – and **Domenico Scarlatti** (1685-1757) for the harpsichord. The talented Venetian, **Vivaldi** (1675-1741), composed a wealth of lively music greatly admired by Bach, particularly his concertos divided into three parts, *allegro/adagio/allegro* and with descriptive interludes as in the *Four Seasons*. Baldassare Galuppi (1706-85), a native of Burano near Venice composed the music for the librettos of Goldoni as well as sonatas for harpsichord with a lively tempo. Although Venice was in its final period of glory, her musical reputation grew with the **Marcello** brothers, Benedetto (1686-1739) and Alessandro (1684-1750). The latter composed a famous concerto for oboe, stringed instruments and organ with a splendid adagio. The instrumental compositions of **Tomaso Albinoni** (1671-1750) are reminiscent of Vivaldi's masterpieces.

---

1) Ut queant laxis/Resonare fibris/Mira gestorum/Famuli tuorum/Solve polluti/Labreatum/Sancte Johannes.

In the 18C important Italian composers worked outside Italy. In the field of chamber music, Luigi Boccherini, a native of Lucca working in Spain, was famous for his melodies and minuets. He also wrote a powerful symphony, *The House of the Devil*.

Antonio Salieri (1750-1825) from the Veneto was an active composer and a famous tutor who taught Beethoven, Schubert and Liszt. Towards the end of his life, he became mentally disturbed and blamed himself for Mozart's death. This episode is the theme of the film *Amadeus* by Milos Forman (1984). The Piedmontese Giovanni Battista Viotti (1755-1824), Salieri's contemporary, enriched the violin repertory with 29 fine violin concertos. He lived in

Vivaldi

Paris and London and died after the failure of his wine business.

Although not a musician, **Lorenzo Da Ponte** deserves a mention for his poetic contribution to great musical works. His love of adventure took him not only to New York where he died but also to Vienna, Europe's musical capital at that time. He collaborated with Mozart and wrote librettos for *The Marriage of Figaro*, *Don Giovanni* and *Così fan tutte* which won him great fame.

This great period ended with the Romantic movement which is wonderfully celebrated by the great violinist **Niccolò Paganini** (1782-1840) although by that time the piano had become more popular than the violin. His adventurous life, genius of interpretation and legendary virtuosity as well as his slim, tall build turned him into a demonic figure. His most famous works include 24 **Capricci** and six concertos; the finale of the second concerto is the well-known *Campanella*.

Opera – Modern opera, which originated with **Monteverdi** (1607, *Orfeo*) who heralded a musical idiom combining words and music, was immediately very successful and became a popular pursuit which influenced the whole cultural scene in Italy.

At the end of the 17C, Neapolitan opera with **Alessandro Scarlatti** established the distinction between arias which highlight virtuoso singing and recitatives which are essential for the development of the action. In the 18C, **Pergolese**, **Cimarosa** and **Paisiello** were the leading composers of comic opera *(opera buffa)*, which is in a lighter vein and entirely sung.

In the 19C there were few great composers of instrumental music apart from Paganini, as lyrical art was made to reflect the intense passions of the Risorgimento. **Rossini** (1782-1868) marked the transition from the classical to the romantic period *(Othello, William Tell* and the comic operas *The Italian Girl in Algiers, The Thieving Magpie* and *The Barber of Seville)*. **Bellini** (1801-35) composed rather average orchestral music but admirable melodies which are successful as such *(La Somnambula, Norma)*. His rival **Gaetano Donizetti** (1797-1848) wrote several melodramas *(Lucia di Lammermoor)* where the action takes second place to the singing, as well as some charming comic operas: *L'Elisir d'Amore, Don Pasquale.* The greatest composer of the genre during the troubled period of the fight for independence from Austria was **Guiseppe Verdi** (1813-1901) with his dramatic yet romantic works: *Nabucco, Rigoletto, Il Trovatore, La Traviata, Aida* etc; he also wrote an admirable *Requiem*. The realist movement *(verismo)* then became popular, with Mascagni *(Cavalleria Rusticana)*, Leoncavallo *(I Pagliaci)*, and especially **Puccini** (1858-1924) whose *Tosca, Madame Butterfly, La Bohème* and other works crowned this lyrical era.

Modern music – In reaction, the next generation concentrated on orchestral music, like **Ottorino Respighi** (1879-1937) who composed symphonic poems *(The Fountains of Rome, The Pines of Rome, Roman festivals)*. 20C composers include Petrassi who explored all musical forms and **Dallapiccola** (1904-75), the leader of the dodecaphonic movement (the 12 notes of the scale are used) in Italy. The sensitive and passionate Luigi Nono (1924-90) is an exponent of serial music to express his political and liberating message; he wrote instrumental, orchestral, vocal and choral works.

La Scala c 1830

Venues and artists – The recent unification of the country accounts for the numerous and famous opera houses and concert halls: the prestigious Scala in Milan, for which Visconti created marvellous sets, the Rome Opera House, the San Carlo theatre in Naples, the Poncielli in Cremona, the Politeama in Palermo, the Fenice in Venice (destroyed by fire in January 1996), the Carlo Fenice in Genoa and the Regio and the modern Lingotto in Turin. In spring Florence hosts a renowned music festival, and in summer splendid performances are held in the amphitheatre at Verona and in Caracalla's Baths in Rome.

Among the great orchestras and chamber music groups, the Orchestra of the Accademia di Santa Cecilia in Rome, the Filarmonica of La Scala in Milan, the Solisti Veniti and the Orchestra of Padua and the Veneto are noteworthy.

Among the great Italian conductors, Arturo Toscanini was renowned for the verve and originality of his interpretations. Other famous names include De Sabata and nowadays, Claudio Abbado, Gian Carlo Giulini, Riccardo Muti, Guiseppe Sinopoli who perform all over the world. Artists of international reputation include the violinists Accoardo and Ughi, the pianists Campanella, Ciccolini, Lucchesini and Maria Tipo and the cellists Brunello and Filippini.

The famous singers Teresa Berganza, Bruson, Fiorenza Cossotto, Cecilia Gasdia, Katia Ricciarelli, Renata Scotto, Lucia Valentini Terrani as well as Ruggiero Raimondi and Luciano Pavarotti are worthy successors to La Malibran, Renata Tebaldi, Maria Callas, Caruso and Beniamino Gigli.

Cinema

Early years – The Italian cinema industry was born in Turin at the beginning of the 20C and grew rapidly (50 production companies in 1914) with great successes on the international scene. Film makers specialised first in historical epics, in the 1910s they turned to adventure films and in the 1930s to propaganda and escapist films subsidised by the State, which distracted spectators temporarily from the reality of the Fascist State.

Neo-Realism – In 1935 the Cinecittà studios and the experimental cinematographic centre which numbered Rossellini and De Santis among its pupils were founded in Rome.

During the years of Fascist rule the cinema had become divorced from real life and to bridge the gap film directors advocated a return to realism and close observation of daily life. The first major theme of **neo-realism** was the war and its aftermath. **Rossellini** denounced Nazi and Fascist oppression in *Rome Open City* and *Germany Year Zero*. **Vittorio De Sica**'s *Sciuscia* (1946) and *Bicycle Thieves* (1948) depicted the unemployment and misery of the post-war years. In *Bitter Rice* (1949) and *Bloody Easter* (1950) **De Santis** portrays the working class divided between the prevailing ideology and revolutionary ambitions.

Neo-realism ended in the early 1950s as it no longer satisfied the public who wanted to forget this bleak period, but its influence was still felt by future generations of film makers.

1960s to the present day – In the' 60s Italian cinema flourished and a large number of films (over 200 a year), generally of very high quality, was made with the support of a strong industrial infrastructure. Three great directors dominated this period.

Fellini (1920-1993) shot the hugely successful *La Strada (The Street)* in 1954 and *La Dolce Vita* in 1960. His fantasy world is reflected in the original camera work.

Antonioni (1912) made his debut in 1959 with *L'Avventura*, and his work *(The Red Desert*, 1960 and *Blow Up*, 1967) underlines the ultimate isolation of the individual.

Visconti (1906-1976) made *Rocco and his brothers* in 1960 and *The Leopard* in 1963. His films which are characterised by splendour and beauty examine closely the themes of impermanence, degradation and death.

During the same period a new generation of film makers made a political and social statement: Pasolini, Olmi, Rosi, Bertolucci and the Taviani brothers.

Cahiers du cinéma

Claudia Cardinale in Visconti's *The Leopard*

Italian cinema won great international success with several masterpieces until the mid-1970s: *Death in Venice* (1970) and *Ludwig* (1972) by Visconti; *Casanova* (1976) by Fellini, *The Passenger* (1974) by Antonioni; *L'Affare Mattei* (1971) by Rosi etc. Since the late 1970s the industry has been in a state of crisis, as it faces competition from television and the collapse of the market. However, some films made by famous directors have won acclaim: *The Night of San Lorenzo* (1982) by the Taviani brothers, *The Ball* (1983) by Ettore Scola, *The Last Emperor* (1987) by Bertolucci, *Cinema Paradiso* (1989) by Tornatore.

The younger generation of film makers (Nanni Moretti, Daniele Luchetti, Pupi Avati, Marco Risi) embraced realism and their protagonists are engaged in the social struggle. The story line is all important.

The main cinematic event in Italy is the Venice Film Festival (late August – early September) for the Golden Lion award which attracts film makers from all over the world.

Food and Wine

Italy is rich in tasty products and its cooking is among the best known in the world. A traditional meal consists of an **antipasto** or hors d'œuvre (raw vegetable salads with a dressing, fine pork-butchers' meats, pickled vegetables), **primo** *(primo piatto:* first course) rice or *pasta* in its numerous forms, plain or combined with various sauces and trimmings; **secundo** (meat or fish course) often accompanied by a **contorno** (vegetable or green salad). After the cheese **(formaggio)** fruit **(frutta)** is served as well as a choice of numerous other desserts: cakes, pastries and sweets **(dolci)**, ices **(gelati)** or frozen cakes **(semi-freddo)**. A young wine is usually served in 1/4 *(quarto)*, half *(mezzo)* or one litre *(litro)* carafes *(sfuso)*. Ask for a wine list if you prefer better quality wines. There is a wide choice of mineral waters available. Traditionally the meal ends with a strong, black espresso coffee. The frothy **cappuccino** dusted with cocoa is also delectable.

SOME REGIONAL SPECIALITIES

Piedmont – Cooking here is done with butter. A popular dish is **fonduta**, a melted cheese dip of milk, eggs and white truffles *(tartufi bianchi)*. *Cardi* (chards) are prepared *alla bagna cauda*, i.e. with a hot sauce containing oil or butter, anchovies, garlic and truffles. The region also produces excellent meat. Monferrato and the Langhe is also famous for its excellent cheese and delicious wines: **Barolo** (used for braising), Barbaresco, **Barbera**, Grignolino, red Freisas, white **Asti**, still or sparkling *(spumante)*, with a strong flavour of grapes.

Lombardy – Milan, where cooking is done with butter, gives its name to several dishes; *minestrone alla milanese*, a soup of green vegetables, rice and bacon; *risotto alla milanese*, rice cooked with saffron; **costoletta** *alla milanese*, a fillet of veal fried in egg and breadcrumbs with cheese; **osso buco**, a knuckle of veal with the marrow-bone. **Polenta**, maize semolina, is a staple food in traditional country cooking. The most popular cheese is the creamy **Gorgonzola**. **Panettone** is a large fruit cake containing raisins and candied lemon peel and **torrone** is a speciality of Cremona. Few wines are produced, apart from those of Valtellina or the Pavia district.

Veneto – As in the Po Plain, the people eat **polenta**, **risi e bisi** (rice and peas), and **fegato alla veneziana** (calf's liver fried with onions). The shellfish, eels and dried cod *(baccalà)* are excellent. Black sphagetti made with squid ink is a popular Venetian dish. **Pandoro**, a star-shaped cake delicately flavoured with orange-flower, is a speciality of Verona. The best wines come from the district of Verona; **Valpolicella** and **Bardolino**, *rosé* or red, perfumed and slightly sparkling, and **Soave**, which is white and strong.

Trentino-Alto Adige, Friuli-Venetia Giulia – In Alto-Adige, **canederli** is a type of gnocchi (dumplings) made with bread and flour served separately or in a broth. There are delicious pastries, in particular the **Strüdel** cake. Friuli is famous for pork-butchers' specialities (ham – **prosciutto di San Daniele**) and fish dishes (**scampi, grancevole** - spider crabs). White wines include Sylvaner and **Pinot Blanc** from Trentino, **Sauvignon** and **Tocai** from Friuli. Red Cabernet and Merlot wines are produced in Friuli, Pinot and Marzemino from Trentino-Alto Adige.

Black pasta

Liguria – The chief speciality of Genoa is **pesto**, a sauce made with olive oil, basil, pine-kernels, garlic and ewes' cheese. It is served with **trenette** (long, thin noodles) and lasagne (flat pasta leaves). The delicious sea-food includes **zuppa di datteri**, a shellfish soup from La Spezia, with which the Ligurians drink Cinqueterre or Pigato, strong white wines.

Emilia-Romagna – The region has a fine gastronomic reputation; its pork-butchers' meat is the most famous in Italy: Bologna **salami** and **mortadella**, Modena **zamponi** (pigs' trotters), Parma **prosciutto** (ham). *Pasta* is varied and tasty when served *alla bolognese* – that is, with a meat and tomato sauce. **Parmesan cheese** *(parmigiano)*, hard and pale yellow, is strong yet delicate in flavour. Emilia produces **Lambrusco**, a fruity, sparkling red wine, and white Albano.

Tuscany – This is where Italian cooking was born, at the court of the Medici. Florence offers its *alla fiorentina* specialities: dried cod **(baccalà)** with oil, garlic and pepper, **bistecca**, grilled steak fillets with oil, salt and pepper, **fagioli all'ucelletto** (beans with quails), or fagioli "al fiasco" with oil, onions and herbs cooked in a round bottle *(fiasco)* on a coal fire.

Leghorn produces **triglie** (red mullet) and **cacciucco** (fish soup) and Siena offers **panforte**, a cake containing almonds, honey and candied melon, orange and lemon. **Chianti** (both red and white) is the most popular wine but there are other notable red (**Brunello di Montalcino, Nobile di Montepulciano**) and white (**Vernaccia di San Gimignano**) wines.

Umbria, Marches – Norcia is the capital of Italian cuisine with the black truffles **(tartufo nero)** and pork dishes. The regional dish is the **porchetta**, a whole sucking pig roasted on the spit. One of the Marches specialities is *vincigrassi*, pasta cooked in the oven with a meat and cream sauce. The wines are white, including the famous **Orvieto** of Umbria, the Verdicchio of the Marches and the delicious Moscato of San Marino.

Chianti Rufina wine

M. Rock/CEPHAS-TOP

Lazio – There are many Roman specialities: **fettucine** or flat strips of pasta, **spaghetti all'amatriciana** (with a spicy sauce) or **alla carbonara** (with a creamy sauce), **gnocchi** alla Romana, **saltimbocca** (a fillet of veal rolled in ham and flavoured with sage, fried in butter and served with a Marsala sauce), and **abbacchio al forno** or roast lamb or *alla cacciatora* (with an anchovy sauce). Vegetables include *carciofi alla Giudia*, artichokes cooked in oil with garlic and parsley. **Pecorino**, ewes' milk cheese, and the famous white wines of Montefiascone and the **Castelli** (Frascati) will satisfy the most discerning gourmet.

Abruzzi, Molise – Among the *pasta* note **maccheroni alla chitarra**, made by hand and cut into strips. **Latticini** (fresh mountain cheeses) are popular.

Campania – Naples is the home of **spaghetti**, which is often prepared with shell-fish *(alle vongole)*. *Trattorie* and *pizzerie* serve *costata alla pizzaiola*, a fillet steak with tomatoes, garlic and wild marjoram, **mozzarella** *in carrozza* (cheese savoury) and especially the **pizza**, a cheese *(mozzarella)* tart topped with tomato and anchovy and flavoured with capers and wild marjoram. Wines from volcanic soil have a delicate, slightly sulphurous taste: red and white Capri, white Ischia, white **Lacryma Christi** and red Gragnano (Vesuvius wines).

Apulia, Basilicata, Calabria – The oysters *(ostriche)* of Taranto are tasty. The most original dish is **capretto ripieno al forno**, a roast kid stuffed with herbs.

Sicily – The island is rich in fruit (lemons, oranges, mandarins, olives, almonds), pastries and ices. The real Sicilian **cassata** is a partly-iced cream cake containing chocolate cream and candied fruits. Other specialities: **cuscusu** (couscous) and fish – tuna, swordfish, anchovies. The best-known wine is **Marsala**, which is dark and strong, but **Malvasia** and the white wines of Etna and Lipari are also delicious.

Sardinia – *See SARDINIA.*

Italy Today

Political and administrative organisation – The referendum of June 1946 set up the Republic and the Constitution of 1 January 1948, a Parliamentary Republic headed by a President who holds office for seven years, with two Houses of Parliament – the Chamber of Deputies and the Senate. Members of both houses are elected by universal suffrage.

The Italian State is unusual in that it is neither unitary nor federal. Political power is shared by two autonomous tiers: the State or central government and the regional councils. The latter are also chosen by the people and enjoy some legislative, administrative and financial powers. Their authority must not exceed those prescribed by the laws passed or approved at national level. The 1948 constitution established 20 regions, although it was not enacted until 1970. Five of these (Sicily, Sardinia, Trentino-Alto Adige, Friuli-Venezia Giulia and Valle d'Aosta) have a special statute and enjoy greater administrative autonomy. The regions are subdivided into 95 provinces, which are themselves composed of districts, each headed by a *Sindaco*.

The socio-political patterns in Italy are dominated by its pronounced regionalism, which is part of its heritage from the time when Italy was composed of a multitude of independent states whose capitals were constantly at war with one another.

Rome is essentially a residential city with a high percentage of civil servants, while Milan is the acknowledged economic capital, and Florence, Bologna and Padua the intellectual centres. The one-time State capitals of Turin, Genoa, Naples and Palermo are now important industrial centres. Venice retains its very own captivating character.

Economy – Far from being hampered by its illustrious past, Italy has transformed its essentially agricultural economy into that of an industrial power which is today one of the most active in Europe and ranks sixth in the world.

In addition to the traditional crops and stock raising, Italy has specialised in rice growing (Po Plain) and the production of **silk** (Lombardy and Venetia). Lacking in raw materials such as coal and iron ore, the Italian industrial sector has been geared to manufacturing industries where cheap labour is more important than raw materials. Italy has always been an important manufacturer of **motor vehicles** and small machines such as sewing machines, typewriters and other domestic appliances. One of its more unusual industries is the making of **pasta**, the national dish, in all its forms to meet both the home market and export requirements.

The southern part of the peninsula is an exception in that it remains economically underdeveloped. The **Mezzogiorno** (impoverished south) as it is known, extends southwards from a line joining the Gulf of Gaeta to the southern edge of the Abruzzi. The economic backwardness of this area has increased ever since the unification of Italy. In 1950 a special organisation and a fund were created to develop both the agricultural (agrarian reform with the subdividing of large estates, soil improvement, land reclamation and reafforestation) and industrial (creation of gigantic complexes often badly integrated, building of dams...) sectors of this area, which has a particularly small working population.

Press – As a general rule the press is decentralised, at least as regards daily newspapers. The Rome *La Repubblica*, the Turin *La Stampa* and the Milan *Il Corriere della Sera* as well as the most important financial daily the Milan *Il Sole 24 ore* are the only papers distributed all over Italy.

The Italian love of sport means that there are three sports dailies: the Milan *La Gazzetta dello Sport* and the Turin *Tuttosport* in the north, and the Rome *Il Corriere dello Sport-Stadio* in the south. In addition the weekly *Guerin Sportivo* has a national circulation.

Fashion – The Italians who are lively and passionate by nature show great fashion flair. Fashion shows are held at yearly intervals in Rome and Florence (Palazzo Pitti) but the fashion capital is undoubtedly Milan where every year the best ready-to-wear collection for women's fashion is awarded the Occhio d'Oro. Many great designers have salons in Milan: Armani, Versace, Gianfranco Ferré, Nicola Trussardi, Mila Schön, Laura Biagiotti, Romeo Gigli as well as the avant-garde stylists Krizia and Moschino. Valentino and the Fendi sisters have set up their operation in Rome. Fashion-related professions and products are part of one of the most successful industrial sectors in Italy.

The clothing industry is concentrated mainly in Lombardy, Venetia (Benetton and Stefanel for knitwear), Tuscany and Emilia-Romagna. Como is famous for silk wear, Prato and Biella for wool products, Florence for leather goods (Gucci) and Vicenza for jewellery.

The Italian way of life – The lively and colourful open-air markets offer an abundance of local produce. Shops which are closed for the mid-day siesta usually remain open late in the evening, especially in the seaside resorts and the south of the country. Italian fashion wear (shoes, clothes and leather goods) and handicrafts (ceramics, glassware, wood and leather work, jewellery, embroidery, fabrics etc) are generally elegant and well designed.

Italian men like to gather on the café terraces in the evening to discuss politics or sport, while the women, children and young people go for the traditional evening stroll *(passeggiata)* and enjoy a chat and ice cream *(gelato)*.

The various traditional festivals with numerous participants dressed in fine local costumes often attract large crowds *(see the Calendar of Events at the end of the guide)*.

J.-P. Langeland/DIAF

Arcades in Piazza della Repubblica, Florence

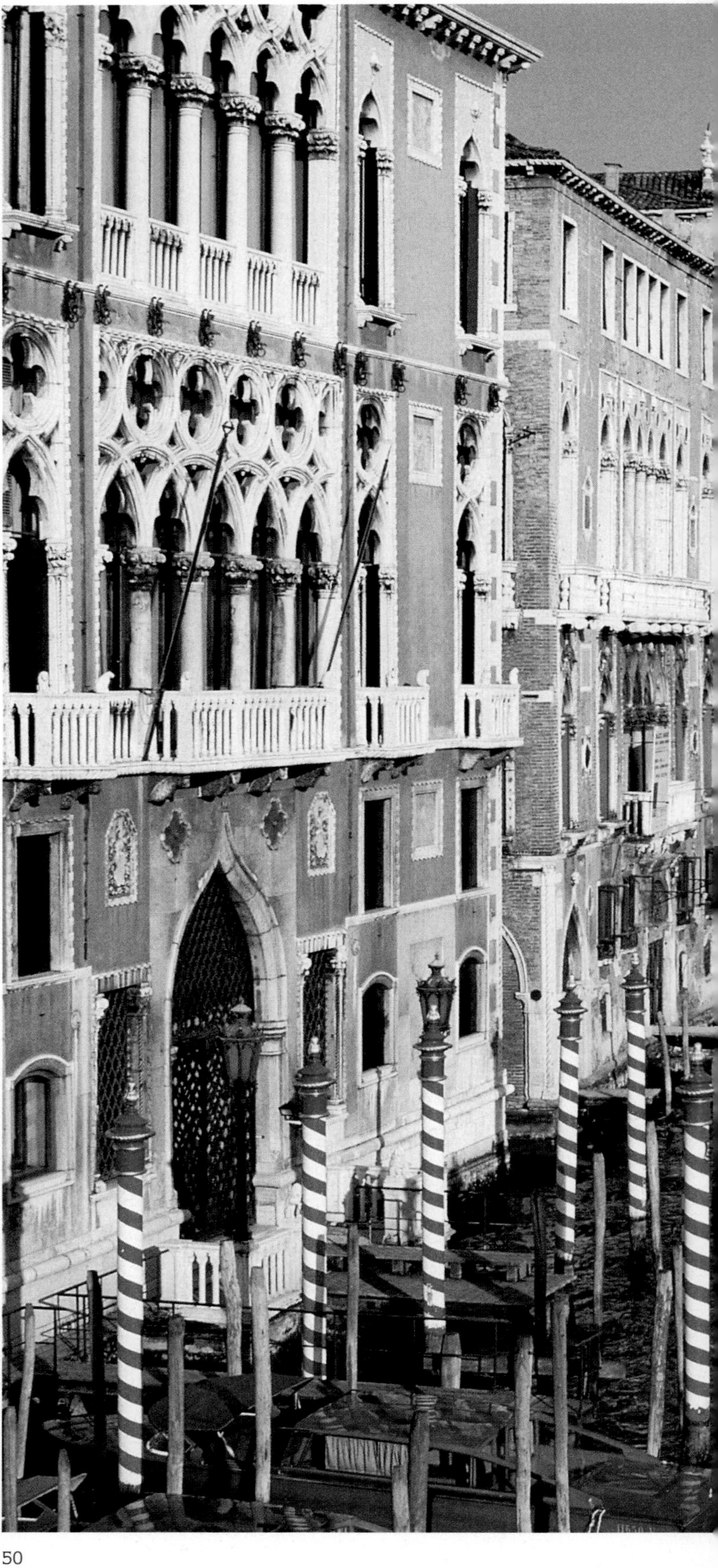

Canal Grande and Santa Maria della Salute, Venezia

Sights

Anne Gaël

Appennino ABRUZZESE★★★

Michelin map 988 folds 26 and 27 or 430 folds 27, 28, 38 and 39.

The Abruzzi Massif, the highest of the Apennine range, is an isolated region with a harsh climate; this has helped to preserve its beautiful landscapes and noble traditions. Bordered to the north by the formidable limestone barrier, the Gran Sasso, the massif which extends from L'Aquila to Sulmona and beyond to Alfedena and the Abruzzi National Park offers a varied landscape: gorges, sheer gullies, lakes, forests, desolate high plateaux and green pastures. In recent years winter sports facilities have proliferated and many resorts now cater for ski enthusiasts from the capital as there is a motorway link from Rome.

Sightseeing – The adjoining map locates the towns and sites described in the guide and also indicates other beauty spots in small black type.

★★ GRAN SASSO

From L'Aquila to Castelli *159km - 99 miles - allow half a day*

This is the highest massif in the Abruzzi and its main peak is **Corno Grande** (alt 2 912m - 9 560ft). On the northern side spines with many gullies slope away gently, while on the southern face Gran Sasso drops abruptly to the great glacial plateaux edged by deep valleys. The lush pastures and tree-covered slopes to the north contrast with the desolate and grandiose expanses to the south.

★ **L'Aquila** – *See L'AQUILA.*

Beyond Paganica the road passes through gorges and climbs to Fonte Cerreto.

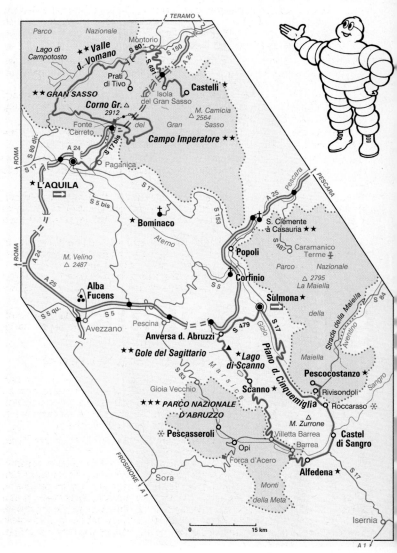

★★ **Campo Imperatore** ⊘ – *Take the road from Fonte Cerreto.* It passes through splendid mountain country grazed by large flocks of sheep or hordes of wild horses. It was from here that Mussolini escaped on 12 September 1943, in a daring raid by German airmen whose plane landed and took off near the hotel in which the Duce had been interned.

Return to Fonte Cerreto.

The road then skirts the lower slopes of the Gran Sasso, as it follows the long green valley, **Valle del Vomano★★**, before entering the magnificent gorges *(5km – 3 miles beyond Tintorale)* which have striking stratified rock walls.

On leaving Montorio, take the S491 to the right, the road to Isola del Gran Sasso.

★ **Castelli** – This town, which stands on a wooded promontory at the foot of Monte Camicia, has been famous since the 13C for its highly colourful and richly decorated faïence (glazed pottery).

GREAT PLATEAUX

Round tour leaving from Sulmona *138km – 86 miles – allow 1 day*

The Great Plateaux with their wide horizons stretch between Sulmona and Castel di Sangro, at a height of over 1 000m – 3 281ft. Cattle graze these expanses and their herdsmen make egg-shaped soft cheese *(scamorza)* which can be purchased at **Rivisondoli.**

★ **Sulmona** – *See SULMONA.*

Beyond, the road runs sometimes along a corniche, in a tunnel or over a viaduct, and leads to the largest of the Great Plateaux, **Piano dei Cinquemiglia**, so-called because it was five Roman miles long (8km – 5 miles).

Near the old village of Rivisondoli, take the S84 to the left.

★ **Pescocostanzo** – This attractive village with its paved streets and old houses is a flourishing craft centre specialising in wrought-iron work, copper, gold and woodwork as well as lace-making.

The Collegiate Church of **Santa Maria del Colle** ⊘ although built to a Renaissance plan has several Romanesque features and baroque additions (organ loft, ceiling and grille of the north aisle).

Castel di Sangro – The town dominates a mountain-rimmed basin. The cathedral, built to the plan of a Greek cross, has Renaissance porticoes.

★ **Alfedena** – The houses of this small town are grouped about the ruined castle. Paths lead northwards to the ancient city of Alfedena with its cyclopean walls and necropolis.

★ **Scanno** – From its high mountain site, Scanno overlooks the lovely Lake Scanno **(Lago di Scanno★)** formed by a landslide which blocked the bed of the river Sagittario. The steep and narrow streets of this attractive holiday resort are lined with old houses and churches.

Women still wear the black local dress which is probably of Oriental origin. In the main street stands a curious 14C fountain decorated in the Byzantine style. Between Lake Scanno and Anversa degli Abruzzi, over a distance of 10km – 6 miles the Sagittario River has hollowed from the grey rock a series of gorges **(Gole del Sagittario★★)** of impressive depth and wildness, which the road follows with many twists and turns.

Anversa degli Abruzzi – The village church has a doorway (dated 1540) with a carved tympanum depicting the Entombment and other sculptures of masks and Biblical figures.

★★★ **PARCO NAZIONALE D'ABRUZZO** (ABRUZZI NATIONAL PARK)

A nature reserve was founded in 1923 in the very heart of the massif to protect the fauna, flora and outstanding landscapes of the region. It extends over an area of approximately 40 000ha – 155sq miles comprising mostly forest (beech and sycamore); local fauna includes royal eagles, Apennine wolves, brown bears, Abruzzi chamois and wild cats and latterly roe deer and red deer.

Access and sightseeing ⊘ – Start either from Gioia Vecchio in the north, Forca d'Acero in the west or Villetta Barrea and Barrea in the east.

Within the confines of the park there are four different protection zones in operation allowing various types of activities, depending on conservation programmes. The visitor is however free to visit a large area of the park using the well-surfaced roads and tracks, and facilities include observation posts, camping and picnic sites as well as visitor centres. The only way to appreciate local fauna or flora is on foot or on horseback in some cases. It is advisable to keep to the signposted footpaths and to be accompanied by an official guide.

❉ **Pescasseroli** – This is the main urban centre in the valley and home to the park's administrative services. The village lies in a basin lined with beech and pine forests. Tourism and timber-related activities are the village's main industries. Pescasseroli is the birthplace of the philosopher and politician, **Benedetto Croce** (1866-1952).

ADDITIONAL SIGHTS

★ **Bominaco** – Two Romanesque churches stand about 500m – 1 640ft above the hamlet of Bominaco, and are all that remain of a Benedictine **monastery** which was destroyed in the 15C. The Church of **San Pellegrino** ⊘ is a 13C oratory decorated with contemporary **frescoes★**, portraying in a rather awkward but detailed way the *Life of Christ* and a giant *St Christopher*. The Church of **Santa Maria★** (11C and 12C) is more characteristic of the local style: it has an elegant chevet and on one of the outer walls an opening flanked by four projecting lions. The bare but well-lit interior has a beautiful 12C raised square **ambo★** from where lessons would be read; it rests on four columns with palm leaf capitals adorned with foliated scrolls and finials.

Corfinio ⊘ – Beyond the village stands the Romanesque **Basilica di San Pelino** or **Basilica Valvense**, with the adjoining 12C Chapel of Sant'Alessandro to the south. Walk round the church to admire the **east end★**. Inside there is a fine 12C pulpit.

Popoli – The main square, Piazza Grande, of this busy market town, is overlooked by the Church of San Francesco, which has a Gothic façade with a baroque crown. The **Taverna Ducale★**, near the square, is an elegant Gothic edifice adorned with coats of arms and bas reliefs which was formerly used for collecting tithes levied by the prince.

Alba Fucens ⊘ – These are the ruins of a Roman colony founded in 303BC. Amidst the gigantic ruins are the remains of a basilica, the forum, baths, the covered market complete with paved streets, wells and latrines.

ALATRI★

Lazio – Population 25 079
Michelin map 988 fold 26 or 430 Q 22

This important city, which was built in the 6C BC, retains several of its cyclopean walls (4C BC). The **acropolis★** which can be reached on foot from the grandiose Porta di Civita is laid out on a trapezoidal plan and is one of the best preserved examples in Italy. It affords a very fine **view★★** of Alatri and the Frosinone Valley.

A maze of steep stairways and alleyways is lined with Gothic houses. The **Palazzo Gottifredi** *(Largo Luigi di Persiis)* is 13C and the Church of St Mary Major **(Santa Maria Maggiore★)** in the transitional Romanesque-Gothic style has a façade with three porches. Inside there is interesting 12C-15C **carved woodwork★**. On the by-pass is the 13C Church of St Sylvester **(San Silvestro)** which is built using the dry-stone technique and contains frescoes dating from the 13C to the 16C.

ALBA

Piedmont – Population 29 354
Michelin map 988 fold 12 or 428 H 6

Alba was the ancient Roman city of Alba Pompeia, the birthplace of the Roman Emperor Pertinax (AD 126-193). It is a gourmet centre famous for its delicious **tartufi bianchi** or white truffles (annual truffle fair in autumn) and its wines (Barolo, Barbaresco and Barbera). The town boasts several **towers of nobility**, churches and medieval houses. Inside the Gothic cathedral **(Duomo San Lorenzo)** are Renaissance stalls inlaid with intarsia work of very delicate craftsmanship.

To the south of Alba is the **Langhe** region, an area of limestone hills and clay soils planted with vineyards. Take the Alba-Ceva road which hugs the crests affording **views★** of both slopes and passes through picturesque hilltop villages.

The chapter on art and architecture in this guide gives
an outline of artistic achievement in the country
providing the context of the buildings and works of art
described in the Sights section
This chapter may also provide ideas for touring
It is advisable to read it at leisure

ALTILIA SAEPINUM ★

Molise

Michelin map 988 fold 27 or 430 R 25 – 25km – 16 miles to the south of Campobasso

The ruins of Roman **Saepinum** spread over 12ha – 30 acres of the fertile plain which lies at the foot of the Matese Mountains and near the village of Altilia, built with stone quarried from the ruins. This Samnite settlement was occupied by the Romans who gave it the status of a municipium (the people had the rights of Roman citizens) and then fortified it in the 1C BC. Saepinum, which reached the height of its glory at the end of the 5C BC, was destroyed by the Saracens in the 9C.

TOUR ⊙ *1 1/2 hours (start in the southwest)*

Porta di Terravecchia – This ruined gateway commands the southern end of the north-south Cardo Maximus, one of the city's two main streets.

★ **Basilica, foro, tempio** – The basilica, forum and temple are to be found at the junction of the Cardo Maximus and the Decumanus Maximus, a paved street crossing the city from east to west. To the left rise the 20 Ionic columns of the **basilica's** peristyle. To the right are the forum, a vast rectangular paved area, and the Decumanus Maximus *(turn right into this street)* which is lined by the ruined senate house *(curia)*; a temple dedicated to Jupiter, Juno and Minerva and a semicircular recess belonging to the "house of the oil presses" with four brick oil containers still visible. Beyond lie the remains of a fountain carrying the sculpture of a mythical griffin and a Samnite house with an impluvium.

Porta di Benevento – The gate stands at the eastern end of the Decumanus Maximus. The outer face of this arch is decorated with a helmet-clad head. The adjoining museum (**museo**) gives an account of the excavations and has displays on the first floor of sculpture, steles and mosaic fragments.

Mausoleo di Ennius Marsus Volmarso – This beautiful crenellated semicircular mausoleum, honouring Ennius Marsus Volmarso, stands beyond the Benevento Gate. The square plinth is guarded by two very badly damaged lions.

Return to the main crossroads and continue up the Decumanus Maximus.

This is a residential area with the remains of shops on the right.

★ **Porta di Boiano** – This gate with its semicircular main arch is flanked by two round towers. It was dedicated to the future Emperor Tiberius and his brother Drusus. From the top there is a good view of the western part of the fortifications and the ruins of the central part of the city.

Fortified ramparts – The wall built of finely-worked stones in a diamond pattern (total length of 1 250m – 1 367yds) describes a rectangle. It is punctuated by 25 round towers, now reduced to the height of the wall, and four fortified gateways. The western part is the best-preserved section.

Mausoleo di Numisius Ligus – *Once beyond the wall, turn right.* The tomb of Numisius Ligus, crowned by four acroteria, has an elegant simplicity.

★ **Teatro** – The small, semicircular theatre built against the inner face of the wall has kept its monumental entrance of white stone.

Museo – *In front of the theatre.* On the ground floor of the museum, interesting sculptures decorate the sarcophagi and the funerary monuments *(cippi)*. Upstairs there is a display of photographs and documents relating to the excavation work.

From the far side of the theatre return to the Cardo Maximus and turn left.

Porta Tammaro – This simple archway leads to the village of Sepino.

AMALFI★★

Campania – Population 5 594

Michelin map 988 fold 27 or 431 F 25

Amalfi, which has given its name to the beautiful Amalfi Coast *(see below)*, is a rather Spanish-looking little town with its tall white houses built on slopes facing the sea in a wonderful **setting**★★★. Amalfi enjoys a very mild climate, making it a popular holiday resort.

The Maritime Republic of Amalfi – This is Italy's oldest republic founded in 840; by the end of the 9C it came under the rule of a doge. It enjoyed its greatest prosperity in the 11C, when shipping in the Mediterranean was regulated by the *Tavole Amalfitane* (Amalfi Navigation Tables), the oldest maritime code in the world. Amalfi traded regularly with the Orient, in particular Constantinople, and the Republic had an arsenal where many large galleys were built. This fleet of galleys played a large part in carrying Crusaders to the Levant.

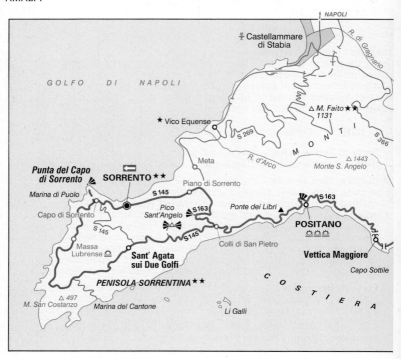

SIGHTS

★ **Duomo di Sant'Andrea** – Founded in the 9C, enlarged in the 10C and 13C and subsequently altered numerous times, the cathedral is a good example of the Oriental splendour favoured by maritime cities. The crypt enshrines relics of St Andrew (Sant'Andrea) which had been removed from Patras to Constantinople, from whence they were transferred in 1206 to Amalfi.

The façade, rebuilt in the 19C on the original model, has a great deal of character: it is the focal point at the top of a stairway and its varied geometrical designs in multicoloured stone are striking. The campanile, on the left, is all that remains of ·the original church. A beautiful 11C bronze **door**★, cast in Constantinople, opens onto the vast atrium which precedes the church.

The interior of the cathedral is in the baroque style. Two antique columns, two candelabra decorated with mosaics and two 12C ambos are of special interest. The atrium leads into the Cloisters of Paradise (**Chiostro del Paradiso**★★) ⊘ which date from 1268. The architecture combines Romanesque austerity and Arab fantasy. The arcades shelter some fine sarcophagi.

★ **Via Genova and Via Capuano** – These two attractive streets starting from the Piazza del Duomo are the main shopping arteries

Costiera Amalfitana

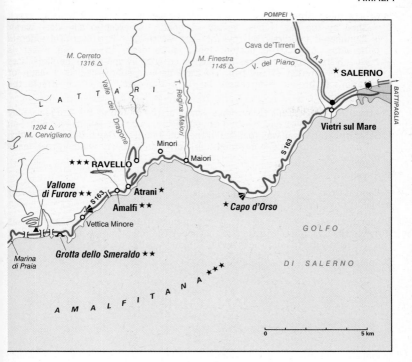

with varied shop fronts, balconies and flower-bedecked niches. Many alleys, stairways and vaulted passageways lead off the main streets into little squares with fountains.

Piazza Flavio Gioia – This square takes its name from the native of Amalfi who is said to have perfected the mariner's compass. The workshops of the **arsenal** stood to the left of the gateway, Porta della Marina.

★★ COSTIERA AMALFITANA (AMALFI COAST) *79km – 49 miles – allow 1 day*

The corniche road follows the indentations of the rocky coast between Sorrento and Salerno which is Italy's finest coastline, namely the Amalfi Coast. For over 30km – 19 miles its innumerable bends afford constantly changing views of enchanting landscapes, wild, fantastically-shaped rocks plunging vertically into a crystal-clear sea, deep gorges spanned by dizzy bridges and Saracen towers perched on jagged rock stacks. The Amalfi Coast, with its wild and rugged landscape, is formed by the jagged fringe of the Lattari Mountains, a deeply-eroded limestone range. Contrasting with these awe-inspiring scenes are the more charming views of fishing villages and the luxuriant vegetation, a mixture of orange, lemon, olive and almond trees, vines and all the Mediterranean flora. The region is very popular with foreigners and artists. A significant part of the attraction is the local cuisine with abundant seafood (fish, crustaceans and shellfish), and the local *mozzarella* cheese washed down with the red Gragnano or white Ravello and Positano wines.

Sightseeing – The map below locates the towns and sites described in the guide, and also indicates other beauty spots in small black type.

★★ **Sorrento and the Sorrento Peninsula** – *See SORRENTO.*

Positano – This fishermen's village is one of the busiest resorts on the coast. The small white cubic houses which reveal a strong Moorish influence and are set in lush gardens, are dotted on the slopes.

Vettica Maggiore – Its houses are scattered over the slopes. From the esplanade there is a fine **view**★★ of the coast and sea.

★★ **Vallone di Furore** – The Furore Valley, between two road tunnels, is the most impressive section of the coast owing to the dark depths of its steep, rocky walls and, in stormy weather, the thunder of wild, rough seas. A fishermen's village has, nevertheless, been built where a small torrent gushes into the sea. The houses clinging to the slopes and vividly-coloured boats drawn up on the shore are an unexpected feature in this bleak landscape.

Those who wish to explore the spot on foot should take the path that goes along one side of the gorge.

★★ **Grotta dello Smeraldo** ⊙ - This marine cave at the end of a rocky creek washed by the sea is best visited by boat. The exceptionally clear water is illuminated indirectly by rays of light which give it a beautiful emerald *(smeraldo)* colour. The bottom looks quite near, though the water is 10m - 33ft deep, but it was not always covered by the sea. Fine stalactites add to the interest of the trip. The cave became submerged as a result of variations in ground level caused by the volcanic activity which affects the whole region.

★ **Atrani** - This pleasant fishermen's village at the mouth of the Dragon Valley (Valle del Dragone) has two old churches: Santa Maria Maddalena and San Salvatore. The latter was founded in the 10C and has a fine bronze door which is very similar to the one in Amalfi Cathedral. An excellent winding road leads to Ravello.

★★★ **Ravello** - *See RAVELLO.*

★ **Capo d'Orso** - The cape with its jagged rocks affords an interesting view of Maiori Bay.

Vietri sul Mare - At the eastern end of this stretch of coastline, the houses of Vietri sul Mare are terraced up the slope. The town is known for its ceramic ware. It affords magnificent **views**★★ of the Amalfi Coast.

★ **Salerno** - *See SALERNO.*

ANAGNI★

Lazio – Population 19 313

Michelin map 988 fold 26 or 430 Q 21 – 65km – 40 miles southeast of Rome

Anagni is a small medieval town, built on a rocky spur, overlooking the Sacco Valley. This was the birthplace of several popes, including Boniface VIII who excommunicated the French King, Philip the Fair. Dante consigned Boniface to Hell for misusing his authority.

★★ **Cattedrale** - The town's most important building stands on the site of the former acropolis. This Romanesque cathedral was built in the 11C and 12C and remodelled in the 13C with Gothic additions. Walk round the outside to admire the three Romanesque apses with Lombard mouldings and arcades, the 14C statue of Boniface VIII over the loggia on the north side and the detached massive Romanesque campanile. The interior comprises a nave and two aisles; the 13C **paving**★ was the work of the Cosmati *(see ART: Middle Ages)*. The high altar is surmounted by a **Romanesque ciborium** or canopy. The **paschal candelabrum** with a spiral column is adorned with multicoloured incrustations; it rests on two sphinxes and is crowned by an infant holding a cup. The work, like the nearby **episcopal throne**, is by Pietro Vassaleto and bears strong similarities with the style of the Cosmati. The **crypt**★★★ ⊙ with its beautiful pavement by the Cosmati also has magnificent 13C **frescoes** depicting the story of the Old Testament, scenes from the lives of the saints and men of science such as Galen and Hippocrates. The **treasury** ⊙ contains some fine liturgical items, notably Boniface VIII's cope of embroidered red silk.

★ **Medieval Quarter** - This quarter consists almost entirely of 13C buildings and is particularly evocative. The façade of **Boniface VIII's Palace** has two pierced galleries one above the other. One has wide round-headed arches while the other consists of attractive twinned windows with small columns. In the Piazza Cavour is the 12C-13C **Palazzo Comunale** with a great **vault**★ at ground level. The rear façade is in the Cistercian style.

ANCONA★

Marches – Population 101 185

Michelin map 988 fold 16 or 430 L 22

Town plan in the current Michelin Red Guide Italia

Ancona, the chief town in the Marches, an Adriatic region of Italy, is built in the form of an amphitheatre on the slopes of a rocky promontory, forming an acute angle from which the name of the town is derived (Greek *ankon* - elbow). It was founded in the 4C BC and became an independent maritime republic in the Middle Ages. It is today a busy port and the main embarkation point for the former Yugoslavia and Greece. The town specialises in the production of accordions, electronic organs and guitars.

SIGHTS

★ **Duomo San Ciriaco** – The cathedral was dedicated to St Cyriacus, 4C martyr and patron saint of Ancona. The Romanesque building combines Byzantine (the Greek cross plan) and Lombard (mouldings and arcades on the outside walls) architectural features. The façade is preceded by a majestic Gothic **porch** in pink stone supported by two lions. The interior is articulated by monolithic marble columns with Romanesque-Byzantine **capitals**. Under the dome, note the clever transition from the square base to the 12-sided drum supporting the dome. The tomb (1509) of Cardinal Giannelli in the chancel is the work of the Dalmatian sculptor Giovanni da Traù.

★ **Loggia dei Mercanti** – This 15C hall for merchants' meetings has a Venetian Gothic façade which was the work of another Dalmatian, Giorgio Orsini.

★ **Santa Maria della Piazza** ⊙ – This small 10C Romanesque church has a charming façade (1210) adorned with amusing popular figures. It was built over the site of two earlier (5C and 6C) **churches** which retain fragments of mosaic pavements.

Museo Nazionale delle Marche ⊙ – *At the southern end of Piazza del Senato.* The museum, installed in the Palazzo Ferretti, has interesting prehistoric and archeological collections on view.

Galleria Comunale Francesco Podesti ⊙ – *Via Ciriaco Pizzecolli.* The public gallery displays works by Crivelli, Titian, Lorenzo Lotto, C. Maratta and Guercino. The gallery of modern art has canvases by Luigi Bartolini, Massimo Campigli, Bruno Cassinari and Tamburini.

San Francesco delle Scale – *Via Ciriaco Pizzecolli, not far from the Galleria Comunale.* This 15C church has a splendid Venetian Gothic doorway by Giorgio Orsini.

Arco di Traiano – The arch was erected at the northern end of Lungomare Vanvitelli in honour of the Emperor Trajan who built the port in AD 115.

EXCURSIONS

★ **Portonovo** – *12km – 8 miles southeast.* Portonovo lies in a picturesque setting formed by the rocky coastline of the **Conero Massif**. A private path leads through woodland to the charming 11C Church of **Santa Maria**★ ⊙, built on an almost square plan inspired by Norman churches.

Jesi – *32km – 20 miles southwest.* The medieval town has a picture gallery **(pinacoteca★)** ⊙ with an important collection of works by Lorenzo Lotto, a Venetian artist of the early 16C, who was influenced by German art. **Palazzo della Signoria**★ is an elegant Renaissance structure built by Francesco di Giorgio Martini, a pupil of Brunelleschi.

ANZIO ⚓

Lazio – Population 33 787
Michelin map 988 fold 26 or 430 R 19

Anzio backs against a promontory facing out to sea and forms with **Nettuno**⚓ a pleasant modern seaside resort. It has a popular yachting harbour.
Anzio is the Antium of antiquity, a Volscian city where Coriolanus took refuge, having abandoned his original intention of engaging in a fratricidal struggle with Rome. Antium was also the birthplace of Nero, in whose villa were found the statues of the Apollo Belvedere, the Fanciulla (young girl) of Anzio and the Borghese Gladiator, now respectively in the Vatican, the National Roman Museum in Rome and the Louvre in Paris.
The name of Anzio is also remembered for the Anglo-American landing of 22 January 1944, which, after a long struggle, ended in the taking of Rome on 4 June 1944. Several military cemeteries, monuments, memorials and museums recall those who gave their lives during this operation.

EXCURSION

★ **Isola di Ponza** – *Access: see the current Michelin Red Guide Italia.* This volcanic island, lying beyond the Gulf of Gaeta, has a verdant ridge and white or blue-grey cliffs, which either are bordered by narrow beaches or drop abruptly into the sea. At the southeast end of the island is the village of **Ponza**⚓⚓ with its serried ranks of cubic and gaily-painted houses in a semicircle around a small harbour. The latter is busy with fishing boats, coasting vessels, pleasure craft and the ferries which ply back and forth to the mainland. The island is popular with underwater fishermen.

AOSTA★

Valle d'Aosta – Population 36 184
Michelin map 988 fold 2, 219 fold 2 or 428 E 3/4
Town plans in the current Michelin Red Guide Italia

Aosta stands in the valley of the same name and is the capital of the region. It has retained the geometric plan of a military camp *(castrum)* and some interesting monuments from the Roman period. Aosta, an active religious centre in the Middle Ages, was the birthplace of the theologian St Anselm, who became Archbishop of Canterbury where he died in 1109. Today it is an active industrial town and, since the opening of the Mont Blanc Tunnel in 1965, an important tourist centre, at the junction of the transalpine routes to France and Switzerland via the St Bernard Tunnel.

★ **Roman buildings** - These are grouped in the centre of Aosta and include a gateway **(Porta Pretoria)**, a majestic arch **(Arco di Augusto)**, both dating from the 1C BC, a **Roman bridge**, a **theatre** and the ruins of an **amphitheatre**.

Collegiata di Sant'Orso ⊙ - The church, dedicated to St Orso, has some lovely carved 15C **stalls** and a baroque rood screen. Beside the 11C **crypt** a doorway opens onto charming little Romanesque **cloisters★** with historiated **capitals★★** illustrating Biblical and secular scenes. The **Priorato di Sant'Orso** is a Renaissance-style priory with elegant **windows★**.

Cattedrale ⊙ - The cathedral was built in the 12C and has been remodelled several times; it now boasts a neo-classical façade (1848). The chancel has 12C mosaic paving, 15C Gothic stalls and the 14C tomb of Thomas II of Savoy. The sacristy contains a rich **treasure** ⊙. The cloisters are 15C.

★★ VALLE D'AOSTA

The Valle d'Aosta comprising the Dora Baltea and adjacent valleys is surrounded by high peaks of both the French and Swiss Alps: Mont Blanc, the Matterhorn (Cervino), Monte Rosa, Grand Combin, Dent d'Hérens, Gran Paradiso and Grande Sassière. Owing to its marvellous situation there are some splendid **viewpoints★★★**.

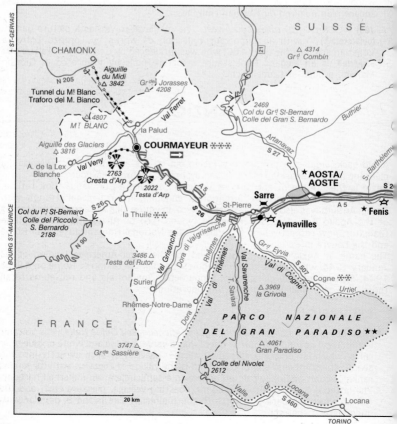

With its secluded valleys, numerous castles, villages with balconied and stone-roofed houses, and a traditional way of life, as well as numerous excursions by cable-car, motor-car or on foot, and scenic routes leading up to glaciers, the Valle d'Aosta is one of the most attractive tourist areas in Italy.

The inhabitants of the high valleys are deeply religious and remain strongly attached to their customs and freedom as well as to the Provençal language. Since 1948 the Valle d'Aosta has been, for administrative purposes, an autonomous district. The people live in houses roofed with flat stone slabs *(lauzes),* raise cattle and produce a cheese called *fontina* which is often used for a cheese fondue. During the long winter evenings many still carve wood as a pastime.

Sightseeing – The map below locates the towns and sites described in the guide, and also indicates other beauty spots in small black type.

★★ Parco Nazionale del Gran Paradiso ⊙ – This national park covering an area of almost 70 000ha – 270sq miles includes an area previously preserved as a royal hunting ground. It can be reached by the Rhêmes, Savarenche, Cogne and Locana valleys or the Nivolet Pass road. The park is rich in wildlife and is important as a reserve for endangered species, such as the ibex, and some of the rarest specimens of Alpine flora.

FROM COURMAYEUR TO IVREA *162km – 101 miles – allow 1 day*

❄❄ **Courmayeur** – *Town plan in the current Michelin Red Guide Italia.* This well-known mountaineering and winter sports resort is a good excursion centre. Take a cable-car to the Cresta d'Arp and to cross the Mont Blanc Massif and make a short detour into France *(for the area beyond La Palud see the Michelin Green Guide Alpes du Nord, in French).* By car explore one of the following valleys: Veny, Ferret or Testa d'Arpi and the road to the Little St Bernard Pass, one of the busiest transalpine routes which was used by the Romans in ancient times.

The route follows the Dora Baltea Valley. Once through St-Pierre and past the road south up the Cogne valley, on the left stands **Castello di Sarre**, the former summer residence of the Counts of Savoy. Further on, to the right, is the 14C

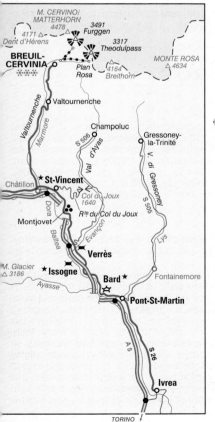

Fortezza di Aymavilles, impressively quartered with great round crenellated towers.

★ **Aosta** – *See AOSTA.*

★ **Castello di Fenis** ⊙ – This imposing fortress contains fine carved furniture in the local style. The inner courtyard has remarkable frescoes portraying the Golden Legend.

❄❄❄ **Breuil-Cervinia** – This winter sports resort is admirably situated at 2 050m – 6 822ft. Cable-cars ⊙ climb up to the Rosa Plateau (Plan Rosa) and the Furggen Pass at 3 491m – 11 453ft.

★ **St-Vincent** – The Casino de la Vallée in its fine park is very popular.
The road passes two castles: Castello di Montjovet and the 14C **Castello di Verrès** which curiously enough has no keep or corner towers.

★ **Castello di Issogne** – The castle was built at the end of the 15C by Georges de Challant. It has a fine courtyard with a fountain surmounted by a wrought-iron pomegranate tree. The arcaded gallery is painted with 15C frescoes and inside the furniture is typical of the Val d'Aosta area.

★ **Fortezza di Bard** – The colossal fortress, dismantled on the orders of Napoleon in 1800 and rebuilt during the 19C, commands the upper Dora Baltea Valley.

Pont St-Martin – This village is named after the Roman bridge which was guarded by a chapel dedicated to St John Nepomucene.

Ivrea – This busy industrial town stands at the mouth of the Valle d'Aosta. To the east of Ivrea is the largest moraine in Europe, the Serra d'Ivrea.

AQUILEIA

Friuli – Venezia Giulia – Population 3 378
Michelin map 988 fold 6 or 429 E 22

While the plan of the town was being outlined (181 BC) with a plough, according to Roman custom, an eagle *(aquila)* hovered overhead: hence its name. Aquileia was a flourishing market under the Roman Empire and was used as general headquarters by Augustus during his conquest of the Germanic tribes. The town then became one of Italy's most important patriarchates (554-1751) ruled by bishops.

★★ **Basilica** – The Romanesque church was built in the 11C on the foundations of a 4C building and restored in the 14C. It is preceded by a porch and flanked by a campanile.
The interior with its nave and two aisles is in the form of a Latin cross. The splendid 4C mosaic **paving★★**, which is one of the largest and richest in western Christendom, depicts religious scenes. The timber ceiling and the arcades are both 14C, the capitals are Romanesque and the decoration of the transept Renaissance. The 9C Carolingian crypt **(Cripta degli affreschi)** ⊘ is decorated with fine Romanesque **frescoes★★**.
The **Cripta degli Scavi** ⊘ is reached from the north aisle. Finds from the excavations are assembled here, notably admirable 4C mosaic **paving★★**.

★ **Roman Ruins** ⊘ – Excavations have uncovered the remains of Roman Aquileia: behind the basilica, the Via Sacra leading to the river port, houses and the forum. The Archeological and Paleo-Christian Museums **(Musei Archeologico e Paleocristiano)** ⊘ contain an important collection of finds from local excavations. The remarkable series of portraits, including those of Tiberius and of Augustus as a youth, in the archeological museum is noteworthy.

AREZZO★★

Tuscany – Population 91 578
Michelin map 988 fold 15 or 430 L 17

After being first an important Etruscan city and then a rich Roman one, Arezzo became an independent commune in the 11C and was annexed by Florence in 1384, following a protracted struggle. The town has many reminders of its past and was the birthplace of several famous men: Guido d'Arezzo (c997-c1050) the inventor of the musical scale, Petrarch the poet (1304-74), Aretino the author (1492-1566), Giorgio Vasari *(see Index)* and probably Maecenas (c70-80 BC), the legendary patron of art and letters.

SIGHTS

San Francesco (ABY) – This large aisleless church was designed for preaching; it was built for the Franciscans in the 14C in the Gothic style and remodelled in the 17C and 18C.

★★★ **Frescoes of Piero della Francesca** – The frescoes depicting the Legend of the Holy Cross were executed from 1452 to 1466 on the walls of the apse. This fresco cycle is undoubtedly a milestone in the history of art. Scenes include the death and burial of Adam, Solomon and the Queen of Sheba, the dream of Constantine, the victory of Constantine over Maxentius, the invention of the Cross, the victorious Heraclius overcoming Chosroes and the announcement of Christ's death to Mary. Piero della Francesca, a pupil of the Florentine school, wrote two treatises on perspective and geometry in later life, and the cycle is the result of his wide-ranging experimentation with two-dimensional space and volume; the poses and expressions of the figures are treated with great realism in a strict composition and reflect the Renaissance ideals of serenity and timelessness. The subtle light suffusing the scenes reveals the influence of Domenico Veneziano, who was the artist's master.

★ **Santa Maria della Pieve** (BY) – This lovely 12C Romanesque church is flanked by a powerful campanile. The Pisan Romanesque-style **façade**★★ is articulated by three tiers of small columns, adorned with various motifs, whose ranks become closer as the height increases. On the high altar is a 14C polyptych by the Sienese, Pietro Lorenzetti.

★ **Piazza Grande** (BY) – This square, behind the above church, is surrounded by medieval houses, Renaissance palaces and the Logge or galleries designed by Vasari (16C). The square is the setting for the **Saracen's Tournament**, when costumed horsemen attack a dummy figure, the Saracen, with lances *(see the Calendar of Events at the end of the guide)*.

Duomo (BY) – The cathedral was built from the 13C onwards on the town's highest point. Inside are some fine **works of art**★: stained glass by the French artist Guillaume de Marcillat (1467-1529), a fresco of Mary Magdalene by Piero della Francesca and the tomb of St Donatus (13C).

San Domenico (BY) – This 13C church, dedicated to St Dominic, has frescoes by the Duccio school and an admirable painted **crucifix**★★ (c1260) attributed to Cimabue.

Casa del Vasari (AY) ⊘ – The house was sumptuously decorated by **Giorgio Vasari** (1511-74), painter, sculptor, architect and early art historian. Also exhibited are works by Tuscan Mannerists.

★ **Museo d'arte medievale e moderna** (AY M¹) ⊘ – The medieval and modern art collections are housed in the Renaissance Palazzo Bruni-Ciocchi and include sculpture, furniture, gold and silver objects, paintings from the Middle Ages to the 19C; **maiolica**★ from Umbria; arms and coins.

Traffic restricted in town centre

M¹ Museo d'arte medievale e moderna   M² Museo archeologico

Museo archeologico (**AZ M²**) ⊙ – The archeological museum overlooks the 1C-2C **Roman amphitheatre** (**ABZ**). There is a remarkable collection of 6C BC-3C AD Etruscan and Roman bronzes, as well as ceramics from the Hellenistic and Roman periods. The Attic vases **(Euphronius vase)** and red vases made in Arezzo are of special interest.

Santa Maria delle Grazie – *1km – 1/2 mile to the south via Viale Mecenate* (**AZ**). In front of the church rises a graceful **portico**★ by the Florentine, Benedetto da Maiano (15C). Inside is a marble **altarpiece**★ by Andrea della Robbia.

Promontorio dell'ARGENTARIO★

Tuscany

Michelin map 988 folds 24, 25 or 430 ○ 15

This ancient promontory, now linked to the mainland by strips of coastline formed by a build-up of sand *(tomboli)*, consists of the small limestone hill called **Monte Argentario** which rises to a height of 635m and is skirted by a road which affords attractive views. Its name, originally *Promontorio Cosano* from the nearby town of Cosa, may be a reference to the shiny, silvery appearance of its rocks or to the bankers *(argentarii)* who once owned it.

Orbetello – Built on the central dike in the lagoon, it is situated at the end of the main access road to the peninsula (SS 440). The town was originally called Urbis Tellus, literally the territory of the city i.e. Rome, probably because it was given in AD 805 to the Abbazia delle Tre Fontane in Rome by Charlemagne. The **fortifications** are a reminder of the influence of the Sienese and, later, the Spaniards (16C - 17C) who made the town the capital of a small state. The **cathedral** was built in the late 14C on the site of an older building and was enlarged by the Spaniards in the 17C. The facade dates from the Gothic period.

≙≙ **Porto Santo Stefano** – It is the main town in the peninsula, and the embarkation point for trips to the island of Giglio. Its houses are built up the hillside on each side of a 17C Aragon-style fort from which there is a superb **view**★ over the harbour and the Talamone Gulf.

Porto Ercole

⌂⌂ **Porto Ercole** – This seaside resort has a tiny old urban district beyond a medieval gateway with hoardings and machicolations that is linked to the fortress above the town by two parallel crenelated walls. From the Piazza Santa Barbara lined by the arcading of the former Palazzo del Governatore (Governor's Palace, 16C), there is a view over the harbour, the bay and the two old Spanish forts perched on Monte Filippo.

★ **Ancient town of Cosa** – On the mainland (near Ansedonia), at the far end of the southernmost bar, Tombolo di Feniglia, the ancient **ruins** ⊙ crown a promontory affording fine views of the Orbetello lagoon and Monte Argentario. This ancient Roman colony, surrounded by walls made of huge blocks of stone, flourished from the 3C BC to the 4C AD. Near the shore is a tower in which Giacomo Puccini composed part of his opera, *Tosca*.

ASCOLI PICENO★★

Marches – Population 53 505
Michelin map 988 fold 16 or 430 N 22
Town plan in the current Michelin Red Guide Italia

Ascoli, an austere but picturesque town, lies in a narrow valley at the confluence of the Castellano and the Tronto. This walled town has a medieval quarter which is rich in churches, palaces, houses and picturesque streets.

★★ **Piazza del Popolo** – The main square, elongated and well-proportioned and paved with large flagstones, is surrounded by Gothic and Renaissance buildings. It is a popular meeting-place and is the setting for the town's main festivities. The People's Captains' Palace (**Palazzo dei Capitani del Popolo**★) is an austere 13C building with an imposing Renaissance doorway, surmounted by a statue of Pope Paul III which was added in 1549 by Cola dell'Amatrice. At the far end of the square St Francis' Church (**San Francesco**★) was begun in 1262 and consecrated in 1371; it has several Lombard features. Abutting the south front is the Merchants' Loggia (**Loggia dei Mercanti**★), a graceful early-16C building showing Tuscan influence, particularly in the capitals.

★ **Centro Storico** – The historic quarter lies between the Tronto River and the **Corso Mazzini**★ lined with old mansions, in particular no 224 the 16C Malaspina Palace. At the beginning of **Via delle Torri** is the Renaissance façade of St Augustine's (**Sant'Agostino**) ⊙ which has a moving fresco of Christ bearing the Cross by Cola dell'Amatrice. The Via delle Torri ends at the 14C Church of St Peter the Martyr (**San Pietro Martire**). Behind is the Romanesque Church of Sts Vincent and Anastasius (**Santi Vincenzo ed Anastasio**★) ⊙ with its curious compartmented façade dating from the 14C. The Ercolani Tower (**Torre Ercolani**) in Via Soderini, is the tallest of the feudal towers of Ascoli. Adjoining is the 12C Lombard Romanesque mansion, **Palazzo Longobardo**. Through the medieval gateway, a single-arched Roman bridge, the **Ponte romano di Solestà**★ ⊙, spans the Tronto at a height of 25m – 82ft. From the far end there is an attractive view of the old quarters.

Duomo ⊙ – The grandiose façade of this 12C cathedral was the work of Cola dell'Amatrice. Inside there is a superb **polyptych**★ (1473) by **Carlo Crivelli**. This Venetian artist famous for his meticulous realism settled in Ascoli Piceno in 1470 and he was a motivating force in the development of a local art movement. The **baptistery**★, square at the base and octagonal above, stands to the left of the cathedral; it is one of the finest in Italy.
Near the baptistery, in Via Buonaparte, is the **Palazzo Buonaparte**, a fine example of 16C Renaissance architecture.

Pinacoteca ⊙ – The picture gallery is housed in the town hall (Palazzo Comunale) in Piazza Arringo and the collections include works by Crivelli and his pupils, Carlo Maratta, Titian, Van Dyck, Bellotto, Guardi and Callot. A precious, delicately-worked 13C English relic, the cope of Nicholas IV, is a prized exhibit.

*Admission times and charges
for the sights described
are listed at the end of the guide
Every sight for which there are times and charges
is identified by the clockface symbol ⊙
in the Sights section of the guide*

ASSISI★★★

Umbria – Population 24 567

Michelin map 988 fold 16 or 430 M 19 – Town plan below

The walled city of Assisi is prettily spread across the slopes of Monte Subasio and retains its medieval character. It is closely associated with **St Francis**, as related in the numerous accounts of his life and work. Under the influence of the Franciscan Order of Minors founded by St Francis, a new, essentially religious, artistic movement developed which marked a turning-point in Italian art.

St Francis Preaching to the Birds
by an unknown 13C master, Maestro di San Francesco
(Basilica inferiore)

Born in 1182 Francis was a rich and brilliant youth who dreamed of military glory; he was converted following an illness in 1201. He witnessed several apparitions of the Virgin and of Christ; the most famous is that of La Verna *(see Index)* during which he received the stigmata. But this mystic also had a deeply poetic soul and was a lover of the beauties of nature, which he praised in texts written in the Umbrian language. In addition, he befriended a young woman of rare beauty, Clare, who founded the Order of Poor Clares. St Francis himself died in 1226 after having founded, in 1210, the Order of Minors, mendicant monks known thereafter as Franciscans.

The son of the rich Assisi draper preached poverty, humility and mysticism, and his teachings gave rise to a new artistic vision which found its expression in the purity and elegance of Gothic art. During the 13C the stark, austere churches which were designed for preaching, were embellished with a new splendour to reflect the tender and profound love of St Francis for nature and its creatures, as described in the tales of St Bonaventure. From the end of the 14C famous masters came from Rome and Venice to Assisi to work on the Basilica of St Francis. These artists abandoned for ever the rigid traditions of Byzantine art in favour of a more dramatic art imbued with a spiritual atmosphere. Cimabue and later Giotto were its most powerful exponents.

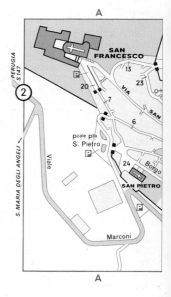

★★★ BASILICA DI SAN FRANCESCO
(ST FRANCIS' BASILICA) (A) *1 1/2 hours*

The basilica consists of two superimposed churches, resting on a series of immense arches. The whole building, erected after the death of St Francis to the plans of Brother Elias, was consecrated in 1253. It was this monk who influenced the Franciscans to use more splendour and decoration.

Basilica inferiore – Beyond the long narthex, the walls of the dark, sombre four-bay nave are covered with 13C and 14C **frescoes★★★**. From the nave, enter the first chapel on the left with **frescoes★★** by Simone Martini (c1284-1344) illustrating the life of St Martin. These are remarkable for their delicate drawing, graceful composition and bright colours. Further along, above the pulpit is a fresco of the *Coronation of the Virgin* attributed to Maso, a pupil of Giotto (14C).

66

The choir **vaulting**★★ is painted with scenes symbolising the Triumph of St Francis and the virtues practised by him. They are the work of one of Giotto's pupils. The north transept is decorated with **frescoes**★★ of the Passion. Those on the ceiling, attributed to pupils of Pietro Lorenzetti, are valued for their narrative design and charm of detail; those on the walls, probably by Lorenzetti himself, are striking for their dramatic expression *(Descent from the Cross)*. In the south transept is the majestic work by Cimabue, a *Madonna with Four Angels and St Francis*★★.

From the north transept make for the Renaissance main cloisters and the **treasury**★★ ⊘ with its many valuable pieces and the **Perkins collection** of 14C to 16C paintings.

At the bottom of the steps, beneath the centre of the transept crossing, is **St Francis' Tomb** which is both impressive and evocative.

Basilica superiore – This accomplished Gothic work with its tall and graceful nave, bathed in light, contrasts with the lower church. The apse and transept were decorated with frescoes (many have since been damaged) by Cimabue and his school. In the north transept Cimabue painted an intensely dramatic *Crucifixion*★★★. Between 1296 and 1304 **Giotto** and his assistants depicted the life of St Francis in a famous cycle of **frescoes**★★★. There are 28 clearly defined scenes, each showing a greater search for realism. They mark a new dawning in the figurative traditions of Italian art, which was to reach its apogee during the Renaissance.

Step out of the basilica onto the esplanade to admire the harmonious façade with its doorway and rose window in Cosmati work *(see ART: Middle Ages)*.

ADDITIONAL SIGHTS

★★ **Rocca Maggiore** (B) ⊘ – The medieval castle is a good example of 14C military architecture. From the top of the keep there is a splendid **view**★★★ of the town of Assisi and the surrounding countryside bathed in golden light.

★★ **Santa Chiara**(BC) – From the terrace in front of the Church of St Clare there is a pretty view of the Umbrian countryside. The church was built from 1257 to 1265 and closely resembles the Gothic Upper Basilica of St Francis'. Inside there are numerous works of art including 14C frescoes depicting the life and history of St Clare; these were influenced by Giotto.

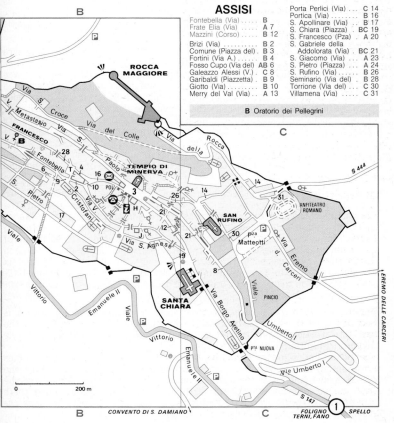

ASSISI

B Oratorio dei Pellegrini

The Byzantine Crucifix brought here from St Damian's Monastery *(below)*, which is said to have spoken to St Francis and caused his conversion to the Christian faith, can be seen in the small Church of St George, which adjoins the south aisle. The crypt enshrines the remains of St Clare.

★ **Duomo San Rufino** (C) – The cathedral was built in the 12C and its Romanesque **façade★★** is one of the finest in Umbria, with a harmonious arrangement of its openings and ornamentation.
The interior, on a basilical plan, was rebuilt in 1571. To the right at the entrance is the baptismal font used for the baptism of St Francis, St Clare and Frederick II.

★ **Piazza del Comune** (B 3) – This square with its attractive fountain occupies the site of the forum: the **Tempio di Minerva★**, a temple converted into a church, with its portico of six Corinthian columns, is one of the best-preserved in Italy.

★ **Via San Francesco** (AB) – This picturesque street is lined by medieval and Renaissance houses. At no 13A the Pilgrims' Chapel (**Oratorio dei Pellegrini – B B**) ⊙ is decorated inside with 15C frescoes, notably by Matteo da Gualdo.

★ **San Pietro** (A) – A Romanesque church, dedicated to St Peter, built by the Benedictines from 1029 to 1268.

EXCURSIONS

★★ **Eremo delle Carceri** ⊙ – *4km – 2 miles east.* The hermitage stands in a beautiful site at the heart of a forest of age-old green oaks. It is said that, having been blessed by St Francis, a huge flock of birds flew out of one of the trees, symbolising the spread of the Franciscan Order throughout the world. The hermitage was founded here by St Bernardino of Siena (1380-1444). The spot derives its name from the fact that Francis and his followers liked to retire from the world here as if they had been put into prison (*carcere* in Italian) in order, according to one of his biographers, to chase out "from the soul the tiniest speck of dust left in it by contact with mankind". Narrow passageways clearly indicating the structure of the monastery (built around the outline of the rock) lead to St Francis' Cave and the old refectory with its 15C tables.

★ **Convento di San Damiano** ⊙ – *2km – 1 mile south of the gateway, Porta Nuova.* St Damian's Monastery and a small adjoining church stand alone amidst olive and cypress trees and are closely associated with St Francis, who received his calling here and composed his *Canticle of the Creatures*, and also with St Clare who died here in 1253. The humble and austere interior is a moving example of a 13C Franciscan monastery.

★ **Basilica di Santa Maria degli Angeli** ⊙ – *5km – 3 miles southwest.* The basilica of St Mary of the Angels was built in the 16C around the **Porziuncola**, a small chapel named after the small plot (*piccola porzione* in Italian) of land on which it was built before the year 1 000 AD. It was in the Porziuncola that St Francis named Clare the "Bride of Christ". It contains a **fresco★** (1393) representing episodes from the history of the Franciscan Order *(above the altar)*. It was in the adjacent chapel, Capella del Transito, that Francis died on 3 October 1226. The St Mary Major Crypt contains an enamelled terracotta **polyptych★** by Andrea della Robbia (c1490). Near the church is the rose bush said to have lost its thorns when the saint threw himself onto it to escape temptation, and the cave in which he used to pray. In the corridor leading to the rose bush is a statue of the saint holding a nest where doves roost.

★ **Spello** – *12km – 8 miles southeast.* A quiet, picturesque little town in which the bastions and gateways bear witness to its past as a Roman settlement. The Church of St Mary Major (Santa Maria Maggiore) contains **frescoes★★** *(chapel on the left)* by Pinturicchio depicting the Annunciation, the Nativity, the Preaching in the Temple *(on the walls)* and the Sybils *(on the vaulting)*. To each side of the high altar are frescoes by Perugino. Nearby, in St Andrew's Church (**Sant'Andrea**), which was built in 1025, is a painting by Pinturicchio and a Crucifix attributed to Giotto. The village is also famous for its Flower Festival *(Le infiorate)* held on the Feast of Corpus Christi *(see the Calendar of Events at the end of the guide)*.

Foligno – *18km – 11 miles to the southeast.* Piazza della Repubblica is overlooked by the 14C **Palazzo Trinci** ⊙, built by the local overlords, and the cathedral (**Duomo**) with its magnificent doorway decorated with Lombard-style geometric decoration.
Foligno is famous for the **Game of the Quintana** when horsemen in 17C costumes representing the ten different quarters of the town must carry away, with the points of their spears, a ring which is hung from the outstretched hand of the Quintana, an early-17C wooden statue. On the day before this tournament there is a procession with over 1 000 participants also in 17C costumes *(see the Calendar of Events at the end of the guide)*.

ATRI

Abruzzi – Population 11 390

Michelin map 988 fold 27 or 430 ○ 23

The inland town of Atri has a beautiful situation looking out to sea. To the west lies the strange **landscape**★★ known as the **Bolge** of Atri, which resulted from the fluvial erosion of a Tertiary plateau. The flat-topped hills with steep sides and gullies are covered with vegetation.

★ **Cattedrale** ○ – Built in the 13C-14C on the foundations of a Roman edifice, the cathedral is in the transitional Romanesque-Gothic style. A Romanesque doorway with a rose window above adorns the otherwise sober and compartmented façade. The lower part of the campanile is square but becomes recessed and polygonal in its upper part. Inside, there are tall Gothic arches and, in the apse, **frescoes**★ by the Abruzzi artist, Andrea Delitio (1450-73), illustrating in a very realistic way and in detail the Lives of the Virgin and of Jesus.

BARI

Puglia – Population 342 710

Michelin map 988 fold 29 or 431 D 32 – Town plan overleaf

Plan of the built-up area in the current Michelin Red Guide Italia

Bari, the capital of Apulia and an agricultural and industrial centre, is first and foremost a port with shipping connections with both Croatia and Greece. The Levantine Fair *(Fiera del Levante)*, held in September, is an important trade fair which was inaugurated in 1930 to encourage trade with other Mediterranean countries.

Bari comprises the old town, clustered on its promontory, and the modern town with wide avenues, laid out on a grid plan in the 19C. Bari was the capital of Byzantium's possessions in Italy and a very prosperous city in the Middle Ages due partly to its role as a pilgrimage centre to St Nicholas' shrine and as a port of embarkation for the Crusades. It declined under the Sforza of Milan and Spanish rule in the 16C.

★ CITTÀ VECCHIA (CDY) *1 1/2 hours*

★★ **Basilica di San Nicola** (DY) – The basilica in the heart of the old town (*città vecchia*), also known as Nicholas' stronghold, was begun in 1087 and consecrated in 1197 to St Nicholas, Bishop of Myra in Asia Minor, who achieved fame by resurrecting three children, whom a butcher had cut up and put in brine. St Nicholas' relics were brought home by sailors from Bari and it was decided to build a church to him. The building is one of the most remarkable examples of Romanesque architecture and it was the model for many churches built locally. The plain but powerful façade, flanked by two towers, is relieved by several twinned openings and a sculptured doorway with bulls supporting the flanking columns. On the north side there is the richly decorated 12C Lions' Doorway.

Inside, the nave and two aisles with a triforium were reroofed in the 17C with a fine coffered ceiling. A large 12C ciborium (canopy) surmounts the high altar behind which is an unusual 11C **episcopal throne**★ in white marble. In the north apse hangs a painting of the *Virgin and Saints* by the Venetian, Bartolomeo Vivarini, and opposite *St Jerome* by Costantino da Monopoli. The tomb of St Nicholas lies in the crypt. The marble columns are crowned by richly-decorated capitals.

★ **Cattedrale** (DY B) – This 11C-12C Romanesque cathedral was added to and then altered at a later date. Inside, the nave and two aisles have oven-vaulted apses and there is a false triforium above the arches. The works of art include a pulpit made up of 11C and 12C fragments, and a baldachin rebuilt from 13C fragments.

In the north aisle is displayed a copy of the *Exultet* (the original is kept in the sacristy), a precious 11C Byzantine parchment scroll in Beneventan script, typical of medieval southern Italy. The illustrations are on the reverse side so that the congregation could see them as the parchment was unrolled for the choristers.

★ **Castello** (CY) ○ – The Emperor Frederick II of Hohenstaufen built the castle in 1233 over the foundations of earlier Byzantine and Norman buildings. The irregular but four-sided courtyard and two of the original towers date from the Swabian period. The castle's defences were strengthened in the 16C.

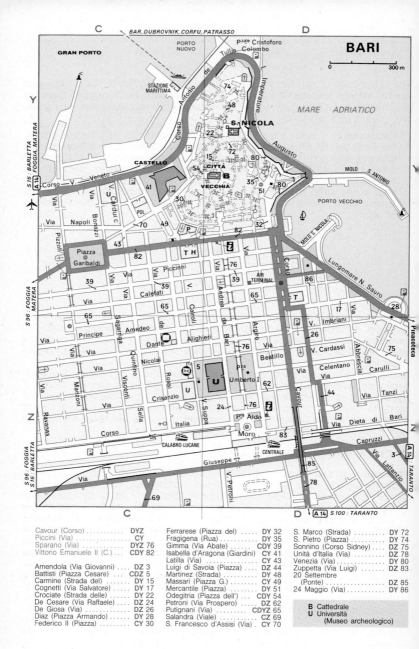

ADDITIONAL SIGHTS

Pinacoteca ⊙ – *On Lungomare Nazario Sauro* (**DY**) *beyond Piazza A. Diaz*. The gallery, on the fourth floor (lift) of the Palazzo della Provincia, comprises Byzantine works of art (sculpture and paintings), a 12C-13C painted wood statue of **Christ★**, *The Martyrdom of St Peter* by Giovanni Bellini and canvases by the 17C-18C Neapolitan school.

Museo archeologico (**DZ U**) ⊙ – *First floor of the university*. The archeological museum displays Greco-Roman collections from excavations made throughout Apulia.

EXCURSION

The road from Bari to Barletta passes through many small but attractive coastal towns which were fortified against invasion by the Saracens during the Middle Ages and the Turks at the end of the 15C. These include **Giovinazzo** with its small 12C cathedral dominating the fishing harbour; **Molfetta** pinpointed by the square towers of its Apulian Romanesque cathedral in white limestone; and **Bisceglie**, a picturesque fishing village, with its cathedral finished in the 13C. The main doorway is flanked by two lions.

BARLETTA ⏏

Puglia – Population 89 578
Michelin map 988 folds 28 and 29 or 431 D 30
Town plan in the current Michelin Red Guide Italia

In the 12C and 13C the town of Barletta was an embarkation port for the Crusades and many military or hospitaller Orders chose this as the site for an institution.

Now a commercial and agricultural centre, the town has a fine historic nucleus comprising several medieval religious or secular buildings.

The symbol of the town is a statue dating back to the Roman era. The Colossus (**Colosso**★★ or Statua di Eraclio) is a gigantic statue over 4.5m – 15ft tall of a Byzantine emperor whose identity is uncertain (Valentinian?). Probably 4C, this work is of interest as it marks the transition from decadent Roman to early Christian art. The stiffness of the figure is offset by the intense expression.

The statue stands in front of the Basilica of the Holy Sepulchre (**San Sepolcro**) ⊘ *(at the junction of Corso Vittorio Emanuele and Corso Garibaldi)* which dates from the 12C-14C and possesses a fine **reliquary**★, with Limoges enamels on the base, for a fragment of the True Cross.

The castle (**Castello**★) ⊘ is an imposing fortress built by the Emperor Frederick II of Hohenstaufen and later remodelled especially by Charles V in the 16C. The latter is responsible for its curious plan with four pointed corner bastions; inside are two large superimposed semi-circular blockhouses. The castle houses a gallery (**pinacoteca**) ⊘ exhibiting a fine series of paintings by the local artist, Giuseppe de Nittis (1846-84) who worked mainly in Paris.

In Via Cialdini, on the ground floor of the 14C Palazzo di Don Diego de Mendoza is the **cellar** where was issued the famous Barletta challenge (**la disfida di Barletta**).

Further along is the 17C **Palazzo della Marra**; its façade is richly decorated in the Baroque style.

The Barletta challenge

In 1503 the town which was held by the Spanish was besieged by French troops. The Italians accused of cowardice by a French prisoner issued a challenge, following which 13 Italian knights led by Ettore Fieramosca met and defeated 13 French knights in single combat.

In the 19C this deed was deemed a fine example of patriotism and Ettore Fieramosca became a heroic figure. In 1933 the author Massimo d'Azeglio based a novel on this event.

EXCURSION

Canne della Battaglia – *12km – 8 miles southeast*. The strategic importance of the site in late Antiquity is evidenced by a famous battle in AD 216 when the Carthaginians led by Hannibal won a decisive victory over the Roman army under the leadership of Scipio. There are ruins of a medieval necropolis and of an Apulian village; and on the opposite slope, a stronghold where the main Roman axis, the *decumanus*, intersected by streets *(cardini)* is still visible, as well as the remains of a medieval basilica and of a Norman castle.

BASSANO DEL GRAPPA ★

Veneto – Population 38 810
Michelin map 988 fold 5 or 429 E 17

Bassano del Grappa, a pottery town which also produces brandy *(grappa)*, is built on the banks of the Brenta River. The town is attractive with narrow streets lined by painted houses and the squares bordered by arcades. In the centre, Piazza Garibaldi is dominated by the 13C square tower, Torre di Ezzelino, and overlooked by the Church of St Francis (**San Francesco**). The church, which dates from the 12C-14C, has an elegant porch (1306). Inside, the 14C Christ is by Guariento. The covered bridge (**Ponte Coperto**) is well known in Italy. Originally built in the 13C, it has been rebuilt many times since.

★ **Museo Civico** ⊘ – The municipal museum is housed in the monastery next to the church of St Francis. The **picture gallery**, on the first floor, has several works by the local da Ponte family. Jacopo da Ponte, otherwise called **Jacopo Bassano** (1510-92), was the best-known member. His works were marked by a picturesque realism and contrasts of light and shade. *St Valentine baptising St Lucia* is his masterpiece.

Other Venetian painters include Guariento, Vivarini, Giambono (14C and 15C), Pietro Longhi, Tiepolo and Marco Ricci (18C). There are also two lovely canvases by the Genoese painter Magnasco (18C) and a gallery devoted to the sculptor Canova.

EXCURSIONS

★★★ **Monte Grappa** – 1 775m – 5 823ft. *32km – 20 miles north.* The road up passes through fine forests and bare mountain pastures, before reaching the summit, from where there is a magnificent **panorama** reaching as far as Venice and Trieste. The monument is a First World War ossuary.

★ **Asolo** – *14km – 9 miles east.* The streets of this attractive little town, dominated by its castle, are lined with palaces painted with frescoes.
The town is closely associated with Robert Browning and Duse, the famous Italian tragic actress who interpreted the works of Gabriele D'Annunzio. Duse is buried in the peaceful cemetery of Sant'Anna.

Marostica – *7km – 4 miles west.* The main square (**Piazza Castello★**) of this charming small medieval city serves as a giant chessboard for a highly original game of chess (**partita a scacchi**) with costumed people as the chessmen *(see the table of Principal Festivals at the end of the guide).*

Cittadella – *13km – 8 miles south.* This stronghold was built by the Paduans in 1220 to counter the Trevisans' construction of Castelfranco. Cittadella is encircled by fine brick **walls★**.

Possagno – *8km – 11 miles northwest.* This was the birthplace of the sculptor **Antonio Canova** (1757-1822), known for his neo-classical works. The **house** where he was born and a sculpture gallery (**Gipsoteca**) ⊙ nearby are open to the public. The temple (**Tempio di Canova**) ⊙ designed by the master himself, crowns an eminence. Inside are the sculptor's tomb and his last sculpture, a *Descent from the Cross★*.

BELLUNO★

Veneto – Population 35 541

Michelin map 988 fold 5 or 429 D 18

Town plan in the current Michelin Red Guide Italia

This pleasant town stands on a spur at the confluence of the Piave and the Ardo rivers and is surrounded by high mountains. To the north are the Dolomites with the Belluno Pre-Alps in the south. An independent commune in the Middle Ages, Belluno came under the aegis of the Venetian Republic from 1404.

Walk along Via Rialto through the 13C gateway, Porta Dojona (remodelled in the 16C), across the **Piazza del Mercato★**, bordered with arcaded Renaissance houses and adorned with a 1409 fountain, along Via Mezzaterra and Via Santa Croce to the gateway, Porta Rugo. Via del Piave offers an extensive **view★** of the Piave Valley and the surrounding mountains. The **Piazza del Duomo★** is surrounded by the late-15C Venetian-style Rectors' Palace (**Palazzo dei Rettori★**), the Episcopal Palace (**Palazzo dei Vescovi**) and the cathedral (Duomo), dating from the 16C with its baroque campanile by Juvara. Inside, there are several good pictures by the Venetian school, notably by Jacopo Bassano and, in the crypt, a 15C **polyptych★** by the Rimini school. The Jurists' Palace (Palazzo dei Giuristi) houses the municipal museum (**Museo civico**) ⊙ with an art gallery (local and Venetian works), a rich coin collection and documents on the Risorgimento *(see HISTORY).*

EXCURSION

Feltre – *31km – 19 miles southwest.* Feltre, grouped around its castle, has kept part of its ramparts and in **Via Mezzaterra★**, old houses, adorned with frescoes in the Venetian manner. **Piazza Maggiore★** is a beautiful square with its noble buildings, arcades, stairways and balustrades. The municipal museum *(Museo civico, 23 Via Lorenzo Luzzo, near the Porta Oria)* ⊙ displays works by Lorenzo Luzzo, a local artist, Marescalchi, Bellini, Cima da Conegliano, Ricci and Jan Massys. The museum also includes a historical section on Feltre and an archeological collection.

BENEVENTO

Campania – Population 62 534

Michelin map 988 fold 27 or 430 S 26 or 431 D 26

This was the ancient capital of the Samnites, who hindered the Roman expansion for some considerable time. In 321 BC they trapped the Roman army in a defile known as the Caudine Forks (Forche Caudine) between Capua and ancient Beneventum. The Romans occupied the town following the defeat in 275 BC of Pyrrhus *(see HISTORY)* and his Samnite allies. During the reign of Trajan, the town knew a period of glory and it was designated as starting-point for the Trajan Way (Via Traiana) leading to Brindisi. Under Lombard rule, it became the seat of a duchy in 571 and later a powerful principality. Following the Battle of Benevento in 1266, Charles of Anjou who had defeated Manfred the then king of Naples and Sicily, supported by Pope Urban IV, claimed the kingship.

★★ **Arco di Traiano** – *At the junction of Via Traiano and Corso Garibaldi.* This is Italy's best-preserved triumphal arch built in AD 114. The low reliefs dedicated to the glory of the Emperor Trajan are of an exceptionally high standard.

★ **Museo del Sannio** ⊙ – Behind the church (**Santa Sophia**) in Piazza Matteotti stands the Samnium Museum, an 8C edifice rebuilt in the 17C on a polygonal plan. The columns of the **cloisters**★ support Moorish-style arches. Adjoining the cloisters, the museum has an important archeological section and works from the Neapolitan school.

Teatro Romano ⊙ – *Near Via Port'Arsa.* This is one of the largest Roman theatres still in existence; it was built in the 2C during the reign of the Emperor Hadrian.

BERGAMO★★

Lombardy – Population 114 887
Michelin map 988 fold 3 or 428 E 10/11

Bergamo, one of the principal towns of Lombardy, is situated on the northern edge of the Lombardy plain at the confluence of the Brembana and Seriana valleys. It is an art centre as well as a busy business and industrial centre.

The modern **lower town** is pleasant while the old **upper town** is quiet, picturesque and evocative of the past. It also has many delightful, old cakeshops whose windows are filled with the small yellow cakes that are a local speciality, the *"polenta e osei"*.

From Roman city to Venetian rule – Around 1200 BC the Ligurians occupied the site of the upper town. The Gauls seized the settlement in c AD 550 and called it Berghem. It was renamed Bergomum by the Romans when they took over in 196 BC. The city was destroyed by the Barbarians before enjoying a period of peace under the Lombards and in particular in the reign of Queen Theodolinda. An independent commune from the 11C to the 13C, it then joined the Lombard League in its struggle against the Emperor Frederick Barbarossa. The town suffered during the struggles between the Guelphs (followers of the pope) and the Ghibellines (followers of the emperor). Under the rule of **Bartolomeo Colleoni** (1400-75), the town fell first to the Visconti family from Milan and then to the Republic of Venice which the famous mercenary leader served successively. Bergamo came under Austrian rule in 1814 and was liberated by Garibaldi in 1859.

Bergamo and its artists – In addition to a large group of local artists, namely Previtali, Moroni, Cariani, Baschenis and Fra Galgario, numerous others worked in the town, including Lorenzo Lotto, Giovanni da Campione and Amadeo.

Scapino   Pantaloon   Fracasso   Pulcinella   Scaramouch   Mezzetino

Masks and Bergamasques – The **Commedia dell'Arte** originated at Bergamo in the 16C. The comedy consists of an improvisation *(imbroglio)* based on a pre-arranged theme *(scenario)*, with gags *(lazzi)* uttered by masked actors representing stock characters: the valet (Harlequin), a stubborn but wily peasant from the Brembana Valley, the braggart (Pulcinella) the lady's maid (Columbine), the lover (Pierrot), the knave (Scapino), the old fox (Scaramouch), the clown (Pantaloon) and the musician (Mezzetino). Its element of caricature sometimes springs from triviality. This form of theatre was popular in France in the 17C and 18C. Bergamo is also the home of the composer Donizetti (1797-1848). The vivacity of the people is displayed in the local musical folklore: the Bergamasque, a lively dance, is accompanied by pipers playing their *pifferi*.

BERGAMO

"Città Alta": traffic restrictions

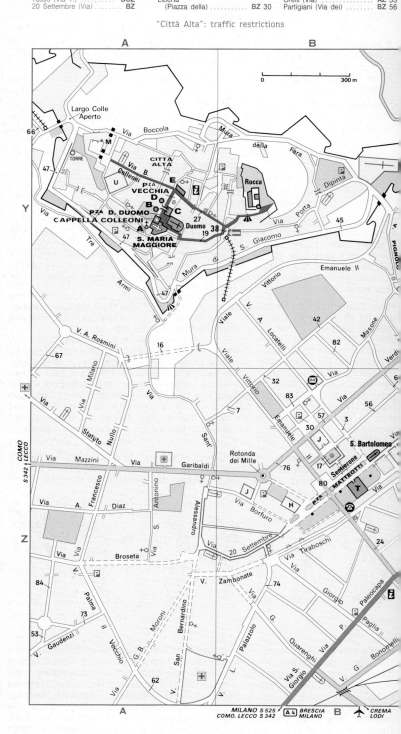

A Tempietto di Santa Croce	C Palazzo della Ragione	E Palazzo Scamozziano
B Battistero	D Torre	T Teatro Donizetti

★★★ CITTÀ ALTA (UPPER TOWN) (ABY)

No cars allowed in this part of the town – 3 hours

When going by car, park outside the walls *(see above)*, or take the funicular *(station in Viale Vittorio Emanuele II)* which ends in **Piazza del Mercato delle Scarpe** (Square of the Shoe Market) **(BY 38)**.

The Upper Town, with its 16C Venetian perimeter wall, its strategically-placed castle, and its winding alleyways lined with old houses, boasts Bergamo's finest buildings.

★★ **Piazza del Duomo (AY)** – This attractive square lined with fine structures is linked to the Piazza Vecchia by the arcades of the Palazzo Ragione.

★★ **Capella Colleoni** ⊘ – The architect of the Carthusian monastery at Pavia, **Amadeo**, designed the chapel (1470-76), a jewel of Lombard-Renaissance architecture, as a mausoleum for Bartolomeo Colleoni, who directed that it should be built on the site of the sacristy of the basilica of St Mary Major. The funerary chapel opens into and is embedded in the north side of the basilica. The domed main structure is adjacent to the north porch which is skilfully used to counterbalance the recess.

The elegant **façade** is faced with precious multi-coloured marble and lavishly decorated with delicate sculptures: figures of children *(putti)*, fluted and wreathed columns, sculptured pilasters, vases and candelabra, medallions and low reliefs combining sacred and secular elements after the contemporary fashion (allegories, scenes from the Old Testament, mythological figures including scenes from the life of Hercules with whom Colleoni identified himself).

The interior is sumptuously decorated with low reliefs of extraordinary delicacy, frescoes by Tiepolo and Renaissance **stalls** with intarsia work. The **Colleoni monument**, also by Amadeo, is surmounted by an equestrian statue of the leader in gilded wood and is delicately carved. The low reliefs of the sarcophagi represent scenes from the New Testament separated by niches housing statues of the Virtues. Between the two sarcophagi are portraits of the leader's children. His favourite daughter, Medea, who died at the age of 15, lies near him *(to the left)*, in a tomb by Amadeo which is a marvel of delicacy and purity.

★ **Basilica di Santa Maria Maggiore** ⊘ – This church, dedicated to St Mary Major, is 12C but the two lovely north and south **porches** with loggias and supported by lions in the Lombard Romanesque style were added in the 14C by Giovanni da Campione.

The interior, remodelled in the baroque style (late 16C-early 17C), is richly decorated with stucco and gilding. The walls of the aisles and the chancel are hung with nine splendid Florentine **tapestries★★** (1580-1586), beautifully designed after cartoons by Alessandro Allori which relate the Life of the Virgin. On the west wall of the nave hangs the sumptuous Flemish tapestry depicting the **Crucifixion★★**. It was woven in Antwerp between 1696 and 1698 after cartoons by L Van Schoor. This part of the church also contains Donizetti's tomb (1797-1848). Note also the curious 18C baroque confessional in the north aisle and the interesting 14C frescoes in the transept. Incorporated in the chancel screen are four superb **panels of intarsia work★★** depicting scenes from the Old Testament. They were made in the 16C after the designs of Lorenzo Lotto.

Maps and town plans in Michelin Guides are oriented with north at the top

Leave by the door giving onto Piazza di Santa Maria Maggiore to admire the 14C south porch, as well as the charming **Tempietto Santa Croce** (**A**) which was built c1000 on the quatrefoil plan in the early-Romanesque style. To return to the Piazza del Duomo walk round the basilica's **east end★** with its radiating chapels decorated with graceful arcading.

★ **Battistero** (**B**) – This charming octagonal baptistery is encircled by a red Verona marble gallery with graceful, slender columns and 14C statues representing the Virtues. It is a reconstruction of Giovanni da Campione's original work dating from 1340. It originally graced the east end of the nave of St Mary Major but was deemed too cumbersome and was demolished in 1660 and rebuilt on its present site in 1898.

Duomo – The cathedral has a richly-decorated interior (18C). The very lovely baroque stalls were carved by the Sanzi.

★ **Piazza Vecchia** (**AY**) – This is the historic centre of the town. The **Palazzo della Ragione** (**AY C**), the oldest town hall in Italy, dates from 1199 but was rebuilt in the 16C. It has graceful arcades and trefoil windows and a central balcony surmounted by the Lion of St Mark symbolising Venetian rule. A 14C covered stairway leads to the majestic 12C **bell tower** (**D**) ⊘ with its 15C clock. The **Palazzo Scamozziano** (**AY E**) opposite is in the Palladian style. The fountain in the centre was offered to Genoa in 1780 by the Doge of Venice, Alvise Contarini.

Via Bartolomeo Colleoni (**AY**) ⊘ – This street is lined with old mansions including the Colleoni Mansion, at Nos 9 and 11, which contains frescoes to the glory of the mercenary leader.

Rocca (**BY**) – Built in the 14C the fortress *(rocca)* was remodelled by the Venetians. There are interesting **views★** of the upper and lower towns.

★ CITTÀ BASSA (LOWER TOWN) *1 1/2 hours.*

The Carrara Academy is in the heart of a district of attractive alleyways, while Piazza Matteotti is at the centre of the present-day business and shopping district in the lower town *(città bassa)*.

★★ **Accademia Carrara** (**CY**) ⊘ – This collection of 15C-18C Italian and foreign paintings is housed in a neo-classical palace.
Beyond the early-15C works, which still recall the International Gothic style *(see ART: Middle Ages)*, hang two important portraits of **Giuliano de'Medici** by Botticelli and the elegant and refined one of **Lionello d'Este** by Pisanello. These are followed by works of the Venetian school: by the Vivarini family, Carlo Crivelli, Giovanni Bellini (gentle Madonnas with dreamy expressions which are similar to those of his brother-in-law, Mantegna), Gentile Bellini (delicate but penetrating portraits), Carpaccio *(Portrait of the Doge Leonardo Loredan)* and by Lorenzo Lotto. Next come the late-15C and early-16C works represented by Cosimo Tura, master of the Ferrarese school (a very realistic *Virgin and Child* showing the influence of Flemish art), by the Lombard, Bergognone (soft light), and by the Bergamask, Previtali.
The 16C covers works by the Venetian Lorenzo Lotto (including a splendid *Holy Family with St Catherine*), the fine Bergamask portraitist Cariani, and the Venetian masters, Titian and Tintoretto. The colours and delicate draughtsmanship of Raphael greatly influenced Garofalo (Benvenuto Tisi) who was nicknamed the Ferrara Raphael, while the Piedmontese Gaudenzio Ferrari and Bernardino Luini, the main exponents of the Renaissance in Lombardy, were inspired by Leonardo da Vinci. The 16C **portraits** are a particularly rich group, with the Ferrarese school which specialised in this art and the Bergamask, Moroni (1523-78). Foreign artists include Clouet *(Portrait of Louis de Clèves)* and Dürer. The 17C-18C Bergamask school is represented by Baschenis (1617-77) and excellent portraits by Fra Galgario (1655-1743). The 17C Flemish and Dutch section (Rubens, Van Dyck, Brueghel...) is dominated by a delightful Van Goyen seascape.
The museum also exhibits 18C Venetian painting: scenes of domestic interiors by Pietro Longhi, topographical views by Carlevarijs, Bernardo Bellotto, Canaletto and Francesco Guardi.

★ **Old quarter** – The main street of this quarter is **Via Pignolo★** (**BCYZ**) which winds among old palaces, mostly 16C and 18C and churches containing numerous works of art. The Church of **San Bernardino** (**CY**) has in the chancel a *Virgin and Saints* (1521) by Lorenzo Lotto. **Santo Spirito** (**CZ**) contains a *St John the Baptist surrounded by saints* and a polyptych by Previtali, a polyptych portraying the Virgin by Bergognone and a *Virgin and Child* by Lorenzo Lotto.

★ **Piazza Matteotti** (**BZ**) – This immense square in the centre of the modern town is overlooked by the **Church of San Bartolomeo** (a superb *Virgin and Saints* by Lorenzo Lotto), the **Donizetti Theatre** (**T**) and is bordered by one of the Bergamasks' favourite promenades, the **Sentierone**.

EXCURSIONS

★ **Museo del Presepio** ⊙ – *Brembo di Dalmine, 8km – 5 miles southwest. 4km from the Dalmine motorway exit. Follow directions for the museum.*
An outstanding collection of some 800 nativity scenes *(presepio)* which come from many different places and range in size from one set out in a hazelnut shell to the enormous 18C Neapolitan creche featuring some delightful street scenes. Note too the electronic nativity scene which, in just 15 minutes, presents a diorama of Biblical events that took place on or around Christmas Eve, with background music. The varied materials include card, papier-maché, ceramic, plaster, wood, stone, and even the modest but highly colourful and striking tinfoil of the Polish nativity scenes. Sometimes the little figures have been made using the most unlikely materials such as pins, matches and even the tiny hinges which fix the material to the ribs in an umbrella. Apart from the scenes themselves the interiors of the houses in the various exhibits reveal the great care and attention paid to the realistic depiction of the various countries.

★ **Val Brembana** – *25km – 16 miles north.* For the Brembana Valley leave Bergamo by the S 470 which follows an industrial development zone. Note the curious two-toned limestone strata of the valley. The important thermal spa of **San Pellegrino Terme**‡‡ lies in a lovely mountain setting.

BOLOGNA★★

Emilia-Romagna – Population 403 397
Michelin map 988 folds 14 and 15 or 429, 430 I 15/16
Plan of the conurbation in the current Michelin Red Guide Italia

Situated on the southern edge of the Po Plain, on the lower slopes of the Apennine foothills, Bologna, the capital of Emilia-Romagna, is a city of many facets: its medieval towers, churches, long arcaded streets lined by sumptuous 14C to 17C palaces recall the former political and cultural importance of this once independent city.
Bologna is famous for its university, one of the oldest in Europe, which already numbered 10 000 students in the 13C and produced many scholars, including Guglielmo Marconi (1874-1937).
In addition to being a gastronomic centre, Bologna is an important industrial and commercial town well-placed on both the national rail and road networks. The city hosts numerous international fairs, shows and exhibitions.

HISTORICAL AND ARTISTIC NOTES

The Etruscan settlement of Felsina was conquered in the 4C BC by the Boïan Gauls, who were driven out in their turn by the Romans in 190 BC. Roman *Bononia* fell under the sway of the Barbarians and did not recover until the 12C. From the 13C onwards the city enjoyed the status of an independent commune and developed rapidly. A fortified city wall, towers, palaces and churches were built and the university flourished and acquired an excellent reputation for its teaching of Roman law. In the struggle which confronted the Ghibellines, supporting the emperor, and the Guelphs, partisans of communal independence, it was the latter who prevailed when in 1249 they defeated the Imperial Army of Frederick II at Fossalta. The emperor's son, Enzo, was taken prisoner and remained at Bologna until his death 23 years later.
In the 15C, following a period of violent struggles between rival families, the city was ruled by the **Bentivoglio** family. Bologna was greatly influenced by the Tuscan Renaissance during the reign of Giovanni II Bentivoglio. The Bentivoglio family was in its turn vanquished in 1506 by **Pope Julius II** and the city remained under papal control until the arrival of Napoleon Bonaparte in 1797. In the early 19C several insurrections were severely repressed by the Austrians and in 1860 Bologna was united with Piedmont.
Famous citizens include the Popes, Gregory XIII, who established our present Gregorian calendar (1582), Gregory XV (17C) and Benedict XIV (18C). In 1530, following the defeat of François I at Pavia and the sack of Rome, the Emperor Charles V obliged Pope Clement VII to crown him in the Basilica of St Petronius in Bologna.

Bologna School of Painting – This term covers the artistic movement founded by the **Carracci**, a Bolognese family of painters, as a reaction to the excessive formalism of Tuscan Mannerism. Their aim was to create simpler compositions and a greater realism of subject matter. Numerous artists, including their Bolognese followers Albani, Guercino, Domenichino and Guido Reni, followed this movement known as the Academy of the Eclectic *(Incamminati)*, whose main teaching precept was the study of nature.

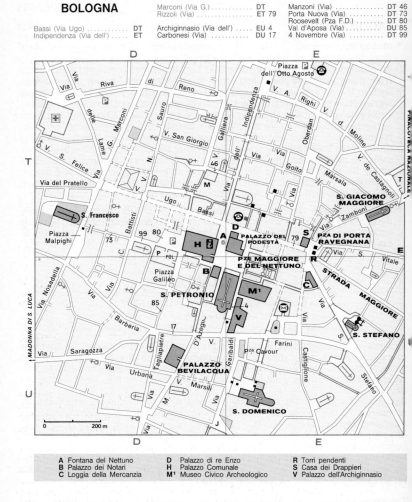

BOLOGNA

A Fontana del Nettuno
B Palazzo dei Notari
C Loggia della Mercanzia
D Palazzo di re Enzo
H Palazzo Comunale
M¹ Museo Civico Archeologico
R Torri pendenti
S Casa dei Drappieri
V Palazzo dell'Archiginnasio

The work of Annibale Carracci, the decorator of the Farnese Palace in Rome and the most famous member of his artistic family, had a decisive influence on this new artistic movement. Annibale was a precursor of baroque art with his purity of tone and the vitality of his decorative schemes.

★★★ CITY CENTRE *1 day*

The two adjoining squares, **Piazza Maggiore** and **Piazza del Nettuno**★★★, together with **Piazza di Porta Ravegnana**★★, the heart of Bologna, form a harmonious ensemble.

★★ **Fontana del Nettuno** (DT A) – The fountain is the work of the Flemish sculptor known as Giambologna or Giovanni Bologna. The muscular bronze Neptune (Nettuno), nicknamed the Giant, is surrounded by four sirens spouting water from their breasts. The group has a rather rough vigour in tune with the town's character.

★ **Palazzo Comunale** (DT H) ⊙ – The façade of the Town Hall is composed of buildings of different periods: 13C to the left, 15C on the right; in the centre the main doorway is 16C (the lower section is by Alessi) and is surmounted by a statue of Pope Gregory XIII. Above and to the left of the doorway is a statue of the *Virgin and Child* (1478) in terracotta by Niccolò dell'Arca. At the far end of the courtyard, under a gallery on the left, rises a great ramp, the so-called *Scala dei cavalli* (at one time climbed by horse-drawn carriages) leading to the richly decorated first-floor rooms, then up again to the second floor.
Opening off the vast Farnese Gallery with 17C frescoes are the splendid rooms, at one time Cardinal Legato's rooms, which now display the town's art collections **(Collezioni comunali d'arte)** ⊙ with a sculpture section and a fine selection of Emilian **paintings**★. They also house a museum **(Museo Morandi)** ⊙ which boasts an extensive collection of works by the painter and engraver from Bologna (1890-1964).
To the left of the Palazzo Comunale stands the severe 14C-15C Notaries' Palace **(Palazzo dei Notari)** (DU B).

★ **Palazzo del Podestà** (ET) ⊘ – The Renaissance façade of the Governor's Palace facing Piazza Maggiore has arcades separated by Corinthian columns on the ground floor and is surmounted by a balustrade. The upper storey is punctuated by pilasters and is crowned by an attic pierced by oculi or round windows.

The 13C King Enzo's Palace **(Palazzo di Re Enzo)** (ET D) stands next to the Governor's Palace. It has a fine inner courtyard and a magnificent staircase leading up to a gallery, to the left of which is a courtyard overlooked by the Arengo Tower and the Podestà Chamber, to the left.

★★ **Basilica di San Petronio** (DEU) – Building on the basilica, dedicated to St
Petronius, began in 1390 to the plans
of Antonio di Vincenzo (1340-1402)
and was fully completed only in the
17C when the vaulting was finished.
The façade, the upper part of which
lacks its marble facing, is remarkable
chiefly for the main **doorway★★** on
which the Sienese Jacopo della Quercia
worked from 1425 to 1438. The lintel,
uprights and embrasures are adorned
with small, expressive low reliefs,
rather pagan in spirit.

This immense building has many **works
of art★** including frescoes by Giovanni
da Modena (15C) in the first and the
fourth chapels off the north aisle.
Particularly striking is the fourth chapel, the right wall of which depicts *the
Journey of the Kings* and the left wall
an impressive *Inferno* and *Paradise*.

Central doorway of Basilica
di San Petronio, Bologna

Additional works include a *Martyrdom of St Sebastian* by the late-15C Ferrara school in the fifth chapel; a *Madonna* (1492) by Lorenzo Costa and the tomb of Elisa Baciocchi, Napoleon's sister, in the seventh chapel; and at the high altar a canopy (baldachin) by Vignola (16C). The 15C organ on the right is one of the oldest in Italy.

★★ **Museo Civico Archeologico** (EU M¹) ⊘ – The atrium and inner courtyard of the municipal museum house an archaeological collection and the adjacent wing houses the plaster casts gallery. On the first floor is an extensive collection of funerary artefacts (7C BC) from the tombs in the graveyard in Verucchio (near Rimini), one of the major centres of Villanovian culture in Emilia. Also representative of this civilisation is the **askos Benacci**, thought to be an unguent and perfume jar. The museum also has prehistoric, Egyptian, Greek and Roman (fine Roman copy of the **head of Athena Lemnia**, the bronze statue by Phidias) and Etruscan-Italian sections.

Near the museum is the 16C Bishop's Palace **(Palazzo dell'Archiginnasio)** ⊘ (EU V), the home of an extensive library (10 000 manuscripts) and the 17C-18C Anatomy Theatre **(Teatro Anatomico).**

★★ **Torri pendenti** (ET R) – There are two tall leaning towers which belonged to noble families in the attractive Piazza di Porta Ravegnana. They are symbols of the continual conflict between rival Guelph and Ghibelline families in the Middle Ages. The taller, **Torre degli Asinelli** ⊘, nearly 100m – 328ft high, dates from 1109. 486 steps lead to the top from where there is an admirable **panorama★★** of the city. The second, known as **Torre Garisenda**, is 50m - 164ft high and has a tilt of over 3m - 10ft. No 1 in the square is the Renaissance Linen Drapers' Hall **(Casa dei Drappieri)** (ET S).

The 14C **Mercanzia★** (EU C) or Merchants' House, in the next square, bears the coats of arms of the various guilds and several small statues.

★ **Basilica di Santo Stefano** (EU) – The basilica comprises four buildings overlooking the square with its Renaissance mansions: the Church of the Crucifix **(Crocifisso)** 11C but remodelled; the 12C Church of the Holy Sepulchre **(Santo Sepolcro)** with its polygonal plan and the shrine of Bologna's patron saint, St Petronius. Go through the Church of the Holy Sepulchre to reach the charming 12C Court of Pilate and Romanesque cloisters transformed into a museum **(museo)** ⊘ (paintings, statues and liturgical objects).

At the far end of the courtyard is the 13C Church of the Trinity **(Chiesa della Trinità)** with a curious 14C multicoloured group representing the Adoration of the Magi.

The 8C-11C church **Santi Vitale e Agricola** is plain and massive.

ADDITIONAL SIGHTS

★★ **Pinacoteca Nazionale** ⊙ - *Take Via Zamboni* (ET). The Bologna school is well represented in this art gallery. The school's characteristics were: in the 14C, gold background, bright colours and Gothic preciosity (affectation), all typical of Byzantine art; under the Renaissance, mannerism, idealism, strict composition; during the baroque period, with the Carracci, realism, vigour and colour; and with the pupils of the Carracci, an academic style.

The first rooms are devoted to the 14C Bolognese painters: Vitale da Bologna (lovely frescoes), Simone De'Crocifissi and Giovanni da Modena. Note, too, the polyptych of the *Madonna Enthroned and Child* the only one of Giotto's works created during his time in Bologna to have survived to the present day.

Next are displayed early Renaissance works: the Venetian school (the Vivarini family and Cima da Conegliano), the Ferrara school with its markedly realistic works (Ercole de'Roberti, Francesco del Cossa and Lorenzo Costa), Bolognese artists such as Francia *(The Adoration of the Child)*.

Note *St Cecilia*, a famous picture of truly classical beauty by Raphael.

The 17C Bologna school is represented by works by the Carracci brothers, Guido Reni, Albani Domenichino and pupils, as well as Guercino with his outstanding masterpiece *St William*, rich in clever light effects.

★ **San Giacomo Maggiore** (ET) - The church, dedicated to St James Major, was founded in 1267. On the north side is a fine Renaissance portico (1481). In the chapel **(Cappella Bentivoglio★)** is a late-15C altarpiece that is considered to be one of Francia's best pieces and frescoes which are in part attributed to the Ferraran, Lorenzo Costa. Opposite the chapel, in the ambulatory, stands the **tomb★** of the jurist, Antonio Bentivoglio, by Jacopo della Quercia. In St Cecilia's Chapel are remarkable **frescoes★** ⊙ (1506) by Francia and Lorenzo Costa.

★ **Strada Maggiore** (EU) - The street is lined with crenellated Gothic and classical palaces. No 44, a palace dating from 1658, houses the **Museo d'Arte industriale** ⊙ and the **Galleria Davia Bargellini** ⊙: 16C-18C Bolognese furniture, 18C puppet theatre, a collection of door handles and locks, and paintings including several on the Madonna and Child theme by the Vivarini family, Garofalo, Francia and Vitale da Bologna.

★ **San Domenico** (EU) - The church, dedicated to St Dominic, was built at the beginning of the 13C and remodelled in the 18C. The famous and beautiful **tomb★★** (arca) of the saint by Nicola Pisano (1267) was crowned with an arch (1468-73) by the sculptor Niccolò da Bari, who was afterwards known as Niccolò dell'Arca. The two saints and a kneeling angel (1494) were by Michelangelo. The chapel south of the choir has a fine painting by Filippino Lippi: the *Mystic Marriage of St Catherine* ★ (1501).

★ **Palazzo Bevilacqua** (DU) - This, the finest palace in Bologna, is in the Florentine-Renaissance rusticated style.

San Francesco (DT) - At the high altar is a magnificent marble **altarpiece★** (1392), a Gothic work by the Venetian sculptor Paolo dalle Masegne.

EXCURSION

Madonna di San Luca - *5km - 3 miles southwest. Leave the city centre by Via Saragozza* (DU). The 18C church is linked to the city by a **portico★** (4km long) of 666 arches. In the chancel is the *Madonna of St Luke*, a painting in the 12C Byzantine style. There is a lovely **view★** of Bologna and the Apennines.

Help us in our constant task of keeping up-to-date
Please send us your comments and suggestions

Michelin Tyre PLC
Tourism Department
Green Guides
38 Clarendon Road
WATFORD
Herts WD1 1SX
Tel: 01923 415 000
Fax: 01923 415 250

BOLSENA

Lazio – Population 4 057
Michelin map 988 fold 25 or 430 O17

Bolsena, the ancient Etruscan city of Volsinii, stands on the banks of Italy's largest lake of volcanic origin; its level is continually changing owing to earth tremors. Its shady shores welcome many visitors attracted by a gentle and limpid light. In the old part of the town its sombre-coloured houses cluster upon a small hill; there is a good view from the S2, the Viterbo-Siena road.

The Miracle of Bolsena – A Bohemian priest had doubts about the Transubstantiation, that is, the incarnation of Christ in the Host. According to legend, as he was celebrating mass in St Christina's Church, the Host began to bleed profusely at the moment of Consecration. The priest no longer doubted the mystery and the Feast of Corpus Christi was instituted.

★ **Santa Cristina** ⊙ – The 3C Saint Christina is said to have belonged to the Bolsena region. She was a victim of the persecutions of Diocletian. Although the church is 11C the façade, articulated by gracefully carved pilasters, is Renaissance. The columns inside are Roman. The north aisle leads to the **Chapel of the Miracle**, where the pavement stained by the blood of the Host is revered, and then to the Grotto of St Christina. In the latter is the Altar of the Miracle and a reclining statue of the saint attributed to the Della Robbia.

BOLZANO★

Bozen – Trentino-Alto Adige – Population 98 059
Michelin map 988 fold 4, 429 C 15/16 – Local map see DOLOMITI
Town plan in the current Michelin Red Guide Italia

Bolzano, the capital of the Alto Adige, lies on the Brenner transalpine route at the confluence of the Isarco and the Adige. The surrounding slopes are covered with orchards and vineyards. The architecture of the town shows a marked Tyrolean or Austrian influence which was exercised between the 16C and 1918. This industrial and commercial town is now also a busy tourist centre owing to its proximity to the Dolomites. There are some lovely houses in the town centre from **Piazza Walther** to **Via dei Portici★**.

★ **Duomo** – The cathedral is built of pink sandstone and roofed with multicoloured glazed tiles. Construction work was carried out during various periods including the paleo-Christian Era (5C – 6C), the Carolingian Era (8C – 9C), the Romanesque (late 12C) and the Gothic periods (13C). The campanile (1501-1519) rises to a height of 62m and includes late Gothic bays. On the north side is the "Small Wine Portal" *(porticina del vino)* on which all the decorative features have a connection with vines and grape harvesting. It indicates the privilege enjoyed by this particular church – an exclusive right to sell wine at this doorway. Inside, there are traces of 14C and 15C frescoes and a fine Gothic, carved sandstone **pulpit★** (1514).

Chiesa dei Dominicani ⊙ – *Piazza Domenicani.* The Dominican Church was built in the early 14C in the Gothic style with a deep presbytery that is separated from the nave by a rood screen. The church was later altered and was subsequently damaged after the secularisation of 1785. To the right beyond the rood screen is St John's Chapel **(San Giovanni)** which is covered in frescoes from the Giotto School and is reminiscent of the Scrovegni Chapel in Padua. The frescoes depict scenes from the lives of the Blessed Virgin Mary, St John the Baptist, St Nicholas and St John the Evangelist. Another set of frescoes, by Friedrich Pacher (15C), can be seen in the cloisters **(chiostro)** to the right of the church.

Chiesa dei Francescani ⊙ – *1, via Francescani.* Burnt down in 1291, the Franciscan Church was rebuilt in the 14C and the gothic vaulting added in the 15C. The **Nativity altar★** is a remarkable wooden altarpiece carved by Hans Klocker (16C). The delightful little cloisters have elegant fan-vaulting decorated with frescoes by the Giotto School.

Antica parrochiale di Gries – *Access via the Corso Libertà beyond Sant'Agostino.* The original Romanesque building was replaced by a 15C Gothic parish church containing a Romanesque wooden Crucifix (opposite the door) and, to the right of the high altar, a side altar with an **altarpiece★** carved by Michael Pacher (c1430-1498), an Austrian painter and sculptor from the Tyrol. It depicts the Crowning of the Virgin between Archangel Gabriel who is about to strike the devil and St Erasmus who is holding out the winch that kills him by tearing out his guts. The back features the work of a Bavarian artist (1488). A particularly curious detail is the pair of glasses worn by the person at the bottom of the painting to the right.

Riviera del BRENTA★★

Veneto

Michelin map 988 fold 5 or 429 fold 15 – 35km – 22 miles east of Padua

Standing alongside the Brenta Canal between Strà and Fusina are numerous lovely classical **villas**★ by Palladio *(see Index)*. These were the summer residences of the Venetian nobility who used to lay on sumptuous night-time festivities to music by Vivaldi, Pergolesi or Cimarosa.

Sightseeing ⊙ – Boat trips leave from both Venice and Padua. By car take the road which follows the Brenta passing through Strà, Dolo, Mira and Malcontenta.

> **Strà** – The **Villa Nazionale**★ ⊙ has a majestic garden with a delightful vista and basin. The spacious **apartments**★ of this 18C palace were decorated by various artists including Giovanni Battista Tiepolo who painted his masterpiece, *The Apotheosis of the Pisani Family*★★.

> **Mira** – The **Palazzo Foscarini** and **Villa Widmann-Foscari-Rezzonico** ⊙ are both 18C. The **ballroom**★ of the latter is entirely decorated with frescoes.

> **Malcontenta** – Palladio built the **Villa Foscari**★ ⊙ in 1574. G. B. Zelotti and B. Franco were responsible for the frescoes.
> The villa was named after the wife of a Foscari who was ill-pleased *(malcontenta)* at being consigned to the villa.

BRESCIA★

Lombardy – Population 194 037

Michelin map 988 fold 4, 428 and 429 F 12

The important industrial town of Brescia lies at the foot of the Lombard Pre-Alps. It has retained the regular street plan of the Roman camp *(castrum)* of Brixia. The town is dominated to the north by a medieval castle (Castello) and its bustling centre has many fine buildings from all periods: Roman, Romanesque, Renaissance and baroque.

HISTORICAL NOTES

Brixia flourished under the Empire and the remains of Roman monuments include the Capitoline Temple and the forum.
In the 8C Brescia became a Lombard duchy and then in the 12C and 13C a free commune and member of the Lombard League *(see Index)*.
The town was one of the most prosperous in Italy, owing to the manufacture of arms and armour. Brescia supplied all Europe until the 18C. From 1426 to 1797 Brescia was under Venetian rule and acquired numerous secular and religious buildings. A group of artists formed the Brescia school and the most important members were, in the 15C, Vincenzo Foppa and in the 16C, Romanino and Moretto, Savoldo and Civerchio.

SIGHTS

★ **Piazza della Loggia** (BY 9) – The **Loggia** (BY H), now the town hall, was built from the end of the 15C to the beginning of the 16C. Sansovino and Palladio were amongst those involved in the building of the upper storey. The **Clock Tower** opposite the Loggia is topped by two clockwork figures (Jacks) that strike the hours. On the south side of the square stand the graceful palaces, **Monte di pietà vecchio** (1484) and **Monte di pietà nuovo** (1497) (BY B). To the north of the square is a picturesque popular quarter with arcades and old houses.

Piazza Paolo VI (BY 16) – The 17C New Cathedral **(Duomo Nuovo)** in white marble seems to crush the Old Cathedral **(Duomo Vecchio★)**, a late 11C Romanesque building which succeeded an earlier sanctuary known as the rotunda after its shape.

Inside, there is a magnificent sarcophagus in rose-coloured marble surmounted by the recumbent figure of a bishop, and in the chancel paintings by local artists, Moretto and Romanino. The organ was built in 1536 by Antegnati. To the left of the Duomo Nuovo, the **Broletto (P)** is an austere Romanesque building dominated by a massive square tower. Proclamations were made from the balcony on the façade.

★ **Pinacoteca Tosio Martinengo (CZ)** ⊘ – The art gallery displays works of the **Brescia school**, characterised by richness of colour and well-balanced composition: religious scenes and portraits by Moretto, more sumptuous religious scenes in the Venetian manner by Romanino and other works, as well as canvases by Vincenzo Foppa and Savoldo. The works of Clouet, Raphael, the Master of Utrecht, Lorenzo Lotto and Tintoretto are also on view.

★ **Via dei Musei (CY)** – This picturesque street has two interesting museums. The Roman Museum **(Museo romano★)** in the ruins of the **Capitoline Temple★** (AD 73) contains a magnificent **Winged Victory** and six bronze Roman **busts**. Beyond the remains of the forum is the monastery of **San Salvatore and Santa Guilia★**

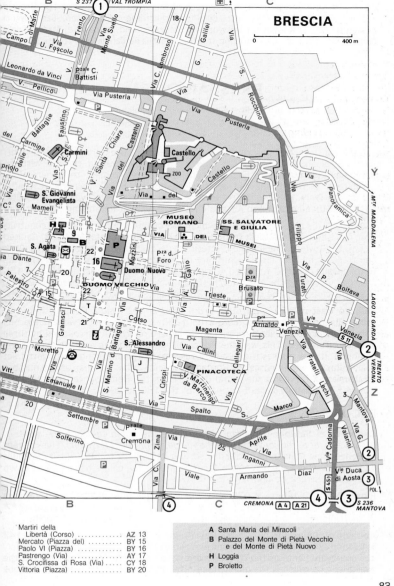

A Santa Maria dei Miracoli
B Palazzo del Monte di Pietà Vecchio
    e del Monte di Pietà Nuovo
H Loggia
P Broletto

founded in AD 753 by Ansa, the wife of the last King of the Lombards, Desiderio. Tradition has it that Desiderio's daughter, Ermengarda, wife of Charlemagne, who later repudiated her, died here. The 9C San Salvatore Basilica still has its original decoration of frescoes and stucco work. The Church of Santa Guilia, in which the dome is decorated with a fresco of God the Father giving His blessing against a star-studded sky, contains **Desiderio's Cross**★★ (8C-9C). It is richly decorated with precious stones, cameos, and coloured glass and includes a portrait thought to be that of Galla Placidia *(see RAVENNA)* and his sons (3C-4C).

Castello (CY) – Built in 1343 for the Viscontis over the remains of a Roman temple, the castle was given additional bastions in the 16C and its entrance is decorated with the lion representing St Mark. It now houses the **Museo delle armi Luigi Marzoli** ⊙, an interesting collection of arms and armour from the 14C to 18C. Roman remains can be seen inside the museum.

Churches – Brescia boasts several Romanesque, Renaissance and baroque churches and nearly all contain paintings of the Brescia school. The 13C **San Francesco**★ (AY) has a 14C *Pietà* by Giotto's followers, *Three saints* by Moretto and a *Virgin and Saints* altarpiece by Romanino. The 15C and 16C **Santa Maria dei Miracoli** (AYZ **A**) features a lovely marble façade★.

San Nazaro – San Celso (AZ) contains Moretto's masterpiece, the *Coronation of the Virgin*★ and a polyptych by Titian. **Sant'Alessandro** (BZ) displays a 15C *Annunciation*★ by Jacopo Bellini and a *Descent from the Cross*★ by Civerchio. **Sant'Agata** (BY) with its rich **interior**★ adorned with a polyptych of the *Virgin of Pity*★ by the 16C Brescia school, as well as a *Virgin with Coral*★, a charming 16C fresco. **San Giovanni Evangelista** (BY) is known for its works by Moretto and Romanino, **Madonna delle Grazie** (AY) for its baroque interior and the **Madonna del Carmini** (BY) for its oriental silhouette.

BRESSANONE★

Brixen – Trentino-Alto Adige – Population 17 010
Michelin map 988 folds 4 and 5 or 429 B 16 – Local map see DOLOMITI
Town plan in the current Michelin Red Guide Italia

Set at the confluence of the rivers Rienza and Isarco, Bressanone is an elegant, typically Tyrolean little town that enjoys a dry, invigorating climate with an exceptionally high number of hours of sunshine. There are many reminders of its eventful past. It was conquered by the Romans in 15 BC, was the seat of a Prince-Bishop from 1027 to 1803, became Bavarian for seven years from 1806 to 1813, and then belonged to Austria until 1919 when it became an Italian town.

Duomo – This baroque cathedral which was orginally a Romanesque construction, has a neo-classical west front designed by Jakob Pirchstaller (1783) flanked by two bell-towers. The luminous interior is decorated with marble, stucco work and frescoes by Paul Troger which are more striking for the gold leaf. The fine Romanesque **cloisters**★ feature 14C ribbed vaulting and interesting 14C and 15C frescoes. Access to the 11C church of San Giovanni Battista *(closed to visitors)* is via the cloisters. The church has 13C Romanesque and 14C Gothic frescoes.

Palazzo Vescovile ⊙ – *Entrance from the Via Vescovado.* Commissioned by Prince-Bishop Bruno de Kirchberg after 1250, the palace underwent numerous alterations in later years but retained its superb **courtyard**★ surrounded by three storeys of arcades. This was the Prince-Bishop's residence and the seat of the bishopric. It now houses the vast **Museo diocesano**★ ⊙ containing a wonderful set of polychrome **wood carvings**★★ (Romanesque and Gothic Tyrolean art), a number of **altarpieces**★ carved in the round dating from the Renaissance, the cathedral **treasure**★ and **Nativity scenes**★ dating from the 18C to 20C.

EXCURSIONS

Convento di Sabiona ⊙ *10km south. Leave the car in the car park north of Chiusa. To get to the convent from the village, go on foot (1/2 hour).* This convent of Benedictine nuns in its attractive setting dates back to the 17C. It was built on the rock where the bishop's palace had stood, the palace having burnt down after being struck by lightning in 1535.

★★★ **Plose** ⊙ – *Alt 2 446m – 8 025ft. To the southeast.* The cable-car from Valcroce and then another from Plose enable visitors to enjoy a wonderful **panorama**★★★ of the Dolomites to the south and the Austrian mountains to the north.

★★ **Abbazia di Novacella** ⊙ – *3km – 2 miles north.* The abbey was founded in 1142 by Bishop Artmanno of Bressanone and run by monks of the Augustinian Order. The courtyard contains the **Well of Wonders** decorated with "eight" wonders of the world, one of which is the abbey itself. The **church** built in the Bavarian baroque style is surprising for the ornateness and brilliance of the interior. Some of the detail in the painting, such as the leg of one of the characters which literally extends out of the fresco, is also striking. The **cloisters**, which were originally Romanesque, are covered with frescoes from a later period and whitewashed over after the plague in the 17C. The memorial stones date back to the 18C. The magnificent Rococo **library** contains 76 000 books including very early books and illuminated manuscripts.

✷✷ **Brunico** - *27km - 17 miles northeast.* This is the main town in the Pusteria Valley. There is an interesting **ethnography museum**★ ⊙ in **Teodone** covering an area of three hectares and including various types of rural building: country house, grain store, farm, hayloft, oven, mill. They provide an effective illustration of the lifestyles and activities of peasants and noblemen in bygone days.

BRINDISI

Puglia - Population 92 531
Michelin map 988 fold 30 or 431 F 35
Town plan in the current Michelin Red Guide Italia *

This important naval and trading port, on the Adriatic side of the 'boot's heel', has a daily shipping connection with Greece. Ever since antiquity the town has played the important role of trading-post with the rest of the Mediterranean basin. It was Trajan who replaced the old Appian Way beyond Benevento with the new Via Traiana which increased the importance of Brindisi from AD 109 onwards. After the Norman conquest the town became a port of embarkation for the Crusades to the Holy Land, and in particular saw the departure of the Sixth Crusade (1228). Along with Taranto and Bari, Brindisi makes up the triangle delimiting the Mezzogiorno, an area of industrial redevelopment.

★ **Colonna Romana** - This Roman marble column near the harbour marked the end of the Appia-Traiana Way. It is crowned by a capital carved with figures.

. **Museo archeologico** ⊙ - *Piazza Duomo.* The archeological museum presents the numerous finds from excavations and a precious collection of vases made by early Italic peoples, the Apulians and Messapii.

CALABRIA★

Michelin map 988 folds 38, 39, 40 or 431
folds 22, 23, 26, 27, 31, 34, 35, 38, 39, 42, 43

Calabria covers the extreme southwestern 'toe' of the Italian peninsula from the Gulf of Policastro to Reggio di Calabria. This mountainous region lacked a good road network, which made it difficult to visit until the motorway to the south was extended as far as the regional capital. For this particular reason the region remained isolated but it would have been a mistake to consider, as a French traveller did at the beginning of the 19C, that "Europe ended at Naples". In fact the opposite is true since the first colonies founded by the Greeks in the 8C BC were located on the Ionian coast of present-day Calabria. It is not always possible - as it is in Sicily at Segesta, Agrigento or Selinunte - to discover the traces of Magna Graecia in the peninsula but the museums of Reggio, Taranto and Naples have collections recalling this period of Greek influence. It lasted until the 3C BC when Rome undertook the conquest of southern Italy, without however establishing a complete and peaceful domination until Sulla reorganised the administration of these provinces in the 1C BC.

After the fall of the Roman Empire, Calabria and the neighbouring regions fell under the sway of the Lombards, Saracens and Byzantines before being reunited with the Norman kingdom of the Two Sicilies and finally becoming part of a unified Italy in 1860.

The mountainous massifs which occupy the interior of the peninsula are fringed by narrow coastal plains. Between these physically-distinct regions there are considerable differences of vegetation and climate according to the seasons. The Sila Massif comprises rugged mountains and alpine prairies; the Aspromonte is covered with chestnut forests; there are stony and abrupt valleys along the coastline and coastal plains covered with fruit trees bordering the Gulf of Taranto. Following the recent agrarian reform emigration has slowed down and the region is emerging from its isolation.

★★ **Massiccio della Sila** - North of Catanzaro and several miles inland, the high granite plateau of the Sila Massif is covered with Italy's most extensive forest of pine, evergreen oak and beech, which alternates with pastures and tranquil, lonely lakes. As a result of the recent agrarian reform this once-inaccessible region is now a holiday destination in both summer and winter.

To the east of the massif, the capital, **San Giovanni in Fiore**, grew up around the abbey founded by Joachim of Fiore for his new religious order, stricter than that of the Cistercians. La Badia Fiorense has a remarkable pointed doorway and some Cistercian windows in the apse. The small holiday village and ski resort of Lorica has been developed on the indented and wooded shores of the immense **Lake Arvo★**.

★ **Aspromonte** – The Aspromonte Massif forms the southern tip of Calabria and culminates in a peak of 2 000m – 6 561ft. The face overlooking the Tyrrhenian coast drops in terraces to the shore while the slope on the Ionian coast descends more gently down to the sea. The forest cover includes chestnut trees, oaks and beeches. The massif serves as a catchment area from which radiate deep valleys eroded by fast-flowing torrents *(fiumare)*. The wide river beds are dry in summer but may fill up rapidly and the waters become destructive. The S 183 between the S 112 and Melito di Porto Salvo runs through attractive scenery and affords numerous and often quite spectacular **panoramas★★★**.

★ **Costa Viola** – The most southern part of the Tyrrhenian coast from Gioia Tauro to Villa San Giovanni, the coast takes its name from the dark purple (*viola*) of its rocky mountain slopes.

⌂ **Gioia Tauro** – This seaside resort backs onto a hinterland of centuries-old olive groves.

Palmi – This small town perched high above the sea has a small fishing harbour and a lovely sandy beach.
The **Museo comunale** ⊙ *(Casa della Cultura, Via San Giorgio)* has an **ethnographic section★** evoking the life and traditions of Calabria: local costumes, handicrafts, ceramics etc.

★ **Bagnara Calabra** – In a picturesque site looking out to sea, Bagnara is the main fishing port for swordfish.

★ **Scilla** – This small fishing-town stands at the foot of a rock which is said to be a mythical female monster, Scylla. According to Homer's *Odyssey*, it was on this rock that ships often came to grief having successfully avoided the whirlpool of Charybdis near Taormina on the Silician coast. Hence the expression "between Scylla and Charybdis".

Villa San Giovanni – This is the car-ferry *(traghetti)* terminal for Sicily.

★ **Rocca Imperiale** – *25km – 16 miles north of Trebisacce*. This picturesque village has grown up around a castle built by the Emperor Frederick II.

⌂⌂ **Tropea** – This ancient small town, built on the clifftop, had its hour of glory under Angevin and Aragonese rule. The lovely Norman-style **cathedral★** (cattedrale) has three apses encrusted with polychrome stones.

Altomonte – *30km – 19 miles south of Castrovillari*. The large market town is dominated by an imposing 14C Angevin cathedral dedicated to **Santa Maria della Consolazione**. The façade is embellished with a doorway and an elegant rose window. Inside there are no aisles and the east end is flat. The fine **tomb★** is that of Filippo Sangineto. The small museum **(museo civico)** ⊙ beside the church has several precious works of art in addition to a statue of *St Ladislas★* attributed to Simone Martini.

Catanzaro – *Town plan in the current Michelin Red Guide Italia*. Catanzaro stands perched on a hilltop, at some distance from the sea, away from the danger of invading forces and malaria-infested waters. The town was founded in the 9C by the Byzantines and it prospered until the end of the 15C thanks to its university and its silk industry, for which it was famous throughout Europe. After having successfully resisted the French troops of Marshal de Lautrec in 1528, the town began to decline in the 17C, owing partly to the Black Death and partly to numerous earthquakes in the 18C and 19C. However the modern town, traversed by Corso Mazzini, has a certain charm.
The **Villa Trieste★** is a terraced public garden with plenty of shade. The church of **San Domenico** (or of the Rosary) contains a very fine altarpiece of the *Madonna of the Rosary★*, which is probably the work of the 17C Neapolitan school.

Cosenza – *Town plan in the current Michelin Red Guide Italia*.
The modern town is overlooked by the old town where streets and palaces recall the prosperity of the Angevin and Aragonese periods. Cosenza was then considered the artistic and religious capital of Calabria. The 12C-13C **cathedral** (Duomo) has recently been restored to its original aspect. Inside is the **mausoleum★** containing the heart of Isabella of Aragon, the wife of Philip III, King of France and son of Louis IX (St Louis who died in Tunis). She died in 1271 outside Cosenza on the way back from Tunis with the sainted king's body and was buried in St-Denis Basilica in France.

Crotone – *See CROTONE*.

Gerace – *Northwest of Locri on the S 111.* This was the inland refuge of the people from Locri at the time of the Saracen raids. It was abandoned in favour of the coastal area when the latter was rid of malaria. The **cathedral** (Cattedrale) is one of the largest in Calabria and dates back to the time of the Norman Robert Guiscard (11C). Although remodelled several times it has retained its basilical plan with a nave and two aisles separated by lovely antique piers. Quite near stands the church of **San Francesco** with a lovely doorway and a 17C **altarpiece★** in polychrome marble.

Locri – *On the east coast of the Aspromonte Massif.* This modest seaside resort was founded by the Greeks in the 7C BC. The town was ruled by the severe laws decreed by Zaleucos and was one of the rival cities of Crotone which she defeated during the battle of Sagra. Locri repelled all annexation attempts by the Syracusan "tyrants". After having sided with Hannibal, along with the other towns on the Ionian coast during the Second Punic War, it declined in importance and was destroyed by the Saracens in the 9C AD. Most of the town's antiquities can be seen in the museum in Reggio di Calabria. There is an interesting excavation site to the south of the town.

Paola – St Francis of Paola was born here around 1416. A monastery **(convento)** ⊙ visited by numerous pilgrims stands 2km – 1 mile away up the hillside. This large group of buildings includes the basilica with a lovely baroque façade which enshrines the relics of the saint, cloisters and a hermitage hewn out of the rock which contains striking votive offerings.

★ **Pentedattilo** – *10km – 6 miles northwest of Melito di Porto Salvo.* In a sun-scorched valley this little village nestles at the foot of a gigantic and highly-eroded rock which resembles a hand pointing upwards to the sky (*pentedattilo* in Greek means five fingers).

Reggio di Calabria – *See REGGIO DI CALABRIA.*

Rossano – *96km – 60 miles northwest of Crotone.* The town spreads over a hillside clad with olive groves. In the Middle Ages it was the capital of Greek monasticism in the west, where expelled or persecuted Basilian monks came for refuge, living in the cells which can still be seen today. The perfect little Byzantine church **San Marco** dates from this period. The flat east end has three projecting semicircular apses with graceful openings. To the right of the cathedral (Cattedrale) a museum **(Museo Diocesano)** ⊙ in the former archbishop's residence has a valuable *Purpureus Codex★*, a 6C evangelistary with brightly-coloured illuminations. 20km – 12 miles to the west of the town is a small church, **Santa Maria del Patire**, the only remaining building of a large Basilian monastery. The church has a nave and two apses ornamented with blind arcading and inside, mosaics portraying various animals.

Serra San Bruno – Between the Sila and Aspromonte Massifs, amidst the Calabrian mountains covered with oak and pinewood **forests★**, this small market town grew up around a **hermitage** founded by St Bruno. The 12C charterhouse *(1km – 1/2 mile from the town)* and the cave which served as hermitage *(4km – 2 1/2 miles southwest of the latter)* recall the memory of St Bruno who died in 1101.

Sibari – *15km – 9 miles south of Trebisacce.* The town was founded in the 8C BC in a very fertile plain which was the source of the exceptional prosperity of the ancient city of **Sybaris.** It was razed in 510 BC by the neighbouring city of Crotone. There is a small archeological museum **(Museo Archeologico)** ⊙ and an excavation site **(Scavi)** ⊙ to the south of the town.

Stilo – *15km – 9 miles west of Monasterace Marina.* On the rocky side of a deep valley this town was the bastion of the Basilian monks and is famous for its Byzantine church, **La Cattolica★** ⊙. Small in size but of perfect proportions in the form of a Greek cross, it is in the pure Byzantine style and is roofed with five domes. Inside, four ancient columns support the elegant arches and vaulting.

La Cattolica, Stilo

Val CAMONICA

Lombardy

Michelin map 988 fold 4, 428 folds 7 and 17 or 429 fold 12

The valley, which stretches from Lovere to Edolo, is industrial in its lower reaches and becomes more picturesque towards its head with several ruined castles guarding its slopes. Many rock engravings dating from prehistory to the Roman era have been discovered in an area 60km – 37 miles long.

★★ **Rock engravings** – The rock faces of Camonica Valley, smoothed by glacial erosion 10 000 years ago, present an even surface ideally suited to decoration. The engravings, made by pitting or scratching the stone, reveal scenes of the daily life of the peoples who lived on the site: in the Paleolithic Era (about 8000 to 5000 BC) they lived solely from the hunt, then took up agriculture in the Neolithic period, and later metalworking in the Bronze Age (from 1800 BC) and the Iron Age (900 BC). There are mainly four types of scenes: the hunt (stags); ox-teams and ploughs; arms and warriors; religious scenes (praying figures, symbols and idols).

The rock engravings are readily accessible in the **Parco Nazionale delle Incisioni Rupestri di Naquane** ⊙ *(2 hours – access from Capo di Ponte)* and in the **Riserva Naturale Regionale di Ceto, Cimbergo e Paspardo** ⊙; for access apply to the **museum** ⊙ at Nadro in Ceto which is devoted to the rock engravings.

Breno – The main town of the valley has a 10C castle and two interesting churches: the 14C-15C Sant'Antonio and San Salvatore.

Palazzo Farnese di CAPRAROLA★

Lazio

Michelin map 988 fold 25 or 430 P 18 – 19km – 12 miles southeast of Viterbo

The **mansion** was built on a pentagonal plan from 1559 to 1575 for Cardinal Alessandro Farnese to the designs of Vignola, and is a good example of the late-16C Mannerist style.

Palazzo ⊙ – The five storey-tall ranges surround a delightful circular inner courtyard. To the left of the entrance hall is Vignola's **spiral staircase★★** which rises majestically through tiers of 30 paired Doric columns, and is decorated with grotesques and landscapes by Antonio Tempesta.

The paintings which adorn several rooms are by the Zuccaro brothers, Taddeo (1529-66) and Federico (c1540-1609) as well as Bertoja (1544-74). These are typical of the refined and sophisticated Mannerist style of the late Italian Renaissance period.

Park – This 18ha – 44 acre park with its terraces and monumental fountains, is embellished by a charming **palazzina** also designed by Vignola.

Isola di CAPRI★★★

Campania – Population 7 074

Michelin map 988 fold 27 or 431 F 24 – Local map overleaf
Access: see the current Michelin Red Guide Italia

Capri, the Island of Dreams, has always been an enchanting place, with its ideal situation off the Sorrento Peninsula *(see local map under Golfo di NAPOLI)*, its beautiful rugged landscape, mild climate and luxuriant vegetation.

Capri captivated two Roman emperors: Augustus moved from Ischia to Capri, and Tiberius spent the latter part of his life here. Since the late 19C the island has attracted numerous celebrities: artists, writers, musicians and actors, in all seasons. Capri is one of the high spots of international tourism.

★ MARINA GRANDE

This is the main port on the northern side of the isle. The houses, some white, some in varied hues, nestle around the bay framed by spectacular cliffs.
A funicular railway goes to Capri (Piazza Umberto I). There is a bus service to Anacapri with a stop at Capri (Via Roma).

BOAT TRIPS

★★ **Grotta Azzurra** ⊙ – *Boats leave from Marina Grande. It is also possible to go by road (8km – 5 miles from Capri).* The Blue Grotto is the most famous among the many marine caves on the island. The light enters, not directly, but by refraction through the water, giving it a beautiful blue colour.

Faraglioni, Capri

★★ **Tour of the isle** ⓥ – *Leave from Marina Grande.* Visitors will discover a rugged coastline, pierced with caves and small peaceful creeks, fringed with fantastically shaped reefs and lined with sheer cliffs dipping vertically into the sea.

The island is quite small: barely 6km – 4 miles long and 3km – 2 miles wide. The particularly mild climate favours the growth of a varied flora: pine, lentisk, juniper, arbutus, asphodel, myrtle and acanthus.

The boats go in a clockwise direction and the first sight is the Sea Ox Cave **(Grotta del Bove Marino)**, which derives its name from the roar of the sea rushing into the cave in stormy weather. Beyond is the headland (Punta del Capo) dominated by Mount Tiberius **(Monte Tiberio)**. Once past the impressive cliff known as Tiberius' Leap *(see below)*, the headland to the south, Punta di Tragara, is fringed by the famous **Faraglioni**, rocky islets eroded into fantastic shapes by the waves. The Arsenal Cave **(Grotta dell'Arsenale)** was used as a nymphaeum during the reign of Tiberius.

Continue past the small port of Marina Piccola *(see below)* to reach the more gentle west coast. The last part of the trip covers the north coast and includes the visit to the Blue Grotto *(see above)*.

★★ CAPRI

Capri is like a stage setting for an operetta with its small squares, little white houses and its quite Moorish-looking alleyways. Another of its charms is that wild and lonely spots can still be found near crowded and lively scenes.

★ **Piazza Umberto I** – This famous piazzetta is the centre of town and the spot where fashionable crowds gather. The busy narrow side streets, such as **Via Le Botteghe★ (BZ 10)**, are lined with souvenir shops and smart boutiques selling luxury goods.

★★ **Belvedere Cannone** – To reach the belvedere take the **Via Madre Serafina★ (BZ 12)**, which is almost entirely vaulted. The belvedere presents the peaceful and mysterious aspect of Capri with its covered and winding stepped alleys.

★★ **Belvedere Tragara** – *Access by Via Camerelle and Via Tragara.* There is a magnificent view of the Faraglioni.

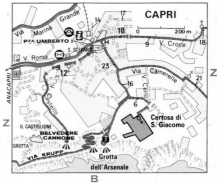

Camerelle (Via)	BZ		Madre Serafina	
Croce (Via)	BZ		(Via)	BZ 12
Fuorlovado (Via)	BZ 9		S. Francesco (Via)	BZ 14
Le Botteghe (Via)	BZ 10		Serena (Via)	BZ 16
Umberto I (Pza)	BZ		Sopramonte (Via)	BZ 17
Vittorio Emanuele			Tiberio (Via)	BZ 18
(Via)	BZ 23		Tragara (Via)	BZ 21
Certosa (Via)	BZ 6			
Fenicia (Scala)	BY 8		**B** Giardini d'Augusto	

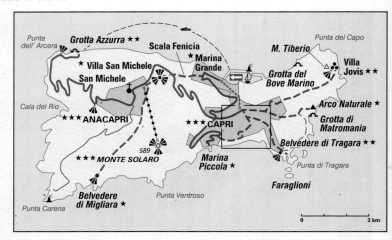

★★ Villa Jovis ⊘ – Jupiter's Villa was the residence of the Emperor Tiberius. Excavations have uncovered servants' quarters, the cisterns that supplied the baths, and the Imperial apartments with a loggia overlooking the sea.

From the esplanade overlooked by a church, there is a lovely **panorama★★** of the whole island.

Take the stairway behind the church to enjoy a view of Tiberius' Leap **(Salto di Tiberio★)**, the impressive cliff from which the emperor is said to have had his victims thrown.

★ Arco Naturale – The sea has created this gigantic natural rock arch which rises well above sea level. Lower down is the **Grotta di Matromania**, a cave where the Romans venerated the goddess Cybele.

Certosa di San Giacomo ⊘ **and Giardini d'Augusto** (BZ B) – This 14C Carthusian Monastery of St James has two cloisters. In the smallest are displayed Roman statues taken from the nymphaeum of the Blue Grotto.

From Augustus' Gardens there is a beautiful **view★★** of Punta di Tragara and the Faraglioni *(see above)*. Lower down, **Via Krupp★**, clinging to the rock face, leads to Marina Piccola.

★ Marina Piccola – There are beautiful small beaches and a haven for fishing boats.

★★★ ANACAPRI

Town plan in the current Michelin Red Guide Italia

Take the Via Roma and a beautiful corniche road to reach Anacapri, a delightful village with shady streets, which is much less crowded than Capri.

★ Villa San Michele ⊘ – *Access from Piazza della Vittoria.*

The villa was built at the end of the 19C for the Swedish doctor-writer, Axel Munthe (d 1949), who lived here up to 1910 and described the atmosphere of the island in his *Story of San Michele*. The house contains 17C and 18C furniture, copies of antique works and some original Roman sculptures. The pergola at the end of the beautiful **garden** giddily overhangs the sea and provides a splendid **panorama★★★** of Capri, Marina Grande, Mount Tiberius and the Faraglioni.

Just below the villa is a stairway, **Scala Fenicia**, which numbers nearly 800 steps and leads down to the harbour. It was for a long time the only link between the town and its port. This is where Axel Munthe met the old Maria "Porta-Lettere" who delivered the mail although she could not read, and who is depicted in his novel.

San Michele – The fine majolica **pavement★** (1761) represents the Garden of Eden after a cartoon by Solimena.

★★★ Monte Solaro ⊘

★★★ Monte Solaro ⊘ – The chairlift swings pleasantly above gardens and terraces brimming over with a luxuriant vegetation. From the summit there is an unforgettable **panorama★★★** of the whole island and the Bay of Naples as far as the island of Ponza, the Apennines and the mountains of Calabria to the south.

★ Belvedere di Migliara – *1 hour on foot Rtn. Pass under the chairlift to take Via Caposcuro.* There is a remarkable **view★** of the lighthouse on the headland, Punta Carena, and of the sheer cliffs.

CAPUA

Campania – Population 18 844

Michelin map 988 fold 27 or 431 D 24 – 38km – 24 miles north of Naples

The present town stands quite near to the ancient Roman Capua where Hannibal grew soft in luxury. This small triangular town, enclosed within ramparts, has a certain charm with its narrow alleys, arches, old palaces and churches, many of which are built with material quarried from the numerous Roman ruins.

Duomo – The cathedral, which dates from the 9C, has been destroyed and rebuilt several times since. The Lombard-style campanile incorporates some ancient fragments at its base. The columns of the atrium have lovely **Corinthian capitals**, dating from the 3C.
Basilical in plan, the cathedral has numerous works of art.

★ **Museo campano** ⊙ – *At the corner of Via Duomo and Via Roma.*
The archeological section in this museum has an astonishing collection of **earth goddesses** dating from the 7C to 1C BC and a charming **mosaic**. The medieval section groups some lovely **sculptures** from the imposing gateway built by the Emperor Frederick II of Hohenstaufen around 1239, to mark the boundary of his kingdom.
The lovely **Piazza dei Giudici** is bordered by the baroque church of Sant'Eligio, a loggia surmounted by a Gothic arch, and the 16C town hall.

CARRARA

Tuscany – Population 67 092

Michelin map 988 fold 14 or 430 J 12

Lying in a fertile basin on the edge of the limestone massif of the Apuan Alps, Carrara owes its fame to the white **marble** which has been quarried here since ancient times. Michelangelo used to come in person to choose blocks from which he carved his masterpieces.

Duomo – The façade is in the Romanesque-Gothic style, adorned with a delicately-carved marble rose window and flanked by an elegant 13C campanile. Inside, there are interesting 14C statues.

LARA PESSINA

Marble quarries

Cave di marmo – The wild countryside and the gigantic nature of the quarrying operations afford a spectacular sight. The impressive quarries, **Cave dei Fantiscritti**★★ *(5km - 3 miles northeast)* in a wild site, and the **Cave di Colonnata**★ *(8.5km - 5 miles east)* in a greener setting, are both actively worked and regularly despatch quantities of marble *(marmo)*. **Marina di Carrara** *(7km - 4 miles southwest)* is the main port, where marble blocks are stacked high.

EXCURSION

★ **Sarzana** - *16km - 10 miles north.* The busy town of Sarzana was once an advanced base of the Republic of Genoa, a rival of Pisa, and its numerous historic buildings bear witness to its past importance. The **cathedral** (Cattedrale) has a marble **altarpiece**★ (1432) delicately carved by Riccomani. In a chapel to the right of the chancel is a phial which is said to have contained the Blood of Christ. In the chapel to the left is a *Crucifixion*★ (1138), a Romanesque masterpiece of the artist, Guglielmo, probably from Lucca.

The **Fortezza di Sarzanello**★ ⊙ (1322) is a fortress built on a height to the northeast of the town, by the *condottiere* (leader of a mercenary army) from Lucca, Castruccio Castracani. It is a curious example of military architecture with deep moats and massive curtain walls guarded at intervals by round towers. From the top of the keep there is a magnificent **panorama**★★ of the town and the Apennine foothills.

Abbazia di CASAMARI★★

Lazio

Michelin map 988 fold 26 or 430 Q 22

Casamari Abbey ⊙ standing in a lonely site was originally a Benedictine foundation and was consecrated in 1217 by Pope Honorius III. It was later taken over by the Cistercians who rebuilt the abbey, modelling it on the abbey at Fossanova *(see Abbazia di FOSSANOVA)* and in accordance with the rules of austerity and self-sufficiency laid down by St Bernard, the founder of the Cistercian Order.

This is a lovely example of early Italian Gothic architecture. Above the entrance porch of the abbey church is a gallery of twinned openings, which served as the abbots' lodging during the Renaissance. The simplicity of the façade is typically Burgundian with a round-headed doorway, the rose window, and rising above all the transept tower.

The interior is spacious, austere and solemn. Built to a Latin cruciform plan, it has a nave and two aisles separated by massive cruciform piers with engaged columns supporting the lofty pointed vaulting. The later canopy seems out of place in the shallow chancel. The apse and arms of the transept are lit by windows with a wheel window above.

On the south side of the church are the cloisters with their twin columns, a well and a lovely flower garden. On the east side, in its traditional position, is the remarkable chapterhouse with delicate ribbed, pointed vaulting supported by clustered columns.

CASERTA★

Campania – Population 68 869

Michelin map 988 fold 27 or 431 D 25

Caserta, the Versailles of the Kingdom of Naples, stands in the heart of a fertile plain.

★★ **La Reggia** ⊙ - This immense palace was begun in 1752 by Vanvitelli for the Bourbon King, Charles III, who dreamed of another Versailles. The palace, one of Italy's most grandiose, was built five floors high on a rectangular plan 249m – 273yds long and 190m – 208yds wide. The façades, each with a projecting colonnaded centrepiece, are grand but rather monotonous. In all there are some 250 windows. The buildings are arranged around four well-proportioned inner courtyards. A magnificent entrance hall leads to the courtyards and the main **staircase**★. The sumptuously-decorated apartments are furnished in the Empire style.

★ **Park** ⊙ - The gardens and park were also designed by Luigi Vanvitelli and his son. The main vista is a succession of fountains and basins studded with statues. The group of Diana and Actaeon is by Vanvitelli himself. The focal point is the monumental **cascade**★★ (78m – 256ft tall) with to the right a picturesque **English garden**★★ ⊙ created for Maria-Carolina of Austria.

★ **Caserta Vecchia** - *10km - 6 miles north.* This small town is dominated by the ruins of its 9C castle. The town has a certain charm with its almost deserted narrow alleyways lined by old buildings with their brown tufa walls.

CASTELFRANCO VENETO★

Veneto – Population 29 496
Michelin map 988 fold 5 or 429 E 17

Castelfranco is a pleasant citadel surrounded by moats. It has a few pretty arcaded houses and is the birthplace of the artist Giorgione. The cathedral **(Duomo)** contains his masterpiece, the *Madonna and Child with Saints*★★.

Born c1477, **Giorgione** died young at the age of 32, probably of the Black Death. His 20 or so masterpieces influenced not only Venetian artists (Titian, who was his pupil and probably completed several of the master's canvases, Giovanni Bellini in his later works, Sebastiano del Piombo, Palma Vecchio, Savoldo, Dosso Dossi etc) but also all of European art, with his masterful handling of light.

Giorgione accomplished in his short lifetime an admirable synthesis of the human figure and nature with his flowing draughtsmanship and his skilful use of colour. The cathedral's work is among his earlier achievements and it already shows a preoccupation with achieving this fusion, as the figures are set on two different planes: the two saints in the shadow of the paved room while the Virgin enthroned on high stands out from the landscape background.

The artist's birthplace, **(Casa natale di Giorgione)** ⊘ *(Piazza del Duomo)* is now arranged as a museum.

CASTELLAMMARE DI STABIA⚓

Campania – Population 68 332
Michelin map 988 fold 27 or 431 E 25 – Local map under Golfo di NAPOLI

This was the ancient Roman spa town of Stabiae. Occupied successively by the Oscans, the Etruscans, the Samnites and finally the Romans in the 4C, Stabia rebelled against Rome but was crushed by Sulla in the 1C BC. The town was rebuilt in the form of small clusters of houses, while luxury villas for rich patricians spread over the high ground. In the AD 79 eruption of Vesuvius the new town was wiped out along with Herculaneum and Pompeii. The naturalist Pliny the Elder who came by boat to observe the phenomenon at close range perished by asphyxiation.

In the 18C the Bourbons undertook excavations, repaired the port, and built shipyards which are still in use.

★ **Antiquarium** ⊘ – *2 Via Marco Mario.* The finds from the excavations are displayed here and include a magnificent series of **mural paintings** from the villas and some very fine stucco **low reliefs.**

Roman villas – *2km - 1 mile to the east by the Gragnano road.*
Ariadne's Villa **(Villa di Arianna)** ⊘ was one of the luxurious villas facing the sea with an incomparable view of the bay and of Vesuvius. The architectural refinement of **Villa San Marco** ⊘ with its two storeys was enhanced by gardens and swimming pools. It was probably a sumptuous country residence.

CASTELLI ROMANI★★

Lazio
Michelin map 988 fold 26 or 430 fold 36

Castelli Romani, or Roman Castles, is the name given to the region of the Alban Hills (Colli Albani), which are of volcanic origin and lie to the southeast of Rome. In the Middle Ages, while anarchy reigned in Rome, the noble families sought refuge in the outlying villages which they fortified. Each of these villages was strategically set on the outer rim of an immense crater, itself pitted with small secondary craters, some of which now contain lakes (Albano and Nemi). Pastures and chestnut groves cover the upper slopes while lower down there are olive groves and vineyards, which produce an excellent wine.

Nowadays the Romans readily leave the capital in summer for the "Castelli" where they find peace, fresh air, good walking country and pleasant country inns.

ROUND TOUR STARTING FROM ROME

122km - 76 miles - allow a whole day

Leave Rome by the Via Appia in the direction of **Castel Gandolfo**★★, now the Pope's summer residence. It is thought that Castel Gandolfo was built on the site of ancient Alba Longa, the traditional and powerful rival of Rome. Their rivalry led to the famous combat of the Horatios for Rome and the Curiaces for Alba, as recounted by the Roman historian Livy. **Albano Laziale** was built on the site of Domitian's villa. Today the town boasts an attractive church, **Santa Maria della**

Rotonda★, large public gardens (Villa Comunale★) and not far from Borgo Garibaldi, the so-called tomb of the Horatios and the Curiaces. **Ariccia** has a lovely square designed by Bernini, a palace which belonged to the Chigi banking family, and the Church of the Assumption. **Velletri** is a prosperous town lying south of the Alban Hills in the heart of a wine-producing region.

Take Via dei Laghi out of Velletri.

This scenic road winds through groves of chestnut and oak trees to reach **Nemi**, a small village in a charming **setting**★★ on the slopes of the lake of the same name. The road then climbs to **Monte Cavo** (alt 949m - 3 124ft) which was crowned by the Temple of Jupiter. First a monastery and now a hotel have occupied the buildings. From the esplanade there is a fine **view**★ of the Castelli region with Rome on the horizon. Beyond the attractively-set **Rocca di Papa**, facing the Alban lakes, the road passes through **Grottaferrata** with its **abbey**★ which was founded in the 11C by Greek monks. **Tusculo** was the fief of the powerful Counts of Tusculum who governed the Castelli region. Next comes **Frascati** ⊙ pleasantly situated on the slopes facing Rome. It is known for its wines and its 16C and 17C villas, particularly the **Villa Aldobrandini**★ ⊙ set above its terraced gardens.

The road back to Rome passes **Cinecittà**, the Italian Hollywood.

CERVETERI

Lazio – Population 20 614
Michelin map 988 fold 25 or 430 Q 18

The ancient Caere was a powerful Etruscan centre, which stood on an eminence to the east of the present town of Cerveteri. Caere attained great prosperity in the 7C and 6C BC and was renowned as an important cultural and religious centre. In the 4C BC Caere began to decline. It was only at the beginning of the 20C that excavation work began on this site. Most of the finds are now displayed in the Villa Giulia in Rome.

★★ **Necropoli della Banditaccia** ⊙ – The admirable necropolis which is to be found 2km – 1 mile to the north of Cerveteri testifies to the Etruscans' belief in an afterlife. It is laid out like a city with numerous tumuli lining a main street. The site is pervaded by a great sense of peace. The tombs generally dating from the 7C BC add a strange note to the scene. These conical earth mounds, often grass-covered, rest on a stone base, which is sometimes decorated with mouldings, with the burial chambers underneath. Other tombs consist of underground burial chambers reached through simply-decorated doors. A vestibule leads into the burial chambers which often contain two funeral beds placed side by side: one is adorned with a small column if the deceased was a man (the breadwinner) and the other with a small canopy in the case of a woman (guardian of the home).

One of the tombs without a tumulus is the **Tomba delle Rilievi**★★ with its painted low-relief stuccoes giving a realistic picture of everyday Etruscan life.

CHIAVENNA

Lombardy – Population 7 362
Michelin map 988 fold 3, 428 D 10

Ancient Chiavenna owes its name to its key *(chiave)* position in the Splügen and Maloja transalpine passes between Italy and Switzerland.

The Collegiate Church of St Lawrence (**Collegiata di San Lorenzo**), built during the Romanesque period and reconstructed in the 16C after a fire, contains two paintings, one by Pietro Ligari (1738) *(2nd chapel on the right)* and one by Giuseppe Nuvoloni (1657) *(1st chapel on the left)*. The **baptistery** ⊙ has a Romanesque **font**★ (1156) in *ollare* stone: the name of the stone being a reference to it being used to make *olle* (urns and vases). The low reliefs illustrate a baptismal scene depicting various social classes (nobleman hunting with his falcon, soldier and craftsman), a child with his godfather, a priest and acolyte, and members of the clergy. The inscription reveals the identity of the sponsors of the work.

The **treasury** *(temporarily closed to visitors)* houses a wonderful 12C **binding for an evangelistary**.

Nearby, above the Palazzo Balbini (15C) is **Il Paradiso**, a rock that was once a fortified site and is now set out as a pleasant garden, the **Giardino botanico e archeologico** ⊙.

See also the strange frescoes decorating the exterior of the Palazzo Pretorio and the entrances in the Via Dolzino on which the inscriptions date back to the days of the Reformation.
Chiavenna is also famous for its **"crotti"**, restaurants housed in natural caves and serving local specialities (found only in Valtellina) such as *pizzoccheri* (buckwheat pasta served with melted cheese) and *bresaola* (dried meat).

EXCURSION

★★ **Strada del Passo dello Spluga** - *30km - 19 miles from Chiavenna to the pass.* The Splügen Pass Road is one of the boldest and most spectacular in the Alps. The **Campodolcino-Pianazzo section**★★★ is grandiose as it climbs the sheer mountainside in tight hairpin bends.

CHIETI

Abruzzi - Population 55 940
Michelin map 988 fold 27 or 430 O 24
Town plan in the current Michelin Red Guide Italia

Chieti is built on the summit of a hill planted with olive trees and offers varied panoramas. Corso Marrucino is the town's busiest street.

Museo archeologico Nazionale d'Abruzzo ⊘ - The archeological museum is housed in a building of the town hall **(Villa Comunale)** set in lovely **gardens**★. There are numerous works which were produced locally from the 6C BC to the 4C AD, in particular the marble statue of Hercules, discovered at Alba Fucens *(see Index)*, a portrait of Sulla, a fine bronze of Hercules and especially the famous *Warrior of Capestrano*★, a strange 6C BC limestone statue, and several rare examples of Picenum art. The Picenes occupied the central part of the Italian peninsula prior to the rise of the Romans.

Roman remains - Three adjoining minute **temples** (Templi Romani) were discovered in 1935 near the post office and Corso Marrucino. Further to the east, water tanks cut out of the hillside supplied the baths, also fairly well preserved.

CHIUSI★

Tuscany - Population 9 089
Michelin map 988 fold 15 or 430 M 17

Standing on a hill covered with olive groves, Chiusi is today a quiet and hospitable little town. It was once one of the 12 sovereign cities of Etruria.

★ **Museo archeologico** ⊘ - *Via Porsenna.* The museum presents the various finds from the burial grounds in the neighbourhood: sarcophagi, rounded tombstones *(cippi)*, alabaster and stone funerary urns, burial urns *(canopae)* in the shape of heads, clay ex-votos as well as a variety of utensils, vases, lamps and jewellery. The objects all display the Etruscan taste for fantasy and realism.
Visitors with a car can visit some of the **Etruscan tombs** ⊘ 3km - 2 miles out of town, as long as they are accompanied by a museum warden.

Cattedrale di San Secondiano - The cathedral was rebuilt in the 12C over the ruins of a 6C Paleo-Christian basilica. The nave and side aisles are separated by 18 ancient columns taken from a number of Roman buildings.

Museo della cattedrale ⊘ - The cathedral museum houses Etruscan, Roman and Paleo-Christian remains discovered beneath the cathedral and in its vicinity. Fine collection of illuminated religious books dating from the 15C and 16C and brought here from the Abbey of Monte Oliveto Maggiore. The collection includes gold artefacts, reliquaries, religious objects etc.

To plan a special itinerary:
  - consult the Map of Touring Programmes which indicates the tourist regions, the recommended routes, the principal towns and main sights
  - read the descriptions in the Sights section which include Excursions from the main tourist centres
Michelin Maps nos 428 to 433 indicate scenic routes, places of interest, viewpoints, rivers, forests...

CINQUE TERRE★★

Liguria

Michelin map 988 fold 13 or 428 J 11 – Local map see The RIVIERA

Lying northwest of the Gulf of La Spezia, the Cinque Terre (Five Lands) is, even today, an isolated region with no good access road. This rugged coast is wild but hospitable, with its vineyards and fishing villages where the people remain strongly attached to their old customs and traditions.

★★ **Vernazza** – This is the most attractive village with its tall colourful houses and its church clustered together at the head of a well-sheltered cove.

Manarola, Cinque Terre

★ **Manarola** – This fishing village with its small 14C church is set in a landscape of terraced vineyards. Starting from the station there is a splendid **walk**★★ *(1/4 hour on foot)* which offers lovely views of the coast and the other villages.

★ **Riomaggiore** – *Take the branch road off the La Spezia-Manarola road.* The old houses of this medieval village lie in a narrow valley. This tiny fishing harbour backs against the strange black rock strata, typical of the region.

CIVIDALE DEL FRIULI★

Friuli – Venezia Giulia – Population 11 187

Michelin map 988 fold 6 or 429 D 22 – 17km – 11 miles northeast of Udine

This is the ancient Forum Julii, which gave the town situated high above the Natisone river its modern name. The Lombards, who came from Scandinavia, settled here in the 6C and founded the first of their many duchies in northern Italy. The town later became the residence of the Patriarchs of Aquileia. From the 15C onward it belonged to Venice. Since the 1976 earthquake, Cividale has been rebuilt.

Duomo – It was extensively rebuilt in the 16C in the Renaissance style by Piero Lombardo (1435-1515) but retains some Gothic features on the façade and in the interior. The high altar has a 12C Veneto-Byzantine silver-gilt altarpiece. The small **Museo cristiano** ⊙, a museum of Lombard art *(opening off the south aisle)*, contains numerous valuable items: the octagonal baptismal font of the Patriarch Callisto, rebuilt in the 8C using Byzantine fragments, and the 8C "altar" of Duke Ratchis in marble with carved sides depicting scenes from the Life of Christ.

★★ **Museo archeologico nazionale** ⊙ – *To the left of the cathedral.* Housed in a superb late-16C palace said to have been designed by Palladio, the museum displays on the second floor the numerous items discovered in Lombard graveyards in Cividale and the surrounding area. They include women's and men's jewellery (including some gold and silver items), weaponry and everyday objects that provide an excellent insight into Lombard culture and art in the 6C, during the Carolingian era. Note the Roman sarcophagus which was re-used at a later date, and the objects taken from the grave of Duke Gisulfo (7C). On the ground floor are archeological exhibits, mainly from the Roman and Lombard periods.

★★ **Tempietto** ⊙ – *Near the Piazza San Biagio.* This elegant 8C Lombard building is a square chamber with quadripartite vaulting and an admirable Lombard **decoration** of friezes and stylised stuccos. It is a unique example of the architecture of this period.

CIVITAVECCHIA

Lazio – Population 51 274
Michelin map 988 fold 25 or 430 P 17

Civitavecchia, the Roman Centumcellae, has been the port of Rome since the reign of Trajan and now handles maritime traffic with Sardinia. The port is guarded by the Fort of Michelangelo, a massive Renaissance construction which was begun by Bramante, continued by Sangallo the Younger and Bernini, and completed by Michelangelo in 1557. Henri Beyle, known under the pen-name Stendhal (1783-1842), was appointed French Consul at Civitavecchia in 1831. In his leisure time Stendhal wrote numerous works, including *The Charterhouse of Parma* (1839).

Museo nazionale archeologico ⊙ – *2A, Largo Plebiscito.* The museum has Etruscan and Roman collections composed of finds from local sites. There is an amazing collection of Roman anchors.

Terme di Traiano or **Terme Taurine** ⊙ – *3km – 2 miles northeast.* There are two groups of baths (*terme*): the first (to the west) dates from the Republican period and the second, the better preserved, was built by Trajan's successor, the Emperor Hadrian.

COMACCHIO

Emilia-Romagna – Population 21 159
Michelin map 988 fold 15, 429 H 18

Comacchio is built on sand and water and in many ways it resembles Chioggia. The main activity of the townspeople is eel fishing. Its brightly-coloured fishermen's houses, its canals spanned by some curious bridges, including an unusual triple bridge, and the fishing boats all lend it a special charm.

★ **Polesina** – This area around the Po delta was once a malaria-infested marshy district. Land reclamation and drainage have since turned it into a fertile agricultural area. The Chioggia to Ravenna road *(90km – 56 miles)* traverses these flat expanses stretching away to the horizon and interrupted only by large solitary farms. Clumps of poplars and umbrella pines add touches of colour, especially in spring, to the monotony of this countryside where eel fishing is still common on the numerous canals which crisscross the area. At **Mesola** *(28km – 17 miles north of Comacchio)* there is a massive brick castle dating from 1583 which once belonged to the Este family. In the southern part of the area the **Valli di Comacchio**, Italy's most important zone of lagoons, has its own special melancholy beauty.

COMO★

Lombardy – Population 90 799
Michelin map 988 fold 3 or 428 E 9 – Local map see Regione dei LAGHI
Town plan in the current Michelin Red Guide Italia

The city was already prosperous under the Romans but reached its zenith in the 11C. It was destroyed by the Milanese in 1127, rebuilt by the Emperor Frederick Barbarossa and from 1355 onwards shared the fortunes of Milan.

The "**maestri comacini**" known as early as the 7C, were masons, builders and sculptors who spread the Lombard style *(see ART)* throughout Italy and Europe. Their name "comacini" has been variously said to refer to their native town, to the fact that they worked in association or that they worked with machines ("cum machinis").

★★ **Duomo** – Begun in the late 14C the cathedral was completed during the Renaissance and crowned in the 18C with an elegant dome by the Turin architect, Juvara. It has a remarkable **façade**★★ which was richly decorated from 1484 onwards by the **Rodari brothers**, who also worked on the **north door**, known as the Porta della Rana because of the frog *(rana)* carving on one of the pillars. They were also responsible for the exquisitely-delicate **south door.**

The **interior**★, full of solemn splendour, combines Gothic architecture and Renaissance decoration. In addition to the curious banners, hung between the pillars, and the magnificent 16C-17C **tapestries**★, there are canvases by B Luini *(Adoration of the Magi Virgin and Child with Saints★)*, and G Ferrari *(Flight into Egypt)*, in the south aisle as well as a *Descent from the Cross★* (1489) carved by Tommaso Rodari in the north aisle. Note also the organ in five parts, comprising 96 registers and 6 000 pipes. Various 17C artists were involved in its construction although its current form is the work of the organ-makers Balbiani and Vegezzi-Bossi.

Adjoining the façade is the **Broletto**★★, or 13C town hall, with an arcade at street level and a lovely storey of triple-arched windows above.

★ **San Fedele** – In the heart of the picturesque old quarter, this church is in the Romanesque Lombard style. The nave and two aisles are terminated by a splendid polygonal Romanesque **chancel**★ with radiating chapels. The whole east end is graced by two storeys of arcading.

★ **Basilica di Sant'Abbondio** – This masterpiece of Romanesque Lombard architecture was consecrated in 1093. The noble but severe **façade**★ has a lovely doorway. The nave and four aisles are separated by columns. The remarkable 14C **frescoes**★ evoke the Life of Christ.

Villa Olmo ⊙ – *3km* – *2 miles north by the S 35 and then the S 340 to the right.* This is a large neo-classical building dating from the late 18C, with a small theatre and gardens, from which there is a lovely **view**★ of Como in its lakeside setting.

CONEGLIANO

Veneto – Population 35 580

Michelin map 988 fold 5 or 429 E 18 – 28km – 17 miles north of Treviso

Conegliano is surrounded by pleasant hills clad with orchards and vineyards, which produce an excellent white wine. This was the birthplace of **Cima da Conegliano** (1459-1518), an admirer of Giovanni Bellini, and a superb colourist who introduced idealised landscapes bathed in a crystal-clear light. The cathedral (**Duomo**) ⊙ has a fine *Sacra Conversazione★* by this artist. The **castello** ⊙ houses two small **museums** and affords a lovely **panorama**★ of the town and its setting. Next to the cathedral the walls of the **Scuola dei Battuti** are decorated with 15C and 16C **frescoes**★ in both the Venetian and Lombard styles.

CORTINA D'AMPEZZO✳✳✳

Veneto – Population 7 104

Michelin map 988 fold 5 or 429 C 18 – Local map see DOLOMITI
Town plan in the current Michelin Red Guide Italia

Cortina, the capital of the Dolomites *(see DOLOMITI)*, is a winter sports and summer resort with a worldwide reputation. Set in the heart of the Dolomites, Cortina makes a good excursion centre for discovering the magnificent **mountain scenery**★★★.

★★★ **Tondi di Faloria** ⊙ ⊥ From the summit a grand panorama may be enjoyed. There are excellent ski slopes.

★★★ **Tofana di Mezzo** ⊙ – A cable-car climbs to 3 244m - 10 743ft, from where there is a superb panorama over the surrounding mountains.

★★ **Belvedere Pocol** ⊙ – Lying to the southwest, this viewpoint affords a lovely view of Cortina which is best at sunset.

The star ratings are allocated for various categories:
- *regions of scenic beauty with dramatic natural features*
- *cities with a cultural heritage*
- *elegant resorts and charming villages*
- *ancient monuments and fine architecture*
- *museums and art galleries*

CORTONA★★

Tuscany – Population 22 591
Michelin map 988 fold 15 or 430 M 17
Town plan in the current Michelin Red Guide Italia

The quiet town of Cortona with its medieval ramparts clings to the steep slopes of a hill clad with olive groves. It affords good views as far as Lake Trasimeno. As early as the 14C Cortona attracted artists including the Sienese, Fra Angelico. Cortona was the birthplace of **Luca Signorelli** (1450-1523), who with his dramatic temperament and sculptural modelling, was the precursor of Michelangelo; he died as a result of a fall from scaffolding when he was decorating the Villa Passerini to the east of Cortona. In the 16C Cortona gave France an architect, Domenico Bernabei, known as **Il Boccadoro** (Mouth of Gold) who designed the Hôtel de Ville in Paris for François I. **Pietro da Cortona** (1596-1669), painter and architect with a lively imagination, was one of the masters of Roman baroque and a talented decorative painter. The latest famous artist was the painter **Severini** (1883-1966) who was linked to the Futurist movement.

SIGHTS

Piazza del Duomo, close up against the ramparts, affords a lovely view over the valley. The Romanesque cathedral **(Duomo)**, remodelled at the Renaissance, contains some works of art.

★★ **Museo diocesano** ⊙ – *Opposite the cathedral.* This former church houses a remarkable collection of paintings: a beautiful *Annunciation* and *Madonna and Saints* by Fra Angelico; works from the Sienese school by Duccio, Pietro Lorenzetti and Sassetta; an excellent group of works by **Signorelli**; and a remarkable *Ecstasy of St Margaret* by the Bolognese artist, G M Crespi (1665-1747). Note also the fine 2C Roman sarcophagus (*Battle of Lapiths and Centaurs*).

★ **Palazzo Pretorio** – The Praetorian Palace was built in the 13C but altered during a later period. Its **façade★** is original and is decorated with coats-of-arms while the façade overlooking the Piazza Signorelli, which is preceded by a grand staircase, dates from the 17C. Inside, the **Museo dell'Accademia Etrusca★** ⊙ displays Etruscan exhibits as well as Roman, Egyptian, medieval and Roman items. Among the Etruscan objects is a strange 5C BC bronze **oil lamp★★** with 16 burners shaped like human figures. The museum also displays works and memorabilia relating to Severini, bequeathed by the artist to his native town.

Santuario di Santa Margherita – This enshrines the fine Gothic **tomb★** (1362) of St Margaret. The Via Santa Margherita leads off to the south of the church. Severini decorated the street with mosaics representing the **Stations of the Cross.**

San Domenico – *Largo Beato Angelico.* The church is dedicated to St Dominic. In the south apse is a *Madonna with angels and saints* by Luca Signorelli, a polyptych by Lorenzo di Niccolò at the high altar and a fresco by Fra Angelico.

★ **Santa Maria del Calcinaio** – *3km – 2 miles west.* Santa Maria, built from 1485 to 1513 by Francesco di Giorgio Martini, strongly resembles the work of Brunelleschi. The church is remarkable for the grace and harmony of its design and its well-balanced proportions. The domed church is built on the Latin cross plan and the lofty interior is well lit.
In the oculus of the façade is a remarkable stained-glass **window** (1516) designed by a French artist, **Guillaume de Marcillat** (1467-1529).

CREMONA★

Lombardy – Population 73 991
Michelin map 988 folds 13 and 14, 428 or 429 G 11/12

Cremona is an important agricultural market town in the heart of a fertile agricultural region. Town life centres on Piazza Roma. The original Gallic settlement became a Latin city before emerging as an independent commune in the Middle Ages. It suffered from the Guelph and Ghibelline troubles of the period. In 1334 the town came under Visconti rule and was united with the Duchy of Milan in the 15C. At the Renaissance the town was the centre of a brilliant artistic movement. In the 18C and 19C the French and Austrians fought for supremacy over Cremona until the Risorgimento *(see Index)*.
From the late 16C the stringed-instrument makers of Cremona gained a reputation as violin and cello makers. The International School of Violin Making carries on this tradition. The Cremonese composer **Claudio Monteverdi** (1567-1643) created modern opera with his *Orfeo* and *The Coronation of Poppea*.

★★ PIAZZA DEL COMUNE (BZ 7) *1 hour*

★★★ **Torrazzo** ⓥ – The remarkable late-13C campanile is linked to the cathedral by a Renaissance gallery. Its massive form is elegantly crowned by an octagonal 14C storey. From the top (112m – 367ft) there is a lovely **view**★ over the town. The astronomical clock, which dates from 1471, has undergone a number of alterations in its history, the last being in the 1970s. It is notable for its illustrations of the stars and the constellations of the zodiac.

★★ **Duomo** – This magnificent Lombard cathedral was begun in the Romanesque and completed in the Gothic style (1107 to 1332). The richly-decorated white marble façade is preceded by a porch. Numerous decorative features were later additions, namely the frieze by the followers of Antelami, the large 13C rose window and the four statue-columns of the central doorway.
The spacious **interior** is decorated with **frescoes**★ by the Cremona school (B. Boccaccino, the Campi, the Bembo, Romanino da Brescia, Pordenone and Gatti). Also of interest are the lovely 17C Brussels **tapestries**★ and at the entrance to the chancel the **high reliefs**★★ by Amadeo, the architect-sculptor of the Carthusian Monastery at Pavia.

★ **Battistero** (L) – This harmonious octagonal baptistery, preceded by a Lombard porch and decorated with a gallery, was remodelled during the Renaissance.

Palazzo comunale (H) ⓥ – This 13C palace was remodelled at a later date. Inside are displayed the most famous violins in the world: the *Charles IX of France* (Amati), the *Hammerle* (Amati), the *Quarestani* (Guarneri), the *Cremonese* 1715 (Antonio Stradivarius) and the *Stauffer* (Guarneri del Gesu).
To the left of the palace is the lovely 13C **Loggia dei Militi** (**K**).

CREMONA

B Sant'Agostino	**E** Palazzo Stanga	**H** Palazzo	**K** Loggia dei Militi
D Palazzo Fodri	**F** Palazzo Raimondi	del Comune	**L** Battistero

ADDITIONAL SIGHTS

★ **Museo civico** (ABY) ⊙ – Installed in a 16C palace this municipal museum has several different sections, notably the **picture gallery** with works of the Cremona school, minor arts (French **ivories**), the **cathedral's treasure** and a **Stradivarius museum** (wooden models and tools belonging to Stradivarius, as well as stringed instruments from the 17-20C).

Renaissance Architecture – The town is embellished with numerous Renaissance palaces including the **Palazzo Fodri**★ (BZ D), the **Palazzo Stanga** (AY E) and the **Palazzo Raimondi** (AY F), as well as churches like **Sant'Agostino** (AZ B) rich in works of art: **portraits**★ of Francesco Sforza and his wife by Bonifacio Bembo and an **altarpiece**★ by Perugino.

On the Casalmaggiore road *(2km – 1 mile out of town by no ③ on the town plan)* is the church of **San Sigismondo** with its lavishly-decorated **interior**★. The frescoes are by the 16C Cremona school (Campi, Gatti, Boccaccino).

The violin town

Cremona was the birthplace of the greatest violin-makers of all time and their instruments are still highly sought after by famous violinists today. The first of the famous violin-makers of Cremona was **Andrea Amati**, from whom King Charles IX of France commissioned instruments in the 16C. His work was continued by his sons and his nephew, Nicolò, master of Andrea Guarneri and the most famous of all of them, **Antonio Stradivarius** (c1644-1737), who made more than 1000 instruments. **Andrea Guarneri** was the first of another renowned dynasty in which the most skilled violin-maker of them all was Giuseppe Guarneri (1698-1744), better known as Giuseppe del Gesù because of the three letters IHS (Jesus, Saviour of Mankind) inscribed on all his violins. Knowledgeable music lovers will find it easy to distinguish between the crystal-clear tones of a stradivarius and the deeper, powerful tones of a Guarneri de Gesù.

CROTONE

Calabria – Population 58 999

Michelin map 988 fold 40 or 431 J 33

The ancient town of Croton was an Achaean colony of Magna Graecia, founded in 710 BC and celebrated in antiquity for its riches, the beauty of its women and the prowess of its athletes, such as Milo of Croton, so admired by Virgil. Around 532 BC Pythagoras founded several religious communities which devoted themselves to the study of mathematics and which once they had become too powerful were expelled northwards towards Metapontum (present-day Metaponto). The rival city of Locari defeated Croton in the mid-6C BC, which in turn defeated its other rival Sybaris. The city welcomed Hannibal during the Second Punic War before being conquered by Rome. Crotone is today a prosperous seaport and industrial centre as well as a popular holiday resort.

Museo archeologico ⊙ – *Via Risorgimento.* The archeological collections include local finds from other colonies of Magna Graecia: displays of ceramics, terracottas, coins and sculpture.

EXCURSIONS

Capo Colonna – *40km – 25 miles south.* At the extremity of this promontory stands a Doric column, the last remaining vestige of a vast temple dedicated to Hera Lucinia (6C or 5C BC).

★ **Santa Severina** – *34km – 21 miles to the northwest.* The 13C cathedral has a remarkable 8C circular **baptistery**★ which shows a strong Byzantine influence. The Norman Castle is also of interest.

The annual Michelin Red Guide Italia
revises its selection of establishments which
  – serve carefully prepared meals at a reasonable price
  – include service on the bill or in the price of each dish
  – offer a menu of simple but good food at a modest cost
  – provide free parking
It is well worth buying the current edition

CUMA★

CUMAE – Campania
Michelin map 988 fold 27 or 431 E 24 – 7km – 4 miles north of Pozzuoli
Local map see Golfo di NAPOLI

Cumae, one of the oldest Greek colonies, was founded in the 8C BC. The city soon dominated the whole Phlegrean area *(see Golfo di NAPOLI)* including Naples, leaving an important Hellenic heritage. Its splendour was at its height under the tyrant Aristodemus. After its capture by the Romans in 334 BC, decline then set in and continued until AD 915 when it was pillaged by the Saracens.

The ancient city of Cumae stands in a serene and solemn setting near the sea. Visitors have access to the ruins of the upper town – the acropolis – where most of the temples stood. In the lower town, excavations have revealed the remains of an amphitheatre, a temple dedicated to the Capitoline Triad (Jupiter, Juno and Minerva) and baths.

★★ **Acropoli** ⊘ – The acropolis is built on a hill of volcanic material (lava and tufa) in a lonely site and is reached by an alley lined with laurels. After the vaulted passageway, the path to the left leads to the Sibyl's Cave **(Antro della Sibilla★)**, one of the most venerated places of Antiquity. Here the Sibyl delivered her oracles. The cave was hollowed out of the rock by the Greeks in the 6C or 5C BC and it is rectangular in shape with three small niches.

Take the stairway up to the sacred way (Via Sacra). From the belvedere there is a good **view★** of the sea. Some finds from the excavations are on display. On the right are the remains of the Temple of Apollo **(Tempio di Apollo)** which was later transformed into a Christian church. Further on is the Temple of Jupiter **(Tempio di Giove)** which was also converted by the early Christians. In the centre stands a large font and there are several Christian tombs near the sanctuary.

★ **Arco Felice** – *Take the minor road in the direction of Naples.* This triumphal arch was erected on the Via Domitiana; there are still traces of the paved way.

The Cumaean Sibyl

In Antiquity the Sibyls were virgin priestesses dedicated to the cult of Apollo and deemed to be semi-divine creatures with powers of divination. According to tradition they went into a trance conducive to delivering their prophesies with the help of Apollo. The oracles were couched in obscure terms which could have different interpretations, hence the adjective sibylline in reference to words with a mysterious or hidden meaning.

The Sibyl from Cumae (one of the main centres of Greek civilisation in Italy) was a famous prophetess. She is reputed to have sold the Sibylline Books, collections of the Sibyls' prophesies, to the Etruscan King of Rome, Tarquin the Elder or Tarquin the Superb (6C BC). The oracles were later used by the rulers to answer their subjects' petitions and expectations. One of the best known depictions of the Cumaean Sibyl by Michelangelo adorns the ceiling of the Sistine Chapel in the Vatican *(see ROME)*.

DOLOMITI★★★

This rugged and grandiose limestone massif is enhanced by yellow and pink tints, harsh or soft depending on the light. The Dolomites extend mostly over the Alto-Adige region, also known as Southern Tyrol, which is German-speaking and of Austrian tradition. The massif is a favourite haunt of skiers and mountaineers. For holidaymakers, the Dolomites provide excellent roads, good paths, immense panoramas and a large selection of hotels.

GEOGRAPHICAL NOTES

The Dolomites are bounded roughly by the Adige River and its tributary, the Isarco, in the west, the Brenta Massif in the south, the Piave Valley in the east and the Rienza (Val Pusteria) in the north. Most of the range is formed of limestone rocks called "dolomites" after a French geologist, Gratet de Dolomieu, who was the first to study their formation at the end of the 18C. A few nuclei of volcanic rock are to be found in the centre and west, and schists in the southwest (Cima d'Asta). The nature of the soil and erosion have created a distinctive landscape: steep, rugged rocks shaped as towers, belfries or domes with gentler slopes at their base covered with alpine pastures, conifers or crops. The steepness of the upper slopes prevented the formation of glaciers.

The various massifs – To the southeast rise Monte Pelmo (3 168m – 10 394ft) and Monte Civetta (3 220m – 10 564ft) while to the south, near the Cima della Vezzana, the Pale di San Martino, which are deeply fissured, are divided into three chains separated by a high plateau. The Massifs of the Latemar (2 842m – 9 324ft) and the Catinaccio (2 981m – 9 780ft), from which rise the well-known Towers of Vaiolet (Torri del Vaiolet), enclose the Passo di Costalunga north of which are the Sasso Lungo and the vast Sella Massif (Gruppo di Sella), skirted by a road. To the east, the chief summits in the Cortina Dolomites are the Tofana di Mezzo, the Punta Sorapiss and Monte Cristallo. Finally in the heart of the range stands the formidable **Marmolada Massif** (Gruppo della Marmolada, 3 342m – 10 964ft), which rises to the highest point in the Dolomites.

The **Cadore** district prolongs the Dolomites to the east and southeast of Cortina; its axis is the Piave Valley and its capital Pieve di Cadore. Here the highest summits are Antelao (3 262m – 10 705ft) and the triple peak Tre Cime di Lavaredo (2 998m – 9 836ft).

Fauna and flora – Birds and animals are those of the Alps: royal eagle, chamois, deer, hawks, and woodcock in the coniferous forest. In spring the prairies are covered with brightly-coloured flowers: edelweiss, deep-blue gentian, white or mauve crocus, six-petalled anemones, starry white saxifrage or five-petalled rock flowers, fringed mauve soldanellas and purplish-pink Turk's Cap lilies. Market gardens and vineyards flourish in valleys dotted with large farmhouses with wooden balconies.

Sightseeing – The map below locates the towns and sites described in the guide, and also indicates other beauty spots in small black type.

★★ DOLOMITE ROAD

From Bolzano to Cortina *210km – 131 miles – allow 2 days*
The main touring route in the Dolomites is the great Dolomite Road, which is a wonderful and world-famous example of road engineering, linking Bolzano and Cortina d'Ampezzo as it follows the central depression of the massif. It runs through a landscape which is always majestic and varied. The road was already used during the Renaissance by merchants travelling from Venice to Germany. It began to be modernised in 1895, was used for military purposes in 1915-18 and was improved after the Second World War.

★ **Bolzano** – *See BOLZANO.*

★ **Val d'Ega** – This narrow gorge, the Ega Valley, with pink sandstone walls, is guarded by the **Castello di Cornedo.**

★ **Nova Levante** – Catinaccio Massif rises up behind this attractive village with its bulbous belfry and pretty houses overlooking the Ega.

★ **Lago di Carezza** (or **Karer See**) – This tiny lake is set in a dark expanse of fir trees with the jagged peaks of the Latemar and the Catinaccio Massifs in the background.

Tre Cime di Lavaredo, Dolomiti

Aerfoto/ARTEPHOT

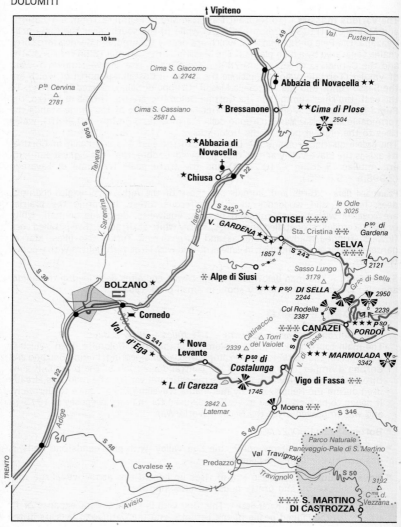

Italian and German place-names:

Adige/Etsch
Alpe di Siusi/Seiseralm
Badia/Abtei
Badia (Val)/Gadertal
Bolzano/Bozen
Braies (Lago di)/Pragser Wildsee
Bressanone/Brixen
Brunico/Bruneck
Campo Fiscalino/Fischleinboden
Carezza (Lago di)/Karersee
Catinaccio/Rosengarten

Cervina (Punta)/Hirzerspitze
Chiusa/Klausen
Cornedo/Karneid
Corvara in Badia/Kurfar
Costalunga (Passo di)/Karerpaß
Croda Rossa/ Hohe Geisel
Dobbiaco/Toblach
Ega (Val d')/Eggental
Gadera/Gaderbach
Gardena (Passo)/Grödnerjoch
Gardena (Val)/Grödnertal

★ **Passo di Costalunga** – From this pass on the Dolomite Road, also called the Passo di Carezza, there is a **view**★ over the Catinaccio on one side and the Latemar on the other. The soft terrain on the slopes of the pass has been stabilised with brushwood.

❀❀ **Vigo di Fassa** ⊙ – This resort, in a picturesque **site**★ in the famous Val di Farsa, is a mountaineering and excursion centre in the Catinaccio Massif *(cable-car).*

❀❀❀ **Canazei** – Canazei lies deep in the heart of the massif, framed between the Catinaccio, the Towers of Vaiolet (Torri del Vaiolet), the Sella Massif and the Marmolada. This is the usual base for most of the excursions and difficult climbs in the Marmolada range. The church has a shingle roof, a bulbous belfry and a painted façade.

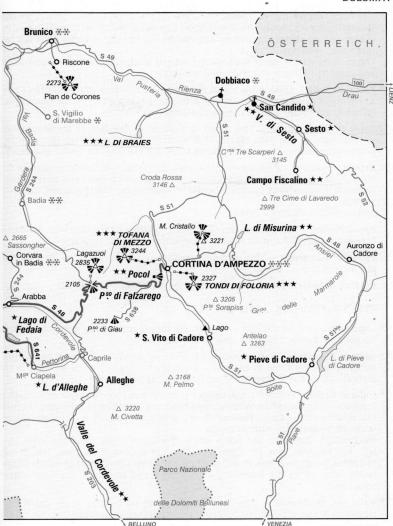

Isarco/Eisack
Lavaredo (Tre Cime di)/Drei Zinen
Nova Levante/Welschnofen
Odle (le)/Geislerspitze
Ortisei/St-Ulrich
Plan de Corones/Kronplatz
Plose (Cima d.)/Plose Bühel
Rienza/Rienz
Riscon/Reischach
San Candido/Innichen
San Cassiano (Cima)/Kassianspitze

San Giacomo (Cima)/Jakobspitze
San Vigilio di M./St. Vigil
S.-Cristina/St-St-Christina
Sarentina (Valle)/Sarntal
Sasso Lungo/Langkofel
Sella (Passo)/Sellajoch
Selva in Val Gardena/Wolkenstein im Grödnerta
Sesto (Val di)/Sextental
Talvera/Talfer
Tre Scarperi (Cima)/Dreischusterspitze
Vipiteno/Sterzing

At Canazei turn right into the S 641.

This road affords very fine **views**★★ of the Marmolada range and its glacier. As one comes out of a long tunnel a lake, **Lago di Fedaia**★ suddenly appears, dominated by the Marmolada range.

★★ **Gruppo della Marmolada** – This is the highest massif in the Dolomites and it has its own glacier and very fast ski-runs.
The **cable-car** ⏱ from Malga Ciapela goes up to 3 265m – 10 712ft offering admirable **panoramas**★★★ of the Cortina peaks (Tofana and Cristallo), the sugar-loaf forms of Sasso Lungo, the enormous tabular mass of the Sella Massif and in the background the summits of the Austrian Alps including the Grossglockner.

Return to Canazei then after 5.5km – 3 miles turn left.

The road follows the **Val Gardena**★★★, one of the most famous valleys in the Dolomites for its beauty, its winter sports facilities and as an excursion centre in summer. Its slopes are covered with coniferous forests, waterfalls and typical mountain dwellings.
The inhabitants still speak the Ladin dialect and retain their traditional costumes and customs. They are skilful wood-workers.

★★★ **Passo di Sella** – Linking the Val di Fassa and Val Gardena this pass offers one of the most extensive and most characteristic **panoramas**★★★ in the Dolomites, including the Sella, Sasso Lungo and Marmolada Massifs.

✵✵✵ **Selva di Val Gardena** – This resort is situated at the foot of the impressive vertical mass of the Sella Massif. It is an active craft centre: wooden objects, pewterware and enamels. In the **church** there is a Flamboyant Gothic **altarpiece**★.

✵✵✵ **Ortisei** – Halfway up the valley is the linear settlement of Ortisei amidst its fir trees. A cable-car climbs up to Alpe di Siusi✵, a winter sports resort and an excursion centre in summer, in a delightful **setting**★★ overlooking the Isarco and Gardena Valleys.
Return to the Dolomite Road.

Passo Pordoi – The highest pass (2 239m – 7 346ft) on the Dolomite Road lies between huge blocks of rock with sheer sides and shorn-off tops.

Passo di Falzarego – This wild and desolate pass offers a good view of the Marmolada and its glacier.

✵✵✵ **Cortina d'Ampezzo and excursions** – *See CORTINA D'AMPEZZO.*

OTHER TOWNS AND SIGHTS

★★★ **Lago di Braies** – Alt 1 495m – 4 905ft. The lake is encircled by grim mountains. Its winding banks fringe the clear green waters.

★★ **Lago di Misurina** – This popular lake in rolling parkland is overlooked to the north by the Tre Cime di Lavaredo. A private toll-road ⊙ leads through larch plantations to a wild **scenery**★★★ of jumbled, jagged rocks.

★★ **Valle di Sesto** – This attractive valley has numerous Tyrolean-style villages, the main one being **Sesto**★. A winding road branches southwards following the Val Fiscalino to end at **Campo Fiscalino**★★ in a grandiose setting, a mountain cirque enclosed by jagged mountain peaks.
San Candido★ stands at the point where the Sesto Valley joins the main valley, Val Pusteria, not far from the Austrian border. This town has three interesting churches: one in the mountain style with shingle roof and bulbous belfry, another in the Austrian baroque style and the third, a Romanesque structure.

★★ **Valle del Cordevole** – The road from Caprile to Bulluno is an extremely picturesque one with its hilltop villages and impressive gorges.
Alleghe on the bank of a pale green **lake**★ is a good excursion centre.

✵✵✵ **San Martino di Castrozza** – In its superb setting, San Martino is an excellent excursion centre with a strong cultural tradition (costumes).

★ **Bressanone** – *See BRESSANONE.*

★ **Chiusa** – A charming Tyrolean-looking village.

★ **Pieve di Cadore** – This town is pleasantly set at the head of a reservoir. It was the birthplace of the great artist, **Titian**. One of his works is to be found in the church, and the house where he was born is now a **museum** ⊙.

★ **San Vito di Cadore** – This attractive village with its shingle-roofed churches is overshadowed by the Antelao.

✵ **Dobbiaco** – In the centre of this village there is an Austrian-style baroque church.

Vipiteno – *30km – 19 miles northwest of Bressanone.* The picturesque **main street**★ has 15C-16C Tyrolean houses with arcades, oriel windows and wrought-iron signs.

The current edition of the annual Michelin Red Guide Italia
offers a selection of pleasant and quiet hotels in convenient locations
It gives their amenities (swimming pools, tennis courts, private beaches and gardens)
as well as their dates of annual closure
The selection also includes establishments which offer good cooking: carefully prepared meals at reasonable prices; Michelin stars for excellent cuisine

Isola d'ELBA★★

ELBA – Tuscany – Population 29 411
Michelin map 988 fold 24 or 430 N 12/13

With its beaches, solitary places, peacefulness and mild, dry climate, the Isle of Elba is a good place for a stay rather than an excursion. In the distant geological past Elba was part of the vanished continent of Tyrrhenia. This, the largest island in the Tuscan Archipelago, like Corsica, Sardinia, the Balearics and the Maures and Estérel Massifs on the French Riviera coast, has an indented coastline with small creeks, caves and beaches. The vegetation is typically Mediterranean with palms, eucalyptus, cedars, magnolias and, in great quantity, olives and vines. The wines produced (white Moscato and red Aleatico) are heady with a strong bouquet. The granitic relief culminates in Monte Capane. East of the island the iron mines worked by the Etruscans are no longer exploited.

Elba is closely associated with Napoleon who was exiled here following his abdication. Between 3 May 1814 and 26 February 1815 the fallen emperor ruled over his small court and the island, which was garrisoned by about 1 000 soldiers.

Sightseeing – Start from Portoferraio and follow one of the two itineraries indicated on the map below: **western Elba** *(about 70km - 44 miles, about 5 hours)* and **eastern Elba** *(68km - 42 miles, about 3 hours)*.

⌂ **Portoferraio** – The island's capital, guarded by ruined walls and two forts, lies at the head of a beautiful bay. In the upper part of the town is the Napoleonic Museum **(Museo Napoleonico)** ⊙ housed in the Villa dei Mulini, a simple house, with a terraced garden, which Napoleon sometimes occupied. His personal library and various mementoes are kept here. Beyond the great sandy beach at **Biodola**, the road goes towards **Marciana Marina**, a small port protected by two piers, one of which is dominated by a round tower, and climbs the wooded slopes of Monte Capanne.

★★ **Monte Capanne** ⊙ – 1 018m - 3 339ft. *Cable-cars leave from Marciana*. From the summit not far from the terminus there is a splendid **panorama**★★ of Elba, the Tuscan coast to the east and the coast of Corsica to the west.

Marciana – From this attractive village there is a lovely **view**★ of **Poggio**, perched on its rocky spur, Marciana Marina and the Bay of Procchio. There is a small museum **(museo archeologico)** ⊙ with displays of prehistoric items, Greek vases etc.

Madonna del Monte – Take the road up to the castle which dominates Marciana and from there a rocky path leads up to this sanctuary, built on the northern slope of Monte Giove. Beside the 16C chapel there is a curious semicircular fountain dated 1698 and a "hermitage" where Napoleon and Maria Walewska spent a few days in 1814.

Marina di Campo – This small fishing port with its popular beach lies at the head of a lovely bay backed by a hinterland plain of olive groves and vineyards.

★ **Villa Napoleone di San Martino** ⊙ – In a setting of silent hills, planted with groves of evergreen oaks and vineyards, this modest house was the ex-emperor's summer residence. There is a lovely view of the Bay of Portoferraio.

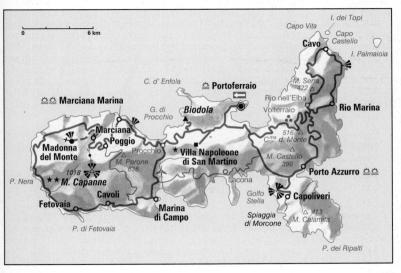

Golfo Stella

Capoliveri - From a spot to the west of this village there is a **panorama★★** of three bays: Portoferraio, Porto Azzurro and Golfo Stella.

Porto Azzurro - This port is overlooked by a fort which now serves as a prison.

Rio Marina - A pleasant port and mining village protected by a crenellated tower. Beyond **Cavo**, a small port sheltered by the Castello headland, the return **journey★★** to Portoferraio is by a high altitude **road★★** affording remarkable views of the ruins of Volterraio, the Bay of Portoferraio and the sea.

ERCOLANO★★

HERCULANEUM - Campania - Population 61 111

Michelin map 988 fold 27 or 431 E 25 - Local map see Golfo di NAPOLI

Herculaneum was founded, according to tradition, by Hercules. Like Pompeii the Roman town was overwhelmed during the AD 79 eruption of Vesuvius.
It was a less important and more peaceful town than Pompeii. Its port was frequented by fishing boats, there were numerous craftsmen and many rich and cultured patricians were drawn to the resort of Herculaneum because of its beautiful setting, overlooking the Bay of Naples. The five quarters of the town were divided by three main streets *(decumani)*. The town has various examples of different types of dwellings, all of which were overwhelmed by the sea of mud which seeped into every nook. The particular interest of a visit to Herculaneum is that all timber structures (frameworks, beams, doors, stairs and partitions) were preserved by a hard shell of solidified mud, whereas at Pompeii they were consumed by fire. The houses were empty, but death caught up with the inhabitants as they tried to flee the city.

RUINS ⏲ *2 hours*

From the access road *(go on foot)* there is a good view of the luxurious villas overlooking the sea.

Casa dell' Albergo - This vast patrician villa was about to be converted into apartments for letting, hence its name. It was one of the most badly damaged by the eruption.

★★ **Casa dell' Atrio a mosaico** - The atrium of this villa is paved with a chequered mosaic. The garden on the right is surrounded by a peristyle. On the left are the bedrooms and at the far end, a pleasant *triclinium* (dining-room). The terrace, flanked by two small rest rooms, offers an attractive view of the sea.

★★ Casa a Graticcio - The house gets its name from the wooden trellis frame work *(graticcio)* of the walls. It is a unique example of this type of house from antiquity.

★ Casa del Tramezzo carbonizzato - The façade is remarkably well preserved. This is a good example of a patrician dwelling which housed several families. The atrium is separated from the *tablinium* (living-room) by a wooden partition *(tramezzo)*. Only the sides of the partition remain standing.

Next door is the dyer's shop (**A**) containing an interesting wooden clothes-press.

★★ Casa Sannitica - The house was built on the very simple plan typical of the Samnites (an Italic people of the Sabine race). The splendid **atrium** is surrounded by a gallery with Ionic columns. The rooms are decorated with frescoes.

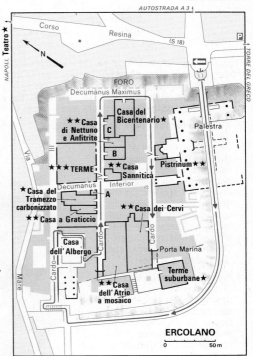

Casa: *House*	Teatro: *Theatre*
Foro: *Forum*	Terme: *Baths*
Porta: *Gate*	Palestra: *Palestra*

★★★ Terme - The baths of Herculaneum which are in excellent condition were built at the time of Augustus. They are not sumptuous but they show a remarkable degree of practical planning. In the **men's baths** visit the *palestra*, the cloakroom (**a**), the *frigidarium* (**b**) with frescoes on the ceiling, the *tepidarium* (**c**) and the *caldarium* (**d**). The **women's baths** include the waiting-room (**e**), the cloakroom *(apodyterium* - **f**), adorned with a mosaic pavement depicting Triton, the *tepidarium* (**g**) with a fine floor mosaic representing a labyrinth, and the *caldarium* (**k**).

★ Casa del Mobilio carbonizzato (B). - This small but rather elegant house has the remains of a charred *(carbonizzato)* bed in one room.

★★ Casa del Mosaico di Nettuno e Anfitrite - This house is equipped with a **shop★**; its counter opened onto the street. Mosaics depicting Neptune and Amphitrite adorn the nymphaeum.

★ Casa del Bel Cortile (C). - This is one of the most original houses in Herculaneum with its courtyard *(cortile)*, stone staircase and balcony.

★ Casa del Bicentenario - This house was laid bare in 1938, two hundred years after digging officially started.
The house has fresco decorations and a small cross incorporated in a stucco panel. This is one of the oldest Christian relics which has been brought to light in the Roman Empire.

★★ Pistrinum - An inscription states that this bakery belonged to Sextus Patulus Felix. In the shop and back room may be seen flour mills, storage jars and a large oven.

★★ Casa dei Cervi - This rich patrician mansion, probably the most beautiful among those overlooking the bay, is adorned with numerous frescoes and works of art, including an admirable sculptured group of stags *(cervi)* being attacked by dogs.

★ Terme Suburbane - These baths, situated near the Sea Gate, are elegantly decorated.

★ Teatro - *Corso Resina.* The theatre could accommodate at least 2 000 spectators.

FAENZA

Emilia-Romagna – Population 54 124
Michelin map 988 fold 15, 429 430 J 17
Town plan in the current Michelin Red Guide Italia

Faenza has given its name to the ceramics known as **faïence**, which have been produced locally since the 15C. In Italy faïence is also known as majolica, because during the Renaissance Faenza potters were inspired by ceramics which were imported from Majorca in the Balearic Isles. Faenza ceramics feature fine clay, remarkable glaze, brilliant colours and a great variety of decoration.

★★ **Museo internazionale delle Ceramiche** ⊙ – These vast collections present the development of ceramic-making throughout the world. On the first floor is a very fine collection of Italian Renaissance majolica, examples of the local ware, popular Italian pieces and an oriental section. On the ground floor, as well as the contemporary Italian collection, there are fine pieces by Matisse, Picasso, Chagall, Léger, Lurçat and the Vallauris school.

★ **Pinacoteca comunale** ⊙ – This important collection includes works by Giovanni da Rimini, Palmezzano, Dosso Dossi, Rossellino, and other canvases from foreign schools (portraits by Pourbus).

Cattedrale – The 15C cathedral was built by Florentine architect Giuliano da Maiano but the façade is unfinished. It

Faïence plate (late 15C)
(Museo Internazionale delle Ceramiche, Faenza)

contains the tomb (1471) of Bishop St Savinus by Benedetto da Maiano. In Piazza della Libertà stands a charming 17C baroque fountain.

Piazza del Popolo – The unusual elongated square has arcades surmounted by galleries. Around it are the 12C governor's house, Palazzo del Podestà and the 13C-15C Palazzo del Municipio.

FANO ⚓

Marches – Population 53 867
Michelin map 988 fold 16 or 430 K 21
Town plan in the current Michelin Red Guide Italia

This town, now a favourite seaside resort, was ruled by the Malatesta family from Rimini in the 13C-15C. The French philosopher Montaigne passed through Fano in April 1581 and provoked a controversy concerning the reputed beauty of the local women.

★ **Corte Malatestiana** – This 15C Renaissance ensemble includes a courtyard-garden and palace, and it would make an ideal theatrical set. The palace houses a museum, **Museo civico** ⊙ with sections on archeology, coins and medals and 14C-18C sculpture and painting. The latter includes Guercino's well-known work, the *Guardian Angel* (1641).

Santa Maria Nuova – 16C-18C. This contains **works**★ by Perugino, which are admired for their fine draughtsmanship and their delicate colours: an exquisite *Madonna and Child* (1497) (third altar on the right) and a graceful *Annunciation* (1498) (second altar on the left).

Fontana della Fortuna – This fountain in Piazza 20 Settembre presents the protecting goddess, Fortune, perched on a pivoting globe, with her billowing cloak acting as a weathervane.

Arco d'Augusto – *At the far end of the street of the same name.* This 1C arch has a main opening and two side ones for pedestrians. A low relief on the façade of the church of St Michael (San Michele) nearby portrays the arch in its original form. To the left of the arch are the remains of the Roman wall.

FERMO★

Marches – Population 35 093
Michelin map 988 fold 16 or 430 M 23

Fermo is one of the artistic and cultural centres of the Marches. It stands in a pleasant **site**★ on the slopes of a hill overlooking the countryside and facing the sea.

★ **Piazza del Duomo** – From this esplanade in front of the cathedral there are splendid **views**★★ of the Ascoli area, the Apennines, the Adriatic and Conero Peninsula.

Duomo ⊘ – The Romanesque-Gothic cathedral (1227) has a majestic **façade**★ in white Istrian stone. A delicately-carved doorway shows Christ with the Apostles on the lintel, and symbolic scenes or figures on the uprights. In the 18C interior are the 14C sarcophagus of Giovanni Visconti, overlord of the town; a 5C mosaic paving in front of the chancel, a 13C-14C Byzantine icon of the Virgin; and a 4C sarcophagus with high reliefs in the crypt.

Piazza del Popolo – This square in the centre of town is surrounded with arcades and elegant porticoes. Numerous palaces including the 15C Palazzo Comunale and the 16C Palazzo degli Studi line the square. Running between these two palaces is the Corso Cefalonia, a picturesque street lined with towers of nobility, palaces and ancient churches.

EXCURSION

Montefiore dell'Aso ⊘ – *20km - 12 miles south.* Carlo Crivelli (1430-95), a painter of courtesans and fair virgins, on being sentenced at Venice in 1457, took refuge in the Marches, and Montefiore thus gained a masterpiece. The church contains a splendid **polyptych**★★, which although incomplete, is finely chiselled and highlighted with gold representing six saints. The most successful panel shows the sinner Mary Magdalene richly apparelled in gold and silk brocade, holding the symbolic box of ointment.

FERRARA★★

Emilia-Romagna – Population 1,43 736
Michelin map 988 fold 15 or 429 H 16

In the heart of the fertile Po Plain, Ferrara is a tranquil town which is best explored in a leisurely manner, on foot or by bicycle. The streets are lined with red-brick houses, austere palaces and charming squares; their secret, melancholy atmosphere was a source of inspiration to the 20C metaphysical painters, De Chirico and Carrà. Ferrara, which was a splendid cultural centre during the Renaissance, remains one of the major artistic and cultural centres in Italy.

A discerning dynasty of patrons of the arts – Initially an independent commune, Ferrara belonged to the **House of Este** from 1208 to 1598, and despite numerous family dramas, often bloodthirsty, the Estes embellished their native city with fine buildings and patronised both men of letters and artists. **Niccolò III** (1393-1441) murdered his wife and her lover but he begat **Lionello** and **Borso**, who became generous administrators and enlightened patrons. **Ercole I** (1431-1505), who was responsible for his nephew's murder encouraged artists, as did his two famous daughters, Beatrice and Isabella d'Este. **Alfonso I** (1475 – 1534), the son of Ercole, became the third husband of Lucrezia Borgia, and Ercole II (1508-59) married Renée of France, the protector of the Calvinists.

After the demise of **Alfonso II** (1533-97) who left no heirs, Ferrara came under the rule of the Papacy and the Estes retired to the Duchy of Modena. Owing to the secular university (founded in 1391) and the patronage of the Este dynasty, the town witnessed a prodigious literary and artistic flowering. Three artists benefitted from the Estes' largesse: **Matteo Maria Boiardo** (1441-94), who wrote *Orlando Innamorata (Roland in love)*, **Ludovico Ariosto** (1474-1533) and **Torquato Tasso** (1544-95). **Ariosto** (1474-1533) spent his lifetime in the service of the Estes, in particular with Alfonso I, and his rare spare time was spent writing his masterpiece *Orlando Furioso (Roland the Mad)*. In relating the adventures of the knight Orlando and Angelica, the poet gives free reign to his imagination. **Tasso** (1544-95), a native of Sorrento, made several visits to Ferrara. During the first he wrote his epic poem *Gerusalemme Liberata (Jerusalem Delivered)* recounting the capture of Jerusalem by the Christians, enlivened by the love-story of Rinaldo and Armida.

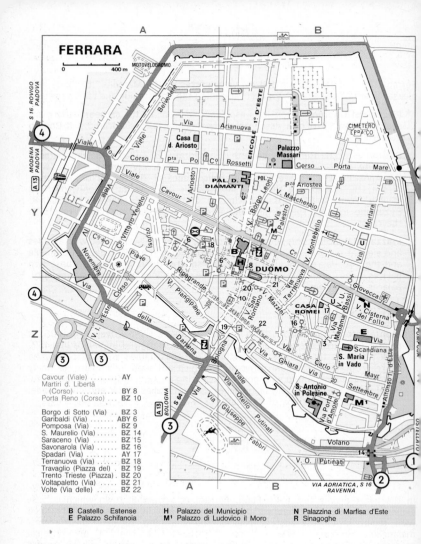

FERRARA

B Castello Estense	**H** Palazzo del Municipio	**N** Palazzina di Marfisa d'Este
E Palazzo Schifanoia	**M¹** Palazzo di Ludovico il Moro	**R** Sinagoghe

Ferrara School of Painting – The leader of this local school was **Cosmé (Cosimo)** Tura (c1430-95) with his strong personality, and its main characteristic was a meticulous realism, borrowed from the Northern schools. It was combined with a rather grim expressionism which derived from Mantegna, and powerful modelling reminiscent of Donatello. The main members were **Francesco del Cossa** (1435-77), who tempered the severity and the metallic sense of form of Tura and whose free and luminous style is evocative of Piero della Francesca; **Ercole de' Roberti** (1450-96), who conversely adopted Tura's strong modelling tradition; and **Lorenzo Costa** (1460-1535) who moved his studio to Bologna where prevailed the dark tones of the Umbrian and Tuscan schools. In the 16C the colourist **Dosso Dossi** and **Garofalo** favoured a greater harmony of colour in line with the Venetian style and allied to the classical tradition of Raphael and the Roman school.

OLD TOWN

★ **Castello Estense (BY B)** ⊙ – This massive castle, guarded by moats and four fortified gateways with drawbridges, was the seat of the Estes. On the *piano nobile*, where the orangery is, visitors may view the apartments decorated with frescoes by the Filippi and others.

★★ **Duomo (BYZ)** – The cathedral was built in the 12C in the Romanesque-Gothic Lombard style and presents a triple façade★★ with a splendid porch. On the tympanum is depicted the *Last Judgement* recalling the decoration of French Gothic cathedrals and the lunette above the central door, the sculpture of St George, is by Nicholaus, an artist of the school led by the Romanesque master, Wiligelmo, who was responsible for the carved decoration of Modena cathedral. On the south side there are two tiers of galleries on the upper section; below is the Loggia dei Merciai, a portico occupied by shops in the 15C. Here stood the Portal of the Months; the panels are kept in the cathedral museum. The bell-tower which was never completed was designed by Leon Battista Alberti. The semi-circular apse with its decorative brickwork is by Biagio Rossetti.

The interior, which was rebuilt in the 18C, contains a number of works of art including an altarpiece by II Guercino in the south arm of the transept and, above the Galilee porch, a **museum**★ ⊙ containing the **panels**★★ of the cathedral's former organ painted by **Cosmé Tura** representing *St George slaying the Dragon* and *The Annunciation*. It also houses the 12C **sculptures**★ from the Portal of the Months and two statues by Jacopo Della Quercia.

The 13C town hall, **Palazzo del Municipio** (**BY** H), facing the cathedral, was once the ducal palace.

Medieval streets – **Via San Romano**, which is still a commercial artery, linked the market square (Piazza Trento e Trieste) and the port (now via Ripagrande). It is lined with several houses with porticoes, an unusual feature in Ferrara. **Via delle Volte**, which has a distinctive character, has become one of the symbols of the town. Covered alleyways *(volte)* linked the houses of the merchants and their warehouses, thus making more habitable space available.

Sinagoghe – Via Mazzini 95. The synagogue was a gift of the Roman banker, Ser Samuel Mele, in 1481 to the Jewish community. The building comprises three temples for different rites: the Italian and German tradition and that from Fano in the Marches.

★ **Palazzo Schifanoia** (**BZ** E) ⊙ – This 14C palace is where the Estes used to come to relax (*schifanoia* means carefree). It now houses the municipal museum (**Museo Civico**). There are interesting archeological and Renaissance exhib-

> **The Jewish community of Ferrara**
>
> The Jewish community flourished in the 14C and 15C owing to the policy of the Estes, who welcomed Jews from Rome, Spain and Germany. The ghetto was instituted under Papal rule in 1624: five gates closed at dusk sealing off the area bounded by Via Mazzini, Vignatagliata e Vittoria. The gates were taken down under the new Italian Kingdom in 1859.
> The Jewish community of Ferrara is portrayed in the novel, The Garden of the Finzi-Contini, by Giorgio Bassani which was turned into an award-winning film in 1970 by Vittorio De Sica.

its and splendid frescoes in the Room of the Months (**Salone dei Mesi**★★). This complex cycle to the glory of Borso d'Este unfortunately retains only some of the 12 months. The three levels illustrate three different themes, notably everyday life at court, astrology and mythology. Several artists, including Francesco del Cossa (March, April, May) and Ercole de' Roberti (September), worked under Cosimo Tura. The frescoes, which demonstrate an extraordinary delicacy when portraying detail and a marvellous vivacity in both the use of colour and draughtsmanship, attest to Ferrara's great cultural achievements during the Renaissance.

The palace houses a museum, the **Museo Civico di Arte Antica**, which displays archeological collections, medals, bronzes, marquetry and ivories. The museum is part of the **Lapidario** situated near a former church Santa Libera.

The 15C-16C church, **Santa Maria in Vado**, near the palace, is decorated inside with frescoes and paintings.

★ **Palazzina di Marfisa d'Este** (**BZ** N) ⊙ – This elegant single-storey residence (1559), formerly surrounded by loggias, pavilions and gardens, is where Marfisa d'Este entertained her friends, among whom was the poet Tasso. The interior is remarkable for the ornate ceiling decoration including grotesques, and elegant 16C-17C furniture. Pass into the garden to visit the Orangery (Loggia degli Aranci); the vault features a mock pergola complete with vine shoots and animals.

★ **Casa Romei** (**BZ**) ⊙ – This is a rare example of a 15C bourgeois residence combining late-Gothic features such as the decoration of the rooms on the ground floor (**Room of the Sibyls**, Room of the Prophets) and Renaissance elements like the portico of the **main courtyard**.

★ **Palazzo di Ludovico il Moro** (**BZ** M¹) ⊙ – This palace, built in the late 15C for Ludovico Sforza the Moor, husband of Beatrice d'Este, is the home of an **archeological museum** with an important collection of 5C-4C BC **Attic vases**★ found at Spina.

Sant'Antonio in Polesine (**BZ**) ⊙– The convent founded in 1257 by Beatrice II d'Este, who joined the Benedictine order, stands in an isolated and peaceful setting.

The **church** has three chapels decorated with fine 14C-16C **frescoes**★ by the Giotto and Emilian schools.

THE RENAISSANCE TOWN

In 1490 Ercole I d'Este commissioned Biagio Rossetti to extend the town to the north. The extension (**Addizione Erculea**) built around two main axes – Corso Ercole I d'Este and Corso Porta Pia, Bragio Rossetti and Porta di Mare – is a great Renaissance town featuring parks and gardens. With this grandiose town-planning scheme Ferrara became the first modern city in Europe, according to the art historian, Jacob Burckhardt.

★ **Corso Ercole Iº d'Este (BY)** – The street lined with splendid Renaissance palaces but lacking any shops retains its original residential aspect. The focal point is the **Quadrivio degli Angeli** at the intersection with the other main axis, emphasised by three palaces with a rich angular decoration, including the Palazzo dei Diamanti.

★★ **Palazzo dei Diamanti (BY)** – The palace takes its name from the marble façade of 12 500 diamond bosses; the angle of the facets varies thus creating a distinctive picture. The palace was designed for a diagonal view: the central feature is therefore the corner embellished with **pilasters** and a balcony.
On the first floor is a gallery, the **Pinacoteca Nazionale**★ ⊘, displaying paintings showing the development of the Ferrarese, Emilian and Venetian Schools from the 13C to 18C. Among the masterpieces are two **tondi** dedicated to San Maurelio by Cosmé Tura, a *Death of the Virgin* by the Venetian Carpaccio, a *Descent from the Cross* by Ortolano, an **altarpiece** by Garofalo and **frescoes** from churches in Ferrara. The Sacrati Strozzi Collection includes paintings of the Muses **Erato** and **Urania** from Leonello d'Este's Studiolo in Palazzo di Belfiore which was situated near the present Corso Ercole I d'Este and was later dismantled when the town was under Papal rule. At no 17 in Corso Ercole I d'Este a museum (Museo Michelangelo Antonioni) presents the pictorial and photographic work of the great Ferrarese film-director.

Palazzo Massari (BY) – This superb late-16C palace now houses the **Museo Boldini** ⊘ containing oils, pastels and drawings that are representative of the artist's development (1842-1931) during the time he spent in Ferrara, Florence and Paris. There are a few works by other artists from Ferrara, including Previati.

Casa dell'Ariosto (AY) ⊘ – *Via Ariosto no 67*. Ariosto's house is now a library but it still has the garden where the poet tended his roses and jasmine.

FIESOLE★

Tuscany – Population 15 077
Michelin map 988 folds 14 and 15, or 430 K 15 – 8km – 5 miles north of Florence
Town plan in the current Michelin Red Guide Italia

The road from Florence winds uphill to Fiesole through olive-clad slopes, past luxuriant gardens and long lines of cypress trees, and affords views of this incomparable **countryside**★★★, so often depicted by the masters of the Italian Renaissance. The Etruscans founded this city in the 7C or 6C BC, strategically built high in the hills with a healthy climate. Fiesole was the most important city in northern Etruria and it dominated its neighbour and rival Florence until the 12C.

★ **Convento di San Francesco** ⊘ – The climb up to the convent which starts in front of the Duomo offers a splendid **view**★★ over Florence (from a small terrace about half-way up). This humble Franciscan convent, with its charming small cloisters, is admirably set on the hilltop.

★ **Duomo** – Founded in the 11C and enlarged in the 13C and 14C, the cathedral was extensively restored in the late 19C. The austere **interior**★, on a basilical plan with raised chancel, has columns supporting antique capitals. There are two handsome **works**★ by the sculptor Mino da Fiesole.

Zona archeologica ⊘ – This archeological site, in its enchanting **setting**★, comprises a **Roman theatre**★ (**1**) (c80 BC), which is still used for performances, a small **Etruscan temple** (**2**) and the remains of **baths** (**3**) built in the 1C BC by the Romans. The museum (**museo archeologico**★) (**4**) exhibits its finds dating from the Etruscan to the medieval period.

FIESOLE

San Domenico ↘ *FIRENZE*
Badia Fiesolana

Antiquarium Costantini (5) ⊙ – *Entrance near the archeological site.* Fine collection of Greek and Etruscan vases. In the basement are the results of the archeological digs carried out on the museum site (Roman murals).

Museo Bandini ⊙ – *Opposite the entrance to the archeological site.* The museum houses a collection of 14C and 15C Tuscan paintings. Note, on the first floor, Petrarch's masterpiece *Triumphs* illustrated by Jacopo del Sellaio.

San Domenico di Fiesole – *2.5km – 1 1/2 miles southwest. See the plan of the built-up area of Florence in the current Michelin Red Guide Italia.* It was in this 15C church, remodelled in the 17C, that Fra Angelico took his vows. In the first chapel on the north side is a ***Madonna and Saints*★** by the artist. In the second chapel on the south is a ***Baptism of Christ*** by Lorenzo di Credi.

Badia Fiesolana – *3km – 2 miles southwest. See the plan of the built-up area of Florence in the current Michelin Red Guide Italia.* This former Benedictine convent was partially rebuilt in the 15C thanks to the generosity of Cosimo the Elder who often stayed here. The Romanesque **façade**★ of the original church, with its decorative green and white marble geometrical motifs, was incorporated in the new building, left unfinished on the death of Cosimo the Elder. The interior and cloisters are typical of Brunelleschi's style.

FIRENZE★★★

FLORENCE – Tuscany – Population 402 211
Michelin map 988 folds 14 and 15, or 430 K 15 – Town plan below
Plans of the conurbation in the current Michelin Red Guide Italia

Florence is without doubt the city where the Italian genius has flourished with the greatest display of brilliance and purity. For three centuries from the 13C to the 16C, the city was the cradle of an exceptional artistic and intellectual activity from which evolved the precepts which were to dictate the appearance of Italy at that time and also the aspect of modern civilisation throughout Europe. The main characteristics of this movement, which was later to be known as the **Renaissance**, were partly a receptivity to the outside world, a dynamic open-minded attitude which encouraged inventors and men of science to base their research on the reinterpretation of the achievements of ancient Rome, and on the expanding of the known horizons. The desire to achieve universality resulted in a multiplication of the fields of interest.

View of Florence

Dante was not only a great poet but also a grammarian and historian who did much research on the origins and versatility of his own language. He was one of Florence's most active polemicists. **Giotto** was not only a painter but also an architect. **Lorenzo the Magnificent** was the prince who best incarnated the spirit of the Renaissance. An able diplomat, a realistic politician, a patron of the arts as well as a poet himself, he regularly attended the Platonic Academy in the Medici villa at Careggi, where philosophers such as Marsilio Ficino and Pico della Mirandola and men of letters like Politian and others established the principles of a new humanism. This quest to achieve a balance between nature and order had its most brilliant exponent in **Michelangelo**, painter, architect, sculptor and scholar whose work typifies a purely Florentine preoccupation.

Florence is set in the heart of a serenely beautiful **countryside★★★** which is bathed by a soft, amber light. The low surrounding hills are clad with olive groves, vineyards and cypresses which appear to have been harmoniously landscaped to please the human eye. Florentine architects and artists have variously striven to recreate this natural harmony in their works, whether it be the campanile of La Badia by Arnolfo di Cambio, or that of the cathedral by Giotto, the façade of Santa Maria Novella by Alberti or the dome of Santa Maria del Fiore by Brunelleschi. The pure and elegant lines of all these works of art would seem to be a response to the beauty of the landscape and the intensity of the light. The Florentine preoccupation with perspective throughout the Quattrocento (15C) is in part the result of this fascination for the countryside and that other great concern of the period, the desire faithfully to recreate what the eye could see.

This communion of great minds, with their varied facets and fields of interest, expressed a common desire to push their knowledge to the limits, and found in the flourishing city of Florence an ideal centre for their artistic and intellectual development. The city's artists, merchants, able administrators and its princely patrons of the arts all contributed to the creation of just the right conditions for nurturing such an intellectual and artistic community, which for centuries was to influence human creativity.

HISTORICAL NOTES

The colony of Florentia was founded in the 1C BC by Julius Caesar on the north bank of the Arno at a spot level with the Ponte Vecchio. The veteran soldiers who garrisoned the colony controlled the Via Flaminia linking Rome to northern Italy and Gaul.

The Middle Ages – It was only in the early 11C that the city became an important Tuscan centre when Count Ugo, Marquis of Tuscany, took up residence here, and again towards the end of the same century when the Countess Matilda affirmed its independence. During the 12C Florence prospered under the influence of the new class of merchants who built such fine buildings as the baptistery and San Miniato. This period saw the rise of trades organised in powerful guilds *(arti)*, which soon became the ruling class when Florence became an independent commune. In the 13C one third of Florence's population was engaged in either the wool or the silk trades, both of which exported their products to the four corners of Europe and were responsible for a period of extraordinary prosperity. These tradesmen were ably supported by the Florentine moneyhouses which succeeded the Lombard and Jewish institutions, and themselves acquired a great reputation by issuing the first-ever bills of exchange and the famous florin, struck with the Florentine coat of arms. The latter was replaced in the late-15C by the Venetian ducat. The main banking families were the Bardi-Peruzzi who advanced huge sums to England at the beginning of the Hundred Years War; they were soon to be joined in the forefront by the Pitti, Strozzi, Pazzi and of course the Medici.

The Guelph cause – Despite its prosperity, Florence did not escape the internal strife between the Ghibellines who were partisans of the Holy Roman Emperor and the Guelphs who supported the Pope. The Guelphs at first had the advantage; but the Ghibellines on being driven out of Florence, having allied themselves with other enemies of Florence, notably Siena, regained power after the Battle of Montaperti in 1260. The Guelphs counter-attacked and retook Florence in 1266. Under their rule the physical aspect of the city changed considerably, notably with the destruction of the fortified tower houses built by the Ghibelline nobility. They created a republic and established government by a single individual or family; lordship *(signoria)* and committees which in Florence were known as *priori*. There then occurred a split between the Black Guelphs and the White Guelphs who opposed the Papacy. During this latter tragedy Dante, who supported the White Guelphs, was exiled for good in 1302. In 1348 the Black Death killed more than half the population and put an end to the period of internal strife.

A glorious era (15C) – Among the numerous wealthy families in Florence, it was the **Medici** who gave the city several leaders who exercised their patronage both in the sphere of fine arts and finance. The founder of this illustrious dynasty was Giovanni di Bicci, a prosperous banker who left his fortune in 1429 to his son **Cosimo the Elder**, who in turn transformed his heritage into the city's most flourishing business. He discreetly exercised his personal power through intermediaries, and astutely juggled his own personal interests with those of the city, which assured Florence a kind of peaceful hegemony. His chief quality was his ability to gather around him both scholars and artists, whom he commissioned for numerous projects.

Cosimo the Elder was a passionate builder and Florence owes many of her great monuments to this "Father of the Land". His son, Piero II Gottoso (the gouty) survived him by five years only and he in turn bequeathed all to his son **Lorenzo the Magnificent** (1449-92). Having escaped the Pazzi Conspiracy Lorenzo reigned like a true Renaissance prince, although it was always unofficially. He distinguished himself by his skilful politics and managed to retain the prestige of Florence amongst its contemporaries while ruining the Medici financial empire. This humanist and man of great sensitivity was a great patron of the arts, and he gathered around him poets and philosophers, who all contributed to make Florence the capital of the early Renaissance.

A turbulent period – On Lorenzo's death, which had repercussions throughout Europe, the Dominican monk **Savonarola**, taking advantage of a period of confusion, provoked the fall of the Medici. This fanatical and ascetic monk, who became the Prior of the Monastery of St Mark, preached against the pleasures of the senses and of the arts, and drove the citizens of Florence to make a "bonfire of vanities" in 1497 in Piazza della Signoria, on which musical instruments, paintings, books of poetry etc were burnt. A year later Savonarola himself was burnt at the stake on the same spot.

The Medici family returned to power with the help of the Emperor Charles V and they reigned until the mid-18C. **Cosimo I** (1519-74) brought back to Florence some of the splendour which she had lost, conquered Siena and he himself became Grand Duke of Tuscany. He continued the tradition of patron of the arts protecting numerous artists.

117

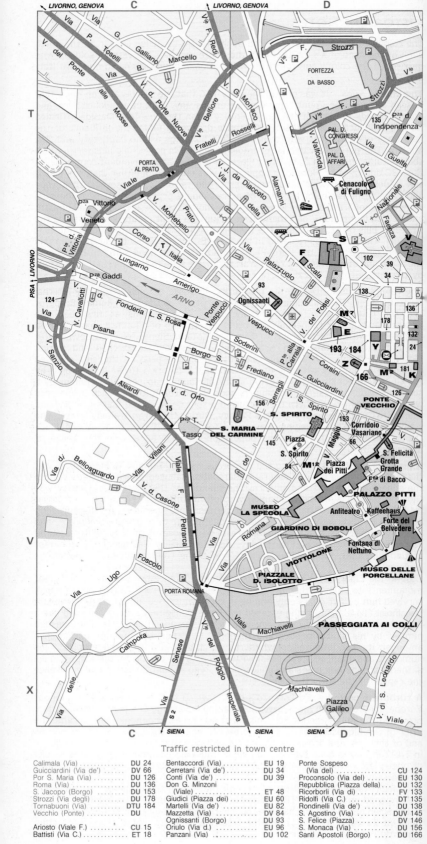

Traffic restricted in town centre

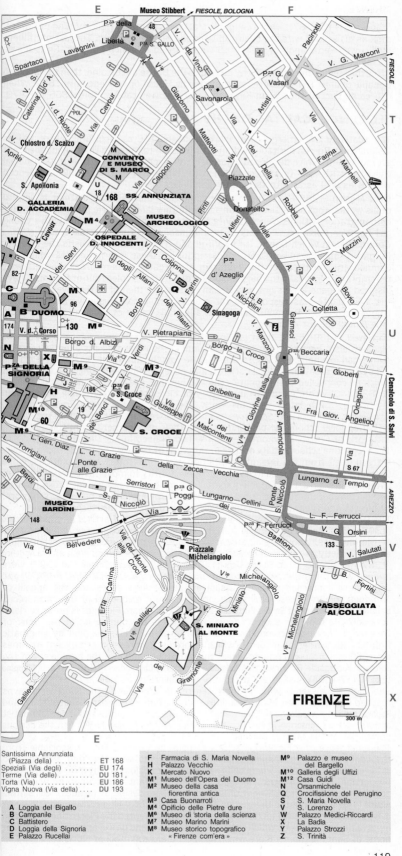

FIRENZE

Francesco I (1541-87), whose daughter Maria was to marry Henri IV King of France, took as his second wife the beautiful Venetian Bianca Cappello. The last prominent Medici was Ferdinand I (1549-1609) who married a French princess, Christine de Lorraine.

After the Medici, the Grand Duchy passed to the House of Lorraine, then to Napoleon Bonaparte until 1814, before returning to the House of Lorraine until 1859. When it became part of the Italian Kingdom, Florence was capital from 1865 to 1870.

FLORENCE, CAPITAL OF THE ARTS

The relatively late emergence of Florence in the 11C as a cultural centre and its insignificant Roman heritage no doubt contributed to the growth of an independent art movement, which developed vigorously for several centuries. One of its principal characteristics was its preoccupation with clarity and harmony which influenced writers as well as architects, painters and sculptors.

Dante Alighieri (1265-1321) established the use of the Italian vernacular in several of his works, thus superseding Latin as the literary language. He made an admirable demonstration with his *New Life (Vita Nuova)*, recounting his meeting with a young girl Beatrice Portinari who was to be the inspiration for his ***Divine Comedy*** *(Divina Commedia)*, in which Dante, led by Virgil and then by Beatrice, visits the Inferno, Purgatory and Paradise. Dante's description of these infernal circles where the damned are chastised, of the mountain of Purgatory where great crowds await redemption, and finally the dazzling vision of the divine splendour of Paradise, have inspired for generations not only Italian writers but men of letters everywhere. In the 14C Dante was responsible for creating an exceptionally versatile literary language to which Petrarch *(see Index)* added his sense of lyricism and Boccaccio *(see Index)* the art of irony.

Machiavelli (1469-1527), born in Florence, was the statesman on whose account Machiavellism became a synonym for cunning; he recounted his experiences as a statesman in a noble and vigorous prose. He was the author of ***The Prince*** (Il Principe – 1513), an essay on political science and government dedicated to Lorenzo II in which he counselled that in politics the end justifies the means. **Francesco Guicciardini** (1483-1540) wrote an important history of Florence and Italy, while **Giorgio Vasari** (1511-74), much later, with his work *The Lives of the Most Eminent Italian Architects, Painters and Sculptors*, was the first real art historian. He studied and classified local schools of painting, tracing their development from the 13C with the work of Cimabue, whom even Dante had praised in his *Divine Comedy*.

The Florentine school had its origins in the work of **Cimabue** (1240-1302) and slowly it freed itself from the Byzantine tradition with its decorative convolutions, while **Giotto** (1266-1337) in his search for truth gave priority to movement and expression. Later **Masaccio** (1401-28) studied spatial dimension and modelling. From then on perspective became the principal preoccupation of Florentine painters, sculptors, architects and theorists who continually tried to perfect this technique.

The Quattrocento (15C) saw the emergence of a group of artists like **Paolo Uccello** (1397-1475), **Andrea del Castagno** (1423-57), **Piero della Francesca** *(see Index)* a native of the Marches, who were all ardent exponents in the matters of foreshortening and the strictly geometrical construction of space; while others such as **Fra Angelico** (1387-1455), and later **Filippo Lippi** (1406-69) and **Benezzo Gozzoli** (1420-97) were imbued with the traditions of International Gothic *(see ART: GOTHIC PERIOD)* and were more concerned with the visual effects of arabesques and the appeal of luminous colours. These opposing tendencies were reconciled in the harmonious balance of the work of **Sandro Botticelli** (1444-1510), whom Florence is proud to claim as a son. He took his subjects from antiquity as the humanists in the court of Lorenzo de' Medici recommended, and he invented fables peopled by enigmatic figures with subtle linear forms, which created an impression of tension. At times a certain melancholy seems to arrest the movement and dim the luminosity of the colours. Alongside Botticelli the **Pollaiuolo** brothers, **Ghirlandaio** (1449-94) and **Filippino Lippi** (1457-1504) ensure the continuity and diversity of Florentine art.

The High Renaissance with its main centres in Rome and other northern towns reached Florence in the 16C. **Leonardo da Vinci** *(see Index)*, **Michelangelo** *(see Index)* and **Raphael** *(see Index)*, all made their debut at Florence, and inspired younger Mannerist artists such as **Pontormo, Rosso Fiorentino, Andrea del Sarto** (1486-1530) and the curious portraitist of the Medici, **Bronzino** (1503-72).

The emergence of a Florentine school of painting is, however, indissociable from the contemporary movement of the architects who were creating a style, also inspired by antiquity, which united the classical traditions of rhythm, a respect for proportion and geometric decoration. The constant preoccupation was with perspective in the arrangement of interiors and the design of façades. **Leon Battista Alberti** (1404-72) was the theorist and grand master of such a movement. However it was **Filippo Brunelleschi** (1377-1446) who best represented the Florentine spirit, and he gave the city buildings which combined both rigour and grace, as in the magnificent dome of Santa Maria del Fiore which has become the symbol of Florence.

Throughout the Quattrocento (15C), buildings were embellished with admirable sculptures which became a harmonious part of the architectural whole. The doors of the baptistery were the object of a competition in which the very best took part. If **Ghiberti** (1378-1455) was finally victorious, **Donatello** (1386-1466) was later to provide ample demonstration of the genius of his art, so full of realism and style, as did **Luca della Robbia** (1400-82) and his dynasty who specialised in glazed terracotta decoration, **Verrocchio** (1435-88) and numerous other artists who adorned the ecclesiastical and secular buildings of Florence. In the 16C **Michelangelo**, who was part of this tradition, confirmed his origins with his New Sacristy (1520-55) of San Lorenzo, which he both designed and decorated with sculpture. Later **Benvenuto Cellini** (1500-71), Giambologna or **Giovanni Bologna** (1529-1608) and **Bartolomeo Ammannati** (1511-92) maintained this unity of style which was responsible for the exceptional beauty of the city of Florence.

SIGHTSEEING

Florence is such an important art centre that it takes at least four days to see the main sights. These are, however, situated fairly closely together in the city centre which is not adapted to heavy traffic. It is therefore advisable to do the sightseeing on foot and establish a visiting programme which takes into account the opening times.

★★ **PIAZZA DEL DUOMO** *1/2 day*

In the city centre, the cathedral along with the campanile and baptistery, form an admirable group of white, green and pink marble monuments, which demonstrate the traditions of Florentine art from the Middle Ages to the Renaissance.

★★ **Duomo** (EU) ⊙ – **Santa Maria del Fiore**, one of the largest cathedrals in the Christian world, is a symbol of the city's power and wealth in the 13C and 14C. It was begun in 1296 by Arnolfo di Cambio and was consecrated in 1436.
This essentially Gothic cathedral is an outstanding example of the Florentine variant of this style, with its sheer size, the predominance of horizontal lines and its polychrome decoration.

Exterior – Walk round the cathedral starting from the south side to admire the marble mosaic decoration and the sheer size of the **east end★★★**. The harmonious **dome★★★** by Brunelleschi took 14 years to build. To counteract the excessive thrust he built two concentric domes which were linked by props. The façade dates from the late 19C.

Interior – The bareness of the interior contrasts sharply with the sumptuous decoration of the exterior. Enormous piers support sturdy arches which themselves uphold the lofty Gothic vaulting. The great octagonal **chancel★★** under the dome is surrounded by a delicate 16C marble balustrade. The dome is painted with a huge **fresco** of the Last Judgement. It is possible to go up to the inner gallery which offers an impressive view of the nave, and then climb to the top of the dome ⊙ (464 steps) for a magnificent **panorama★★** of Florence.
The sacristy doors on either side of the high altar have tympana adorned with pale blue terracottas by Luca della Robbia representing the Resurrection and the Ascension. In the new sacristy (left), there are inlaid armorial bearings by the Maiano brothers (15C).
A dramatic episode of the **Pazzi Conspiracy** took place in the chancel. The Pazzi, who were rivals of the Medici, tried to assassinate Lorenzo the Magnificent on 26 April 1478, during the Elevation of the Host. Lorenzo, though wounded by two monks, managed to take refuge in a sacristy, but his brother Giuliano fell to their daggers.
The axial chapel contains a masterpiece by Ghiberti, the sarcophagus of St Zanobi, the first Bishop of Florence. One of the low reliefs shows the saint resurrecting a child. The frescoes in the north aisle include: in the first bay near the choir, one showing Dante explaining the *Divine Comedy* to the city of Florence (1465); further along to the right, two equestrian portraits of leaders of mercenary armies *(condottieri)* by Paolo Ucello (1436) and Andrea del Castagno (1456).
A stairway on the other side of the nave, between the first and second pillars, leads to the **Crypt of Santa Reparata**, the only remaining part of a Romanesque basilica which was demolished when the present cathedral was built. The basilica itself was formerly an early Christian church (5C-6C). Excavations have revealed traces of mosaic paving belonging to the original building and Brunelleschi's tomb (behind the railing-enclosed chamber, at the bottom of the stairs, on the left).

★★ **Campanile** (EU B) ⊙ – The tower is tall (82m – 269ft) and slender and is the perfect complement to Brunelleschi's dome, the straight lines of the former balancing the curves of the latter. Giotto drew the plans for it and began building in 1334, but died in 1337.

The Gothic campanile was completed at the end of the 14C; its geometric decoration with its emphasis on horizontal lines is unusual. The admirable low reliefs at the base of the campanile have been replaced by copies. Those on the lower band were executed by Andrea Pisano and Luca della Robbia and those on the upper band by pupils of Andrea Pisano, but the overall design was by Giotto. The original low reliefs are in the Cathedral Museum.

From the top of the campanile (414 steps) there is a fine **panorama**★★ of the cathedral and town.

★★★ **Battistero** (EU C) ⊙ – The baptistery is faced in white and green marble in a sober and well-balanced Romanesque style. The **bronze doors**★★★ are world-famous.

The South Door *(entrance)* by Andrea Pisano (1330) is Gothic and portrays scenes from the life of St John the Baptist *(above)*, as well as the Theological Virtues (Faith, Hope, Charity) and the Cardinal Virtues *(below)*. The door-frames which show great skill are by Vittorio Ghiberti, son of the designer of the other doors. The North Door (1403-24) was the first done by Lorenzo Ghiberti. He was the winner of a competition in which Brunelleschi, Donatello and Jacopo della Quercia also took part. Scenes from the Life of Christ are evoked with extraordinary nobility and harmony of composition.

The East Door (1425-52), facing the cathedral, is the one that Michelangelo declared worthy to be the **Gate of Paradise**. In it Ghiberti recalled the Old Testament; prophets and sibyls adorn the niches. The artist portrayed himself, bald and malicious, in one of the medallions.

Interior – With its 25m – 82ft diameter, its green and white marble and its paving decorated with oriental motifs, the interior is grand and majestic. The dome is covered with magnificent **mosaics**★★★ of the 13C. The Last Judgement is depicted on either side of a large picture of Christ the King; on the five concentric bands that cover the other five panels of the dome, starting from the top towards the base, are the Heavenly Hierarchies, Genesis, the Life of Joseph, scenes from the Life of the Virgin and of Christ, and the Life of St John the Baptist.

On the right of the apse is the tomb of the Antipope John XXIII, friend of Cosimo the Elder, a remarkable work executed in 1427 by Donatello assisted by Michelozzo. Under the 14C Gothic **Loggia del Bigallo** (EU A) to the south of the baptistery, lost or abandoned children were exhibited.

★★ **Museo dell'Opera del Duomo** (EU M¹) ⊙ – The museum contains items from the cathedral, campanile and baptistery; note models of Brunelleschi's dome on the ground floor. On the mezzanine is the famous *Pietà*★★ which Michelangelo left unfinished. In the large room on the first floor are two famous statues by **Donatello** – an impressive repentant *Magdalene*★ carved in wood, and the prophets Jeremiah and Habakkuk, the latter being nicknamed *Zuccone* (vegetable marrow) because of the shape of his head.

In the same room are the famous **Cantorie**★★, choristers' tribunes from the cathedral, by Luca della Robbia and Donatello. The museum also houses the famous silver **altarpiece**★★ depicting the life of St John the Baptist, a 14C-15C masterpiece and the admirable **low reliefs**★★ from the campanile: those by Andrea Pisano and Luca della Robbia depict scenes from the Book of Genesis and various human activities.

★★ **PIAZZA DELLA SIGNORIA** (EU) *1 day*

★★ **Piazza della Signoria** – This was, and still is, the political stage of Florence, with a wonderful backcloth formed by the Palazzo Vecchio, the Loggia della Signoria and in the wings the Uffizi Museum. The many statues make it virtually an open-air museum of sculpture: near the centre of the square, the equestrian statue of Cosimo I, after

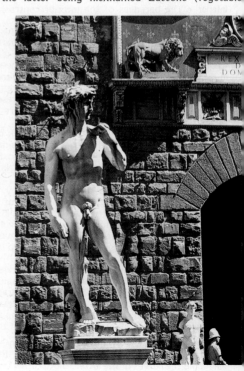

David by Michelangelo, Piazza della Signoria

Giovanni Bologna, and at the corner of the Palazzo Vecchio, the Fountain of Neptune (1576) by Ammannati. In front of the Palazzo Vecchio are copies of the proud *Marzocco* or *Lion of Florence* by Donatello and Michelangelo's *David*.

★★ Loggia della Signoria (EU D) – The Loggia, built at the end of the 14C, was the assembly hall and later the guardroom of the Lanzi (foot soldiers) of Cosimo I. It contains ancient (Classical) and Renaissance statues: the *Rape of a Sabine* (1583), *Hercules and the centaur Nessus* by Giovanni Bologna and the wonderful *Perseus*★★★ holding up the severed head of Medusa, a masterpiece executed by Benvenuto Cellini from 1545 to 1553.

★★ Palazzo Vecchio (EU H) ⊘ – The Old Palace's powerful mass is dominated by a lofty bell-tower, 94m – 308ft high. Built from 1299 to 1314 probably to plans by Arnolfo di Cambio, it is in a severe Gothic style without any openings at ground level, a series of twinned windows above and battlements, parapet walk and crenellations on top with the tower.

The refinement and splendour of the Renaissance interior is a complete contrast. The **courtyard★** was restored by Michelozzo in the 15C and decorated in the following century by Vasari. The 16C fountain is surmounted by a delightful winged goblin, a copy of a work by Verrocchio (the original is housed in the palace).

Initially the seat of government (Palazzo della Signoria), the palace was then taken over in the 16C by Cosimo I as his private residence, as it was better suited to accommodating his large court. Most of the redecoration work done by Giorgio Vasari dates from this period. When Cosimo I abandoned the palace in favour of the Pitti Palace it was renamed Palazzo Vecchio. The apartments were lavishly decorated with sculptures by Benedetto and Giuliano da Maiano (15C) and with paintings by Vasari and Bronzino (16C) to the glory of Florence and the Medici.

On the first floor the great Sala dei Cinquecento, painted with frescoes by several artists including Vasari, contains a group carved by Michelangelo, *The Genius of Victory.* The walls of the magnificent **studiolo★★** or study of Francesco de' Medici, which was designed by Vasari, were painted by Bronzino, who was responsible for the medallion portraits of *Cosimo I* and *Eleanora of Toledo*. Leo X's apartment was decorated by Vasari and his assistants with scenes illustrating episodes of the Medici history.

On the second floor, Cosimo I's apartments are open to the public. They are known as the Apartment of the Elements because of the allegories decorating the first chamber. The decoration was designed by Vasari around the theme of ancient mythology.

Beyond these chambers are Eleonora of Toledo's apartments, again designed by Vasari with the exception of the chapel which is decorated with frescoes by Bronzino. Finally, in the apartments of the Priors of the Arts, the best-known chamber is the Chamber of Lilies **(Sala degli Gigli★)** which has a magnificent coffered **ceiling** by Guiliano da Maiano and the dressing-room **(Sala del Guardaroba★)** lined with 16C maps.

★★ UFFIZI (EU M¹⁰) ⊘

This is one of the finest art museums in the world. These collections were assembled by several generations of Medici and the visitor can follow the evolution of Italian art from its beginnings to the 17C.

The early nucleus was gathered together by Francesco I (1541-87) to which were added the collections of the Grand Dukes Ferdinand I, II and Cosimo III. In 1737 the last member of the Medici dynasty, Anna Maria Luisa, Electress Palatine, bequeathed the Medici collection to her native city of Florence.

The Uffizi Museum was then housed in the Renaissance palace, designed by Vasari in 1560, which contained the offices *(uffizi)* of the Medici adminis-tration.

The rich collections of drawings and paintings are on the first floor; paintings and sculpture are exhibited in 45 rooms which are linked by two galleries on the second floor.

Galleries – The first gallery *(east)* is essentially dedicated to Florentine and Tuscan artists: there are works by Cimabue, Giotto, Duccio, Simone Martini (the *Annunciation*, a masterpiece of Gothic art), Paolo Uccello **(Battle of San Romano)** and Filippo Lippi. The **Botticelli Room★★★** houses the artist's major works: the allegories of the **Birth of Venus** and **Spring** and the *Madonna with Pomegranate*. Other exhibits in the gallery include the **Adoration of the Magi** and the **Annunciation** by Leonardo da Vinci and a series of Italian and foreign paintings from the 15C and 16C (Perugino, Cranach, Dürer, Bellini, Giorgione, Correggio etc).

The first 11 rooms of the second gallery *(west)* contain works from the Italian Cinquecento (16C): *Tondo Doni* by Michelangelo, *Madonna and the Goldfinch* and *Leo X* by Raphael, *Madonna and the Harpies* by Andrea del Sarto, *Urbino Venus* by Titian and *Leda and the Swan* by Tintoretto. The other rooms are dedicated to both Italian and foreign paintings from the 17C and 18C: included in the collection are *Isabella Brandt* by Rubens, **Caravaggio**'s *Adolescent Bacchus* and works by **Claude Lorrain** and **Rembrandt**.

★★ PONTE VECCHIO (DU)

As its name suggests, this is the oldest bridge in Florence. It has been rebuilt several times and spans the narrowest point of the Arno. Its orginal design includes a line of jewellers' shops and the **Corridoio Vasariano**,

Pallas and the Centaur by Botticelli

a passageway which was built by Vasari to link the Palazzo Vecchio to the Pitti Palace and passes overhead.

★★ PALAZZO PITTI (DV)

This 15C Renaissance building, of rugged but imposing appearance, with pronounced rustication and many windows, was built to the plans of Brunelleschi for the Pitti family, the rivals of the Medici. It was Cosimo I's wife, Eleanora di Toledo, who enlarged the palace by the addition of two wings. The court moved to the palace in 1560.

★★★ **Galleria Palatina** – *First floor*. This gallery houses a marvellous collection of paintings: groups★★★ of works by Raphael (*Portrait of a Lady* or *La Velata*, *Madonna del Granduca* and *Madonna della Seggiola*) and Titian (portraits of *La Bella*, *The Aretino*, *The Concert* and the *Grey-eyed Nobleman*).
On the first floor are the State Apartments (**Appartamenti reali**★) ⊘ The building also houses a modern art gallery (**Galleria d'Arte Moderna**★) ⊘ which mainly displays Tuscan works from the 19C and 20C. The section devoted to the **Macchiaioli** movement *(see INDEX)* is represented by an exceptional series★★ by Fattori, Lega, Signorini, Cecioni. This wing also houses a Costume Museum (**Galleria del Costume**) *(access by lift located near the ticket office)* which displays Italian costumes dating from the 18C to the present day. In the other wing is the Silver Museum (**Museo degli Argenti**★★) ⊘ presenting items largely from the Medici collections.

★ GIARDINO DI BOBOLI (DV)

This Italian-style terraced garden, behind the Pitti Palace, was designed in 1549 by Tribolo and is ornamented with antique and Renaissance statues. At one end of an avenue to the left of the palace is the **grotta grande**, a grotto created in the main by Buontalenti (1587-97). Cross the amphitheatre to reach the highest point of the garden from which, on the right, the **Viottolone**★, an avenue of pines and cypresses, runs down to **Piazzale dell'Isolotto**★, a circular pool with a small island, planted with citrus trees and adorned with a fountain by Giovanni Bologna. A pavilion houses a Porcelain Museum (**Museo delle Porcellane**★). A fort (**Forte del Belvedere**), at the top of the hill, affords a splendid panorama★★ of Florence and the celebrated Florentine countryside. The elegant villa which dominates the bastion was designed by Buontalenti.

★★★ PALAZZO E MUSEO NAZIONALE DEL BARGELLO (EU M⁹) ⊘

This austere palace was formerly the residence of the governing magistrate *(podestà)* and then became police headquarters *(bargello)*. It is a fine example of 13C-14C medieval architecture planned round a majestic **courtyard**★★ with a portico and loggia. The Volognona tower (57m – 188ft) soars above the building. The palace is now a museum of sculpture and decorative arts with particularly good sections on Italian and Florentine Renaissance sculpture.

The rooms on the ground floor are devoted to the works of 16C Florentine sculptors: **Brutus** and the *Pitti Tondo* (a marble medallion depicting the Virgin and Child with St John) by Michelangelo; **low reliefs** from the pedestal of the Perseus bronze by Benvenuto Cellini.

There is an exceptional collection *(first floor)* of **sculpture★★★** by **Donatello** which includes his *Marzocco* (the Florentine heraldic lion), the bronze *David*, as well as the low-relief of *St George* from Orsanmichele.

The rooms on the second floor display terracottas by Giovanni and Andrea della Robbia and works by **Verrocchio**, including the famous bronze statue of *David*.

★★ SAN LORENZO (DU V)

This was the Medici family parish church near the Medici Palace, and it was here that most of the family was buried. The **church★★** was begun by Brunelleschi c1420. The interior is a perfect example of the sobriety of style introduced by **Brunelleschi** and typical of his thoughtful, measured, rigorous architectural style and its human dimension. His great achievement is the **Old Sacristy★★** *(at the far end of the north transept).* Donatello was responsible for part of the decoration of the latter and also the two **pulpits★★** in the nave with bronze panels, which are works of admirable virtuosity and full of a great sense of drama.

★★ **Biblioteca Medicea Lauren-ziana** ○ – Cosimo the Elder's library was added to by Lorenzo the Magnificent. Access is from the north aisle of the church or through the charming 15C **cloisters★** *(entrance to the left of the church).* The vestibule was designed as an exterior and is occupied by a magnificent **staircase★★**, supremely elegant as the curved steps of the central flight lead up to the library proper. The staircase was built by Ammannati to Michelangelo's designs. The library, also by Michelangelo, displays in rotation some of the 10 000 manuscripts.

★★ **Cappelle Medicee** ○ – Entrance on Piazza Madonna degli Aldobrandini. The Medici Chapels include the Princes' Chapel and New Sacristy.

The **Princes' Chapel** (17C-18C), grandiose but gloomy, is faced with semi-precious stones and marbles and is the funerary chapel for Cosimo I and his descendants.

The **New Sacristy** was Michelangelo's first architectural work and despite its name was always intended as a funerary chapel. Begun in 1520, it was left unfinished when the artist left Florence in 1534. Michelangelo achieved a great sense of rhythm and solemnity by using contrasting materials, dark grey sandstone *(pietra serena)* and the white of the walls and marbles.

The famous **Medici tombs★★★** were also the work of Michelangelo.

The Procession of the Magi by Benozzo Gozzoli
(detail showing Lorenzo the Magnificent)

Giuliano, Duke of Nemours (d 1516), is portrayed as Action, surrounded by allegorical figures of Day and Night; and Lorenzo II, Duke of Urbino (d 1519), as a Thinker with Dawn and Dusk at his feet.

Of the plans for Lorenzo the Magnificent's tomb only the admirable group of the Madonna and Child flanked by saints was completed. In the plain tomb underneath lie Lorenzo the Magnificent and his brother Giuliano.

★★ PALAZZO MEDICI-RICCARDI (EU W) ⊘

This noble but austere building is typical of the Florentine Renaissance with its mathematical plan and rustication, massive at ground level and lighter on the upper level. The palace which has a square arcaded courtyard was begun in 1444 by Michelozzo on the orders of his friend Cosimo the Elder.

From 1459 to 1540 it was a Medici residence, and Lorenzo the Magnificent held court here, attended by poets, philosophers and artists alike. In the second half of the 17C the palace passed to the Riccardi who made extensive alterations to the building.

★★★ **Chapel** – *First floor: entrance by the first stairway on the right in the courtyard.* This tiny chapel was decorated with admirable **frescoes** (1459) by **Benozzo Gozzoli**. *The Procession of the Magi* is a vivid picture of Florentine life with portraits of the Medici and of famous dignitaries from the East who had assembled for the Council of Florence in 1439.

★★ **Luca Giordano Gallery** – *First floor: entrance by the second stairway on the right in the courtyard.* The entire roof of this gallery built by the Riccardi at the end of the 17C and splendidly decorated with gold stucco, carved panels and great painted mirrors, is covered by a brightly-coloured baroque fresco of the Apotheosis of the second Medici dynasty, masterfully painted by Luca Giordano in 1683.

★★ SAN MARCO (ET) ⊘

The museum in a former Dominican monastery, rebuilt c1436 in a very plain style by Michelozzo, is virtually the **Fra Angelico Museum★★★**. Fra Angelico took orders in Fiesole before coming to St Mark's, where he decorated the walls of the monks' cells with edifying scenes. Humility, gentleness and mysticism were the qualities expressed by this artistic monk in a technique influenced by the Gothic tradition. His refined use of colour, delicate draughtsmanship and timid handling of the subject-matter imbued these frescoes with a pacifying power, particularly appropriate for this oasis of calm and place of meditation.

The former guest hall, opening off the cloisters on the right, contain many of the artist's works on wood, especially the triptych depicting the *Descent from the Cross*, the famous *Last Judgement* and other religious scenes. The chapter-house has a severe *Crucifixion* while the refectory contains an admirable *Last Supper★* by Ghirlandaio.

The staircase leading to the first floor is dominated by his well-balanced and sober masterpiece, the *Annunciation*. The monks' cells open off three corridors, with lovely timber ceilings. Along the corridor to the left of the stairs are the *Apparition of Christ to the Penitent Magdalene (1st cell on the left)*, the *Transfiguration (6th cell on the left)* and the *Coronation of the Virgin (9th cell on the left)*.

At the far end of the next corridor are the cells of Savonarola, who was prior of St Mark's. Off the corridor on the right is the **library★**, one of Michelozzo's finest achievements.

★★ GALLERIA DELL'ACCADEMIA (ET) ⊘

The museum gives the visitor some idea of the extraordinary personality of **Michelangelo** and the conflict between the nature of his raw materials and his idealistic vision. The **main gallery★★★** contains the powerful figures of *Four Slaves* (1513-20) and *St Matthew* (all unfinished) who would seem to be trying to struggle free from the marble. At the far end of the gallery, in a specially designed apse (1873), is the monumental figure of *David* (1501-04), the symbol of youthful but well-mastered force and a perfect example of the sculptor's humanism. The **picture gallery★** has works by 13C-15C Tuscan masters, including a painted chest by Adimari and two Botticellis.

★★ SANTA MARIA NOVELLA (DU S)

The Church of Santa Maria Novella and the adjoining monastery were founded in the 13C by the Dominicans. The church overlooks an elongated square which was originally the setting for chariot races.

The **church★★**, begun in 1279, was completed only in 1360, except for the **façade**, with harmonious lines and geometric patterns in white and green marble, which was designed by Alberti (upper section) in the 15C.

It is a large church (100m – 328ft) designed for preaching. On the wall of the third bay in the north aisle is a famous **fresco★★** of the Trinity with the Virgin, St John and the donors in which Masaccio, adopting the new Renaissance theories, shows great mastery of perspective. At the far end of the north transept, the Strozzi di Mantora Chapel (raised) is decorated with **frescoes★** (1357) by the Florentine Nardo di Cione depicting the Last Judgement on a grand scale. The **polyptych★** on the altar is by Nardo's brother, Orcagna di Cione. The sacristy contains a fine **Crucifix★** *(above the entrance)* by Giotto and a delicate glazed terracotta **niche★** by Giovanni della Robbia.

In the Gondi Chapel *(first on the left of the high altar)* is displayed the famous **Crucifix★★** by Brunelleschi, which so struck Donatello that he is said, on first seeing it, to have dropped the basket of eggs he was carrying.

The chancel is ornamented with admirable **frescoes★★★** by **Domenico Ghirlandaio** who, on the theme of the Lives of the Virgin and of St John the Baptist, painted a dazzling picture of Florentine life in the Renaissance era.

The church is flanked by two cloisters. The finest are the Green Cloisters (**Chiostro Verde★**) ⊙, so-called after the dominant colour of the frescoes painted by Paolo Uccello and his school (scenes from the Old Testament). Opening off these to the north is the Spaniards' Chapel (**Cappellone degli Spagnoli**) with late-14C **frescoes★★** by **Andrea di Bonaiuto** (also known as Andrea da Firenze). With an intricate symbolism the frescoes depict the Church Triumphant and the glorification of the action of the Dominicans. To the east is the refectory which houses the church's treasure.

★★ SANTA CROCE (EU) ⊙ *1hour*

The church and cloisters of Santa Croce give onto one of the town's oldest squares. This is the church of the Franciscans. It was started in 1294 and completed in the second half of the 14C. The façade and the campanile date from the 19C.

The **interior** is vast (140m by 40m – 460ft x 130ft) as the church was designed for preaching and consists of a single spacious nave and slender apse with fine 15C stained glass windows. The church is paved with 276 tombstones and along the walls are ornate tombs.

South aisle: By the first pillar, a *Virgin and Child* by A Rossellino (15C); opposite, the tomb of Michelangelo (d 1564) by Vasari; opposite the second pillar, the funerary monument (19C) to Dante (d 1321, buried at Ravenna); by the third pillar, a fine **pulpit★** (1476) by Benedetto da Maiano and facing it the monument to V. Alfieri (d 1803) by Canova; opposite the fourth pillar, the 18C monument to Machiavelli (d 1527); facing the fifth pillar, an elegant low relief of the *Annunciation*★★ carved in stone and embellished with gold by Donatello; opposite the sixth pillar, the **tomb of Leonardo Bruni★★** (humanist and chancellor of the Republic, d 1444) by B. Rossellino, and next to it the tomb of Rossini (d 1868).

South transept: At the far end, the Baroncelli Chapel with **frescoes★** (1338) depicting the Life of the Virgin by Taddeo Gaddi and at the altar the **polyptych★** of the Coronation of the Virgin from Giotto's studio.

★ **Sacristy** ⊙ *(access by the corridor on the right of the chancel):* This dates from the 14C and is adorned with **frescoes★** including a Crucifixion by Taddeo Gaddi and, in the fine Rinuccini Chapel, with scenes from the Life of the Virgin and of Mary Magdalene by Giovanni da Milano (14C). At the far end of the corridor is the harmonious Medici Chapel (1434) built by Michelozzo, with a fine **altarpiece★** in glazed terracotta by Andrea della Robbia.

Chancel: The first chapel to the right of the altar contains evocative **frescoes★★** (c1320) by Giotto depicting the life of St Francis; in the third chapel is the tomb of Julie Clary, the wife of Joseph Bonaparte. The chancel proper is covered with **frescoes★** (1380) by Agnolo Gaddi relating the legend of the Holy Cross.

North transept: At the far end is a famous *Crucifixion*★★ by Donatello, which Brunelleschi tried to surpass at Santa Maria Novella.

North aisle *(coming back)*: Beyond the second pillar, a fine **monument to Carlo Marsuppini★** by Desiderio da Settignano (15C); facing the fourth pillar the tombstone of L. Ghiberti (d 1455); the last tomb (18C) is that of Galileo (d 1642).

★★ **Cappella dei Pazzi** ⊙ – *At the far end of the first cloisters; entrance to the right of the church.* This chapel by Brunelleschi is entered through a domed portico, and is a masterpiece of the Florentine Renaissance remarkable for its original conception, its pure, rigid lines, its skilful proportions and the harmony of its decoration (glazed terracotta from the Della Robbia workshop).

Great cloisters – *Entrance at the far end of the first cloisters, on the right.* These very elegant cloisters were designed by Brunelleschi shortly before his death (1446) and were completed only in 1453.

Museo dell'Opera di Santa Croce ⊙ – The museum is installed in the buildings around the first cloister and in particular in the former refectory. The museum contains a famous *Crucifixion*★ by Cimabue which was seriously damaged by the 1966 floods which particularly affected Santa Croce.

★★ PASSEGGIATA AI COLLI

See plans of the built-up area in the Michelin Red Guide Italia. 2 hours on foot or 1 hour by car.

For a drive to the hills take the road to the east along the south bank of the Arno to the medieval tower in Piazza Guiseppe Poggi. Poggi laid this fine road to the hills from 1865 to 1870. Take the winding pedestrian street to Piazzale Michelangiolo for a splendid view★★★ of the whole city.

Not far from here, in a splendid setting★★ overlooking the town, the Church of San Miniato al Monte★★, built from the 11C to 13C, is one of the most remarkable examples of Florentine Romanesque architecture. Its very elegant façade is decorated with geometric designs in green and white marble, not unlike those of the baptistery. The harmonious interior also ornamented with multicoloured marble contains a 13C pavement. The Chapel of Cardinal James of Portugal★ opening out of the north aisle is a fine Renaissance structure. In the centre of the nave is a Chapel of the Crucifix by Michelozzo. The pulpit and chancel screen *(transenna)* form a remarkable ensemble★★ beautifully inlaid with marble (early 13C). In the apse is a mosaic depicting Christ giving His Blessing. The frescoes★ (1387) in the sacristy are by Spinello Aretino. The 11C crypt has delicate columns with antique capitals.

ADDITIONAL SIGHTS

★★ **Frescoes of Santa Maria del Carmine** (DU) ⊙ – In the Cappella Brancacci is a fresco cycle (1427) by **Masaccio** depicting Original Sin and the Life of St Peter. It was finished by Filippino Lippi. *Cindy ree'*

La Badia (EU X) – 10C church of a former abbey *(badia)* with an elegant campanile★. The interior has a sumptuous coffered ceiling★★ and houses several works of art including Filippino Lippi's **Virgin appearing to St Bernard**★, a delicate relief★★ sculpture in marble by Mino da Fiesole and the tombs★ carved by the same artist.

★ **Casa Buonarroti** (EU M³) ⊙ – Michelangelo Buonarroti owned this house although he never lived here. There are several of the sculptor's works on display inside (*Battle of the Centaurs* and *Madonna della Scala*).

Cenacolo di Sant'Apollonia (ET) ⊙ – In the former refectory hangs a *Last Supper*★ by Andrea del Castagno.

★ **Cenacolo di San Salvi** ⊙ – *East of Florence* FU. The former refectory of the abbey contains a splendid fresco★★ of the Last Supper (1520) by Andrea del Sarto.

Ognissanti (DU) ⊙ – This church was built in the 13C and remodelled in the 17C. Inside are fine frescoes by Botticelli (*St Augustine*) and Ghirlandaio (*St Jerome*). The latter is also responsible for the **Last Supper**★ in the refectory adjacent to the church.

★ **Santo Spirito** (DUV) – The church was built from 1444 onwards to plans by Brunelleschi. It contains fine works of art★.

Santa Trinità (DU Z) – The Cappella dell'Annunziazione★ in this church is decorated with frescoes by Lorenzo Monaco (*Life of the Virgin*); those in the Capella Sassetti★★ are by Ghirlandaio (*Life of St Francis*).

★ **Loggia del Mercato Nuovo** (DU K) – This gallery (loggia) with its elegant Renaissance arcades was built in the 16C in the heart of the commercial district. It now serves as a market for Florentine crafts.

★★ **Museo Archeologico** (ETU) ⊙ – The museum has an important collection of Egyptian, Greek (François vase★★, found in an Etruscan tomb but of ancient origin), Etruscan (Arezzo Chimera★★, a 5C BC masterpiece) and Roman art.

★★ **Museo della Casa Fiorentina Antica** (DU M²) ⊙ – Artefacts and furniture evoke the life of a rich Florentine family of the period. The museum is housed in Palazzo Davanzati, a tall medieval-style 14C building with an inner courtyard.

Museo Marino Marini (DU M¹) ⊙ – Displayed in this museum are works of the famous Florentine sculptor and painter who died in 1980.

★ **Museo di Storia della Scienza** (EU M⁴) ⊙ – Presentation of a rich collection of scientific instruments including the lens used by the mathematician and astronomer Galileo.

★ **Opificio delle Pietre dure** (ET M⁴) ⊙ – Lorenzo the Magnificent was responsible for reviving the ancient tradition of decorating with semi-precious stones in the form of mosaics *(pietre dure)*. This workshop now specialises in restoration work and there is a small museum.

★ **Orsanmichele** (EU N) – Originally a grain storehouse, Orsanmichele was rebuilt in the 14C. There are works by Donatello, Ghiberti, Verrocchio etc. Inside, there is a splendid Gothic tabernacle★★ by Orcagna.

★★ **Palazzo Rucellai (DU E)** – The palace was designed by Leon Battista Alberti and built in the 15C. The façade is the first cohesive example of the three ancient orders placed one on top of the other.

★★ **Palazzo Strozzi (DU Y)** – The building dates from the end of the 15C and is one of the finest palaces in Florence with its rusticated stonework, cornice and arcaded courtyard.

★ **Piazza della Santissima Annunziata (ET 168)** – This fine piazza is enhanced by Giambologna's equestrian statue of Ferdinando I de'Medici and two baroque fountains.

Chiesa della SS. Annunziata (ET) – The church dates from the 15C. In the chancel are some fine **frescoes★** by Rosso Fiorentino and Pontormo which were completed by Franciabigio. The interior is in the Baroque style; the north arm of the transept gives access to the Renaissance Cloister of the Dead **(Chiostro dei Morti)**. The vault by the door is adorned with the *Madonna with the Sack★* by Andrea del Sarto (16C).

★ **Ospedale degli Innocenti (ET)** – Brunelleschi's **portico★★** is decorated by terracotta **medallions★★** by Andrea della Robbia. The Foundlings' Hospital houses a gallery **(Pinacoteca)** ⊘ displaying Florentine works.

EXCURSIONS

See the plan of the conurbation in the current Michelin Red Guide Italia.

★★ **Ville Medicee** – In the 15C and 16C, the Medici built several elegant villas throughout the Florentine countryside.

★ **Villa della Petraia** ⊘ – *3km – 2 miles north.* In 1576 Cardinal Ferdinand de' Medici commissioned the architect Buontalenti to convert this former castle into a villa. In the 16C **garden**, there is a remarkable fountain by N. Tribolo with a bronze statue of Venus by Giovanni Bologna.

★ **Villa di Castello** ⊘ – *5km – 3 miles north in Castello.* This villa was embellished by Lorenzo the Magnificent and restored in the 18C. It has a very fine garden adorned with statues and fountains.

★★ **Villa di Poggio a Caiano** ⊘ – *17km – 11 miles north by the Pistoia road, the S 66.* Sangallo designed this villa for Lorenzo the Magnificent. The loggia is decorated by the Della Robbia. The magnificent drawing-room has a coffered ceiling and **frescoes** by Pontormo representing Vertumnus and Pomona, gods of orchards and fruit.

S. Chirol

Ponte Vecchio

★ **Villa "La Ferdinanda"** – *26km – 16 miles west in Artimino.* This villa was commissioned from Buontalenti by Grand Duke Ferdinand I at the end of the 16C. Its many chimneys, its double spiral stairway and its magnificent setting overlooking the Arno valley give it a striking appearance. It is not open to the public, but there is a **museum of Etruscan archeology** ⊙ in the basement, which contains evidence of Etruscan settlement in this area.

★★ **Certosa del Galluzzo** ⊙ – *6km – 4 miles south by the Siena road.* The grandiose Carthusian monastery was founded in the 14C and underwent successive alterations until the 17C. The adjoining palace contains frescoes by Pontormo. The monks' cells are grouped around the Renaissance **cloisters**.

The great centres of Renaissance art: Florence, Rome, Siena, Padua, Venice, Milan, Parma, Perugia.

FORLÌ

Emilia-Romagna – Population 110 334
Michelin map 988 fold 15, 429, 430 J 18

Forlì is set on the Via Emilia and it was an independent commune ruled by an overlord in the 13C and 14C. The citadel was heroically defended in 1500 by Caterina Sforza against Cesare Borgia.

Basilica di San Mercuriale – *Piazza Aurelio Saffi.* The basilica is dominated by an imposing Romanesque campanile. The lunette of the doorway is adorned with a 13C **low relief**. The numerous works of art inside include several paintings by Marco Palmezzano and the tomb of Barbara Manfredi by Francesco di Simone Ferrucci.

Pinacoteca ⊙ – *72 Corso della Repubblica.* The art gallery includes works by local 13C-15C artists. There is a delicate *Portrait of a Young Girl* by Lorenzo di Credi.

EXCURSIONS

Cesena – *19km – 12 miles southeast by the Via Emilia.* The town lies at the foot of a hill on which stands the great 15C castle of the Malatestas. It contains the Renaissance library, **Biblioteca Malatestiana**★ ⊙ *(Piazza Bufalini).* The interior of the library comprises three long aisles with vaulting supported on fluted columns capped with fine capitals. On display are valuable manuscripts, including some from the famous school of miniaturists at Ferrara, as well as the Missorium, a great silver-gilt plate probably dating from the 4C.

Bertinoro – *14km – 9 miles southeast.* This small town is famous for its panorama and its yellow wine (Albana). In the middle of the town is a "hospitality column" fitted with rings, each corresponding with a local home. The ring to which the traveller tethered his horse would determine which family should be his hosts. From the nearby terrace there is a wide **view**★ of Romagna.

Abbazia di FOSSANOVA★★

FOSSANOVA Abbey – Lazio
Michelin map 988 fold 26 or 430 R 21

Standing, as the rule prescribes, in a lonely site, the Cistercian Abbey of Fossanova ⊙ is the oldest of the Order in Italy. Monks from Cîteaux in France settled here in 1133. In 1163 they began to build their abbey church, which was to serve as a model for many Italian churches (Casamari for instance). Although rather heavily restored, Fossanova has kept its original architecture and plan intact. It was designed in accordance with the rules of austerity laid down by St Bernard. The buildings are laid out to suit the activities of the monks and lay-brothers.

Church – The church (consecrated in 1208) is in the Burgundian style but such decoration as there is recalls the Lombard tradition with traces of the Moorish style. As regards the exterior, the Latin cross plan with flat east end, the octagonal transept crossing tower, the rose windows and the triple-bayed window of the east end are typically Cistercian. The well-lit and lofty interior has a central nave balanced by aisles with groined vaulting.

Cloisters – These are picturesque with three Romanesque sides and the fourth or south side in the late-13C pre-Gothic style (transitional Romanesque Gothic style). The small columns are Lombard in form and decoration. The fine Gothic chapterhouse opens into the cloisters through wide twin bays. It was in the guest house, which stands apart, that the teacher and scholar St Thomas Aquinas died on 7 March 1274.

GAETA★

Lazio – Population 22 331
Michelin map 988 fold 27 or 430 S 22

This former fortress, still partly walled, is admirably sited on the point of a promontory bounding a beautiful **bay★**. The coastal road round the bay affords magnificent views. Gaeta has a pleasant beach of fine sand, Serapo Beach, facing south.

Duomo – The cathedral is interesting, especially for its 10C and 15C Romanesque Moorish campanile adorned with glazed earthenware and resembling the Sicilian or Amalfi bell-towers. Inside, the late-13C **paschal candelabrum★** is remarkable for its size and for its 48 low reliefs depicting scenes from the Lives of Christ and St Erasmus, the patron saint of sailors.
A picturesque medieval quarter lies near the cathedral.

Castello – The castle, dating from the 8C, has been altered many times. The lower castle was built by the Angevins, while the upper one was the work of the Aragonese.

Monte Orlando ⊙ – Standing on the summit is the tomb of the Roman Consul Munatius Plancus (Mausoleo di Lucio Muniazio Planco), a friend of Caesar who founded the colonies of Lugdunum (Lyons) and Augusta Raurica (Augst near Basle).

EXCURSION

⌂ **Sperlonga** – *16km – 10 miles northwest.* The village stands on a rocky spur, pitted with many caves, up in the Aurunci mountains.

Grotta di Tiberio e Museo Archeologico ⊙. – The cave *(grotta)* lies below the Gaeta-Terracina road *(left after the last tunnel)*. It was in this cave that the Emperor Tiberius narrowly escaped death when part of the roof fell in.
In the **museum**, by the roadside, there are 4C-2C BC statues, outstanding heads and busts and some realistic theatrical masks. There is also a reconstruction of a colossal group depicting the punishment meted out to the Cyclops Polyphemus by Ulysses.
At the Gaeta end of the tunnel are the charred ruins of Tiberius' Villa.

Promontorio del GARGANO★★★

GARGANO Promontory – Puglia
Michelin map 988 fold 28 or 431 folds 2, 6

The Gargano Promontory, shining white under a blue sky, projects like a spur from the "boot" of Italy. It is one of the most attractive natural regions of Italy with its wide horizons, its deep and mysterious forests and its lonely, rugged coastline. This paradise for amateurs of sun and sea is marred by one drawback: most of the beaches and bays are private as they belong to camping sites and hotels and are not easily accessible.
Geologically, Gargano is quite independent from the Apennine Mountains; it is a limestone plateau fissured with crevices into which water runs. Originally an island, Gargarno was connected to the mainland by an accumulation of deposits brought down by the rivers from the Apennines. Today the massif is riven by high-altitude valleys, with fertile valley floors, and is heavily afforested in the east. The scanty pastures and moors on the plateaux support flocks of sheep and goats and herds of black pigs.
The picturesque islands, the **Isole Tremiti** *(see Isole TREMITI)* belong to the same geological formation *(access: see the current Michelin Red Guide Italia).*

131

TOUR

Leave from Monte Sant'Angelo and follow the itinerary indicated on the local map (146km – 91 miles – allow 1 day).

★ **Monte Sant'Angelo** – *See MONTE SANT'ANGELO.*

★★ **Foresta Umbra** – Forests are rare in Apulia and this vast expanse of venerable beeches, elders, pines, oaks, chestnuts, linden trees as well as ancient yews, covers over 11 000ha – 24 958 acres of undulating countryside. Visitors are welcome and the forest is well equipped with recreational facilities. Shortly after the turning to Vieste there is a forestry lodge (Casa Forestale) which now serves as the **visitor centre.**

⌂⌂ **Peschici** – Well-situated on a rocky spur jutting out into the sea, this fishing town is now a seaside resort.

⌂⌂ **Vieste** – In a similar setting to Peschici, this small but ancient town, crowded on the clifftop, is dominated by its 13C cathedral. In the town centre there is an interesting Shell Museum **(Museo Malacologico)** ⊙ displaying a large collection of shell from all over the world.
To the south is a vast sandy beach with a limestone sea-stack, **Faraglione di Pizzomunno**, standing offshore.
Between Vieste and Mattinata there is a very fine **scenic stretch★★** of corniche road, overlooking the indented coastline. After 8km – 5 miles the square tower in **Testa del Gargano** marks the easternmost extremity of the massif: fine **view★** of the inlet, **Cala di San Felice**, which is spanned by a natural arch at the seaward end.
Beyond the popular holiday resort of **Pugnochiuso**⌂⌂, there is another beauty spot, the Bay of Zagare **(Baia delle Zagare★)**.

⌂⌂ **Mattinata** – From the road running down towards Mattinata there is a fine **view★★** of this agricultural market town, a white mass amid a sea of olive groves encircled by a rim of mountains.

GENOVA★★

GENOA – Liguria – Population 676 069
Michelin map 988 fold 13 or 428 I 8
Local maps see La RIVIERA – Town plan overleaf
Plan of the built-up area in the current Michelin Red Guide Italia

Genoa the superb, the greatest seaport in Italy, spreads over a mountain amphitheatre. It is a city of surprises and contrasts, where the most splendid palaces stand side by side with the humblest alleyways, known as *carruggi*.

HISTORICAL NOTES

Genoese expansion was based on a strong fleet, which already in the 11C ruled supreme over the Tyrrhenian Sea, having vanquished the Saracens. By 1104 the fleet already comprised 70 ships, all built in the famous dockyards, making it a formidable power much coveted by foreign rulers such as the French Kings, Philip the Fair and Philip of Valois.
The Crusaders offered the Genoese an opportunity of establishing trading posts on the shores of the Eastern Mediterranean. Following the creation of the Republic of St George in 1100, seamen, merchants, bankers and money lenders united their efforts to establish the maritime supremacy of Genoa.
Initially Genoa allied itself with Pisa in the struggle against the Saracens (11C) and then became her enemy in a conflict concerning Corsica (13C). Finally it became the most persistent rival of that other great maritime republic, Venice (14C), disputing with her the trading rights for the Mediterranean. Genoa had colonies as far afield as the Black Sea.
In the 14C the Genoese merchant seamen controlled the trade in precious cargoes from the Orient; in particular they had the monopoly in the trading of alum used in the dyeing trade to fix colours.
Limited partnership companies flourished. Founded in 1408 the famous Bank of St George, grouping the maritime state's lending houses, administered the finances of the trading posts. The merchants became ingenious money lenders and instituted such modern methods as bills of credit, cheques and insurance to increase their profits.
Following continual struggles between the rival families of Genoa the decision was taken in 1339 to elect a doge for life and to seek, essentially in the 15C, foreign protection.

In 1528 the great admiral **Andrea Doria** (1466-1560) gave Genoa its aristocratic constitution which gave it the status of a mercantile republic. The enterprising and independent Andrea was one of Genoa's most famous sons: he was an admiral, a legislator and an intrepid and wise leader who distinguished himself against the Turks in 1519 and, while serving François I, by covering the French retreat after their defeat at Pavia (1525). In 1528, indignant at François I's unjust treatment of him, he entered the service of Charles V, who plied him with honours and favours. Following his death and the development of ports on the Atlantic coast, Genoa declined as a port and it was Louis XIV who destroyed the harbour in 1684. In 1768 by the Treaty of Versailles Genoa surrendered Corsica to France. Later, under the leadership of Giuseppe Mazzini, it became in 1848 one of the cradles of the Risorgimento *(see Index)*.

Andrea Doria by Sebastiano del Piombo

Fine Arts in Genoa – As in many countries, the decline of commercial prosperity in the 16C and 17C coincided with intense artistic activity, evidenced in the building of innumerable palaces and the arrival at Genoa of foreign artists, especially the Flemish. In 1607 Rubens published a work on the *Palazzi di Genova (Palaces of Genoa)* and from 1621 to 1627 Van Dyck painted the Genoese nobility. Puget lived at Genoa from 1661 to 1667, working for patrician families such as the Dorias and the Spinolas.

The art of the Genoese school, characterised by dramatic intensity and the use of muted colours, is represented by Luca Cambiaso (16C), Bernardo Strozzi (1581-1644), the fine engraver Castiglione, and especially Alessandro Magnasco (1667-1749) whose sharp and colourful brushwork marks him out as a precursor of modern art.

In the field of architecture, Galeazzo Alessi (1512-72), when at his best, was the equal of Sansovino and Palladio in the nobility and ingenuity of his designs when integrating isolated buildings in the existing urban landscape.

★★ OLD TOWN *allow 1 day*

A picturesque maze of narrow streets extends east of the old port to Via Garibaldi and Piazza De Ferrari.

★★ **Port** (EXY) – From the raised road (*Strada Sopraelevata* – EXYZ) which skirts the port, there are good views of Italy's principal port. To the east the old port (Porto Vecchio) includes a pleasure boat harbour, shipyards, and quays for ferries leaving for the islands or Africa. To the west the modern port (Porto Nuovo) is fringed by an industrial zone with steel and chemical plants as well as oil refineries. This busy port handles imported raw materials (oil and petrol, coal, minerals, cereals, metal and wood) and exports manufactured goods such as machines, vehicles and textiles. There are organised **boat trips** ⊙ to visit the port.

★ **Sailors' Quarter** (FY) – At the centre of this district is the 13C Palazzo San Giorgio which was the headquarters of the famous Bank of St George. The building was remodelled in the 16C.
Behind the palace on Piazza Banchi (of the banks) is the Loggia dei Mercanti which is now a fruit and vegetable market.

★ **Piazza San Matteo** (FY) – In the city centre, this small but harmonious square is lined with 13C-15C palaces that belonged to the Doria family. No 17 is a Renaissance building presented to Andrea Doria by a grateful republic.
The **Chiesa di San Mateo** has a Genoese-style façade with alternating courses of black and white stone. The tomb and sword of Andrea Doria are in the crypt.

★ **Cattedrale di San Lorenzo**(FY) – The cathedral, built from the 12C to the 16C, has a splendid Gothic **façade**★★ typical of the Genoese style. French influence appears in the placing of the 13C doorways and the large rose window.

GENOVA

0   200 m

NERVI   LA SPEZIA   S. Maria di Carignano

H   Palazzo Municipale
M   Museo Chiossone

The carving on the central doorway represents a Tree of Jesse and scenes from the Life of Christ *(on the piers)* and the Martyrdom of St Lawrence and Christ between the Symbols of the Evangelists *(on the tympanum)*. The early-13C knifegrinder, at the right corner of the façade, resembles the angel of the sundial at Chartres and performs the same function. The transept crossing is crowned with a dome designed by Alessi. The severe and majestic **interior**★ has marble columns in the nave. The **Chapel of St John the Baptist**★ allegedly contains the bones of St John.

The **treasury**★ ⊙ includes the famous **Sacro Catino** which, according to legend, is said to be the Holy Grail.

★ **Via Garibaldi** (FY) – This street of palaces, once known as Via Aurea, was built to designs by Alessi in the 16C. It is one of the loveliest streets in Italy.
At No 1 is Alessi's **Palazzo Cambiaso** (1565); No 3 is the **Palazzo Parodi** (1578); No 4 the **Palazzo Carrega-Cataldi** ⊙ (1588), also by Alessi, has a delightful entrance hall and a dazzling gilded **gallery**★. Both No 6, **Palazzo Doria**, and No 7, **Palazzo Podestà** (1565-67), are by the same architect, G B Castello. The **Palazzo Municipale** (Town Hall) (**H**) ⊙, the former Palazzo Doria Tursi, at No 9, has a lovely arcaded courtyard. The collections include the violin of Paganini and manuscripts by Christopher Columbus. No 11, **Palazzo Bianco** ⊙, contains a very

fine **art gallery**★ (Flemish and Dutch paintings by Provost, Van der Goes, Gerard David, Van Dyck, Rubens, also French and Spanish works as well as canvases by the Genoese, Strozzi).

The **Palazzo Rosso** ⊘ at No 18 also houses a **picture gallery**★ with works by the Venetian (Titian, Veronese and Tintoretto) and Genoese schools, a canvas by Dürer and some remarkable **portraits**★ by Van Dyck. In addition there are sections on baroque sculpture, Ligurian ceramics and medals.

Via Balbi (EX) – This street is joined to Via Garibaldi by Via Cairoli and is lined with palaces. The Royal Palace **(Palazzo Reale)** ⊘, formerly the Balbi Durazzo, at No 10, dates from 1650 and contains a Van Dyck room. The imposing 17C University Palace **(Palazzo dell'Università**★**)** at No 5 has a court and a majestic staircase. The 17C Palazzo Durazzo Pallavicini is at No 1.

★ **Galleria Nazionale di Palazzo Spinola** (FY) ⊘ – The beautifully decorated rooms of this 16C-18C mansion with their period furnishings make an ideal setting for the works of art. The fine frescoes (17C-18C) on the **ceilings**★ are by Tavarone, L Ferrari and S Galeotti.

The **art collection**★ comprises works by painters of the Italian and Flemish Renaissance: an *Ecce Homo* by Antonello da Messina, a *Madonna* and especially a sumptuous polyptych of the *Adoration of the Magi*★★ by Joos Van Cleve, and finally a *Crucifixion* by Brueghel the Younger. From the 17C there are canvases by Strozzi, Castiglione Genovese and a ravishing *Portrait of a Child* by Van Dyck.

★ **Acquario** (EY) ⊘ – The aquarium has a modern, instructive layout. Illuminated panels describe (in Italian and English) the species and explain the varied habitats recreated in the tanks.

The visit begins with a film that provides an introduction to the underwater world. Then, a computerised system offers an opportunity for a "hands-on" experience and various observation points give visitors the impression that they are in amidst the fish and marine mammals. There are also reconstructions of the underwater environments of the Mediterranean and the Red Sea, a tropical forest and a coral reef. Of particular interest are the seals, reptiles, dolphins, sharks, penguins and muraena.

ADDITIONAL SIGHTS

Piazza De Ferrari (FY) – This square is bordered by the remains of the Opera House, partly destroyed in 1944, and numerous palaces including the mansion, Palazzo Ducale (1778) with its monumental façade overlooking Piazza Matteotti. **Chiesa del Gesù** was built by Tibaldi in 1597. The splendid interior of the church is the setting for an *Assumption* by Guido Reni and a *Circumcision* and a *St Ignatius Healing* by Rubens.

San Donato (FZ) – This 12C-13C church has an attractive octagonal **campanile**★ in the Romanesque style. The Romanesque interior is also quite charming. A 14C Virgin and Child stands to the right of the chancel in the chapel.

Santissima Annunziata (EFX) – This 17C church is one of the most splendid in Genoa. The sumptuous decoration inside is a happy mixture of gilding, stucco and frescoes and is a good example of the Genoese baroque style.

Santa Maria di Carignano – *Take Via Ravasco* (FZ **39**). This vast church was built in the 16C to plans by Alessi. Inside, there is a fine statue of **St Sebastian**★ by Puget.

Villetta Di Negro (GXY) – On higher ground to the northwest of Piazza Corvetto, this is a sort of belvedere-labyrinth with palm trees, cascades and artificial grottoes.

From the terrace there a lovely **view**★ over the town and the sea. Standing on the summit is the **Museo Chiossone**★ ⊘ (**M**), a museum including sections on Chinese art and Japanese arms and armour, a remarkable collection of prints, ivories and lacquerwork.

Castelletto (FX) – From the terrace *(reached by lift)* there is a fine **view**★ of the town.

★ **Cimitero di Staglieno** – *1.5km – 1 mile north. Leave from Piazza Corvetto* (GY), *see the town plan in the current Michelin Red Guide Italia.* In this curious cemetery there are ornate tombs and simple clay tumuli.

The palaces of the former maritime republics of Genoa and Venice reflect their past glory and opulence.

GRADO ≙≙

Friuli-Venezia Giulia – Population 9 105
Michelin map 988 fold 6 or 429 E 22

At the time of the Barbarian invasions the inhabitants of Aquileia founded Grado which was from the 5C to the 9C the residence of the Patriarchs of Aquileia. Today Grado is a busy little fishing port and seaside resort with a growing reputation. The town situated in the middle of the lagoon is an imposing sight.

★ **Old Quarter** - This is a picturesque district with a network of narrow alleys *(calli)* running between the canal-port and the cathedral. The cathedral, Duomo di Santa Eufemia, is on the basilical plan and dates from the 6C. It has marble columns with Byzantine capitals, a 6C mosaic pavement, a 10C ambo and a valuable silver-gilt **altarpiece★**, a Venetian work of the 14C. Beside the cathedral stands the 6C Basilica of St Mary of Grace (Santa Maria delle Grazie) which has some original mosaics and fine capitals.

GROSSETO

Tuscany – Population 71 329
Michelin map 988 folds 24 and 25 or 430 N 15

This modern-looking provincial capital is situated in the fertile Ombrone Plain. The old town is encircled with late-16C ramparts and their powerful bastions built by the Medici.

★ **Museo Archeologico della Maremma** - Piazza Baccarini. The archeological museum presents a collection of Bronze Age jewellery and pottery, a fine set of Etruscan and Roman sculptures (carved funeral urns, steles, sarcophagi), amphorae, busts of emperors, marble statues dating from the Roman Era and small bronzes. Also on display are outstanding **Greek and Etruscan vases** dating from the 6C to 2C BC.

San Francesco - *Piazza dell'Indipendenza.* This 13C abbey church contains small frescoes by the 14C Sienese school and a lovely painted 13C crucifix.

EXCURSION

Ruins of Roselle ⊘ - *12km - 8 miles northeast. Leave Grosseto by the Siena road and after 10km - 6 miles turn right into an unsurfaced road.* Important excavation work has uncovered the Etruscan city of Roselle which was conquered by Rome in the 3C.

GUBBIO ★★

Umbria – Population 30 758
Michelin map 988 fold 16 or 430 L 19

The small town of Gubbio, spread out over the steep slopes of Monte Ingino, has preserved almost intact its rich cultural and artistic heritage. Encircling ramparts, buildings of warm yellow stone roofed with Roman tiles, and distinctive towers and palaces outlined against a burnt and austere landscape make it one of the Italian towns in which the harsh atmosphere of the Middle Ages is most easily imagined. In the 11C and 12C the free commune of Gubbio, a strong supporter of the Ghibelline cause *(see Index)*, enjoyed a period of expansion before being governed by the Montefeltro family in the 15C and then by the Della Roveres. The town came under papal rule from 1624.

Since medieval times the artisans of Gubbio have specialised in ceramics. In the early 16C Mastro Giorgio produced the famous iridescent red lustre – the secret of which was never discovered by nearby towns.

The town is also famous for the wolf which ravaged the country at a time (early 13C) when St Francis lived in Gubbio. The saint set off and reproached the wolf for its misdeeds, whereupon the repentant wild animal laid its paw in St Francis' hand and swore that it would do no more harm. The people then adopted and fed their friend, the wolf, to the end of its life.

Gubbio has its traditional festivals; the most spectacular is the **Candle Race**. Three "candles", or *"ceri"*, strange wooden poles 4m - 13ft tall, each topped with the statue of a saint (including St Ubald, patron saint of the town), are carried through the crowded streets in a frenzied race covering a distance of 5km - 3 miles, from the historical town centre to the basilica of Sant'Ubaldo situated at an altitude of 820m - 2.665ft. During the race the "candle"-carriers, dressed in ancient costumes, demonstrate their skill by attempting not to drop their "candles" and carrying St Ubald into the church first, before the doors are slammed shut after the other two statues have arrived. These three strange *"ceri"*, whose origins date back to the pre-Christian era, grace Umbria's coat-of-arms *(see also the Calendar of Events at the end of the guide)*.

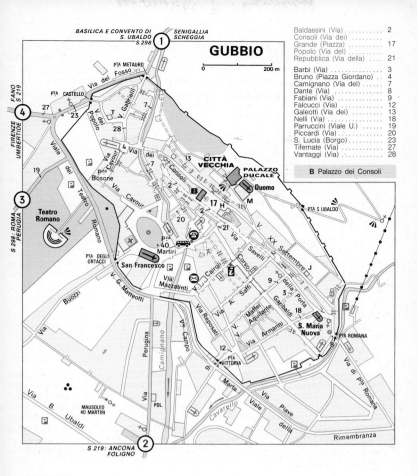

SIGHTS

★★ **Città vecchia** – Piazza Grande stands at the heart of this charming but austere area of the old town with its steep, narrow streets, sometimes stepped, spanned by arches converted into living quarters. The houses, flanked by palaces and towers of nobility, are often used as ceramic artists' workshops. The façade, often built of a mixture of brick, rubblework and dressed stone, sometimes has two doors; one narrower than the main door is known as the Door of Death through which coffins were brought out.

The most picturesque streets are Via Piccardi, Baldassini, dei Consoli, 20 Settembre, Galeotti and the embankments along the River Camignano leading to Piazza 40 Martiri.

★★ **Palazzo dei Consoli** (**B**) ⊘ – Overlooking Piazza Grande, this imposing Gothic building, supported by great arches rising above Via Baldassini, has a majestic façade which reflects the palace's internal plan. The stairway leads up to the vast hall *(Salone)* where popular assemblies were held and which contains collections of statues and stonework.

Next is a museum, Museo Civico, where the **Tavole eugubine** have pride of place. The bronze tablets (2C-1C BC) are inscribed in the ancient language of Umbria. This document is unique in the fields of linguistics and epigraphy. The tablets record the political organisation and religious practices of the region in Antiquity.

★ **Palazzo Ducale** ⊘ – The Ducal Palace, which dominates the town, was built from 1470 onwards for Frederico de Montefeltre. The design is attributed to Laurana, although it was probably finished by Francesco di Giorgio Martini, who was inspired by the ducal palace at Urbino. The elegant courtyard is delicately decorated. The rooms are adorned with frescoes and lovely chimmeypieces; the Salone is particularly interesting.

Teatro romano – This fairly well-preserved Roman theatre dates from the reign of Augustus.

San Francesco – The inside walls of the north apse are covered with remarkable early-15C **frescoes★** by the local painter, Ottaviano Nelli. The church is dedicated to St Francis.

137

Duomo – The plain façade of the cathedral is adorned with low reliefs showing the Symbols of the Evangelists. The interior consists of a single nave. The **Episcopal Chapel** ⊘ opens to the right. It is a luxurious sitting-room decorated in the 17C, from which the bishop could follow the services.

Chiesa di Santa Maria Nuova – The church contains a charming **fresco★** by Ottaviano Nelli.

EXCURSIONS

Fabriano – *36km – 22 miles east by* ②. The industrial town of Fabriano has manufactured paper since the 13C. This was the birthplace of two delightful artists, **Allegretto Nuzi** (c1320-73) and **Gentile da Fabriano** (c1370-1427), who were both exponents of the International Gothic style *(see Index)*. **Piazza del Comune★** in the centre of Fabriano, with its elegant Gothic fountain, is overlooked by the grim 13C Governor's Residence (Palazzo del Podestà). A stairway leads to the quiet and charming **Piazza del Duomo★** bordered by the 15C hospital and the cathedral (Duomo) decorated with frescoes by Allegretto Nuzi.

★★ **Grotte di Frasassi** – *50km – 31 miles northeast by* ①. A tributary of the River Sentino has formed a vast network of underground caves (*grotte*). The largest, the **Grotta del Vento★★**, is composed of seven chambers where the visitor may admire stalagmites, stalactites and other diverse forms in a variety of colours.

Isola d'ISCHIA★★★

ISCHIA – Campania – Population 45 757

Michelin map 988 fold 27 or 431 E 23 – Local map see Golfo di NAPOLI
Access: see the current Michelin Red Guide Italia

Ischia, known as the Emerald Island because of its luxuriant vegetation, is the largest island in the Bay of Naples and one of its major attractions. A clear, sparkling light plays over a varied landscape: a coast covered with pinewoods, indented with bays and creeks sheltering villages with their colourful cubic houses; the slopes covered with olive trees and vineyards (producing the white or red Epomeo wine); and an occasional village with its quaint white houses. The cottages, sometimes roofed with a dome and with an outside staircase, often have walls covered with vines.
The island rose out of the sea during the Tertiary era at the time of a volcanic eruption, and has many hot springs with various medicinal properties. The soil is volcanic in origin.

TOUR

The map below locates the towns and sights described in the guide, and also indicates other beauty spots in small black type.
A tour of the island, which is fairly small, can be done in a matter of hours *(40km – 25 miles: follow the itinerary on the map)*. The narrow road, as it winds between rows of vines, offers numerous fine viewpoints of the coast and the sea.

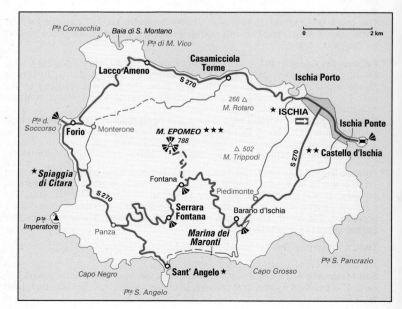

★ **Ischia** – *Town plan in the current Michelin Red Guide Italia.* The capital is divided into two settlements, **Ischia Porto** and **Ischia Ponte.** The Corso Vittoria Colona, an avenue lined with cafés and smart shops, links the port, in a former crater, and Ischia Ponte. The latter owes its name to the dyke built by the Aragonese to link the coast with the rocky islet on the summit of which stands the **Castello d'Ischia**★★. This is a group of buildings comprising a castle and several churches. On the outskirts are a large pinewood and a fine sandy beach.

★★ **Monte Epomeo** – *Access is by a path which branches off in a bend of the road once level with the public gardens. 1 1/2 hours on foot Rtn or by donkey.* From the summit of this tufa peak there is a vast **panorama** of the entire island and the Bay of Naples.

Serrara Fontana – Not far from this settlement a belvedere offers a plunging **view**★★ of the site of Sant'Angelo with its beach and peninsula.

★ **Sant'Angelo** – The houses of this peaceful fishing village cluster round the small harbour. Nearby is the vast Maronti Beach **(Marina dei Maronti)** which has been transformed by the opening of many thermal establishments *(access by a footpath).*

★ **Spiaggia di Citara** – This fine beach is sheltered by the majestic headland, Punta Imperatore. Another thermal establishment, Giardini di Poseidone, is laid out with numerous warm-water swimming pools amidst flowers and statues.

Forio – The town centre is Piazza Municipio, a tropical garden overlooked by old buildings.

Lacco Ameno – *Town plan in the current Michelin Red Guide Italia.* This was the first Greek colony on the island and was called Pithecusa (meaning lots of monkeys). It is now a holiday resort. The Church of Santa Restituta *(Piazza Santa Restituta)* was built on the remains of an early-Christian basilica and a necropolis. There is a small archeological museum. The tour of the island ends with the important thermal spa of **Casamicciola Terme.**

★ **Isola di PROCIDA**

Access: see the current Michelin Red Guide Italia.

Procida is formed by craters levelled by erosion and has remained the wildest island in the Bay of Naples. The fishermen, gardeners and winegrowers live in delightful and colourful houses with domes, arcades and terraces.

Regione dei LAGHI★★★

LAKE DISTRICT

Michelin map 988 folds 2, 3 and 4, 219 folds 6 to 10, 428 folds 4 to 6 and 14 to 18 or 429 folds 11 to 13 – Local maps below

The Lake District extends from Piedmont to Veneto and from Switzerland to Trentino in the north. Narrow and long, these lakes are all of glacial origin and their banks are covered with a varied and luxuriant vegetation which flourishes in the particularly mild climate.

This fairyland of blue waters at the foot of shapely mountains has always been a favourite haunt of artists and travellers. The charm and originality of these Pre-Alpine lakes are due to the juxtaposition of Alpine and southern scenery, the numerous villas with attractive gardens on the lakesides, the great variety of flowers throughout the year, the small sailing villages with their flotilla of boats where fresh fish is the speciality. Each lake has its own specific character, making it quite different from its neighbour.

Sightseeing ⊙ – The maps below locate the towns and sites described in the guide, and also indicate other beauty spots, in smaller black type. *For places in Switzerland see the Michelin Green Guide Switzerland (in French and English).*

★★ **LAGO MAGGIORE**

Lake Maggiore is the most famous of the Italian lakes, in part for its legendary beauty at times both majestic and wild, and also for the Borromean Islands. It is fed by the Ticino River, which rises in Switzerland, and its waters change from a jade green in the north to a deep blue in the south. The mountains of the Alps and Pre-Alps shelter the lake which enjoys a constantly mild climate in which a luxuriant and exotic vegetation flourishes.

Take one of the **boat trips** ⊙ on the lake, as the views from the lakeside road with its heavy traffic are often screened.

Isola dei Pescatori, Lago Maggiore

★ **Angera** - This wonderful holiday resort stands in the shadow of the **Rocca Borromeo** ⊙. There is a vast panoramic view from a tower, the **Torre Castellana**. Known since the days of the Lombards (8C), the Rocca still has Law Courts decorated with admirable 14C **frescoes**★★ depicting the life of Archbishop Ottone Visconti. The fortress also houses the Doll Museum **(Museo della bambola★)** ⊙ with an extensive collection of exhibits showing the development of the doll (*bambola*) since the early 19C. The dolls are made from various materials such as papier maché, wax, porcelain, felt, celluloid, metal, fabric and plastic. There are French, German, English and Italian dolls with very animated expressions. The museum also presents dolls' furniture and miniature accessories including dinner services and kitchen utensils along with models of places where they might be used, eg, in school or a shop.

Arona - The chief town on Lago Maggiore is overlooked by the gigantic statue, **Colosso di San Carlone★** ⊙, of St Charles Borromeo, the Cardinal Archbishop of Milan who distinguished himself by the authority he showed in re-establishing discipline and morals in the Church and by his heroic conduct during the plague of 1576. The statue is 24m high with a 12m – 39ft base.
At the summit of the old town the Church of St Mary **(Santa Maria)** contains a lovely **polyptych★** (1511) by Gaudenzio Ferrari.
From the ruined castle **(Rocca)** there is a **view★** of Lake Maggiore, Angera and its mountain setting.

★ **Baveno** - This quiet holiday resort, once visited by Queen Victoria, has a Romanesque church and an octagonal Renaissance baptistery.

★★★ **Isole Borromee** ⊙ - *Town plan in the Michelin Red Guide Italia, under Stresa.*
A large area of the lake was given to the princely Borromeo family in the 15C but only gradually did they purchase all the islands in the tiny archipelago. In the 17C, Charles III established a residence on **Isola Bella★★★**, named after his wife, Isabella. The palace, built in the Lombard Baroque style, has several state rooms – medals room, state hall, music room, Napoleon's room, ballroom and Hall of Mirrors.
The most unusual feature is the caves where those living in the palace could find cooler air on very hot days. The decoration of light and dark coloured stones and shells is designed to represent an underwater world. The gardens, filled with a variety of exotic plants, form an amazing baroque composition, a truncated pyramid of ten terraces ornamented with statues, basins, fountains and architectural perspectives simulating stage sets. At the top of the garden is the shell-shaped "amphitheatre" providing an extraordinary scenic effect.
Boat trips are available to the **Isola dei Pescatori★★★** with has retained its original charm and the **Isola Madre★★★**, an island totally covered with a splendid garden of flowers and rare or exotic plants. In the palazzo, note the Puppet Theatre that once belonged to the House of Borromeo.

★★ **Cannero Riviera** - The houses of this resort rise in tiers above the lake amid olive trees, vineyards, orange and lemon groves.

★ **Cannobio** – Cannobio is a small resort near the Swiss border. In addition to the Renaissance Church of the Madonna della Pietà there are several other fine old houses. 3km – 2 miles out of town *(on the Malesco road)* is the **Orrido di Sant'Anna★**, a precipice formed by the torrent.

★ **Cerro** – This peaceful village on a well-shaded part of the lakeside has a tiny fishing port and an interesting **ceramics museum** ⊙.

Laveno Mombello ⊙ – From here a cable-car climbs up to the summit of **Sasso del Ferro★★** from where there is a vast **panorama** over the entire Lake District.

★★ **Pallanza** – Everywhere flowers deck and scent this wonderful resort. Its **quays★★**, sheltered by magnolias and oleanders, offer lovely views of the lake. On the outskirts of the town on the Intra road is the **Villa Taranto★★** with its famous **gardens** ⊙ featuring azaleas, heathers, rhododendrons, camelias, dahlias, maples etc.

Santa Caterina del Sasso – *About 500m – 547yds from Leggiuno.* This hermitage was founded in the 13C by an anchorite, Alberto Besozzo. In a picturesque setting, the building clings to a rock overlooking the lake.

★★ **Stresa** – *Town plan in the current Michelin Red Guide France.* This pleasant resort, which attracts many artists and writers, enjoys a magnificent situation on the west bank of Lago Maggiore facing the Borromean Islands, and is a delightful place with all the amenities of both a holiday resort in spring, summer and autumn and a winter sports resort.
The ski slopes are on **Mottarone★★★** ⊙ *(take the Armeno road: 29km – 18 miles; the scenic toll-road from Alpino: 18km – 11 miles; or the cable-car)* which from its summit provides a magnificent **panorama** of the lake, the Alps and the Monte Rosa massif.
Standing on the outskirts of the town, off the Arona road, is the **Villa Pallavicino★** ⊙ with its wildlife park.
From Stresa, follow the Vezzo Gignese direction. At **Gignese** *(8km – 5 miles southwest)* there is a small, interesting museum **(Museo dell'ombrello e del parasole)** ⊙ which illustrates the history, from 1850 to the present day, of the umbrella and sunshade, an accessory largely linked to fashion, when suntans were not always in vogue, and the emancipation of women.

★★ LAGO D'ORTA

Lake Orta, one of the smallest Italian lakes, is separated from Lake Maggiore by the peak, Il Mottarone rising to the northeast. It is perhaps the most delightful and the most gracious of all the lakes with its setting of wooded hills and the tiny islet, Isola San Giulio.
The lakesides have been inhabited since earliest times and in the 4C the people were converted to Christianity by St Julius.

★★ **Madonna del Sasso** – *5km – 3 miles from Alzo.* From the church terrace there is a magnificent view of the lake in its verdant mountain setting.

★★ **Orta San Giulio** – This small resort has a delightful site on the tip of a peninsula. The alleyways are lined with old houses adorned with elegant wrought-iron balconies. The **Palazzotto★** or 16C town hall is decorated with frescoes.

★ **Sacro Monte d'Orta** – *1.5km – 1 mile from Orta.* This sanctuary dedicated to St Francis of Assisi and set on a hilltop comprises 20 chapels. These are decorated in the Baroque style and the frescoes serve as background to groups of lifelike terracotta statues.

★★ **Isola di San Giulio** ⊙ – *Boats leave from Orta.* On this jewel of an island, 300m – 328yds long and 160m – 175yds wide, stands the **Basilica di San Giulio** ⊙ which is said to date from the lifetime of St Julius.
Inside there is a lovely 12C **ambo★**, decorated with frescoes by the school of Gaudenzio Ferrari (16C). Note also, in the crypt, the shrine containing the relics of St Julius.

Varallo – *About 20km – 12 miles west.* This industrial and commercial town in the Val Sesia is famous for its pilgrimage to the **Sacro Monte★★** with its 43 chapels. Again these are decorated with frescoes and groups of life-size terracotta figures (16C-18C) which illustrate the Fall and scenes from the Life of Christ. They were the work of several artists including Gaudenzio Ferrari (1480-1546), a local painter who was a pupil of Leonardo da Vinci. Ferrari showed definite originality and picturesque realism in his work.

★★ LAGO DI LUGANO

Most of **Lake Lugano**, also known as Lake Ceresio by the Italians, is in Swiss territory. Lugano is wilder than Lakes Maggiore and Como and with its irregular outline has none of the grandeur or majesty of the others. Its mild climate and its steep mountain countryside make it an ideal place for a holiday.
There are **boat trips** ⊙ on the lake.

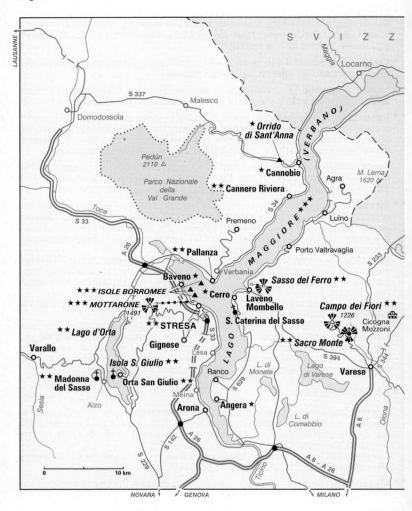

★ **Campione d'Italia** – An Italian enclave in Switzerland, Campione is a colourful, smiling village which is highly popular on account of its casino. A chapel, Oratorio di San Pietro, is a graceful building dating from 1326. It was the work of the famous **maestri campionesi** *(see Index),* who vied with the *maestri comacini* in spreading the Lombard style throughout Italy.

★ **Lanzo d'Intelvi** – Set in the heart of a pine and larch forest, this resort (alt 907m – 2 976ft) is also a ski centre in winter. 6km – 4 miles away is the **Belvedere di Sighignola★★★**, also known as the "balcony of Italy" because of its extensive view of Lugano, the Alps as far as Monte Rosa and on a clear day Mont Blanc.

Varese – *13km – 8 miles southwest of Porto Ceresio. Town plan in the current Michelin Red Guide Italia.* This busy but pleasant modern town stands not far from the lake of the same name. One of its advantages is a mild and sunny climate due to its proximity to the Italian lakes.
8km – 5 miles to the northwest rises the hilltop, **Sacro Monte★★**, with its important pilgrimage church dedicated to the Virgin. The road up to the basilica is lined with 14 chapels decorated with frescoes in *trompe-l'œil* and groups of life-size terracotta figures. From the summit there is a magnificent **view★★** of the lakes and surrounding mountains.
10km – 6 miles to the northwest is the long mountainous ridge, **Campo dei Fiori★★**, which raises its forest-clad slopes above the plain. There is a vast **panorama★★** of the Lake District.

Villa Cicogna Mozzoni, Bisuschio ⊘ – *8km – 5 miles northeast of Varese on the road to Porto Ceresio.* The villa, set in fine Italian terraced gardens, was originally a hunting lodge in the 15C which was extended in the 16C with the addition of a residence. In the first floor rooms complete with furnishings, the upper part of the walls and the ceilings are adorned with fine frescoes in the Renaissance style.

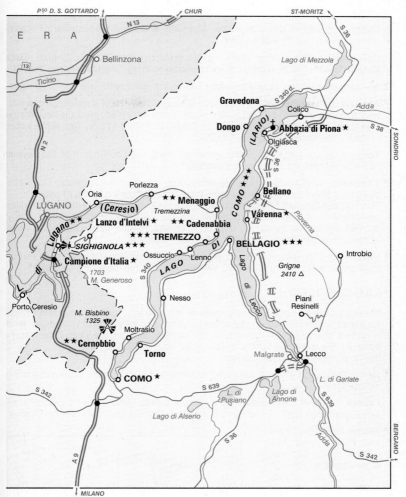

★★ LAGO DI COMO

Set entirely within Lombardy, **Lake Como**, of all the Italian lakes, has the most variety. Pretty villages, tiny ports, villas in shady exotic gardens succeed one another along the banks of this Pre-Alpine lake. Bellagio stands on a promontory at the confluence of its three arms. This lake may also be visited by **boat** ⊙.

★★ **Bellagio** – Bellagio occupies a magnificent site on a promontory dividing Lake Lecco from the southern arm of Lake Como. It has a worldwide reputation for the friendliness of its people and its excellent amenities. The splendid lakeside **gardens★★** of **Villa Serbelloni** ⊙ and **Villa Melzi** ⊙ with their fragrant and luxuriant vegetation are the main sights in Bellagio. It is pleasant to stroll up and down the pretty, steep little streets on the hillside.

Bellano – This small industrial town stands on the Pioverna River at the mouth of the valley (Valsassina), with the great mass of the Grigne towering behind. The attractive 14C **church** with a façade by Giovanni da Campione is in the Lombard Gothic style.

★★ **Cadenabbia** – This delightful resort occupies an admirable site opposite Bellagio. A splendid avenue of plane trees, Via del Paradiso, links the resort with the Villa Carlotta and Tremezzo.
From a chapel, **Capella di San Martino** *(1 1/2 hours Rtn on foot)* there is a good **view★★** of Bellagio on its promontory, Lakes Como and Lecco and of the Grigne.

★★ **Cernobbio** – This splendid location is famous for the **Villa d'Este**, the opulent 16C residence now transformed into a hotel and surrounded by fine parkland *(access to both the villa and the park is limited to hotel guests)*. The best view of the villa (from the ground) is from Piazza del Risorgimento, near the landing stage with the Liberty-style roof.

★ **Como** - *See COMO.*

Dongo - It was in this village that Mussolini and his mistress, Clara Petacci, were captured on 27 April 1945.

Gravedona - This fishing village has an attractive Romanesque Church, **Santa Maria del Tiglio★**. The 5C baptistery was remodelled in the Lombard style in the 12C.

★★ **Menaggio** - Favoured by a cool summer breeze, this is one of the lake's smart resorts.

★ **Abbazia di Piona** - *2km - 1 mile from Olgiasca.* This graceful monastery, which was founded in the 11C by Cluniac monks, and which adopted Cistercian rule a century later under St Bernard of Clairvaux (1090-1153), has remarkable Lombard Romanesque **cloisters★** (1252).

Torno - On the outskirts of this attractive port, the 14C Church of **San Giovanni** has a fine Lombard Renaissance **doorway★**.

★★★ **Tremezzo** - A mild climate and a beautiful site combine to make Tremezzo a favourite place for a stay. The terraced gardens, **Parco comunale★**, are a haven of peace. The 18C **Villa Carlotta★★★** ⊘ *(entrance beside the Grand Hotel Tremezzo)* occupies an admirable site facing the Grigne Massif. The numerous statues include a copy by Tadolini of the famous group of Love and Psyche by Canova. The main attraction is, however, the beautiful terraced **gardens**.

★ **Varenna** - This delightful town with its many gardens and cypresses stands on a small promontory. The 16C **Villa Monastero** ⊘ has beautiful **gardens★★**.

★ LAGO D'ISEO

Though **Lake Iseo** is not very well known, its wild scenery, its high mountain fringe, its banks sometimes steep and often indented and its peaceful villages, all lend a certain charm to this small lake. From the midst of the deep blue waters emerges the island of Monte Isola (alt 600m - 1 969ft).
There are **boat trips** ⊘ on the lake.

★ **Iseo** - The church, Pieve di Sant'Andrea, with its 13C campanile faces a charming square.

Lovere - In this small industrial town the **Galleria Tadini** ⊘ has a collection of arms, paintings (Bellini and Parmigianino), porcelain and sculpture by Canova.

★★ **Monte Isola** ⊘ - From the Chiesa della Madonna della Ceriola, crowning the summit of this green island, there is a vast **panorama★★** of the lake and the Alps near Bergamo.

★ **Pisogne** - This small port has an attractive lakeside setting. The church, **Santa Maria della Neve**, is adorned with 16C **frescoes★** by Romanino du Brescia.

★★★ LAGO DI GARDA

Lake Garda, the largest lake, is also considered one of the most beautiful. Its many assets include low-lying banks which are alluvial in the south, steep slopes on the west bank, and the mountain chain of Monte Baldo to the east. The Dolomites to the north shelter the lake from the cold north winds, creating a very mild climate which already earned it the name of "beneficent"

lake *(Il Benaco)* in ancient times. It had both strategic and commercial importance and throughout history has been coveted by neighbouring powers.

Artistically, both as regards painting and architecture, the region was greatly influenced by the Venetian Republic which ruled the region from the 15C to the 18C. Even in Roman times the banks of the lake were appreciated as a place to stay and today's travellers have a large number of resorts from which to choose. There are **boat trips** ⊙ on the lake.

Bardolino – This village famous for its red wine has an elegant Romanesque **church**★ dating from the 11C, which is dedicated to St Severinus.

Campione del Garda – The Bishops of Trento, Brescia and Verona met here to bless the lake.

Desenzano del Garda – The old port, the picturesque Piazza Malvezzi and the neighbouring old quarter are all good places to stroll through. The 16C parish church **(Parrocchiale Santa Maria Maddalena)** has a very intense *Last Supper*★ by Tiepolo. To the north of the town in Via Scavi Romani, the **Villa Romana** ⊙ boasts remarkable multicoloured **mosaics**★ dating from the Roman period.

★ **Garda** – This popular resort which gave its name to the lake shows a strong Venetian influence. Both the Palazzo dei Capitani and the Palazzo Fregoso are 15C.

★★ **Gardone Riviera** – This small resort enjoys many hours of sunshine and offers the tourist a wide choice of hotels. 1km - 1/2 mile from the town is the **Vittoriale**★ ⊙ estate which belonged to the poet **Gabriele D'Annunzio** (1863-1938) who is buried here. The neo-Classical villa, La Priora ⊙, is full of the solemn atmosphere which this writer-aesthete so cultivated. The museum and park display mementoes of his turbulent life.

Gargnano – This charming resort is surrounded by great expanses of glasshouses for the growing of lemon and citron trees.

The Church of **San Francesco** has lovely 15C cloisters with curious Moorish-style galleries featuring capitals carved with oranges and lemons, recalling the fact that it was probably the Franciscan monks who introduced citrus fruits to the area. The lakeside promenade leads to the neo-Classical **Villa Feltrinelli** *(not open)* which served as Mussolini's headquarters during the Fascist Republic (1943-45).

★ **Limone sul Garda** – This is one of the lake's most attractive villages. Terraced lemon groves often under glass stretch along the lake shores. From Limone a **panoramic route**★★ climbs up to the Tremosine plateau before descending to Tignale. It offers superb **views**★★★ of the lake and its mountainous setting.

★ **Malcesine** – This attractive town stands on a promontory at the foot of Monte Baldo and is dominated by the crenellated outline of the **Castello Scaligero**★. This 13C-14C castle belonged to the Scaligers of Verona.

The 15C Palazzo dei Capitani in the Venetian style stands on the edge of the lake. From the summit of **Monte Baldo** ⊙ (cable-car) there is a splendid **panorama**★★★ of the lake and to the north the Brenta and Adamello Massifs.

★★ **Punta di San Vigilio** – This headland is in a romantic setting. The 16C **Villa Guarienti** *(not open)* was built to the plans of Sanmicheli for the Veronese humanist, Agostino Brenzoni.

★ **Riva del Garda** – This small resort is dominated to the west by a rocky escarpment. Already in ancient times it was an important trading and communication centre set on the route between Verona and the Alps. Today the picturesque **old town**★ is a maze of narrow shopping streets.

The castle **(Rocca)** ⊙ houses a museum **(Museo civico)** with its archeological and historical collections.

★ **Salò** – This was the seat of the Venetian Captain under the Venetian Empire and from this period of splendour it has retained its 15C cathedral **(Duomo)**. Inside are a large gilt **polyptych**★ (1510) in wood and several works by Moretto da Brescia and Romanino.

San Martino della Battaglia ⊙ – An **ossuary-chapel**, a museum and a tall **tower** commemorate the battle of 24 June 1859 at Solferino *(see below)*, and the wars of the Risorgimento *(see Historical Table and Notes)* waged by the Italians to win their independence from Austria.

★★ **Sirmione** – This important resort has been well known since the beginning of the century as a spa. It is said to be particularly effective in the treatment of respiratory disorders. The houses cluster around the 13C castle, **Rocca Scaligera**★ ⊙, at the tip of the narrow Sirmione peninsula, as it stretches out into the lake. The small 15C Church of Santa Maria Maggiore has interesting 15C-16C frescoes.

On the rocky tip of the peninsula are the remains of a vast Roman villa which belonged to the poet Catullus. The excavation site is known as the **Grotte di Catullo** ⊙ and it is possible to distinguish the remains of buildings in this attractive **site**★★.

Solferino – A chapel (**capella ossario**) and a museum (**museo**) ⊙ recall the battle of 24 June 1859 (the field of battle extended as far as San Martino, *see above*) when the French and Piedmontese troops defeated the Austrians and brought about Italy's independence *(see Historical Table and Notes)*. The heavy casualties (11 000 dead and 23 000 wounded) led to the founding of the **Red Cross** by Henri Dunant. A **monument** on the site marks the event.

Torbole – This pleasant resort was the venue for a most unusual event in 1439. Venice, in an attempt to rescue the town of Brescia, under siege by the Visconti of Milan, armed a fleet which sailed up the Adige and crossed the mountains towards Torbole on Lake Garda. From there the fleet set sail to occupy Maderno on the west bank. The following year Venice was able to capture Riva and finally achieve suzerainty over the lake.

Valeggio sul Mincio – *Exit the Milan-Venice motorway at Peschiera. Follow signs for Parco Giardino Sigurtà which is 10km – 6 miles south of Peschiera.* Having been granted the right to pump up spring water from the Mincio, Carlo Sigurtà (1898-1983), an industrial pharmacist who spent 40 years of his life working on the properties of thermal springs, completely transformed the 17C villa used by Napoleon III as his headquarters in 1859. Now, the beautifully maintained park (50ha – 123 acres), **Parco Giardino Sigurtà**★★ ⊙, can only be visited by car. Thirteen car parks have been set out along the 7km – 4 mile route. They mark the start of interesting footpaths. In addition to its magnificent location on the Mincio, the park has a wonderful range of Mediterranean flora, vast grassy swards, architectural and natural features, and, in certain areas, the gentle sound of classical music.

Fine gardens: Villa d'Este (Tivoli), Hanbury Gardens (Ventimiglia), Boboli Gardens (Florence), Villa Nazionale (Strà).

L'AQUILA★

Abruzzi – Population 66 826

Michelin map 988 fold 26 or 430 fold 27 – Local map under Appenino ABRUZZESE
Town plan in the current Michelin Red Guide Italia

L'Aquila was founded in the 13C by the Emperor Frederick II of Hohenstaufen who gave it an imperial eagle as its emblem. Charles I of Anjou took control of the town in 1266 and was responsible for building part of the fortifications. The town has many Romanesque or Renaissance churches and palaces, built of golden stone, often marked with the initials IHS (*Iesus Hominum Salvator* – Jesus Saviour of Mankind) after the preaching and motto of St Bernardino of Siena. The saint died here in 1444.

★★ **Basilica di San Bernardino** ⊙ – This superb edifice, built from 1454 to 1472, was given a remarkable façade by Cola dell'Amatrice in 1527. The interior, in the form of a Latin cross, is spacious and well-lit and roofed with a lovely baroque wooden ceiling.
The **mausoleum**★ of St Bernardino is adorned with figures by the local sculptor, Silvestro dell'Aquila, as is the elegant **tomb**★ of Maria Pereira.

★ **Castello** – This square castle, quartered with powerful bastions, is a good example of 16C military architecture. The great rooms now house a museum, the **Museo Nazionale d'Abruzzo**★★ ⊙, with its archeological, medieval (mainly interesting examples of local craftsmanship) and modern sections.

★ **Basilica di Santa Maria di Collemaggio** ⊙ – This Romanesque basilica, which dominates a vast square, was begun in 1287 on the initiative of Pietro da Morone, founder of the Celestine Order and future Pope Celestine V. The wonderful **façade**★★ of white and pink stone is pierced with three rose windows and round-headed doorways, all added in the 14C.

★ **Fontane delle 99 cannelle** – This imposing fountain was remodelled in the 15C. Ninety-nine masks spout water into its basins. This figure corresponds to the legend which relates the miraculous founding of the town with its 99 quarters, 99 castles, 99 squares and 99 fountains. Even today a bell in the tower of the Law Courts tolls 99 times every evening.

Gourmets...
The chapter on food and drink in the Introduction to this guide
describes gastronomic specialities and the best local wines
The annual **Michelin Red Guide Italia**
offers an up-to-date selection of good restaurants

LECCE★★

Puglia – Population 100 893
Michelin map 988 fold 30 or 431 F 36
Town plan in the current Michelin Red Guide Italia

Set in the very heart of the Salento region, Lecce was in Roman times the prosperous town of Lupiae. The Norsemen greatly favoured the town and made it the capital of the region known as Terra d'Otranto.

From the 16C to the 18C, Lecce knew a period of great splendour during which it was embellished with Renaissance, Rococo and Baroque monuments. The local finely-grained limestone was particularly easy to work, and the town's numerous Baroque buildings are remarkable for the abundance of decorative work which has earned the city the nickname of "the Baroque Florence". When seen at night the whole decked in lights resembles a sumptuous theatrical set.

The most inventive artists came from the Zimbalo family: their work is to be found in both churches and palaces and is widespread throughout the Salentina Peninsula.

★★BAROQUE LECCE

Time: 1 hour

Façade of Basilica di Santa Croce, Lecce

★★ **Santa Croce** – Although several architects worked on this basilica in the 16C and 17C, it is the best example of the Baroque style of Lecce. The façade is sumptuously decorated without being overbearing.

The interior is light and airy and the plainer architectural style is reminiscent of the Florentine Renaissance idiom. There is also an abundant Baroque decoration of great delicacy. The side chapel contains a fine **high altar** with sculptured low reliefs by Francesco Antonio Zimbalo.

Palazzo del Governo – Adjoining the basilica the Governor's residence, a former Celestine monastery, has a rusticated façade with a frieze above and intricately-decorated window surrounds, especially at first-floor level.

★★ **Piazza del Duomo** – The unity of the buildings bordering this square makes it one of the finest in southern Italy. The **campanile** (1661-82) and the cathedral **(Duomo)** (1659-82) are by Giuseppe Zimbalo, the 17C **Palazzo Vescovile** and the **Seminario** dating from 1709 by Giuseppe Cino.

In the courtyard of the latter there is an ornately-decorated **well★** by the same sculptor.

ADDITIONAL SIGHTS

★ **Museo Provinciale Sigismondo Castromediano** ⊘ – Housed in a modern building, the museum has a rich archeological section *(ground floor)* and a very important **ceramics collection★★** *(first floor)*. Of particular interest are the proto-Italiot and Italiot vases decorated with painted figures. There is an art gallery on the third floor.

★ **San Mateo** – This church with its harmonious façade by Achille Carducci shows the distinct influence of Borromini and his Roman work, the Church of San Carlo alle Quattro Fontane.

★ **Chiesa del Rosario (or San Giovanni Battista)** – This church was Giuseppe Zimbalo's last work and the façade features an abundance of decoration which is both intricately detailed and yet gracious.

The **interior★** is adorned with several altarpieces which are very ornate.

Santi Nicolò e Cataldo – *North of the town near the cemetery.* The church was built in 1180 by the Norman Tancred and rebuilt in 1716, probably by Giuseppe Cino who retained intact the central part of the Romanesque façade with its small rose window and Norman doorway. There is an attractive Baroque structure in the 16C cloisters.

Sant'Irene (or Chiesa dei Teatini) – The church was built by Francesco Grimaldi for the monks of the Theatine Order and it contains splendid **altarpieces★** which are attributed to Francesco A Zimbalo.

Chiesa del Gesù (or **Chiesa del Buon Consiglio**) – *Via Francesco Rubichi*. The austere style of the church, built by the Jesuits from 1575 to 1579, makes a sharp contrast with the other churches of the town.

Sant'Angelo – *Via Manfredi*. Although unfinished, this façade is typical of Francesco Giuseppe Zimbalo (1663) and is decorated with garlands, cherubs, angels etc.

Piazza Sant'Oronzo – This busy square forms the town centre and is dominated from on high by the statue of the town's patron saint, St Oronzo, who crowns one of the two columns which used to mark the end of the Appian Way in Brindisi *(see BRINDISI)*.
On the south side of the square, parts of the Roman amphitheatre have been uncovered.

*Admission times and charges
for the sights described
are listed at the end of the guide
Every sight for which there are times and charges
is identified by the clockface symbol ⊘
in the Sights section of the guide*

LIGNANO ☆☆

Friuli – Venezia Giulia – Population 5 693
Michelin maps 988 fold 6 or 429 E/F 21

Lignano, the largest seaside resort on the coastline of Friuli, lies on a long, sandy peninsula covered with pine woods. Stretching east from the mouth of the Tagliamento, it closes off part of the Marano Lagoon, an angling reserve. Its **beach**★★ ⊘, facing Grado, the Trieste Gulf and the coastline of Istria (which is often visible), is popular for its 8km – 5 miles of fine, golden sand that slopes very gently into the sea; it is a safe holiday resort for families with children.
The resort comprises three areas. At the tip of the peninsula is **Lignano Sabbiadoro**, the oldest part of the town and a convivial place with old houses, shopping streets and a large yachting marina (the *darsena*). Separated from Sabbiadoro by a large expanse of pine wood that belongs to the Vatican and is reserved for children's holiday camps is **Lignano Pineta**, an elegant, modern part of the town laid out like a spiral and divided off by streets radiating out from the central square. **Lignano Riviera** gets its name from the nearby Tagliamento. The water offshore from its beach is slightly colder but the vegetation is thicker here. Inland, holidaymakers can enjoy the 18-hole golf course and visit the zoo, the **Parco zoo Punta Verde** ⊘, which presents animals from all over the world.

LIVORNO

LEGHORN – Tuscany – Population 167 087
Michelin map 988 fold 14, 428 fold 37 or 430 L 12
Town plan in the current Michelin Red Guide Italia

The important seaport of Leghorn deals mainly in timber, marble, alabaster, cars and craftwork from Florence. Cosimo I de' Medici started rebuilding the harbour to replace the silted-up Porto Pisano, and it was finished in 1620 under Cosimo II. The main streets are Via Grande lined with arcaded buildings, Via Cairoli and Via Ricasoli. In the Piazza Micheli, from which the Fortezza Vecchia (Old Fortress) can be seen, stands the **monument**★ to the last prominent Medici, the Grand Duke Ferdinand. The four bronze Moors (1624) were the work of Pietro Tacca.

EXCURSION

Montenero – *9km – 6 miles south*. The 18C pilgrimage church dedicated to Our Lady of Grace consists of a richly decorated Baroque church, a monastery and behind railings the *famedio*, a series of chapels reserved for the burial of distinguished citizens of Livorno.

LORETO⭐

Marches – Population 10 775
Michelin map 988 fold 16 or 430 L 22
Town plan in the current Michelin Red Guide Italia

The small city of Loreto is grouped around its well-known church which is the scene of a famous pilgrimage to the "House of Mary". The old quarter is partially encircled by massive brick ramparts dating from the 16C. It is said that the Santa Casa (Holy House) or House of Mary was miraculously carried from Nazareth in several stages by angels and set down in a wood of laurels (*lauretum* in Latin), which gave its name to Loreto. In fact three walls of the House of Mary were transported in 1294 by the Angeli (angels in Italian), a noble family which ruled over Epiros where Nazareth is located. Loreto which is located near the port of Ancona was chosen as it was part of the Papal States which could extend its protection to the sacred relics.

The most popular pilgrimages take place on the Feast of the Virgin, the Nativity (8 September) and the Translation of the Santa Casa (10 December) *(see the Calendar of Events at the end of the guide)*.

The Venetian painter **Lorenzo Lotto** (1486-1556), who imbued his portraits with a new psychological meaning, lived at Loreto from 1535 until his death. Towards the end of his life he became an Oblate in the Santa Casa.

⭐⭐ SANTUARIO DELLA SANTA CASA ⊙ *1 hour*

Many famous architects, painters and sculptors contributed to the building and decoration of this church, the Sanctuary of the Holy House. Construction started in 1468 and was only completely finished in the 18C. The architects included firstly Giuliano da Sangallo, then Bramante who built the side chapels, and finally Vanvitelli who designed the bulbous campanile. Go round the outside of the church to admire the lovely triple **apse**⭐⭐ and Sangallo's elegant dome. The sober and harmonious façade with its double buttresses surmounted by clocks at the corners is typical of the late Renaissance.

The three **bronze doors**⭐⭐ are adorned with fine late-16C and early-17C statues. The interior has a nave and two aisles. At the end of the south aisle the **Sacristy of St Mark**⭐ (San Marco) is crowned by a dome painted with frescoes (1477) by Melozzo da Forli with an exceptional sense of foreshortening, showing angels carrying the Instruments of the Passion. In the **Sacristy of St John**⭐ (San Giovanni) is a lavabo designed by Benedetto da Maiano under a vault painted with frescoes by Luca Signorelli. Standing at the transept crossing is the **Santa Casa**⭐⭐ which was sumptuously faced with marble carved in the 16C by Antonio Sansovino and other sculptors. The north transept leads to a room decorated by Pomarancio (1605-10).

Piazza della Madonna⭐, in front of the basilica, is lined by the unfinished portico of the Palazzo Apostolico, which now houses a picture gallery **(pinacoteca)** ⊙. This contains a remarkable collection of **works**⭐ by Lorenzo Lotto, paintings by Simon Vouet and Pomarancio. The Flemish tapestries were woven to designs by Raphael and there is a superb collection of Urbino faïence vessels.

EXCURSION

Recanati – *7km – 4 miles southwest.* This little town, perched on a hill, was the birthplace of the poet **Giacomo Leopardi**, the most perceptive but melancholy of men whose work was very melodious. The **Palazzo Leopardi** ⊙ contains mementoes of the writer. The **Pinacoteca Civica** ⊙ has several important works by Lorenzo Lotto, including an Annunciation.

MICHELIN GUIDES

The **Green Guides** *(fine art, historic monuments, scenic routes)*

Austria – Belgium and Luxembourg – Brussels – California – Canada – Chicago –
England-The West Country – Europe – France – Germany – Great Britain –
Greece – Ireland – Italy – London – Mexico – Netherlands – New England –
New York City – Paris – Portugal – Quebec – Rome – Scandinavia-Finland –
Scotland – Spain – Switzerland – Thailand – Tuscany – Venice – Wales –
Washington DC

... and the collection of regional guides for France

The **Red Guides** *(hotels and restaurants)*

Benelux – Deutschland – España Portugal – Europe – France – Great Britain and Ireland – Italia – Switzerland

LUCCA★★★

Tuscany – Population 87 577
Michelin map 988 fold 14, 428, 429 or 430 K 13

Situated in the centre of a fertile plain, Lucca has preserved within its girdle of ramparts, often tree-topped, a rich heritage of churches, palaces, squares and streets which gives the town a charming air, unscathed by contemporary developments.

HISTORICAL NOTES

Lucca was colonised by the Romans in the 2C BC and it has retained the plan of a Roman military camp, with the two principal streets perpendicular to one another. During the Middle Ages a complicated system of narrow alleys and oddly-shaped squares was added to the original network. The town became an independent commune at the beginning of the 12C and flourished until the mid-14C with the silk trade as its main activity. In the early 14C the town enjoyed a great period of prosperity and prestige under the control of the mercenary leader Castruccio Castracani (d 1328). Lucca's finest religious and secular buildings date from this period. Luccan architects adopted the Pisan style to which they added their own characteristic refinement and fantasy. From 1550 onwards the town became an important agricultural centre and with this new prosperity came a renewed interest in building. The countryside was dotted with villas, the town encircled by ramparts and most of the houses were either rebuilt or remodelled. In the early 19C, Elisa Bonaparte ruled the city for a brief period from 1805 to 1813. Following Napoleon's Italian campaigns he bestowed the titles of Princess of Lucca and Piombino on his sister. She showed a remarkable aptitude for public affairs and ruled her fief with wisdom and intelligence, encouraging the development of the town and the arts.

The Legend of the Holy Cross – The **Volto Santo** (Holy Visage) is a miraculous Crucifix kept in the cathedral. It is said that after Christ had been taken down from the Cross, Nicodemus saw the image of his face on it. The Italian Bishop Gualfredo, when on pilgrimage in the Holy Land, succeeded in tracing the Volto Santo and embarked in a boat without a crew or sails which drifted ashore on the beach at Luni, near La Spezia. As the worshippers at Luni and Lucca disputed possession of the Holy Image, the Bishop of Lucca had it placed on a cart drawn by two oxen; they immediately set off towards Lucca.
The fame of the Volto Santo, spread by merchants from Lucca, gained ground throughout Europe. A most unusual commemorative procession, **Luminara di Santa Croce**, passes through the illuminated town after dark (see the Calendar of Events at the end of the guide).

THE IMPORTANT CHURCHES
3 hours

From the great **Piazza Napoleone** (car park) make for the Piazza San Giovanni, overlooked by the church of the same name, and then the Piazza San Martino, bordered on the left side by the 16C Palazzo Micheletti designed by Ammannati with pretty terraced gardens.

★★ **Duomo**(C) – The cathedral, dedicated to St Martin, was rebuilt in the 11C. The exterior was remodelled almost entirely in the 13C, as was the interior in the 14C and 15C. The strength and balance of the green and white marble **façade★★**, designed by the architect Guidetto da Como, are striking despite its

Traffic

Battistero (Via del)	B 6
Fillungo (Via)	BC
Roma (Via)	B 31
Vittorio Veneto (Via)	B 50
Anfiteatro (Pza dell')	C 2
Angeli (Via degli)	B 3
Antelminelli (Pza)	C 4
Asili (Via degli)	B 5
Battisti (Via C.)	B 7
Beccheria (Via)	B 8

B Battistero e chiesa
    dei Santi Giovanni e Reparata
C San Cristoforo

asymmetry. The upper section with its three superimposed galleries is the first example of the Pisan Romanesque style *(see PISA)* as it developed in Lucca; the idiom is characterised by lighter, less rigid lines and by inventive ornamentation. The ornate sculpture and marble-inlaid designs are of great interest.

The slim and powerful campanile harmoniously combines the use of brick and marble, and the number of openings increases with the height.

The sculptural decoration of the porch is extremely rich: pillars with naïvely-carved columns, arcading, friezes and a variety of scenes (barking dogs, Roland sounding his horn, a man wrestling with a bear and another stroking his beard). The Gothic **interior** has elevations where the round-headed main arches with their robust piers contrast with the delicacy of the elegant triforium. On the west wall is an unusual Romanesque sculpture of St Martin dividing his cloak. The classical and sober lines of this sculpture herald the style of Nicola Pisano. In the north aisle is the lovely shrine *(tempietto)* built by the local artisan Matteo Civitali (1436-1501) to house the Volto Santo. The great 12C figure of **Christ★** in wood blackened through time shows a distinctly Oriental influence because of its hieratic aspect. It is said to be a copy of the legendary one.

In the north transept is one of the masterpieces of Italian funerary sculpture by the Sienese artist, Jacopo della Quercia (1406): the **tomb★★** of Ilaria del Carretto, wife of Paolo Guinigi, lord of Lucca in the early 15C. The recumbent figure wears a long, delicately-draped robe and at her feet lies a small dog, a symbol of fidelity.

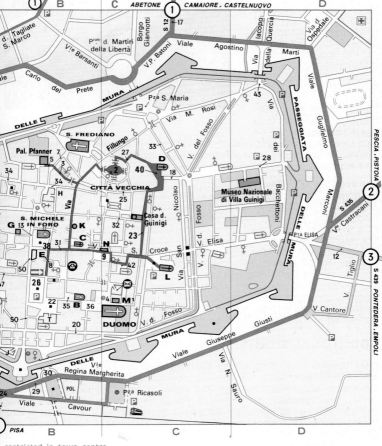

restricted in town centre

Bernardini (Pza dei) .... C 9	Indipendenza	S. Gemma Galgani (Via) ... C 33
Boccherini (Pza L.) .... A 10	(Piazza dell') .... B 24	S. Giorgio (Via) .... B 34
Cadorna (Viale) .... D 12	Mordini (Via A.) .... C 25	S. Giovanni (Pza) .... B 35
Calderia (Via) .... B 13	Napoleone (Pza) .... B 26	S. Martino (Pza) .... B 36
Catalani (Via) .... A 15	Portico (Via del) .... C 27	S. Michele (Pza) .... B 38
Civitali (Via M.) .... C 17	Quarquonia	S. Pietro (Pza) .... C 40
Fratta (Via della) .... C 18	(Via della) .... D 28	Servi (Pza dei) .... C 42
Garibaldi	Repubblica (Viale) .... B 29	Varanini (Pza L.) .... D 43
(Corso) .... AB 20	Risorgimento	Verdi (Pzale G.) .... A 45
Giglio (Pza dell) .... B 22	(Pza) .... B 30	Vittorio Emanuele II
Guinigi (Via) .... C 23	S. Andrea (Via) .... C 32	(Via) .... AB 47

D San Pietro Somaldi	**G** Casa natale di Puccini	**M¹** Museo
E Palazzo Pretorio	**K** Torre Civica delle Ore	della cattedrale
F San Paolino	**L** Santa Maria Forisportam	**N** Palazzo Bernardini

Other works of art include a *Presentation of the Virgin in the Temple* by Bronzino *(north aisle)* and the large-scale **Last Supper★** with its subtle lighting by Tintoretto *(south aisle).*

★★ **San Michele in Foro** (B) – The white mass of the 12C-14C church on the site of the Roman forum dominates the adjoining square which is lined by old mansions and the Palazzo Pretorio.

The exceptionally tall **façade★★** (the nave itself was to have been taller) is a good example of the Lucca-Pisan style, despite the fact that the lower part was remodelled last century. The four superimposed galleries surmount blind arcading and are decorated with varied motifs.

At the top, two instrument-playing angels flank a statue of the Archangel Michael slaying the dragon.

The simplicity of the Romanesque **interior** is a direct contrast to the or-

San Michele in Foro

nate exterior. On the first altar of the south aisle is a **Madonna★** by Andrea della Robbia. The south transept is adorned with a lovely **painting★** with brilliant colours by Filippino Lippi.

★ **San Frediano** (B) – This great church, dedicated to St Frigidian, was rebuilt in the original Lucca-Romanesque style in the 12C before the influence of the Pisan school was felt. The sober façade is faced with white marble from the Roman amphitheatre. The upper middle section, remodelled in the 13C, is dominated by a Byzantine-style mosaic depicting the Ascension by local artists.

The interior comprises a nave and two aisles with wooden ceilings (flanked by Renaissance and Baroque side chapels) on the plan of the early-Christian basilicas: the nave which ends in a semicircular apse is articulated by antique columns crowned with fine capitals.

To the right on entering is a curious Romanesque **font★** (12C) with low reliefs depicting the story of Moses. The chapel of Sant'Agostino is decorated with frescoes by the Ferraran painter Amico Aspertini: one of these depicts the translation of the Volto Santo from Luni to Lucca.

ADDITIONAL SIGHTS

★ **Città Vecchia** (BC) – The streets and squares of old Lucca are full of atmosphere with their Gothic and Renaissance palaces, their towers of nobility, old shops, sculptured doorways and coats of arms, elegant wrought-iron railings and balconies. Starting from Piazza San Michele, follow Via Roma and Villa Fillungo to Piazza del Anfiteatro situated inside the Roman amphitheatre. From here go towards Piazza San Pietro (12C-13C church) and then take Via Guinigi where at No 29 stands **Casa dei Guinigi** ⊘ (C) with its tower (**panorama★** of town from the top) crowned with trees which rises above the great façade with Gothic windows. The houses opposite at Nos 20 and 22 also belonged to the Guinigi family. Continue to the Romanesque Church of **Santa Maria Forisportam** (C L), so-called because it stood outside the Roman walls.

Via Santa Croce, Piazza dei Servi and Piazza dei Bernardini, where the 16C palace of the same name stands (C N), lead back to Piazza San Michele.

★ **Passeggiata delle Mura** – A walk is laid out along the ramparts (4km – 3 miles long) which give the town a special charm. They were built in the 16C and 17C and include 11 bastions, linked by curtain walls, and four gateways.

Museo Nazionale di Palazzo Mansi (A) ⊙ – The **apartments** of this 17C palace have a remarkable interior **decoration★** (17C-18C). The **Pinacoteca** includes works by 17C Italian artists (Salimbeni and Barocci) and foreign paintings.

Museo Nazionale di Villa Guinigi (D) ⊙ – *Via della Quarquonia. Closed for restoration.* The villa which once belonged to Paolo Guinigi now contains archeological, sculpture (Romanesque, Gothic and Renaissance) and painting (Lucca and Tuscan) sections. There are some remarkable panels of intarsia work.

EXCURSIONS

Villa Reale di Marlia ⊙ – *8km – 5 miles north. Leave by ① on the town plan.* The Villa Reale is surrounded by magnificent 17C **gardens★★** modified by Elisa Bonaparte. Unusual features include a lemon grove, a 17C nymphaeum and an open-air theatre.

Villa Mansi ⊙ – *Segramigno, 11km – 7 miles north. Leave by ① on the town plan.* This 16C villa, transformed in the 18C, has a façade covered with statues and a vast shady **park★** where statue-lined alleys lead to a lovely pool.

Villa Torrigiani (or **Camigliano**) ⊙ – *12km – 8 miles northeast. Leave by ① on the town plan.* This 16C villa was converted in the 17C into an elegant summer residence by Marques Nicolao Santini, ambassador of the Lucca republic to the Papal Court and to the Court of Louis XIV. The gardens designed by Le Nôtre, are adorned with fountains, grottoes and nymphaea. The villa, which has a delightful rococo façade, contains rooms adorned with frescoes.

MANTOVA★★

MANTUA – Lombardy – Population 56 821
Michelin map 988 or 428, 429 G 14
Town plan in the current Michelin Red Guide Italia

Mantua is set in the heart of a flat fertile plain which was formerly marshland on the southeastern border of Lombardy. It is encircled to the north by three lakes formed by the slow-flowing Mincio. This active and prosperous town has important mechanical and petrochemical industries. The region is also the first producer of hosiery worldwide.

HISTORICAL NOTES

Although, according to a legend quoted by Virgil, Mantua was founded by Monto, daughter of the divine Tiresias, its origins would seem to be Etruscan dating back to the 6C or 5C BC. It passed to the Gauls before becoming Roman in the 3C BC. In 70BC **Virgil** (Publius Virgilius Maro), the great poet, was born in the Mantua area. Author of the *Aeneid* in which he recounts the wanderings of Aeneas, the exiled Trojan prince, and the foundation of the earliest settlement, from which Rome was to spring, Virgil describes his beloved Mantuan countryside, with its soft misty light, and the pleasures of rural life in his own harmonious but melancholy style in the *Eclogues* or *Bucolica* and in the *Georgics*.

In the Middle Ages Mantua was the theatre for numerous struggles between rival factions which successively sacked the town, before it became an independent commune in the 13C and finally the domain of Luigi Gonzaga, nominated Captain General of the People. Under the **Gonzaga** family, who were enlightened rulers and patrons of the arts

Gastronomy in Mantua

The rich Mantuan cuisine boasts many specialities including the delicious *tortelli*, fritters stuffed with pumpkin, macaroons, mustard and nuts, and *Sbrisolona*, a succulent cake which owes its curious name from the fact that it is impossible to taste it without eating every morsel.

The lagoon of Mantua

From the Middle Lake and the Lower Lake, near Castel San Giorgio, motorboats leave daily for wonderful trips along the lower course of the Mincio. Visitors who plan a stay in Mantua from mid-July to late August, should not miss the opportunity for an enchanting excursion in a small boat on the river decked with pink and white lotus blooms. *It is advisable to enquire in advance about the flowering time from the park authorities.* ☎ *0376 689 166.*

and letters, Mantua became an important intellectual and artistic centre in northern Italy of the 15C and 16C. Thus Gian Francesco Gonzaga (ruled 1407-44) placed his children in the charge of the famous humanist Vittorio da Feltre (1379-1446) and commissioned the Veronese artist **Pisanello** (1395-1440?) to decorate his ducal palace. His son Ludovico III (1444-78), a mercenary army leader by profession, was a typical Renaissance patron: he gave land to the poor, built bridges and favoured artists. The Sienese humanist Politian (1454-94), the Florentine architect Leon Battista Alberti (1404-72) and the Paduan painter **Mantegna** (1431-1506) all belonged to his court. Francesco II (1484-1519) married Isabella d'Este, a beautiful and wise woman who contributed to the fame of Mantua. Their son Federico II was made duke by the Emperor Charles V in 1530 and he commissioned the architect and artist **Giulio Romano** (1499-1546), Raphael's pupil, to embellish his native town; the artist worked on the ducal palace and cathedral and the Palazzo del Te.

In 1627 Vicenzo II died without heirs and the succession passed to the Gonzaga-Nevers family, the cadet line, but the Habsburg Emperor Ferdinand II opposed the French succession, and in 1630 sent an army which sacked the town and deserted it following a plague which decimated Milan and Lombardy (the background to these dramatic events is explained in the novel *I Promessi Sposi* by Manzoni). The Gonzaga-Nevers, however, restored the fortunes of the town until 1707 when they were deposed and Mantua became part of the Austrian Empire which ruled until 1866, except for a period under Napoleonic rule (1787-1814), when it joined the Kingdom of Italy.

★★★ PALAZZO DUCALE (BY) ⏱ 1 1/2 hours

The Ducal Palace comprises buildings from various periods: the Magna Domus and the Palazzo del Capitano erected in the late 13C by the Bonacolsi, Lords of Mantua from 1272 to 1328; the Castello di San Giorgio, a 14C fortress, and other inner sections built by the Gonzaga in the 15C-16C, including the 15C ducal chapel of Santa Barbara.

★★★ Apartments – Start from the 17C Ducal Stairway which gives access to the first floor. One of the first rooms displays *The Expulsion of the Bonacolsi and the Triumph of the Gonzaga on 16 August 1328* by Domenico Morone (1442-1517). The painting shows the medieval aspect of Piazza Sordello with the old façade of the cathedral. The Pisanello rooms on the first floor have fragments of frescoes and remarkable **sinopie**★★ (rough sketches using a red earth pigment), which were discovered in 1969 and are a good example of the refined and penetrating work of Pisanello. These lyrical scenes draw inspiration from the feats of the Knights of the Round Table and the fantastic and timeless world of medieval chivalry. The **Tapestry Room** (Appartamento degli Arazzi), formerly known as the Green Apartment (Appartamento Verde), in the neo-Classical style, is hung with nine splendid Brussels tapestries after Raphael. The **Room of the Zodiac** (Camera dello Zodiaco) leads to the **Moors Room** (Stanzino dei Mori), in the Venetian style, and to the **Hall of the Rivers** (Sala dei Fiumi) which overlooks the **Hanging Garden** (Giardino Pensile). The giants depicted on the walls represents the rivers of Mantua. The **Moors Corridor** (Corridoio dei Mori) leads into the famous **Hall of Mirrors** (Sala degli Specchi) used for dance and music. In the elegant **Archers' Room** (Sala degli Arcieri), the antechamber to the ducal apartments, hang paintings by Rubens and Domenico Fetti. The **Ducal Apartments** (Appartamento Ducale) comprise a suite of rooms remodelled for Vincenzi I in the early 17C by Antonio Maria Viani, and including the **Paradise Room** (Appartamento del Paradiso) and the tiny **Dwarfs' Room**

Ceiling, Palazzo Ducale, Mantua

MANTOVA

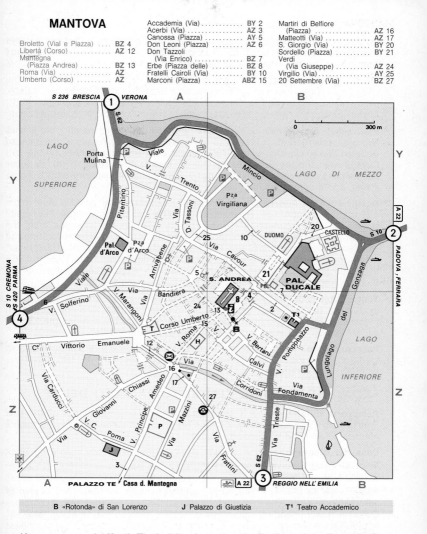

B «Rotonda» di San Lorenzo   **J** Palazzo di Giustizia   **T¹** Teatro Accademico

(Appartamento dei Nani). The building known as the **Rustica** and the **Equestrian Court** (Cortile della Cavallerizza) are by Giulio Romano; the courtyard is lined by a **gallery**, Galleria della Mostra, built in the late 16C by Antonio Maria Viani to house Vicenzo I's art collection, and by the **Hall of the Months** (Galleria dei Mesi) erected by Giulio Romano. In the Castello di San Giorgio may be viewed the celebrated **Spouses' Room** (Camera degli Sposi) - so-called because this is where marriages were recorded - executed from 1465 to 1474 by **Andrea Mantegna**. The walls are covered with a cycle of frescoes to the glory of the superb and refined world of the Gonzaga court. Mantegna creates an illusion of space with his knowledge of foreshortening and perspective and his skilful use of volume and materials. The painted *trompe-l'œil* and carved stucco decoration and garlands of foliage and fruits are typical. On the north wall look for Ludovico II turned towards his secretary, and his wife Barbara seated full-face. The children cluster round their parents, as do other members of the court including an enigmatic dwarf.

On the west wall the fresco presents Ludovico with his son, Cardinal Francesco, against the background of a town with splendid monuments, which could well be Rome as imagined by Mantegna who had not yet visited the city. Mantegna has portrayed himself as the figure in purple which can be glimpsed on the right of the dedication. His great mastery of *trompe-l'œil* culminates in the ceiling oculus from which gaze cupids and servants. This invention was highly successful and introduces a note of wry humour and even strangeness to this otherwise rather solemn ensemble.

HISTORIC CENTRE

★ **Piazza Sordello (BY 21)** - This square, which was the centre of old Mantua, has retained its medieval aspect. To the west is the 13C Palazzo Bonacolsi - the tall Torre della Gabbia (Tower of the Cage) still bears on its façade the cage *(gabbia)* in which wrongdoers were exhibited - and the 18C Palazzo Vescovile where telamones adorn the 18C façade. To the east are the oldest buildings of the Palazzo Ducale: the Magna Domus and the crenellated Palazzo del Capitano.

On the north side stands the Cathedral (Duomo) which features varied elements and styles: the neo-Classical façade, the late-Gothic right wing and a Romanesque campanile. The 16C interior was designed by Giulio Romano.

Piazza Broletto (BZ 4) – This was the centre of public life at the time of the commune (13C) when was built the Palazzo Broletto, a 13C communal palace, partly remodelled in the 15C. On its façade it has a seated statue of Virgil (1225). At the right corner rises the Torre Comunale, a tower later converted into a prison.

★ **Piazza delle Erbe** (BZ 8) – The Square of Herbs derives its name from a fruit and vegetable market. It is lined to the north by the rear façade of the Palazzo Broletto and to the east by the 13C Palazzo della Ragione, flanked by the 15C Clock Tower and the Romanesque church, **Rotonda di San Lorenzo**★ (B) ⊙. Sober and elegant, this circular building has a colonnaded ambulatory with a loggia above, and a dome crowning all.

★ **Basilica di Sant'Andrea** (BYZ) – The basilica dedicated to St Andrew, built in the 15C to the plans of Alberti, is a masterpiece of the Italian Renaissance. The façade retains Classical architectural features: the tympanum, the triumphal arch, the niches between the pilasters. The interior has a single nave. The barrel-vaulting and walls are painted in trompe-l'œil. The first chapel on the left contains the tomb of Mantegna. The transept crossing is crowned by a dome built from 1732 to 1765 by Filippo Juvara. In the crypt two urns housed in a reliquary contain a relic of the Blood of Christ brought to Mantua by the Roman soldier Longinus.

Teatro Bibiena (BZ T') ⊙ – *47 Via Accademia*. This tiny but graceful 18C theatre by Bibiena has a curious stage set in imitation marble with four orders in pasteboard and a monochrome decor. The theatre which welcomed the 13-year old Mozart on 13 December 1769, is still used for concerts.

Palazzo d'Arco (AY) ⊙ – *Piazza d'Arco*. This neo-Classical palace in the Palladian tradition *(see VICENZA)* contains interesting collections of 18C furniture, paintings and ceramics.

FROM THE HISTORIC CENTRE TO PALAZZO DEL TE

Palazzo di Giustizia (AZ J) – *Via Poma*. The monumental façade of the Law Courts with caryatids is early 17C. At No 18 in the same street is Romano's house built in 1544 to his own designs.

Casa del Mantegna (AZ) – *47 Via Acerbi*. This rather severe-looking brick building was undoubtedly built to designs by Mantegna himself in 1476. It has a delightful courtyard.

★★ **Palazzo del Te** (AZ) ⊙ – This large country mansion was built on the plan of a Roman house by Giulio Romano for Federico II from 1525 to 1535. It combines Classical features and melodramatic invention, such as the amazing "broken" entablature in the main courtyard, and is a major achievement of the Mannerist style. The interior was ornately decorated by Giulio Romano and his pupils. In the **Room of Psyche** (Sala di Psiche) used for banquets, the sensual and lively style of Guilio Romano is the best illustration of the hedonistic character of the palace. The frescoes in the **Giants' Room** (Sala dei Giganti), the most distinctive room of the palace, depict the wrath of Jupiter against the Titans. The overall decoration which covers the walls and ceiling creates an indefinite spatial illusion and the dome above gives a sense of artificiality in sharp contrast to the effect sought by Mantegna in the Camera degli Sposi in the Palazzo Ducale.

MASSA MARITTIMA★★

Tuscany – Population 9 494
Michelin map 988 fold 14 or 430 M 14

The name *Massa*, which is of Latin origin, has been linked to *Marittima*, the meaning of which is probably associated with the coastal area and hinterland. It may also be a reference to the nearby *Maremma* region. The town, in a pleasant setting, has a rich historic past and was particularly important during the Middle Ages.

★★ **Piazza Garibaldi** – This lovely square is lined by some fine medieval buildings, three of which are of Romanesque origin – Palazzo del Podestà with its many double-windowed bays, the crenellated Palazzo Comunale and the cathedral.

★★ **Duomo** – The cathedral was probably built in the early 11C. In addition to the Romanesque style, Gothic-style features were added in 1287 by **Giovanni Pisano**. The majestic building is adorned with blind arcades in the lower part and dominated by a fine campanile, at one time crenellated but now surmounted by a spire with four bellcotes, pierced with windows which increase in number with the height.

The interior, in the form of a Latin cross, comprises three aisles which are divided by two rows of columns crowned with capitals of different styles. The inside wall of the façade is decorated with striking pre-Romanesque low reliefs revealing the Byzantine influence (10C). There is an unusual baptismal font (1267). In the chapel to the left of the choir stalls is the panel of the *Virgin of the Graces* which has been attributed to **Duccio di Buoninsegna** and the remains of the *Presentation of Christ at the Temple* by Sano di Pietro (1406-81). In the chapel to the right of the choir stalls is the *Crucifixion* by Segna di Bonaventura (recorded from 1298 to 1327).

Palazzo del Podestà – The palace, which dates back to 1225-30, was the residence of the town's most eminent magistrate *(podestà)*. The façade is decorated with the coat of arms of the *podestà*. The building now houses the **Museo archeologico** ⊙: exhibits include an interesting stele by Vado dell'Arancio and the splendid *Virgin in Majesty* by Ambrogio Lorenzetti (1285-c1348).

★ **Fortezze dei senesi** and **Torre del Candeliere** ⊙ – The Sienese fortress was built in 1335. The nearby tower, Torre del Candeliere, is all that remains of the fortress built in 1228. The tower is linked to the fortress by an arch 22m across.

Sant'Agostino – The Church of St Augustine, which dates from the early 14C, has a Romanesque façade, a lovely Gothic apse and a 17C crenellated campanile added in the 17C. To the left are the remaining two wings of the Romanesque cloisters.

Museo di Storia e Arte delle Miniere ⊙ – The museum, which is situated near Piazza Garibaldi, evokes the mining activities in the 700 metres of tunnels in the surrounding area; note the supporting timberwork and extraction techniques.

EXCURSION

★★ **Abbazia** and **eremo di San Galgano** – *32km – 20 miles northeast.* This ruined, but still impressive, Gothic Cistercian Abbey was built by monks from 1224 to 1288, and dedicated to **St Galgan** (1148-81). The remains of the old monastery include the cloisters, the chapter house and the scriptorium.

The hermitage, a circular Romanesque construction, overlooks the abbey from 200m away. The splendid **cupola** (1181-85) was inspired by the Etruscan-Roman tombs and is an ideal point of reference between the ancient and Renaissance worlds. The church was erected to house the rock where in 1180 Galgano Guidotti plunged the sword turning it into the symbol of the cross. There are frescoes by Ambrogio Lorenzetti in the chapel to the left of the altar.

MATERA★★

Basilicata – Population 54 869
Michelin map 988 fold 29 or 431 E 31

Matera overlooks a ravine separating it from the Murge Hills in Puglia. This provincial capital stands in the heart of a region dissected by deeply eroded gorges - a desolate landscape with wide horizons. Modern Matera, the town's centre of activity, is laid out on a plateau overlooking the lower town with its many rock dwellings *(sassi)*, now mostly abandoned. In the town and surrounding area there are some 130 churches hewn out of the rock. These date back to the 8C BC and the arrival of oriental (non-Latin) monastic communities who settled locally and in Puglia. They were adept in this form of underground architecture which shows a Byzantine influence.

★★ **The Sassi** – The two main troglodyte quarters are on either side of the rock crowned by the cathedral. The roofs on some houses serve as walkways while the lower storeys are hewn out of the rock. Little white-ashed houses and stairways overlap and overhang one another in a labyrinth which is difficult to unravel.

★★ **Strada dei Sassi** – This panoramic street skirts the wild gorge and runs round the cathedral rock. The natural rock walls are riddled with both natural and man-made caves.

★ **Duomo** – The cathedral was built in the 13C Apulian-Romanesque style; the façade has a lovely rose window and a projecting gallery above the single doorway. The walls are embellished with blind arcades. On the south side are two richly-sculpted doorways. The interior was remodelled in the 17C and 18C. The Byzantine fresco portraying the Madonna dates from the 12C-13C, the Neapolitan crib is 16C and the lovely carved stalls of the choir are 15C. The **Chapel of the Annunciation**★ *(the last one on the south side)* has a beautiful Renaissance decoration.

San Pietro Caveoso ⊘ - This Baroque church stands at the foot of Monte Errone, which has several churches hewn out of the rock and decorated with frescoes, namely Santa Lucia alle Malve, Santa Maria de Idris and San Giovanni in Monterrone.

Musio Nazionale Ridola ⊘ - This museum in a former monastery has an interesting collection of archeological finds, which were discovered locally.

★★ **Views of Matera** - *4km - 2 1/2 miles by the Altamura road then the road to Taranto and finally a right turn to follow the signpost "chiese rupestri" (rock churches).* The road leads to two belvederes affording splendid views of Matera. On the left below the parking area are several churches hollowed out of the rock face.

MERANO★★

Trentino-Alto Adige – Population 33 547
Michelin map 988 fold 4, 218 fold 10 or 429 B/C 15
Town plan in the current Michelin Red Guide Italia

Merano, lying at the start of the wider upper valley of the Adige, known as the Val Venosta, is an important tourist centre and spa. It is blessed with a mild climate. There are numerous cable-cars and chairlifts up to **Merano 2000**, a good winter sports centre also popular in summer for excursions into the mountains.

★★ **Passeggiate d'Inverno e d'Estate** - These winter and summer promenades run along the Passirio River. The winter one, facing south, is shady and flower-decked and attractively lined with shops, cafés and terraces and is by far the busier. It is prolonged by the Passeggiata Gilf which ends near a powerful waterfall. The summer promenade, on the opposite bank, meanders through a lovely park planted with pines and palm trees.

★★ **Passeggiata Tappeiner** - This magnificent promenade (4km - 2 1/2 miles long) winds high above Merano affording remarkable viewpoints as far as the Tyrol.

Duomo di San Nicolò - This Gothic cathedral has a huge belfry and a west front with a crenellated gable. The right-hand side is decorated with a 14C statue of St Nicholas and a gigantic statue of St Christopher that was repainted in the 19C. The interior, roofed with beautiful ribbed **Gothic vaulting★**, includes two 15C stained glass windows and two painted wooden **Gothic polyptychs★** (16C) by Knoller, a native of the Tyrol. In the neighbouring **Cappella di Santa Barbara** standing at the start of the old footpath leading to Tirolo is a 16C high relief of the *Last Supper.*

★ **Via Portici (Laubengasse)** - This arcade-lined street is overlooked by houses with painted façades and oriel windows. The shops have curiously-sculpted façades.

★ **Castello Principesco** ⊘ - Built in the 14C and extended in the 15C, this castle has crenellated gables and a tower with a pepper-pot roof. It was used by the Princes of Tyrol as their residence when they stayed in the town. It has some fine apartments that are stylishly if austerely furnished.

EXCURSIONS

★ **Avelengo (Hafling)** - *10km - 6 miles to the southeast.* A scenic road leads to the plateau of Avelengo which dominates the Merano valley.

★ **Merano 2000** ⊘ - *Access by cable-car from Val di Nova, 3km - 1.9 miles east.* This conifer-clad plateau is a winter sports centre. It also makes a good centre for excursions into the mountains in summer.

The Alto-Adige

The region has retained its tradition and remains unspoilt. Laws are strictly enforced: for instance, there are no advertising hoardings along the road contrary to the practice in the rest of the country. Traditions are kept alive, especially during the Christmas and New Year celebrations. Chimneysweeps in costume call to offer greetings, the village band strikes up a traditional tune in front of every house. An inscription in chalk of the letters K M B and a date on some doorways represents the mark of the Three Wise Men who have blessed the houses.

★ **Tirolo** – *4km – 2 miles north. It can also be reached by skilift from Merano.* This charming Tyrolean village in the middle of vineyards and orchards is dominated by its castle **(Castel Tirolo)** ⓥ built in the 12C by the Counts of Val Venosta. **Castel Fontana** (also known as the **Brunnenburg**) is a strange set of 13C fortifications rebuilt at a later date. The American poet Ezra Pound worked on his *Cantos* here after 1958, when the accusation of collaboration with the Nazi regime based on his radio programmes was lifted.

★ **Val Passiria** – *50km – 31 miles to the Rombo Pass; 40km – 25 miles to the Monte Giovo Pass.* The road follows the Passiria Valley as far as the attractive Tyrolean village of **San Leonardo**, which clusters round its church. The **Rombo Pass Road★** (Timmelsjoch), steep and often cut out of the living rock, offers impressive views of the mountain peaks on the frontier. The **Monte Giovo Pass Road★** (Jaufenpass) climbs amidst conifers. On the way down, there are splendid **views★★** of the snow-capped summits of Austria.

MILANO★★★

MILAN – Lombardy – Population 1 367 733
Michelin map 988 fold 3, 219 fold 19 or 428 F 9
Town plan in the current Michelin Red Guide Italia

Milan, the lively capital of Lombardy, is the second city in Italy as regards population, politics and cultural affairs, and first in the field of commerce, industry and banking. Set in the heart of northern Italy at the foot of the Alps, the enterprising spirit of its people has combined with certain historic circumstances to make Milan one of the country's most dynamic towns which is even today in full expansion.

The town is bounded by two concentric boulevards: the shorter, enclosing the medieval centre, has replaced the 14C ramparts, of which traces remain, among them the Porta Ticinese (**JY**) and the Porto Nuovo (**KU**). The outer wall marks the town's expansion during the Renaissance. After 1870 Milan expanded rapidly beyond its fortifications, particularly along the main communication axes.

HISTORICAL NOTES

Milan is probably Gallic (Celtic) in origin, but it was the Romans who subdued the city of Mediolanum in 222 BC and ensured its expansion. At the end of the 3C Diocletian made Milan the seat of the rulers of the Western Empire, and in 313 Constantine published the **Edict of Milan** which gave freedom of worship to the Christians. In 375 **St Ambrose** (340-396), a Doctor of the Church known for his eloquence, became bishop of the town, thus adding to its prestige.

The Barbarian invasions of the 5C and 6C were followed by the creation of a Lombard Kingdom with Pavia as capital. In 756 Pepin, King of the Franks, conquered the area, and his son Charlemagne was to wear the Iron Crown of the Kings of Lombardy from 774. In 962 Milan once again became capital of Italy.

In the 12C Milan allied itself to other cities to form the Lombard League (1167) to thwart the attempts of the Emperor Frederick Barbarossa to conquer the region. With the decisive victory at **Legnano** the cities of the league achieved their independence. In the 13C the **Visconti**, Ghibellines and leaders of the local aristocracy, seized power. The most famous member was **Gian Galeazzo** (1347-1402), an able war leader, man of letters, assassin and pious builder of Milan's Cathedral and the Carthusian Monastery of Pavia. His daughter, Valentina, married Louis, Duke of Orleans, the grandfather of Louis XII of France. This family connection was the reason for the later French expeditions into Italy.

After the death of the last Visconti, Filippo-Maria (d 1447), and three years of the Ambrosian Republic, the Sforza took over the rule of Milan, thanks to Francesco, the son of a simple peasant and son-in-law of Filippo-Maria Visconti. The most famous figure in the **Sforza** family, **Ludovico il Moro** (1452-1508) made Milan a new Athens by attracting to his court the geniuses of the time, Leonardo da Vinci and Bramante. However, Louis XII of France proclaimed himself the legitimate heir to the Duchy of Milan and set out to conquer the territory in 1500. His successor François I renewed the offensive but was thwarted at Pavia by the troops of the Emperor Charles V. From 1535 to 1713 Milan was under Spanish rule. During the plague, which ravaged the town from 1576 to 1630, members of the Borromeo family, St Charles (1538-84) and Cardinal Federico (1564-1631) distinguished themselves by their religious and humanitarian work.

Under Napoleon, Milan became the capital of the Cisalpine Republic (1797) and later of the Kingdom of Italy (1805). In 1815 Milan assumed the role of capital of the Venetian-Lombard Kingdom.

MILANO

Borgogna (Via)	KX 36	Curie (Viale P.N.)	HV 77
Borgonuovo (Via)	KV 38	Dugnani (Via)	HY 80
Calatafimi (Via)	JY 45	Fatebenefratelli	
Caradosso (Via)	HX 49	(Via)	KV 92
Ceresio (Via)	JU 59	Ghisleri (Via A.)	HY 101
Circo (Via)	JX 63	Giardini (Via dei)	KV 102
Coldi Lana (Viale)	JY 65	Guastalla (Via)	KX 110
Col Moschin (Via)	JY 66	Maffei (Via A.)	LY 135
Conca del Naviglio (Via)	JY 69	Melzo (Via)	LU 152
Cordusio (Piazza)	KX 73	Mercato (Via)	JV 158

Dante (Via) .... JX
Manzoni (Via A.) .... KV
Monte Napoleone (Via) ..... KV

Aurispa (Via) .... JY 14
Battisti (Via C.) .... KLX 20
Bocchetto (Via) .... JX 30

Traffic is restricted in the central zone divided into sectors outlined in green

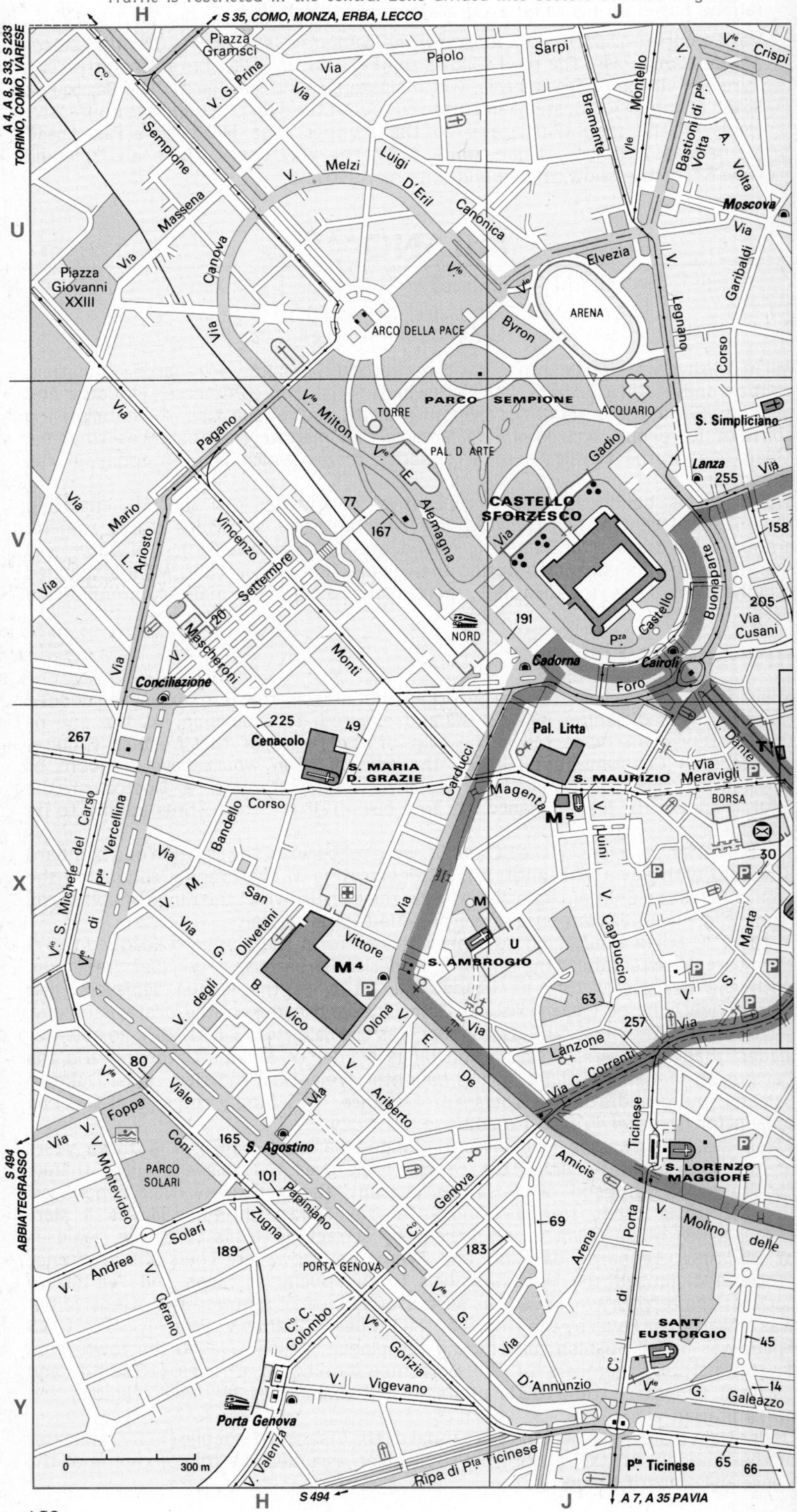

S 35, COMO, MONZA, ERBA, LECCO

A 4, A 8, S 33, S 233
TORINO, COMO, VARESE

S 494
ABBIATEGRASSO

S 494

A 7, A 35 PAVIA

160

To pass from one sector to another return to the perimeter road

LIFE IN MILAN

The most frequented parts of Milan are around Piazza del Duomo (**MZ**), Via Dante (**JX**) and Via Manzoni (**KV**). At the **Galleria Vittorio Emanuele II**★ (**MZ**), which was laid out in 1877 to the plans of Giuseppe Mengoni, the Milanese come to talk, read their *Corriere della Sera* or drink coffee side by side with the tourists. For visitors looking for luxury items or just wanting to stroll through the most fashionable districts in the city, the Corso Vittorio Emanuele II (**NZ**), the Piazza San Babila (**NZ**), the Corso Venezia (**LV**), and the Via Monte Napoleone (**NZ 171**) and Via della Spiga (**KV**) – where the couture houses are – are pleasant areas to explore. The picturesque Brera District (**KV**), which is popular with artists and full of art galleries, is particularly busy in the evening. The Corso Magenta (**HJX**) and the streets around Sant'Ambrogio (**HJX**) have retained all the charm of the Milan of another age with old houses and winding, narrow streets lined with old cafes and antique shops.

Further artistic attractions include the excellent concerts and recitals at **La Scala** and the Conservatory (**Conservatorio NZ T²**). There are also numerous theatres (**Piccolo JX T¹**, Lirico, Manzoni, Carcano).

Milanese cooking is famous for its fillets of veal in breadcrumbs *(scaloppina alla milanese)*, marrow bone (shin of veal) with its meat *(osso buco)*, saffron-tinted *risotto* and vegetable and pork soup *(minestrone)*. The perfect accompaniment is the Valtellina wines or those from the Pavia region.

FINE ARTS

The Cathedral (Duomo) marks the climax of architecture of the Gothic period. Prominent architects during the Renaissance were the Florentine, Michelozzo (1396-1472) and especially **Donato Bramante** (1444-1514), favourite master mason of Ludovico il Moro before he left for Rome. An admirer of Classical art, he was both a classicist and a man of great imagination who invented the **rhythmic articulation** (a façade with alternating bays, pilasters and niches) which imparted much of their harmony to many Renaissance façades.

The Lombard school of painting sought beauty and grace above all else. Its principal exponents were Vincenzo Foppa (1427-1515), Bergognone (1450-1523) and Bramantino (between 1450 and 1465-1536). The works of Andrea Solario (1473-c1520), Boltraffio (1467-1516) and especially the delicate canvases of **Bernardino Luini** (c1480-1532) attest to the influence of **Leonardo da Vinci** who stayed in Milan for some time.

Today Milan is the capital of Italy's publishing business and is an important centre, with its numerous art galleries, for contemporary art.

★★★ DUOMO (CATHEDRAL) (MZ) AND PRECINCTS

1 1/2 hours

Parking is difficult in the centre of town. There are however paying car parks in Piazza Diaz (MZ), Via San Marco (KUV) and Via Santa Radegonda (MZ 237). Cars may also be parked in the outer boulevards or in the car parks built beside certain underground stations on the outskirts of the town.

★★★ **Exterior** – This Gothic marvel of white marble, both colossal and ethereal, bristling with belfries, gables, pinnacles and statues, stands at one end of a great paved esplanade teeming with people and pigeons. Whilst they are part of the setting, the pigeons are largely responsible for the building's deterioration. Its recent restoration was a lengthy and highly technical process.

View of roofs, Duomo, Milano

It should be seen late in the afternoon in the light of the setting sun. Building began with the chevet in 1386 on the orders of Gian Galeazzo Visconti, and continued in the 15C and 16C under the direction of Italian, French and German master masons. The façade was finished only between 1805 and 1809, on the orders of Napoleon. Walk round the cathedral to view the **east end** with three vast bays of curved and counter-curved tracery and wonderful rose windows. The overall design is the work of a French architect, Nicolas de Bonaventure, and of a Modenese architect, Filippino degli Organi.

From the 7th floor of the Rinascente store in Corso Vittorio Emanuele there is an interesting close-up view of the architectural and sculptural features of the roofs.

★★ **Interior** – In contrast with the exterior this is bare, severe and imposing, an impression further strengthened by the dim light. The nave and four aisles are separated by 52 pillars of tremendous height (148m – 486ft). The width across the transepts is 91m – 299ft. The windows of the nave, aisles and transept have fine stained glass, which dates in part back to the 15C and 16C.

The mausoleum of Gian Giacomo Medici in the south arm of the transept is a fine work by Leoni (16C). In the north arm is the curious statue of St Bartholomew (who was flayed alive), by the sculptor Marco d'Agrate. Pass under the dome and in front of the monumental chancel (1570-90) with the high altar by Pellegrino Tibaldi. The magnificent bronze candelabrum in the north transept is a French work of the 13C. In the crypt **(cripta)** and treasury **(tesoro)** ⊘, visitors can see the silver urn containing the remains of St Charles Borromeo, Bishop of Milan, who died in 1584, as well as ivories and gold and silver church plate. On the way out, you can see the entrance to the Paleo-Christian baptistery **(batistero)** and the 4C basilica of Santa Tecla whose outline has been marked out on the parvis.

★★ **Visita ai Terrazzi** ⊘ – Take a walk on the roof to view the 135 pinnacles, numerous white marble statues (2 245 in all!), full of grace and elegance, and the Tiburio or central tower (108m – 354ft), surmounted by a small gilt statue, the Madonnina (1774).

★★ **Museo del Duomo** (MZ M¹) ⊘ – Housed in the royal palace built in the 18C by Piermarini, the cathedral museum shows the various stages in the building and restoration of the cathedral, and houses sculptures, tapestries and old stained glass windows. Also of note are the splendid **Aribert Crucifix★** (1040), the original support for the Madonnina (1772-73), and the large wooden **model★** *(modellone)* of the cathedral made to a scale of 1:20 in the 16C-19C.

★ **Via and Piazza Mercanti** (MZ 155) – In Via Mercanti stands the Palace of Juriconsults (Palazzo dei Giureconsulti **C**), built in 1564 with a statue of St Ambrose teaching on the façade. The Piazza Mercanti is quiet and picturesque. The charming Loggia degli Osii (1316) is decorated with heraldic shields, statues of saints and the balcony from which penal sentences were proclaimed. To the right of the loggia is the Baroque palace of the Palatine schools, with statues of the poet Ausonius and St Augustine in the niches. Opposite is the town hall, the **Palazzo della Ragione** or Broletto Nuovo (**D**) which was built in the 13C and extended in the 18C. The **equestrian statue** on the façade is of the governing magistrate *(podestà)* Oldrado da Tresseno. It is a Romanesque work by Antelami.

★★ **Teatro alla Scala** (MZ) – Traditionally recognised as being the most famous opera in the world, La Scala surprises people seeing it for the first time because of the simplicity of its exterior, which gives no hint of the magnificence of its auditorium. Built from 1776 to 1778 with six levels of boxes, it can seat an audience of 2 000 people.

The **Museo del teatro★** ⊘ presents memorabilia relating to Toscanini and Verdi, including busts, portraits and stage costumes. From the museum, you can go into one of the boxes and see the auditorium.

★★ MUSEUMS

Milan boasts numerous museums with rich and varied collections.

★★ **Pinacoteca di Brera**(KV) ⊘ – The gallery is housed in a 17C palace. In the courtyard is a statue of Napoleon (1809) depicted as a victorious Roman emperor by Canova. The picture collection is one of the most extensive in Italy.

The tour of the gallery starts with the Jesi collection which introduces the main artistic movements of the first-half of the 20C: note the sense of movement and dynamism of the futurist painters (Boccioni's *La Rissa in galleria*), the deconstruction of form of the Cubists and the clean geometry of the metaphysical works by Carrà *(The metaphysical muse)* and Morandi *(Still Life)*. The sculpture collection is dominated by three artists: Medardo Rosso, Arturo Marini and Marino Marini. Along the passage to the left, it is possible to admire the Maria Theresa Room and the library, Biblioteca Braidense.

The Cappella Mocchirolo gives a brief review of Italian painting from the 13C to 15C (*polyptych of Valle Romita* by Gentile da Fabriano).

MILANO

C	Palazzo dei Giureconsulti
D	Palazzo della Ragione
M¹	Museo del Duomo
M⁷	Casa del Manzoni
T²	Conservatorio

Traffic is restricted in the central zone divided into sectors outlined in green
To pass from one sector to another return to the perimeter road

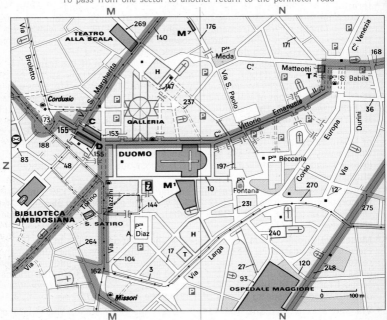

The Brera holding of **Venetian paintings** is the largest and most important one after Venice. Masterpieces include the *Pietà*★★ by Giovanni Bellini and the famous *Dead Christ*★★★ by Mantegna, an admirable meditation on death with a realism given added pathos by the artist's skill in foreshortening. In the Napoleon Rooms hang major works by Tintoretto *(Miracle of St Mark★)*, Veronese *(Dinner at the house of Simon)* and Giovanni and Gentile Bellini *(St Mark preaching at Alexandria in Egypt)*.

The **Lombard school** is well represented and pride of place is given to a *polyptych with Madonna and Saints*★ by Vicenzo Foppa and the *Madonna of the rose garden*★★★ by Bernardino Luini.

The *Montefeltro altar-piece*★★★ by Piero della Francesca and the splendid *Marriage of the Virgin Mary*★★★ by Raphaël in which the perspective focuses on a circular Bramante-style building, are masterpieces of Italian Renaissance art. Further along, Caravaggio's *Meal at Emmaus*★★★ is a fine example of the artist's use of strong contrast between light and shade and of his realism.

In the Room of 18C Venetian painting *Rebecca at the Well*★★ by Piazzetta is an exquisite portrayal of the girl's gaze, with expressions of both astonishment and innocence, even though the portrait is in profile.

The last rooms are dedicated to 19C-20C painting. Paintings on display include the *Carro rosso* by Fattori. Amongst the foreign artists are Hayez *(The Kiss)*, Ribera, Van Dyck, Rubens and Reynolds.

★★★ **Castello Sforzesco (JV)** ⏱ – This huge brick quadrilateral building was the seat of the Sforza, Dukes of Milan. The **municipal art collections** are now on display in the castle.

★★ **Museo di Scultura** – *Ground floor.* The minimalist approach of the museum's layout is particularly effective. Romanesque, Gothic and Renaissance works are mainly by Lombard sculptors. Interesting works include the **tomb of Bernabò Visconti**★★ (14C) surmounted by his equestrian statue from the Romanesque period; and the **reclining figure of Gaston de Foix** with accompanying **statues**★★ (1523) by Bambaia in his usual classical and harmonious style, as well as the unfinished *Rondanini Pietà*★★★ by Michelangelo, both from the Renaissance.

★ **Pinacoteca** – *1st floor.* The gallery displays works by Mantegna, Giovanni Bellini, Crivelli, Bergognone, Luini, Moretto, Moroni, Magnasco, Tiepolo, Guardi, Lotto etc.

★ **Museo degli strumenti musicali** – An extensive collection of stringed instruments, some of which are made to resonate by the use of a bow and others which are plucked, wind instruments and keyboards.

Museo archeologico – *In the vault under the Rochetta courtyard.* The museum includes a prehistory collection, Egyptian art and a lapidary exhibition. Another section of the museum is housed in the monastery of San Maurizio *(see below)*.

★★ **Biblioteca Ambrosiana** (MZ) ⊘ – The library is in a palace built in 1609 for Cardinal Frederico Borromeo. In addition to the many manuscripts there is an art gallery **(pinacoteca)** on the first floor. Of interest are Italian Renaissance works (Ghirlandaio, Bartolomeo Vivarini and Bergognone), **low reliefs★★** from the tomb of Gaston de Foix *(see above)* by Bambaia, allegorical paintings and the delightful *Mouse with a Rose★* by Velvet Brueghel (1568-1625), several canvases by Luini and a portrait by Giorgione. There are two remarkable **portraits★★★**, one of the musician Gaffurio by Leonardo da Vinci, the other of Beatrice d'Este by Ambrogio de Predis. The lovely *Basket of Fruit★* is by Caravaggio and the *Nativity★* by the Mannerist artist Barocci.
Room 10 contains Raphael's splendid **cartoons★★★** for the frescoes of the School of Athens in the Vatican. Another room has the collection of reproductions from the drawings in the great *Codex Atlanticus*, where the universal genius of Leonardo is powerfully displayed.

★★ **Museo Poldi Pezzoli** (KV M²) ⊘ – Attractively set out in an old mansion, the museum displays collections of weapons, fabrics, paintings, **clocks★**, and small bronzes. Among the paintings on the 1st floor (at the top of an old staircase built into an irregular, octagonal-shaped stairwell) are works by the Lombard School (Bergognone, Luini, Foppa, Solario, Boltraffio), **portraits★★** of Luther and his wife by Lucas Cranach and, in the Golden Hall decorated with a **Persian carpet**, the famous *Portrait of a Woman★★★* by Piero del Pollaiolo, a *Descent from the Cross* and a *Madonna and Child★★* by Botticelli, and a *Dead Christ★* full of pathos by Giovanni Bellini. The other rooms are hung with works by Pinturicchio, Palma il Vecchio *(Portrait of a Courtesan)*, Francesco Guardi, Canaletto, Tiepolo, Perugino, and Lotto.

Galleria d'Arte Moderna (LV M³) ⊘ – *16 Via Palestro.* The Modern Art Gallery has been set out in the Villa Reale built in 1790 which also houses the Marino Marini Museum and the Grassi Collection. It includes *The Fourth Estate* by Pelliza da Volpedo, works by Giovanni Segantini *(The Two Mothers, The Angel of Life)*, a famous *Portrait of Alexander Manzoni* by Francesco Hayez, and sculptures by the Milanese sculptor, Medardo Rosso (1858-1928). The **Carlo Grassi Collection** comprises works by Gaspare Van Wittel, Pietro Longhi, Cézanne, Van Gogh, Manet, Gauguin, Sisley, Corot, Toulouse-Lautrec, Boccioni and Balla. The **Marino Marini Museum** displays sculptures and paintings by the artist. The **Contemporary Art Pavilion** (PAC) *(14 Via Palestro)* has been designed for temporary exhibitions *(additional charge)*.

★ **Casa di Manzoni** (MZ M⁷) ⊘ – *1 Via G. Morone.* It was in this luxurious mansion that Manzoni lived for 60 years. On the ground floor, visitors can see the library with the writer's books and desk. On the first floor are memorabilia, photographs, portraits, letters and illustrations of his most famous novel, *The Betrothed*. The bedroom where he died still has its original furniture.

★ **Museo civico di Storia Naturale** (LV M⁶) ⊘ – *55 Corso Venezia.* The Natural History Museum contains interesting geological, paleontological and zoological collections. The instructive layout with numerous dioramas is particularly suitable for children.

★★ **Palazzo Bagatti Valsecchi** (KV L) ⊘ – The façade of the palace is divided into two parts: they are connected by a loggia *(1st floor)* surmounted by a balcony. All that can be seen of the present residence *(opposite)* of the Bagatti Valsecchi family is the beautiful internal courtyard.

Museum – At the top of the flight of steps embellished with a wrought iron railing is the piano nobile of the residence of Fausto and Giuseppe Bagatti Valsecchi, who, at the end of the 19C, decided to furnish their house in the Renaissance style, as was customary at the time. They used authentic pieces and faithful reproductions, adding their own personal touch. The two private apartments, belonging to Fausto and Giuseppe, are open to the public as well as the reception rooms.
Fausto's rooms comprise: the **fresco room** (depicting the *Madonna of Mercy* (1496)), the **library** decorated with two splendid 16C leather globes (the blue one is a particularly fine example) and various objects including a 17C German roulette set and the **bedroom** which is dominated by a magnificent bed carved

with *Christ's Ascent to Calvary* and various battle scenes. The bathroom is particularly charming: the bath is set in a Renaissance-style niche. The **labyrinth passage**, which is aptly named after the ceiling decoration, leads to the **domed gallery**, an area that serves to link the various rooms on the floor. The **room** containing a stove from Valtellina (sala della stufa valtellinese) gives access to Giuseppe's apartment: the warm atmosphere is due to the fine wood panelling embellished with a sculpted frieze with human figures, animals and floral patterns. The **red room**, used by Giuseppe and Carolina Borromeo, his wife, contains children's furniture including a baby walker, commode and two cradles as well as a 17C Sicilian bed; Giuseppe's room, all in green, has a fine sculpted ceiling.

Access to the formal rooms is via the domed gallery: the huge **reception hall**, heated by an impressive chimney, the **arms room** with its fine collection of bayonets and the **dining room** decorated with 14C Flemish tapestries, paintings and 17C ceramics.

★ **Museo Nazionale della Scienza e della Tecnica Leonardo da Vinci** (HX M⁴) ⊘
– This vast museum exhibits interesting scientific documents. In the **Leonardo da Vinci Gallery**, visitors can see models of the Tuscan artist's inventions. The other sections of the museum deal with acoustics, chemistry, telecommunications, and astronomy. Large pavilions are given over to displays relating to the railways, aircraft and shipping.

ADDITIONAL SIGHTS

★ **Santa Maria delle Grazie** (HX) – This Renaissance church erected by the Dominicans from 1465 to 1490 was finished by Bramante. The interior (restored), is adorned with frescoes by Gaudenzio Ferrari in the fourth chapel on the right, and the impressive **dome**★, gallery and cloisters all by Bramante. The best view of the **east end**★ is to be had from Via Caradosso (HX 49).

Cenacolo ⊘ – In the former refectory *(cenacolo)* of the monastery is the famous painting of *The Last Supper*★★★ by **Leonardo da Vinci**, a fresco painted between 1485 and 1497 at the request of Ludovico il Moro. The fresco has deteriorated badly as a result of the passing years, and this together with certain mistakes on the part of the artist (he chose the coldest wall in the room) meant that long-term restoration work had to be instigated in 1976.

Opposite the fresco is a superb *Crucifixion*★ (1495) by Montorfano.

★★ **Basilica di Sant'Ambrogio** (HX) – The basilica was founded at the end of the 4C by St Ambrose and it is a magnificent example of the 11C-12C Lombard-Romanesque style with its pure lines and fine **atrium**★ adorned with capitals. The façade pierced by arcading is flanked by a 9C campanile to the right and a 12C one to the left. The doorway was renewed in the 18C and has 9C bronze panels. In the crypt, behind the chancel, lie the remains of St Ambrose, St Gervase and St Protase.

Inside the basilica there is a magnificent Byzantine-Romanesque **ambo**★ (12C) to the left of the nave, and at the high altar a precious gold-plated **altar front**★★ which is a masterpiece of the Carolingian period (9C). In the chapel of San Vittore in Ciel d'Oro *(at the end of the south transept)* there are remarkable 5C **mosaics**★. From the far end of the north transept one can gain access to Bramante's portico.

★ **Sant'Eustorgio** (JY) – The Romanesque basilica, dedicated to St Eustorgius, was founded in the 9C and belonged to the Dominicans. The side chapels were added in the 15C. Behind the choir is a chapel, the **Cappella Portinari**★★, a jewel of the Renaissance style by the Florentine, Michelozzo. The architecture, frescoes illustrating the life and martyrdom of St Peter by Vincenzo Foppa, and sculpture (richly carved marble tomb, 1339) by Giovanni di Balduccio, are all in complete harmony.

★ **Basilica di San Satiro** (MZ) – With the exception of the 9C square campanile and the west front, which dates from 1871, the basilica, like the baptistery, was designed by Bramante. The architect adopted a totally Classical idiom to solve the problem posed by lack of space, skilfully integrating gilded stucco and *trompe-l'œil* work to create the impression of a chancel. The **dome**★ is also remarkable. The basilica also includes a small Oriental-style chapel on the plan of a Greek Cross, decorated with a 15C painted terracotta statue of the *Descent from the Cross* and fragments of 9C-12C frescoes.

★ **Ca'Granda-Ex Ospedale Maggiore** (NZ) – The hospital, founded by Francesco Sforza in 1456, was completed in the 17C and is at present occupied by various University faculties. It is composed of three different ranges and five courtyards; the loggias of the façades are decorated with the busts of famous men.

In the Brera district, the church of **San Marco** (KV) is also open to the public. It was rebuilt in 1286 over much older foundations. It houses an interesting black and white fresco painted by the Leonardo da Vinci School *(north aisle)* representing a *Madonna and Child with St John the Baptist*. It was discovered in 1975.

Not far away is the **Basilica di San Simpliciano (JV)**, built in 385 AD on the orders of St Ambrose, Bishop of Milan. A few extensions were made to the Paleo-Christian basilica during the Early Middle Ages and the Romanesque period. On the vaulting in the apse is a *Coronation of the Virgin* by Bergognone (1481-1522).

Both these churches host excellent concerts.

★★ **San Maurizio** (or **Monastero Maggiore**) **(JX)** – This is a monastery church built in the Lombard-Renaissance style (early 16C). The bare façade, which often goes unnoticed on Corso Magenta despite the narrowness of the pavement, conceals an interior divided into two, well-lit sections and entirely decorated with **frescoes**★ by Bernardino Luini. To reach the chancel (where concerts are held), take the passageway situated to the left at the back of the church.

Opposite is the **Palazzo Litta** with its 18C façade.

Museo Civico di Archeologia (JX M⁵) ⊘ – *15 Corso Magenta.* The museum housed in the extant buildings of the great Benedictine monastery is divided into five sections: Roman and Barbarian art on the ground floor and Greek, Etruscan and Indian (Gandhara) art in the basement. The most outstanding Roman exhibits are the 4C **Trivulzio cup**★ with fine openwork cut from a single piece of glass, and the large **silver platter from Parabiago**★ (4C) featuring the festival of the goddess Cybele.

There are interesting remains of the 3C Roman wall in the garden.

★ **Basilica di San Lorenzo Maggiore (JY)** – The basilica was founded in the 4C and rebuilt in the 12C and 16C. It has kept its original octagonal plan. In front of the façade is a majestic **portico**★ of 16 Roman columns, all that remains of the Roman town of Mediolanum. The majestic interior is in the Byzantine-Romanesque style and has galleries exclusively reserved for women, a vast dome and spacious ambulatory. From the south side of the chancel pass through the atrium and then a 1C Roman doorway to a chapel, the **Cappella di Sant'Aquilino**★ ⊘ dating from the 4C. It has retained its original plan and the paleo-Christian mosaics.

Further on, the **Porta Ticinese (JY)**, a vestige of the 14C ramparts, leads to the attractive quarter (Naviglio Grande), where the artists gather.

EXCURSION

★ **Abbazia di Chiaravalle** ⊘ – *7km – 4 miles southeast. Leave by Porta Romana* (**LY**) *then consult the plan of the built-up area in the current Michelin Red Guide Italia.*

The abbey, founded by St Bernard of Clairvaux (hence Chiaravalle) in 1135, is dominated by an elegant polygonal **bell tower**★. It is an early example of Gothic architecture in Italy. Brick and white stone are combined in the typical Cistercian style. The porch was a 17C addition. Inside, there are a nave and two aisles and 14C frescoes on the dome. Another fresco in the south transept represents the Tree of the Benedictine Saints. The small cloisters are delightful.

Book well in advance
accommodation is often scarce in the high season

MODENA★

Emilia-Romagna – Population 177 121
Michelin map 988 fold 14, 428, or 429 I 14
Town plan in the current Michelin Red Guide Italia

Modena, situated between the Secchia and Panaro Rivers, at the junction of the Via Emilia and the Brenner Autostrada, is an active commercial and industrial centre (manufacture of shoes and cars and railway engineering) and one of the most important towns in Emilia-Romagna. However, Modena with its archbishopric and university, remains a quiet town whose old quarter in the vicinity of the cathedral is adorned by several spacious squares lined with arcades. It is in this part of the town that one finds such gastronomic specialities as *zamponi* (stuffed pigs' trotters) and Lambrusco, a sparkling red wine which is produced locally.

The original Roman colony of Mutina then became independent before becoming part of the Lombard League *(see Index)*, falling under the domination of the Estes from Ferrara to avoid being ruled by Bologna. In 1453 the duchy of Modena was created for Borso d'Este. In 1598 they were expelled from Ferrara by the pope and they took refuge at Modena which reached the peak of its prosperity during the 17C.

SIGHTS

★★★ **Duomo** – The cathedral is dedicated to St Geminian and is one of the best examples of Romanesque architecture in Italy. Here the Lombard architect, Lanfranco, gave vent to his sense of rhythm and proportion. The *maestri campionesi (see (Index)* put the finishing touches to his work. Most of the sculptural decoration is due to Wiligelmo, a 12C Lombard sculptor.

The façade is divided into three parts, reflecting the interior with its nave and two side aisles. It is crowned by the Angel of Death carrying a fleur-de-lys, a work carried out by the *"campionesi"* masters. Above the Gothic rose window designed by Anselmo da Campione (13C) the symbols of the four Evangelists surround a sculpture of the Saviour. A gallery with 12 columns topped with decorated capitals and punctuated by triple bays flanks a small structure. The central portal is enhanced by a porch supported by two lions by Wiligelmo whose name can be seen on one of the stones to the left of the portal. The doorway also includes the date 1099, the year in which the church was founded. The low reliefs above the side doors and to each side of the central portal depict episodes from the Book of Genesis: the Creation and the life of Adam and Eve, Cain and Abel, and Noah's Ark. The south side overlooking the square is remarkable for its architectural rhythm. From left to right, are the Prince's Doorway carved by Wiligelmo, the Royal Entrance, a gem carved by the *campionesi* masters in the 13C and a 16C pulpit decorated with the symbols of the four Evangelists. To reach the other side of the church, walk under the Gothic arches linking the cathedral to the huge Romanesque campanile built of white marble (88m – 286ft) known as Ghirlandina because of the bronze garland on its weather-vane. On the north side is the Fishmarket Door, so-called because it used to lie near the fish market at the bishop's palace; it was carved by the Wiligelmo School. The recessed orders of the arches are decorated with episodes from the Breton cycle, the architrave with imaginary animals. On the inside of the pilasters are the Labours of the months.

The interior of the cathedral reveals the ebullience of Gothic churches and the simplicity of Romanesque architecture. It has ogival vaulting. The great arches are supported on alternating mighty brick pillars and on more slender pillars. The walls are punctuated with a gallery broken up by triple bays. In the north aisle beyond the Statuine Altar (with small statues), there is a 14C pulpit and, opposite this, a rough wooden seat traditionally said to have been used by the public executioner. The choir stalls in the presbytery, the work of Lendinara, date from the 15C. The **rood screen★★★**, a Romanesque masterpiece, surmounted by a 12C Crucifix is supported by Lombardy lions and the pulpit rests on small telamones; they are both works by *"campionesi"* masters dating from 12C-13C. The parapet is decorated with scenes from Christ's Passion.

The crypt has a large number of slender columns. It contains a terracotta sculpture group of the *Holy Family* (15C) and St Germiniano's tomb. In the south aisle of the church is an exquisite 16C terracotta Nativity scene.

A museum **(museo del Duomo)** ⊘ contains the famous 12C **metopes★★**, low reliefs which used to surmount the flying buttresses. They represent wandering players or symbols incomprehensible today, but whose modelling, balance and style have an almost classical air.

Palazzo dei Musei – This 18C palace contains the two most important art collections gathered by the Este family.

★ **Biblioteca Estense** ⊘ – *1st floor, staircase on the right.* This is one of the richest libraries in Italy, containing 600 000 books and 15 000 manuscripts, the most interesting of which are on display. The prize exhibit is the **Bible of Borso d'Este**. It has 1 020 pages illuminated by a team of 15C Ferrara artists, including Taddeo Crivelli.

★★ **Galleria Estense** ⊘ – This excellent gallery comprises 14C Emilian, 15C Venetian (Cima da Conegliano), Ferrarese (notably the astonishing *St Anthony* by Cosima Tura) and Florentine (Lorenzo di Credi) works. The 16C is represented by Veronese, Tintoretto, Bassano, El Greco, Correggio, Il Parmigianino, Dosso Dossi, as well as by the local artist, Nicolò dell' Abbate. The 17C is illustrated by the Emilian painters, the Carracci and the followers of Caravaggio, while the 18C includes Venetian landscape painters. The foreign schools are also well represented. Among the sculptures, note a powerful bust of Francesco I d'Este by Bernini.

The glass cabinets display around 100 **coins and medals**, several of which were executed by the Verona artist Pisanello. These form only a fraction of the remarkable collection (35 000 items) belonging to the Gallery.

★ **Palazzo Ducale** – This noble and majestic building, the ducal palace, was begun in 1634 for Francesco I d'Este and has an elaborately elegant design. Today it is occupied by the Infantry and Cavalry schools.

EXCURSIONS

Abbazia di Nonantola ⊙ - *11km - 7 miles north*. The abbey was founded in the 8C and flourished during the Middle Ages. The 12C abbey church has some remarkable **Romanesque sculpture★** carved by Wiligelmo's assistants in 1121.

Carpi - *18km - 11 miles north*. This attractive small town has a 16C Renaissance cathedral by Peruzzi, overlooking **Piazza dei Martiri★**. The **Castello dei Pio★** ⊙, an imposing building bristling with towers, includes a courtyard by Bramante and contains a small museum. The 12C-16C Church of Sagra has a tall Romanesque campanile, **Torre della Sagra**.

Abbazia di MONTECASSINO★★

MONTE CASSINO ABBEY – Lazio
Michelin map 988 fold 27 or 430 R 23

The access road to one of the holy places of Roman Catholicism climbs in hairpin bends, affording remarkable views of the valley. The monastery of Monte Cassino, the mother house of the Benedictines, was founded in 529 by St Benedict (d 547). It was here that the saint drew up a complete and precise set of rules combining intellectual study and manual labour with the virtues of chastity, obedience and poverty. In the 11C under Abbot Didier the abbey's influence was at its height. The monks were skilled in the arts of miniatures, frescoes and mosaics and their work greatly influenced Cluniac art.

The abbey has been destroyed four times since its foundation, including at the **Battle of Cassino** (October 1943 - May 1944). After the Allies had taken Naples, the Germans made Cassino the key stronghold in the system of defences guarding the approaches to Rome. The assaults against this bastion failed, despite the great heroism and heavy losses of the Polish Corps. This brought about heavy bombardment from the air by the Americans and the destruction of the abbey. Then the 5th US Army proceeded to attack but without breaking the deadlock. Following a crucial action by the French army which suffered heavy casualties, and an attempt by British troops to surround the German position, the final assault, with the Polish Corps as the spearhead, was launched on 17 May. After a raging battle, the Germans abandoned Cassino on the following day, allowing the Allies to join forces and leaving open the road to Rome. The abbey has been rebuilt to the original plans as a truncated square building with massive underpinnings, and once again crowns the summit of Monte Cassino.

★★ **Abbey** ⊙ - It is preceded by a suitably solemn suite of four communicating cloisters. The bare façade of the basilica quite belies the sumptuousness of the **interior★★** where marble, stucco, mosaics and gilding create a dazzling if somewhat austere ensemble in the 17C-18C style. The chancel has lovely 17C walnut stalls and the marble tomb enshrining the remains of St Benedict.

★★ **Museo** ⊙ - The museum presents documents on the abbey's history and works of art which survived the 1944 bombing.

On the way down to Cassino are a museum, the **Museo archeologico nazionale** ⊙, and the neighbouring excavation site (amphitheatre, theatre and tomb of Umidia Quadratilla).

MICHELIN GREEN GUIDES

Art and Architecture
Ancient monuments
Scenic routes
Landscape
Geography
History
Touring programmes
Plans of towns and buildings

A selection of guides for holidays at home and abroad

MONTECATINI TERME‡‡‡

Tuscany – Population 20 671

Michelin map 988 fold 14, 428, 429, 430 K 14

Town plan in the current Michelin Red Guide Italia

Montecatini is one of Italy's most frequented and most fashionable thermal spas and specialises in treating stomach, intestinal and liver ailments. There is an interesting museum of modern art **(Museo dell'Accademia d'Arte)** ⊘ which has works by Italian artists (Guttaso, Primo Conti, Messina) and some of the personal belongings of Verdi and Puccini.

Montecatini Terme

EXCURSION

★★ **Collodi** – *15km – 9 miles west.* Collodi was the pen-name adopted by Carlo Lorenzini, the author of *Pinocchio*, whose mother was born in the village. A park, **Parco di Pinocchio★** ⊘, in the form of a maze is laid out on the banks of the Pescia River.

★★ **Villa Garzoni** ⊘ – The villa is an amazing building dating from the Baroque period and the 17C. In the **gardens★★★** are vistas, pools, clipped trees, grottoes, sculpture and mazes creating a charming and imaginative spectacle.

MONTEFALCO★

Umbria – Population 5 486

Michelin map 988 fold 16 or 430 N 19

14C ramparts still girdle this charming little town, which lies among vineyards and olive groves. It is perched – as its name suggests – like a falcon on its nest and has been called the Balcony of Umbria. Owing to its strategic position it was destroyed by the Emperor Frederick II and then coveted for two centuries by the popes. Montefalco, won over to Christianity in 390 by St Fortunatus, has its own saint, Clara, not to be confused with the companion of St Francis of Assisi.

The ring road (Circonvallazione) affords remarkable views of the Clitumnus Basin.

Torre Comunale ⊘ – From the top (110 steps) of the Communal Tower there is a beautiful **panorama★★★** of nearly the whole of Umbria.

San Francesco ⊘ – This Franciscan church has been converted into a museum. The mid-15C **frescoes★★** by the Florentine Benozzo Gozzoli are full of freshness and colourful realism. In addition there are frescoes by Perugino and Francesco Melanzio (15C-16C), a native of Montefalco.

Santa Illuminata – The church is Renaissance in style. The tympanum of the main doorway and several niches in the nave were painted by Francesco Melanzio.

Sant'Agostino – *Corso G. Mameli*. The church, dedicated to St Augustine, is Gothic with frescoes by Umbrian painters of the 14C, 15C and 16C.

San Fortunato – *1km – 1/2 mile south*. The church is preceded by a small 14C colonnaded courtyard. On the tympanum of the doorway Benozzo Gozzoli painted a **fresco★** showing the Madonna between St Francis and St Bernardino. Inside, the south altar is adorned with another fresco by Gozzoli of St Fortunatus.

Abbazia di MONTE OLIVETO MAGGIORE★★

MONTE OLIVETO MAGGIORE ABBEY – Tuscany

Michelin map 988 fold 15 or 430 M 16 – 36km – 22 miles southeast of Siena

The extensive rose-coloured brick buildings of this famous **abbey** ⊙ lie hidden among cypresses, in a countryside of eroded hillsides. Monte Oliveto is the Mother House of the Olivetans, a congregation of the Benedictine Order which was founded in 1313 by Blessed Bernard Tolomei of Siena.

Chiostro Grande – The great cloisters are decorated with a superb cycle of 36 **frescoes★★** depicting the life of St Benedict by **Luca Signorelli** from 1498 and by **Il Sodoma** from 1505 to 1508. The frescoes begin on the right by the west door at the great arch, with two of Sodoma's masterpieces: Christ of the Column and Christ bearing His Cross. The majority of the frescoes are by Il Sodoma, a refined artist, who was influenced by Leonardo da Vinci and Perugino *(see Index)* and shows great interest in the flattering representation of different human types, landscapes and picturesque details, as illustrated in the following frescoes: no 4 depicting St Benedict receiving his hermit's robe; no 12 the saint greeting two young men in a crowd – the people are shown in different poses; no 19 voluptuous courtesans have been sent to seduce the monks (splendid architectural elements open onto a long perspective). Signorelli *(see Index)*, who completed only eight frescoes, is more concerned with the powerful, sculptural nature of the figures and the dramatic effect of the compositions where landscape is only secondary: in no 24 St Benedict resuscitates a monk who has fallen off a wall.

The cloisters lead to the refectory (15C), the library and the pharmacy.

Chiesa abbaziale – The interior of the abbey church was remodelled in the Baroque style in the 18C. The nave is encircled by inlaid **stalls★★** (1505) by Fra Giovanni da Verona. Access to the crib is to the right of the chancel.

MONTEPULCIANO★★

Tuscany – Population 13 846

Michelin map 988 fold 15 or 430 M 17

Montepulciano, perched on the crest of a hill of volcanic rock, with impressive **views★★** in between valleys, has numerous religious and secular buildings influenced by the Florentine Renaissance. Inhabitants of Chiusi, fleeing from the Barbarian invasion, founded the town in the 6C. This was the birthplace of **Politian** (1454-94), one of the most exquisite Renaissance poets. The poet was a great friend of Lorenzo de' Medici, whom he called Lauro (Laurel) and whom he saved from assassination during the Pazzi Conspiracy *(see Duomo in FIRENZE)*. The *Stanzas*, Politian's masterpiece, describe a sort of Garden of Delight haunted by attractive women. Politian's verse matches the painting of his friend Botticelli.

★ **Città antica** – Beyond the gateway, Porta al Prato, the high street, the first part of which bears the name Via Roma, loops through the monumental area in the old town. At no 91 Via Roma stands the 16C **Palazzo Avignonesi** attributed to Vignola; no 73, the palace of the antiquarian Bucelli, is decorated with stone from Etruscan and Roman buildings; further along, the **Renaissance façade★** of the church of **Sant'Agostino** was designed by Michelozzo (15C); a tower opposite has a Pulcinello as Jack. At the Logge del Mercato (Grain Exchange) bear left into Via di Voltaia nel Corso: Palazzo Cervini (no 21) is a fine example of Florentine Renaissance architecture with its rusticated stonework and curvilinear and triangular pediments designed by Antonio da Sangallo, a member of an illustrious family of architect-sculptors, who designed some of the most famous buildings in Montepulciano. Continue along Via dell'Opio nel Corso and Via Poliziano (no 1 is the poet's birthplace).

★★ **Piazza Grande** - Forming the centre of the city, this square with its irregular plan and varying styles avoids architectural monotony while blending into a harmonious whole. The Town Hall **(Palazzo Comunale★)** is a Gothic building which was remodelled in the 15C by Michelozzo. From the top of the square tower **(torre)** ⊘ there is an immense **panorama★★★** of the town and its environs. The majestic Renaissance **Palazzo Nobili-Tarugi★** facing the cathedral is attributed to Antonio da Sangallo the Elder. The palace has a portico and great doorway with semicircular arches; six Ionic columns, standing on a lofty base, support the pilasters of the upper storey. The square also has an attractive **well★** adorned with an admirable sculpture of lion supporters holding aloft the Medici coat of arms. Inside the 16C-17C cathedral **(Duomo)** to the left of the west door lies the recumbent figure of Bartolomeo Aragazzi, secretary to Pope Martin V; the statue was part of a monument by Michelozzo (15C), as were the low reliefs of the two first pillars and the statues flanking the high altar. The monumental **altarpiece★** (1401) above the high altar is by the Sienese artist, Taddeo di Bartolo.

Museo civico-Pinacoteca Crociani ⊘ - *Via Ricci.* There is a fine collection of glazed terracotta by Andrea della Robbia; Etruscan remains and paintings dating from the 13C to 18C.

Continue along the high street to Piazza San Francesco for a fine **view** of the surrounding countryside and of the church of San Biagio. Walk down Via del Poggiolo and turn right into Via dell'Erbe to return to the Logge del Mercato.

★★ **Madonna di San Biagio** - *1km - 1/2 mile. Leave by the Porta al Prato and then take the Chianciano road before turning right.* This splendid church built in pale-coloured stone and consecrated in 1529 is an architectural masterpiece by **Antonio da Sangallo.** The building, which was greatly influenced by Bramante's design for St Peter's in Rome (it was not executed in full owing to Bramante's death - *see ROME : St Peter's Basilica*), is a useful example of Bramante's concepts. San Biagio's design is simpler although it is planned in the shape of a Greek cross and is crowned by a dome. Two campaniles flank the main façade; one is unfinished and the other includes the three architectural orders (Doric, Ionic and Corinthian). The south transept is prolonged by a semicircular sacristy. The interior gives the same impression of majesty and nobility. To the left of the west door is a 14C Annunciation. The 16C marble high altar is imposing. Opposite the church stands the Canonica (canonry), an elegant porticoed building.

EXCURSION

♯♯ **Chianciano Terme** - *10km - 6 miles southeast.* This fashionable thermal spa is pleasantly situated with many hotels. The healing properties of its waters were known to the Etruscans and the Romans. There are some fine shady parks.

MONTE SANT'ANGELO★

Puglia - Population 15 051

Michelin map 988 fold 28 or 431 B 29 - Local map p 105

Monte Sant'Angelo stands in a wonderful **site★★**. The town is built on a spur (803m - 2 634ft) dominated by the massive form of its castle and overlooks both the Gargano Promontory and the sea. It was in a nearby cave between 490 and 493 that the Archangel Michael, chief of the Heavenly Host, appeared three times to the bishop of Siponto. After a further apparition in the 8C it was decided to found an abbey. During the Middle Ages all the Crusaders came to pray to the Archangel Michael, the saintly warrior, before embarking at Manfredonia.

On 29 September the annual feast day includes the procession of the Archangel's Sword.

★ **Santuario di San Michele** - The church dedicated to St Michael, designed in the transitional Romanesque-Gothic style, is flanked by a detached octagonal campanile dating from the late 13C. Opposite the entrance a long covered stairway leads up to the very beautiful and richly worked **bronze door★** which is of Byzantine origin and dates from 1076. It gives access to both the nave with pointed vaulting which opens onto the cave (to the right) in which St Michael is said to have made his apparition. The marble statue of the saint is by Andrea Sansovino (16C) and the 11C episcopal throne is decorated in a style characteristic of Puglia.

★ **Tomba di Rotari** ⊘ - *Go down the stairs opposite the campanile.* The tomb is to the left of the apse of the ruined Church of St Peter's. Above the entrance are scenes from the Life of Christ. Inside, the tower rises in stages through a square, an octagon and finally a triangle to the dome. The tomb was supposed to contain the remains of Rotharis, a 7C King of the Lombards, but is really a 12C baptistery.

Santa Maria Maggiore - *Left of Tomba di Rotari.* The church built in Apulian Romanesque style boasts a fine doorway. Inside there are traces of the Byzantine frescoes which covered the walls. Note the figure of St Michael in the south aisle.

MONZA

Lombardy – Population 120 464
Michelin map 988 fold 3, 219 fold 19 or 428 F 9

Monza is quite an attractive industrial town specialising mainly in textiles. It stands on the edge of the Brianza, a lovely green hilly area dotted with lakes, attractive towns and villas set in lovely gardens.

★ **Duomo** – This cathedral was built in the 13C-14C and has an attractive Lombard **façade**★★ (1390-96) in alternating white, green and black marble, which is remarkable for its harmonious proportions and variety of openings. It was the work of Matteo da Campione, one of the famous *maestri campionesi (see Index)*, who spread the Lombard style throughout Italy.
The **interior**★ was remodelled in the 17C. The splendid silver gilt **altar front**★ dates from the 14C. To the left of the chancel is the Chapel of the Queen of the Longobards, Theodolinda (6C-7C), with its fascinating 15C **frescoes**★ depicting scenes in the life of this pious sovereign.
The treasury **(tesoro)**★ ⊙ has the famous 5C-9C **Iron Crown**★★ of the Kings of Lombardy, which was offered by Pope Gregory I the Great to the queen. In addition there are fine pieces of 6C to 9C plate, 17C reliquaries and 16C tapestries.

★★ **Parco di Villa Reale** – The majestic neo-Classical royal villa was the residence of Eugène de Beauharnais and Umberto I of Italy, who was assassinated at Monza by an anarchist in 1900. This vast park is landscaped in the English manner. In the northern part of the park there are several sporting facilities and the Monza racing circuit which is the venue for the annual Grand Prix Formula One race.

NAPOLI★★★

NAPLES – Campania – Population 1 068 927
Michelin map 988 fold 27 or 431 E 24 – Local map see Golfo di Napoli
Plan of built-up area in the current Michelin Red Guide Italia

The beauties and surprises of Naples have been praised by innumerable poets and writers. The lovely bay, with its horizon bounded by Posillipo, the islands, the Sorrento Peninsula and lofty Vesuvius, is one of the most beautiful in the world. Its fame has also been enhanced by the area's attractive climate and the special atmosphere evoked by the streetlife, a world of fantasy and superstition, magic and fate. This is why it is important to experience the everyday life of the Neopolitans (so vital, vivacious yet fatalistic and sad) as well as the sights of historical interest. It is Naples' streetlife which gives this town its theatrical character.
Even if the chaotic traffic and the industrial quarters to the East might be disappointing, it is a city rich with artistic interest waiting to be explored and it is well worth persevering. However, when visiting areas of historical interest like Spaccanapoli or via Tribunale visitors are vulnerable to petty crime: visitors are advised to avoid attracting undue attention to themselves by either behaviour or dress, to leave nothing of value in the car and to be on the alert at all times.

HISTORICAL NOTES

According to legend, the siren Parthenope gave her name to a town which had sprung up round her tomb, which is why Naples is called the Parthenopaean City. In fact, Naples originated as a Greek colony named Neapolis, conquered by the Romans in the 4C BC. Rich inhabitants of Rome like Virgil, Augustus, Tiberius, Nero etc used to spend the winter there, but the Neapolitans themselves retained the Greek language and customs until the decline of the Empire.
Since the 12C seven princely families have reigned over Naples: the Normans, Hohenstaufens, Angevins, Aragonese, Spanish and Bourbons. The French Revolution of 1789 brought in French troops, and in 1799 a **Parthenopaean Republic** was set up, followed by a French kingdom (1806-15) under Joseph Bonaparte (Napoleon's brother) and afterwards Joachim Murat (Napoleon's brother-in-law), both of whom promoted excellent reforms. From 1815 to 1860 the restored Bourbons remained in power in spite of the 1820 and 1848 revolts.

ART IN NAPLES

A royal patron of the arts – Under the princes of the House of Anjou, Naples was endowed with many ecclesiastical buildings, which were greatly influenced by the French Gothic style. "**Good King Robert" of Anjou** (1309-43) attracted poets, scholars and artists from various regions of Italy to his court in Naples. Boccaccio spent part of his youth in Naples where he fell in love with Fiammetta, whom some believe to have been the king's own daughter. His friend Petrarch also spent some time

Ferdinand of Aragon's fleet in Naples harbour (15C)

in this city. In 1324 Robert the Wise brought the Sienese sculptor Tino di Camaino to adorn many of the churches with his monumental tombs. Other churches were embellished with frescoes by the Roman artist Pietro Cavallini, slightly later by Giotto whose works have unfortunately disappeared, and by Simone Martini.

The Neapolitan School of Painting (17C - early 18C) – The busiest period in Neapolitan painting was the 17C which began with the arrival in Naples in 1607 of the great innovator in painting, **Caravaggio**. The master's style was bold and realistic: he often used real people as models for his crowd scenes. He used chiaroscuro with dramatic effect with light playing a fundamental part. So a new school of painting flourished, its members greatly inspired by the master. The principal followers were Artemisia Gentileschi, the Spaniard **José Ribera** alias Spagnoletto, **Caracciolo** and the Calabrian Mattia Preti. One pupil who differed greatly from the others was **Luca Giordano** whose spirited compositions were full of light. His decorative work heralds the painting of the 18C. **Francesco Solimena** perpetuated the former's style but he was also influenced by the more sombre style of Mattia Preti and by Classicism drawing inspiration from Arcadia. His paintings are characterised by chiaroscuro effects which lend solidity to shapes and a strong balance to the use of space. There are examples of this artist's works in several churches in Naples including the Church of San Nicola alla Carità (**KY**).

Original works – Numerous were the architects who built fine Baroque buildings in Naples and the surrounding area. **Ferdinando Sanfelice** (1675-1748) had a highly inventive and theatrical approach to staircases, which he placed at the far end of the courtyard where they became the palace's most important decorative feature. It was, however, **Luigi Vanvitelli** (1700-73) who was the great Neapolitan architect of the 18C. The Bourbon King, Charles III, entrusted Vanvitelli with the project to build another Versailles at Caserta *(see CASERTA)*.
It was in the 17C that Naples began to specialise in the marvellous **cribs** *(presepi)* which were to become very famous.

Music and theatre – Neapolitans have always shown a great love of music, be it for **opera** where great importance is placed on the virtuosity of the singer, or for more **popular music**, sometimes joyful, sometimes melancholy, practised to the accompaniment of a guitar or a mandolin. Naples gave the character Scaramouch (old fox) to the *Commedia dell' Arte (see BERGAMO)* as well as Pulcinella which is the true Neapolitan face.

Religious festivals – In Naples these are sumptuous and the best known are the Festivals of Madonna di Piedigrotta, Santa Maria del Carmine and especially the Feast of the Miracle of St Januarius. Between Christmas and Epiphany (Twelfth Night) the local churches are adorned with splendid cribs. *See the Calendar of Events at the end of the guide.*

IN THE STREETS OF NAPLES

The Neapolitans, who often bear a striking resemblance to the Greeks, speak a very expressive dialect in a sing-song way. They have lively imaginations (they fear the Evil Eye – *jettatura*) and readily give vent to their emotions. Religious festivals are numerous and very popular and even sporting events, in particular football matches, become a pretext for outrageous behaviour.

There are numerous novels and films which have captured the peculiarities of the Neapolitans and their way of life. Popular scenes which used to charm the tourists are now a thing of the past. Traffic is hectic. The town with its narrow streets is ill-suited to heavy traffic but cars weave in and out frenetically and only the genius for improvisation, the daring and virtuosity of Neapolitan drivers compensate for their lack of discipline.

The quarters – The busy port handles more passengers than any other in Italy but is second to Genoa in goods traffic. The city centre extends around **Piazza del Plebiscito** and the **Galleria Umberto I** (**JKZ**). The working-class quarters, with their streets set close together and hung with washing, are to be found in the Spaccanapoli (Old Naples) and in the area to the west of the Via Toledo (**KY**), the Spanish quarter where the steep narrow streets run parallel to each other. To the west of the town lie the residential areas spread over the hillsides of **Vomero** and **Posillipo** *(see Index)*.

B. Morand/DIAF

Galleria Umberto I, Napoli

★★ CITY CENTRE *2 1/2 hours*

★★ **Castel Nuovo** (or **Maschio Angiono**) (**KZ**) ⊙ – This imposing castle, surrounded by deep moats, was built in 1282 by Pierre de Chaulnes and Pierre d'Agincourt, the architects of Charles I of Anjou. It was modelled on the castle at Angers. A remarkable **triumphal arch**★★ embellishes the entrance on the town side. This masterpiece bearing sculptures to the glory of the House of Aragon, was built to designs by Francesco Laurana in 1467. Access to the **Sala dei Baroni** is via the staircase in the inner courtyard *(at the far end on the left)*. The fine vaulting is star shaped, formed by the tufa groins intersecting with other architectural features. The **Cappella Palatina** (14C) features an elegant Renaissance doorway which was previously surmounted by Laurana's splendid *Virgin* now kept, along with other works by the same artist in the sacristy. The internal walls of the chapel are decorated with frescoes which have come from the Castello di Casaluce in Caserta.

★ **Teatro San Carlo** (**KZ T¹**) ⊙ – The theatre was built under Charles of Bourbon in 1737 and rebuilt in 1816 in the neo-Classical style. The opera house is an important institution in the Italian world of music.
The splendid auditorium, with boxes on six levels and a large stage, is built entirely of wood and stucco to achieve perfect acoustics.

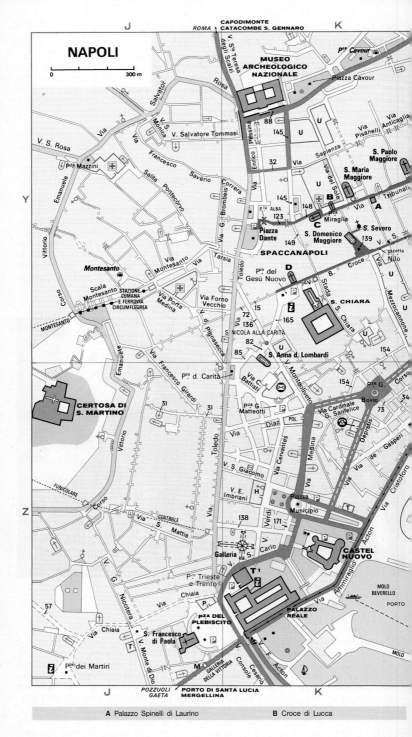

A Palazzo Spinelli di Laurino   B Croce di Lucca

★ **Piazza del Plebiscito** (JKZ) – This noble semicircular "square" (19C) is enclosed on one side by the royal palace, on the other by the neo-Classical façade of the Church of St Francis of Paola (**San Francesco di Paola**), built on the model of the Pantheon in Rome and prolonged by a curving colonnade. The equestrian statues of Ferdinand I and Charles III of Bourbon are by Canova.

★ **Palazzo Reale** (KZ) ⊘ – The royal palace was built at the beginning of the 17C by the architect Domenico Fontana and has been remodelled several times. The façade retains more or less its original appearance. Since the late 19C the niches on the façade contain eight statues of the most famous Kings of Naples. A huge **staircase** with twin ramps and crowned by a coffered dome leads to the

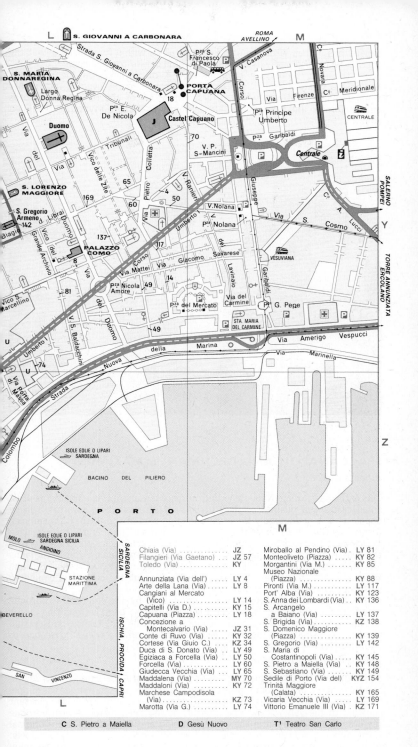

apartments★ and the sumptuously decorated **royal chapel**. It was only after 1734 that royalty lived in the apartments. The richly ornamented rooms have retained their numerous works of art, tapestries, paintings, period furniture and fine porcelain. Of particular interest are the splendid **door knockers**★ made of wood: putti, nymphs and animals are set off against a gilded background in a floral pattern.

★★ **Porto di Santa Lucia** - *Town plan in the current Michelin Red Guide Italia.* Santa Lucia is the name of the small suburb that juts out towards the sea. It is best known as the name of a tiny port, immortalised by a famous Neapolitan song, nestling between a rocky islet and the jetty linking it to the shore. **Castel dell'Ovo** is a severe edifice built by the Normans and remodelled by the Angevins in 1274.

177

Legend has it that Virgil hid a magic egg (*uovo*) within its walls and that the destruction of the egg would result in a similar fate for the castle.

From the jetty there is a splendid **view★★** of Vesuvius on the one hand and of the western side of the bay on the other. In the evening, go further along to Piazza Vittoria which offers a **view★★★** of the residential suburbs on the Vomero and Posillipo hillsides, brightly lit up by a myriad of twinkling lights.

Castel dell'Ovo

★★ SPACCANAPOLI AND DECUMANUS MAXIMUS

4 hours on foot

This is the heart of old Naples. With its numerous churches, dilapidated palaces, small crafts and businesses, and its ancient streets where swarms a lively populace, it is undoubtedly the most engaging part of the town. Its main axis, formed by the Via S. Benedetto Croce, S. Biagio dei Librai and Vicaria Vecchia is nicknamed Spaccanapoli, meaning the street which bisects Naples. It follows the course of one of the main roads through ancient Naples, the Decumanus Maximus which now more or less forms the Via Tribunali (**KLY**). Strolling through these streets is to witness Naples' evolution through the centuries, beginning with the Greeks and the Romans.

In Piazza del Gesù Nuovo, which is dominated by the impressive Baroque monument of the Virgin, is the **Church of Gesù Nuovo (KY D)** ⊘ with its fine façade and diamond pointed facing, a unique testimony to the 15C Palazzo Sanseverino nearby. The inside of the façade is decorated with Solimena's *Chasing Heliodorus from the Temple*.

Enter Via Benedetto Croce.

★ **Santa Chiara (KY)** ⊘ – Sancia of Majorca, the wife of Robert the Wise of Anjou, had this Church of the Poor Clares built in the Provençal-Gothic style. The simple façade is preceded by a porch in peperine, the grey colour of which is in pleasant contrast to the yellow tufa. The interior, having been restored with Baroque features, was destroyed in the 1943 bombing and then rebuilt in its original form. A bare, lofty nave, lit by tall, narrow twin windows, opens onto 9 chapels. At the end, in place of an apse, a long wall is lined with memorials to the Anjou dynasty: including the **tomb★★** of Robert the Wise, the work of Florentine sculptors, and the tomb of Charles of Anjou, attributed to Tino di Camaino who is also responsible for the **tomb★** of Marie de Valois *(near the south wall)*.

★ **Cloisters** – The current lay-out is the work of Domenico Antonio Vaccaro who, in the 18C, transformed the interior of the cloisters into a garden. It was divided into four parts with two covered avenues that intersect at the centre to form a cross. He was also responsible for embellishing the wall of the portico, the seats and the columns lining the avenues with fine **majolica decoration★** which features floral motifs, landscapes, pastoral scenes and mythological subjects.

San Domenico Maggiore (KY) – The church apse gives onto a square ornamented with a small Baroque votive monument *(guglia)* to St Dominic. The interior of the church has both Gothic (**caryatids** by Tino di Camaino support a huge paschal candelabrum) and Baroque features. In the side aisle to the right, the second chapel is decorated with frescoes by Pietro Cavallini (1309). The 18C sacristy lined with panelling contains numerous coffins of members of the court of Aragon.

Cappella Sansevero (KY) ⊘ – This 16C chapel was completely restored in the 18C by Raimondo de Sangro, an eccentric whose passion for alchemy and scientific study gave rise to a certain notoriety. There are even two skeletons complete with "petrified" circulatory system *(in an underground chamber, access from the south aisle)*.
In the chapel there are fine marble **sculptures★**: on either side of the choir are *Chastity* (the veiled woman) and *Despair* (the latter being symbolised by a man struggling with a net); the central one depicts the splendid *Christ covered by a shroud*, a masterpiece by Giuseppe Sammartino. The folds of a thin shroud are draped on the peaceful recumbent figure.
Just before Via S. Biagio dei Librai, is the charming **Piazzetta del Nilo**, adorned with a statue of the Nile from which it derives its name. A little further along, to the left, is the attractive Via S. Gregorio Armeno. It is lined with small shops and workshops where the small figurines for the Nativity scenes *(presepio)* are produced. The skills required have been handed down from father to son since the 19C. These days the statuettes include modern figures. The area is particularly charming around Christmas time. At the end of the street, at the bend, rises the campanile of the church of San Gregorio Armeno.

Neapolitan cuisine and specialities

Pasta, pizza, ricotta, mozzarella (buffalo milk cheese), fish and shellfish are ingredients which are commonly found in Neopolitan cooking. Typical dishes might include spaghetti served *al dente* (lightly cooked) with clams *(vongole)*, a thin, crusty pizza, deep-fried fish or a plate of sea-food such as clams and mussels. Restaurants open late into the night as Neopolitans usually dine after 10 o'clock. The famous Neopolitan pastry eaten at Christmas and Easter is filled with candied peel and ricotta and laced with a special sweet wine called *Lacrima Christi* (tears of Christ). **Scaturchio** in Spaccanapoli is the place to go for good coffee and pastries such as *sfogliatella* (flaky pastry filled with ricotta, candied fruit and spices) and *babà* which is very popular with the locals.
The local vines are grown in volcanic soil and the wines include Falerno, red and white wines from Capri, as well as the white from Ischia.

San Gregorio Armeno (LY) ⊘ – This church is dedicated to St Gregory. A spacious atrium leads onto the **interior★** of the church which is opulently Baroque in style. The frescoes along the nave and in the cupola are the work of Luca Giordano. At the end of the nave are two huge Baroque **organs**. Of particular interest in the presbytery is the high altar with intarsia work in polychrome marble and, to the right, the *comunichino*, a brass screen from behind which the nuns followed mass. The beautiful ceiling, in gilded wood, features medallions decorated by Teodoro di Enrico.
The **cloisters** (*access via the steps in the monastery*) have a splendid fountain (*centre*) decorated with statues of Christ and the Samaritan (late 18C).
At the end of Via S. Gregorio Armeno is Via dei Tribunali which runs into the Decumamo Maggiore that dates back to ancient Rome. Access to the **ruins** ⊘ is through the church of San Lorenzo Maggiore. The ruins reveal Naples' Greco-Roman history: along with the forum there are traces of the treasury, bakery and *macellum* (large covered market).

San Lorenzo Maggiore (LY) ⊘ – The Church of St Lawrence was built in the 14C over an early Christian church, the remains of which include the perimeter walls, two mosaics and the columns from the nave. Restored in the Baroque style, it was eventually returned to its original appearance after recent restoration work.

... Where to go

There are many typical pizzerie in Naples. Two of the most famous are **Trianon** at 46 Via Colletta and **Brandi** at 1 Salita Sant'Anna di Palazzo.
Of the many restaurants listed in the **Michelin Red Guide Italia**, **Ciro a Mergellina** (at 21 Via Mergellina) and **Da Ciro** (at 71 Via S.Brigida) are recommended. Both have menus which include traditional specialities. Diners are sometimes treated to live mandolin or guitar music.
For good coffee and pastries try **Gambrinus** in Piazza Trieste e Trento, **Scaturchio** in Piazza S.Domenico Maggiore, **Caflish** at 143 Via Chiaia, **La Caffettiera** in Piazza dei Martiri and **Motta** at 152 Via Toledo.

It is built on the plan of a Latin cross with an elegant **arch**★ that spans the transept crossing. The nave, a simple, austere rectangular space (except for a chapel on the west wall which has kept its splendid Baroque additions) is a testament to the Franciscan influence. The **polygonal apse**★ is an interesting specimen of French Gothic architecture in southern Italy. It is surmounted by elegant arches crowned by twin bays and terminates in an ambulatory onto which open chapels with frescoes by disciples of Giotto. The north transept houses a large chapel dedicated to St Anthony and, at the altar, a painting of the saint surrounded by angels (1438), on a gold background. To the right of the high altar is the remarkable **tomb**★ of Catherine of Austria, attributed to Tino di Camaino.

The **chapter-house** *(access from the south transept)*, with its frescoed walls and vault, houses a unique "illustrated bible" – terracotta figurines placed inside nutshells which date from the 1950s.

★★ **Decumanus Maximus** (KY) ⊘ – Turn right to get to **Pio Monte della Misericordia** (17C) which houses six panels; the themes are linked to the charitable works carried out by the institute. Of particular interest are *St Peter freed from Prison* by Caracciolo and the fine *The Seven Works of Mercy*★★★ by **Caravaggio**.

Then return to the Girolamini monument and, a little further on, to the Church of **San Paolo Maggiore**. In front is a splendid flight of steps; the interior is Baroque and very ornate; note the polychrome altar. The sacristy houses two fine frescoes by **Solimena**: *The Fall of Simon Magus* and *St Paul on the road to Damascus*. Further along, to the right, is the Church of **Santa Maria delle Anime del Purgatorio** with its tiny underground cemetery (cimitero sotterraneo) where, until recently, the unique practice of cleaning the bones was carried out for the purposes of receiving grace, a widespread practice in Naples.

At no 362 is **Palazzo Spinelli di Laurino** (**A**) with a curious elliptical courtyard embellished by one of Sanfelice's staircases.

On the parvis of the Church of **Santa Maria Maggiore**, also known as Pietrasanta, with its beautiful flooring in brick and majolica (1764) rise, to the left, the Renaissance chapel, Cappella Pontano, and, to the right, a fine campanile which dates back to the original church (11C).

Beyond **Croce di Lucca** (**B**), a 17C church with coffered ceiling of gilded wood, is the Church of **San Pietro a Maiella** (**C**). It has Gothic overtones but was restored in the 17C. Features include the fine carved choir stalls and the frescoes in the apse.

The tour ends in Piazza Bellini which is a pleasant place to spend the evening. In the centre are the ruined Greek walls. A little further on is **Piazza Dante**, overlooked by a semicircular range of buildings, the work of Vanvitelli.

★★★ MUSEO ARCHEOLOGICO NAZIONALE (KY) ⊘ *2 hours*

The National Archeological Museum occupies a 16C building which was originally intended to house the royal cavalry, and then became the seat of the university from 1610 to 1777. The collections comprise mainly works of art belonging to the Farnese family and treasures discovered at Pompeii and Herculaneum. It is one of the richest museums in the world for Greco-Roman antiquities.

★★★ **Greco-Roman sculpture** – This department is on the ground floor.

Galleria dei Tirannicidi – *Turn right on entering.* The Tyrant-Slayers' Gallery is devoted to Archaic art. The *Aphrodite Sosandra* with a fine, proud face and elegantly-draped robe is a splendid copy of a Greek bronze (5C BC), while the powerful marble group of the *Tyrant-Slayers*, a copy of a Greek bronze, represents Harmodios and Aristogiton who delivered Athens from the tyrant, Hipparchus, in the 6C BC.

Galleria dei Grandi Maestri – *Access from the Galleria dei Tirannicidi.* In the Great Masters' Gallery, Room II contains the majestic statue of the Farnese Pallas (Athena) and Orpheus and Eurydice bidding each other farewell, a low relief of touching simplicity copied from an original by Phidias (5C BC). In Room III is the *Doryphorus*, the spear-bearer, a copy of the famous bronze by Polyclitus.

Galleria del Toro Farnese – Access to the Farnese Bull Gallery is via the Galleria della Flora which houses the famous *Callipygian Venus* (1C) and two copies of *Aphrodite crouching* by Doidalsas (3C).

In the centre is the colossal *Flora farnese*. The *Warrior and Child* on the left is admirable, and in front a fine *Nike (Victory)* or statue of a woman in basalt. In the last room is the impressive sculptured group called the *Farnese Bull* depicting the death of Dirce, a legendary queen of Thebes. It was carved from a single block of marble. It is a 2C Roman copy, which like many works in the Farnese collection has undergone much restoration, thereby altering its original characteristics. In the right wing is the *Farnese Hercules*, resting after his famous labours.

Galleria dei Marmi Colorati – *To be relocated.* The most famous of the works in coloured marble is the statue of *Artemis of Ephesus* (2C) in alabaster and bronze, representing the deity venerated at the famous temple by the Aegean Sea. She is sometimes considered as a nature goddess in the oriental tradition and is represented with numerous breasts symbolising her motherly nature.

Grande Atrio – In the Great Hall, against the second pillar on the right is the statue of the priestess Eumachia, discovered at Pompeii. The robe is beautifully draped and the face expressive.

Galleria dei Ritratti greco-romani – *To be located on the right at the far end of the hall.* The Greek and Roman Portrait Gallery contains the portrait busts of Socrates, Homer, Euripides and fine portraits of Roman emperors.

★★ **Mosaics** – *To the left on the mezzanine.* Although most of these come from Pompeii, Herculaneum and Stabia they offer a wide variety of styles and subject matter. There are two small works (*Visit to a Fortune-Teller* and *Roving Musicians*) by Dioscurides of Samos along with the *Actors on stage* found in Room of the Tragic Poet *(Room LIX)*. Mosaics including a *frieze with festoons and masks* and the splendid mosaic of the **Battle of Alexander and Darius** *(Room LXI)* which paved the floor of the House of the Faun at Pompeii, are housed in Rooms LX and LXI. The latter reveals a remarkable sense of depth (rear view of a horse in the foreground) and movement (the horses champing at the bit, the lances crossed and the Persian king prostrate in front of Alexander). The collection also includes some fine examples of *opus sectile* *(Room LVII)*.

★★★ **Napoli Antica Gallery** – *To the right on the mezzanine.* The exhibits illustrate events from the ancient history of the city and include detailed descriptions, images and finds (including the two impressive **statues** from the temple of the Dioscuri, now San Paolo Maggiore). There is also a fine series of female terracotta **heads**★ (probably votive offerings) with different head-dresses *(2nd room)*. Particular attention has been paid to the description of the underground cemeteries and hypogea *(5th room)*. There is also an exhibition of utensils including bowls, amphorae, pitchers, balsam jugs and vases.

★★★ **Works from Villa di Pisone or dei Papiri** – *First floor, on the right.* The villa, which was discovered at Herculaneum in the 18C but was later reburied, is thought to have belonged to L Calpurnius Pison who was Julius Caesar's father-in-law. The owner had turned the house into a museum. The documents and splendid works of art from his collections are priceless. The Sala dei Papiri Room (CXIV) contains photographs of some of the 800 papyri from the library. In Room CXVI are exhibited **bronze statues** that adorned the peristyle of the villa: the **Drunken Faun** lost in euphoria, a **Sleeping Satyr** with a beautiful face in repose; the two lifelike **Wrestlers** are inspired from Lysippus (4C BC); the famous **Dancers from Herculaneum** are probably in fact water-carriers; the famous **Hermes at Rest**, with a tall strong figure, reflects Lysippus' ideal.

In Room CXVII, in addition to the **portrait** mistakenly identified as that of **Seneca** and one of the most remarkably expressive works handed down from antiquity, are exhibited an "Ideal Head" identified as Artemis, and the majestic statue of Athena Promachos (1C BC).

★★ **Small bronzes, silver, glass and ivory gallery** – *First floor, on the left.* These rooms are mostly dedicated to finds brought back from Pompeii and Herculaneum. Exhibits include silver found in the House of Menander, ivory ornaments, Greek arms, glass objects and small bronzes including everyday utensils *(the latter are to be redisplayed)*.

★★★ **Sala del Tempio di Iside** – *First floor, on the left, after the room above.* The room features objects and pictures from the Temple of Isis discovered behind the Great Theatre at Pompeii. Three areas have been partially reconstructed to evoke the original structure: the portico, the *ekklesiasterion* (the assembly room where the worshippers of Isis met) and the *sacrarium* (sanctuary). The frescoes on the walls illustrate a still life (figs, grapes, geese and doves are all elements linked to the worship of this Egyptian goddess and were part of the Isis cult). Of particular interest are the beautiful large panels which are well preserved and depict sacred rights and scenes illustrating the myths surrounding Io (Isis).

★★★ **Sala degli affreschi** – *First floor, on the left, at the far end.* The collection includes some splendid frescoes from Pompeii, Herculaneum and Stabiae in particular. The diversity of style and colour is a testament to the richness of this form of decorative art practised by the Romans *(see POMPEI)*. Exhibits include beautiful paintings with mythological subjects such as Heracles and Ariadne, the tragic Medea and Iphigenia, and epic poems including episodes from the Trojan war which are often inserted in architectural perspectives, friezes of cupids, satyrs and maenads. The female figures found at Stabia which represent *Leda, Medea, Flora* and *Artemis* are notable for their grace and gentleness. The medallions depicting pastoral scenes were originally in a villa at Boscotrecase.

★★ CERTOSA DI SAN MARTINO (JZ) ⊘ *1 hour*

This immense Carthusian Monastery of St Martin is beautifully situated on a spur of the Vomero hill. The **Castel Sant'Elmo**, a massive structure with bastions, overlooks the monastery to the west; it was rebuilt by the Spaniards in the 16C and was for a long time used as a prison *(now used to house temporary exhibitions)*. From the drill square *(access on foot or by lift)* there is a wonderful view over the city and the bay. The monastery was founded by the Anjou dynasty in the 14C and was almost completely remodelled in the 16C and 17C. The monastic buildings can be visited, as well as the museum which is arranged in the buildings overlooking the Procurators' Cloisters.

Church – The **interior**★★ is lavishly Baroque and is adorned with paintings by Caracciolo, Guido Reni and Simon Vouet. To the left of the choir, beyond the sacristy with its superb furnishings embellished with inlay, is the treasury decorated with frescoes by Luca Giordano and a painting by Ribera, *La Pietà*.

Great Cloisters – This harmonious ensemble is the work of the architect-sculptor Cosimo Fanzago.

★ **Museum** – The section devoted to festivals and costumes contains an exceptional collection of figurines and Neapolitan **cribs**★★ *(presepi)* in polychrome terracotta from the 18C and 19C. The collection is a wealth of objects (from baskets of fruit and vegetables in wax to animals and utensils) widely used in Neopolitan cribs: the four cribs on display are fine examples. The tour concludes with a large, impressive crib from the late 19C (some of the figures date back to the 18C). To the left of the cloisters there is also an interesting **sculpture** section including works by Tino di Camaino.

★★ PALAZZO AND GALLERIA NAZIONALE DI CAPODIMONTE ⊘ *2 hours*

The **Capodimonte Palace and Art Gallery** are on the northern outskirts of Naples: take the Via S. Teresa degli Scalzi (**JKY**).
This former **royal estate**★ extends over high ground to the north of the city. The whole includes a massive and austere palace which was built from 1738 to 1838, an extensive park, and the remains of the famous 18C porcelain factory. The palace itself has an art gallery in addition to the royal apartments.

Reorganisation of the museum is in progress; works on display range from the 12C to the 19C.

★★ **Pinacoteca** – *Main floor.* The nucleus of the holding is the Farnese collection which has been enriched over the years. The works are presented mostly in chronological order and trace the main trends in the evolution of Italian painting; there are also important works by foreign artists.
The Primitives include a dramatic *Crucifixion* by Masaccio.
The figure of Mary Magdalene in a bright red dress with arms stretched towards the cross is a fine example of perspective heralding the Renaissance, which is exemplified by the works of Botticelli *(Madonna and Child with Saints)*, Filippino Lippi and Raphael. A fine example of the Venetian school is the **Transfiguration** by Giovanni Bellini; the soft colours and light convey a sense of serenity which suffuses the landscape. Among the main exponents of Mannerism are Sebastiano del Piombo (*The Veiled Madonna* and a remarkable *Clement VII*), Pontormo and Rosso Fiorentino. Titian's study of light is exemplified in the sensual *Danae* and in the works of his pupil El Greco: light is an important feature in the *Boy lighting a candle with a firebrand*. Serenity and tenderness are evoked in a small canvas, *The Mystic Marriage of St Catherine*, by Correggio and in the *Holy Family* by Parmigianino, which stresses the essential role of the mother: the child is only partly shown. The section devoted to foreign artists includes two fine works by the Flemish master, Peter Breugel the Elder (*The Misanthrope* and *The Parable of the Blind*).
The Mystic Marriage of St Catherine by Annibale Carracci is remarkable for its harmony and elegance. In Atalanta and Hypomene, Guide Reni combines a Classical theme with movement and study of light which are typical of the 18C. Among the 17C masterpieces are a remarkable *Flagellation* by Carravaggio and *The Scourging of Christ* by Caracciolo which are housed temporarily in the Drawings and Etchings Room on the ground floor.

Royal apartments – *1st floor.* The rooms have fine furnishings. There is a Chinese-style **porcelain room**★★ executed in the 18C at Capodimonte for the royal summer residence at Portici. Of particular interest is a small **room**★ with walls faced in porcelain and decorated with flowers and scenes of Chinese inspiration. Also on view are a fine porcelain collection including the elegant Procession of Aurora in unglazed porcelain dating from the 19C, and the royal armoury.

ADDITIONAL SIGHTS

★ **Mergellina** – *Plan of the built-up area in the current Michelin Red Guide Italia.* Mergellina, at the foot of the Posillipo hillside with the small port of Sannazzaro, is one of the few places in Naples ideal for a stroll. It affords a splendid **view**★★ of the bay: the Vomero hillside, crowned by Castel Sant'Elmo, slopes down gently towards the Santa Lucia headland and Egg Castle beyond, with Vesuvius in the distance.

★ **Villa Floridiana** – *To the west of Naples. Town plan in the current Michelin Red Guide Italia.* This graceful small white palace *(palazzina)* in the neo-Classical style stands high up on the Vomero hillside and is surrounded by a fine park. The façade overlooks the gardens which afford a splendid **panorama**★.

★ **Museo Nazionale di Ceramica Duca di Martina** ⊙ – An interesting museum, housed inside the villa, displays a collection of enamels, ivories, faïence and especially porcelain.

★★ **Catacombe di San Gennaro** ⊙ – *North of Naples. Plan of the built-up area in the current Michelin Red Guide Italia.* The catacombs dug in the volcanic rock extend over two floors and consists of vast galleries illuminated by a gentle light. The galleries open out to form a "baptistery" in the lower section and a spacious basilica with three aisles (4C-6C) in the upper section. The tomb of St Januarius, whose remains were transferred here in the 6C, is decorated with frescoes of the saint. There are beautiful paintings in the niches (3C-10C). In the upper section, the vault of the atrium is adorned with early Christian work and portraits of the dead adorning the family tombs. The Bishops' Crypt above the tomb of St Januarius, contains fine mosaics depicting the bishops.

★ **Santa Maria Donnaregina** (LY) – Go through the cloisters adorned with 18C faïence. A Baroque church of the same name precedes the small 14C Gothic church which shows a French influence. Inside is the **tomb**★ of the founder, Mary of Hungary, widow of Charles II of Anjou, by Tino di Camaino. The walls of the nuns' chancel are decorated with 14C **frescoes**★.

★ **San Giovanni a Carbonara** (LY) – An 18C stairway leads to the elegant Gothic doorway of this 14C church. Inside are the tomb of Ladislas of Anjou (15C) and many works of art in two chapels, the Carracciolo del Sole behind the choir and the Carracciolo del Vico, to the left of the previous one.

★ **Porta Capuana** (LMY) – This is one of the fortified gateways in the walls built in 1484 to the plans of Giuliano da Maiano. The Capuan Castle **(Castel Capuano)** (LY) nearby was the former residence of the Norman princes and the Hohenstaufens.

Duomo (LY) – Built in the 14C, the cathedral was considerably altered at a later date. Held in great veneration by the people, the Chapel of St Januarius **(Cappella di San Gennaro)** ⊙, in a rich baroque style, is preceded by a remarkable 17C bronze grille: behind the high altar are two glass phials containing the saint's blood which is supposed to liquefy, failing which disaster will befall the town. The Feast of the **Miracle of St Januarius** is held twice annually on the first Sunday in May and on 19 September.
The dome is decorated with a Lanfranco fresco showing an admirable sense of movement. A door in the middle of the north aisle gives access to the 4C **Basilica di Santa Restituta** ⊙, which was transformed in the Gothic period and again in the 17C. At the far end of the nave, the 5C baptistery of St John (San Giovanni) is a fine structure containing mosaics of the same period.

★ **Palazzo Como** (LY) – This majestic late-15C palace, with its rusticated stonework, is a reminder of the Florentine Renaissance. It contains the **Museo Civico Filangieri** ⊙ which displays collections of arms and armour, ceramics and porcelain, furniture and paintings by Ribera, Carracciolo, Mattia Preti etc.

Sant'Anna dei Lombardi (KYZ) ⊙ – This Renaissance church, dedicated to St Anne of the Lombards, is rich in contemporary Florentine **sculpture**★. Inside is the tomb of Mary of Aragon *(1st chapel on the left)* by Antonio Rossellino and an *Annunciation (1st chapel on the right)* by Benedetto da Maiano. In the oratory to the right of the choir is a *Descent from the Cross*, a late-15C terracotta by Guido Mazzoni who introduced this style of rather theatrical realism to Naples which was to become very popular in southern Italy. The former sacristy has lovely stalls which are attributed to Fra Giovanni da Verona (1457-1525).

Villa Comunale – *Town plan in the current Michelin Red Guide Italia.* Vanvitelli laid out these public gardens along the waterfront in 1780. They are very popular with the Neapolitans for the evening walk. An aquarium stands within the gardens.

Acquario ⊙ – The aquarium presents a large variety of sea creatures to be found in the Bay of Naples.

NAPOLI

Museo Principe di Aragona Pignatelli Cortes ⊙ - *Riviera di Chiaia, in front of the Villa Comunale. Town plan in the current Michelin Red Guide Italia.* The ground floor of the summer residence of the Princess Pignatelli (she lived here until the 1950s) is open to visitors. Furnishings date back to the 19C. In the garden, the old stables house an interesting collection of carriages from the same period. The vehicles which have been very well preserved are of English, French and Italian origin.

Golfo di NAPOLI★★★

Bay of NAPLES – Campania

Michelin map 988 fold 27 or 431 E 24/25

The Bay of Naples, extending from Cumae to Sorrento, has a rich history and is one of the most beautiful Italian gulfs. It is an area of striking contrasts where one may find in close proximity isolated places conducive to meditation, such as the archeological sites, the bare slopes of Vesuvius, the Sibyl's Cave or Lake Averno, and others bustling with activity, noisy, crowded with traffic,

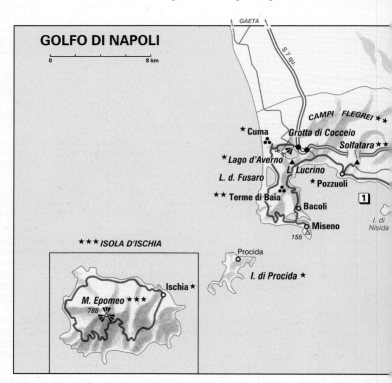

enlivened by a population which lives with the ever-present fear of earthquakes and a new volcanic eruption. Its legendary beauty is somewhat marred by the uncontrolled sprawl of industrial development which has reached the outskirts of Naples. However, its islands, capes and mountains offer unforgettable excursions.

Sightseeing – Follow the itineraries indicated on the local map below.

★★ 1 FROM NAPLES TO CUMAE

Campi Flegrei *45km – 28 miles – about 6 hours*

This volcanic area, the Phlegrean Fields, which received its name from the ancients ("phlegrean" is derived from a Greek word meaning "to blaze"), extends in an arc along the Gulf of Pozzuoli. Hot springs, steam-jets and sulphurous gases rise from the ground and from the sea, and are proof of an intense underground activity. Lakes have formed in the craters of extinct volcanoes. This stretch of coastline is subject to variations in ground level due to volcanic activity.

★★★ **Naples** – *See NAPOLI.*

★ **Posillipo** – This famous hill forms a promontory and separates the Bay of Naples from Pozzuoli Bay. Posillipo, dotted with villas and their lovely gardens and modern buildings, is Naples' main residential area. It affords splendid views of the bay.

★ **Marechiaro** – This small fishermen's village built high above the sea was made famous by a Neapolitan song *Marechiare*.

Parco Virgiliano (or **Parco della Rimembranza**) – From the Garden of Remembrance there are splendid **views**★★ over the Bay of Naples, from Cape Miseno to the Sorrento Peninsula, as well as the islands of Procida, Ischia and Capri.

★ **Pozzuoli** – *See POZZUOLI.*

★★ **Solfatara** – *See POZZUOLI: Solfatara.*

Lago Lucrino – In antiquity, oyster farming was practised here on the lake and the banks were lined with elegant villas. One of these belonged to Cicero and another was the scene of Agrippina's murder, on the orders of her son Nero.

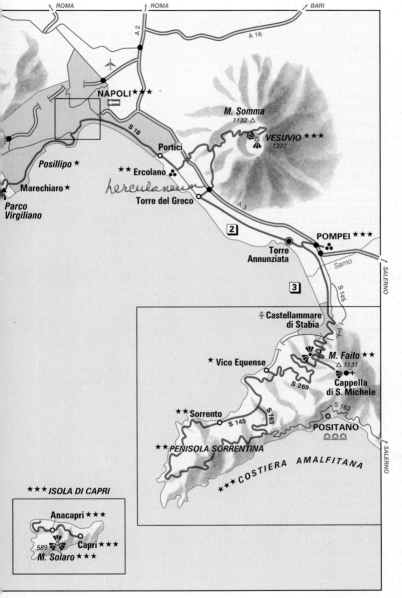

★★ **Terme di Baia** ⊙ – This Greek colony was in Roman times a fashionable beach resort, as well as a thermal spa (*terme*) with the most complete equipment in the world for hydrotherapy. The Roman emperors and patricians had immense villas, all of which disappeared under the sea after a change in ground level. However, ruins of the famous baths remain on the hilltop overlooking the sea. Facing the hill, these include from left to right the baths of Venus, Sosandra and Mercury.

Bacoli – On the high ground in the old town rises the **Cento Camerelle**★ ⊙ *(Via Cento Camerelle, to the right of the church)*. This huge reservoir, which belonged to a private villa, is built on two levels: the grandiose upper level built in the 1C has four sections and immense arches; the lower part, built much earlier, has a network of narrow galleries forming a cross, that emerge high above sea level. The famous **Piscina Mirabile**★ ⊙ *(at the church take the road to the left, Via Ambrogio Greco, and then Via Piscina Mirabile to the right)* was an immense cistern designed to supply water to the Roman fleet in the port of Miseno. It is 70m long, 25m wide and nearly 15m high (230ft×82ft×49ft) and is divided into five sections with 48 pillars supporting the roof. There are remarkable light effects.

Miseno – This name is given to a lake, a port, a promontory, a cape and a village. Lake Miseno, a former volcanic crater, was believed by the ancients to be the Styx, across which Charon ferried the souls of the dead. Under the Emperor Augustus it was linked by a canal to the port of Miseno, which was the base of the Roman fleet. The village of Miseno is dominated by Monte Miseno, on which Misenus, the companion of Aeneas, is said to have been buried. The slopes of the promontory were studded with luxurious villas, including the one where in AD 37 the Emperor Tiberius choked to death.

Lago del Fusaro – A lagoon with a small island on which Vanvitelli built a hunting lodge for King Ferdinand IV of Bourbon in 1782.

★ **Cumae** – *See CUMAE.*

★ **Lago d'Averno** – *The lake lies below the Cumae-Naples road: belvedere on the right approximately 1km – 1/2 mile beyond Arco Felice.* This lake within a crater is dark, still and silent and wrapped in an atmosphere of mystery, which was all the more intense in antiquity as birds flying overhead were overcome by fumes and dropped into the lake to be swallowed up. Homer and Virgil regarded it as the entrance to the Underworld. Under the Roman Empire, Agrippa, a captain in the service of the Emperor Augustus, developed it as a naval base and linked it by canal with Lake Lucrino *(see above)*, which in turn was linked to the open sea. An underground gallery 1km – 1/2 mile long, known as Cocceio's Cave (**Grotta di Cocceio**), connected Avernus with Cumae, and was used by chariots.

★★★ ② **FROM NAPLES TO TORRE ANNUNZIATA**

Vesuvius *44km – 27 miles – allow 1 day*

The coast road relieves the Salerno motorway across a densely-populated industrial zone, once a favoured resort of the Neapolitan aristocracy (18-19C). There are two important sites located a short distance from the road.

Portici – The road crosses the courtyard of the **royal palace** built in 1738 for the Bourbon King Charles III. Today the palace buildings are the home of the Naples Faculty of Agronomy. In his opera *The Mute Girl of Portici (Muette de Portici)*, the French composer, Auber, features the 17C revolt against the Spaniards, instigated by Masaniello, a young fisherman from Portici.

★★ **Herculaneum** – *See ERCOLANO.*

★★★ **Vesuvio** – The outline of Vesuvius, one of the few still active volcanoes in Europe, is an intrinsic feature of the Neapolitan landscape. It has two summits: to the north **Monte Somma** (alt 1 132m – 3 714ft) and to the south Vesuvius proper (alt 1 277m – 4 190ft). In time the volcanic materials on the lower slopes have become fertile soil with orchards and vines producing the famous *Lacryma Christi* wine.

The eruptions of Vesuvius – Until the earthquake of AD 62 and the eruption of AD 79 which buried Herculaneum and Pompeii, Vesuvius seemed extinct; its slopes were clothed with famous vines and woods. By 1139, seven eruptions had been recorded. Then came a period of calm during which the slopes of the mountains were cultivated. On 16 December 1631 Vesuvius had a terrible awakening, destroying all the settlements at its foot: 3 000 people perished. The eruption of 1794 devastated Torre del Greco. The volcano had minor eruptions in 1858, 1871, 1872, from 1895 to 1899, 1900, 1903, 1904, a major eruption in 1906, 1929, and one in 1944 altering the shape of the crater. Since then, apart from brief activity linked with the 1980 earthquake, Vesuvius has emitted only a plume of smoke.

Ascent ⊙ – *From Herculaneum and via Torre del Greco: 27km – 17 miles plus 3/4 hour on foot Rtn. Wear stout walking shoes.* A good road leads to a junction in the midst of lava flows. Take the left fork *(car park further on).* The path is an easy but most impressive climb up the volcano, scattered with cinders and lapilli.

From the summit there is an immense **panorama★★★** over the Bay of Naples enclosed by the Sorrento Peninsula in the south and Cape Miseno in the north. Beyond is the Gulf of Gaeta. The crater affords an unforgettable sight for its sheer size and the desolation of the slopes of its jagged walls, for the great yawning crater, which takes on a pink colour in the sun, and the spouting steamjets.

Torre del Greco – This town which has been repeatedly destroyed by the eruptions of Vesuvius, is well known for its ornaments made of coral and volcanic stone, and cameos.

Torre Annunziata – This town is the centre of the famous Neapolitan pasta industry. It has been buried under the lava of Vesuvius seven times. Here is the sumptuous Villa di Oplontis which is open to the public.

★★ **Villa di Oplontis** ⊙ – This fine example of a Roman suburban villa is thought to have belonged to Poppea, wife of Nero. The vast building, in which can be identified the slaves' quarters (to the east) and the area given over to the imperial apartments (to the west), has many well-preserved examples of beautiful original **wall paintings**. In particular, there are landscape scenes featuring architectural elements, portrait medallions and still-lifes, including a basket of figs and details of fruit (in the two recesses or *triclinia* to the east and west of the atrium respectively). Of the various animals depicted, the peacock appears so frequently as to have supported the theory that the name of the villa was derived from it. Within the villa, the kitchens are easily identified (with ovens and sink), as are the latrines which represent an advanced drainage system. The area to the west of the piscina, perhaps used as a conservatory, has fine wall paintings with foreshortened flowers and fountains.

★★ ③ FROM TORRE ANNUNZIATA TO SORRENTO

69km – 43 miles – allow 1 day

Torre Annunziata – *See above.*

★★ **Pompeii** – *See POMPEI.*

★ **Castellammare di Stabia** – *See CASTELLAMMARE DI STABIA.*

★★ **Monte Faito** – *Toll-road.* Monte Faito is part of the **Lattari range**, a headland which separates the Bay of Naples from the Gulf of Salerno and forms the Sorrento Peninsula. Its name is derived from the beech trees (*fagus* in Latin) which offer shade in summer. The steeply-winding road leads to a roundabout (Belvedere dei Capi) for a splendid **panorama★★★** of the Bay of Naples, then upwards to a chapel, **Cappella San Michele**, which affords another **panorama★★★** – the wild landscape of the Lattari mountains contrasts strongly with the smiling scenery of the Bay of Naples and the Sarno plain. There is a fine run down towards Vico Equense.

★ **Vico Equense** – A small health and seaside resort on a picturesque rocky site.

★★ **Sorrento and Sorrento Peninsula** – *See SORRENTO.*

★★ ISLANDS

★★ **Capri** – *See Isola di CAPRI.*

★★ **Ischia** – *See Isola d'ISCHIA.*

★ **Procida** – *See Isola d'ISCHIA: Procida.*

To plan a special itinerary:
  – consult the Map of Touring Programmes which indicates the tourist regions, the recommended routes, the principal towns and main sights
  – read the descriptions in the Sights section which include Excursions from the main tourist centres
Michelin Maps nos 428 to 433 indicate scenic routes, places of interest, viewpoints, rivers, forests...

NOVARA

Piedmont – Population 100 973

in map 988 folds 2 and 3, 219 fold 17 or 428 F 17
Town plan in the current Michelin Red Guide Italia

Novara is situated on the borders of Piedmont and Lombardy to the north of the Lomellina, a vast rice-growing area. It is a busy commercial and industrial town as well as an important road junction in the road network of northern Italy.

★ **Basilica di San Gaudenzio** – Built from 1577 to 1659 to the designs of the Lombard architect, Pellegrino Tibaldi, it was crowned with a tall slender **dome**★★ (1844-78), an audacious addition by a local architect, A Antonelli. Inside are several interesting works of art, including paintings by Morazzone (17C) and Gaudenzio Ferrari (16C) and the silver **sarcophagus**★ of the city's patron saint (St Gaudentius).

Cortile del Broletto – This lovely courtyard has several interesting buildings including the 15C Palazzo Podestà, the 13C Broletto (Town Hall) and the Palazzo degli Paratici, now the **Museo Civico** (art gallery and archeological section).

Duomo – This neo-Classical cathedral by Antonelli has a 6C-7C paleo-Christian baptistery. The chancel is adorned with a black and white Byzantine-style mosaic **pavement**★.

EXCURSION

La Lomellina – This region lying between the Ticino and the Po is the great rice-growing area of Italy and a landscape of vast stretches of flooded land divided by long rows of willows and poplars.
The chief towns of artistic interest are: **Vigevano** with its outstanding elliptical **Piazza Ducale**★★ at the foot of the Palazzo Sforza; **Mortara** has a 14C Church of San Lorenzo with interesting paintings by G Ferrari; **Lomello**, after which the region is named, boasts the attractive 11C Church of Santa Maria with its 8C baptistery.

Use the Index to find more information about a subject mentioned in the guide
  – people, towns, places of interest, isolated sites, historical events
  or natural features...

ORVIETO★★

Umbria – Population 21 378
Michelin map 988 fold 25 or 430 N 18

This important Etruscan centre later became a papal stronghold and it was here that Clement VII took refuge in 1527 when Rome was sacked by the troops of the French King, Charles V.
Orvieto is a pleasant city with its wealth of historic buildings and it enjoys a particularly remarkable **site**★★★ on the top of a plug of volcanic rock. Those arriving by the Bolsena or Montefiascone roads have particularly good views of this site. The region produces a pleasant, white wine, the cool and fragrant Orvieto.

★★★ DUOMO *1 hour*

In the heart of the town the quiet Piazza del Duomo, of majestic proportions, is lined with several interesting buildings. The cathedral, a perfect example of the transitional Romanesque-Gothic style, was begun in 1290 to enshrine the relics of the Miracle of Bolsena *(see BOLSENA)*. Over 100 architects, sculptors, painters and mosaicists took part in the building of the cathedral which was completed only in 1600. The austere Palace of the Popes **(Palazzo dei Papi★) (M²)** ⊘ now houses the Cathedral Museum.

★★★ **Façade** – This is the boldest structure and the richest in colour among Italian Gothic buildings. The vertical lines are accentuated by the slender gables and especially by the soaring buttresses, which are clad with small panels of coloured marble, elongated in shape and further prolonged by pinnacles. The sumptuous decorative effect is obtained by the use of sculptures lower down with multicoloured marbles and mosaics above. The façade was designed by the Sienese, Lorenzo Maitani (1310-30), and continued by Andrea Pisano, Orcagna and Sanmicheli.

Façade, Duomo, Orvieto

Maitani was also the artist responsible for the astonishing **low reliefs**★★ adorning the pillars. The second shaft to the right of the main doorway has a very realistic *Last Judgement*. Orcagna was the designer of the rose window, fitted into a square frame, further adorned with niches containing the Apostles and the Prophets.

Interior – A nave and two aisles built in alternating courses of black and white stone rest on semicircular arches supported by lovely bracketed capitals. A moulding projects above the arches. The nave and aisles are roofed with a timber ceiling, while Gothic vaulting covers the transepts and the chancel. The paving slopes up towards the chancel, reducing the perspective. Alabaster window-panes let in plenty of light. At the entrance stand the 15C stoup and the Gothic font. A fresco of the *Virgin and Child* (1425) in the north aisle is by Gentile da Fabriano.

In the north transept under the 16C monumental organ is the entrance to a chapel, the **Cappella del Corporale**, which enshrines the relics of the Miracle of Bolsena and notably the linen cloth (corporal) in which the bleeding Host was wrapped. A tabernacle encloses the **Reliquary**★★ of the Corporal, a masterpiece of medieval goldsmiths' work (1338) encrusted with enamels and precious stones. In the chapel on the right is a *Madonna of Pity* (1320) by the Sienese painter, Lippo Memmi.

A fine Gothic stained glass **window**★ in the chancel illustrates the Gospel with recognisable figures of theologians and prophets.

The south transept gives access, beyond a wrought-iron grille (1516), to the famous chapel, **Cappella della Madonna di San Brizio**, painted with admirable **frescoes of *the Apocalypse***★★. These were begun in 1447 by Fra Angelico with the help of Benozzo Gozzoli and were entrusted from 1499 to 1504 to **Luca Signorelli**; they are considered to be the latter's masterpiece. As the human figure was his main interest while landscape and colour remained secondary considerations, the theme of the frescoes enabled him to perfect his talent. Although he lacked a spiritual dimension, with his precise draughtsmanship, his careful portrayal of human anatomy and his dramatic compositions, he was the precursor of Michelangelo. On the ceiling, Fra Angelico painted Christ among angels and prophets; the apostles, doctors, virgins, martyrs and patriarchs are by Signorelli. The latter was responsible for the wall frescoes of extraordinary power: the *Preaching of the Antichrist* (first lunette on the left) containing portraits of Signorelli and Fra Angelico; the *End of the World* (on the west wall) and the *Resurrection of the Body* (first lunette on the right). The end wall of the chapel is devoted to the *Last Judgement*. There is a *Pietà* of astonishing power in a niche in the right-hand wall.

ORVIETO

ADDITIONAL SIGHTS

★★ **Pozzo di San Patrizio** ⊘ - St Patrick's Well was dug in the volcanic rock by order of Pope Clement VII de' Medici to supply the town with water in case of siege. Sangallo the Younger was entrusted with the work. Two spiral staircases, lit by 72 windows, wind up and down without meeting. The well is over 62m – 203ft deep and its water cold and pure.

★ **Palazzo del Popolo** - The town hall is built of volcanic rock in the Romanesque-Gothic style. The façade has a majestic balcony, elegant windows and curious fluted merlons.

★ **Quartiere Vecchio** – This quiet, unfrequented quarter has retained its old houses, medieval towers and churches. At the western extremity stands the Church of **San Giovenale;** the Gothic apse is decorated with 13C-15C frescoes.

Museo archeologico Faina (M¹) ⊘ – This important **Etruscan Collection**★ includes splendid painted vases, carved terracotta funerary urns and a rare 4C sarcophagus.

San Bernardino – A charming Baroque church dedicated to St Bernard with the refined decoration of a theatre. The oval interior is delightfully decorated and has an organ carved with figures.

Piazza della Repubblica – It stands on the site of the ancient forum, dominated by the Church of Sant'Andrea, dedicated to St Andrew, with its lovely 12-sided Romanesque tower.

OSTIA ANTICA★★

Lazio

Michelin map 430 Q 18 – 24km – 15 miles southwest of Rome

Ostia, at the mouth of the Tiber, takes its name from the Latin word *ostium* meaning mouth. According to Virgil, Aeneas landed here but its foundation dates in reality back to the 4C BC when Rome embarked on her conquest of the Mediterranean. From that time on, Ostia's development has reflected that of Rome: a military port during the period of expansion, a commercial port once Rome had established an organised system of trade. At first there was simply a castle to protect the port from pirates but by 1BC Ostia had become a real town around which Sulla built ramparts in 79BC. Like Rome, Ostia began to decline in the 4C.

Slowly the harbour silted up and malaria decimated the population. Ostia was soon covered by alluvium deposited by the Tiber. It was 1909 before Ostia was discovered and regular excavations began.

On this extensive site the visitor can discover a variety of interesting remains: warehouses *(horrea)*; baths; sanctuaries; the substantial dwelling-house, the *domus* built around its atrium or courtyard; and the more usual block of flats, several storeys high *(insula)*. They were nearly all built of brick and unrendered. Some had elegant entrances framed by a triangular pediment resting on two pillars. Here and there a porch or a balcony added interest to the street front.

In addition there are the numerous meeting-places for both business and pleasure, and the forum which was the hub of both political and social life. During the empire Ostia was a town with a population of 100 000 which included a large number of foreigners.

Forum and Capitol, Ostia Antica

TOUR OF THE EXCAVATIONS ⊘ *3 hours*

Follow the itinerary outlined on the map which includes many other places of interest in addition to the ones described. For a more detailed description consult the current **Michelin Red Guide Rome**.

Once past the **Via delle Tombe**, just outside the **Porta Romana** (the main entrance to the town coming from Rome) is the **Decumanus Maximus**, the east-west axis of all Roman towns; in Ostia it was paved with large slabs and lined with porticoed houses and shops.

On the right are the **Terme di Nettuno**. This 2C building has a terrace with a view of the fine **mosaics★★** which depict the marriage of Neptune and Amphitrite. A little further on, on the opposite side is the **Horrea di Hortensius★**, grand 1C warehouses built round a pillared courtyard which is lined with shops. The theatre has been much restored but is nevertheless very evocative of life in a Roman city.

★★ Piazzale delle Corporazioni – Under the portico in the square were the offices of the 70 trading corporations which represented the trading links with the Roman world. The mosaic pavement portrays their emblems, which in turn indicate the commodity they traded in and the country of origin. The temple in the centre of the square is sometimes attributed to Ceres, goddess of corn and the harvest.

On the right is the Casa di Apuleio and then the Mitreum **(Mitreo)**, a temple to Mithras and one of the best preserved in Ostia.

★★ Thermopolium – This bar with a marble counter served hot drinks (hence its name).

★ Casa di Diana – This is a striking example of an *insula* (block of flats) with rooms and passages arranged around an inner courtyard.

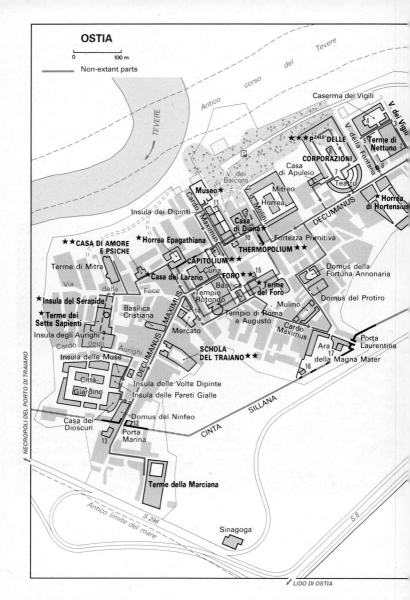

OSTIA

0 — 100 m

Non-extant parts

★ **Museo** ⊙ – The museum displays objects found in Ostia: crafts, oriental religious cults (numerous in Ostia), sculptures and **portraits**★, and examples of the rich interior decoration found in Ostia.

★★ **Capitolium** and **Foro** – The **Capitol** was the largest temple in Ostia, built in the 2C and dedicated to the Capitoline triad: Jupiter, Juno and Minerva. Some of the pillars of the surrounding portico in the **forum** (extended in the 2C) are still standing. At the far end stands the 1C Temple of Rome and Augustus (Tempio di Roma e Augusto), faced with marble.
Beyond the **Casa del Lario**★ so-called because of the red and ochre brick decoration is the **Horrea Epagathiana**★, a warehouse with a fine doorway featuring columns and frontispiece.

★★ **Casa di Amore e Psiche** – This 4C building, facing the seashore, has interesting remains of mosaic and marble floors and a lovely nymphaeum.

Terme – There is a series of baths *(terme)* starting with the **Terme di Mitra** with traces of the steps and *frigidarium*. Further along are the **Insula del Serapide**★ and the **Terme dei Sette Sapienti**★ – there is a handsome mosaic floor in the large circular room. Beyond the walls are the **Terme della Marciana** with a beautiful **mosaic**★ in the *frigidarium*.

★★ **Schola del Traiano** – This impressive 2C to 3C building was the headquarters of a guild of merchants. Inside can be seen several porticoed courtyards and a rectangular basin.

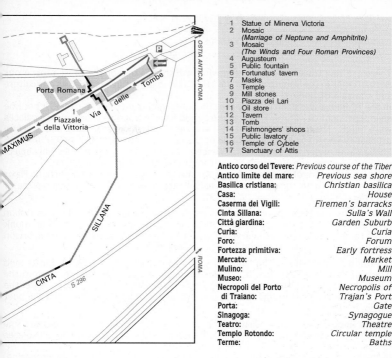

1	Statue of Minerva Victoria
2	Mosaic *(Marriage of Neptune and Amphitrite)*
3	Mosaic *(The Winds and Four Roman Provinces)*
4	Augusteum
5	Public fountain
6	Fortunatus' tavern
7	Masks
8	Temple
9	Mill stones
10	Piazza dei Lari
11	Oil store
12	Tavern
13	Tomb
14	Fishmongers' shops
15	Public lavatory
16	Temple of Cybele
17	Sanctuary of Attis

Antico corso del Tevere:	*Previous course of the Tiber*
Antico limite del mare:	*Previous sea shore*
Basilica cristiana:	*Christian basilica*
Casa:	*House*
Caserma dei Vigili:	*Firemen's barracks*
Cinta Sillana:	*Sulla's Wall*
Città giardina:	*Garden Suburb*
Curia:	*Curia*
Foro:	*Forum*
Fortezza primitiva:	*Early fortress*
Mercato:	*Market*
Mulino:	*Mill*
Museo:	*Museum*
Necropoli del Porto di Traiano:	*Necropolis of Trajan's Port*
Porta:	*Gate*
Sinagoga:	*Synagogue*
Teatro:	*Theatre*
Templo Rotondo:	*Circular temple*
Terme:	*Baths*

Make for the **Basilica cristiana**, a 4C Christian basilica; a row of columns separates the aisles which end in apses. An inscription on the architrave of a colonnade marks the entrance to what has been identified as the baptistery.

A little further on are the **Terme del Foro★** which are the largest baths in Ostia. Along one side is a good example of a public lavatory. In the rectangular enclosure of the **Campo della Magna Mater** are the remains of a temple dedicated to Cybele (or the Magna Mater, the Great Mother. The sanctuary, Sacello di Attis, has a statue of the goddess in the apse and two fauns flanking the entrance.

OTRANTO

Puglia – Population 5 114

Michelin map 988 fold 30 or 431 G 37

Otranto lies on the Adriatic coast of the "heel" of the peninsula. This fishing port was once capital of "Terra d'Otranto", the last remaining Byzantine stronghold, and resisted the Lombards and then the Normans for some considerable time. In the 15C when the town was besieged by the troops of Mohammed II the townspeople took refuge in the cathedral where they were massacred. Survivors were taken prisoner and killed on the summit of a hill, Colle della Minerva, where a sanctuary was built to the memory of the martyrs.

Città vecchia – There is a good view of the old town from the northeast pier; to the left is the 15C **Castello Aragonese** flanked by its massive cylindrical towers. To reach this stronghold perched on the clifftop pass through the gateways Porta di Terra and the 15C Porta Alfonsina.

★ **Cattedrale** – This 12C cathedral was altered in the late 15C. Inside, antique columns separate the nave from the two aisles and there is a remarkable mosaic **pavement★★★** dating from 1165. It was the work of a local craftsman, Pantaleone. The stylisation of the figures, the vivacity of their poses and attitudes, the freshness of the colours and variety of the symbols make this a fascinating illustrated story.

EXCURSION

★ **The coast to the south** – Between Otranto and Santa Maria di Leuca *(51km – 32 miles)* the road offers fine views of this wild and indented coastline. At the head of an inlet is the cave, **Grotta Zinzulusa** ⓥ, with concretions and two lakes, one salt water and the other fresh, which are inhabited by rare marine species.

PADOVA★★

PADUA – Veneto – Population 215 017

Michelin map 988 fold 5 or 429 F 17

There are few traces of ancient Patavium which was one of the most prosperous Roman cities in the Veneto during the 1C BC owing to its fluvial trade, its agriculture and the sale of horses.

In the 7C Padua was destroyed by the Lombards, and from the 11C to 13C it became an independent city-state. This was the period when numerous churches and palaces were built. The city underwent its greatest period of economic and cultural prosperity under the enlightened rule of the lords of Carrara (1337-1405). In 1405 Padua came under the sway of the Venetian Republic and remained a loyal subject until 1797 when the Venetian Constitution was abolished by Napoleon.

The historic centre of Padua, a busy town and an art and pilgrimage centre, is **Piazza Cavour** (**DY 15**), with the neo-Classical **Caffè Pedrocchi**, which was a meeting-place of the liberal élite in the Romantic period.

St Anthony the Hermit – The saint is venerated in Padua. He was born in Lisbon in 1195 and died at the age of 36 in the environs of Padua. This Franciscan monk was a forceful preacher. His help was invoked by the shipwrecked and those in prison and he is generally represented holding a book and a lily.

A famous university – The University of Padua founded in 1222 is the second oldest in Italy after Bologna. It expanded rapidly and attracted students from the whole of Europe. Galileo was a professor and among its students were the Renaissance scholar Pico della Mirandola, the astronomer Copernicus and the poet Tasso.

Art in Padua – In 1304, **Giotto** came to Padua from Florence to decorate the Scrovegni Chapel. He painted a cycle of frescoes which is one of the masterpieces of Italian art.

In the 15C the Renaissance in Padua was marked by Donatello, another Florentine, who stayed in the city from 1444 to 1453.

Also in the 15C Paduan art flourished under the guiding influence of the Paduan artist, **Andrea Mantegna** (1431-1506). A painter of powerful originality, he was fascinated by anatomy and archeology and was also a technical innovator in the field of perspective.

ARTISTIC CENTRE *2 1/2 hours*

★★★ **Frescoes by Giotto** – The cycle of 39 frescoes was painted c1305-10 by Giotto on the walls of the **Cappella degli Scrovegni** (**DY**) ⊘. The chapel, built in 1303, illustrates the lives of Joachim and Anna, Mary and Jesus: the *Flight into Egypt*, *Judas' Kiss* and the *Entombment* are among the most famous. On the lower register, the powerful monochrome figures depict the Vices *(left)* and Virtues *(right)*. The *Last Judgement* on the west wall completes the cycle.

This work shows an exceptional unity and is Giotto's masterpiece, displaying great dramatic power, harmonious composition and intense spirituality. On the altar stands a **Virgin**★ by the Tuscan sculptor Giovanni Pisano.

★★ **Frescoes in the Chiesa degli Eremitani** (**DY**) – The 13C Church of the Hermits was badly damaged by bombing in 1944 but has been rebuilt in the original Romanesque style. In the Cappella Ovetari *(the second on the right of the Cappella Maggiore*) are fragments of frescoes by **Mantegna**. The various scenes *(Martyrdom of St James* on the north wall, *Assumption* in the apse and *Martyrdom of St Christoper* on the south wall) display his powerful visionary talent and his careful attention to perspective and architectural detail. The Lady Chapel (Cappella Maggiore) has splendid frescoes by **Guariento**, Giotto's Venetian pupil.

★ **Museo Civico agli Eremitani** (**DY M**) ⊘ – The municipal museum in the Hermitage of St Augustine (Sant'Agostino) comprises several collections: archeology (Egyptian, Etruscan, Roman and Pre-Roman), coins (Bottacin Bequest) and 15C-18C Venetian and Flemish paintings (Emo Capodilista collection).

The museum also contains the extensive collection from the former Art Gallery including not only furniture, ceramics and sculptures but also **paintings**★★, most of them from the Venetian School (14C-18C). In particular, note works by Giotto, Guariento, Giovanni Bellini, Veronese, and Tintoretto and the splendid 15C tapestry entitled *The Expedition of Uri*.

PILGRIMAGE CENTRE *1 1/2 hours*

★★ **Basilica del Santo** (**DZ**) ⊘ – This important pilgrimage church dedicated to St Anthony overlooks the square in which Donatello erected an **equestrian statue**★★ of the Venetian mercenary leader **Gattamelata** (nickname of Erasmo di Nardi who died in Padua in 1443) (**A**). This bronze was the first of its size to be cast in Italy.

PADOVA

Altinate (Via) .... **DYZ**
Cavour (Piazza e via) ..... **DY** 15
Dante (Via E.) .... **CY**
Filiberto (Via E.) .... **DY** 24
Garibaldi (Corso) .... **DY** 27
Ponti Romani
 (Riviera dei) .... **DYZ** 53
Roma (Via) .... **DZ**

S. Fermo (Via) .... **DY**

Carmine (Via del) .... **DY** 10
Cesarotti (Via M.) .... **DZ** 17
Erbe (Piazza delle) ...... **DZ** 20
Eremitani (Piazza) .... **DY** 21
Frutta (Piazza della) ..... **DY** 25
Garibaldi (Piazza) .... **DY** 28
Gasometro (Via dell' ex) .. **DY** 29
Guariento (Via) .... **DY** 35
Insurrezione (Piazza) ..... **DY** 39

Monte di Pietà (Via del) ... **CZ** 45
Petrarca (Via) .... **CY** 50
Ponte Molino (Vicolo) ..... **CY** 52
S. Canziano (Via) .... **DZ** 57
S. Lucia (Via) .... **DY** 59
Vandelli (Via D.) .... **CZ** 66
Verdi (Via G.) .... **CY** 67
Vittorio Emanuele II
 (Corso) .... **CZ** 70
8 Febbraio (Via) .... **DZ** 74
58 Fanteria (Via) .... **DZ** 75

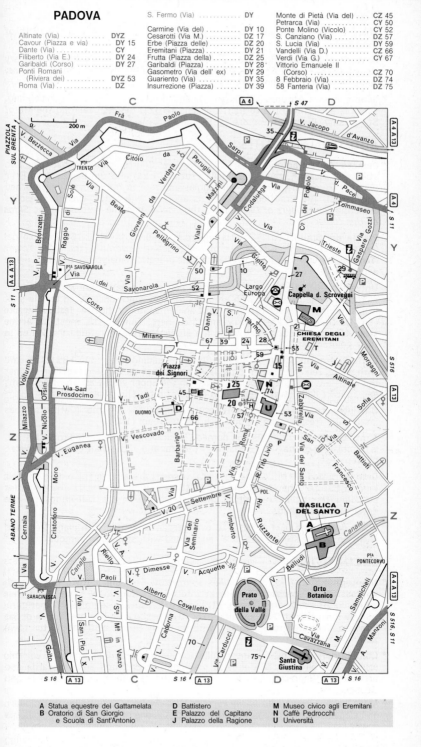

A Statua equestre del Gattamelata	**D** Battistero	**M** Museo civico agli Eremitani
B Oratorio di San Giorgio e Scuola di Sant'Antonio	**E** Palazzo del Capitano	**N** Caffè Pedrocchi
	J Palazzo della Ragione	**U** Università

The basilica with its eight-tiered bulbous domes was built from 1232 to 1300 in the transitional Romanesque-Gothic style and brings to mind St Mark's in Venice. The imposing **interior**★★ contains numerous works of art: off the north aisle is the **Cappella del Santo**★★, a Renaissance masterpiece, which contains the tomb-cum-altar of St Anthony (Arca di Sant'Antonio) by Tiziano Aspetti (1594); on the walls are magnificent 16C **high reliefs**★★ by several artists. In the chancel the **high altar**★★ is adorned with bronze panels (1450) by Donatello. The third chapel, off the south aisle, has **frescoes**★ by Altichiero (14C), an artist from Verona.

There is a fine **overall view**★ of the building from the cloisters to the south of the basilica.

★ **Oratorio di San Giorgio** (DZ B) ⊘ – St George's Oratory was built as a funerary chapel and is decorated with 21 **frescoes**★ (1377) by Altichiero and his pupils, depicting various religious scenes.

★ **Scuola di Sant'Antonio** (DZ B) ⊘ – A chamber on the first floor of this building, which is adjacent to the former, contains 18 16C **frescoes**★ relating the life of St Anthony. Four of these are by Titian.

ADDITIONAL SIGHTS

★ **Palazzo della Ragione** (DZ J) ⊘ – The Law Courts, standing between two attractive **squares**★, the Piazza della Frutta (DZ 25) and the Piazza delle Erbe (DZ 20), are remarkable for their loggias and roof in the form of an upturned ship's keel. The first-floor **Salone**★★ is adorned with a 15C cycle of frescoes depicting the *Labours of the Months*, the *Liberal Arts*, the *Trades* and the *Signs of the Zodiac*.

Piazza dei Signori (CYZ) – This square is lined by the 14C-15C Palazzo del Capitano (E), one-time residence of the Venetian Governors, the Clock Tower (**Torre dell'Orologio**★) with its arcade, and the graceful Renaissance gallery, Loggia del Consiglio.

Università (DZ U) ⊘ – The University is housed in a palace known as the "Bo" from the name of an inn with an ox as its sign which once stood on the site. It has retained a lovely 16C courtyard and an anatomy theatre, **Teatro Anatomico** (1594). University life is very animated here. One of the most attractive spectacles is graduation day when the students are celebrating, dressed up in their pointed hats.

Caffè Pedrocchi (DZ N) – This neo-Classical building, erected in 1831, is a café with white, red and green rooms. It was here that the student rebellion against the Austrians was played out in 1848. On the upper storey are meeting rooms and concert halls (**sale**) ⊘ built in a range of different styles.

Battistero (CZ D) – The baptistery adjoining the Duomo (Cathedral) has interesting frescoes and a polyptych by Menabuoi (14C).

Santa Giustina (DZ) – This 16C domed Classical church, dedicated to St Justina, is reminiscent of the Saint's Basilica. At the far end of the chancel is an **altarpiece**★ by Veronese.

Orto Botanico (DZ) ⊘ – The botanical gardens are among the oldest of their kind in Europe. They were laid out in 1545 and contain many exotic species including the palm tree which inspired Goethe in his reflections on the development of plants.

Prato della Valle (DZ) – This 17C oval garden is planted with plane trees and encircled by the still waters of a canal, lined with statues of famous men.

EXCURSIONS

★ **Montagnana** – *47km – 29 miles southwest*. This small town is girt with impressive 14C **ramparts**★★ with at intervals 24 polygonal towers and four gateways. The cathedral (**Duomo**), attributed to Sansovino, contains a Transfiguration by Veronese at the high altar, 16C frescoes and stalls. The Church of **San Francesco**, dedicated to St Francis, with its lovely Gothic belfry abuts the town wall.

★ **Colli Euganei** – The Euganean hills to the south of Padua are of volcanic origin. This pleasant hilly area is planted with orchards and vineyards and was already appreciated in Roman times for its numerous hot springs and its wines.

‡‡‡ **Abano Terme** – *Town plan in the current Michelin Red Guide Italia*. This modern and elegant thermal spa well-shaded by pines is one of Italy's most famous spa towns.

‡‡ **Montegrotto Terme** – Although less important than Abano it is rapidly growing in importance. This was the ancient *Mons Aegrotorum* (mountain of the sick).

★ **Monselice** – This town, whose Latin name *Mons Silicis* bears witness to its importance as a mining community during Roman times, has retained a large section of its walls and is dominated by the ruins of a castle. From Piazza Mazzini, go up the picturesque Via del Santuario to reach the 13C-14C castle, the Romanesque cathedral (Duomo), the early-17C Sanctuary of the Seven Churches and the Villa Balbi with its Italian garden. The upper terrace affords a lovely **view**★ of the region.

★ **Arquà Petrarca** – *6.5km – 4 miles northwest of Monselice.* It was here, in these tranquil, medieval surroundings, that **Petrarch** (1304-1374) died. He was born in Arezzo in 1304 but his stormy life took him to various places in Italy and abroad. In a church in Avignon, he met Laura, the woman with whom he fell in love for all time and whom he immortalised in his collection of sonnets entitled the *Canzoniere*. His works became a reference throughout Europe for lyric poetry and, during the Renaissance, they gave rise to attempts at imitation after the poet had become virtually a cult figure.

The house **(casa★)** ⊙ where he lived and died is open to the public. It has 16C frescoes and the original coffered ceiling. Exhibits include memorabilia of the poet and autographs of famous visitors such as Carducci or Byron. His pink marble tomb was erected on the church square in 1380.

Este – Cradle of the Este family, rulers of Ferrara, the town still has an attractive section of **town wall★** to the north. The **Museo Nazionale Atestino★** ⊙, housed in the 16C Mocenigo Palace, has an extensive archeological collection relating to local farming from the Paleolithic to the Roman eras. The collection is displayed chronologically. *Ateste* was the name of the town during Roman times. The Duomo (cathedral), on an elliptical plan, contains a large canvas (1759) by Tiepolo.

★ **Riviera del Brenta** – *See Riviera del BRENTA.*

PAESTUM★★★

Campania

Michelin map 988 fold 28 or 431 F 26/27

One of Italy's most important archeological sites, Paestum was discovered by chance around 1750, when the Bourbons started to build the road which crosses the area today.

The initial settlement was an ancient Greek colony founded around 600 BC under the name of Poseidonia by colonists from Sybaris *(see SYBARIS)*. Around the year 400 BC the city fell to a local tribe, the Lucanians. It became Roman in the year 273 BC but began to decline towards the end of the Empire because of the malaria which finally drove out its inhabitants.

Paestum is also a seaside resort; its beach is sheltered by a fine pinewood.

TOUR *2 hours*

★★ **Museo** ⊙ – The masterpieces in this museum include the famous **metopes★★**, 6C BC low reliefs in the Doric style which adorned both the temple of Hera *(10km – 6 miles north near the mouth of the Sele River)*, and the small temple next to it. The Tomb of the Diver **(Tomba del Tuffatore★★)** has unique Greek funerary paintings.

★★★ **Rovine** ⊙ – *Itinerary indicated on the accompanying plan*. The temples, built of a fine yellow limestone, stand amidst the ruins (rovine) of dwellings sheltered by cypresses and oleanders. Take the Porta della Giustizia through the 5km – 3 mile-long city wall **(Cinta muraria★)** and follow the **Via Sacra** which leads to the Temple of Hera.

★★ **Basilica** – The rear of the "Basilica", so-called by 18C archeologists, stands to the right of the Via Sacra. This mid-6C BC temple was dedicated to Hera (Juno). The peristyle comprises 50 archaic fluted columns with a slight swell. The porch *(pronaos)* leads into the central chamber divided into two aisles.

★★★ **Tempio di Nettuno** – When Paestum was first discovered this well-preserved temple was thought to have been dedicated to Neptune (or Poseidon in

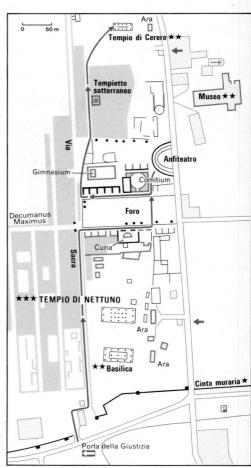

Anfiteatro:	Anphitheatre	Museo:	Museum
Ara:	Altar	Tempietto	Underground
Cinta muraria:	Wall	sotterraneo:	temple
Foro:	Forum	Tempio:	Temple

Greek, hence the town's name Poseidonia). It has since been proved that it was dedicated to Hera. Dating from the mid-5C BC it is in an admirably pure Doric style. The entablature and the two triangular pediments are almost intact. Inside, the central chamber is divided into three aisles.

The forum (**foro**), surrounded by a portico and shops, is in the centre of the city. The Roman amphiteatre (**anfiteatro**) built at the end of the Republic, is today divided by the main road. The small Underground Temple (**Tempietto Sotterraneo**) contained superb bronze vases.

★★ **Tempio di Cerere** – Originally erected in the late 6C BC in honour of Athena, the Temple of Ceres retains 34 columns and parts of its pediments. Nearby is the sacrificial altar.

PARMA ★★

Emilia-Romagna – Population 170 178

Michelin map 988 fold 14, or 428 and 429 H 12/13

Parma, at the junction of the Via Emilia and the Mantua-La Spezia road, is an important market town and industrial centre with a rich heritage. The town has a certain refined charm and is often bathed in a diaphanous light. Piazza Garibaldi (**BZ 9**) is a popular meeting-place for the townspeople. The famous 20C conductor Arturo Toscanini was born in Parma.

HISTORICAL NOTES

A settlement was founded on this site by the Etruscans in 525 BC and it became a Roman station on the Via Emilia in 183 BC. It declined but revived in the 6C under the Ostrogoth King, Theodoric. After having been an independent commune from the 11C-13C, it became a member of the Lombard League *(see Index)*. After the fall of the commune's government in 1335, Parma was governed in turn by the Visconti, the Sforza and, later, the French before being annexed by the papacy in 1513. In 1545 Pope Paul III Farnese gave two papal territories, Parma and Piacenza, having made them a duchy, to his son Pier Luigi Farnese, who was assassinated in 1547. However, the Farnese dynasty continued to reign until 1731 and several members of the house were patrons of the arts and letters, collectors and great builders.

When it passed to the Bourbons, its first sovereign was Charles, successively King of Naples then King of Spain. When Don Philip, the son of Philip V of Spain and Elizabeth Farnese, married Louise Elizabeth, the favourite daughter of Louis XV, the town underwent a period (1748-1801) of great French influence in several domains (customs, administration and the arts).

Numerous Frenchmen came to work in Parma while others like Stendhal chose to live here; he made Parma the setting of his well-known novel, *The Charterhouse of Parma*. The Bourbon-Parma had their Versailles at Colorno, north of the town. The last major historical figure was Marie-Louise of Habsburg, Napoleon's second wife, who reigned from 1814 to 1847.

The Parma School – The school is represented by two main artists, Correggio and Il Parmigianino, whose works formed the transition between the Renaissance and Baroque art. Antonio Allegri (1489-1534), known as **Correggio**, was a master of light and chiaroscuro; his work shows a gracefully sensual and optimistic vision which seemed to herald 18C French art. Francesco Mazzola (1503-40), or **Il Parmigianino** (The Parmesan) as he was commonly known, was a more troubling and melancholy personality. His elongated forms and new, rather cold, colours were characteristic of Mannerism *(see ART:Mannerism)*. His canon of feminine beauty influenced the Fontainebleau school and all the other European Mannerists of the 16C, through the intermediary of Niccolò dell'Abbate and Il Primaticcio.

★★ **CITY CENTRE** *1/2 day*

This historic core of the city comprises the Romanesque **Episcopal Centre** ★★★ (**CYZ**) including the cathedral and baptistery, the Baroque Church of St John and the surrounding palaces as well as the Palazzo della Pilotta (16C-17C) and Correggio's Room.

★★ **Duomo** (**CY**) – The cathedral is in the Romanesque style and is flanked by an elegant Gothic campanile. The façade includes a Lombard porch supported by lions and surmounted by a loggia and three tiers of galleries with little columns. Inside, the dome is decorated with the famous **frescoes** painted by Correggio from 1522 to 1530. The ascending rhythm of the *Assumption of the Virgin* with the central figure amidst a swirling group of cherubim is remarkable. The artist's mastery of perspective and movement is expressed in an original and exuberant style virtually Baroque in spirit. A ***Descent from the Cross*** (1178) by the sculptor Antelami stands in the south transept.

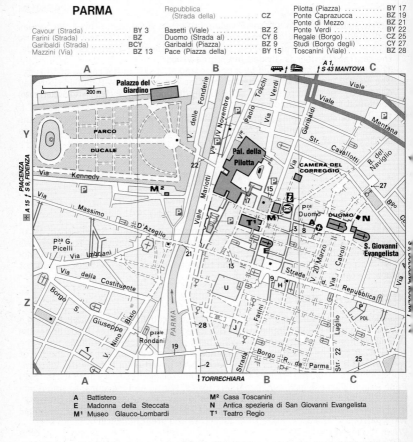

A   Battistero
E   Madonna della Steccata
M¹ Museo Glauco-Lombardi

M² Casa Toscanini
N   Antica spezieria di San Giovanni Evangelista
T¹ Teatro Regio

Despite the solemnity of the figures, the influence of the Provençal School is obvious. In the nave, the frescoes are by Gambara (1530-1574); on the vaulting they were painted by Bedoli (16C). The gilded *Angel* (1284) which crowned the spire of the bell-tower is now on the third pillar to the left of the nave.

★★★ **Battistero (CY A)** – This is Italy's most harmonious medieval monument. The octagonal baptistery in Veronese rose-coloured marble was started in 1196 and the architecture and carved decoration, which show great unity of style, date from the 13C. The baptistery is attributed to the sculptor Antelami who was also responsible for the sculptures; his signature appears on the lintel of the north door, dedicated to the Virgin. Inside (the interior is a 16-sided polygon), the admirable 13C **frescoes** of Byzantine inspiration depict scenes from the *Life of Christ* and the *Golden Legend*.

San Giovanni Evangelista (CYZ) – This Renaissance church, dedicated to St John the Evangelist, has a Baroque façade. Inside, the **frescoes on the dome**★★, painted by Correggio (1520-24), depict the *Vision of St John at Patmos* and the *Translation of St John the Evangelist*. Those on the arches of the chapels to the north (1st, 2nd and 4th) were executed by Parmigianino.
In the convent next door are the Renaissance **cloisters** ⊘.

Antica Spezieria di San Giovanni Evangelista (CY N) ⊘ – *1 Borgo Pipa.* This 13C pharmacy was started by the Benedictine monks. The furnishings date from the 16C.

Palazzo della Pilotta (BY) – The palace was so-called because the game of fives *(pilotta)* was played in its courtyards. This rather austere building, erected by order of the Farnese from 1583 to 1622, now houses two museums, the Palatine Library and the Farnese Theatre.

★ **Museo nazionale di Antichità** ⊘ – The National Museum of Antiquities displays pre-Roman and Roman artefacts including the finds made in the excavation of Velleia to the west of Parma.

★★ **Galleria nazionale (Pinacoteca)** ⊘ – The well-laid out gallery exhibits Emilian, Tuscan and Venetian paintings of the 14C, 15C and 16C by: Leonardo da Vinci *(La Scapigliata)*, Fra Angelico, Dosso Dossi, El Greco, Canaletto, Bellotto, Piazzetta and Tiepolo. Il Parmigianino is represented by his astonishing portrait *Turkish Slave*, which is of considerable elegance, and Correggio by one of his master-pieces, *The Virgin with St Jerome* (1528), as well as other works.

★ **Teatro Farnese** ⊘ – This imposing theatre was built in wood in 1619 by G B Aleotti, following the model of Palladio's Olympic Theatre in Vicenza *(see VICENZA)*. Inaugurated for the marriage of Margaret de' Medici and Odoardo Farnese, the theatre was almost totally destroyed in 1944 and was rebuilt exactly as before in the 1950s.

★ **Camera del Correggio** (CY) ⊘ – Correggio's Room, also known as St Paul's Room **(Camera di San Paolo)**, was the dining-room of the Abbess of St Paul's Convent. The ceiling frescoes depicting mythological scenes with a luminous quality are Correggio's first major work (1519-20). The garlands of flowers and trelliswork and the reliefs and architectural detail at the base of the vault reveal the influence of Mantegna, whom he met in his youth in Mantua *(see MANTOVA)*. The next room was decorated by Araldi (1504).

ADDITIONAL SIGHTS

★ **Museo Glauco-Lombardi** (BY M¹) ⊘ – The Glauco-Lombardi museum is chiefly devoted to life in the Duchy of Parma Piacenza in the 18C and 19C. It contains paintings and mementoes of the former Empress Marie-Louise who governed the duchy. There are numerous works by French artists: Nattier, Mignard, Chardin, Watteau, Fragonard, Greuze, La Tour, Hubert Robert, Vigée-Lebrun, David and Millet.

Madonna della Steccata (BZ E) ⊘ – This 16C church, designed by the architects Bernardino and Zaccagni, contains fine **frescoes**★ by Il Parmigianino representing *the Foolish and the Wise Virgins*, between Adam and Moses, and Eve and Aaron. The mausoleum of Neipperg, husband of the former French Empress Marie-Louise who became Duchess of Parma, is on the left, and the tombs of the Farnese family and the Bourbon-Parma are in the crypt.

Teatro Regio (BY T¹) – The Royal Theatre, built between 1821 and 1829 at the request of Marie-Louise of Habsburg, has a Classical frontage. The inaugural performance was of Bellini's opera, *Zaira*. The acoustics are excellent.

Palazzo del Giardino (BY) – The ducal garden **(parco ducale★)** was landscaped by the French architect Petitot and adorned with statues by another Frenchman, Boudard.

★ **Casa Toscanini** (BY M²) ⊘ – The birthplace of the famous conductor (1867-1957) houses interesting documents for anybody with a love of music: distinctions and decorations granted to the musician, sculptures and objects connected with the Toscanini family, Verdi and Wagner, letters from Mazzini, Garibaldi, D'Annunzio and Einstein, and numerous reminders of the master's work in America. There is also an audiovisual presentation of the conductor's career.

EXCURSIONS

★ **Torrechiara** ⊘ – *17km – 11 miles south by the Langhirano road*. This 15C fortress, built on a hilltop, is powerfully fortified by double ramparts, massive corner towers, a keep and machicolated curtain walls. The upper rooms (the Gaming and Gold Rooms) have remarkable **frescoes**★. From the terrace there is a superb **view**★ which reaches as far as the Apennines.

Fidenza – *23km – 14 miles west. Leave Parma by Via Massimo D'Azeglio* (AY). This attractive agricultural town has a remarkable 11C cathedral **(Duomo★)** which was completed in the Gothic style in the 13C. The lovely sculptured decoration of the **central porch**★★ is most likely the work of the Parmesan sculptor, Antelami. The three fine Romanesque doors are adorned with lions, a typically Emilian feature (see Reggio, Modena, Ferrara, Parma).

Fontanellato – *19km – 12 miles to the northwest by the Fidenza road and then the road to Soragna, to the right*. The vast moat-encircled castle, **Rocca San Vitale** ⊘, stands in the centre of town. The ceiling of one of the rooms is decorated with a **fresco★** depicting Diana and Actaeon by Il Parmigianino. The fine furnishings date from the 17C.

PAVIA*

Lombardy – Population 76 792

Michelin map 988 fold 13 or 428 G 9

Town plan in the current Michelin Red Guide Italia

This proud city on the banks of the Ticino River is rich in buildings from the Romanesque and Renaissance periods. The many old feudal towers dotted around the city were built by the noble families of Pavia, often as a public sign of their wealth – the taller the tower, the richer the family.

This important military camp under the Romans then became, successively, the capital of the Lombard Kings, rival of Milan in the 11C, famous intellectual and artistic centre during the 14C under the Visconti, a fortified town in the 16C and one of the most active centres of the 19C independence movements. The university one of the oldest and most famous in Europe, was founded in the 11C and its students included Petrarch, Leonardo da Vinci and the poet Ugo Foscolo *(The Las Letters of Jacopo Ortiz)*.

The dreams of conquest of the French kings ended at Pavia when, after his victory at Marignano (1515), François I was defeated and taken prisoner by the Emperor Charles V at the Battle of Pavia on 24 February 1525.

SIGHTS

* **Castello Visconteo** ⊙ – This impressive brick building was built by the Visconti It now houses the **Musei Civici★**, the municipal collections, which are rich in archeological finds, medieval and Renaissance sculpture and particularly paintings. The picture gallery **(pinacoteca★)**, on the first floor, has numerous masterpieces including a lovely altarpiece by the Brescian artist Vincenzo Foppa a *Virgin and Child* by Giovanni Bellini and a very expressive *Christ bearing the Cross* by the Lombard artist, Bergognone. The last room contains a 16C model of the cathedral by Fugazza after plans by Bramante.

* **Duomo** – This vast cathedral, surmounted by one of Italy's largest domes, was begun in 1488: both Bramante and Leonardo da Vinci are said to have worked on the plan. The façade is 19C. To the left of the façade stood an 11C municipal tower, which fell down in March 1989, while opposite is the 16C Bishop's Palace The adjoining Piazza Vittoria is overlooked by the 12C **Broletto** or town hall. The square affords an interesting view of the cathedral's chevet.

* **San Michele** – This lovely Romanesque church, dedicated to St Michael, has a pale-coloured sandstone **façade★** which is quite remarkable for the balance and variety of its sculptural ornamentation. An impressive Romanesque doorway on the south side has a lintel on which Christ is seen giving a papyrus volume to St Paul and the Keys of the Church to St Peter. Inside, there are interesting architectural features (dome on squinches, the friezes and modillions beneath the galleries, the elevated chancel, mosaics, capitals etc). The apse is decorated with a lovely 15C **fresco★** portraying the *Coronation of the Virgin*.

San Pietro in Ciel d'Oro – This Lombard-Romanesque church, dedicated to S Peter, which was consecrated in 1132, has a richly decorated west **door★**. In the chancel is the **Arca di Sant'Agostino★** (the tomb of St Augustine – 354-430), the work of the *maestri campionesi (see Index)*.

San Lanfranco – *2 km – 1 mile west.* In the chancel of this church, a **cenotaph★** (late 15C) by Amadeo commemorates Lanfranc, who was born in Pavia and became Archbishop of Canterbury, where he is buried (d 1098).

Certosa di PAVIA★★★

PAVIA CARTHUSIAN MONASTERY – Lombardy

Michelin map 988 fold 13 or 428 G 9 – 9km – 6 miles to the north of Pavia

The "Gra Car", Gratiarum Cartusia (Charterhouse of the Graces), is one of the most remarkable and characteristic examples of Lombard art. It was founded as a family mausoleum in 1396 by Gian Galeazzo Visconti of Milan. Most of the monastery was built in the 15C and 16C to the plans of successive architects. The former palace of the Dukes of Milan (1625) is on the right of the courtyard, and on the left are the studios of the sculptors in charge of the decoration.

*** **Façade** – Even unfinished, the façade is nevertheless famous for the care and richness of its decoration. The more ornate lower part (1473-99) was the work of the Mantegazza brothers, the famous architect and sculptor Amadeo, who worked also in Bergamo, and his pupil, Briosco. The upper part was completed in 1560 by another architect and sculptor, Cristoforo Lombardo.

The façade is adorned with multicoloured sculptures in marble, with medallions copied from antiquities, at the base, statues of saints in the niches and an endless

R. Bouquet/DIAF

Certosa di Pavia

variety of foliage, garlands and ornaments. Round Amadeo's famous windows are scenes from the Bible, the Life of Christ and the life of Gian Galeazzo Visconti. The low reliefs round the central doorway by Briosco depict events in the history of the Carthusians. Before entering the church, walk round to the left for a general view of the late Lombard-Gothic style, with its galleries of superimposed arcades.

★★ **Interior** ⊙ – The interior has a certain solemn grandeur and, although it is essentially Gothic, the beginnings of the Renaissance can be detected in the transept and the chancel.

There are numerous works of art. The chapels of the south aisle are decorated with late-15C frescoes by Bergognone who was also responsible for a *Crucifixion*, an altarpiece and a polyptych. The second chapel on the north side contains a **polyptych** of *God the Father* by Perugino. The north transept has an *Ecce Homo* by Bergognone, superb candelabra (1580) by Fontana and the famous **reclining figures** (1497) of Ludovico il Moro and Beatrice d'Este by Cristoforo Solari. The doorway to the former sacristy was the work of Amadeo. In the lavatorium there is a splendid Renaissance marble **lavabo** and a **fresco** by Luini. In the south transept stands the magnificent **tomb of Gian Galeazzo Visconti** by Cristoforo Romano dated 1497.

There are two **cloisters**. The smaller one is decorated with charming terracottas and a Baroque fountain. The larger one with 122 richly decorated arcades is bordered by 24 cells.

PERUGIA★★

Umbria – Population 150 576
Michelin map 988 fold 15 or 430 M 19

Perugia was one of the 12 Etruscan city-states known as *lucumonies* which comprised the federation of Etruria in the 7C and 6C BC. The massive Etruscan wall with its gateways gives some idea of the splendour of that age. The town also has numerous ecclesiastical and secular buildings from the Middle Ages. Today the capital of Umbria is an industrial and commercial centre and a university town.

Umbrian Painting – In harmony with their peaceful countryside, the Umbrian painters had gentle, mystic souls. They loved landscapes with pure lines, punctuated with trees; and in their stylised compositions, the women are depicted with a tender gracefulness, sometimes too mannered. Their technique is characterised by extremely delicate draughtsmanship and soft colours. The masters were Giovanni Boccati (1410-c1485), Fiorenzo di Lorenzo (d 1520) and especially Pietro Vannucci alias **Perugino** (1445-1523), the teacher of Raphael. His favourite subjects were religious; in them he showed his sense of space, atmosphere and landscape, marred only by a touch of mannerism. The historical artist **Pinturicchio** (1454-1518) was influenced by Perugino but his charmingly realistic scenes were painted more naïvely than those of his predecessor.

★★ PIAZZA 4 NOVEMBRE (BY) *2 hours*

This square in the heart of Perugia is one of the grandest in Italy. Here are grouped the chief buildings of the glorious period as an independent commune: the Priors' Palace, the Great Fountain and the Cathedral. Leading off from the far end of the square is the picturesque **Via Maestà delle Volte★** (**ABY 29**) with its medieval houses and vaulted passageways.

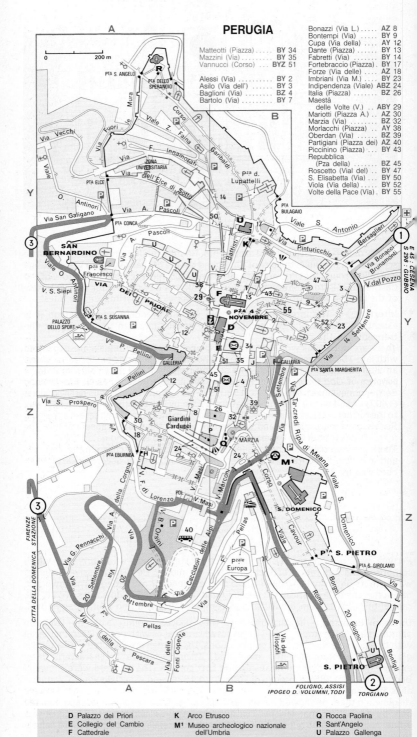

PERUGIA

Matteotti (Piazza)	BY 34
Mazzini (Via)	BY 35
Vannucci (Corso)	BYZ 51
Alessi (Via)	BY 2
Asilo (Via dell')	BY 3
Baglioni (Via)	BZ 4
Bartolo (Via)	BY 7

Bonazzi (Via L.)	AZ 8
Bontempi (Via)	BY 9
Cupa (Via della)	AY 12
Dante (Piazza)	BY 13
Fabretti (Via)	BY 14
Fortebraccio (Piazza)	BY 17
Forze (Via delle)	AZ 18
Imbriani (Via M.)	BY 23
Indipendenza (Viale)	ABZ 24
Italia (Piazza)	BZ 26
Maestà delle Volte (V.)	ABY 29
Mariotti (Piazza A.)	AZ 30
Marzia (Via)	BZ 32
Morlacchi (Piazza)	AY 38
Oberdan (Via)	BY 39
Partigiani (Piazza dei)	AZ 40
Piccinino (Piazza)	BY 43
Repubblica (Pza della)	BZ 45
Roscetto (Vial del)	BY 47
S. Elisabetta (Via)	BY 50
Viola (Via della)	BY 52
Volte della Pace (Via)	BY 55

D	Palazzo dei Priori	**K**	Arco Etrusco
E	Collegio del Cambio	**M¹**	Museo archeologico nazionale dell'Umbria
F	Cattedrale	**Q**	Rocca Paolina
		R	Sant'Angelo
		U	Palazzo Gallenga

** **Fontana Maggiore** – The Great Fountain was built to the designs of Fra Bevignate (1278) and is admirably proportioned. The sculpted panels are the work of Nicola Pisano (lower basin) and his son Giovanni (upper basin). Copies replace some of the originals, which are on display in the National Gallery of Umbria.

** **Palazzo dei Priori** (BY D) – The Priors' Palace was begun in the 13C and enlarged in the following centuries. It forms an ensemble of impressive grandeur. The façade overlooking the square has a majestic outside staircase leading up to a marble pulpit from which the priors harangued the people. The Corso Vannucci (BY 51) façade boasts a fine 14C doorway. Inside, the palace rooms are decorated with either 14C frescoes or beautifully carved 15C panelling in the Notaries' Chamber and college of the Mercanzia.

** **Galleria Nazionale dell'Umbria** ⊙ – The National Gallery of Umbria, housed on the top floor of the Priors' Palace, presents a large selection of Umbrian art showing its development from the 13C to the late 18C.
On display are: a *Madonna* by Duccio, a *Crucifix* by the unknown master, Maestro di San Francesco, a *polyptych of St Anthony* by Piero della Francesca and works by Fra Angelico, Boccati and Fiorenzo di Lorenzo.
Masterpieces by Pinturicchio and Perugino include a *Dead Christ* with its black background and an admirable *Madonna of Consolation*. Note also the marble statuettes by Nicola and Giovanni Pisano from the Great Fountain, and other works by Arnolfo di Cambio. The 17C is represented by Federico Barocci, Pietro da Cortona and Orazio Gentileschi.
The 15C Priors' Chapel is dedicated to the city's patron saints: St Herculanus and St Louis of Toulouse, whose story is told by Benedetto Bonfigli (d 1496) in a remarkable cycle of **frescoes**. The museum also has some lovely 13C and 14C French enamels and ivories.

* **Cattedrale** (BY F) – The cathedral is Gothic, but the Piazza Dante façade was completed with a Baroque doorway.
The south chapel contains an interesting *Descent from the Cross* by Barocci, which inspired Rubens in his *Antwerp Descent*. In the north chapel is a ring said to be the Virgin's wedding ring. In both these chapels, note the superb **stalls** with 16C marquetry work.

ADDITIONAL SIGHTS

** **San Pietro** (BZ) – To reach the church, dedicated to St Peter, go through the **Porta San Pietro**★ (BZ), a majestic but unfinished work of the Florentine Agostino di Duccio. The church was built at the end of the 10C and remodelled at the Renaissance. Inside are 11 excellent canvases by Vassilacchi, alias Aliense, a Greek contemporary of El Greco. Also of note are: the **carved tabernacle** by Mino da Fiesole and the marvellous 16C **stalls**★★.

* **San Domenico** (BZ) – An imposing Gothic church dedicated to St Dominic. The interior was altered in the 17C. To the right of the chancel is the 14C **funerary monument** of Benedict XI.

** **Museo Archeologico Nazionale dell'Umbria** (BZ M') ⊙ – The National Archeological Museum comprises prehistoric, Etruscan and Umbrian sections. The remarkable collections include funerary urns, sarcophagi and Etruscan bronzes.

* **Collegio del Cambio** (BY E) ⊙ – The Exchange was built in the 15C for the money-changers. In the Audience Room are the famous **frescoes**★★ of Perugino and his pupils. These frescoes display the humanist spirit of the age, which sought to combine ancient culture and Christian doctrine. The statue of Justice is by Benedetto da Maiano (15C).

** **Oratorio di San Bernardino** (AY) – To reach the church of St Bernardine, walk along the picturesque **Via dei Priori**★. This Renaissance jewel (1461) by Agostino di Duccio is exquisite in its harmonious lines, the delicacy of its multicoloured marbles and its sculptures. The low reliefs on the façade depict St Bernardine in glory on the tympanum, the life of the saint on the lintel and delightful angel musicians on the shafts. Inside the church, the altar consists of a 4C Paleo-Christian sarcophagus.

* **Via delle Volte della Pace** (BY 55) – The picturesque medieval street is formed by a long 14C Gothic portico as it follows the Etruscan town wall.

* **Sant'Angelo** (AY R) – This small church is circular in plan and dates from the 5C-6C. The interior includes 16 ancient columns.

* **Rocca Paolina** (BZ Q) ⊙ – *Access via Porta Marzia*. These are the remains of a fortress built in 1540 on the orders of Pope Paul III; hence the name "Pauline". The impressive interior still has huge walls, streets and wells dating from the 11C to 16C. Escalators have been built to facilitate access within the fortress.

PERUGIA

★ **Arco Etrusco (BY K)** – This imposing Etruscan Arch is built of huge blocks of stone. A 16C loggia surmounts the tower on the left.
Alongside, the majestic 18C **Palazzo Gallenga (U)** serves as a summer school for foreign students.

Giardini Carducci (AZ) – There is a superb view★★ from the Carducci Gardens, dominating the San Pietro quarter, over the Tiber Valley.

EXCURSIONS

★ **Ipogeo dei Volumni** ⊙ – *6km – 4 miles southeast. Leave by* ② *on the town plan.* This Etruscan hypogeum hewn out of the rock, comprises an atrium and nine burial chambers. The Volumnian tomb is the largest; it contains six rounded tombstones *(cippi)*, the biggest being that of the head of the family (2C BC).

Torgiano – *16km – 10 miles southeast. Leave by* ② *on the town plan.* This village dominating the Tiber Valley, has an interesting wine museum **(museo del vino★)** ⊙ (Lungarotti Foundation) describing wine-growing traditions in Umbria and Italy since the days of the Etruscans: excellent historical and photographic documents.

PESARO ⚌⚌

Marches – Population 88 475
Michelin map 988 fold 16, 429 fold 36 or 430 K 20
Town plan in the current Michelin Red Guide Italia

Pesaro is on the Adriatic coast at the mouth of the smiling Foglia Valley, which is terraced with vineyards, orchards and Italian poplars. The town was the birthplace of the composer **Gioacchino Rossini** (1792-1868), whose house (**casa natale** ⊙ no 34 Via Rossini) is now a museum.

★ **Musei Civici** ⊙ – The **picture gallery** in the Municipal Museum contains several works by the Venetian Giovanni Bellini *(see index)*. The famous **Pala di Pesaro** (1475) is an immense altarpiece representing the Virgin being crowned on the central panel, and numerous other scenes on the predella.
In the **ceramics section★★**, the Umbrian potteries are well represented but there are also examples of work from the Marches region.

Palazzo Ducale – The great mass of the Ducal Palace, built for a member of the Sforza family in the 15C, overlooks the Piazza del Popolo with its fountain adorned with tritons and sea horses. The crenellated façade has an arcaded portico with, above, windows adorned with festoons and cherubs.

Museo Oliveriano ⊙ – *97 Via Mazza.* There is an interesting collection of archeological items of varied origins: Italic, Greek, Etruscan and Roman.

Antica Chiesa di San Domenico – *In Via Branca behind the post office.* All that remains of the church, dedicated to St Dominic, is the 14C façade with a lovely pointed doorway flanked by spiral columns and sculpture.

EXCURSION

Gradara – *15km – 9 miles northwest.* Gradara is a medieval town, almost intact, surrounded by walls and battlemented gateways. The **Rocca★** ⊙, built on a square plan with corner towers, is a well-preserved example of military architecture in the 13C and 14C. It is here that Gianni Malatesta is said to have surprised and then murdered his wife, Francesca da Rimini, and her lover, Paolo Malatesta. Dante portrayed the inseparable couple in his *Divine Comedy*.

PIACENZA★

Emilia-Romagna – Population 102 051
Michelin map 988 fold 13 or 428 G 11
Town plan in the current Michelin Red Guide Italia

Piacenza was originally built by the Romans at the end of the Via Emilia on the south bank of the Po. It flourished in the Middle Ages and became a member of the Lombard League *(see Index)*. In 1545 Pope Paul III Farnese gave Piacenza and its neighbour Parma to his son along with the title of duke. After this its destiny was linked with that of Parma.

SIGHTS

★★ **Palazzo del Comune** – Also called "Il Gotico", this building is a masterpiece of Lombard-Gothic architecture and has a severe but harmonious appearance. There is a curious contrast between the marble lower part and the brick upper storeys, the great openings and the elegantly decorated windows. Standing in the square in front are two remarkable 17C **equestrian statues★★** of Alessandro Farnese and Ranuccio I Farnese.

★ Duomo ⊙ – This remarkable Lombard-Romanesque cathedral dates from the 12C-13C. The façade is pierced with three doorways and a rose window. The interior on the plan of a Latin cross is simple and forceful. Some of the dome frescoes are by Guercino.

San Savino ⊙ – *Near the junction of Via G. Alberoni with Via Roma*. The crypt of this 12C church, with its very pure architectural lines, has a magnificent mosaic pavement from the 11C-12C.

San Sisto ⊙ – *At the northern end of Via San Sisto*. This is a rather curious 16C building. The façade is preceded by an atrium and a doorway with rustication and grotesque masks. The interior has an interesting Renaissance decoration.

Madonna di Campagna ⊙ – *Via Campagna*. This 16C church, in the form of a Greek cross, contains interesting frescoes, notably by the 16C Venetian Pordenone.

Basilica di Sant'Antonino – *Piazza Sant'Antonino*. This former early-Christian basilica dedicated to St Anthony was remodelled in the 11C and has interesting features: an octagonal tower (40m – 131ft high), lanterns and the north "Paradise" vestibule (1350) in the Gothic style.

Palazzo Farnese ⊙ – This imposing late-Renaissance building was never completed but it now houses a museum **(Museo Civico)**. The paintings include a *Madonna* by Botticelli and two cycles of frescoes, richly framed in stucco, depicting the stories of Alessandro Farnese and Pope Paul III by Draghi and Ricci. There are also collections of Murano glass, ceramics (17C-18C), Romanesque sculpture (12C), frescoes of the Lombard school (14C-15C), coats of arms and ancient arms, and an archeological section *(reorganisation in progress)*. A **collection of carriages** (16C-17C) and a **Museo del Risorgimento** are also of interest to visitors.

Galleria d'Arte Moderna Ricci Oddi ⊙ – *No 13 Via S. Siro*. The modern art collections include Italian paintings from the various regions ranging from the Romantic period to the 20C: works by the landscape painter Antonio Fontanesi, the Macchiaioli (Fattori), artists influenced by the Impressionist school (Boldoni, Zandomeneghi), works in an oriental and figurative idiom (De Pisis), Futurist (Boccioni) and metaphysical (De Chirico, Carrà) paintings. There are also sculptures (Medardo Rosso) and works by foreign artists such as Klimt who influenced Italian art.

Galleria Alberoni ⊙ – *No 77 Via Emilia, opposite the university*. The gallery is situated within the precincts of a college founded in the 18C by Cardinal Alberoni, and comprises 17C-18C Flemish and Italian **tapestries** and a collection of 15C-19C paintings including an *Ecce Homo* by Antonello da Messina, and works by Flemish (Jan Provost) and 17C-18C Italian artists (Guido Reni, Baciccia, Luca Giordano).

PIENZA★★

Tuscany – Population 2 325

Michelin map 988 fold 15 or 430 M·17 – 52km – 32 miles southeast of Siena

The former town of Corsignano was renamed in honour of its most famous son, the diplomat and humanist poet, Eneo Silvio Piccolomini (1405-64), who became Pope Pius II in 1458. He commissioned the Florentine architect, **Bernardo Rossellino** (1409-82), a pupil of Alberti, to build in his native village a square which would be the focal point of an **ideal city** and would bring together the civil and religious authorities. The architectural unity of the square, which was the first example of Renaissance town planning, was intended to reflect the city's harmony. The principal monuments line the town's main axis: the town hall opposite the cathedral has a ground-floor loggia. The other sides of the square are framed by the Bishop's Palace (simply restored in the 15C) and the Palazzo Piccolomini; a pretty well in front of the latter enhances the overall plan.

There is a fine **view★** over Orcia Valley from behind the cathedral.

★ Cattedrale – The cathedral, which was completed in 1462, has a Renaissance façade. The interior (restored) shows Gothic influences and contains several paintings by the Sienese school, including an *Assumption★★*, a masterpiece by Vecchietta.

Museo della Cattedrale ⊙ – The Cathedral Museum contains pictures of the 14C and 15C Sienese school and a remarkable 14C historiated cope made in England.

PIENZA

* **Palazzo Piccolomini** ⊙ – Rossellino's masterpiece was greatly influenced by
the Palazzo Rucellai in Florence *(see FIRENZE)*. The three sides facing the
town are similar; the fourth overlooking Orcia Valley has three tiers of loggias
and gives onto hanging gardens which are among the earliest to have been
created. The elegant inner courtyard features slim Corinthian columns. The
palace still has its armoury, and the incunabula and a Baroque bed from the
papal bedchamber.

Pienza and Val d'Orcia

EXCURSIONS

* **Montalcino** – *24km – 15 miles west.* In addition to part of its 13C walls, this
small hillside town still has a magnificent fortress **(fortezza★★)** built in 1361, a
consummate example of defensive forts at that time. It is shaped like a pentagon
and its tall walls, with machicolations and parapet walk, are punctuated by five
towers. One of them was used as officers' quarters and, in case of siege, could
be used by the nobility. The ordinary people would seek shelter within the outer
walls. It was here that the government of Siena took refuge when the town was
captured by Holy Roman Emperor Charles V in 1555.
Montalcino is also famous for its **Brunello**, a red wine of excellent quality produced
in a small vineyard. The town is a picturesque labyrinth of medieval streets
leading to a Romanesque and Gothic church, to the 13C town hall (**Palazzo
Comunale★**) flanked by a loggia and topped by a tall tower, or to the small museum
(**museo diocesano**) ₋ paintings and sculptures from the 14C-15C Siena School,
ceramics from Montalcino, and antique remains.

** **Abbazia di Sant'Antimo** ⊙ – *35km – 22 miles southwest.* The abbey, which
was founded in the 9C, stands in an isolated hill **site★** amid cypress and olive
groves. Its prosperity was at its peak in the 12C when the **church** was built. It
is a fine example of Cistercian Romanesque architecture with Burgundian (ambulatory and apsidal chapels) and Lombard (porch, belltower with Lombard bands and
façades) influences. The interior is spacious and austere. Columns topped by fine
alabaster capitals divide the nave with its wooden roof from the aisles which have
groined vaulting. Only some of the monastic buildings remain standing.

Michelin publications for a trip to Italy

maps 428, 429, 430, 431 (scale 1: 400 000)
map 988 Italy-Switzerland (scale 1: 1 000 000)
road atlas Italy (scale 1: 300 000)
Green Guide Italy: sights and scenic routes
Green Guide Rome: 29 walks in the Eternal Cily
Green Guide Tuscany: art and architecture, landscape
Green Guide Venice: the fascinating city, the islands in the lagoon,
the Palladian villas along the Brenta
Red Guide Italia: Hotels and restaurants

PISA★★★

Tuscany – Population 98 810

Michelin map 988 fold 14 or 428, 429, and 430 K 13

This calm and pleasant town, near the sea, has splendid buildings recalling the past grandeur of the Pisan Republic.

HISTORICAL NOTES

Sheltered from raiding pirates, Pisa was a Roman naval base and commercial port until the end of the Empire (5C). It became an independent maritime republic at the end of the 9C and continued to benefit from its geographical location. Pisa became the rival of Genoa and Venice, and the Pisans waged war against the Saracens in the Mediterranean basin. It was in the 12C and the beginning of the 13C that Pisa reached the peak of its power and prosperity. This period was marked by the construction of some fine buildings and the foundation of the university. During the 13C struggles between the Emperor and the Pope, Pisa supported the Ghibellines *(see Index)* and thus opposed Genoa on the seas and Lucca and Florence on land. In 1284 the Pisan fleet was defeated at the **naval battle of Meloria.** Ruined and wracked by internal strife, Pisa's maritime empire foundered; Corsica and Sardinia which she had ruled since the 11C were ceded to Genoa. Pisa herself passed under Florentine rule and the Medici took a special interest in the city, especially in the world of science. Its most famous son was the astronomer and physicist **Galileo** (1564-1642). His patron was Cosimo II, Grand Duke of Tuscany. Nevertheless Galileo, aged 70, had to defend his theory of the rotation of the earth before the Inquisition and in fact renounced it.

PISAN ART

The economic prosperity of the powerful maritime Pisan Republic from the 11C to the 13C fostered the development of a new art style which is particularly evident in the fields of architecture and sculpture. The **Pisan-Romanesque style**, with the cathedral as the most rigorous example, is characterised by external decoration: the alternate use of different coloured marbles to create geometric patterns, a play of light and shade due to the tiers of loggias with small columns on the upper parts of the façade, and intarsia decoration showing the strong influence of the Islamic world and of Christian countries of the Near East which had relations with the maritime republic. Alongside architects such as Buscheto, Rainaldo and Diotisalvi there were numerous sculptors to embellish the exteriors. Pisa became an important centre for Gothic sculpture in Italy, thanks to the work of **Nicola Pisano** (1220-c80), originally from Puglia, and his son **Giovanni Pisano** (1250-c1315). Their work included carved pulpits with two good examples in the Baptistery and the Cathedral, which greatly influenced the early Tuscan Renaissance.

★★ PIAZZA DEL DUOMO (AY) *3 hours*

In and around this famous square, also known as **Campo dei Miracoli**, are four buildings which form one of the finest architectural complexes in the world. It is advisable to approach on foot from the west through the Porta Santa Maria to enjoy the best view of the leaning tower.

★★ **Duomo** ⊘ – This splendid cathedral was built with the fantastic spoils captured during the expeditions against the Muslims. Building started in 1063 under Buscheto and was continued by Rainaldo, who designed the façade.
The **west front**★★★ is light and graceful with four tiers of small marble columns and a decorative facing of alternating light – and dark-coloured marble. The church itself is built on the plan of a Latin cross. The original doors were replaced by bronze **doors**★ cast in 1602 to designs by Giovanni Bologna. The south transept door has very fine Romanesque bronze **panels**★★ (late 12C) by Bonanno Pisano, depicting the Life of Christ in a naïve but free creative style.
The **interior**★★, with its nave and four aisles, is impressive for its length (100m – 328ft), its deep apse, its three-aisled transept and the forest of piers which offer an astonishing variety of perspectives. Note in particular the beautiful **pulpit**★★★ of **Giovanni Pisano** on which he worked from 1302 to 1311. It is supported by six porphyry columns and five pillars decorated with religious and allegorical statues.
The eight panels of the pulpit evoke the Life of Christ and group a multitude of personages with dramatic expressions. Near the pulpit is Galileo's lamp, which gave the scholar his original idea for his theory concerning the movement of the pendulum.

★★ **Torre pendente** or **Campanile** – The **Leaning Tower of Pisa** is both a bell-tower and belfry. This white marble tower (58m – 189ft high) was begun in 1173 in a pure Romanesque style by Bonanno Pisano and completed in 1350. Built, like the towers of Byzantium, as a cylinder, the tower has six storeys of galleries with columns which seem to wind round in a spiral because of the slope of the building. On the lower level is the blind arcading decorated with lozenges that is specific to the architecture of Pisa. The tower slowly began leaning in 1178 and it has continued to do so ever since at a rate of between 1 and 2 millimeters a year. It is caused by the alluvial soil on which the tower is built, soil that is insufficiently resistant to bear the weight of the building. Over the years, architects have tried in vain to correct the unfortunate "lean". After the tower was closed to the public in 1990, it was surrounded by two stainless steel cables at first floor level and, in 1993, the base was strengthened by a reinforced concrete "corset", which included 670 tonnes of lead to counterbalance the lean.

★★★ **Battistero** ⊙ – Work on the Baptistery began in 1153 and the two lower storeys are in the Romanesque Pisan style, while the frontons and pinnacles above the first-floor arcades are Gothic. The building is roofed with an unusual dome and has four doorways with fine carving. The majestic interior is full of light and has a diameter of 35m – 115ft. The sober decoration consists of light- and dark-coloured marble; in the centre is a lovely octagonal **font**★ (1246) by an artist from Como, Guido Bigarelli. The masterpiece of the baptistery is the admirable **pulpit**★★ (1260) by Nicola Pisano. It is less ornate than the one done by his son for the cathedral and stands on simple columns. The five panels of the pulpit depict the Life of Christ: its noble, Classical sculptures are no doubt inspired by Roman art and the sarcophagi to be found in the neighbouring Composanto.

★★ **Camposanto** ⊙ – This burial ground was begun in 1277 by Giovanni di Simone, one of the architects of the leaning tower. Work was interrupted by the naval Battle of Meloria *(see Index)* and completed only in the 15C. The large rectangular area is bounded on the outside by a blind portico. Inside, the majestic semicircular arcading includes four delicate lancet windows with Gothic tracery. The soil in the Camposanto (Sacred Field) proper, in the centre, is said to have been brought back from the Hill of Calvary by the Crusaders. There are Greco-Roman sarcophagi in the galleries, which are paved with about 600 tombstones. The majority of the wall frescoes have been destroyed in a fire caused by artillery shelling in 1944. One of the most famous cycles comprising *The Triumph of Death*★★★ and the *Last Judgement*★★ and *Hell*★ by a 14C artist was saved and is displayed in the north gallery. The transience and vanity of wordly pleasures are illustrated with great realism.

★★ **Museo dell'Opera del Duomo** (**M²**) ⊙ – The Cathedral Museum contains works of art from the monuments in Piazza del Duomo: 12C-16C sculptures (Romanesque period influenced by Islamic and Burgundian art, Gothic and Renaissance); cathedral treasure (ivory *Madonna and Child* by Giovanni Pisano) and silver ware. On the first floor are displayed 15C-18C paintings and sculpture; fragments of Renaissance stalls and 12C-13C illuminated manuscripts; episcopal vestments and ornaments; archeological artefacts found in the early 19C in the cemetery by Carlo Lasinio, who made a series of engravings of the Camposanto frescoes.

Piazza del Duomo

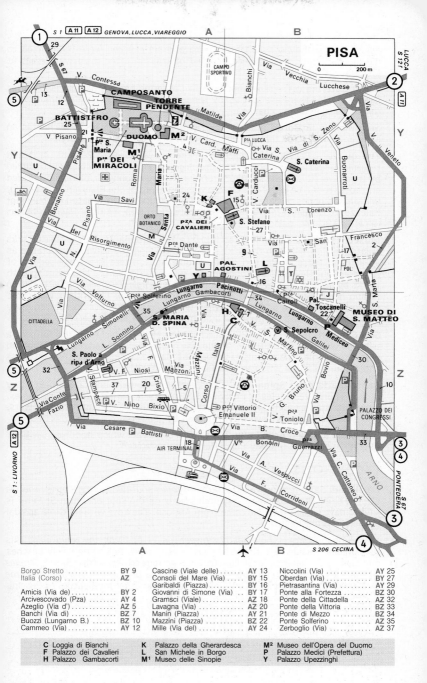

PISA

★ **Museo delle Sinopie** (M¹) ⊙ – This museum contains the sketches or *sinopie* (sketches in a reddish-brown pigment, sinopia, which came from Sinope on the Black Sea) which were under the frescoes and were brought to light by a fire following the 1944 bombing. They have been well restored and give a good idea of the vitality and free draughtsmanship of these 13C-15C painters.

ADDITIONAL SIGHTS

★ **Piazza dei Cavalieri** (AY) – This, the historic centre of Pisa, gets its name from the Cavalieri di Santo Stefano (Knights of St Stephen), a military order which specialised in the struggle against the infidels. Around the square are: the **Palazzo dei Cavalieri** (ABY F) with a **façade**★ decorated by Vasari; the **Chiesa di Santo Stefano** (BY) built in 1569 with its white, green and pink marble façade and dedicated to St Stephen; and the **Palazzo Gherardesca** (AY K) designed in 1607 by Vasari to stand on the site of a former prison, Torre della Fame,

211

where Count Ugolino della Gherardesca and his children were condemned to die by starvation, having been accused of treason after the naval defeat at Meloria.

Santa Caterina (BY) – The Church of St Catherine has a graceful Pisan-Gothic façade★. Inside there are statues by Nino Pisano, in particular an *Annunciation* (on either side of the chancel).

San Michele in Borgo (BY L) – The façade★ of the church of St Michael is an excellent example of the transitional Pisan Romanesque-Gothic style.

The quays – Prestigious palaces line the quays, **Lungarno Pacinotti** (ABY) and **Lungarno Mediceo** (BZ), notably **Palazzo Upezzinghi** (AY Y), a 17C building now occupied by the university; **Palazzo Agostini**★ (ABY), a 15C mansion with a highly-decorated entrance front (the Caffè dell'Ussero was the haunt of the Risorgimento poets), and on the opposite bank the Palazzo Gambacorti (BZ H), a late-14C building; Palazzo Toscanelli (BZ) where Byron wrote *Don Juan;* and the Palazzo Medici (BZ P), a 13C-14C palace.

★★ **Museo Nazionale di San Matteo** (BZ) ⊙ – The National Museum houses works created in Pisa between the 13C and 15C, showing the town's importance as an artistic centre at the end of the Middle Ages. There is a small section of ceramics, but the museum concentrates mainly on sculpture and painting with works by great sculptors such as Andrea Pisano *(Virgin of the Annunciation)* and Nino Pisano *(Virgin Mary Nursing)* and by early Pisan painters or Florentines who came to work in the town in the 14C when work was in progress on the cemetery (Camposanto). Note the **polyptych** by Simone Martini and Masaccio's *St Paul*.

San Sepolcro (BZ) – This 12C Church of the Holy Sepulchre in the form of a pyramid was built by Diotisalvi. Inside, the nobly-proportioned **chancel**★ is roofed with a tall dome. There is also the tomb of Maria Mancini, Louis XIV's mistress and Mazarin's niece who came to Pisa to die in 1715.

★★ **Santa Maria della Spina** (AZ) – This early-14C church, dedicated to St Mary of the Thorn, resembles a finely-worked reliquary shrine with all its gables, pinnacles, statues and statuettes by the Pisano, their assistants and followers. Some of the originals have been replaced by replicas.

San Paolo a Ripa d'Arno (AZ) – The Church of St Paul which stands on the bank of the Arno boasts a lovely Pisan-Romanesque façade★.

EXCURSIONS

★ **Basilica di San Piero a Grado** – *6km – 4 miles southwest. Leave by* ⑤*, the Via Conte Fazio*. This Romanesque church stands on the spot on which St Peter is said to have landed when he came from Antioch. The apse with its three apsidal chapels is remarkable.

⌂⌂ **Viareggio** – *20km – 12 miles northwest. Leave by* ① *on the town plan*. This fashionable seaside resort, on the Tyrrhenian Coast, has some lovely beaches and plenty of amenities for holidaymakers. At **Torre del Lago Puccini** *(5km – 3 miles to the southeast)* the composer Puccini wrote *La Bohème, Tosca* and *Madame Butterfly*. The **Villa Puccini** ⊙ contains the tomb and other mementoes of Puccini.

PISTOIA★★

Tuscany – Population 87 698
Michelin map 988 fold 14, 428, 429 fold 33 and 430 K 14
Town plan in the current Michelin Red Guide Italia

This industrial town has a rich historic centre which is evidence of its importance in the 12C-14C. Both Lucca and Florence coveted Pistoia, but it was Florence and the Medici who annexed it for good in 1530.

★★ PIAZZA DEL DUOMO *1 hour*

This is a most attractive and well-proportioned square lined with elegant secular and religious buildings.

★ **Duomo** – Rebuilt in the 12C and 13C, the cathedral's façade★ is a harmonious blend of the Pisan-Romanesque style (tiers of colonnaded galleries) and the Florentine-Renaissance style (porch with slender columns added in the 14C). The lower part of the campanile is quite massive but it becomes more graceful towards the top with three tiers of colonnaded galleries. The interior was remodelled in the 17C. Inside is the famous **altar of St James**★★★ ⊙, a masterpiece of silversmith work dating from the 13C, which was modified and extended in the following centuries. The saints surround the apostle seated in a niche, with

Christ in Glory above. Scenes from the Old and New Testaments complete the composition. In the chapel to the left of the chancel is a lovely *Madonna in Majesty*★ (c1480) by Lorenzo di Credi.

★ **Battistero** ⊙ – This Gothic octagonal baptistery with polychrome marble facing dates from the 14C. The tympanum of the central doorway bears a statue of the *Virgin and Child* between St Peter and St John the Baptist, attributed to Nino and Tommaso Pisano.

Palazzo Pretorio – This palace was built in the 14C as the residence of the governing magistrate *(podestà)* and remodelled in the 19C.

Palazzo del Comune – The Town Hall was built from 1294 to 1385 and has a graceful arcaded façade with elegant paired windows or triple bays. The palace houses the **Museo Civico** ⊙ with a collection of paintings and sculptures from the 13C-20C Tuscan school.

ADDITIONAL SIGHTS

Palazzo del Tau – *Corso Silvano Fedi.* This former monastery of the Order of the Monks Hospitaller of St Anthony was built in the 14C. It owes its name to the blue enamel "T" that used to adorn the monks' habits. It is now an **Information Centre** ⊙ on the work of the sculptor **Marino Marini** (1901-1980).

Ospedale del Ceppo – The portico on the hospital façade has a magnificent **frieze**★★ in terracotta (1530) by Giovanni della Robbia showing the Seven Works of Mercy.

★ **Sant'Andrea** – This church dedicated to St Andrew is in the pure Pisan-Romanesque style and has a famous **pulpit**★★ executed (1298-1308) by Giovanni Pisano in his dramatic but intensely lively manner: the panels represent five scenes from the Life of Christ. The lovely **crucifix**★ in gilded wood is by Giovanni Pisano *(in a niche beyond the first altar on the right).*

San Giovanni Forcivitas – The Church of St John outside the City, built from the 12C to the 14C, has a long and spectacular **north façade**★ in the Pisan-Romanesque style. Inside, there is a **pulpit**★ (1270) by Fra Guglielmo from Pisa, a polyptych by Taddeo Gaddi *(to the left of the altar)* and an admirable glazed terracotta of the *Visitation*★★ by Luca della Robbia.

EXCURSION

★ **Vinci** – *24km – 15 miles south.* The great Leonardo da Vinci was born not far from this town. The **Museo Leonardiano** ⊙ is housed in the castle in honour of its famous son.
The birthplace (**casa natale** ⊙) of the artist lies 2km – 1 mile to the north amidst olive trees, bathed in a pellucid light.

Golfo di POLICASTRO★★

Gulf of POLICASTRO – Campania – Basilicata – Calabria
Michelin map 988 or 431 G 28

This magnificent gulf extending from the tip of Infreschi to Praia a Mare is backed by high mountains whose sharp, needle-like peaks soar skywards.
The lower slopes are planted with cereals and olive groves with clumps of chestnut trees above. Between Sapri and Praia a Mare the corniche road overlooks the green waters which lap the charming creeks. A series of small villages succeed one another along this enchanting coast.

⌂⌂ **Maratea** – This seaside resort has many beaches and creeks and its hotels and villas are hidden behind a screen of luxuriant vegetation. The village itself is spread over the slopes of Monte Biagio, on the summit of which stands the Basilica of San Biagio and the great white figure of the Statue of the Redeemer (22m – 72ft tall), the work of Innocenti (1965). Nearby there is a superb **panorama**★★ of the Gulf of Policastro and the Calabrian coast.

The Practical Information section at the end of the guide lists:
    – information about travel, motoring, accommodation, recreation
    – local or national organisations providing additional information
    – calendar of events
    – admission times and charges for the sights described in the guide

POMPEI★★★

POMPEII – Campania – Population 25 173

Michelin map 988 fold 27 or 431 E 25 – Local map see Golfo di NAPOLI

Pompeii, the opulent town which was buried in AD 79 in one of the most disastrous volcanic eruptions in history, provides important evidence of the ancient way of life. The extensive and varied ruins of the dead city, in its attractive setting, movingly evoke on a grand scale a Roman city at the time of the Empire.

HISTORICAL NOTES

Pompeii was founded in the 8C BC by the Oscans, but by the 6C BC a Greek influence was already prevalent in the city from its neighbour Cumae, which was then a powerful Greek colony. From the end of the 5C BC, when it came under Samnite rule, to the beginning of the 1C AD the city knew great prosperity; town planning and art flourished. In the year 80 BC, the town fell under Roman domination and then it became a favourite resort of rich Romans. Roman families settled there. Pompeii adopted Roman organisation, language, lifestyle, building methods and decoration. When the eruption of Vesuvius struck, Pompeii was a booming town with a population of about 25 000. The town was situated in a fertile region, trade flourished and there was even some industrial activity; it also had a port. The numerous shops and workshops which have been uncovered, its wide streets and the deep ruts made in the cobblestones by chariot wheels are evidence of the intense activity that went on in the town.

The people had a lively interest in spectacles, games and active politics. In the year AD 62, an earthquake extensively damaged the town but before all could be put to rights, Vesuvius erupted (August AD 79) and also destroyed Herculaneum and Stabiae. In the space of two days Pompeii was buried under a layer of cinders 6m to 7m – 20ft to 23ft deep. Bulwer-Lytton describes these events in *The Last Days of Pompeii*.

It was only in the 18C, under the reign of Charles of Bourbon, that systematic excavations began. The finds had a tremendous effect in Europe, creating a revival of antique art and the development of a so-called Pompeiian style.

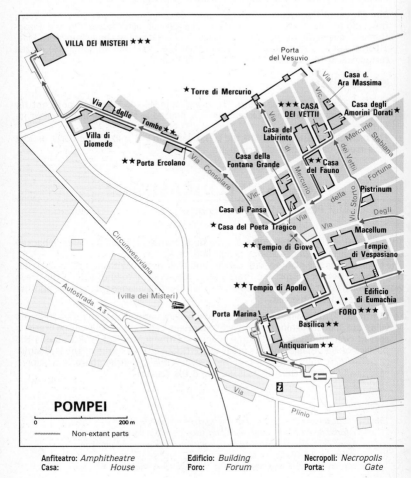

Anfiteatro: *Amphitheatre*	**Edificio:** *Building*	**Necropoli:** *Necropolis*
Casa: *House*	**Foro:** *Forum*	**Porta:** *Gate*

ARCHITECTURE AND DECORATION

Building methods – Pompeii was destroyed before a degree of uniformity in building methods had been achieved and it presents examples of the diverse methods and materials used: **opus quadratum** (large blocks of freestone piled on top of one another, without mortar of any kind); **opus incertum** (irregularly-shaped blocks of tufa or lava bonded with mortar); **opus reticulatum** (small square blocks of limestone or tufa arranged diagonally to form a decorative pattern); **opus testaceum** (walls are faced with triangular bricks laid flat with the pointed end turned inwards). Sometimes the walls were faced with plaster or marble. There are several types of dwelling in Pompeii: the sober and austere house of the Samnites, which became larger and more richly decorated through Greek influence. With the arrival of the Romans and the problems arising from a growing population, a new kind of house evolved in which limited space is compensated for by richness of decoration.

Pompeiian painting – A large number of paintings which adorned the walls of the dwellings have been transferred to the Archeological Museum in Naples. However, a visit to the dead city gives a good idea of the pictorial decoration of the period. There are four different **styles**. The 1st style by means of relief and light touches of colour imitates marble. The 2nd style is by far the most attractive: walls are divided into large panels by false pillars surmounted by pediments or crowned by a small shrine, with false doors all designed to create an illusion of perspective.

The artists show a partiality for the famous Pompeiian red, cinnabar obtained from mercury sulphide, and a dazzling black, both of which make for a very striking style. The 3rd style abandoned false relief in favour of scenes and landscapes altogether more ethereal and painted in pastel colours. Most of the frescoes uncovered at Pompeii belong to the 4th style. It combines elements from the 2nd style with others from the 3rd style to produce ornate compositions.

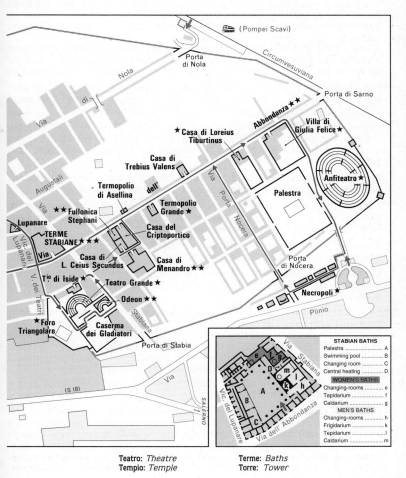

Teatro: *Theatre*　　Terme: *Baths*
Tempio: *Temple*　　Torre: *Tower*

LA CITTÀ MORTA (THE DEAD CITY) ⊘

allow 1 day - access by several gates

Porta Marina - This was the gateway through which the road passed to go down to the sea. There are separate gates for animals and for pedestrians.

★★ **Antiquarium** - This contains historical records, objects in daily use and reconstructions of mills. There are mouldings of human beings and animals in the attitudes in which they died.

Streets - The streets are straight and intersect at right angles. They are sunk between raised pavements and are interrupted at intervals by blocks of stone to enable pedestrians to cross without getting down from the pavement. This was particularly useful on rainy days when the roadway was awash; these stepping-stones were positioned so as to leave enough space for chariots. Fountains, of simple design, adorned square basins all similar.

★★★ **Foro** - The forum was the centre of the town and the setting for most of the large buildings. In this area, religious ceremonies were held, trade was carried out and justice was dispensed. The immense square was paved with broad marble flagstones and adorned with statues of past emperors. A portico surmounted by a terrace enclosed it on three sides.

The **Basilica**★★ is the largest building (67m by 25m - 220ft by 82ft) in Pompeii where judicial affairs and business were conducted.

The **Tempio di Apollo**★★ is a temple dedicated to Apollo which was built before the Roman occupation and stood against the majestic background of Vesuvius. The altar was placed in front of the steps leading to the shrine *(cella)*. Facing each other are copies of the statues of Apollo and Diana found on the spot (the originals are in the Naples Museum). The **Horreum**, a warehouse probably used for storing cereals, has a display of archeological artefacts.

The **Tempio di Giove**★★ has pride of place. The temple dedicated to Jupiter is flanked by two triumphal arches, formerly faced with marble.

The **Macellum** was a large covered market lined with shops. In the centre, a kiosk surrounded by pillars and crowned by a dome contained a basin.

The **Tempio di Vespasiano**, dedicated to Vespasian, contained a marble altar adorned with a sacrificial scene.

A fine doorway with a marble frame decorated with carvings of plants gave access to the **Edificio di Eumachia** (Building of Eumachia), built by the priestess for the powerful guild of the *fullones (see below)* of which she was the patron.

★ **Foro Triangolare** - There are several Ionic columns of a majestic propylaeum which preceded the Triangular Forum. A few vestiges of its small **Doric temple** provide rare evidence of the town's existence in the 6C BC.

★ **Teatro Grande** - The Great Theatre was built in the 5C BC, remodelled in the Hellenistic period (200-150 BC) and again by the Romans in the 1C AD. It was an open-air theatre which could be covered by a canopy and could hold 5 000 spectators.

Caserma dei Gladiatori - The barracks for the gladiators has a large esplanade bounded by a gateway, originally used as a foyer for the theatres.

★★ **Odeon** - Odeons, or covered theatres, were used for concerts, oratorical displays and ballets. This held only 800 spectators. It had a wooden roof and it dates from the early days of the Roman colonisation.

★ **Tempio d'Iside** - This small temple is dedicated to the Egyptian goddess Isis, adopted by the Romans, who were very liberal in their choice of gods.

Casa di L. Ceius Secundus - This is an interesting house *(casa)* with its façade faced with stucco in imitation of stone as in the 1st style, and with its pretty little *atrium*.

★★ **Casa di Menandro** - This large patrician villa named after Menander, was richly decorated with paintings (4th style) and mosaics and had its own baths. Part of the building was reserved for the servants' quarters. There is a Tuscan *atrium (see ANCIENT CIVILISATIONS)* with a *lararium* arranged as a small shrine in one corner. It has a remarkable peristyle with Doric columns faced with stucco, between which stands a low wall adorned with plants and animals.

The house opens onto **Via dell'Abbondanza**★★, a commercial street which is now most evocative with its shops and houses.

Casa del Criptoportico - *No 2, Via dell'Abbondanza.* After passing through the peristyle (note the painting in the *lararium*: Mercury with a peacock, snakes and foliage), go down to the Cryptoporticus, a wide underground passage surmounted by a fine barrel vault and lit by small windows. This type of corridor, which was very popular in Roman villas during the Empire, was used as a passage and for exercise as it was sheltered from the sun as well as from bad weather.

★★ **Fullonica Stephani** – *No 7, Via dell'Abbondanza.* This is an example of a dwelling-house converted into workshops. The clothing industry flourished in Roman times as the full, draped costume required a lot of material. In the *fullonicae*, new fabrics were finished and clothes were laundered. Several of these workshops have been uncovered in Pompeii. The **fullones** (fullers) cleaned the cloths by trampling them underfoot in vats filled with a mixture of water and soda or urine.

Termopolio di Asellina – This was a bar which also sold pre-cooked dishes *(thermopolium).* A stone counter giving directly onto the street formed the shop front; jars embedded in the counter contained the food for sale.

★ **Termopolio Grande** – This bar, which is similar to the previous one, has a painted *lararium.*

Casa di Trebius Valens – The inscriptions on the wall are electoral slogans. At the far end of the peristyle the polychrome fresco is in imitation of a stone wall.

★ **Casa di Loreius Tiburtinus** – This was a rich dwelling, judging from the fine marble *impluvium*, the *triclinium* adorned with frescoes and the **decoration**★ against a white background of one of the rooms, which is among the best examples of the 4th Pompeiian style. But its most luxurious feature was the splendid **garden**★ which was laid out for water displays.

★ **Villa di Giulia Felice** – Built just within the town boundary, it has three main parts: the dwelling, the baths which the owner opened to the public, and a section for letting, including an inn and shops. The large garden is bounded by a fine **portico**★ and embellished by a fine series of basins.

★ **Anfiteatro** – This is the oldest Roman amphitheatre known (80 BC). Alongside is the great **palestra** used as a training ground by athletes.

★ **Necropoli at the Porta di Nocera** – According to custom, tombs line one of the roads leading out of town, via the Nocera Gate.

Take the Via di Porta Nocera to return to the Via dell' Abbondanza, then turn left.

★★★ **Terme Stabiane** – *See plan above and details of Roman baths – see Ancient Civilisations.*
These baths, the best preserved and most complete in Pompeii, are divided into sections for men and women. The entrance is through the gymnasium, *palestra* (**A**) for athletic games, to the left of which is a swimming pool, *piscina* (**B**), with adjacent changing-rooms, *spogliatoio* (**C**).
The **women's baths** begin at the far end on the right, with changing-rooms (**e**) fitted with lockers, a *tepidarium* (lukewarm, **f**) and a *caldarium* (hot, **g**). The central heating apparatus (**D**) is between the men's and women's baths. The **men's baths** have large, well preserved changing-rooms (**h**), a *frigidarium* (cold, **k**), a *tepidarium* (**l**) and a *caldarium* (**m**). There is a fine stucco decoration on the coffered ceiling.

Lupanare – The decorations of the brothel are licentious.

★ **Pistrinum** – Note the baker's oven and flourmills.

★★ **Casa del Fauno** – This vast, luxurious house had two atriums, two peristyles and dining-rooms for all seasons. The bronze original of the famous statuette of the faun that adorned one of the impulviums is in the Naples Museum. The rooms contained admirable mosaics including the famous *Battle of Alexander and Darius* (Naples Museum) which covered the area between the two peristyles.

Casa del Labirinto – One of the rooms opening onto the peristyle has a mosaic of the labyrinth with Theseus killing the Minotaur.

★★★ **Casa dei Vettii** – The Vettii brothers were rich merchants. Their dwelling, the most lavishly decorated in the town, is the finest example of a house and garden that have been faithfully restored. The reroofed *atrium* opens directly onto the peristyle surrounding a delightful garden with statues, basins and fountains.
The **frescoes** in the *triclinium*, on the right of the peristyle, depict mythological scenes and friezes of cupids, and are among the finest from antiquity.

★ **Casa degli Amorini Dorati** – This house shows the refinement of the owner, who probably lived during the reign of Nero, and his taste for the theatre. The glass and gilt medallions depicting cupids (*amorini*) have deteriorated. But the building as a whole, with its remarkable peristyle with one wing raised like a stage, is well preserved. There is an obsidian mirror set in the wall near the passage between the peristyle and *atrium.*

Casa dell'Ara Massima – There are well-preserved **paintings**★ (one in *trompe-l'œil*).

★ **Torre di Mercurio** – A tower on the town wall, dedicated to the god Mercury, now affords an interesting **view**★★ of the excavations.

Casa della Fontana Grande – Its main feature is the large **fountain★** (fontana) shaped as a niche decorated with mosaics and fragments of coloured glass in the Egyptian style.

★ **Casa del Poeta Tragico** – This house takes its name from a mosaic now in the Naples Museum. A mosaic of a watchdog at the threshold bears the inscription *Cave Canem* (Beware of the dog).

Casa di Pansa – A very spacious house partly converted for letting.

★★ **Porta Ercolano** - The Herculaneum Gate was the main gateway of Pompeii, with two gates for pedestrians and one for vehicles.

★★ **Via dei Sepolcri** – A great melancholy feeling pervades this street lined with mounumental tombs and cypresses. There are examples of all forms of Greco-Roman funerary architecture: tombs with niches, small round or square temples, altars resting on a plinth, drum-shaped mausoleums, simple semi-circular seats or exedrae.

Villa di Diomede – This important dwelling dedicated to Diomedes has a loggia overlooking the garden and the swimming pool.

★★★ **Villa dei Misteri** – *Access possible by car.* Standing outside the city walls, this patrician villa, although it has lost much of its ornamentation, still comprises numerous rooms. Near the present entrance were the outbuildings *(partly excavated)*. These were reserved for all domestic or agricultural work and as the servants' quarters.
In the main dwelling, the room on the right contains the splendid **fresco** for which the villa is famous. This vast composition, which fills the whole room, depicts against a Pompeiian red background the initiation of a young bride to the mysteries *(misteri)* of the cult of Dionysus (Child reading the rites; scenes of offerings and sacrifices; flagellation; nuptials of Ariadne and Dionysus; dancing Bacchante; dressing of the bride). The mistress of this house was probably a priestess of the cult of Dionysus, which was then very popular in southern Italy. There is a fine peristyle and an underground passage *(criptoportico)*.

Help us in our constant task of keeping up-to-date
Please send us your comments and suggestions

Michelin Tyre PLC
Tourism Department
Green Guides
38 Clarendon Road
WATFORD
Herts WD1 1SX
Tel: 01923 415 000
Fax: 01923 415 250

Abbazia di POMPOSA★★

POMPOSA ABBEY – Emilia-Romagna

Michelin map 988 fold 15 or 429 H 18 – 49km – 30 miles east of Ferrara

Pomposa ⊙, a Benedictine abbey founded in the 6C, enjoyed great fame in the Middle Ages, especially from the 10C to the 12C, when it was distinguished by its Abbot, St Guy (Guido) of Ravenna, and by another monk, Guido d'Arezzo, the inventor of the musical scale.
The fine Pre-Romanesque **church★★** in the style typical of Ravenna is preceded by a narthex whose decoration exemplifies the Byzantine style. To the left, an admirable Romanesque campanile (1063) is remarkable for the progression in the number and size of its windows, and the elegant simplicity of the Lombard bands and arches adorning its nine storeys; and finally, the variety of geometric decoration obtained by the use of bricks.
The nave has some magnificent mosaic **paving** and two Romanesque stoups, one in the Romanesque style and the other in the Byzantine style. The walls bear an exceptional cycle of 14C **frescoes** based on the illuminator's art. From right to left the upper band is devoted to the Old Testament while the lower band has scenes from the Life of Christ; the corner pieces of the arches depict the *Apocalypse*. On the west wall are a *Last Judgement* and in the apsidal chapel *Christ in Majesty*.
Opposite the church stands the Palazzo della Ragione, where the abbot dispensed justice.

Promontorio di PORTOFINO★★

PORTOFINO PENINSULA – Liguria
Michelin map 988 fold 13 or 428 J 9

This rocky, rugged promontory offers one of the most attractive landscapes on the Italian Riviera. The coastline is dotted with small villages in sheltered bays. Part of the peninsula has been designated as a nature reserve **(Parco Naturale)** to protect the fauna and flora. By taking the corniche roads and the numerous footpaths the visitor can discover the secret charms of this region.

★★ PORTOFINO

To reach the port which gave the peninsula its name, take the road that passes via **Santa Margherita Ligure**⌂⌂ *(5km - 3 miles)*, a fashionable seaside resort, and then the **corniche road**★★ (Strada Panoramica) which affords lovely views of the rocky coast. This small fishing village with its gaily-coloured houses lies at the head of a sheltered creek. The **walk to the lighthouse**★★★ *(1 hour on foot Rtn)* is beautiful, especially in the evening, when the setting sun shines on the Gulf of Rapallo. Wonderful views unfold between the olive trees, yews and sea pines.

From the castle **(castello** ⊙**)** – formerly Castello San Giorgio *(take the stairway which starts near the harbour and the Church of San Giorgio)* – there are splendid **views**★★★ of Portofino and the Gulf of Rapallo. Continue along the pathway to the lighthouse, from where the view extends right round the coast as far as La Spezia.

EXCURSIONS

San Lorenzo della Costa – *10km – 6 miles north.* At Santa Margherita Ligure take the **scenic road**★★ which offers a succession of lovely views over the Gulf of Rapallo. The Church of **San Lorenzo** contains a **triptych**★ (1499) by an artist from Bruges. It may have been the work of Gerard David (Gheeraert Davit) who spent some time in Genoa.

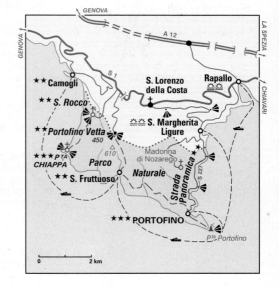

★★ **Portofino Vetta** ⊙ – *14km - 9 miles north-west by a toll road.* From this elevated site (450m - 1 476ft) there is a lovely view of the peninsula and the Ligurian coast.

★★ **San Fruttuoso** – *There is no road suitable for cars to this village.*

On foot: *take the sign-posted footpath starting in Portofino (4 1/2 hours Rtn) or another from Portofino Vetta, but the final stages are difficult (3 hours Rtn).*

By boat: ⊙ *services oper-* ate from Rapallo, Santa Margherita Ligure, Portofino and Camogli. This delightful fishing village stands at the head of a narrow cove in the shadow of Monte Portofino.

★★ **Belvedere di San Rocco** – *13km – 8 miles northwest.* From the terrace beside the church there is a view of Camogli and the western coast from the headland, Punta della Chiappa, right round to Genoa. A path leads to **Punta della Chiappa**★★★ *(2 1/2 hours on foot Rtn by a stepped footpath which starts to the right of the church).* There are unforgettable views of the peninsula and, from the chapel, of the Genoa Coast.

★★ **Camogli** – *15km - 9 miles northwest.* Tall houses crowd round a small harbour.

The towns and sights described in this guide are indicated in black lettering on the local maps and town plans

POTENZA

Basilicata – Population 65 577
Michelin map 988 fold 28 or 431 F 29
Town plan in the current Michelin Red Guide Italia

Potenza overlooks the upper Basento Valley with wide mountain views. The ancient town, founded by the Romans, flourished during the Empire. Today it is an active town, the growth of which was favoured by the development of the road and rail networks in the region. Its tall, modern buildings, curiously terraced, make an unusual sight which is quite dazzling by night. The old town suffered extensive damage in the 1980 earthquake. The 13C Church of **San Francesco**, with its lovely Renaissance **doorway★** carved in wood, contains a marble Renaissance tomb and a 13C Madonna.

Potenza is situated in **Lucania**, an indescribably wild region ravaged by erosion.

POZZUOLI★

Campania – Population 75 002
Michelin map 988 fold 27 or 431 E 24 – 16km – 10 miles west of Naples
Local map see Golfo di Napoli

Pozzuoli, which is of Greek origin, became an active trading port under the Romans. As the town is at the centre of the volcanic area known as the Phlegrean Fields *(see Index)* and is constantly affected by changes in the ground level which occur in this region, the town centre has been evacuated.

The town has given its name to *pozzolana*, a volcanic ash with a high silica content which is used in the production of certain kinds of cement.

★★ **Anfiteatro Flavio** ⊙ – *Corso Terracciano.* This amphitheatre is one of the largest in Italy and dates from the reign of Vespasian, the founder of the Flavian dynasty. It could accommodate 40 000 spectators. Built of brick and stone, it is relatively well preserved: note the outer walls, the entrances and the particularly well-preserved **basements★★**.

★ **Tempio di Serapide** – *Set back from Via Roma.* The temple, dedicated to Serapis, which is situated near the sea, was really the ancient market place and was lined with shops. There is a sort of apse in the end wall which contained the statue of Serapis, the protecting god of traders. The central edifice shows the effects of variations in ground level: the columns reveal signs of marine erosion.

★ **Tempio di Augusto** – The temple, dedicated to Augustus, dated from the early days of the Empire and was converted into a Christian church in the 11C. A recent fire has revealed a grandiose marble colonnade with its entablature.

★★ **Solfatara** ⊙ – *2km – 1 mile northeast by the Naples road.* Although extinct, this crater still has some of the features of an active volcano such as jets of steam charged with sulphurous fumes, strong-smelling and with traces of yellow, miniature volcanoes spitting hot mud and bubbling jets of sand. The ground gives a hollow sound and the surface is hot. The sulphurous vapours have been used for medicinal purposes since Roman times.

PRATO★★

Tuscany – Population 165 735
Michelin map 988 fold 14, 429 fold 33 or 430 K 15

In spite of the peaceful and provincial air of its old quarter, Prato is a bustling and important town which has developed with the textile industry since its early beginnings in the 13C. For a long time Prato was in conflict with Florence, but in 1351 she fell under the sway of her illustrious neighbour and remained thus until the 18C. In the 14C a fortified wall in the form of a hexagon was erected around the old town.

SIGHTS

★ **Duomo** (B) – The cathedral, built in the 12C and 13C and extended in later centuries, presents a harmonious blend of the Romanesque and Gothic styles. The façade, with its partial facing of white stone and green marble, owes its elegance to its lofty central part, its finely carved decoration and the graceful circular pulpit with a canopy (15C) by Michelozzo. The south side has blind arcading in the true Pisan tradition. The campanile has a Gothic upper storey.

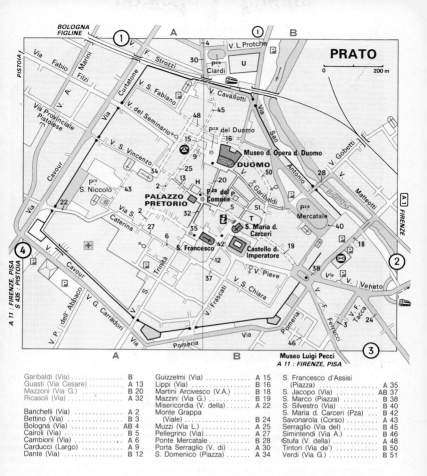

The interior of the church, sober in style, has massive columns of green marble and numerous works of art: the Chapel of the Holy Girdle (**Capella del Sacro Cingolo**) contains the precious relic which, legend has it, the Virgin had given to Thomas as proof of her Assumption. The girdle was brought from Jerusalem by a citizen of Prato in the 12C. The chapel is enclosed by two delicately-worked bronze **screens**★ and decorated with frescoes (1392-95) by Agnolo Gaddi and his pupils. The ***Virgin and Child***★ (1317) is by the sculptor Giovanni Pisano. The **frescoes**★★ by **Filippo Lippi** in the axial chapel form a striking picture of the lives of St Stephen and St John the Baptist. From 1452 to 1465 this artistic monk, renowned for his libertine ways, painted this masterpiece with its pleasantly fresh colours and spontaneous attitudes; the graceful melancholy of the feminine figures in two scenes, the ***Banquet of Herod***★★★ and *Salome's Dance*, are more typical of the work of one of his pupils, Botticelli. On the walls of the chapel to the right are **frescoes**★ started by Paolo Uccello and completed by Andrea di Giusto. Note also the marble **pulpit**★ with the original shape of a chalice, and in a niche a moving ***Virgin with an Olive***★, a terracotta statue (1480) by Benedetto da Maiano.

Museo dell'Opera del Duomo (B) ⊙ – The Cathedral museum is housed in several rooms overlooking a delightful courtyard. Amongst the exhibits are the seven **panels**★ carved from 1428 to 1438 by Donatello for the pulpit from which the Holy Girdle used to be displayed. The pulpit was set on the corner of the cathedral's west front. Also on display are pieces of ecclesiastical plate and paintings by Filippino Lippi (1457-1504), the son of Filippo, and by Carlo Dolci (1616-1686).

★ **Palazzo Pretorio** (A) – This austere and massive building, a curious mixture of the Romanesque and Gothic styles, overlooks a charming small square, **Piazza del Comune**, with a gracious bronze fountain (1659) by Tacca. Three floors of the building are occupied by the Municipal Gallery (**Galleria Comunale**) which presents works by the 14C and 15C Tuscan school and notably an important collection of **polyptychs**★ by Bernardo Daddi, Lorenzo Monaco, Filippo Lippi etc. There are also works by the Neapolitan Caracciolo (17C) and the Dutchman Van Wittel the Elder.

221

Michelozzo's pulpit on the exterior of the Duomo

Castello dell'Imperatore (B) – This is one of the rare existing examples in northern and central Italy of a castle built by the Emperor (Imperatore) Frederick II of Hohenstaufen. This imposing structure, on a square plan around a central courtyard, has massive walls with very few openings and enormous projecting towers. The castle is modelled on Castel del Monte *(see Index)* in the south. With its cleft Ghibelline crenellations, this fortified stronghold guarded the route between the Emperor's northern empire and his Kingdom of Sicily in the south.

Santa Maria delle Carceri (B) – This attractive late-15C building was designed by Giuliano da Sangallo. The **interior** displays both a severity and a nobility typical of Florentine architecture as influenced by Brunelleschi.

Chiesa di San Francesco (AB) – This church, dedicated to St Francis, was built from the 13C to the 15C. The chapterhouse has **frescoes**★ by Nicolo di Pietro Gerini, a Florentine artist who was influenced by Giotto.

PUGLIA★

Michelin map 988 folds 28, 29 and 30

This region takes its name from the ancient Roman province of Apulia. It extends from the spur of the Italian "boot" right down to the heel, all along the Adriatic coast in the south of the country. With the exception of the Gargano Promontory and the limestone Murge Hills which rise behind Bari, it is a flat plain planted with cereals, olive trees, vines or in pasture.

Away from the main tourist haunts, Puglia offers the visitor its beautiful yet severe scenery, quiet beaches and some marvellous architectural gems, both religious and military.

HISTORICAL NOTES

As early as the late 8C BC Greeks from Laconia and Sparta founded the towns of Gallipoli, Otranto and most significantly Taranto on the Apulian coast. In the 5C and 4C BC Taranto was the most prosperous town in Magna Graecia. The local tribe, the Lapyges, tenaciously resisted Greek colonisation; in the 3C BC the Greek cities and the Italiots both came under Roman domination.

Taranto declined as Brindisi, a trading-post facing the eastern part of the Mediterranean, flourished. The latter was linked to Rome when Trajan prolonged the Appian Way. The Roman colonisation greatly benefited this area by introducing improved communications and political organisation. Christianity was first introduced to the area in the 3C and was strengthened in the 5C with the appearances of the Archangel Michael at Monte Sant'Angelo.

The area was occupied successively by the Byzantines, Lombards and Arabs before Puglia sought help in the 11C from the Normans who then dominated the entire area. Puglia greatly increased its trade and its architectural heritage during both the early Crusades, most of which embarked from the Apulian ports, and the reign of Roger II of Sicily (1095-1154).

It was under the Emperor Frederick II of Hohenstaufen, an unusual, authoritarian and cruel character, an atheist but a cultured and highly intelligent person, that the region knew a period of splendour in the first-half of the 13C. The King was captivated by the country and chose to reside here. This favoured trade, the unification of the country and the establishment of an efficient administration. His son Manfred continued his work but had to submit to Charles of Anjou in 1266. The French lost interest in the region and it began to lose its vitality and prestige. Puglia then passed to the Aragon dynasty who by isolating the region, greatly contributed to its decline.

After a period of Austrian domination, the Bourbons of Naples improved to some small extent the misery and stagnation to which the country had been reduced by the Spanish. The brief Napoleonic period followed a similar policy. In 1860 Puglia was united with the rest of unified Italy.

During the 20C Apulia has progressively emerged from the difficult position of inferiority which was prevalent throughout the rest of the Italian south or Mezzogiorno. The region has achieved a certain independence and vigour and now claims two thriving industrial towns, Taranto and Lecce, a Trade Fair in Bari and several newly-founded universities.

TOWNS AND SIGHTS

★★ **Grotte di Castellana** ⊙ - *40km – 25 miles southeast of Bari, at Castellana-Grotte.* This network of caves was created by the underground rivers which filter down through the limestone of the Murge Hills. The vast chamber, now void of water, was discovered in 1938 and has an infinite variety of magnificent concretions: draperies, richly-coloured stalactites and stalagmites. The White Cave **(Grotta Bianca)**, 70m – 230ft underground, glistens with calcite crystals.

★★ **Gargano Promontory** - *See Promontorio del GARGANO*

★★ **Trulli Region and Alberobello** - *See Terra dei TRULLI.*

★★ **Castel del Monte** ⊙ - *29km – 18 miles southeast of Barletta.* The Emperor Frederick II of Hohenstaufen built this powerful castle *c*1240. It stands, proud and solitary, on the summit of one of the Murge Hills. With its octagonal plan the Castel del Monte is the sole exception in a series of 200 quadrilateral fortresses built by this sovereign on his return from the Crusades. The octagonal plan of the fortress, built in a pale-coloured stone, is strengthened at each of its angles by an octagonal tower (24m – 79ft tall). The overall plan combines balance, logic and strict planning with delicate decoration.

Trulli, Alberobello, Puglia

223

The superb Gothic gateway takes the form of an ancient triumphal arch and opens into the inner courtyard. Arranged around this at ground-floor level are eight vast trapezoidal chambers with pointed vaulting. Above, the eight identical rooms are lit by delicately-ornamented windows. The arrangement of the water conduits is quite ingenious: water runs from the rooftops into the cisterns of the towers and is then piped into the different rooms.

≙ **Gallipoli** – The old town with its attractive small port is set on an island and linked to the modern town by a bridge. Note the **Hellenistic fountain** *(to the left of the bridge)* with a baroque pediment, the Angevin castle, the cathedral with a baroque façade which recalls Lecce and, nearby, the baroque Church of Santa Teresa. The **interior**★ of the **church (la Purissima)** is sumptuously decorated.

★★ **Lecce** – *See LECCE.*

Locorotondo – *See Terra dei TRULLI.*

★ **Martina Franca** – *See Terra dei TRULLI.*

★ **Monte Sant'Angelo** – *See MONTE SANT'ANGELO.*

★ **Ostuni** – *35km – 22 miles west of Brindisi.* This large market town now spreads over several hillsides. At the centre of the old town with its white alleyways and ramparts stands the late-15C cathedral **(Duomo)** built in the Gothic style. The **façade**★ is crowned by an unusual curved gable which is a precursor of the Baroque school.

★ **Taranto** – *See TARANTO.*

★ **Tremiti Islands** – *See Isole TREMITI.*

Altamura – This large market town in the Murge Hills also has its old quarter on a hilltop. The 13C cathedral **(Duomo)** in the transitional Romanesque-Gothic style forms the focal point at the upper end of the main street. The façade is crowned with two bulbous bell-towers, 16C additions, and pierced by a delicately decorated 13C **rose window**★ and a richly-sculptured 14C-15C **doorway**★.

Bari – *See BARI.*

≙ **Barletta** – *See BARLETTA.*

Bitonto – *17km – 11 miles southwest of Bari.* Set amidst a sea of olive groves this small town has a fine cathedral **(Duomo**★**)** which strongly resembles those in Trani and Bari. The three-part façade is enlivened by large, richly-sculptured openings. On the south side an elegant gallery with small columns surmounts the ground-floor arcade. Inside, columns with fine capitals support a gallery with triple openings. The fine pulpit dates from 1229.

Brindisi – *See BRINDISI.*

Canosa di Puglia – *23km – 14 miles southwest of Barletta.* The inhabitants of this Greek, then Roman, city were known for their ceramic vases *(askoi)*. The 11C Romanesque cathedral **(Duomo)** which shows a certain Byzantine influence, was remodelled in the 17C following an earthquake. The façade is 19C. Inside note the 11C episcopal throne and the **tomb**★ of Bohemond, Prince of Antioch (d 1111), the son of Robert Guiscard (1015-85), a Norman adventurer who campaigned in southern Italy. This curious mausoleum is in the form of a domed cube. In the Via Cadorna there are three 4C BC hypogea **(Ipogei Lagrasta)** ⊘ and to the right of the Andria road stand the remains of a Paleo-Christian basilica **(San Leucio)** which was itself built on the site of a Roman temple.

Foggia – *Town plan in the current Michelin Red Guide Italia.*
Foggia is set in the heart of a vast cereal-growing plain, the Tavoliere. This trading and industrial centre was founded in c1050 by the Norman, Robert Guiscard. In 1223 the Emperor Frederick II of Hohenstaufen built a castle which has now disappeared.
The present cathedral **(Duomo)** incorporates parts of an earlier building (13C), notably the lower walls with some blind arcading and a sculptured cornice above, and the crypt. This earlier structure, which was destroyed by the 1731 earthquake, has been rebuilt.

Galatina – This craft and wine-making centre stands on the flat and stony Salento Peninsula. The cathedral with its Baroque façade recalls the gracious style of Lecce. The 14C Church of **Santa Caterina di Alessandria**★ is decorated with a marvellous cycle of **frescoes**★ by several 15C artists. The frescoes in the cloisters are 18C.

Galatone – *24km – 15 miles southwest of Lecce.* The **Chiesa del Crocifisso della Pietà** has a lovely **façade★** embellished in the Baroque style typical of the Lecce area. The sumptuous interior decoration includes gilding and stucco ornamentation.

Lucera – Already important in Roman times, Lucera was ceded by the Emperor Frederick II of Hohenstaufen to the Saracens of Sicily, who in turn were expelled by Charles II of Anjou, the grandson of Louis IX (St Louis). Lucera has an imposing 13C castle **(castello)★** built by the Angevins, which affords a fine **panorama★** of the Tavoliere Plain. The historic centre is dominated by a 14C cathedral **(Duomo)** which overlooks a fine square, the focal point of the town. Nearby stands another imposing Romanesque church with sober architectural lines which is dedicated to St Francis of Assisi but is linked with San Francesco Fasani who lived in the area in the 18C and restored the building. Further along, a fine palace, unfortunately in poor condition, houses a museum **(Museo Civico G. Fiorelli)** ⊘ which displays a marble *Venus★*, a Roman replica of a model by the school of Praxiteles. A short distance from the centre stands a well-preserved Roman amphitheatre **(anfiteatro romano★)** built during Augustus' reign.

≏**Manfredonia** – Manfred, the son of the Emperor Frederick II of Hohenstaufen, founded the port in the 13C. It is guarded by a fine 13C castle **(castello)** and a bastion pierced with pointed openings. The Church of **Santa Maria di Siponto★** *(3km – 2 miles south by the S 89)* is an elegant 11C building in the Romanesque style which shows influences both oriental (square plan and terraced roof hiding the dome), and Pisan (blind arcades with columns enclosing lozenges).
The late-11C Church of **San Leonardo** *(beyond the Church of Santa Maria, take the Foggia road to the right)* has a fine delicately-sculptured **doorway★** dating from the early 13C.

Otranto – *See OTRANTO.*

Ruvo di Puglia – *34km – 21 miles west of Bari.* On the edge of the Murge Hills, Ruvo has an Apulian-style Romanesque cathedral **(Duomo★)** with a sober façade embellished by a rose window, a twin opening, a sculptured doorway and at the very top a frieze of arches. Inside the lofty nave, tall arches carry a deep cornice supported by sculptured corbels. The **Museo Archeologico Jatta** ⊘ has a fine collection of Attic, Italiot and Apulian vases including the superb **Crater of Talos★★**, a red-figured vase with a black background.
Take Via De Gaspari where stands the 16C Clock Tower (Torre dell'Orologio) – opposite is the Renaissance Palazzo Caputi – to reach Piazza Matteotti which is flanked by fine palaces and the ruins of a medieval castle.

Trani – This wine-growing town has an ancient port surrounded by old houses. The 11C-13C Romanesque cathedral **(Duomo★★)** is one of the finest in Puglia and is dedicated to St Nicholas the Pilgrim, a humble Greek shepherd who arrived in Trani on the back of a dolphin.
Blind arcades encircle the building and there is a fine **bronze door★** which was cast in 1180. Beyond the lofty transept the chancel has a delicately-decorated window. To the south rises the bell-tower. Inside, one detects a strong Norman influence. The nave and aisles are slightly raised as they are built over two immense crypts, the lower of which is literally a forest of ancient columns. The upper church is well lit but severe with slender twin columns carrying the main arches and an elegant gallery with triple openings.
From the public gardens **(giardino pubblico★)** to the east of the port there is an attractive view of the old town and its tall cathedral. The castle **(castello –** restored) on the seashore was built by Frederick II.

Troia – *17km – 11 miles southwest of Foggia.* This agricultural market town is well situated on a hilltop overlooking the Tavoliere plain. The Romanesque **cathedral** in the Apulian style was begun in the 11C and completed two centuries later. The façade is embellished with blind arcading and a lovely **rose window★**. A fine 12C **bronze door★** in the Byzantine tradition opens into the nave and two aisles separated by columns with finely-worked capitals. The north doorway has a sculptured **tympanum** depicting Christ flanked by two angels.

The Michelin Green Guide Rome (French and English editions) proposes many walks in the Eternal City visiting:
 – *the best-known sights*
 – *the districts steeped in 3 000 years of history*
 – *the art treasures in the museums and galleries*

RAVELLO★★★

Campania – Population 2 424
Michelin map 988 south of fold 27 or 431 F 25 – Local map see AMALFI

Ravello with its alleys, stairways and roofed passages clings to the steep slopes of the Dragon Hill. The **site★★★**, suspended between sea and sky, is unforgettable. The road from Amalfi climbs in hairpin bends up the narrow Dragon Valley, planted with vines and olive groves.

★★★ **Villa Rufolo** ⊙ – *Like the cathedral it overlooks Piazza Vescovado.* The villa was built in the 13C by the rich Rufolo family of Ravello and was the residence of several popes, of Charles of Anjou and more recently in 1880, of the German composer Wagner. A well-shaded avenue leads to a Gothic entrance tower. Beyond is a Moorish-style courtyard with typical sharply-pointed arches in the Sicilian-Norman style and interlacing above. This was originally cloisters in the 11C. A massive 11C tower overlooks the well-tended gardens and the elegant villa.

From the terraces there is a splendid **panorama★★★** of the jagged peaks as far as Cape Orso, the Bay of Maiori and the Gulf of Salerno.

★★★ **Villa Cimbrone** ⊙ – A charming **alley★** leads from Piazza Vescovado to the villa, passing on the way through the Gothic porch of the convent of St Francis, founded by the saint himself in 1222 (cloisters). On entering the grounds the visitor should see first the charming cloisters and a lovely hall with pointed vaulting and some curious grilles. A wide alley leads through the garden to the belvedere, adorned with marble busts. There is an immense **panorama★★★** over the cultivated, terraced hillsides, Maiori, Cape Orso and the Gulf of Salerno.

Duomo – The cathedral, founded in 1086, was transformed in the 18C. The campanile is 13C. The fine **bronze door★** with its panels of reliefs was cast in 1179 by Barisanus da Trani. In the nave the antique columns have been uncovered and there is a magnificent mosaic-covered **pulpit★★** with a remarkable variety of motifs and fantastic animals (1272). On the left is an elegant 12C **ambo** with green mosaics representing Jonah and the Whale. The small museum **(museo)** ⊙ in the crypt has sculptural fragments, mosaics, a silver **head-reliquary** with the relics of St Barbara.

★ **San Giovanni del Toro** ⊙ – This small 11C church, dedicated to St John, was restored in the 18C. Inside, antique columns support the arches. There is a richly-decorated 11C **pulpit★**, a Roman sarcophagus (south aisle) and 14C frescoes in the crypt.

RAVENNA★★★

Emilia-Romagna – Population 135 807
Michelin map 988 fold 15, 429, 430 I 18

In the peaceful provincial-looking town of Ravenna, the sober exteriors of its buildings belie the wealth of riches accumulated when Ravenna was an imperial city, the Byzantium of the West and an Exarchate of Byzantium. Indeed the many wonderful mosaics which adorn the city's ecclesiastical buildings are the finest in Europe. Their bright colours, richness of decoration and powerful symbolism are evocative of a great spirituality.

After the division of the Empire in 395 by Theodosius, Rome already in decline was abandoned in AD404 by Honorius who made Ravenna the capital of the Roman Empire. Honorius' sister, **Galla Placidia**, lavishly governed the Western Empire before the Barbarian invasions brought the Ostrogoth Kings Odoacer (476-493) and **Theodoric** (493-526) to Ravenna; they also embellished Ravenna in their turn. The strategic location of Ravenna's port, Classis, facing the Greek world, inevitably led to trading with Byzantium which had become capital in 476. Ravenna came under Byzantine rule in 540 in the reign of the Emperor Justinian, and was administered by Exarchs. From then on Ravenna exercised considerable influence over the whole of northern Italy and beyond.

★★★ MOSAICS *one day*

The oldest mosaics are in the Neoni Baptistery and the Galla Placidia Tomb (5C). Next in chronological order are those adorning the Arians' Baptistery, St Apollinaris the New, St Vitalis, and finally St Apollinaris in Classe (6C).

★★ **Mausoleo di Galla Placidia** (Y) ⊙ – This mid-5C mausoleum in the form of a Latin cross has a great architectural harmony and is embellished by wonderful mosaics. The vaulting shining with stellar and floral motifs and the dome are painted a deep blue. On the tympanum and pendentives the symbolic scenes are full of serenity, in particular the Good Shepherd, on the west wall. The sarcophagi at either end of the projecting arms are the tombs of Galla Placidia and her family.

★★ **Basilica di San Vitale** (Y) ⊘ – The basilica consecrated in 547 by Archbishop Maximian is an architectural masterpiece; the splendour, originality and light effects are typical features of the later period of ancient art. The church, dedicated to St Vitalis, has an octagonal plan, two storeys of concave exedrae encircled by an ambulatory and a deep apse. The richly-decorated interior is dazzling: precious marbles, Byzantine capitals splendidly carved, frescoes and especially the **mosaics** of the apse with their brilliant colours. On the sides and the end wall of the chancel are depicted scenes from the Old Testament; on the side walls inside the chancel are wonderful groups representing the **Empress Theodora** with her suite and the **Emperor Justinian** attended by his court. These works display splendour, hieratic power and a strong Byzantine influence. On the ceiling **Christ the King** is enthroned between St Vitalis and Bishop Ecclesio, the founder of the church.

Empress Theodora, Basilica di San Vitale

To the left of San Vitale is the National Museum **(Museo Nazionale)** (Y M¹) ⊘ with its Roman, Oriental, Byzantine, Romanesque and Renaissance collections.

★ **Battistero Neoniano** (Z) ⊘ – The baptistery, erected in the 6C by Bishop Neoni and also known as the Orthodox Baptistery, contains splendid mosaics in brilliant contrasting colours. There are decorative motifs above the bays of the main arches, and the dome portrays the **Baptism of Christ** and the 12 Apostles. The Byzantine low reliefs over the arches of the rotunda represent the prophets.
The 18C cathedral (E), adjacent to the baptistery, is dominated by a 10C-11C round campanile. The 6C marble ambo is adorned with symbolic animals.

★ **Basilica di Sant'Apollinare Nuovo** (Z) ⊘ – This lovely church, built in 519 by Theodoric and dedicated to St Apollinaris the New, has a nave and two aisles separated by Corinthian columns and is adorned with brilliant **mosaics** with a gold background. On the upper walls are scenes from the Life of Christ, then pictures of saints and prophets. Below is the famous **procession of saints** depicting holy virgins leaving the town and port of Classis, behind the Three Kings, bearing offerings to the Virgin. Opposite is a procession of 26 martyrs leaving the palace of Theodoric, moving solemnly towards Christ the King, who is surrounded by angels.

Battistero degli Ariani (Y D) ⊘ – The Arians' Baptistery is thought to have been built by Theodoric in the 6C. The dome is decorated with fine **mosaics** of the Baptism of Christ framed by the 12 Apostles and a throne adorned with a cross.

★★ **Basilica di Sant'Apollinare in Classe** ⊘ – *5km – 3 miles south. Leave Ravenna by ① on the plan, the S 67.* The basilica stands in open country not far from the sea. The basilica was begun in 534 and consecrated in 549; a cylindrical campanile was added in the 11C.
The majestic interior has a nave and two aisles separated by 26 arches on marble columns. In the aisles lie superb early-Christian carved sarcophagi (5C-8C). The triumphal arch and chancel feature magnificent 6C-7C **mosaics** with a marked freedom and simplicity of composition and a lovely harmony of colour. The mosaics, full of symbolism, portray Christ the Saviour and the Transfiguration.

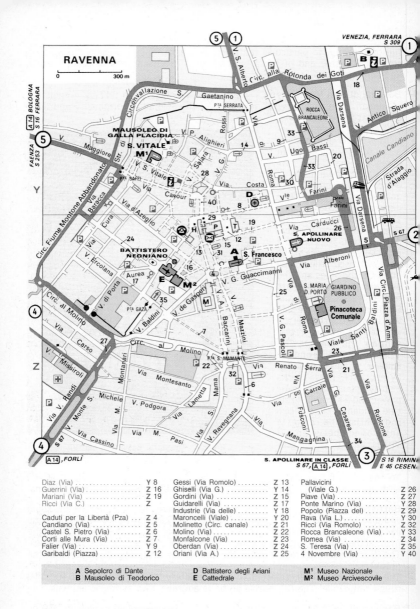

ADDITIONAL SIGHTS

★ **Mausoleo di Teodorico** (Y B) ⊘ – This curious mausoleum, erected by Theodoric around 520, is built of huge blocks of freestone assembled without mortar. The two-storey building is covered by a remarkable monolithic dome 11m – 36ft in diameter in Istrian stone. Inside, the decoration is sober and austere. A Romanesque porphyry basin has been transformed into a sarcophagus.

Museo Arcivescovile (Z M²) ⊘ – The Episcopal Palace museum displays a small lapidary collection and Archbishop Maximian's **throne**★★ (6C), a masterpiece in carved ivory. St Andrew's Chapel (**Sant'Andrea**★★) contains remarkable mosaics.

Pinacoteca Comunale (Z) ⊘ – This municipal picture gallery includes works from most of the Italian schools from the 14C to the 20C. The **recumbent figure**★ (1526) of a young knight, Guidarello Guidarelli, is a masterpiece by Tullio Lombardo.

Sepolcro di Dante (Z A) – Dante was exiled from Florence and took refuge first at Verona and then at Ravenna, where he died in 1321. The classical building in which the tomb now stands was erected in 1780.

San Francesco (Z) – This 10C Romanesque church, dedicated to St Francis, is flanked by a campanile of the same period. Remodelled after the Second World War, it still retains some fine Greek marble columns, a 5C high altar and a 9C-10C crypt.

REGGIO DI CALABRIA

Calabria – Population 177 756
Michelin map 988 fold 39 or 431 M 28
Town plan in the current Michelin Red Guide Italia

Reggio, which backs against the Aspromonte Massif, is a pleasant town of modern appearance, rebuilt after the earthquake of 1908 along the Straits of Messina. Reggio is surrounded by rich groves of olives, vines, orange and lemon trees, and fields of flowers used for making perfume. Half the world production of bergamot (a citrus fruit) comes from Reggio. There are daily boat and car ferry services to Sicily *(see the current Michelin Red Guide Italia)*.

★ **Lungomare** – This long and elegant sea-front promenade lined with palm trees and magnolias affords views of the Sicilian coastline and Etna.

★★ **Museo Nazionale** ⊙ – This modern museum, in the centre of town, contains an important **archeological collection** covering the history of Magna Graecia. There is also an interesting art gallery.
The museum has won great renown since it was selected to display *(ground floor)* the *Riace Warriors*★★★ dating probably from the 5C BC, which were discovered in 1972 off the coast of the small Calabrian harbour of Riace. The two warrior figures are exceptionally well preserved and are striking for their imposing appearance, their harmonious proportions and the refinement of their details. Their origin and the identity of the sculptor remain an enigma. The ground floor also has displays on local prehistory, finds dating from Magna Graecia (especially the excavations at Locri which have uncovered Greek and locally-produced pottery, terracotta votive tablets, a marble group etc).
On the first floor are the Hellenistic works and the coin collection.
The second-floor art gallery **(pinacoteca)** has two remarkable works by **Antonello da Messina**: *St Jerome* and *Three Angels appearing before Abraham.*

EXCURSION

★ **Aspromonte** – *From its junction (bivio Brandano) with the S 112 to Melito di Porto Salvo on the south coast, the S 183 crosses the Aspromonte Massif from north to south, allowing the visitor to discover its many varied aspects. See CALABRIA.*

REGGIO NELL'EMILIA

Emilia-Romagna – Population 131 853
Michelin map 988 fold 14, 428 folds 27 and 28, 429 fold 22 or 430 H 13
Town plan in the current Michelin Red Guide Italia

This rich industrial and commercial centre, set on the Via Emilia, was the birthplace of Ariosto *(see Index)*. Like Modena and Ferrara, it belonged to the Este family from 1409 to 1776. In the town centre are Piazza Prampolini and Piazza Cavour, overlooked by the municipal theatre (19C).

★ **Galleria Parmeggiani** ⊙ – *2 Corso Cairoli*. The collections comprise gold plate, fabrics, costumes, arms, furniture and paintings: works by El Greco and Ribera as well as Flemish and Italian Mannerist artists.

Madonna della Ghiara ⊙ – *Corso Garibaldi*. A lovely 17C church with a dome. The interior was richly decorated by the Bolognese school.

EXCURSION

Brescello – *28km – 17 miles northwest.* The town owes its name (Brixellum) to the Celts who settled in the Po Plain and who, as they had moved along the plain, had already founded the settlements of Bressanone (Brixen) and Brescia (Brixia). Brescello, though, has most recently come back into the headlines for the films of **Don Camillo** and **Peppone**, characters superbly interpreted by Fernandel and Gino Cervi. In addition to the places themselves, which have remained intact, there is in the first chapel to the right of the church the Crucifix which spoke to Don Camillo and, on the outskirts of the village, the Chapel of the Blessed Virgin that Peppone wanted to demolish. A few yards from the main square is a museum **(museo)** ⊙ containing items and posters relating to the films and the objects used during the filming.

Castello di Canossa – *32km – 20 miles southwest. Follow the San Polo d'Enza road and then turn left to Canossa.* Only the romantic ruins, perched on a rock, remain of the imposing stronghold which belonged to the great Countess of Tuscany, Matilda (1046-1115), who supported the pope against the emperor for 30 years during the quarrel over the investiture of bishops and abbots *(see INTRODUCTION)*. The Emperor Heinrich IV of Germany came barefoot and in his shirtsleeves through the snow, to make amends to Pope Gregory VII in 1077. He had to wait three days for his absolution. This is the origin of the expression "to go to Canossa"; that is, to humble oneself after a quarrel.

RIETI

Lazio – Population 43 090

Michelin map 988 fold 26 or 430 O 20 – 37km – 23 miles southeast of Terni

Rieta lies at the junction of several valleys in the heart of a fertile plain and is the geographical centre of Italy. It is also a good excursion centre from which to follow in the footsteps of St Francis of Assisi, who preached locally.

Piazza Cesare Battisti – This is the centre of the town, where the most important buildings are to be found. Take the gateway to the right of the 16C-17C Palazzo del Governo with its elegant loggia to reach the pleasant **public garden★**, from where there is a lovely view of the town and its surroundings.

Duomo – This cathedral has a 15C porch and a lovely Romanesque campanile dating from 1252. Inside, the fresco of the Madonna dates from 1494 while the **crypt** is 12C.

Palazzo Episcopale – *Behind the cathedral.* This 13C episcopal building has heavily-ribbed **vaulting★** over the two vast naves which are now used as a garage.

EXCURSIONS

Convento di Fonte Colombo ⊙ – *5km – 3 miles southwest. Take the Contigliano road and after 3km – 2 miles turn left.* It was in the old monastery that St Francis underwent an eye operation. He dictated the Franciscan Rule in the grotto after having fasted for 40 days. Visitors will see the 12C Chapel of St Mary Magdalene adorned with frescoes depicting the "T", the emblem of the Cross designed by St Francis; the St Michael Chapel and the grotto where he fasted; the tree-trunk in which Jesus appeared to him; the old monastery and the 15C church.

★ **Convento di Greccio** ⊙ – *15km – 9 miles northwest. Take the road via Contigliano to Greccio and continue for 2km – 1 mile. Leave the car on the esplanade at the foot of the monastery.*
This 13C monastery clings to a rocky overhang at an altitude of 638m – 2 093ft. It was here that St Francis celebrated Christmas in 1223 and said mass at a manger *(presepio)* between an ox and an ass, thus starting the custom of making cribs at Christmas.
Visitors have access to the Chapel of the Crib (Cappella del Presepio – frescoes by the school of Giotto) and the areas where St Francis and his companions lived. On the upper floor is the church of 1228 with its original furnishings.

Convento di Poggio Bustone ⊙ – *10km – 6 miles north by the Terni road.* Perched at an altitude of 818m – 2 684ft in a lovely green setting, the monastery consists of a 14C church, much altered, with its 15C to 17C frescoes, charming 15C-16C cloisters, a 14C refectory, and two caves in which St Francis is said to have lived.

Convento La Foresta ⊙ – *5km – 3 miles north.* It was in this mountain retreat that St Francis wrote his *Canticle of the Creatures* and performed the miracle of the vine. In the wine cellar is the vat which was filled by the miraculous grape. The cave where St Francis stayed is also open to visitors.

RIMINI ≜≜≜

Emilia-Romagna – Population 127 884

Michelin map 988 fold 15, 429 fold 36 or 430 J 19

Town plan in the current Michelin Red Guide Italia

Rimini has two faces: that of an ancient city rich in history and that of an international ultra-modern seaside resort with its marina, airport and in particular, a great beach of fine sand.
This Umbrian and Gallic colony, with its strategic situation at the junction of the Via Emilia and the Via Flaminia, flourished during the Empire. In the 13C the town grew to fame with the notoriety of its ruling house, the **Malatesta**. They combined extreme refinement with savagery. Dante immortalised the fate of the tragic lovers, Paolo Malatesta and Francesca da Rimini, who were murdered by Gianni Malatesta, the brother of Paolo and the husband of Francesca. Later Sigismondo I Malatesta, cultured patron of the arts and protector of the humanists, repudiated, poisoned and strangled his first three wives, before making an irregular marriage with his mistress, Isotta. After the fall of the Malatesta, Rimini became a papal town. More recently, Rimini has achieved international fame as the birthplace of the film director, Federico Fellini (1920-1993).

SIGHTS

★ **Tempio Malatestiano** – The church was built in the 13C by the Franciscans and became the Malatesta mausoleum in the 14C. It was remodelled from 1447 by Leon Battista Alberti on Sigismondo I's orders, to house the tombs of the tyrant and of his wife Isotta. The Florentine architect was inspired by the nearby Arch of Augustus and designed an antique façade with a great pediment and a single opening. The Renaissance "temple" was left unfinished but its façade marks the beginning of a new style for religious buildings.

The spacious and imposing interior includes an allegorical decoration of exquisite grace and subtlety, due in large part to Agostino di Duccio. The same motifs are also found in the side chapels. In the reliquary chapel, to the right, Piero della Francesca painted the portrait of *Sigismondo Malatesta*★. In the adjacent chapel, the tomb of Isotta faces an admirable **painted 14C crucifix**★ of the Rimini school. The first chapel on the left contains the cenotaph of Sigismondo's ancestors adorned with low reliefs.

Arco d'Augusto – *Piazzale Giulio Cesare*. The arch of Augustus was built in 27 BC and has a majestic appearance, with fine fluted columns and Corinthian capitals.

Ponte di Tiberio – The bridge was begun under Augustus and completed under Tiberius in AD 21. The building material is massive blocks of Istrian limestone.

EXCURSION

Italia in Miniatura ⊙ – The park (Italy in Miniature) includes a garden, boot-shaped and showing contours and relief to represent the form of Italy. There are about 200 models of its architectural treasures and sites. An area is devoted to Europe and there is also an entertainment section.

La RIVIERA★★

Liguria

Michelin map 988 folds 12 and 13, 195 folds 19, 20 and 29 or 428 folds 24, 25 and 32 to 36

From Ventimiglia to the Gulf of La Spezia, the coast describes a curve backed by the slopes of the Alps and the Ligurian Apennines, with Genoa in the middle.

The enchanting Italian or Ligurian Riviera is like the French Riviera, a tourist paradise. The mild climate makes it particularly popular in winter. The coast is dotted with popular resorts with good amenities and a wide range of hotels. The hinterland provides a large choice of walks for those who prefer solitude.

Sightseeing – The map below locates the towns and sites described in the guide, and also indicates other beauty spots in small black type.

★ ① RIVIERA DI PONENTE (WESTERN RIVIERA)

From Ventimiglia to Genoa *175km – 109 miles – allow a day*

The main road of the Riviera, the Via Aurelia, is of Roman origin. It is difficult, as it is winding and narrow, and carries heavy traffic. Nevertheless, there are remarkable viewpoints from the stretches of corniche road or when the road runs close to the blue waters of the Ligurian Sea. Slightly inland the A10 motorway with its many tunnels and viaducts runs parallel. The road passes through a succession of resorts with villas often screened by luxuriant and varied vegetation, or crosses a stretch of coastal plain traversed by mountain torrents. With its exceptionally good exposure the Riviera specialises in the growing of flowers, often under glass, throughout the year.

The hinterland provides a sharp contrast, with the tranquility of its wild forested landscapes.

Ventimiglia – *Town plan in the current Michelin Red Guide Italia.* Not far from the French border, Ventimiglia has an old quarter (Città Vecchia) crisscrossed by narrow alleyways, an 11C-12C cathedral (Duomo), an 11C octagonal baptistery, an 11C-12C Church of San Michele and the 17C Neri Oratory. The Hanbury Gardens (**Giardini Hanbury**★★) ⊙ in **Mortola Inferiore** *(6km – 4 miles west, in the direction of the French border)* with their varied and exotic vegetation, are laid out in terraces, overlooking the sea.

⌂⌂ **Bordighera** – The villas and hotels of this famous resort are scattered among flower gardens shaded by splendid palm trees. The old town, with its winding alleys, still has several fortified gateways.

⌂⌂ **San Remo** – *See SAN REMO.*

★ **Taggia** – Taggia, set amidst vineyards, orchards and olive groves, commands the Argentina Valley. In the 15C and 16C Taggia was an important art centre frequented by Louis Bréa from Nice, the Piedmontese Canavese, and the Genoese Perino del Vaga and Luca Cambiaso.
The Church of **San Domenico**, dedicated to St Dominic, has a fine collection of **works★** by Louis Bréa (*Virgin of Pity* and the *Baptism of Christ*).

⌂ **Diano Marina** – From here it is possible to visit the fortified village of **Diano Castello** and its 12C Chapel of the Knights of Malta (Cappella dei Cavalieri di Malta) with its multicoloured wooden roof.

⌂ **Albenga** – Albenga lies a short distance inland, in an alluvial plain with rich market gardens. The medieval **old town★** is clustered round the cathedral (**Cattedrale**) with its imposing late-14C campanile. The vaulting of the nave is covered with *trompe-l'œil* frescoes. The octagonal 5C baptistery has a baptismal font and a charming Paleo-Christian mosaic in the style typical of Ravenna.

Grotte di Toirano ⊙ – The caves were inhabited in the late-Neolithic period. There are traces of human footprints, torch marks, bear remains and prints, and mud balls used as missiles. The caves open into a series of chambers bristling with stalagmites and stalactites. The last section is the most interesting: a cave until fairly recently filled with water, which has hollowed it out and given it its round shape.

Finale Ligure – **Finale Marina** has a basilica with a fanciful baroque façade. In **Finale Pia** the abbey church is graced with an elegant late-13C campanile. The old town of **Finale Borgo★**, 2km – 1 mile inland, still has its town walls and its Collegiate Church of San Biagio with its elegant 13C polygonal campanile. Inside are a polyptych of St Catherine (1533) and a 16C painting of St Blaise surrounded by saints.
From **Castello San Giovanni** *(1 hour on foot Rtn, start from Via del Municipio)* there is a **view★** of Finale Ligure, the sea and the hinterland. Higher up, **Castello Gavone** retains a 15C round tower with diamond-shaped rustication.

★ **Noli** – This fishing village still has ancient houses, 13C towers and a Romanesque church with a huge wooden statue of Christ, also of the Romanesque period.

Savona – *Town plan in the current Michelin Red Guide Italia.* Italy's seventh port, Savona handles crude oil, coal, cellulose and Italian cars for export to Britain and the United States. The old town has several Renaissance palaces, a 16C cathedral (Duomo) and on the sea-front a 16C fortress, **Fortezza Priamar**, where the Italian patriot Mazzini was imprisoned in 1830.

⌂ **Albisola Marina** – This town is known for its production of ceramics, which carries on a 13C tradition. At the end of the 16C a Duke of Nevers, a member of the Italian Gonzaga family, summoned the Conrade brothers from Albisola to Nevers to found a faïence factory. The 18C **Villa Faraggiana** ⊙ with its exotic **park★**, now houses the Ligurian Ceramics Centre. The exhibits include: the rich Empire furnishings, ceramic pavements and flooring, and the superb **ballroom★** with its stucco and fresco decoration.

★★ **Genoa** – *See GENOA.*

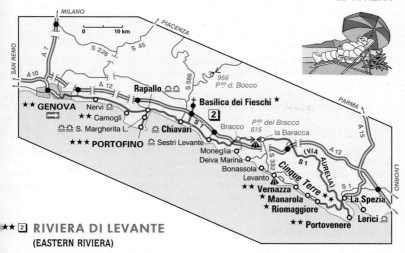

★★ 2 RIVIERA DI LEVANTE
(EASTERN RIVIERA)

From Genoa to La Spezia *173km - 108 miles - allow 1 day*

This stretch of coast has more character and is wilder than the Riviera di Ponente. Sharp promontories, little sheltered coves, tiny fishing villages, wide sandy bays, cliffs, the pinewoods and olive groves of the hinterland, all lend it charm. The road is often winding and hilly but there are fewer stretches of corniche road and the road often runs much further from the coast.

★★ **Genoa** - *See GENOVA.*

★★ **Portofino** - *See Promontorio di PORTOFINO.*

⚓⚓ **Rapallo** - *Town plan in the current Michelin Red Guide Italia.* This sophisticated seaside resort is admirably situated at the head of a bay to the east of the Portofino peninsula. The Lungomare Vittorio Veneto is a lovely palm-shaded **promenade**★ along the sea-front.

⚓ **Chiavari** - This seaside resort has a vast beach and a pleasure-boat harbour. In San Salvatore 2km - 1 mile to the northeast is the small 13C **Basilica dei Fieschi**★ with its alternating courses of black and white marble. The vaulting is pointed. Opposite stands the Palazzo Fieschi, a graceful 13C Genoese Gothic building.

★★ **Cinque Terre** - *See CINQUE TERRE.*

La Spezia - *Town plan in the current Michelin Red Guide Italia.* This naval base and important port comprises Italy's largest naval dockyard and specialises in the manufacture of arms. The **museo navale** ⊙ displays souvenirs, arms and models.

★★ **Portovenere** - This small, severe-looking town is dominated by a 12C-16C citadel. Some of the houses date as far back as the 12C and were in fact once fortified by the Genoese.
The Church of San Lorenzo dates from the 12C, while the Church of San Pietro incorporates parts dating from the 6C. From the terrace there is a very fine view of the Gulf of La Spezia and the Cinque Terre region.

⚓ **Lerici** - At the head of a well-sheltered cove Lerici has an important 13C castle (castello) which was rebuilt in the 16C by the Genoese.
It was near this village that the Shelleys rented a small house in 1822. Percy Bysshe drowned on the return trip from Leghorn to greet Leigh Hunt, who was to edit a new journal with Shelley and Byron. He was cremated on the beach, Il Gombo, north of the mouth of the Arno and his ashes are buried in the Protestant Cemetery in Rome.

This guide, which is revised regularly,
incorporates tourist information provided at the time of going to press
Changes are however inevitable owing to improved facilities and
fluctuations in the cost of living

ROMA★★★

ROME – Lazio – Population 2 773 889
Michelin map 988 fold 26 or 430 Q 19 – Town plan below
Plan of the conurbation in the current Michelin Red Guide Italia

The capital of the Roman Empire to which it owes its name, and the centre of Christendom since the fall of the Empire, Rome is rich in monuments of its ancient history which justify its renown as the Eternal City.

Since 1870 when it became the capital of Italy, Rome has undergone extensive urban development. Then it was a city of barely 200 000 inhabitants while today there are almost 3 million. The treasures of Rome are not always easy to visit, as the city centre is a maze of narrow streets and traffic snarls up easily.

The Roman landscape bathed in a golden light, with its cypresses and pine trees outlined against the beautiful blue sky, is enchanting.

Visitors are advised to use the **Michelin Green Guide Rome** with its itineraries in the various districts, descriptions of selected sights, plans of certain quarters and buildings, and notes on the city's history and its artistic traditions.

HISTORICAL NOTES

The legendary origins of Rome were perpetuated by both Roman historians and poets, such as Livy in his *Roman History* and Virgil in the *Aeneid*. Both claimed that Aeneas, son of the goddess Venus, fled from Troy when it was captured, and landed at the mouth of the Tiber. Having defeated the local tribes he founded Lavinium. His son Ascanius (or Iulus) founded Alba Longa. It was here that Rhea Silvia the Vestal, following her union with the god Mars, gave birth to the twins Romulus and Remus, who were abandoned on the Tiber. The twins came to rest at the foot of the Palatine where they were nursed by a wolf. Later Romulus marked a furrow round the sacred area on which the new city was to be built. Jesting, Remus stepped over the line; Romulus killed him for violating the sacred precinct. Romulus populated his village with outlaws who settled on the Capitol and he provided them with Sabine wives. An alliance grew up between the two peoples who were ruled by a succession of kings, alternately Sabine and Latin, until the Etruscans arrived.

Modern historians emphasise the strategic location of Rome's seven hills especially that of the Palatine, which was a staging-post on the salt road (Via Salaria). This no doubt led to the development of settlements around the Palatine in the 8C BC.

Two centuries later the Etruscans had transformed these villages of shacks into a well-organised town, with a citadel on the Capitol. The last Etruscan king, Tarquin the Superb, was thrown out in 509 BC and the Consulate was instituted.

The Republican era was an ambitious one of territorial expansion. During the 2C and 1C BC the Republican regime tore itself to pieces in a civil war. To restore order disrupted by the rival political factions and rule the newly-conquered territories, it required a clever man of very determined character. **Julius Caesar** (101-44 BC) emerged from amidst the contenders by reason of his audacious strategies (he conquered the whole of Gaul in 51), his grasp of political affairs, his talents as an orator and his unbounded ambition. Appointed consul and dictator for life, he was assassinated on the Ides of March, 15 March 44 BC. He was succeeded by his nephew, **Octavian**, a young man who was of delicate health and had won no military glory. Octavian was to demonstrate tenacity of purpose and political genius and ably rid his path of possible rivals. In 27 BC the Senate granted Octavian the title **Augustus**, which invested him with an aura of holiness. He soon became the first Roman emperor. His achievements were considerable: he extended Roman government and restored peace to the whole of the Mediterranean basin.

Among Augustus' successors there were those who were driven by madness and cruelty (Caligula, Nero and Domitian); and others who continued the good work of Roman civilisation: the good administrator, Vespasian; Titus who was known as the love and delight of the human race; Trajan, the "best of Emperors" and great builder; and Hadrian, an indefatigable traveller and passionate Hellenist.

Christian Rome – As the old order passed away, undermined from within by economic misery and the concentration of authority in the hands of one man, and from without by Barbarian attacks, a new force – Christianity – emerged. It had first reached Rome in the reign of Augustus. The religion of Jesus originated in Palestine and Syria, and was spread throughout the pagan world by his disciples. As the world fell into disarray, Christianity preached a new doctrine of brotherly love and the hope of happiness after death. During the last years of the 1C and the early years of the 2C the Christian Church became organised, but transgressed the law from the beginning because the Emperor embodied religious power. It was

S. Chirol

Colosseo

not until the **Edict of Milan** (313), which allowed Christians to practise their religion openly, and the conversion of **Constantine** (314) that the Church could come out into the open.

From the first days of Christianity, the bishop was Christ's representative on earth. The bishop of Rome, capital of the Empire, claimed primacy. Gradually the name "**Pope**", which had been used for all bishops, was reserved for the Bishop of Rome alone. For 19 centuries the popes at the head of the Roman church have influenced the history of Christianity and given the Eternal City its particular character. In the 11C **Gregory VII** restored order to the Christian church, which had by then an appalling reputation. He dealt with two scourges: the buying and selling of church property, and the marriage of the clergy. In so doing he started the Investiture Controversy, which opposed the Sovereign Pontiff and the Emperor. During the Renaissance numerous popes were scholarly, ambitious and great patrons of the arts, and greatly contributed to the embellishment of the capital by bringing to their court such artists as Raphael and Michelangelo. They included Pius II, Sixtus IV (who built the Sistine Chapel, Santa Maria della Pace and Santa Maria del Popolo), Julius II (who commissioned Michelangelo to decorate the ceiling of the Sistine Chapel), Leo X (who had a great personal fortune and nominated Raphael as intendant of the arts), Clement VII, Sixtus V (a great builder) and Paul III who built the Farnese Palace.

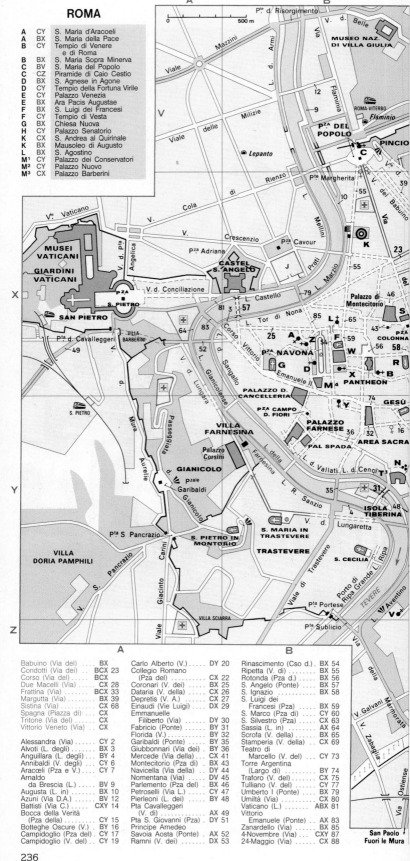

ROMA

A	CY	S. Maria d'Aracoeli
A	BX	S. Maria della Pace
B	CY	Tempio di Venere e di Roma
B	BX	S. Maria Sopra Minerva
C	BV	S. Maria del Popolo
C	CZ	Piramide di Caio Cestio
D	BX	S. Agnese in Agone
D	CY	Tempio della Fortuna Virile
E	CY	Palazzo Venezia
E	BX	Ara Pacis Augustae
F	BX	S. Luigi dei Francesi
F	CY	Tempio di Vesta
G	BX	Chiesa Nuova
H	CY	Palazzo Senatorio
K	CX	S. Andrea al Quirinale
K	BX	Mausoleo di Augusto
L	BX	S. Agostino
M¹	CY	Palazzo dei Conservatori
M²	CY	Palazzo Nuovo
M³	CX	Palazzo Barberini

San Paolo Fuori le Mura

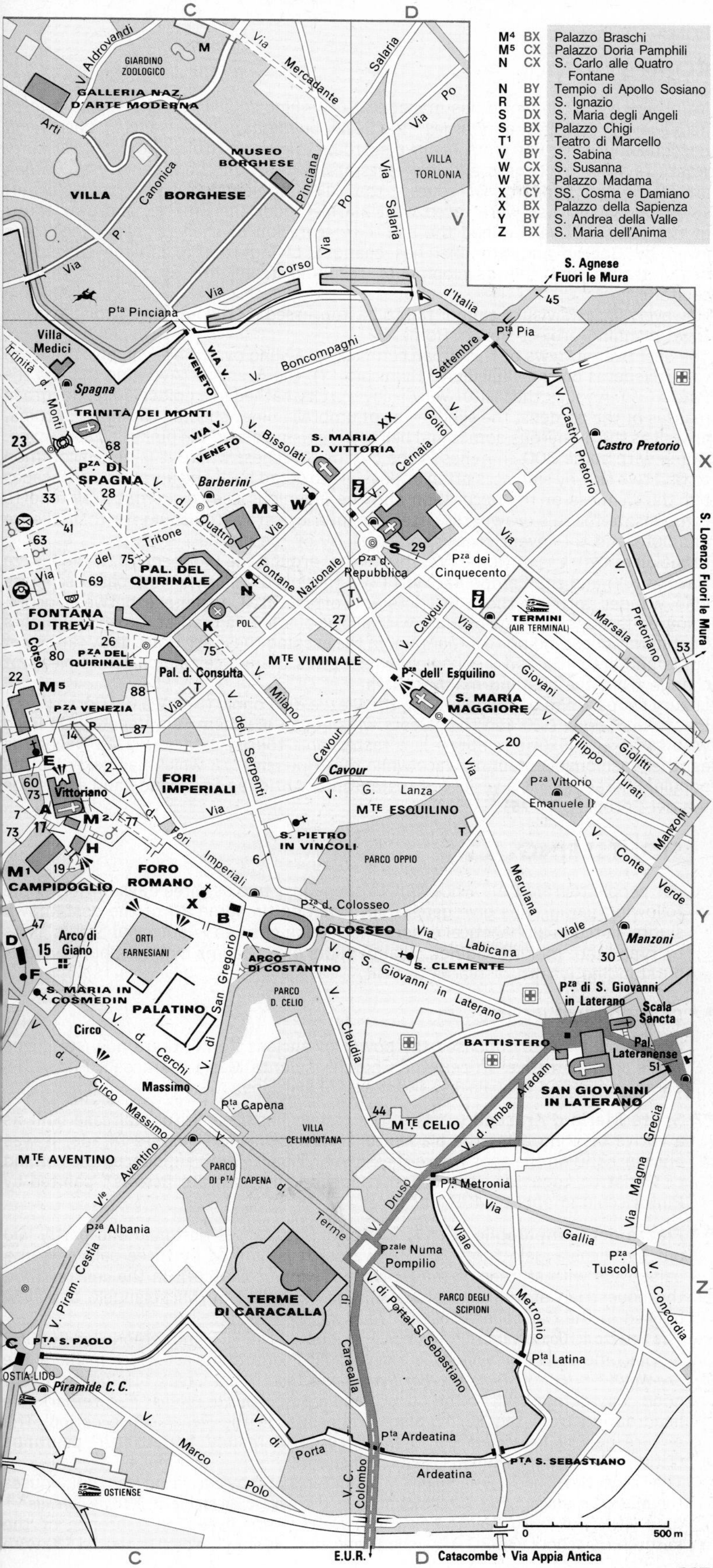

M4	BX	Palazzo Braschi
M5	CX	Palazzo Doria Pamphili
N	CX	S. Carlo alle Quatro Fontane
N	BY	Tempio di Apollo Sosiano
R	BX	S. Ignazio
S	DX	S. Maria degli Angeli
S	BX	Palazzo Chigi
T1	BY	Teatro di Marcello
V	BY	S. Sabina
W	CX	S. Susanna
W	BX	Palazzo Madama
X	CY	SS. Cosma e Damiano
X	BX	Palazzo della Sapienza
Y	BY	S. Andrea della Valle
Z	BX	S. Maria dell'Anima

ROME TODAY

No other city in the world has managed to combine so successfully such a diverse heritage of Classical antiquities, medieval buildings, Renaissance palaces and Baroque churches. Far from being discordant they constitute a logical continuity where revivals, influences and contrasts are evidence of the ingenuity of Roman architects and builders. Of course, the ruins no longer present their former splendour when they were faced with marble under the Empire, and only a few of the palaces have retained the painted decoration of their façades. The Rome loved by Goethe and Stendhal has changed owing to the damage caused by heavy traffic and the developments resulting from the modernisation of a capital city.

However, today's visitor cannot fail to be impressed by the immensity of the great town planning project that is Rome.

The best overall views of this urban complex sprawling over the seven hills are from the belvederes on the Janiculum (Gianicolo **AY**), the Aventine (Aventino **CZ**) and the Pincio (**BV**). At dusk the visitor will discover a city bathed in a golden light, the green masses of the gardens, the silhouettes of umbrella pines shading the areas of ruins, as well as the numerous domes and bell-towers rising above the pink-tiled roofscape.

Rome with some 300 churches is the city of churches, where it is not uncommon to find two side by side. It is often impossible to stand back and admire their façades but the richness of the decoration and the ingenious use of *trompe-l'œil* tend to compensate for this drawback. Often the interiors are astonishing for their silence and light and the inventiveness and audacity of the ultimate design.

In the older districts of Rome (Vecchia Roma) around the Pantheon (**BX**), the Piazza Navona (**BX**) and the Campo dei Fiori (**BY**), there is a wealth of fine palaces. Those who wander through these districts will often catch a glimpse between ochre-coloured façades of a small square with all the bustle of a market, or several flights of stairways descending to a fountain. In the evening these areas are lit by tall street lights and are bathed in a soft glow which gives them a certain charm, a pleasant change from the bustling main arteries.

Luxury shops are to be found around the Piazza del Popolo (**BV**), Via del Corso (**BCX**), Piazza di Spagna (**CX**) and the streets which open off them. Via Veneto (**CX**) lined with cafés and luxurious hotels is a fashionable tourist centre. Piazza Navona is another fashionable meeting-place while the **Trastevere** (**BY**), which has never lost its popular character, has a variety of restaurants. Antique and second-hand shops line Via dei Coronari (**BX 25**).

SIGHTSEEING

For people touring Italy who want to spend just two or three days in Rome, the following paragraphs give general information on some 20 of the best-known sights, listed in alphabetical order. The section entitled "Additional Sights" lists by type other major buildings, beauty spots or museums highlighting the city's outstanding wealth of places to visit.

★★★ CAMPIDOGLIO (CAPITOL – CY)

On the hill which symbolised the power of ancient Rome, there now stand the city's administrative offices, the Church of Santa Maria d'Aracoeli, Piazza del Campidoglio and its palaces, and pleasant gardens.

★★ **Santa Maria d'Aracoeli** (**CY A**) – The church has a beautiful staircase built as a votive offering after the plague of 1346, and a flat, austere façade. It was built in 1250 on the spot where the Sibyl of Tibur (Tivoli) announced the coming of Christ to Augustus. In the first chapel on the right are **frescoes★** painted by Pinturicchio in about 1485.

★★★ **Piazza del Campidoglio** (**CY 17**) – Capitol Square was designed and partly laid out by Michelangelo from 1536 onwards. It is framed by three palaces and a balustrade with statues of the Heavenly Twins or Dioscuri. In the centre stood the equestrian statue of Marcus Aurelius installed by Michelangelo and now housed in the Capitoline Museum *(below)*.

The **Palazzo dei Conservatori★★★** (**CY M¹**) ⊘, built in the 15C and remodelled in 1568 by Giacomo della Porta, houses a **museum★★★** of antique art which includes the **She-Wolf★★★** (6C-5C BC), the **Boy Extracting a Thorn★★**, a Greek original or a very good copy dating back to the 1C BC, and a Bust of **Junius Brutus★★**, a remarkable head dating from the 3C BC placed on a bust in the Renaissance period. The picture gallery (**pinacoteca★** *2nd floor*) contains mainly 14C to 17C paintings (Titian, Caravaggio, Rubens, Guercino, Reni).

The **Palazzo Nuovo** (New Palace) (**CY M²**), built in 1655 by Girolamo Rainaldi, houses the **Museo Capitolino★★** ⊘ which contains: the **equestrian statue of** *Marcus Aurelius★★* (late 2C); the **Dying Gaul★★★**, a Roman sculpture based on a bronze of the Pergamum school (3C-2C BC) ; the Emperors' Room (**Sala degli Imperatori★★**) with portraits of all the emperors; the **Capitoline Venus**★★, a Roman work inspired by the Venus of Cnidus by Praxiteles; and the **Mosaic of the Doves**★★ from Hadrian's Villa at Tivoli.

The **Palazzo Senatorio**★★★ (**CY H**) ⊘ is a 12C building, remodelled between 1582 and 1602 by Giacomo della Porta and Girolamo Rainaldi.

From Via del Campidoglio (**CY 19**) there is a beautiful **view**★★★ of the ruins.

★★★ Terme di CARACALLA (CZ) ⊘

These baths built by Caracalla in AD 212 extend over more than 11 hectares – 27 acres and could take 1 600 bathers at a time. The main rooms *(caldarium, tepidarium* and *frigidarium)* occupy the middle part of the central section whilst the secondary rooms (vestibule, palestra and *laconicum*) are symetrically positioned at the sides. The ruined caldarium for the very hot bath, a circular room (34m – 112ft in diameter), is the setting for operatic performances in summer.

★★★ CASTEL SANT'ANGELO (ABX) ⊘

The imposing fortress was built in AD 135 as a mausoleum for the Emperor Hadrian and his family. In the 6C, Gregory the Great erected a chapel on top of the mausoleum to commemorate the apparition of an angel who, by putting his sword back into its sheath, announced the end of a plague. In the 15C Nicholas V added a brick storey to the ancient building and corner towers to the surrounding wall. Alexander VI (1492-1503) added octagonal bastions.

In 1527, during the sack of Rome, Clement VII took refuge in the castle and installed an apartment which was later embellished by Paul III; the **Popes' Apartment**★ stands isolated at the summit of the fortress and testifies to the graciousness of the popes' life style.

A long passageway (Il Passetto) links the fortress to the Vatican palaces. A fine spiral ramp dating from antiquity leads to the castle. From a terrace at the summit there is a splendid **panorama**★★★ of the whole town.

The Castel Sant'Angelo is linked to the left bank of the Tiber by the graceful **Ponte Sant'Angelo**★ (**BX 57**), which is adorned with baroque angels carved by Bernini and with statues of Sts Peter and Paul (16C).

★★★ CATACOMBE (CATACOMBS)

*Leave Rome by Via di Porta S. Sebastiano (**DZ**). Plan of the built-up area in the current Michelin Red Guide Italia.*

There are numerous underground Christian cemeteries alongside the Via Appia Antica. In use from the 2C they were rediscovered in the 16C and 19C. They consist of long galleries radiating from an underground burial chamber *(hypogeum)* which belonged to a noble Roman family of the Christian faith. They permitted fellow Christians to use the galleries.

The decorations of the catacombs (carvings or paintings of symbolic motifs) are precious examples of early Christian art.

The visitor with little time to spare should visit the following ones:

Catacombe di San Callisto★★★ ⊘ near the Appian Way, famous for its exceptional collection of paintings.

Catacombe di San Sebastiano★★★ ⊘ near the Appian Way.

Catacombe di Domitilla★★★ ⊘ *entrance at no 282 Via delle Sette Chiese.*

★★ COLOSSEO (COLISEUM – CY) ⊘

This amphitheatre, inaugurated in AD 80, is also known as the Flavian Amphitheatre after its initiator, Vespasian, first of the Flavian emperors. With its three superimposed Classical orders (Doric, Ionic and Corinthian), it is a masterpiece of classical architecture. Fights between men and beasts, gladiatorial contests, races and mock naval battles took place in the arena.

Now an integral part of the Coliseum, the **arco di Constantino**★★★ is an arch erected to commemorate Constantine's victory over Maxentius in AD 315. Some of the low reliefs were removed from other 2C monuments.

★★ FORI IMPERIALI (IMPERIAL FORUMS – CY)

These were built by Caesar, Augustus, Trajan, Nerva and Vespasian. There are hardly any remains of the latter two. The Via dei Fori Imperiali, laid out in 1932 by Mussolini, divides the imperial forums.

Of Caesar's Forum (**Foro di Cesare**★★ – *view from Via del Tulliano)* (**CY 77**) there remain three lovely columns from the Temple of Venus Genitrix. Of the Augustan Forum (**Foro di Augusto**★★ – *view from Via Alessandrina)* (**CY 2**) there remain a few columns of the Temple of Mars the Avenger, vestiges of the stairway and of the wall enclosing the forum (behind the temple).

The forum is dominated by the House of the Knights of Rhodes (Casa dei Cavalieri di Rodi), built in the Middle Ages and rebuilt in the 15C amidst the ancient ruins.

The forum seen from the Palatino

All that remains of the largest and finest, Trajan's Forum **(Foro di Traiano★★★)**, is Trajan's column **(Colonna Traiana★★★)** which depicts, in over 100 scenes, episodes of the war waged by Trajan against the Dacians. It is an unrivalled masterpiece. The markets **(mercati★★★** ⊘ – *entrance in Via 4 Novembre* – **CXY 87)**, which have kept their semicircular façade, were a distribution and supply centre. They comprised about 150 shops which were also retail outlets. The Tower of the Militia **(Torre delle Milizie★)** is part of a 13C fortress. It leans slightly as the result of an earthquake in the 14C.

★★★ FORO ROMANO (ROMAN FORUM – CY) ⊘

The remains of the Roman Forum, the religious, political and commercial centre of ancient Rome, reflect the 12 centuries of history which created Roman civilisation. The forum was excavated in the 19C and 20C.
Take the Sacred Way, **Via Sacra★**, along which victorious generals marched in triumph to the **Curia★★**, rebuilt in the 3C by Diocletian. Senate meetings were held here; nowadays it houses Trajan's low reliefs **(Plutei di Traiano★★)**, sculpted panels depicting scenes from the life of the Emperor, and sacrificial animals. Nearby rises an imposing Triumphal Arch, **Arco di Settimio Severo★★**, built in AD 203 to commemorate the Emperor's victories over the Parthians. At the foot of the Capitol stood some remarkable monuments: the late 1C Temple of Vespasian **(Tempio di Vespasiano★★)** of which only three elegant Corinthian columns remain; the Temple of Saturn **(Tempio du Saturno★★★)** which retains eight 4C columns; and the **Portico of the Di Consentes★**, a colonnade of pillars with Corinthian columns dating back to restoration work of AD 367 – the portico was dedicated to the 12 principal Roman deities.
The Column of Phocas **(Colonna di Foca★)** was erected in AD 608 in honour of the Byzantine Emperor Phocas who presented the Pantheon to Boniface IV. The **Basilica Giulia★★**, which has five aisles, was built by Julius Caesar and completed by Augustus. It served as a law court and exchange.
Three beautiful columns with Corinthian capitals remain of the Temple of Castor and Pollux **(Tempio di Castore e Polluce★★★)**. The circular Temple of Vesta **(Tempio di Vesta★★★)** stands near the House of the Vestal Virgins **(Casa delle Vestali★★★)**. The Temple of Antoninus and Faustina **(Tempio di Antonino e Faustina★★)** was dedicated to the Emperor Antoninus Pius and his wife (fresco of grotesques and candelabra). The temple now houses the Church of San Lorenzo in Miranda rebuilt in the 17C.

The grandiose Basilica of Maxentius (**Basilica di Massenzio★★★**) was completed by the Emperor Constantine. The Triumphal Arch of Titus (**Arco di Tito★★**), erected in 81, commemorates the capture of Jerusalem by this emperor, who reigned for only two years.

★★ Chiesa del GESÙ (BY)

The mother-church of the Jesuits in Rome, built by Vignola in 1568, is a typical building of the Counter-Reformation. On the outside, the engaged pillars replace the flat pilasters of the Renaissance, with light and shade effects and recesses. The interior, spacious and ideal for preaching, was lavishly decorated in the baroque style: on the dome, the **Baciccia frescoes★★** illustrate the *Triumph of the Name of Jesus* (1679); the **Cappella di Sant'Ignazio★★★** *(north transept)*, a chapel where the remains of St Ignatius Loyola rest, is the work (1696-1700) of the Jesuit Brother Andrea Pozzo and is sumptuously decorated.

★★ PALATINO (CY)

The Palatine Hill, where Romulus and Remus were discovered, was chosen by Domitian as the site for the Imperial Palace. The building included three main areas: the **Domus Flavia★** or official state apartments, the **Domus Augustana★★** or private imperial apartments, and the **Stadium★**. The House of Livia (**Casa di Livia★★**) probably belonged to Augustus (fine vestiges of paintings). The Farnese Gardens (**Orti Farnesiani**), laid out in the 16C on the site of Tiberius' palace, afford **views★★** of the Forum and town.
Leave the Palatine by an exit alongside the Arch of Titus.

★**Tempio di Venere e di Roma** (CY B) – The Temple of Venus and Rome built between 121 and 136 by Hadrian was the largest in the city (110m – 361ft by 53m – 174ft). It was unique in that it comprised two *cellae* with apses back to back. One was dedicated to the goddess of Rome and faced the Forum; the other was dedicated to Venus and faced the Coliseum.

★★ PANTHEON (BX) ⊘

The Pantheon, an ancient building perfectly preserved, founded by Agrippa in 27 BC and rebuilt by Hadrian (117-125), was a temple which was converted into a church in the 7C.
Access is through a porch supported by 16 single granite columns, all ancient except for three on the left. The doors are the original ones. The **interior★★★**, a masterpiece of harmony and majesty, is dominated by the **antique dome★★★**, the diameter of which is equal to its height. The side chapels, adorned with alternately curved and triangular pediments, contain the tombs of the kings of Italy and that of Raphael *(on the left)*.

★★ PIAZZA DEL POPOLO and PINCIO (BV)

The **Piazza del Popolo** was designed by Giuseppe Valadier (1762-1839). The **Porta del Popolo★** was pierced in the Aurelian wall in the 3C, and adorned with an external façade in the 16C and with an inner façade designed by Bernini in the 17C. The Renaissance Church of **Santa Maria del Popolo★★** (C) was remodelled in the Baroque period. It contains 15C **frescoes★** by Pinturicchio *(first chapel on the right)*; two **tombs★** by Andrea Sansovino *(in the chancel)*; two **paintings★★★** by **Caravaggio**: the *Crucifixion of St Peter* and the *Conversion of St Paul (first chapel to the left of the chancel)*; and the **Cappella Chigi★** *(2nd on the left)*, a chapel designed by Raphael. The Egyptian obelisk, which was brought to Rome in the reign of Augustus, was erected in the centre in the 16C by Pope Sixtus V.
Leading off the Piazza del Popolo is the main street of central Rome, **Via del Corso★★** (BCX), lined with handsome Renaissance palaces and fashionable shops.

Pincio (BV) – This fine public park was laid out in the 19C by Giuseppe Valadier. It affords a magnificent **view★★★** particularly at dusk when the golden glow so typical of Rome is at its mellow best.
Viale della Trinità dei Monti (BCVX) leads southwards and is overlooked by the **Villa Medici** (CX), now the home of the French Academy.

★★ PIAZZA DI SPAGNA (CX)

This square, a popular tourist attraction, was so named in the 17C after the Spanish Embassy occupied the Palazzo di Spagna. It is dominated by the majestic Spanish Steps (**Scala della Trinità dei Monti★★★**) built in the 18C by the architects de Sanctis and Specchi, who adopted the baroque style of perspective and *trompe-l'œil*. At the foot of the stairway are the Boat Fountain (**Fontana della Barcaccia★**) by Bernini's father, Pietro (17C), and Keats' House where the poet died in 1821. At the top of the stairs, Holy Trinity on the Hill (**Trinità dei Monti★**) (CX) is the French church built in the 16C and restored in the 19C. It contains a *Deposition from the Cross★* *(2nd chapel on the left)* dating from 1541 by Daniele da Volterra, a great admirer of Michelangelo.

Leading off from this square is **Via dei Condotti** (**BCX 23**) lined with elegant shops. It was also renowned for the Caffè Greco, a famous establishment which was opened in 1760 and frequented by celebrities (Goethe, Berlioz, Wagner, Stendhal etc).

★★★ PIAZZA NAVONA (BX)

The square built on the site of Domitian's stadium retains its shape. A pleasant and lively pedestrian precinct, it is adorned at the centre with Bernini's Baroque masterpiece, the Fountain of the Four Rivers (**Fontana dei Fiumi★★★**), completed in 1651. The statues represent the four rivers – Danube, Ganges, Rio de la Plata and Nile – symbolising the four corners of the earth.
Among the churches and palaces lining the square are **Sant'Agnese in Agone★★** (**BX D**) with a baroque façade by Borromini (attractive **interior★** on the plan of a Greek cross), and the adjoining 17C **Palazzo Pamphili.**

★ PIAZZA VENEZIA (CXY)

The Piazza in the centre of Rome is lined with palaces: Palazzo Venezia, Palazzo Bonaparte, where Napoleon's mother died in 1836, and the early 20C Palazzo delle Assicurazioni Generali di Venezia.

★ Palazzo Venezia (**CY E**) ⊙ – This palace, built by Pope Paul II (1464-71), is one of the first Renaissance buildings. A **museum**, on the first floor, presents collections of medieval art (ivories, Byzantine and Limousin enamels, Italian Primitive paintings on wood, gold and silver work, ceramics and small bronzes (15C-17C). The Basilica of St Mark (**Basilica di San Marco**), which was incorporated within the palace in the 15C, has a fine Renaissance **façade★** overlooking Piazza di San Marco (**CY 60**).

Vittoriano (**CY**) – This huge memorial by Giuseppe Sacconi, begun in 1885 in honour of the first king of a united Italy, Victor Emanuel II, overshadows the other monuments of Rome by its sheer size and dazzling white colour. It affords a **view★★** of the Eternal City.

★★★ Basilica di SAN GIOVANNI IN LATERANO (DY) ⊙

St John Lateran, the cathedral of Rome, is among the four major basilicas in Rome. The first basilica was founded by Constantine prior to St Peter's in the Vatican. It was rebuilt in the Baroque era by Borromini and again in the 18C.
The main façade by Alessandro Galilei dates from the 18C and the central door has bronze panels that originally belonged to the Curia of the Roman Forum (modified in the 17C). The vast and grandiose interior has a 16C **ceiling★★** which was restored in the 18C. In the nave the **Statues of the** *Apostles★* by pupils of Bernini stand in niches built by Borromini. The elegant **Cappella Corsini★** *(first in the north aisle)* was designed by Alessandro Galilei. The transept **ceiling★★** dates from the end of the 16C. The Chapel of the Blessed Sacrament (**Cappella del SS Sacramento** – *north transept*, has fine ancient **columns★** in gilded bronze. The pretty cloisters (**chiostro★**) are the work of the Vassalletto (13C), marble-masons who were associates of the Cosmati *(see Index)*. The baptistery (**Battistero★**), built in the 4C, is decorated with beautiful 5C and 7C mosaics.
In **Piazza di San Giovanni in Laterano** rises a 15C BC Egyptian obelisk, the tallest in Rome.
The Lateran Palace (**Palazzo Lateranense**), rebuilt in 1586, was the papal palace until the papal court returned from Avignon. The staircase, **Scala Sancta**, is a precious vestige from the medieval papal palace and is traditionally identified as the one Christ used in the palace of Pontius Pilate. Worshippers climb the stairs on their knees. At the top is the papal chapel (Sancta Sanctorum) with its many precious relics.

★★★ SANTA MARIA MAGGIORE (DX) ⊙

It is one of the four major basilicas in Rome. It was built by Sixtus III (AD 432-440) and is dedicated to St Mary Major. It has since undergone extensive restoration. The campanile, erected in 1377, is the highest in Rome. The façade is the work of Ferdinando Fuga (1743-1750). The adjoining **loggia** ⊙ is decorated with **mosaics★** by Filippo Rusuti (end 13C), much restored in the 19C.
The impressive **interior★★★** contains remarkable **mosaics★★★**: in the nave, those above the entablature are among the most ancient Christian mosaics in Rome (5C) and depict scenes from the Old Testament; on the 5C trimphal arch are scenes from the New Testament; in the apse, the mosaics are composed of 5C elements but were completely redone in the 13C.
The coffered **ceiling★** is said to have been gilded with the first gold brought from Peru. The floor, the work of Cosmati (12C) was subject to much restoration in the 18C. The **Cappella di Sisto V** *(south aisle)* and the **Cappella Paolina** *(north aisle)* were both built in the form of a Greek cross and surmounted by a cupola. Another chapel was added at the end of the 16C and one in the 17C: they were richly decorated in the Baroque style. Sistus V, Pius V of Clemente and Paul V are buried here.

Leave the church by the door at the far end of the south aisle.
From **Piazza dell'Esquilino**, with its Egyptian obelisk, there is a **view**★★ of the imposing 17C chevet.

★★ Basilica di SAN PAOLO FUORI LE MURA (BZ) ⊙

Leave by Via Ostiense. Plan of the built-up area in the current Michelin Red Guide Italia.

One of the four major basilicas. It was built by Constantine in the 4C on the site of St Paul's tomb. It was rebuilt in the 19C, after it had been wholly destroyed by fire in 1823, on the original basilical plan of early Christian churches.
The impressive **interior**★★★ contains: an 11C bronze door cast in Constantinople *(at the entrance of the first south aisle)*; and a Gothic **ciborium**★★★ (1285) by Arnolfo di Cambio, placed on the high altar which stands above a marble plaque inscribed with the name Paul and dated 4C. In the Chapel of the Blessed Sacrament (**Cappella del SS. Sacramento**★) *(left of the chancel)* are: a 14C wooden figure of Christ attributed to Pietro Cavallini; a statue of St Brigitta kneeling, by Stefano Maderno (17C); a 14C or 15C statue of St Paul; and the **paschal candelabrum**★★, a 12C Romanesque work of art by the Vassalletto.
The cloisters (**chiostro**★) are also attributed, at least in part, to this same family of artists.

★★ Fontana di TREVI (TREVI FOUNTAIN – CX)

This late-Baroque creation was commissioned from Nicola Salvi in 1762 by Pope Clement XIII. The central figure, the Ocean, rides in a chariot drawn by two sea-horses and two tritons.
Tourists continue the tradition of throwing two coins over their shoulders into the fountain – one coin to ensure their return to Rome and the other for the fulfilment of a wish.

VATICANO (VATICAN – AX) ⊙

The Vatican City is bounded by a wall, overlooking Viale Vaticano, and to the east by the colonnade of St Peter's Square. This makes up the greater part of the Vatican state as laid down in 1929 in the Lateran Treaty. The Vatican City, now reduced to only 44 hectares – 109 acres and with less than a thousand inhabitants, stems from the Papal States, a donation made in the 8C by Pepin the Short to Pope Stephen II, and lost in 1870 when Italy was united into one Kingdom with Rome as its capital. The Vatican State, with the Pope as ruler, has its own flag and anthem; it prints stamps and mints its own coinage which is legal tender throughout Italy. In 1970, Pope Paul VI dissolved the armed forces, retaining only the Swiss Guard who wear a colourful uniform said to have been designed by Michelangelo.
The Pope, who is the Head of State, is also the Supreme Head of the Universal Church, and from this very small state, the spiritual influence of the church radiates throughout the world through the person of the Sovereign Pontiff. When the Pope is in residence, he grants public audiences (**udienza pubblica**) ⊙.

★★ **Giardini Vaticani** ⊙ – The vast, magnificent gardens are adorned with fountains and statues, gifts from various countries. Of particular interest is the Casina of Pius IV, a fine 16C building decorated with stucco work and paintings. From the gardens are glorious views of the cupola.

★★ PIAZZA DI SAN PIETRO (ST PETER'S SQUARE – AX)

This architectural masterpiece was begun in 1656 by Bernini, master of the Baroque. The two semicircles of the colonnade which adorn the square and frame the façade of the basilica form an ensemble of remarkable sobriety and majesty. At the centre of the square stands a 1C BC obelisk brought from Heliopolis in Egypt to Rome in AD 37 by order of Caligula. It was erected here in 1585 on the initiative of Sixtus V by Domenico Fontana. At the top is a relic of the Holy Cross.

★★ Basilica di SAN PIETRO (ST PETER'S BASILICA – AX) ⊙

Constantine, the first Christian Emperor, decided in AD 324 to build a basilica on the site where St Peter was buried after he had been martyred in Nero's circus. In the 15C it proved necessary to rebuild.
For two centuries, the plan of the new basilica was constantly revised. The plan, of a Greek cross surmounted by a dome designed by Bramante and adopted by Michelangelo, was altered to a Latin cross at the behest of Paul V in 1606, when he instructed Carlo Maderna to add two bays and a façade to Michelangelo's square plan. From 1629 onwards, the basilica was decorated in a sumptuous Baroque style by Bernini.
The **façade** (115m – 377ft long and 45m – 151ft high) was completed in 1614 by Carlo Maderna; it is surmounted by colossal figures, and masks the dome. In the centre is the balcony from which the Sovereign Pontiff gives his benediction *Urbi et Orbi* (to the City and the World).

Basilica di San Pietro

Under the **porch**, the first door on the left has bronze panels carved by Giacomo Manzù (1964); the bronze central door dates from the Renaissance (1455); the door on the right or Holy Door is opened and closed by the Pope to mark the beginning and end of a Jubilee Year.

Inside, it is customary to approach the stoups in the nave which at first glance appear of normal size but are in fact huge. Such size emphasises the gigantic dimensions of the basilica, otherwise not apparent because of the harmony of its proportions. The length of St Peter's can be compared to that of other great basilicas throughout the world by means of markers inlaid in the pavement of the nave.

The first chapel on the right contains the *Pietà*★★★, the moving and powerful masterpiece carved by Michelangelo in 1499-1500, which shows his creative genius.

In the right aisle, adjoining the Cappella del SS Sacramento, **Gregory XIII's Monument**★ is adorned with low reliefs illustrating the institution of the Gregorian calendar devised by that pope. Immediately beyond the right transept, **Clement XIII's Monument**★★★ is a fine neo-Classical design by Canova dating from 1792.

The apse is dominated by St Peter's Throne **(Cattedra di San Pietro**★★★**)** by Bernini (1666), a great carved throne in bronze encasing a 4C episcopal chair but symbolically attributed to St Peter, and surmounted by a glory in gilded stucco. In the chancel of the right is **Urban VIII's Monument**★★★, again by Bernini (1647), a masterpiece of funerary art. On the left stands **Paul III's Monument**★★★ by Guglielmo della Porta (16C), a disciple of Michelangelo.

St Leo the Great's Altar *(chapel to the left of the chancel)* has a fine Baroque **altarpiece**★ carved in high relief by Algardi. Nearby, **Alexander VII's Monument**★, characterised by extreme exuberance, is a late work

Pietà by Michelangelo

A. Gaël

by Bernini (1678) assisted by his pupils. The **baldaquin**★★★ which crowns the pontifical altar and is 29m – 95ft tall (the height of the Farnese Palace) was strongly criticised: partly because the bronze had been taken from the Pantheon and partly because it was thought to be too theatrical and in bad taste. It does, however, fit in well with the overall architectural plan.

The **dome**★★★ designed by Michelangelo, which he himself built as far as the lantern, was completed in 1593 by Giacomo della Porta and Domenico Fontana. From the **summit** ⊘ *(leave the basilica by the right aisle for access)* there is a **view**★★★ of St Peter's Square, the Vatican City and Rome from the Janiculum to Monte Mario.

The 13C bronze **Statue of St Peter**★★ overlooking the nave is attributed to Arnolfo di Cambio and is greatly venerated by pilgrims, who come to kiss its feet.

Innocent VIII's Monument★★★ *(between the second and third bays in the left aisle)* is a Renaissance work (1498) by Antonio del Pollaiuolo. The **Stuart Monument** *(between the first and second bays in the left aisle)* carved by Canova is adorned with beautiful **angels**★ in low relief.

The Historical Museum **(Museo Storico**★**)** ⊘ *(entrance in the left aisle, opposite the Stuart Monument)* has many treasured items including **Sixtus IV's tomb**★★★ (1493) by Pollaiuolo.

★★ MUSEI VATICANI (VATICAN MUSEUMS – AX) ⊘

Entrance: Viale Vaticano.

The museums of the Vatican occupy part of the palaces built by the popes from the 13C onwards, which have been extended and embellished to the present day.

These include on the first floor the **Museo Pio-Clementino**★★★ (Greek and Roman antiquities) with its masterpieces: the **Belvedere Torso**★★★ (1C BC), greatly admired by Michelangelo; the **Venus of Cnidus**★★, a Roman copy of Praxiteles' Venus; the **Laocoon Group**★★★, a 1C BC Hellenistic work; the **Apollo Belvedere**★★★, a 2C Roman copy; **Perseus**★★, a neo-Classical work by Canova, which was purchased by Pius VII; **Hermes**★★★, a 2C Roman work inspired by the work of Praxiteles; and the **Apoxyomenos**★★★, the athlete scraping his skin with a strigil after taking exercise, a 1C Roman copy of the Greek original by Lysippus.

245

The **Museo Etrusco★**, on the second floor, has a remarkable 7C BC gold **fibula★★** adorned with lions and ducklings in high relief *(Room II)* and the *Mars*★★ found at Todi, a rare example of a large bronze statue from the 5C BC (*Room III*). The **Sala della Biga** derives its name from the **two-horse chariot** *(biga)*, a 1C Roman work reassembled in the 18C.

The four Raphael Rooms **(Stanze di Rafaello★★★)**, the private apartments of Julius II, were decorated by Raphael and his pupils from 1508 to 1517. The result is a pure Renaissance masterpiece. The frescoes are remarkable: the *Borgo Fire*, the *School of Athens*, *Parnassus*, the *Expulsion of Heliodorus from the Temple*, the *Miracle of the Bolsena Mass* and *St Peter delivered from prison*. The **Collezione d'Arte Moderna Religiosa★★** assembled by Pope Paul VI, is displayed in the apartment of Pope Alexander VI.

On the first floor the Sistine Chapel **(Cappella Sistina★★★)** is open to the public; its splendid vault, painted by Michelangelo from 1508 to 1512, illustrates the Bible, the Creation, the Flood and above the altar the Last Judgement which was added by the artist in 1534. The lowest sections of the side walls were decorated by Perugino, Pinturicchio and Botticelli. The Picture Gallery **(Pinacoteca★★★)** also contains some first-class works: three **compositions★★★** by **Raphael** (*The Coronation of the Virgin, The Madonna of Foligno* and *The Transfiguration* – Room VIII); *St Jerome*★★ by Leonardo da Vinci *(Room IX)* and a **Descent from the Cross★★** by Caravaggio *(Room XII)*.

ADDITIONAL SIGHTS

Churches

★ **Chiesa Nuova** (BX G) – This church dates from the Counter-Reformation. Alongside is the **Oratorio dei Filippini** with an elegant **façade★** by Borromini.

★★ **Sant'Andrea al Quirinale** (CX K) – This masterpiece by Bernini has an elliptical **interior★★**.

★ **Sant'Andrea della Valle** (BY Y) – This early-17C church has a **façade★★** by Rainaldi (17C) and a lovely **dome★★** by Carlo Maderna, painted by Lanfranco. Domenichino decorated the **apse★**.

★ **Sant'Agnese fuori le Mura** – *Take Via Nomentana* (DV). *Town plan in the current Michelin Red Guide Italia.*
A **mosaic★** adorns the apse. The Church of **Santa Costanza★**, originally a 4C mausoleum, also boasts a fine **mosaic★**.

★ **Sant'Agostino** (BX L) – The church of St Augustine contains Jacopo Sansovino's **Madonna del Parto★**, Raphael's fresco of the **Prophet Isaiah★** and Caravaggio's **Madonna of the Pilgrims★★★**.

★★ **San Carlo alle Quattro Fontane** (CX N) – **Borromini's** masterpiece with an intricate façade which reveals the torment of the architect, and an **interior★★** on an elliptical plan.

★ **Santa Cecilia in Trastevere** (BY) ⊘ – A much-altered 9C building. The statue of *St Cecilia★* (1599) is by Stefano Maderno and the **Last Judgement★★★** (c1293) is the work of Pietro Cavallini.

★★ **San Clemente** (DY) – The basilica is arranged over several levels. There are 12C **mosaics★★★** in the apse and **frescoes★** by Masolino.

★★ **Sant'Ignazio** (BX R) – The façade and central ceiling **frescoes★★** are by the Jesuit, Andrea Pozzo.

★★ **San Lorenzo fuori Le Mura** – *Take Via dei Ramni* (DX 53). *Town plan in the current Michelin Red Guide Italia.*
The basilica of St Lawrence Without the Walls dates from the 6C and the 13C: 5C-6C **harvest sarcophagus**, 13C **ambos★** and a 13C **papal throne★**.

★★ **San Luigi dei Francesi** (BX F) – This is the French church in Rome. It contains **frescoes★** by Dominichino and **paintings★★★** by Caravaggio.

★★ **Santa Maria degli Angeli** (DX S) – This prestigious church was built amidst the ruins of Diocletian's baths. The **transept★** gives a good idea of the solemn magnitude of the ancient building.

Santa Maria dell'Anima (BX Z) – One of Rome's rare Gothic interiors.

★★ **Santa Maria in Cosmedin** (CY) – Elegant 12C **campanile★**. In the porch is the **Bocca della Verità** (Mouth of Truth).

★★ **Santa Maria Sopra Minerva** (BX B) – The church has numerous works of art: **frescoes★** by Filippino Lippi and both Gothic and Baroque **tombs★**.

★ **Santa Maria della Pace** (BX A) – The four **Sibyls★** are by Raphael.

Eestasy of St Theresa by Bernini

★★ **Santa Maria in Trastevere (BY)** – 12C basilica with 12C-13C **mosaics**★★★ in the chancel.

★★ **Santa Maria della Vittoria (CX)** – This is Carlo Maderna's masterpiece. The sumptuous **interior**★★★ provides the setting for Bernini's *Ecstasy of St Theresa of Avila*★★★ (1652).

★ **San Pietro in Montorio (BY)** – This 15C church has Sebastiano del Piombo's *Flagellation*★ and Bramante's **Tempietto**★ in the courtyard. **View**★★★ of Rome from the esplanade.

★ **San Pietro in Vincoli (CY)** – The church of St Peter in chains contains Julius II's mausoleum and *Moses*★★★ by Michelangelo.

★★ **Santa Sabina (BY V)** – This 5C building is one of Rome's oldest basilicas. Beautiful cypress wood **door**★★ (5C). The **interior**★★ is well proportioned and full of light.

★★ **Santa Susanna (CX W)** – The 9C-16C church has a beautiful **façade**★★★ by **Carlo Maderna**.

Santi Cosma e Damiano (CY X) – 5C church with a beautiful 16C coffered **ceiling**★ and 6C and 7C **mosaics**★.

Monuments from antiquity

Arco di Giano (CY) – Through this public gateway, the Arch of Janus, passed some of Rome's busiest roads.

★★ **Ara Pacis Augustae (BX E)** – The altar is the major work of the Augustan "golden age" and is decorated with magnificent **low-relief carvings**.

★★ **Area Sacra del Largo Argentina (BY)** – These ruins of four temples date from the days of the ancient Roman Republic.

Circo Massimo (CY) – This was the largest circus in Rome and was used exclusively for chariot races.

Mausoleo di Augusto (BX K) – Augustus' mausoleum takes the form of an Etruscan tumulus tomb.

★ **Piramide di Caio Cestio (CZ C)** – Rome's most original mausoleum was erected in the 12C BC by a rich citizen, Caius Cestius.

★★ **Teatro di Marcello (BY T¹)** – One of Rome's largest theatres, it was inaugurated by Augustus in the 11C BC.

★★ **Tempio di Apollo Sosiano (BY N)** – The temple was dedicated to Apollo medicus and retains three elegant fluted **columns**★★.

★ **Tempio della Fortuna Virile (CY D)** – This rectangular and austere temple dates from the late 2C BC.

★ **Tempio di Vesta (CY F)** – An elegant circular construction dating from the Augustan period.

★ **Tomba di Cecilia Metella (DZ)** – A fine example of a noble woman's tomb.

Museums and palaces

★ **Galleria Nazionale d'Arte Moderna** (CV) ⊙ – The National Gallery of Modern Art contains Italian painting and sculpture from the 19C to the present day.

★★★ **Museo Borghese** (CV) ⊙ – Sculptures by Canova and Bernini and paintings by Raphael, Correggio, Titian and Caravaggio.

★★★ **Museo Nazionale Romano** (DX) ⊙ – Greek and Roman antiquities; paintings from various Roman villas.

★★★ **Museo Nazionale di Villa Giulia** (BV) ⊙ – Exceptional collection of antiquities relating to the Etruscan civilisation. The setting is Julius III's elegant country villa.

★★ **Palazzo Barberini** (CX M³) ⊙ – This Baroque palace now houses a remarkable Art Gallery (**Galleria di Pittura★★**) – paintings by Tintoretto, Caravaggio, Raphael, Titian, Quentin Metsys, Holbein etc.

★ **Palazzo Braschi** (BX M⁴) ⊙ – A late-18C papal family palace now housing a museum (**museo★**) tracing the history of Rome from the Middle Ages.

★★ **Palazzo della Cancelleria** (BXY) – An elegant palace built from 1483 to 1513 with a harmonious inner courtyard.

Palazzo Chigi (BX S) – This 16C palace now belongs to the Presidency of the Council of Ministers.

Palazzo della Consulta (CX) – This palace with its façade★ by Ferdinando Fuga (18C) is now the seat of the Constitutional Court.

Palazzo Corsini (ABY) ⊙ – A 15C palace rebuilt in the 18C. **Picture Gallery** (Fra Angelico, Caravaggio).

★ **Palazzo Doria Pamphili** (CX M⁵) ⊙ – A handsome 16C palace with a **collection★★** of paintings by Caravaggio, Velasquez, the Carracci etc.

★★ **Palazzo Farnese** (BY) ⊙ – It is now the French Embassy. It was built from 1515 by several architects: Antonio da Sangallo the Younger, Michelangelo (who designed the upper cornice of the façade, the Farnese coat of arms above the central balcony and the second floor of the inner court), Vignola who collaborated on the inner court and built the palace's rear façade, and Giacomo della Porta who designed the loggia of the same façade.

Palazzo Madama (BX W) – A 16C palace now the seat of the Senate.

Palazzo di Montecitorio (BX) – This 17C palace houses the Chamber of Deputies.

★★ **Palazzo del Quirinale** (CX) – This handsome 16C palace was designed as a summer residence for the popes and is now the official residence of the President of the Republic.

Palazzo della Sapienza (BX X) – A 16C palace with Borromini's masterpiece, the Church of San'Ivo★ with its bell-tower, in the inner courtyard.

★ **Palazzo Spada** (BY) ⊙ – The **Galleria di Pittura★** presents the private collection of the 17C churchman, Cardinal Spada.

★★ **Villa Farnesina** (ABY) ⊙ – This villa was built from 1508 to 1511 for Agostino Chigi who commissioned Raphael and his pupils to decorate the interior.

Squares, streets, sites, parks and gardens

★ **Piazza Bocca della Verità** (CY 15) – A combination of ancient (Arco di Giano, Tempio della Fortuna Virilis and Tempio Totondo known as the Tempio di Vesta), medieval (Santa Maria in Cosmedin) and Baroque buildings, makes a typical Roman scene.

★ **Piazza Campo dei Fiori** (BY) – This well-known square and one of the most popular in Rome is the site of a picturesque food market held every morning.

★ **Piazza Colonna** (BX) – At the centre of this busy square stands the 2C **column★** in honour of Marcus Aurelius.

★★ **Piazza del Quirinale** (CX) – This elegant and gently-sloping square is adorned with a fountain, an obelisk, statues of the Dioscuri and is overlooked by the Palazzo del Quirinale and Palazzo della Consulta *(above)*.

★ **Piazza Sant'Ignazio** (BX 58) – This charming square was designed in imitation of a theatre stage.

★ **Porta San Paolo** (CZ) – This gate opens onto Via Ostiense which led to St Paul's Basilica, from which the gate took its present name.

★ **Porta San Sebastiano** (DZ) – This is Rome's most spectacular gate, in honour of St Sebastian (3C).

★ **Via dei Coronari** (BX 25) - This attractive street known for its second-hand and antique shops is lined with palaces glowing in ochre and stone.

★★ **EUR** - *Take Via Cristoforo Colombo* (DZ) *Town plan in the current Michelin Red Guide Italia.* This new district (1939) to the south of Rome with its colossal modern architecture is the site of the Museum of Roman Civilisation (**Museo della Civiltà Romana★★**) ⊙.

★ **Isola Tiberina** (BY) - This peaceful spot, the Tiber Island, is linked to the bank by the Fabrician Bridge (**Ponte Fabricio**) (BY 31), the only Roman bridge to survive intact.

Gianicolo (AY) - This attractive promenade affords extensive **views★★★** over the city.

★★ **Giardini Vaticani** (AX) - The Vatican Gardens provide a good view of the dome of St Peter's which rises majestically above the gardens.

★★ **Villa Borghese** (CV) - This is Rome's largest public park.

Roman historians generally counted the years as from the foundation of Rome (Ab Urbe Condita). The system of counting from the birth of Christ (AD) was introduced in the 6C by Dionysius Exiguus, a Scythian monk.

SABBIONETA★

Lombardy - Population 4 438
Michelin map 988 fold 14 or 428, 429 H 13
33km - 21 miles southwest of Mantua

The town was built from 1558 by Vespasiano Gonzaga (1531-91), a mercenary leader in the service of Philip II of Spain who conferred on his loyal servants the glorious order of the Golden Fleece. The order was created in 1429 by Philip the Good, Duke of Burgundy. Vespasiano was a cultured man and he wanted to take charge of the building of his ideal town.

★ **Town** ⊙ - Its hexagonal walls, star plan and monuments make Sabbioneta a jewel of Italian Mannerism.
The Garden Palace (**Palazzo del Giardino**) was designed for festivities and its walls and ceilings were richly painted with frescoes by Bernardino Campi and his school. The great **Galleria** (96m - 315ft long) is one of the longest Renaissance galleries.
The Olympic Theatre (**Teatro Olimpico★**), a masterpiece by Vicentino Scamozzi (1552-1616), was built from 1588 to 1590 and is one of the oldest covered theatres in Europe. The interior is decorated with frescoes by the school of Veronese and there is a ducal box adorned with colonnades and statues of the gods.
The Ducal Palace (**Palazzo Ducale**), has finely-carved wooden and coffered ceilings. There are interesting equestrian statues of the Gonzaga family. The Galleria degli Antenati is also noteworthy.
Vespasiano Gonzaga is buried in the **Chiesa dell'Incoronata** with its octagonal plan and dome. Vespasiano's **mausoleum★** is adorned with a bronze statue by Leone Leoni (1509-90); he is depicted as Marcus Aurelius.
The **Museo d'Arte Sacra** displays the **Golden Fleece** discovered in 1988 in Vespasiano's tomb *(see above)* in the church.
The 18C Synagogue (**Sinagoga**) traces the story of the town's Jewish community whose great legacy was the elegant printworks also used by Vespasiano.

SACRA DI SAN MICHELE★★★

Piedmont
Michelin map 988 fold 12 or 428 G 4 - 37km - 23 miles west of Turin

This **Benedictine Abbey** ⊙, perched on a rocky site (alt 962m - 3 156ft), was a powerful establishment in the 13C with over 100 monks and 140 sister houses. It was built at the end of the 10C by Hugues de Montboissier from Auvergne and its layout bears a strong resemblance to that of the Mont St Michel in Normandy. After passing through the iron doors of the entrance gatehouse, climb the great staircase leading to the **Zodiac Door**; its pilasters and capitals were decorated by the famous Master Nicolò (1135). The Romanesque-Gothic **church** built on top of the rocky eminence has 16C frescoes. The early-16C triptych on the high altar is by Defendente Ferrari. The carved capitals are outstanding.
From the esplanade there is a lovely **view★★★** of the Alps, the Dora Valley, the Po and Turin plains.

SALERNO*

Campania – Population 148 969

Michelin map 988 fold 28 or 431 E/F 26 – Local map see AMALFI

Plan of the built-up area in the current Michelin Red Guide Italia

Salerno, lying along the graceful curve of its gulf, has retained a medieval quarter on the slopes of a hill crowned by a castle. The town is now an active port and industrial centre while market gardening is the main activity of the surrounding area.

Salerno was at first Etruscan, then Roman and became a principality under the Lombards. The Norman Robert Guiscard made it his capital in 1077. A rich trading city, Salerno became famous for its university, which attracted some of the greatest scholars of the time, and in particular its school of medicine which flourished from the 11C to 13C. The town acquired the nickname of City of Socrates. With the arrival of the Kings of Anjou Salerno declined and witnessed the rise of its neighbour and rival, Naples. It was just south of Salerno that the 5th US Army landed on 9 September 1943.

★★ **Duomo** ⊙ – The cathedral is dedicated to St Matthew the Evangelist, who is buried in the crypt. It was built on the orders of Robert Guiscard and consecrated by Pope Gregory VII in 1085. The Norman-style building was remodelled in the 18C and suffered considerable damage in the 1980 earthquake. The church is preceded by a delightful arcaded **atrium** built of multicoloured stone with ancient columns. The square tower to the right is 12C. The central doorway has 11C bronze doors cast in Constantinople.

The interior is of impressive dimensions. The two **ambos**★★ encrusted with decorative mosaics and resting on slender columns with marvellously-carved capitals, along with the **paschal candelabrum**, form an outstanding 12C-13C group. The Crusaders' Chapel at the far end of the south aisle is where the Crusaders had their arms blessed. Under the altar is the tomb of Pope Gregory VII who died in exile at Salerno (1085).

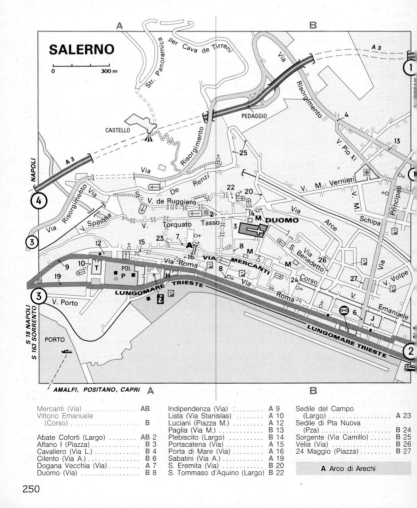

Mercanti (Via) .... AB	Indipendenza (Via) .... A 9	Sedile del Campo
Vittorio Emanuele	Lista (Via Stanislas) .... A 10	(Largo) .... A 23
(Corso) .... B	Luciani (Piazza M.) .... A 12	Sedile di Pta Nuova
	Paglia (Via M.) .... B 13	(Pza) .... B 24
Abate Coforti (Largo) .... AB 2	Plebiscito (Largo) .... B 14	Sorgente (Via Camillo) ...... B 25
Alfano I (Piazza) .... B 3	Portacatena (Via) .... A 15	Velia (Via) .... B 26
Cavaliero (Via L.) .... B 4	Porta di Mare (Via) .... A 16	24 Maggio (Piazza) .... B 27
Cilento (Via A.) .... B 6	Sabatini (Via A.) .... A 19	
Dogana Vecchia (Via) .... A 7	S. Eremita (Via) .... B 20	
Duomo (Via) .... B 8	S. Tommaso d'Aquino (Largo) B 22	**A Arco di Arechi**

In the north aisle stands the tomb of Margaret of Durazzo, the wife of Charles III of Anjou.

★ **Via Mercanti** – This street is one of the most picturesque with its shops, old houses and oratories. At its west end stands an arch, **Arco di Arechi (A A)** built by the Lombards in the 8C.

★ **Lungomare Trieste** – From this promenade, planted with palm trees and tamarisks, there is a wide view of the Gulf of Salerno.

Abbazia di SAN CLEMENTE A CASAURIA★★

SAN CLEMENTE A CASAURIA ABBEY – Abruzzi
Michelin map 988 fold 27 or 430 P 23 – 40km – 25 miles southwest of Pescara
Access: by the A25 motorway and the Torre de' Passeri exit road

The San Clemente Abbey ⊘ was founded in 871 and rebuilt in the 12C by the Cistercians in the transitional Romanesque-Gothic style. The secularised church is all that remains today.

Church – The façade is quite remarkable: a deep portico has three arches resting on lovely capitals; the main doorway is decorated with exceptional sculpture, notably on the uprights, tympanum and lintel (the bronze door was cast in 1191). The interior comprises a nave and two aisles and a semicircular apse, and is typical of the architectural simplicity dear to St Bernard. Both the monumental pulpit and the paschal candelabrum are 13C. The high altar is surmounted by a finely-carved Romanesque **ciborium★★★**. The 9C crypt has survived from the original structure and has vaulting supported by ancient columns.

SAN GIMIGNANO★★★

Tuscany – Population 6 945
Michelin map 988 fold 14, 428 fold 38 or 430 L 15
Town plan in the current Michelin Red Guide Italia

San Gimignano with its many medieval towers stands on a hilltop in the rolling Tuscan countryside where vineyards and olive groves flourish. Its numerous towers of nobility have earned it the nickname of San Gimignano dalle belle torri (of the Fine Towers).

In the 12C the town was an independent commune and it prospered during the next 200 years. The towers of nobility were thought for a long time to have been built for defensive purposes, and as a sign of the power of the noble families who were split in the internecine fighting between the Ghibellines and the Guelphs. The former supported the emperor and the latter the pope.

The holes in the walls served to fix gangways between the towers of allied nobles, enabling them to meet quickly in times of danger. A simpler explanation may be that the towers were linked to the town's past economic success. In the Middle Ages it was an important textile centre which guarded the secret of yellow saffron dye, and to protect the precious cloth (the length determined the value) from the sun and dust, the wealthy manufacturers were forced to build the tall towers as they had no room to spread it out on a flat surface, owing to the town plan. The stairways were fixed on the outside, in holes which are still to be seen, so as not to waste any space inside.

★★ **Piazza della Cisterna** – The square is paved with bricks laid on their edges in a herring-bone pattern and it derives its name from a 13C cistern or well *(cisterna)*. It is one of the most evocative squares in Italy with its tall towers and austere 13C-14C mansions all around.

★★ **Piazza del Duomo** – The Collegiate Church, palaces and seven towers of nobility line this majestic square.

★ **Collegiata di Santa Maria Assunta** ⊘ – This 12C Romanesque Church was extended in the 15C by Giuliano da Maiano. The façade was restored in the 19C. Inside are a *Martyrdom of St Sebastian* (1465) by Benozzo Gozzoli and an *Annunciation* in wood by Jacopo della Quercia *(west wall)*. The walls of the left aisle are adorned with **frescoes★** evoking scenes from the Old Testament by Bartolo di Fredi (14C), while the **frescoes★★** (c1350) of the right aisle are by Barna da Siena and depict scenes from the Life of Christ *(start at the top)*. They display an elegant draughtsmanship and delicate colours. In the **Cappella di Santa Fina** (railings) designed by Giuliano da Maiano, the harmonious **altar★** is by his nephew Benedetto da Maiano and the **frescoes★** (1475) by Domenico Ghirlandaio.

Along the left side aisle of the collegiate church is the charming little **Piazza Pecori**. Beneath a portico is a lovely statue of the *Annunciation* by Ghirlandaio.

★ **Palazzo del Popolo (H)** ⊘ –
The 13C-14C Town Hall is dominated by a tall **tower**, from the top of which unfolds an unusual **view**★★ over the brown roofs and towers of the town. The Council Chamber has a remarkable **Maestà**★ (Madonna and Child enthroned in Majesty) (1317) by Lippo Memmi, which was restored c1467 by Benozzo Gozzoli. A museum **(Museo Civico**★**)** on the second floor presents paintings from the 12C to 15C Florentine and Sienese schools.

Palazzo del Podestà – This 13C Governor's Palace has a vast porch on the ground floor. It also comprises an impressive tower (51m – 167ft high) known as the Torre Rognosa. Close by stands the 13C Palazzo Chigi.

Sant'Agostino – This 13C church has in its chancel a cycle of 17 **frescoes**★★ painted from 1463 to 1467 by Benozzo Gozzoli. The life of the famous theologian St Augustine is depicted with the fresh colour, sense of perspective and love of detail typical of this artist. Near the west door stands the **tomb**★ of St Bartolo by Benedetto da Maiano (15C).

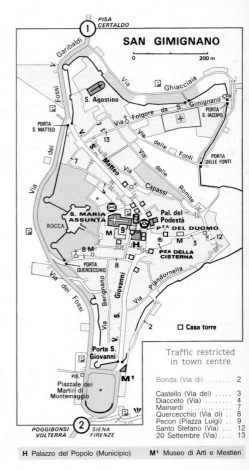

Traffic restricted in town centre

Bonda (Via di) 2
Castello (Via del) 3
Diacceto (Via) 4
Mainardi 7
Quercecchio (Via di) . . 8
Pecori (Piazza Luigi) . . 9
Santo Stefano (Via) . . . 12
20 Settembre (Via) 13

H Palazzo del Popolo (Municipio)   M¹ Museo di Arti e Mestieri

EXCURSIONS

★★ **Volterra** - *29km - 18 miles southeast. See VOLTERRA.*

★ **San Vivaldo** ⊘ - *17km - 10 miles northwest. Leave by* ①. In 1500 Franciscan monks settled here to honour the body of St Vivaldo who died here in 1320. During the next 15 years they built a monastery and a series of chapels (17 are still extant) recreating the holy places of Jerusalem in miniature. The chapels of the **sacro monte** contain painted terracottas which depict nearly-to-scale scenes ranging from the Passion to Whitsuntide.

Certaldo - *13km - 8 miles north.* It was in this village, in the wooded Elsa Valley, that **Giovanni Boccaccio** (1312-75) spent the last years of his life. Along with Dante and Petrarch, he was one of the three great Italian writers.
In the upper town are the **Casa del Boccaccio** ⊘, now converted into a museum, the Church of San Jacopo where the writer is buried and the **Palazzo Pretorio** ⊘, which was rebuilt in the 16C.

Repubblica di SAN MARINO★

SAN MARINO REPUBLIC – Population 23 372
Michelin map 988 fold 15, 429, 430 K 19
Town plan in the current Michelin Red Guide Italia

One of the smallest states in the world (61km² - 23sq miles), San Marino stands in an admirable **site**★★★ on the slopes of the jagged sandstone ridge of Monte Titano. This ancient republic strikes its own coinage, issues its own postage stamps and has its own army and police force.
San Marino is believed to have been founded in the 4C by a pious mason, Marinus, who was fleeing from the persecutions of the Emperor Diocletian. The system of government has changed little in nine centuries, and the leading figures are still the two Captains Regent, who are chosen from among the 60 members of the Grand Council and installed every six months during a colourful ceremony *(see the Calendar of Events at the end of the guide)*. The economy is based on tourism, trade, the sale of postage stamps, craft industries and agriculture. San Marino produces a very pleasant wine, Moscato.

SIGHTS

Palazzo del Governo ⊙ – *Piazza della Libertà.* Government House was rebuilt in the Gothic style in the late 19C. The Great Council Chamber is open to visitors.

Basilica di San Marino – *Piazzale Domus Plebis.* The basilica contains the relics of St Marinus.
In the nearby Church of San Pietro there are two niches hewn in the rock, in which St Marinus and his companion St Leo are said to have slept.

Rocca Guaita; Rocca Cesta or della Fratta; Rocca Montale – These three peaks are crowned with three towers *(torri)* which are linked by a watchpath. From the towers there are splendid **views**★★★ of the Apennines, the plain, Rimini and the sea as far as the Dalmatian coast. In the Torre Cesta there is a museum, **Museo delle Armi Antiche** ⊙, with a collection of 12C to late-medieval arms. It also features gunpowder firearms, as well as guns and rifles dating from the 16C, 17C and 18C.

Museo-Pinacoteca ⊙ – The museum displays paintings by Strozzi, Ribera, Guerchino; Egyptian and Etruscan art; and Roman coins and statues.

Museo di San Francesco ⊙ – 12C to 17C and modern paintings (20C) as well as Etruscan pottery and funerary objects.

Museo Filatelico e Numismatico ⊙ – *At Borgo Maggiore.* Collection of stamps and coins issued by the Republic since the mid-19C.

EXCURSION

★★ **San Leo** – *16km – 10 miles southwest. Leave to the north then take the road to the left leading down to the Marecchia Valley. Just before Pietracuta and the S 258 bear left.*
A steep winding road climbs to the summit of the huge limestone rock (alt 639m - 2 096ft) in an impressive **setting**★★, made famous by Dante in his *Divine Comedy*, with the historic village of San Leo and its 15C fortress **(Forte★)**, perched on the edge of the cliff, where the charlatan Count Cagliostro (18C) was imprisoned and died. It now houses a museum and picture gallery **(museo-pinacoteca)** ⊙: arms, furniture and 15C to 18C paintings.
From the fortress there is an immense **panorama**★★★ of the Marecchia Valley, Montefeltro and San Marino.
The cathedral, which is in the Lombard-Romanesque style (1173), and the pre-Romanesque parish church (restored) are noteworthy.

SAN REMO ♨♨

Liguria – Population 56 035
Michelin map 988 fold 12 or 195 fold 20 or 428 K 5 – Local map see La RIVIERA
Town plan in the current Michelin Red Guide Italia

San Remo curves round its wide bay protected by two headlands, and is backed by a rim of mountains. The luxurious capital of the Riviera di Ponente enjoys a pleasantly warm temperature all the year round and the highest number of sunshine hours on the Ligurian coast. In addition to these advantages San Remo boasts a wide choice of hotels, thermal establishments, a pleasure boat harbour, casino, racecourse, lively festivals and other cultural and sporting events.
San Remo is the main Italian flower market and millions of roses, carnations and mimosa are exported worldwide. The flower market takes place from October to June from 6 to 8am.

Corso Imperatrice – It is Liguria's most elegant seafront promenade and it is particularly known for its Canary palms.

★ **La Pigna** – This is the name given to the old town, because of its pointed shape (*pigna* meaning beak). It has a medieval aspect with its winding alleys lined with tall and narrow houses. From Piazza Castello climb up to the baroque Church of Madonna della Costa, from where there is an attractive **view**★ of the town and bay.

EXCURSIONS

★★ **Monte Bignone** – Alt 1 299m - 4 262ft. *13km - 8 miles to the north.*
From the summit of this pine-covered peak there is a splendid **panorama**★★ which extends as far as Cannes in France.

Bussana Vecchia – *Take the road to Arma di Taggia and turn into a road just beyond San Remo.* The medieval fortified village was destroyed by an earthquake in 1887 and was deserted until the 1960s, when some artists, mostly foreigners, set about restoring the houses and moved in. The paved streets are now lined with shops selling their work and crafts.

SANSEPOLCRO⋆

Tuscany – Population 15 670
Michelin map 988 fold 15 or 430 L 18

This small industrial town (famous for its pasta) still has its old town walls and numerous **old houses**⋆ dating from the Middle Ages up to the 18C, a reminder of its early, but long-lasting, prosperity. The finest streets are the **via XX Settembre** and the **via Matteotti** where there is also an austere Romanesque-Gothic cathedral. However, Sansepolcro's main claim to fame is the birth here in c1415 of the most important artist of the Italian Quattrocento (15C), **Piero della Francesca** *(see Index).* *See the Calendar of Events at the end of the guide.*

⋆⋆ **Museo Civico** ⊘ – *65 via Aggiunti.* The most interesting exhibits in the municipal museum are the admirable **paintings**⋆⋆⋆ by **Piero della Francesca**: his *Resurrection* (an impressive example of a mature style of art), the beautiful polyptych of the *Virgin of Mercy* and two fragments of frescoes, one of *St Julian* and the other of *St Ludovico.* The museum also has works by Bassano, Signorelli, and the Della Robbia School, as well as etchings and a few pieces of church plate. From the upper floor, there is a beautiful view of the via Matteotti and fragments of frescoes and sinopies (red chalk drawings)(14C). The basement contains sculptures and architectural ornamentation dating from the 13C to the 18C.

San Lorenzo – The church, dedicated to St Lawrence, contains a superb *Descent from the Cross*⋆ by the Mannerist artist Rosso Fiorentino.

EXCURSIONS

⋆⋆ **Camaldoli** – *76km – 47 miles northwest.* Camaldoli, situated in a great forest in the heart of the mountains, was the cradle of the Camaldulian Order, founded in the 11C by St Romuald. The monastery, standing at the head of an austere valley, was rebuilt in the 13C. Higher up in a grim, isolated site is the Hermitage **(Eremo**⋆**)**, a cluster of buildings encircled by ramparts. These include St Romuald's cell and a fine 18C church.

⋆ **Convento della Verna** – *36km – 22 miles northwest.* The monastery, pleasantly situated, was founded in 1213 and it was here that St Francis of Assisi received the Stigmata. The visitor can see the Chapel of the Stigmata, St Francis' sleeping place and the enormous projecting rock under which he used to pray. The basilica and the small church of Santa Maria degli Angeli are adorned with terracottas by Andrea della Robbia.

Castello, Poppi

★ **Poppi** - *61km - 38 miles northwest.* This proud and attractive city, formerly the capital of the Casentino, overlooks the Arno Valley. The city itself is crowned by its proud-looking castle **(castello★)**, former seat of the Counts of Guidi. This 13C Gothic palace has a curious **courtyard★** decorated with coats of arms.

Monterchi - *17km - 11 miles south.* The cemetery chapel has a strange but compelling work by Piero della Francesca, the *Madonna del Parto★*, which has been detached and placed above the altar. This is a rare example of the pregnant Virgin in Italian art.

The star ratings are allocated for various categories:
- *regions of scenic beauty with dramatic natural features*
- *cities with a cultural heritage*
- *elegant resorts and charming villages*
- *ancient monuments and fine architecture*
- *museums and art galleries*

SIENA★★★

Tuscany – Population 58 842
Michelin map 988 fold 15 or 430 M 15/16
Plan of built-up area in the current Michelin Red Guide Italia

Siena "the Beloved" is a mystical, gentle, passionate and generous art centre. Siena invites the visitor to stroll through its narrow Gothic streets, lined with palaces and patrician mansions, which converge on the famous Piazza del Campo. It is encircled by massive ramparts.

More than anywhere else Siena conveys the aspect of a medieval city. Its plan extends over three converging red clay hills (from which the colour "burnt sienna" is named) at the very heart of the high Tuscan plateau.

For those wishing to visit the town in more detail, we recommend the Michelin Guide to **Tuscany**.

HISTORICAL NOTES

Siena's greatest period of prosperity was the 13C-14C, when it was an independent republic with a well-organised administration of its own. It flourished essentially on trade and banking. During the Guelphs versus Ghibellines *(see Index)* conflict, Siena was opposed to its powerful neighbour Florence. One of the most memorable episodes of this long struggle was the Battle of Montaperti (1260), when the Sienese Ghibellines resoundingly defeated the Florentine Guelphs. During this troubled time Siena acquired her most prestigious buildings, and a local school of painting evolved which played a notable part in the development of Italian art.

In 1348 the plague decimated Siena's population and the city began to decline as dissension continued to reign among the rival factions. By the early 15C Siena's golden era was over.

The mystical city of Siena was the birthplace in 1347 of **St Catherine**. By the age of seven, it seems, she had decided on her spiritual marriage with Christ. She entered the Dominican Order aged 16 and had many visions and trances throughout her life. She is said to have received the Stigmata at Pisa. In 1377 she helped to bring the popes back from Avignon to Rome, which they had left in 1309. **St Bernardine** (1380-1444) is also greatly venerated in Siena. He gave up his studies to help the victims of the plague in the city. At the age of 22, he entered the Franciscan order and was a leader of the Observants, who favoured a stricter observance of the rule of St Francis. A great preacher, he spent much of his time travelling throughout Italy.

SIENESE ART

It was not only in political matters that Siena opposed Florence. In this, Dante's city, Cimabue and Giotto were innovators, but were greatly influenced by the Roman traditions of balance and realism which led to the development of Renaissance art in all its glory. Siena, on the other hand, remained attached to the Greek or Byzantine traditions, in which the graceful line and the refinement of colour gave a certain dazzling elegance to the composition, which was one of the chief attractions of Gothic painting.

Duccio di Buoninsegna (c1255-1318/19) was the first to experiment with this new combination of inner spirituality and increased attention to space and composition as well as the splendour of the colours.

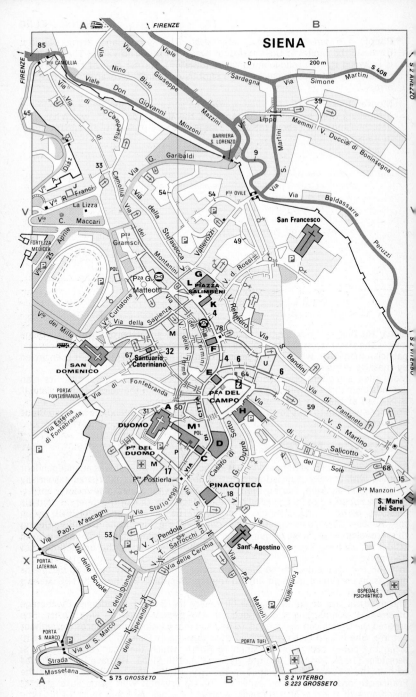

SIENA

Traffic restricted in town centre

A	Battistero S. Giovanni
C	Palazzo Piccolomini
D	Palazzo Chigi-Saracini
E	Loggia dei Mercanti
F	Palazzo Tolomei
G	Palazzo Salimbeni
H	Palazzo Pubblico
K	Palazzo Spannocchi
L	Palazzo Tantucci
M¹	Museo dell'Opera Metropolitana

The length of time given in this guide
*- for **touring** allows time to enjoy the views and the scenery*
*- for **sightseeing** is the average time required for a visit*

Simone Martini (c1284-d 1344 in Avignon) followed in Duccio's footsteps but imitated nature more closely with his exquisite harmonies of colour and taste for detail. He had a considerable reputation in Europe and worked at the Papal Court in Avignon. His contemporaries **Pietro** and **Ambrogio Lorenzetti** introduced an even greater realism with minute delicate details, while at the same time remaining true to the sense of line of their predecessors. One of the favourite themes of the Sienese school was the Virgin and Child.

The Sienese artists of the Quattrocento (15C) continued in the spirit of the Gothic masters. While Florence concentrated on rediscovering antiquity and its myths, minor masters such as **Lorenzo Monaco, Giovanni di Paolo** and **Sassetta** continued to emphasise affectation in figure design, flexibility of line and subtlety of colour which made Siena an ideal refuge for Gothic sensibilities.

In the field of secular architecture, the Gothic style gave Siena its own special character with the use of elements which made for a more graceful aspect. Brick and stone were often associated on the lower storeys, while windows became more numerous, especially in the Sienese style with a depressed triple arch supporting a pointed one.

Building activity was concentrated on the cathedral where construction work and transformations lasted over two centuries. There again the façade is in a unique Gothic style where one can detect the transition from the Romanesque to the Flamboyant Gothic in an interpretation full of affectation.

Sculpture, also influenced by the building of the cathedral, was enriched by the output of two Pisan artists, Nicola and Giovanni Pisano *(see Index)*. The latter decorated the cathedral façade with a series of highly expressive figures and his work influenced **Tino di Camaino**, born in Siena in 1280 but who spent the last years of his life at the Angevin Court in Naples. However, the important figure in Sienese sculpture is **Jacopo della Quercia** (1371-1438), who successfully combined Gothic traditions with the Florentine Renaissance style.

★★ PIAZZA DEL CAMPO (BX) *1 1/4 hours*

This "square" forms a monumental ensemble of almost matchless harmony. It is shaped like a scallop or a fan and is paved with brick and encircled by a ring of stone slabs. The piazza slopes down to the long brick and stone façade of the Palazzo Pubblico. Eight white lines radiate outwards dividing the area into nine segments, each symbolising one of the forms of government which ruled Siena. This consisted of nine members representing trade and banking who ruled the city during its greatest period of prosperity from the late-13C to the mid-14C.

At the upper end is the **Fonte Gaia** (Fountain of Joy) so-called because of the festivities which followed its inauguration in 1348. Fountains were at that time a symbol of the city's power. It was embellished with panels sculpted by Jacopo della Quercia but these, now badly deteriorated, have been replaced by replicas. The Piazza del Campo is the venue twice annually *(see the Calendar of Events at the end of the guide)* for the popular festival **Palio delle Contrade**. The whole town participates in the preparation of this event for weeks beforehand and it recalls the medieval administrative organisation of Siena with its three main quarters, themselves subdivided into parishes *(contrade)*. Stands are put up for spectators around the piazza, and the surrounding houses are decked with pennants.

The festivities begin with a procession of the *contrade* in costume, who then compete in a dangerous horserace round the square. There is much betting on the outcome. The *palio*, a standard bearing the effigy of the Virgin, the city's protectress, is awarded to the winner.

★★ Palazzo Pubblico (BZ H) ⓥ

The Town Hall, built between the late-13C and mid 14C in the Gothic style, is of a rare elegance with its numerous triple bays under supporting arches, which adorn the gently-curved façade. High up on the central part is a circular bronze panel inscribed with the monogram IHS (*Iesus Hominum Salvator* Jesus Men's Saviour) used as a badge by St Bernardine. From one end of the façade rises the slim form of the **Torre del Mangia**, a tower (88m – 289ft high) designed by Lippo Memmi. At the foot of the tower, **Cappella di Piazza** is a chapel in the form of a loggia dating from 1352, built to mark the end of the plague. It was remodelled in the Renaissance style a century later.

This palace was the seat of Siena's successive governments and most of the great artists of the Sienese school contributed to its decoration.

Sala dei Priori – In the Priors' Room, frescoes (1407) by Spinello Aretino recount the struggles between Pope Alexander III and the Emperor Frederick Barbarossa.

★ **Cappella** – The chapel contains frescoes by Taddeo di Bartolo portraying the Life of the Virgin, a very lovely **railing★** and its magnificent early-15C **stalls★★** with intarsia work illustrating the Creed, and on the high altar a Holy Family by Sodoma.

★★ **Sala del Mappamondo** – In the Globe Room the admirable *Maestà*★★ (1315) is Simone Martini's earliest known work, and opposite is the famous *equestrian portrait*★★ of the Sienese general, Guidoriccio da Fogliano, by the same artist. Note the curious contrast between the realism with which the figure is portrayed and the unreality of the background landscape.

★★ **Sala della Pace** – In the Peace Room are the famous frescoes, although badly damaged (1335-40), of Ambrogio Lorenzetti, entitled *Effects of Good and Bad Government*★★, where the artist has achieved a happy combination of a scholarly and noble allegorical approach with that of meticulous narrative detail.

★★ **Torre** ⊘ – From the top of the tower there is a superb **panorama**★★ of Siena's chaotic rooftops and of the gently-rolling Sienese countryside beyond.

Piazza del Campo

★★★ DUOMO (CATHEDRAL AND PRECINCTS) *1 1/2 hours*

★★★ **Duomo** (AZ) ⊘ – The richly-decorated façade of the cathedral was begun in the 13C by Giovanni Pisano who added some remarkably expressive statues. The upper part was modelled on Orvieto Cathedral. The sober Romanesque campanile dates from 1313. The walls of the **interior** are faced with alternating bands of black and white marble. The profusion of pillars provides a multitude of perspectives as one moves about. The 15C-16C **paving**★★★ is unique. About 40 artists including **Beccafumi** worked on the 56 marble panels which portray, either in graffiti or intarsia work, mythological figures such as Sibyls, Virtues and Allegories and scenes from the Old Testament in a lively and delicate manner. In the chancel is a 15C bronze tabernacle by Vecchietta and richly decorated 14C-16C **stalls**★★. At the entrance to the north transept stands the famous **pulpit**★★★ carved from 1266 to 1268 by **Nicola Pisano**, who relates the Life of Christ in seven panels in a grandiose and exceptionally-dramatic style. From the north aisle a charming doorway leads to the famous library, **Libreria Piccolomini**, built in 1495 by Cardinal Francesco Piccolomini, the future Pius III, to house his uncle's books. The Umbrian painter **Pinturicchio** adorned it with **frescoes**★★ (1502-09) depicting episodes in the life of Aeneas Silvius Piccolomini (Pius II). The delicate draughtsmanship is typical of miniatures, while the brilliant colours are more typical of illuminations. In the centre stands the famous marble statue of the *Three Graces*, a 3C Roman sculpture (damaged) showing Hellenistic influence.

★★ **Museo dell'Opera Metropolitana** (ABZ M¹) ⊘ – The museum is in the extant part of the vast building started in 1339. The present cathedral was to have been its transept. The project was abandoned owing to technical problems and especially the terrible plague of 1348. The museum contains Giovanni Pisano's statues which originally adorned the cathedral façade, a low relief by Jacopo della Quercia and the famous *Maestà* (Virgin in Majesty) by **Duccio**. This altarpiece was originally painted on both sides (now separated). The panels of the reverse side depict scenes from the Passion of Christ, with a wealth of intimate details.

★ **Battistero di San Giovanni** (AX A) ⊘ – The baptistery, dedicated to St John, lies below the cathedral, under an extension of the chancel, and dates from the 14C. The façade started in the Gothic style was never completed.
The interior is decorated with 15C frescoes. The **font**★★ is adorned with panels designed by Jacopo della Quercia. The bronze panels were by several Tuscan masters such as Lorenzo Ghiberti and Donatello. Of note is the latter's *Feast of Herod*.

ADDITIONAL SIGHTS

★★ **Pinacoteca** (BX) ⊘ – The extensive collection of 13C-16C Sienese paintings is displayed in the 15C **Palazzo Buonsignori**★.
On the second floor is the rich section of the **Primitives**. Beyond the late-12C to early-13C painted Crucifixes and the works of a local artist, Guido da Siena, are the masterpieces of the Sienese school such as Duccio, with the *Madonna of the Francisans*. The *Virgin and Child* is by Simone Martini. There are also numerous works by the Lorenzetti brothers including the **Pala del Carmine**. Note the *Virgin of Humility* by Giovanni di Paolo.
On the first floor note Pinturicchio's works, a *Birth of the Virgin Mary* by Beccafumi and *Christ on the Pillar* by Sodoma.

S. Chirol

★ **Via di Città (BX), Via Banchi di Sopra (BVX 4)** – These narrow, flagstoned streets bordered by remarkable **palaces★** bustle with life.

Coming from Via San Pietro the visitor will see in the Via di Città, on the left the 15C **Palazzo Piccolomini** or Palazzo delle Papesse (**C**) with the lower part of its façade rusticated in the Florentine manner. Practically opposite stands the long curving Gothic façade of the **Palazzo Chigi-Saracini (D)**, now the home of the Academy of Music. Farther along, on the right, the **Loggia dei Mercanti (E)** or Merchants' Loggia, in the transitional Gothic-Renaissance style with a 17C top storey, is the seat of the Commercial Courts.

Beyond on the left is the 13C **Palazzo Tolomei (F)**, an austere but elegant building. Robert of Anjou, King of Naples, stayed here in 1310. The **Piazza Salimbeni★ (BV)** is enclosed on three sides by buildings with different architectural styles: at the far end the 14C **Palazzo Salimbeni (G)** is Gothic; on the left the 15C **Palazzo Spannocchi (K)** is Renaissance; while the 16C **Palazzo Tantucci (L)** on the left is Baroque.

★ **Basilica di San Domenico (AVX)** – St Catherine had her trances in this 13C-15C Gothic conventual church. Inside, there is an authentic portrait of the saint by her contemporary Andrea Vanni.

In the Cappella di Santa Caterina *(halfway down the south aisle)* is a lovely Renaissance **tabernacle★** carved in marble by Giovanni di Stefano which contains the head of the saint. The **frescoes★** by Sodoma on the walls depict scenes from the life of the saint.

Casa di Santa Caterina (AX) – *Entrance in Via Santa Caterina.* St Catherine's house has been transformed into a series of superimposed oratories. In the basement is the cell where St Catherine lived. Above is the 13C painted crucifix in front of which the saint is said to have received the Stigmata.

Sant'Agostino (BX) – This 13C church, dedicated to St Augustine, has a baroque interior. There is a remarkable *Adoration of the Crucifix★* by Perugino, and the Cappella del Santo Sacramento contains **works★** by Ambrogio Lorenzetti, Matteo di Giovanni and Sodoma.

A Map of Touring Programmes
is given at the beginning of the guide
To plan a special tour
use the preceding Map of Principal Sights

SORRENTO★★

Campania – Population 16 455
Michelin map 988 fold 27 or 431 F 25 – Local map see AMALFI
Town plan in the current Michelin Red Guide Italia

This important southern Italian resort, known for its many beautiful gardens, overlooks the gulf of the same name. Orange and lemon groves are to be found in the surrounding countryside and even encroaching on the town. Local craftsmen produce various marquetry objects. The poet **Torquato Tasso** *(see Index)* was born in Sorrento in 1544.

San Francesco – This Baroque church, dedicated to St Francis, with its bulbous belfry masks delightful 13C **cloisters★**. The capitals are carved with water-leaf motifs while the interlaced arcades are typical of the Sicilian-Arab style *(see SICILY)*.
The public gardens, **Villa Comunale**, next door offer a good **viewpoint★★** for admiring the Bay of Naples.

★ **Museo Correale di Terranova** ⊘ – Housed in an 18C palace, the museum has mementoes of the poet Tasso, a small archeological section and above all a fine collection of 17C and 18C furniture. From the terrace, beyond the orange grove, there is a very fine **view★★** over the Gulf of Sorrento.

EXCURSION

★★ **Penisola Sorrentina** – *Round tour of 33km - 21 miles. Leave Sorrento to the west by the S 145 and at the junction take the road to the right to Massa Lubrense.* This winding road skirts the Sorrento Peninsula and affords fine views of the hillsides covered with olive groves, orange and lemon trees and vines. The last cling to the trelliswork which supports rush matting in winter to protect the citrus from the cold. From the headland **(Punta del Capo di Sorrento)** *(footpath: from the church in the village of Capo di Sorrento take the road to the right and after the college the paved path, 1 hour Rtn)* there is a superb **view★★** of Sorrento. Beyond **Sant'Agata sui Due Golfi**, perched on a crest overlooking both the Gulf of Salerno and the Bay of Naples, the road descends steeply to Colli di San Pietro.
The return to Sorrento by the S 163 offers on the way down some superb **views★★** over the Bay of Naples.

SPOLETO★

Umbria – Population 37 742
Michelin map 988 fold 26 or 430 N 20
Town plan in the current Michelin Red Guide Italia

This former Roman municipium became the capital of an important Lombard duchy from the 6C to the 8C. The town covers the slopes of a hill crowned by the Rocca dei Papi. The city was dear to St Francis, who loved its austere character, tempered by the grace of the narrow winding alleys, the palaces and numerous medieval buildings.
Each summer the town hosts an international arts festival, **Festival dei Due Mondi** *(see Calendar of Events at the end of the guide)*.

★★ **Duomo** – Flanked by a baptistery, the cathedral provides the focal point of **Piazza del Duomo★**. The façade is fronted by a fine Renaissance porch and adorned above by a rose window and 13C mosaic. Inside there are frescoes *(first chapel on the south side)* by Pinturicchio, Fra Lippo Lippi's tomb *(south transept)* commissioned by Lorenzo de' Medici, and in the apse **frescoes** depicting the life of the Virgin by Fra Filippo Lippi and his assistants.

★★ **Ponte delle Torri** – The Bridge of Towers was built in the 13C over a Roman aqueduct which was used as a foundation. The bridge with its ten Gothic arches is guarded by a small fortified gatehouse at one end.

★ **Basilica di San Salvatore** – St Saviour's Basilica, one of the first Christian churches in Italy, was built by Oriental monks in the 4C and modified in the 9C. Roman materials were re-used in the building of the later edifice.

★ **San Gregorio Maggiore** – This 12C Romanesque church, dedicated to St Gregory Major, was modified in the 14C. The 14C baptistery to the left of the entrance porch has walls covered with frescoes *(Massacre of the Innocents)*. The campanile is built of stone from ancient buildings.
The dark, bare nave and aisles rest on massive columns with roughly-hewn capitals. In the chancel there is a 15C fresco and a carved stone cupboard of the same period.

Arco di Druso – This arch was built in AD 23 in honour of Tiberius' son, Drusus.

San Domenico – This lovely 13C and 14C church, dedicated to St Dominic, is built of alternating courses of white and pink stone. The nave is decorated with 14C and 15C frescoes and the south transept contains a canvas by Lanfranco.

EXCURSIONS

★ **Monteluco** – *8km – 5 miles east.* An attractively-winding road leads up to Monteluco. On the way up, the Church of St Peter **(San Pietro)** has a lovely 13C Romanesque **façade**★ with relief sculptures. On the summit, **Monteluco**★ was once the seat of an ancient cult, but is now a health resort. The monastery founded by St Francis still exists.

★ **Fonti del Clitunno** – *13km – 8 miles north.* These crystal-clear waters which surge amid aquatic plants were sacred to the Romans. They plunged animals into the water for purification prior to sacrifice. 1km – 1/2 mile below stands a temple **(tempietto**★) ◷ of Clitumnus, a minuscule early-Christian building dating from the 5C. It boasts columns and a carved pediment.

SUBIACO

Lazio – Population 8 999

Michelin map 988 fold 26 or 430 Q 21

St Benedict, founder of the Benedictine Order, and his twin sister Scolastica retired to this spot at the end of the 5C and built 12 little monasteries before moving to Monte Cassino.

To reach the monasteries of Santa Scolastica and San Benedetto (3km – 2 miles) take the Frosinone road and shortly before the Aniene Bridge turn left.

Monastero di Santa Scolastica ◷ – Standing in the fine site overlooking the Aniene Gorges the monastery has preserved a majestic 11C campanile, its church which was remodelled in the 18C, and three cloisters. The third, the work of the Cosmati *(see Index),* is admirable in its simplicity.

★ **Monastero di San Benedetto** ◷ – This monastery, dedicated to St Benedict, stands above the previous one clinging to the rock face in a wild site, overhanging the gorge. The buildings date from the 13C and 14C.

The church has two storeys. The **upper church** has walls painted with frescoes of the 14C Sienese school and the 15C Umbrian school. The **lower church**, itself with two storeys, is covered with frescoes by Magister Consolus, an artist of the 13C Roman school.

Visitors are admitted to the Sacred Cave **(Sacro Speco)** where St Benedict lived a hermit's existence for three years. A spiral staircase then leads up to a chapel which contains the earliest portrait of St Francis (without Stigmata or halo), painted to commemorate the saint's visit to the sanctuary. The Holy Staircase **(Scala Santa)** leads down to the Chapel of the Virgin (frescoes by the Sienese school) and the Shepherd's Cave. From there the visitor can enter the rose garden where St Benedict threw himself into brambles to resist temptation.

SULMONA★

Abruzzi – Population 25 484

Michelin map 988 fold 27 or 430 P 23 – Local map see Appennino ABRUZZESE

Sulmona, which lies at the head of a fertile basin framed by majestic mountains, was the birthplace of the Roman poet **Ovid**, best known for his long poem *Metamorphoses.* The town has retained its medieval character.

★★ **Palazzo dell'Annunziata** – The palace was built by a Brotherhood of Penitents and has an original façade which displays varying styles: on the left the Gothic doorway has statues of the Virgin and St Michael, while the triple-arched opening with four statues of Doctors of the Church dates from 1415; the central and right-hand parts are both later (1483 and 1522). There is an astonishingly carved frieze halfway up the façade.

In contrast the sober façade of the adjacent church is the work of Pietro Fontana (in 1710).

★ **Porta Napoli** – *Southern town gateway.* This Gothic gate has historiated capitals (14C). The exterior has an unusual decoration of an opening, bosses and rosettes.

Piazza Garibaldi – This square is the scene on Wednesdays and Saturdays of a large and highly-colourful market. The square is bordered on two sides by a medieval aqueduct and overlooked by the Gothic doorway of the Church of St Martin (San Martino) and the Renaissance fountain, **Fontana del Vecchio.**

On Easter Sunday, the **feast of the "Madonna che scappa in piazza"** is celebrated in Piazza Garibaldi: the statue of the Virgin is borne to a meeting with the Risen Christ; as she comes within sight of Him, she sheds her mourning clothes and appears in a resplendent green robe.

TARANTO★

Puglia – Population 231 350
Michelin map 988 fold 29 or 431 F 33
Town plan in the current Michelin Red Guide Italia

Taranto is a well-protected naval base at the end of a great roadstead, closed at the seaward end by two fortified islands. Taranto was founded in the 7C BC and became one of the most important colonies of Magna Graecia. The old quarter lies on an island and is linked to the modern town by a swing bridge.

During Holy Week many impressive ceremonies take place in the town, including several processions between Thursday and Saturday, one lasting 12 hours and another 14 hours, which go from church to church at a very slow pace *(see the Calendar of Events at the end of the guide)*.

★★ **Museo Nazionale** ⊙ – The National Museum has a good collection of local archeological finds which illustrate the history of Magna Graecia. On the first floor, in addition to sculpture, architectural fragments and grave artefacts, is an exceptional **collection of pottery★★★** with vases in the Corinthian, Attic, proto-Italiot and Apulian styles. A large collection of Hellenistic jewellery (4C-3C BC), found in tombs locally, is displayed in the Gold Room **(Sala degli Ori★★★).**

★★ **Lungomare Vittorio Emanuele** – A long promenade planted with palm trees and oleanders.

★ **Giardini Comunali** – From the municipal gardens, a haven of exotic and luxuriant vegetation, there is a magnificent view over the harbour's inner basin, the Mare Piccolo.

Duomo – The 11C-12C cathedral with a Baroque façade has been greatly remodelled. The nave and two aisles are separated by ancient columns with Roman or Byzantine capitals and the ceiling is 17C. The Chapel of **San Cataldo★** was faced with polychrome marble and embellished with statues in the 18C.

TARQUINIA★

Lazio – Population 14 052
Michelin map 988 fold 25 or 430 P 17 – 21km – 13 miles to the northwest of
Civitavecchia

The town of Tarquinia crowns a rocky platform, facing the sea, in a barley- and corn-growing region interspersed with olive groves. Tarquinia is famous for the Etruscan burial ground which lies quite near. According to legend, the town was founded in the 12C or 13C BC. Archeologists have found 9C BC vestiges of the Villanovian civilisation which derived its name from the village of Villanova near Bologna, and developed around the year 1000 BC in the Po Plain, in Tuscany and in the northern part of Latium, where the Etruscans later settled. Standing on the banks of the Marta River, Tarquinia was a busy port and in the 6C BC ruled the coast of Etruria. Under Roman rule, Tarquinia was decimated by malaria in the 4C BC and was sacked by the Lombards in the 7C. The inhabitants then moved to the present site about a mile to the northeast of the original position.

★★ **Necropoli Etrusca** ⊙ – *4km – 2.5 miles southeast.* The burial ground is on a bare, windswept ridge parallel with that on which the former Etruscan city stood. The necropolis extends over an area 5km – 3 miles long and 1km – 0.5 mile wide and contains around 600 tombs dating from the 6C-1C BC. As at Cerveteri there are no visible remains at ground level but there are remarkable **paintings★★★** on the walls of the underground burial chambers. These colourful and lively paintings are of the utmost importance for the light they shed on the Etruscan civilisation. The most important tombs include: the tomb of the Baron **(tomba del Barone)**, dating from the 6C BC; the 5C BC tomb of the Leopards **(tomba del Leopardi)**, one of the finest, in which are depicted leopards as well as scenes of a banquet and dancing; the 6C BC tomb of the Bulls **(tomba dei Tori)** with its erotic paintings; the tomb of the Lionesses **(tomba delle Leonesse)** dating from around 530-520 BC;

the 4C BC Giglioli tomb **(tomba Gigliogi)** decorated with *trompe-l'œil* paintings of costumes and arms; and the late-6C BC tomb with Hunting and Fishing Scenes **(tomba delle Caccia e della Pesca)**, which consists of two chambers displaying the return from the hunt, a banquet and the art of fishing.

★ **Museo Nazionale Tarquiniese** ⊙ – The National Museum is housed in the **Palazzo Vitelleschi**★ built in 1439 and has a most remarkable collection of Etruscan antiquities originating from the excavations in the necropolis. Artefacts include sarcophagi, pottery, ivories, votive offerings and 6C BC Attic kraters and amphorae. The following exhibits are of great interest: two admirable **winged horses**★★★ in terracotta and on the second

The Winged Horses, Tarquinia

floor several reconstructed tombs, notably the tomb with the Funeral Bed **(tomba del Letto Funebre)** (460 BC) and the tomb of the Triclinium **(tomba del Triclinio)** (480-470 BC), one of the finest in the necropolis.

★ **Santa Maria in Castello** – *Take the Via Mazzini, then the Via di Porta Castello beyond the wall.* This Romanesque church (1121-1208), dedicated to St Mary, stands near a tall tower built in the Middle Ages and was part of the fortified citadel guarding the town. It has an elegant doorway decorated with Cosmati work *(see Index)* and an imposing interior.

TERNI

Umbria – Population 108 247

Michelin map 988 fold 26 or 430 O 19

Town plan in the current Michelin Red Guide Italia

Terni, an important industrial centre, has an old town with several fine palaces, the Church of St Francis with its 15C belltower, and St Saviour's Church, which has early-Christian (5C) origins. The bustling town centre comprises Piazza della Repubblica and Via Roma.

EXCURSIONS

★★ **Cascata delle Marmore** ⊙ – *Take the Macerata road the S 209 (7km – 4 miles east of Terni) or the Rieti road, the S 79 (9km – 6 miles to the east plus 1/2 hour Rtn on foot).*
This artificial waterfall created by the Romans falls in three successive drops down sheer walls of marble *(marmore)* to disappear at the bottom of a wooded ravine.

Carsulae: Roman Ruins – *16km – 10 miles northwest. Go via S. Gemini and S. Gemini Fonte.* These are the remains of a Roman town destroyed in the 9C.

Ferentillo – *18km – 11 miles northeast.* This picturesque village is dominated by two ruined castles. From here *(5km – 3 miles north, then 2km – 1/2 mile further by a poor road)* it is possible to reach the solitary **Abbazia di San Pietro in Valle** ⊙, an abbey which was founded in the 7C and rebuilt in the 12C. The cloisters are decorated with 12C frescoes and there are Roman sarcophagi.

The chapter on art and architecture in this guide gives an outline of artistic achievement in the country providing the context of the buildings and works of art described in the Sights section This chapter may also provide ideas for touring It is advisable to read it at leisure

TERRACINA⌂

Lazio – Population 37 044
Michelin map 988 fold 26 or 430 S 21

Terracina stands in an attractive setting at the head of a bay and is backed by a limestone cliff. In the Roman era it was already a fashionable country resort. Terracina has retained part of its medieval wall and some Roman remains.

Duomo – The cathedral overlooks the attractive **Piazza del Municipio** which still has the paving of the Roman forum. It was consecrated in 1075 and is fronted by a portico on ancient columns which support a 12C mosaic frieze. The campanile with its small columns is in the transitional Romanesque-Gothic style.
Inside, the **pulpit** and **paschal candelabrum**★, a lovely 13C work by the Cosmati *(see Index)*, are of special interest.

★ **Tempio di Giove Anxur** – *4km – 2.5 miles plus 1/4 hour on foot Rtn by the Via San Francesco Nuovo.* Although there are few remains other than the foundations, a vaulted gallery and an underground passage *(cryptoporticus)*, it is worth visiting the site of the Temple of Jupiter for its beauty alone and for the extensive **panorama**★★ of the town, the canals and port, Monte Circeo and the Pontine marshes, the plain of Fondi with its lakes, and the coast as far as Gaeta.

EXCURSION

★ **Parco Nazionale del Circeo** – Designated in 1934 this park covers a narrow coastal strip between Anzio and Terracina and includes part of the former Pontine marshes. Some of the most attractive beauty spots are: **Monte Circeo**, the refuge of the wicked witch Circe who transformed Ulysses and his companions into a herd of pigs; **Lago di Sabaudia**, a lake which can be reached by a bridge leading to the town of **Sabaudia**⌂, a pleasant country resort; the **scenic route** *(5km – 3 miles from the San Felice – Torre Cervia road)* is lined with luxury villas and brightened by typically-Mediterranean plants and flowers.

TIRANO

Lombardy – Population 8 914
Michelin map 988 folds 3, 4 or 428, 429 D 12

The Church of **Madonna di Tirano** was built from 1505 onwards on the spot where the Virgin Mary had appeared in a vision. It has a nave and side aisles. The west front dates from 1676 and is enhanced with highly-ornate Baroque decoration including frescoes by Cipriano Valorsa di Grosio (1575-1578), nicknamed the "Raphael of La Valtellina" *(nave)*, a fresco of the Apparition dating from 1513 *(left, above the confessional)*, paintings by a pupil of Morazzone *(chancel)* and a highly-ornate, grandiose 17C **organ**. The loft was made by Giuseppe Bulgarini and the panels on the gallery representing the *Birth of the Infant Jesus, The Adoration of the Magi* and *The Circumcision* were painted by G B Salmoiraghi (1638).

TIVOLI★★★

Lazio – Population 52 392
Michelin map 988 fold 26 or 430 Q 20 – 31km – 19 miles east of Rome
Town plan in the current Michelin Red Guide Italia

Tivoli is a small town on the lower slopes of the Apennines where the river Aniene plunges in cascades into the Roman plain.
The villas testify to Tivoli's importance as a holiday resort from the Roman period through to the Renaissance. Tivoli or Tibur in antiquity came under Roman control in the 4C BC and it was there that a Sibyl prophesied the coming of Jesus Christ to the Emperor Augustus.

★★★ **VILLA D'ESTE** *2 hours*
See the detailed town plan in the Michelin Green Guide Rome.

In 1550 Cardinal Ippolito II d'Este, who had been raised to great honours by François I of France but had fallen into disgrace when the king's son Henri II succeeded to the throne, decided to retire to Tivoli, where he immediately began to convert the former Benedictine convent into a pleasant country seat. The Neapolitan architect, Pirro Ligorio, was invited to prepare plans. The simple

Gardens, Villa d'Este

architecture of the villa contrasts with the elaborate terraced gardens. The statues, pools and fountains enhance the natural beauty with all the grace of the Mannerist style.

To the left of the main entrance stands the old abbey church of St Mary Major **(Santa Maria Maggiore)** with its attractive Gothic façade and a 17C bell-tower. Inside, in the chancel, are two 15C triptychs: above the one on the left is a painting of the Virgin by Jacopo Torriti, who also worked in mosaic at the end of the 13C.

★★ **Palace and gardens** ⊙ – From the former convent cloisters go down through the elaborately-decorated Old Apartments. From the ground-floor level there is a pleasant **view**★ of the gardens and Tivoli itself. A double flight of stairs leads to the upper garden walk. A fountain with a shell-shaped basin, **Fontana del Bicchierone**, is attributed to Bernini. To the left the **Fontana Rometta**, or "Mini Rome", reproduces some of the well-known monuments of Classical Rome. From here a splendid avenue lined with fountains, **Viale delle Cento Fontane**★★★, leads to the Oval Fountain (**Fontana dell'Ovato**★★★) dominated by a statue of the Sibyl. At a lower level the Fishpond Esplanade (**le Peschiere**) is overlooked at one end by the Organ Fountain (**Fontana dell' Organo**★★★) in which a concealed water-powered organ once played music. Right at the very bottom of the garden is the Nature Fountain (**Fontana della Natura**) with a statue of Diana of Ephesus. Return by the central avenue to admire the Dragon Fountain (**Fontana dei Draghi**), built in 1572 in honour of Pope Gregory XIII, then turn right to pass the Bird Fountain (**Fontana della Civetta**) which used to produce bird song, and finally the modernised Fountain of Proserpina (**Fontana di Proserpina**).

★★★ VILLA ADRIANA ⊙

2 1/2 hours

6km - 4 miles south-west by the Rome road, the S 5, and then a local road to the left, 4.5km - 3 miles from Tivoli.

This was probably the richest building project in antiquity and was designed entirely by Hadrian (AD 76-138), who had visited every part of the Roman Empire. He had a passion for both art and architecture and he wished to recreate the monuments and sites he had visited during his travels. In AD 134 the villa was almost finished, but the 58 year-old Hadrian, ill and grief-stricken by the death of his young favourite Antinoüs, was to die four years later. Although later emperors probably continued to visit Tivoli, the villa was soon forgotten and fell into ruin. The site was explored from the 15C to the 19C and the recovered works were dispersed to various museums and private collections. It was only in 1870 that the Italian government organised the excavation of Tivoli, thus revealing this magnificent complex. Before exploring the site it is advisable to study a model of the villa displayed in a room next to the bar. *Follow the itinerary shown on the accompanying plan.*

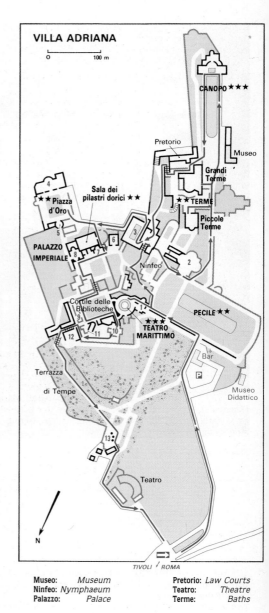

Museo: *Museum*	**Pretorio:** *Law Courts*
Ninfeo: *Nymphaeum*	**Teatro:** *Theatre*
Palazzo: *Palace*	**Terme:** *Baths*

★★ **Pecile** – The water-filled Pecile takes its name from a portico in Athens. It was built in the shape of a large rectangle with slightly curved ends and is lined with a portico; it was oriented so that one side was always in the shade.
The apsidal chamber called the philosophers' room **(Sala dei Filosofi – 1)** was perhaps a reading room.

★★★ **Teatro Marittimo** – The circular construction consists of a portico and a central building surrounded by a canal. It provided an ideal retreat for the misanthropic Hadrian. Bear south to pass the remains of a nymphaeum **(ninfeo)** and the great columns which belonged to a building comprising three semicircular rooms round a courtyard **(cortile – 2)**.

★★ **Terme** – The lay-out of the baths shows the high architectural standards attained in the villa. First come the Small Baths and then the Great Baths with an apse and splendid vaulting.
The tall building, called the Praetorium **(Pretorio)**, was probably a storehouse.

★★★ **Canopo** – Beyond the museum **(museo)** which contains the finds from the most recent excavations is a complex which evokes the Egyptian town of Canope with its famous Temple of Serapis. The route to

Canope from Alexandria consisted of a canal lined with temples and gardens. At the southern end of this site is a copy of the Temple of Serapis. Having reached the ruins overlooking the nymphaeum, turn right before skirting the large **fishpond (3)** surrounded by a portico.

Palazzo Imperiale – The palace complex extended from Piazza d'Oro to the Libraries.

★★ **Piazza d'Oro** – The rectangular piazza was surrounded by a double portico and was an esthetic indulgence serving no useful purpose. On the far side are traces of an octagonal chamber **(4)** and a domed chamber **(5)** opposite.

★★ **Sala dei Pilastri Dorici** – The hall takes its name from the surrounding portico which was composed of pilasters with Doric bases and capitals.
Also visible are the firemen's barracks **(Caserma dei Vigili** – 6)**, remains of a summer dining-room **(7)** and a nymphaeum **(8)**. These buildings overlook a courtyard which is separated from the **library court** by a cryptoporticus, part of a network of underground passages which ran from one villa to another without emerging above ground.
The suite of ten rooms along one side of the library court was an infirmary **(9)**. Note the fine mosaic **paving**★. According to custom the **library** was divided in two for a Greek section **(10)** and a Latin section **(11)**.
The route to the **Terrazza di Tempe** goes past rooms paved with mosaic which belonged to a dining-room **(12)**.
The path runs through the trees on the slope above the valley past a **round temple (13)** attributed to the goddess Venus, and skirts the site of a **theatre**, on the left, before ending at the entrance.

ADDITIONAL SIGHT

★ **Villa Gregoriana** ⊙ – This wooded park has a tangle of paths which wind down the steeply-wooded slopes to the river Aniene where it cascades through the ravine. The waters of the Aniene plunge down at the Great Cascade **(Grande Cascata**★★)**, disappear out of sight at the Siren's Cave **(Grotta della Sirena)** and burst from the rock-face in Neptune's Cave **(Grotta di Nettuno)**. Climb the slope overlooking the ravine to leave the Villa Gregoriana and visit Sibyl's Temple **(Tempio della Sibilla)**, also known as the Temple of Vesta. This elegant Corinthian-style structure dates from the end of the Republic. An Ionic temple stands alongside.

TODI★★

Umbria – Population 16 699
Michelin map 988 folds 25 and 26 or 430 N 19

Todi, a charming old town perched on an attractive **site**, has retained three sets of walls dating from the Etruscan (Marzia Gateway), Roman and medieval periods.

★★ **Piazza del Popolo** – This square in the centre of Todi is surrounded by buildings which are evidence of the town's flourishing commercial life in the Middle Ages. The 13C Gothic **Palazzo dei Priori**★ was formerly the seat of the governor *(podestà)*. Its windows were remodelled at the Renaissance and it is dominated by a curious 14C tower on a trapezoidal plan.
The 13C **Palazzo del Capitano**★ has attractive windows in groups of three flanked by small columns. Both this and the neighbouring building have arcades with round-headed arches and massive pillars at ground level. The adjoining **Palazzo del Popolo**★ ⊙, one of the oldest communal palaces in Italy (1213), houses a lapidary museum, a picture gallery and a museum of Etruscan and Roman antiquities.

★★ **San Fortunato** – *Piazza della Repubblica.* Building on the church, dedicated to St Fortunatus, lasted from 1292 to 1460; the structure combines Gothic and Renaissance features. The **central doorway**★★ catches the eye with the richness and delicacy of its decoration. The well-lit and lofty interior has **frescoes** (1432) by Masolino (fourth chapel to the south) and the tomb of Jacopone da Todi (1230-1307), a Franciscan monk, a poet and author of the *Stabat Mater*.

★ **Duomo** – This great early-12C Romanesque building is preceded by a majestic staircase leading up to its harmonious façade, all in pink and white marble, with a great rose window pierced and fretted in the Umbrian manner. Walk round the building to admire the Romanesque apse. Inside note the Gothic capitals, the Renaissance font and the lovely stalls with intarsia work dating from 1530.

Piazza Garibaldi – This square adjoining the Piazza del Popolo is graced with a monument to Garibaldi. From the terrace, there is a pretty **view**★★ of the valley and distant rounded hills.

Rocca – Pass to the right of St Fortunatus and walk up to the ruins of the 14C castle. There is a well-shaded and pleasant public garden.

★ **Santa Maria della Consolazione** – *1km – 1/2 mile west on the Orvieto road.* This Renaissance church was built of pale stone from 1508 to 1609 by several architects who drew inspiration from the designs of Bramante. The plan is that of a Greek cross; four polygonal apses are reinforced by pilasters with composite capitals. The dome, whose drum is designed in accordance with Bramante's rhythmic principles *(see MILAN: Fine Arts)*, rises roundly from the flat terrace roof. The interior is austere and well lit. The dome was decorated in the 16C and the 12 statues of the Apostles are by Scalza (16C).

TOLENTINO

Marches – Population 18 293
Michelin map 988 fold 16 or 430 M 21

This small town in the Marches region was where Napoleon Bonaparte and Pope Puis VI signed the Treaty of Tolentino ratifying the surrendering of Avignon to France. Tolentino with the Basilica of St Nicholas is known as a pilgrimage centre. Numerous miracles are attributed to this Augustinian hermit who died in Tolentino in 1305.

★★ BASILICA DI SAN NICOLA *1 hour*

The building of this basilica, dedicated to St Nicholas, lasted from 1305 to the 18C and the exterior reflects the different construction periods. The façade, remodelled in the 17C in the Baroque style, has an elegant late-Gothic doorway attributed to Nino di Bartolo (15C).

Interior ⊘ – The vast rectangular nave is striking for the rigour of its plan, the splendour of its marble, gold and stucco decoration and the magnificent coffered ceiling (1628). The side chapels contain numerous works of art: in the first chapel on the south side an admirable canvas by Guercino (1640), and in the fourth on the same side a 14C polychrome recumbent Madonna in wood and an effigy of St Lorenzina.

★ **Cappella delle Sante Braccia** – *South side of chancel.* The Chapel of the Holy Arms has a remarkably rich decoration. Note the high altar with steps, all in chased silver.

★★ **Cappella del Cappellone** – The chapel serves as south transept and is the most famous part of this pilgrimage church, owing to its cycle of 14C **frescoes** by an unknown master of the Rimini school on its vaulting and walls. The lower frescoes recount episodes from the life of St Nicholas of Tolentino while those on the vaulting evoke the Life of Christ.

Chiostro Grande – The Great Cloisters are 13C and 14C. The galleries and the adjoining oratory are decorated with Baroque frescoes (17C) illustrating the life of the saint.

Cripta – *Go back through the Capella del Cappellone.* The crypt, which was completed only in 1932, enshrines the remains of St Nicholas of Tolentino in a reliquary-coffin.

Museums – These include a gallery of votive offerings, a ceramics and archeological section, pottery and Roman objects (municipal museum).

TORINO★★

TURIN – Piedmont – Population 961 512
Michelin map 988 fold 12 or 428 G 4/5 – Town plan below
Plan of the built-up area in the current Michelin Red Guide Italia

Turin stands at the confluence of the Dora Riparia and the Po and is the meeting-place of important transalpine routes from France and Switzerland. The capital of Piedmont is an elegant, lively and prosperous town. Most of the town was built on a regular plan in the 17C and 18C and it has wide avenues, spacious squares and numerous parks.

HISTORICAL NOTES

During the 1C the capital of the Celtic tribe, the Taurini, was transformed by the Romans into a military colony and given the name of Augusta Taurinorum. Converted to Christianity, it became the seat of a bishopric in the early 5C and then a century later a Lombard duchy before passing under Frankish rule. From the 11C onwards and for nearly nine centuries the destiny of Turin was linked to that of the **House of Savoy**. This dynasty descended from Umberto the Whitehanded (d 1056), reigned over Savoy and Piedmont, then Sardinia and all of Italy. It was Italy's reigning royal family from 1861 to 1946. They were skilful rulers, often siding with the pope rather than the emperor, and playing France off against the Dukes of Milan. They slowly extended their rule over the area. It was in the early 18C that Charles Emmanuel II and Victor Amadeus II embellished their adopted city with splendid buildings by Guarini and Juvara. Charles Emmanuel III increased the importance of Turin during his reign (1732-73) by reorganising the kingdom's administration and by establishing in his capital a court with very formal etiquette, similar to the one at Versailles.

In 1798 Charles Emmanuel IV was expelled from Turin by French troops full of the new revolutionary spirit. On the fall of Napoleon Bonaparte, Victor Emmanuel I was restored to his kingdom and he promoted a policy against foreign interference in Piedmontese affairs. Turin then became the centre of the struggle against the Austrians and for the unification of Italy.

Following the reorganisation of the Piedmont by the statesman Camillo Cavour, the Franco-Piedmontese alliance against Austria, the victories at Solferino and Magenta (1859), Victor Emmanuel II was proclaimed King of Italy and Turin became the seat of the Italian government. The House of Savoy reigned over Italy until the proclamation of an Italian Republic in 1946.

ECONOMY

The intense activity of its suburban industries has made Turin the capital of Italian engineering. The people of Turin are born-mechanics and most of the motor engineers come from the Politecnico of Turin University. It is here that the Italian motor industry, represented by FIAT and Lancia, was born. Turin is responsible for about 77 per cent of Italy's car production. Many of the modern FIAT works are established in the southern suburb of Mirafiori.

Important tyre manufacturers and well-known coachbuilders (one of the most famous was Pinin Farina) contribute to the prosperity of the motor industry of Turin itself, whose products are displayed at the Turin Motor Show every even year. The textile and clothing industries are also highly developed.

LIFE IN TURIN

The life of the town is concentrated in Via Roma (CXY), Piazza San Carlo (see overleaf), and Via Po (DXY), which leads to the huge Piazza Vittorio Veneto (DY), built in the classical style. The modern-looking Via Roma is lined with arcades, beneath which are the luxury shops with attractive window displays of refined and highly reputed luxury articles from Turin it self, such as silk, leather goods and fashion.

The Piazza San Carlo, halfway along the Via Roma, is the meeting-place of fashionable women, while connoisseurs linger in the antiquaries' and book-sellers' shops. The large cafés built in the neo-Classical style which open onto the Via Po played a part in the politics of the 19C. The courteous and refined atmosphere of Turin is that of a cultural centre distinguished by many publishing houses, well-known newspapers (La Stampa), a Music Conservatory and a large university. But the town has other attractions, and the people of Turin, with appetites whetted by the famous Vermouths (Martini, Cinzano or Carpano), are partial to good cooking. Cardi in bagna cauda (cardoons in piquant sauce) and tartufi bianchi (white truffles) are specialities eaten with grissini (bread sticks) and accompanied by the delectable wines of the region. Sweetmeats, nougat (torrone piemontese), chocolates and chocolate creams are also excellent.

CITY CENTRE

★★ **Piazza San Carlo** (CXY) – This is a graceful example of town planning. The Churches of **San Carlo** and **Santa Cristina**, symmetrically placed on the south side, frame the Via Roma. The curious façade of Santa Cristina, surmounted by candelabra, was designed by the famous Sicilian-Turinese architect Juvara, who was responsible for many of Turin's lovely buildings. On the east side is the 17C palace which was the French Ambassador's residence from 1771 to 1789. In the centre of the square stands the statue (1838) of Emanuele Filiberto of Savoy.

Palazzo dell'Accademia delle Scienze (CX M') – This 17C palace by Guarini now houses two interesting museums, known as the Academy of Science.

★★ **Museo Egizio** ⊙ – Ground and first floors. The Egyptian Museum is one of the richest collections of Egyptian antiquities in Europe. The basement houses the finds from the excavations carried out in 1911 by the two Italian archeologists, Schiaparelli and Farina.

On the ground floor is the section on **statuary art** with 20 seated or standing figures of the lion-headed goddess Sekhmet from Karnak, and an important series of **statues of Pharaohs** of the New Kingdom (1580-1100 BC), Egypt's Golden Age. The **Rock Temple of Thutmose III** (c1450 BC), a gift from the United Arab Republic,

originated from Elles-
sya 200km – 124 miles
to the south of Aswan.
The collections on the
first floor evoke all as-
pects of Egyptian civil-
isation, in particular:
the **sarcophagi** – simple
examples dating from
the Middle Kingdom
(2100-1580 BC) and
sculpted ones during
the New Kingdom; a
collection of **canopic urns**;
and an important num-
ber of mummies and
copies of funerary pa-
pyri rolls known as the
Book of the Dead. In addition to the recreated
funeral chambers *(masta-
bas)* (Giza 2500 BC),
there is an exceptional
collection of **funerary
steles** dating from the
Middle and New King-
doms. Jewellery and
pottery from the pre-
dynastic civilisations,
known as Nagadian,
date from the 4000-
3000 BC. The influence
of the Greek world
made itself felt from
the 4C BC following the
conquest by Alexander
the Great (masks and
statuettes), followed
by the Romans from
30BC (bronze vases).
Another room is de-
voted to **inscriptions**; the
hieroglyphs (deci-
phered by Champollion
in 1824), and texts in
hieratic script using
cursive on papyrus,
limestone flakes and
fragments of pottery.

★★ **Galleria Sabauda** ⊙ – *Entrance via 2nd floor.*
Set out on two floors,
the gallery houses the
**collections of the House of
Savoy** and has five sec-
tions devoted to paint-
ing: the Venetian
School, the academic
movement *("maniera
internazionale",* late
15C-early 16C), the
Lombard School, the
followers of Caravag-
gio, the Flemish and
Dutch School and its
influences.
Note the strikingly real-
istic *Assumption*
(1623) by Gentileschi,
the works by Albani
(Bologna 1578-1660),
Tintoretto, and Vero-
nese *(The Meal at the
House of Simon)*, the

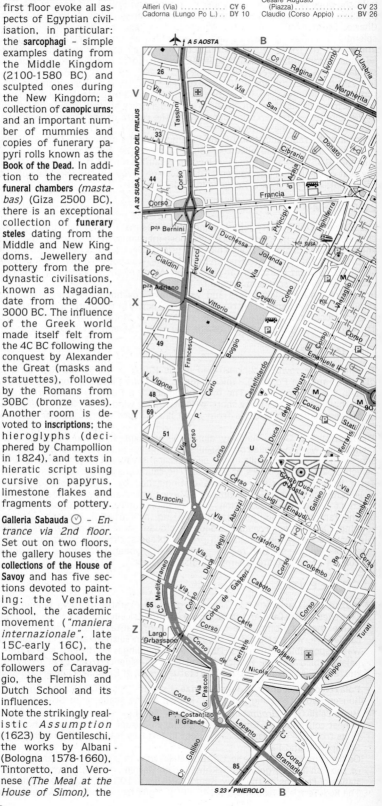

TORINO

Carlo Felice (Piazza)	**CY** 16
Roma (Via)	**CXY**
S. Carlo (Piazza)	**CXY**
Alfieri (Via)	**CY** 6
Cadorna (Lungo Po L.) ..	**DY** 10

Carignano (Piazza)	**CX** 12
Carlo Emanuele II	
(Piazza)	**DY** 13
Casale (Corso)	**DY** 18
Castello (Piazza)	**CX** 19
Cesare Augusto	
(Piazza)	**CV** 23
Claudio (Corso Appio)	**BV** 26

Traffic restricted
in town centre

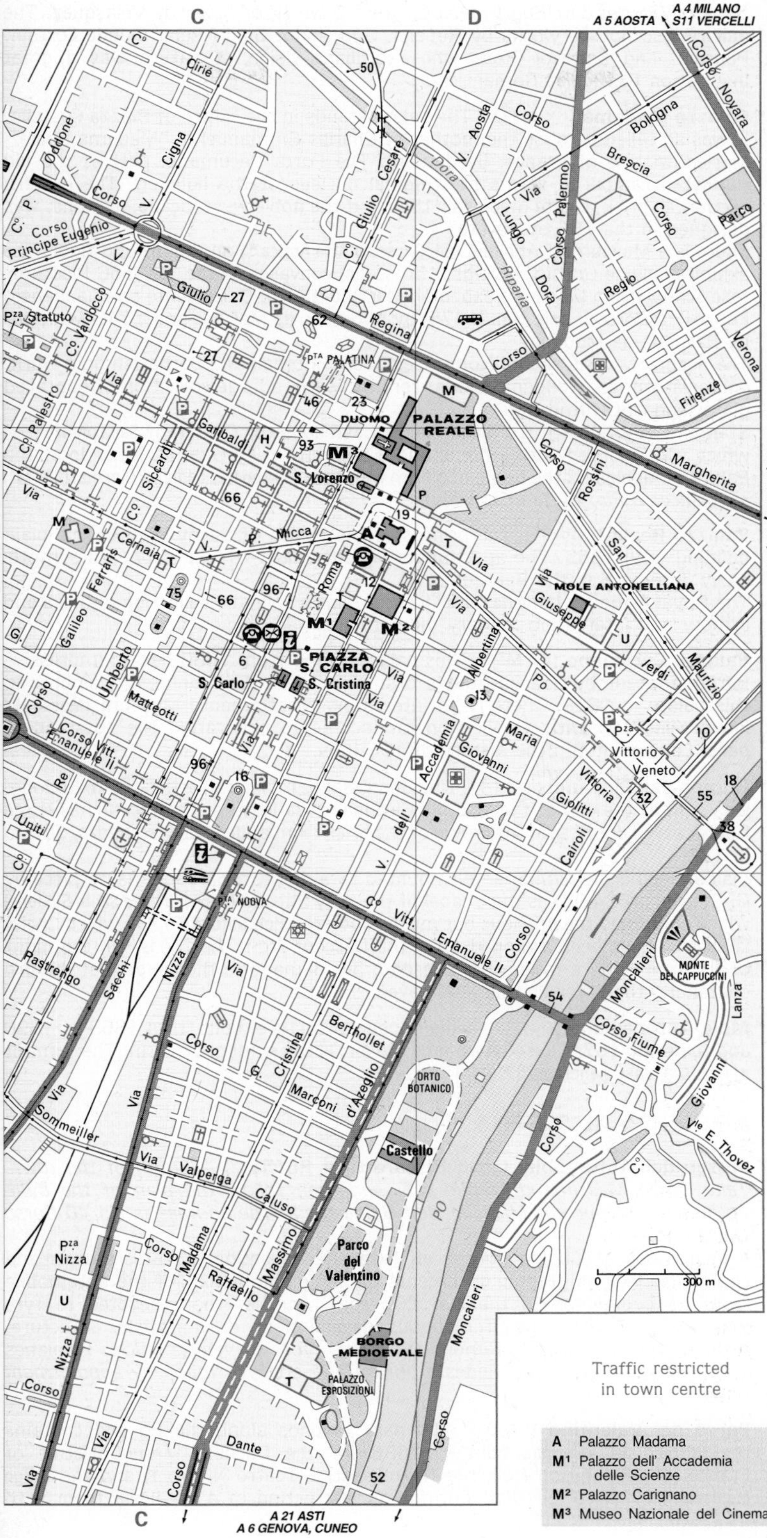

A   Palazzo Madama
M¹ Palazzo dell' Accademia
     delle Scienze
M² Palazzo Carignano
M³ Museo Nazionale del Cinema

great canvases by the Bassano family who were forerunners of Caravaggio in their contrasting use of light and shade, *The Triumph of Aurelius* by Tiepolo, and a beautiful *Madonna* with a wistful expression, a work typical of the Paduan artist Mantegna who influenced the Venetian School during the Renaissance. There is also a large series of official portraits by Van Dyck, including the famous *Sons of Charles I of England*. Note, too, *Philip IV of Spain* by Velasquez. The gallery also houses works by Rubens, Guerchino, Guido Reni, Claude Lorrain, Poussin, and Salvator Rosa whose brilliant vision of nature was a great inspiration to the Pre-Romantics.

★ **Palazzo Madama** (CX A) ⊙ – The palace stands in the centre of Piazza Castello. It was so called because the mother of Charles Emmanuel II, "Madama Reale", Marie-Christine of France, lived there. The Porta Decumana, part of the old Augustan ramparts, forms the original nucleus of the building. The eastern section, in brick, is late medieval (15C), but the noble west façade, in stone, was designed in the 18C by Juvara.

There is a Museum of Ancient Art **(Museo d'Arte Antica★)** on the ground floor. The exhibits include Gothic carvings, 15C stalls, canvases of the 15C-16C Piedmontese school (Gian Martino Spanzotti, Macrino d'Alba, Defendente and Gaudenzio Ferrari), a *Portrait of a Man* (1475) by Antonello da Messina and a 14C *Madonna* by Barnaba da Modena.

The decorative arts section comprises Greek, Roman and Barbarian gold work, enamels, ivories, wooden caskets, ceramic ware, a large collection of engraved glass, and 15C furniture.

Standing slightly back from the Piazza Castello is the Church of **San Lorenzo** (CX) which was adorned with a dome and a bold crown by Guarini. Next door, the Palazzo Chiablese is the home of a Film Museum **(Museo Nazionale del Cinema)** (CX **M³**) *(entrance: 2 Piazza San Giovanni).*

★ **Palazzo Reale** (CDVX) – The princes of the House of Savoy lived in this plain building until 1865. The apartments **(appartementi)** ⊙ *(first floor)* are sumptuously decorated in the Baroque style.

The Royal Armoury **(Armeria Reale★)** ⊙ contains a splendid collection of arms and armour and interesting military memorabilia.

Palazzo Carignano (CX **M²**) – This palace dating from 1680 has an impressive Baroque façade by Guarini. Italy's first king, Victor Emmanuel II, was born in this palace in 1820. There is an interesting Risorgimento Museum **(Museo del Risorgimento★)** ⊙ with a collection of documents illustrating the outstanding people and events in the history of 19C Italy.

★ **Duomo San Giovanni** (CX) ⊙ – This Renaissance cathedral, dedicated to St John, was built at the end of the 15C for Cardinal Della Rovere. The façade has three finely-carved doorways; the crown of the brick campanile was designed by Juvara in 1720.

Inside, behind the high altar surmounted by a dome, a Baroque masterpiece by G. Guarini (1624-83), is the Chapel of the Holy Shroud **(Cappella della Santa Sindone)** which enshrined the precious but much-contested **Holy Shroud★★★** in which Christ is said to have been wrapped after the Descent from the Cross. On the night of 11 April 1997 a raging fire caused grave damage to the chapel but the urn containing the precious relic was saved.

★ **Mole Antonelliana** (DX) ⊙ – This unusual structure, built from 1863 to 1890 and towering 167m – 548ft up into the air, is the symbol of Turin. The summit affords a vast **panorama★★** of Turin.

ADDITIONAL SIGHTS

★ **Museo dell'Automobile Carlo Biscaretti di Ruffia** ⊙ – *South of the town. Take Corso Massimo d'Azeglio (CZ) and then follow the plan of the built-up area in the current Michelin Red Guide Italia. The address is No 40 Corso Unità d'Italia.*

A vast modern building houses an extensive collection of cars, chassis and engines as well as graphic documents outlining the history of the automobile from its beginnings to the last 20 years. Another room devoted to tyre manufacture traces the tremendous development of materials, structure, technology and research, famous car races, types of vehicle (cycles to planes etc). The museum also includes a library and archives *(open by appointment only).*

Parco del Valentino (CDZ) – The park extends along the Po and contains the **Castello del Valentino** built in 1688 for the Duchess Marie-Christine of France, the Exhibition Hall, the New Theatre (Teatro Nuovo **T**) and the **Borgo Medievale★** ⊙, a curious and faithful reconstruction of a medieval town with its castle.

Museo dell'Automobile Carlo Biscaretti di Ruffia

EXCURSIONS

Plan of the built-up area in the current Michelin Red Guide Italia.

★ **Basilica di Superga** – *10km – 6 miles east*. This masterpiece was built by Juvara from 1717 to 1731 on a hill (670m – 2 198ft high). The basilica is circular in plan and roofed with a dome and its most remarkable feature is its monumental façade with its imposing columns and pilasters. The chapel dedicated to the Virgin, in the chancel, is a pilgrimage centre. The basilica is the Pantheon of the Kings of Sardinia.

★ **Tombe dei Reali** ⊙: The royal tombs in the crypt include that of Victor Amadeus II, who built the basilica to fulfil a vow made when his capital was being besieged by a French and Spanish army in 1706. Alongside are the tombs of Charles-Albert and other princes of the House of Savoy. From the esplanade there is a fine view★★★ of Turin, the Po Plain and the Alps.

★ **Colle della Maddalena** – *32km – 20 miles east*. From Superga take the scenic route via Pino Torinese which affords good views★★ of Turin. From Pino Torinese continue to the hilltop, **Colle della Maddalena**, and the **Parco della Rimembranza**, a very popular large public park which commemorates those who died in the First World War.
On the way down there are more lovely views★ of Turin. The **Parco Europa** at Cavoretto overlooks the southern part of the town.

★ **Palazzina di caccia di Stupinigi** or **Palazzina Mauriziana** ⊙ – *11km – 7 miles southwest*. This huge building was a hunting (*caccia*)-lodge built by Juvara for Victor Amadeus II of Savoy. Napoleon stayed here before assuming the crown of Italy. The palace now houses a Fine Arts and Furniture Museum **(Museo d'arte e del mobilio)**. The apartments are richly decorated in the rococo style of the 18C. A magnificent park surrounds the palazzina.

Castello di Rivoli ⊙ – *14km – 8 1/2 miles west*. Victor Amadeus II commissioned Juvara to build a grandiose residence (18C) in the Baroque style. Only the left wing (some rooms are decorated) and the lower part of the central range were built. The château now houses a Museum of Contemporary Art **(Museo d'arte contemporanea)** (1960 to the present day).

★ MONFERRATO

The proposed itinerary *(150km – 93 miles – allow 1 day)* takes the visitor through this attractive region of limestone hills, with its numerous castles and vineyards producing most of the Piedmontese wines, the best known of which is Asti.
Leave Turin to the east by the S 10.

Chieri – This town is known for its cuisine. Its monuments include: a Triumphal Arch (1580), a 15C Gothic cathedral and the 13C-15C Church of San Domenico with its fine campanile.

Asti – *Town plan in the current Michelin Red Guide Italia*. The home town of the tragic poet, Vittorio Alfieri (1749-1803), is the scene of an annual horse race *(palio)* which is preceded by a procession with over 1 000 participants in 14C

and 15C costume *(see the table of Principal Festivals at the end of the guide)*. The 12C baptistery **(Battistero di San Pietro★)**, the 15C Church of San Pietro and the Gothic cloisters form an attractive group. In the heart of the old town the 14C Gothic cathedral **(Cattedrale)** is decorated with Baroque paintings.
Take the S 231 and then the S 456 to reach Ovada.

★ **Strada dei Castelli dell'Alto Monferrato** – Between Ovada and Serravalle Scrivia a scenic route, also known as the wine route, follows the crest of the hillsides covered with vineyards. Along the way there is a series of hilltop villages, each one guarded by a castle.

Isole TREMITI★

TREMITI ISLANDS – Puglia – Population 365
Michelin map 988 fold 28 or 431 A 28
Access: see the current Michelin Red Guide Italia

This tiny archipelago, the only one on the Adriatic coast, lies offshore from the Gargano Promontory *(see Index)* and belongs to the same geological formation. There are two main islands, San Nicola and San Domino as well as two uninhabited isles, Capraia and Pianosa; the latter is much further out in the Adriatic.
The boat trip out from Manfredonia offers unforgettable **views★★★** of the Gargano coastline with its dazzling white limestone cliffs. As the boat rounds the promontory there are also good views of the coastal towns of Vieste, Peschici and Rodi Garganico set on their precipitous sites. On the points of the rocky headlands there are typical platforms *(trabocco)* equipped with square fishing nets.

★ **San Nicola** – High on the clifftop stands the **Abbazia di Santa Maria al Mare** ⊙, an abbey originally founded by the Benedictines in the 9C. A fortified ramp leads up to the abbey. Of particular interest are the remains of an 11C mosaic pavement, a 15C Gothic polyptych and a 13C Byzantine crucifix. From the cloisters there are good glimpses of the second island, San Domino.

★ **San Domino** ⊙ – Take a boat trip round this island and discover the wild beauty of its very indented and rugged coasts covered in pine forests.

TRENTO★

TRENT – Trentino-Alto Adige – Population 101 624
Michelin map 988 fold 4 or 429 D 15
Town plan in the current Michelin Red Guide Italia

Trent (or Trento), capital of Trentino, stands on the Adige not far from the Brenta Massif and is encircled by rocky peaks and valleys. Austrian and Italian influences meet here. This agricultural and industrial centre stands at an important crossroads with the converging of routes from the Brenner Pass, Brescia and Venice.

HISTORICAL NOTES

This Roman colony under the Empire became an episcopal See in the 4C, was occupied successively by the Ostrogoths under Theodoric, and by the Lombards in the 6C before being united to the Holy Roman Empire in the late 10C. From 1004 to 1801 the town was governed by a succession of Prince-Bishops.
The **Council of Trent** (1545-63), called by Pope Paul III to study methods of combating Protestantism, met in the town. These important deliberations marked the beginning of the Counter-Reformation and the findings were to change the character of the Church. The main decisions which aimed at the re-establishment of ecclesiastical credibility and authority, concerned compulsory residence for bishops and the abolition of the sale of indulgences.
After a period of Napoleonic rule in the 19C, Trento was ceded to the Austrians in 1814.
In 1918, the town was liberated, after a long hard struggle, by Italian troops.

★ **CITY OF THE PRINCE-BISHOPS** *2 hours*

★ **Piazza del Duomo** – This cobbled square is the town centre. All around stand the cathedral, the Palazzo Pretorio (13C, restored), the belfry and the Rella houses painted with 16C frescoes.

Duomo – The majestic 12C-13C cathedral is in the Lombard-Romanesque style. The façade of the north transept is pierced with a window forming a Wheel of Fortune which determines man's destiny: Christ stands at the summit, the Symbols of the Evangelists rise towards him.

Inside, note the unusual sweep of the stairway leading to the towers. To the right, in the 17C Chapel of the Crucifix (Cappella del Crocifisso), is a large wooden Christ in front of which the decrees of the Council of Trent were proclaimed. In the south transept is the tomb of the Venetian mercenary leader Sanseverino who was killed in 1486.

The remains of a 5C early-Christian basilica (**Basilica paleocristiana** ⊘) lie beneath the chancel.

★ **Museo Diocesano** ⊘ – The Diocesan Museum installed in the Palazzo Pretorio displays the most important items from the cathedral's treasure, paintings, carved **wooden panels**★, **altarpiece**★ and eight early-16C **tapestries**★ which were woven in Brussels by Pieter Van Aelst.

Via Belenzani – This street is lined with palaces in the Venetian style. Opposite the 16C town hall (Palazzo Comunale) stand houses with walls painted with frescoes.

Via Manci – The Venetian (loggias and frescoes) and mountain (overhanging roofs) styles are intermingled all along the street. No 63, the Palazzo Galazzo with its embossed stonework and huge pilasters is 17C.

★ **Castello del Buon Consiglio** ⊘ – This castle, once the residence of the prince-bishops, now houses an art museum (Museo Provinciale d'Arte di Trento). On the left are the 13C Castelvecchio (Old Castle) and the Torre Grande (known as Tower of Augustus); in the centre is the 16C Renaissance Palazzo Magno, the bishop's residence; and on the extreme right the square Torre dell' Aquila (Eagle Tower).

The interior of the castle gives the impression of being made up of a maze of courts, staircases, passages and sundry buildings. The Castelvecchio has a beautiful court in the Venetian-Gothic style with four tiers of galleries adorned with frescoes, including the portraits of the prince-bishops. The Palazzo Magno leads to the Loggia del Romanino with its 16C frescoes. The loggia overlooks a charming Renaissance courtyard, Cortile dei Leoni. The apartments of the prince-bishops with their coffered ceilings decorated with stucco and frescoes are the perfect setting for rich collections of 16C-18C paintings, furniture and ceramics.

ADDITIONAL SIGHTS

★ **Palazzo Tabarelli** – A remarkable building in the Venetian-Renaissance style with pilasters, pink marble columns and medallions.

Santa Maria Maggiore – Numerous meetings of the Council of Trent were held in this Renaissance church, dedicated to St Mary Major, with a Romanesque campanile. The elegant marble organ loft (1534) in the chancel is by Vincenzo and Girolamo Grandi. At the second altar on the right, in the nave, is a 16C altarpiece of the Madonna and saints by Moroni.

Sant'Apollinare – This small Romanesque church on the west bank of the Adige has a curious pointed roof covering two Gothic domical vaults. It is dedicated to St Apollinaris.

★★ GRUPPO DEL BRENTA

Round tour starting from Trento *233km – 145 miles – allow two days*

The wild limestone Brenta Massif prolongs the Dolomites beyond the Adige Valley. Its characteristic features are deep valleys, solitary lakes and erosion-worn rocks.

Sightseeing – The map below locates the towns and sites described in the guide and also indicates other beauty spots in small black type.

Take the S 45b in the direction of Vezzano.

★ **Lago Toblino** – Th charming lake fringed with tall rushes, stands against a background of rocky walls. An attractive little castle, once the summer residence of the Bishops of Trent, stands on a small peninsula.

★ **Valle Rendena** – This wide valley clad with firs and larches has charming villages with churches covered with frescoes, protected by overhanging roofs.
The Church of **San Vigilio** near Pinzolo has a remarkable *Dance of Death* (1539) by Simone Baschenis.

★★ **Val di Genova** – The valley crosses the granite Adamello Massif and is known for its wild grandeur. The road follows a fast-flowing river as it tumbles and foams along the rock-strewn bed to reach a waterfall (**Cascata di Nardis**★★) where the waters drop over 100m – 328ft.

✦✦ **Madonna di Campiglio** – This pleasant resort and winter sports centre has many hotels and numerous possibilities for excursions.

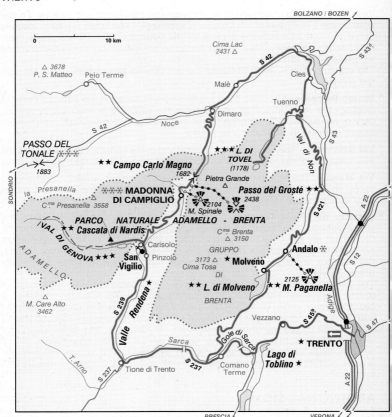

★★ Campo Carlo Magno ⊙ – A supposed visit by Charlemagne gave this place its name. It has become a winter sports centre.
From a pass **(Passo del Grosté)** – *cable-car and then on foot* – there is a fine **panorama★★** of the Brenta Massif.
Continue to Dimaro and Malè and at Cles turn right towards Tuenno.

★★★ Lago di Tovel – Pass through wild gorges to reach this lovely lake fringed by wooded slopes. In hot weather the waters of the lake take on a reddish tinge due to the presence of microscopic algae.

⁕ Andalo – This small holiday resort is set in majestic scenery amidst a great pine forest and overlooked by the crests of the Brenta Massif.
From the summit of **Monte Paganella** ⊙ *(cable-car)* at 2 125m – 6 972ft there is a splendid **panorama★★** of the whole region, and in clear weather as far as Lake Garda.

★ Molveno – This choice resort is situated amid gently-sloping meadows at the north end of a **lake★★** which lies on the floor of a cirque.

TREVISO ★

Veneto – Population 83 315
Michelin map 988 fold 5 or 428 E/F 18
Town plan in the current Michelin Red Guide Italia

Treviso, situated in the rich Venetian plain, is an important agricultural and industrial centre but has retained its old walled town. Ever since the 14C its fortunes have been linked with those of Venice.

★ Piazza dei Signori – This forms the historic centre of Treviso and is bordered by impressive monuments: the Palazzo del Podestà with its tall municipal bell-tower, the **Palazzo dei Trecento★** (1207) and the Renaissance Palazzo Pretorio. Lower down in Piazza del Monte di Pietà is the former pawn shop **(Monte di Pietà)** ⊙ with the Chapel of the Rectors (Cappella dei Reggitori).
In Piazza San Vito there are two adjoining churches: **San Vito** and **Santa Lucia** which is adorned with remarkable **frescoes★** by Tommaso da Modena, one of the finest 14C artists after Giotto.

★ **San Nicolò** – This large Romanesque-Gothic church, dedicated to St Nicholas, contains interesting frescoes, especially those on the columns which are by Tommaso da Modena. In the Onigo Chapel there are portraits of people from Treviso by Lorenzo Lotto (16C). The *Virgin in Majesty* at the far end of the chancel is by Savoldo (16C). In the adjoining monastery (**convento**) the chapter-house has portraits of famous Dominicans by Tommaso da Modena.

★ **Museo Civico Bailo** ⊙ – *22 Borgo Cavour*. In the municipal museum are works by Tommaso da Modena, Girolamo da Treviso (15C) and others of the Venetian school such as Cima da Conegliano, Giovanni Bellini, Titian, Paris Bordone, Jacopo Bassano and Lorenzo Lotto.

Duomo – The 15C and 16C cathedral has seven domes, a neo-Classical façade and a Romanesque crypt. Left of the cathedral stands an 11C-12C baptistery. In the Chapel of the Annunciation (Cappella dell'Annunziata), to the right of the chancel, there are frescoes in the Mannerist style by Pordenone and on the altarpiece an *Annunciation* by Titian.

San Francesco – *Viale Sant' Antonio da Padova*. This church in the transitional Romanesque-Gothic style has a fine wooden ceiling, the tombstone of Petrarch's daughter and the tomb of one of Dante's sons, as well as frescoes by Tommaso da Modena in the first chapel to the left of the chancel. The church is dedicated to St Francis.

EXCURSIONS

Maser ⊙ – *29km – 18 miles northwest by the S 348*. This small agricultural town is known for its famous **villa★★★** built in 1560 by Palladio for the Barbaro brothers: Daniele, patriarch of Aquileia and Marcantonio, ambassador of the Venetian Republic. The interior was decorated from 1566 to 1568 with a splendid cycle of **frescoes★★★** by Veronese. It is one of his best decorative schemes and he used all his amazing knowledge of perspective, *trompe-l'œil*, foreshortening and his sense of movement and colour. Not far from the villa is a **Tempietto**, a graceful circular chapel with a dome which was also the work of Palladio.

Vittorio Veneto – *41km – 26 miles north*. The name of this town recalls the great victory of the Italians over the Austrians in 1918. In Ceneda to the south of the town, a museum (**Museo della Battaglia**) ⊙ which presents documents on this victory is installed in a 16C loggia (Loggia Cenedese) with a frescoed portico by Sansovino. The suburb of Serravalle in the north has retained a certain charm. The Church of **San Giovanni** *(take Via Roma and then Via Mazzini)* has interesting **frescoes★** attributed to Jacobello del Fiore and Gentile da Fabriano (15C).

★ **Portogruaro** – *56km – 35 miles east*. The town grew up from the 11C onwards along the banks of the river Lemene, a trade route that brought the town its wealth. Two fine main streets lined with attractive porticoes flank the river banks and there are numerous palaces built in a style that is typically Venetian, dating from the late Middle Ages and the Renaissance (14C-16C). On the **Corso Martiri della Libertà★★** (the busiest of the shopping streets) not far from the 19C cathedral and its leaning Romanesque campanile is the strange **Palazzo Municipale★** built in a late-Gothic style (14C) on which the façade is crowned with Ghibelline merlons. Behind the palace is the river: note, to the right, the two 15C watermills (now restored) and a small 17C fishermen's chapel (Oratorio del Pesce) with its own landing-stage. In the Via del Seminario (the main street on the opposite bank) stands a museum (**Museo Archeologico Nazionale** – *no 22*) which has Roman exhibits (small bronze of Diane the Huntress) and Paleo-Christian artefacts from Concordia Sagittaria *(3km – 2 miles south)*, a Roman colony founded in 40 BC.

TRIESTE★

Friuli-Venezia Giulia – Population 230 644

Michelin map 988 fold 6 or 429 F 23

Plan of the built-up area in the current Michelin Red Guide Italia

Trieste is a modern town which stands at the head of a bay of the same name and at the foot of the Carso Plateau. The edge of the latter forms a steep coast with magnificent white cliffs as far as Duino in the north. Trieste is the largest seaport on the Adriatic. Its extensive port (12km – 8 miles of quays stretch as far as the Slovenian border) handles more goods from Austria and the former Yugoslavia than from Italy. An oil pipeline links Trieste to refineries in Austria and Bavaria. The vast shipyards, specialising in the building of large vessels, are important to the local economy.

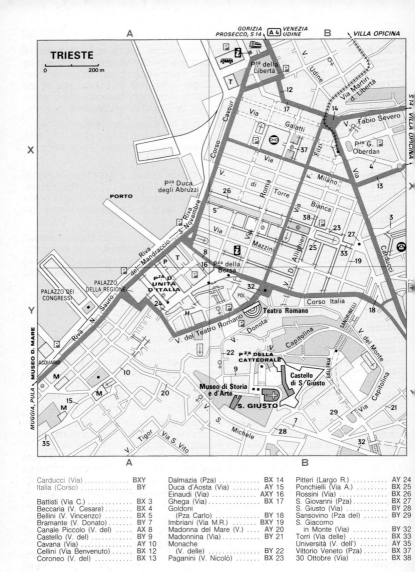

TRIESTE

0   200 m

HISTORICAL NOTES

Trieste is of very ancient origin; the Celts and Illyrians fought over the town before the Romans made it their great trading centre of Tergeste, which had the important role of defending the eastern frontiers of the Empire. In the Middle Ages it came under the sway of the Patriarch of Aquileia and then, in 1202, under Venice. In 1382 Trieste rebelled and placed itself under the protection of Austria and it played the role of mediator between the two powers until the 15C. In 1719 Charles VI declared it a free port and established the headquarters of the French Trading Company (Compagnie d'Orient et du Levant) in the city. Trieste then enjoyed a second period of prosperity and was embellished by numerous fine buildings. Many political exiles sought refuge in Trieste. It was only in 1919 after fierce fighting that Trieste was united with the Kingdom of Italy.

At the beginning of the 20C Trieste boasted an active literary group under the leading influence of the novelist Italo Svevo and the poet Umberto Saba. James Joyce lived in the town for some years until 1914.

★★ COLLE DI SAN GIUSTO *1 hour*

This hilltop was the site of the ancient city and today the **Piazza della Cattedrale★** (BY) is lined with the ruins of a Roman basilica, a 15C-16C castle, a 1560 Venetian column, the altar of the Third Army (1929) and the Basilica of St Justus.

★ **Basilica di San Giusto** (BY) – It was founded in the 5C on the site of a Roman building, but the present buildings date in large part from the 14C. The façade is pierced with a fine Gothic rose window and decorated with a low relief and bronze busts. The massive campanile has fragments of Roman columns built into its lowest storey and bears a 14C statue of St Justus. From the top there is an attractive **view**★ of Trieste.

The **interior**★ comprises a nave and four aisles. The side aisles belonged to two separate basilicas which were joined together in the 14C by the building of the nave. In the south aisle there are: a lovely 13C mosaic and 11C frescoes depicting the life of St Justus. A magnificent 12C **mosaic**★★ in the north apse shows the Virgin in Majesty between the Archangels Michael and Gabriel, and the Apostles.

Castello di San Giusto (BY) ⊘ - The castle houses a **museum** of furniture and a fine collection of **arms**★.

Museo di Storia e d'Arte (BY) ⊘ - The Museum of History and Art contains a remarkable collection of red-figured **Greek vases**★ and charming **small bronzes**★ dating from the Roman Archaic period.

Teatro Romano (BY) - The remains of an early-2C Roman theatre lie at the foot of the Hill of St Justus.

LOWER TOWN *1 hour*

★ **Piazza dell'Unità d'Italia** (AY) - Three early 20C palaces line this square, namely the Palazzo del Governo (Government Palace), Palazzo del Comune (Town Hall) and the offices of Lloyd Trieste.

★ **Museo del Mare** ⊘ - *Via A. Ottaviano. Take Riva Nazario Sauro* (AY). The history of seafaring is traced from its beginnings to the 18C. The **fishing section**★ is of special interest.

EXCURSIONS

Santuario del Monte Grisa - *10km - 6 miles north. Leave by Piazza della Libertà* (BX) *in the direction of Prosecco and then Villa Opicina and follow the signposts to "Monte Grisa".*
This modern sanctuary is dedicated to the Virgin. From the terrace there is a splendid **panorama**★★ of Trieste and its bay.

Villa Opicina ⊘ - *9km - 6 miles north. Leave by Via Fabio Severo* (BX). *After 4.5km - 3 miles turn left off the S 14 to take the S 58. It is also possible to take the funicular which leaves from Piazza Oberdan.*
Villa Opicina stands on the edge of the Carso Plateau (alt 348m - 1 142ft). From the belvedere with its obelisk there is a magnificent **view**★★ over Trieste and its bay.

★ **Castello di Miramare** ⊘ - *8km - 5 miles northwest by the coast road.* Standing on the point of a headland, this castle with its lovely terraced **gardens**★ was built in 1860 for Archduke Maximilian of Austria, who was executed by shooting in Mexico in 1867, and his wife, Princess Charlotte, who died insane.

★ **Grotta Gigante** ⊘ - *13km - 8 miles north. Follow the above directions to Villa Opicina and then turn left in the direction of Borgo Grotta Gigante.*
An impressive stairway leads down to this chamber of amazing size where one can walk among the splendid concretions. There is a speleological museum **(Museo di Speleologia)** at the entrance to the cave.

Muggia - *14km - 9 miles south. Leave by Riva Nazario Sauro* (AY). Facing Trieste, this small Venetian-looking town boasts a 15C Gothic cathedral (Duomo) with an attractive pointed campanile and an elegant façade in Istrian limestone.

Terra dei TRULLI★★★

Puglia

Michelin map 988 fold 29 or 431 E 33

This region extending between Fassano, Ostuni, Martina Franca and Alberobello takes its name from the very curious buildings, the *trulli (photograph see PUGLIA),* which are to be found almost everywhere. These strange, white, dry-stone structures have conical roofs covered with grey stone slabs. Each dome corresponds to a room. The *trulli* usually stand in groups of three or four. A tall chimney crowns the side of the buillding. The external staircase leads to the attic. The doorway stands in a recessed arch surmounted by a gable. Inside, the rooms are domed.

★★ **Alberobello** - This small town has an entire district of *trulli* which often abut one another. They spread over the hillside to the south of the town (Zona Monumentale). On the hilltop stands the Church of **Sant'Antonio** also in the form of a *trullo (take Via Monte Sant'Angelo).* Inside, the transept crossing is covered with a dome, similar to those in the *trulli.* It is possible to visit some of these strange dwellings: from the rooftops there is often a good view of the site. The **Trullo Sovrano**★, a two-storeyed *trullo,* the largest in Alberobello, stands near the principal church on Piazza Sacramento.

Locorotondo - *36km - 22 miles north of Taranto*. This town takes its name from the layout of its alleyways which wind in concentric circles (*loco rotondo:* round place) around the hill on which it is set. The road from Martina Franca offers a splendid **view**★ of a multitude of white houses with tall pointed gables. The road from Martina Franca to Locorotondo follows the **Valle d'Itria**★★, a vast and fertile plain planted with vines and olive trees and dotted with *trulli*, beehive-shaped houses.

★ **Martina Franca** - This white city rises on a hilltop in the Murge Hills. The architecture of the old town, girdled by its ramparts, is an attractive combination of the Baroque and rococo styles.
The pleasant **Piazza Roma** is bordered by the former ducal palace (1668). The Collegiate Church, **Collegiata San Martino**, with its lovely façade embellished with high reliefs is the principal monument in Piazza Plebiscito. Walk down the **Via Cavour**★ which is lined by numerous Baroque palaces.

TUSCANIA★

Lazio – Population 7 732
Michelin map 988 fold 25 or 430 O 17 – 24km – 15 miles west of Viterbo

Tuscania was a powerful Etruscan town, a Roman municipium and an important medieval centre. The town retains fragments of its walls and two superb churches, a little way out of town. Tuscania's artistic heritage was considerably damaged by the earthquake of February 1971.

★★ **San Pietro** - The golden-hued façade of St Peter's stands at the far end of an empty square on the site of the Etruscan acropolis. To the left are two medieval towers and to the right the former bishop's palace. The harmonious façade dates from the early 13C. The symbols of the Evangelists surround a rose window, probably of the Umbrian school. Lower down an atlante (or a dancer?) and a man (Laocöon?) being crushed by a snake probably came from Etruscan buildings.
The interior was built by Lombard masons in the 11C. Massive columns with beautiful capitals support curious denticulated arches. The nave retains its original and highly decorative paving. The frescoes in the apse are 12C. The crypt **(cripta**★★**)** ⊙ is a forest of small columns, all different and of various periods – Roman, Pre-Romanesque and Romanesque – supporting groined vaulting.

★ **Santa Maria Maggiore** - This late-12C church, dedicated to St Mary Major, is modelled on St Peter's. The 13C Romanesque **doorways**★★ are decorated with masterly sculptures.
Inside is an ambo rebuilt with 8C, 9C and 12C fragments. Above the triumphal arch there is a realistic 14C fresco of the *Last Judgement*.

UDINE★

Friuli-Venezia Giulia – Population 98 882
Michelin map 988 fold 6 or 429 D 21
Town plan in the current Michelin Red Guide Italia

This charming town was the seat of the Patriarchs of Aquilea from 1238 to 1420 when it passed under Venetian rule. Udine nestles round a hill encircled by the picturesque lane, Vicolo Sottomonte, with a castle on its summit. The charm of Udine lies in its Gothic and Renaissance monuments, its secluded squares and narrow streets, often lined with arcades. The town was badly damaged, like most of Friuli, by the 1976 earthquake.

★★ **Piazza della Libertà** - This very harmonious square has kept its Renaissance character and is bordered by several public buildings. The former town hall is also known as the **Loggia del Lionello** (1457), from the name of its architect. Its Venetian-Gothic style is characterised by the elegant arcades and its white and rose-coloured stonework. Opposite on a slightly higher level is the 16C **Loggia di San Giovanni**, a Renaissance portico surmounted by a 16C clock tower, with Moorish jacks *(Mori)* similar to the ones in Venice. A 16C fountain plays in the centre of the square, not far from statues of Hercules and Cacus and the columns of Justice and St Mark.

Castello ⊙ - This imposing early-16C castle is preceded by an esplanade from which there is a good view of Udine and the surrounding Friuli countryside. This was the seat of the representatives of the Most Serene Republic (Venice).

Alongside is the 13C Church of **Santa Maria del Castello** with a 16C façade and campanile which bears a statue of the Archangel Gabriel at its summit. Inside, there is a 13C fresco of the *Descent from the Cross*.

Duomo ⊙ – This 14C Gothic cathedral remodelled in the 18C has a lovely Flamboyant-Gothic doorway. The massive campanile has, on one of its faces, statues of the Angel of the Annunciation and of Archangel Gabriel (14C). Inside, there is attractive **Baroque decoration★**: organ loft, pulpit, tombs, altarpieces and historiated stalls. Tiepolo painted the remarkable *trompe-l'œil* frescoes in the Chapel of the Holy Sacrament (Cappella del Santo Sacramento).

The Oratory of Purity **(Oratorio della Purità)**, to the right of the cathedral, has a ceiling decorated with a remarkable *Assumption* (1757) by Tiepolo.

Palazzo Arcivescovile ⊙ – The 16C-18C Archbishop's Palace boasts **frescoes★** by Tiepolo. The ceiling of its grand staircase depicts the *Fall of the Rebel Angels*, while the apartments are decorated with scenes from the Old Testament.

Piazza Matteotti – This lovely square bordered by arcaded houses is the site of a lively open-air market. Also of interest are: the elegant 16C Baroque Church of San Giacomo, a 16C fountain and a 15C column of the Virgin. It is pleasant to stroll in Via Mercato Vecchio and Via Vittorio Veneto with their shops beneath the arcades.

EXCURSION

★★ **Villa Manin** ⊙ – *30km – 18 miles southwest, in Passariano*. Having lived in the Friuli area (territory under Venetian control) since the 13C, the Manins occupied very high-ranking positions in the service of the Republic. The villa was a summer residence, the counterpart of their palace on the Grand Canal. The 16C villa was rebuilt in the 17C and rapidly completed with two wings set at right angles to the main part of the building, recalling the grandeur of Versailles. Finally, it was extended by semi-circular outbuildings based, in design, on St Peter's Square in Rome. This grandiose building was requisitioned by Napoleon Bonaparte when preparing the **Treaty of Campoformio** *(8km – 5 miles southwest of Udine)* which, by a quirk of history, was signed (without being renamed despite the fact that it marked the end of the Republic of Venice) in the palace of the last Doge, Ludovico Manin.

In the right wing of the villa, visitors can see the magnificent chapel and its sacristy, the stables with their 18C and 19C coaches and carriages, and the weapons room (15C-18C arms). The villa itself houses temporary exhibitions every summer, and they provide an opportunity to admire the luxurious decoration and frescoes in its vast chambers. The superb grounds are decorated with statues.

URBINO ★★

Marches – Population 15 111

Michelin map 988 folds 15 and 16, 429 fold 36 or 430 K 19

Town plan in the current Michelin Red Guide Italia

The walled town of Urbino, with its rose-coloured brick houses, is built on two hills overlooking the undulating countryside bathed in a glorious golden light. Urbino was ruled by the Montefeltro family from the 12C onwards and reached its peak in the reign (1444-82) of **Duke Federico da Montefeltro**, a wise leader, man of letters, collector and patron of the arts. Urbino was the birthplace of **Raphael** (Raffaello Sanzio) (1483-1520).

★★ PALAZZO DUCALE (DUCAL PALACE) *1 1/2 hours*

The palace (1444-72), started by order of Duke Federico by the Dalmatian architect Luciano Laurana and completed by the Sienese Francesco di Giorgio Martini, is a masterpiece of harmony and elegance. The design hinges on the panorama to the west of the old town, and the original façade overlooking the valley is pierced by superimposed loggias and flanked by two tall round towers. The severe east wing facing Piazza Rinsacimento has irregularly-spaced windows, while the majestic north façade is punctuated by three great doors at ground level and four rectangular windows on the first floor.

The inner courtyard, inspired by earlier Florentine models, is a classic example of Renaissance harmony with its pure, delicate lines, serene architectural rhythm and subtle combination of rose-coloured brick and white marble.

On the ground floor are a museum (**Museo Archeologico** - lapidary fragments: inscriptions, steles, architectural remains etc), a library (**Biblioteca del Duca**) and cellars (**cantine**).

★★ **Galleria Nazionale delle Marche** ⊙ - The palace's first-floor rooms with their original decoration are the setting for the National Gallery of the Marches which contains several great **masterpieces★★★**: a predella of the *Profanation of the Host* (1465-9) by Paolo Uccello, a *Madonna* di Senigallia and a curious *Flagellation of Christ* by Piero della Francesca *(see Index)*, the *Ideal City (see Pienza)* by Laurana and the famous portrait of a woman, known as *The Mute*, by Raphael. Duke Federico's **studiolo★★★** is decorated with magnificent intarsia panelling. A collection of 16C-17C Italian paintings and 17C-18C maiolica is displayed on the second floor.

To the north of the palace stands the early-19C cathedral built by Valadier.

ADDITIONAL SIGHTS

★ **Casa di Raffaello** ⊙ - *57 Via Raffaello.* Raphael lived here up to the age of 14. This typical 15C house belonged to the boy's father, Giovanni Sanzio or Santi, and contains mementos and period furniture.

Chiesa Oratorio di San Giovanni Battista e San Giuseppe ⊙ - *Via Barocci.* Of these two adjacent churches, the first is 14C and contains curious **frescoes★** by the Salimbene brothers depicting the life of St John the Baptist. The second, dating from the 16C, has in the nave a colossal statue of St Joseph (18C) painted in grisaille, and a very lovely stucco **crib★**, a life-size work by Federico Brandani (1522-75).

★★ **Strada Panoramica** - Starting from Piazza Roma, this scenic road skirts a hillside and affords admirable **views★★** of the town walls, the lower town, Ducal Palace and cathedral: a wonderful scene in various hues of pink brick.

VELIA★

Campania

Michelin map 988 fold 38 or 431 G 27 - 14km - 9 miles northwest of Pisciotta

The extensive ruins of the ancient city of Velia (**Elea**) are situated in the vicinity of Castellammare di Velia in the region of Cilento. Excavations have uncovered only part of the site. This colony was founded in 535 BC by Phocean Greek refugees who had been expelled by the Persians. Before settling in Massalia (Marseilles) they lived in the Corsican settlement of Alalia (Aleria), where they were victorious in a naval battle (*c*538) against the combined Carthaginian and Etruscan fleets. The busy and prosperous port of Velia - known for a long time as Elea - is famous for its school of the Eleatic philosophers (5C). Two of the better-known philosophers were Parmenides and his pupil Zeno.

Lower town - *Pass under the railway line to reach this quarter.* From the entrance there is an interesting view of the ruins which include the former lighthouse, 4C BC town wall, the baths, the south sea-gateway and the 4C BC gateway, **Porta Rosa★**.

Acropolis - A medieval castle abuts the remains of a 5C BC Greek temple. Laid out below are the ruins of the amphitheatre. A small **museum** houses statues of Parmenides, Zeno and Aesculapius which were found amidst the ruins.

Michelin Green Guides for North America

California
Canada
Chicago
Florida
New York City
New England
Quebec
San Francisco
Washington

VENEZIA★★★

VENICE – Veneto – Population 309 041

Michelin map 988 fold 5 or 429 F 18/19 – Town plan below

A fascinating city between sea and sky, like Venus rising from the waves, Venice welcomes tourists from the five continents drawn to her by the charm of her canals, the pellucid light and the coolness of the sea breezes. She also offers the intellectual pleasures to be derived from her masterpieces, which mark the meeting of East and West.

The vanished greatness of Venice accounts for the myth of an artificial, voluptuous and tragic city, the scene of intrigues plotted in an atmosphere of corruption where dreams became nightmares. Many writers, the Romantics especially, have described the disturbing and fascinating atmosphere of the city. They include Thomas Mann in his novel *Death in Venice* which the Italian director Luchino Visconti made into a film.

Today the exceptional setting of Venice threatens its very existence. The nature of the terrain on which it is built and the rising level of the surrounding waters pose a constant threat. Various measures have already been taken and a plan to safeguard and remedy the position has been devised.

ARRIVING IN AND EXPLORING VENICE

By car or by train

The classic approach, is by the Ponte della Libertà. Cars must be left in one of the paying **garages** ⊙ *(autorimesse)* in Piazzale Roma (**AT**), or in the **car parks** ⊙ on the island of Tronchetto. Trains terminate at Stazione di Santa Lucia.

By vaporetti

From the train station or from Piazzale Roma, the *vaporetti* (water-buses) services are a convenient means of transport. Line No 1 (*accelerato*: omnibus service) runs to St Mark's in 1/2 hour, via the Grand Canal and stopping at both sides of the canal or Line No 82 which provides a faster service stops at fewer landing stages.

Seasons

Venice is attractive in all seasons but is especially so in spring and autumn when the colours are more vivid or the light is softer. In summer when the sky is hazy and sightseeing can be rather tiring owing to the high humidity and heat, Venice holds grandiose festivals: the **Festival of the Redeemer** on the island of Giudecca, the historic regatta on the Grand Canal and the International Film Festival. The rejoicing of Carnival marks a high spot during the rigours of winter.

VARIOUS ASPECTS OF VENICE

Venice is built on 117 islands; it has 150 canals and 400 bridges. A canal is called a *rio*, a square a *campo*, a street a *calle* or *salizzada*, a quay a *riva* or *fondamenta*, a filled-in canal *rio Terrà*, a passageway under a house *sottoportego*, a courtyard a *corte* and a small square a *campiello*.

The squares are charming, with their well-curbs often sculpted *(vera da pozzo)*. The hub of public life is the Piazza San Marco *(see below)* where tourists and citizens sit on the terraces of the famous Florian and Quadri cafés. The Florian is the best-known café; founded in 1720 it has received Byron, Goethe, George Sand, Musset and Wagner within its mirrored and allegory-painted walls.

The shops in St Mark's have sumptuous window displays of lace, jewellery, mirrors and the famous glassware from Murano. The **Mercerie (EU)**, shopping streets, lead to the Rialto Bridge.

On the far side of this are the displays of greengrocers' *(erberie)* and fishmongers' shops *(pescherie)*.

In addition to these well-known and busy areas there are the **Frari Quarter (BU)** and that of **Santa Maria Formosa (FTU)**, which have a certain peaceful charm with their brick façades and silent canals. Visitors can also discover the Venice of the Venetians by moving out of the crowds that congregate in and around San Marco or the Rialto.

Meals in the restaurants *(trattorie)* are among the attractions of Venice. The fare consists chiefly of sea-food, squid *(calamaretti)*, cuttlefish, eels and mussels in the Venetian manner but also calf's liver cooked in the Venetian way, with onions. These dishes should be accompanied by the pleasant local wines: Valpolicella, Bardolino and Amarone for red wines, and Soave and Prosecco for the whites.

283

VENEZIA

Gondolas – For centuries gondolas have been the traditional means of transport in Venice. The gondola is an austere and sober craft except for its typical iron hook, which acts as a counterweight to the gondolier. The curved fin is said to echo the dogal *corno* (horn-shaped hat) and the prongs to represent the *sestieri* or districts of the city. The prong on the back of the stern symbolises the Guidecca.

Gondolas

The Venetians – The Venetians are both proud and fiercely traditional, known for their commercial and practical skills. The "bautta" (black velvet mask) and domino (a wide hooded cape), once very popular with the locals and still worn in Venice at Carnival time, add to their elusiveness. Skilled courtesans, diplomats and spies have given Venice a reputation for intrigue and manoeuvring in love and politics. Venetian is a very lively dialect which is used in place of Italian, even in place names.

The Marriage of Venice and the Sea – A sumptuous ceremony that, since the year 1000 (with a few interruptions) has celebrated the capture of the towns of Istria and Dalmatia from the pirates. It is an admirable expression of the link between Venice and the sea, the element that made the city great for many centuries and the one that still gives it its beauty to this day.
In memory of this historic past, every year on the Feast of the Ascension, or "Sensa" in Venetian, the Doge, dressed in cloth of gold, would board *Bucentaur,* his golden state barge, and throw a ring into the sea with the words, "We wed you, o Sea, as a sign of true and perpetual dominion".

HISTORICAL NOTES

Venice was founded in AD 811 by the inhabitants of Malamocco, near the Lido, fleeing from the Franks. They settled on the Rivo Alto, known today as the Rialto. In that year the first Doge – a name derived from the Latin *dux* (leader) – Agnello Partecipazio, was elected and thus started the adventures of the Venetian Republic, La Serenissima, which lasted 1 000 years. In 828 the relics of St Mark the Evangelist were brought from Alexandria; he became the protector of the town.

The Venetian Empire – From the 9C to the 13C Venice grew steadily richer as it exploited its position between East and West. With its maritime and commercial power it conquered important markets in Istria and Dalmatia. The guile of Doge Dandolo and the assistance of the Crusaders helped the Venetians capture Constantinople in 1204. The spoils from its sack flowed to Venice, while trade in spices, fabrics and precious stones from markets established in the east grew apace.
Marco Polo (1254-1324) returned from China with fabulous riches. He related his amazing adventures in French in his *Book of the Wonders of the World* and won great fame throughout Europe.
The 14C war with its rival Genoa ended in victory for the Venetians in 1381.

Glory – The first-half of the 15C saw Venetian power at its peak: the Turks were defeated at Gallipoli in 1416 and the Venetians held the kingdoms of Morea, Cyprus and Candia (Crete) in the Levant.

In mainland Italy, from 1414 to 1428, they captured Verona, Vicenza, Padua, Udine, and then Brescia and Bergamo. The Adriatic became the Venetian Sea from Corfu to the Po.

Decline – The capture of Constantinople by the Turks in 1453 started the decadence. The discovery of America caused a shift in the patterns of trade and Venice had to keep up an exhausting struggle with the Turks who were defeated in 1571 in the naval battle of **Lepanto**, in which the Venetians played an important part. Their decline, however, was confirmed in the 17C when the Turks captured Candia (Crete) after a 25-year siege.

The "Most Serene Republic" came to an end in 1797. Napoleon Bonaparte entered Venice and abolished a thousand year-old constitution. Then, by the **Treaty of Campoformio**, he ceded the city to Austria. Venice and the Veneto were united with Italy in 1866.

The long-lasting oligarchy – The government of the Republic was from its earliest days organised to avoid the rise to power of any one man. The role of doge was supervised by several councils: the Grand Council drew up the laws; the Senate was responsible for foreign affairs, military and economic matters; the Council of Ten, responsible for security, kept a network of secret police and informers which created an atmosphere of mistrust but ensured control of all aspects of city life.

VENETIAN PAINTING

The Venetian school of painting with its marked sensuality is characterised by the predominance of colour over draughtsmanship, and by an innate sense of light in hazy landscapes with blurred outlines. Art historians have often noted the contrast between the scholarly and idealistic art of the Florentines and the freer, more spontaneous work of the Venetians, which later influenced the Impressionists. The real beginnings of Venetian painting are exemplified by the **Bellini** family: Jacopo, the father, and Gentile (1429-1507) and **Giovanni** (or **Giambellino**, 1430-1516), his sons. The latter, who was the younger son, was a profoundly spiritual artist and one of the first Renaissance artists to integrate landscape and figure compositions harmoniously. In parallel, their pupil **Carpaccio** (1455-1525) recorded Venetian life with his usual imagination and care for detail while **Giorgione** remained a major influence. His pupil, **Lorenzo Lotto**, was also influenced by the realism of Northern artists.

The Renaissance came to a glorious conclusion with three great artists: **Titian** (c1490-1576) who painted dramatic scenes where dynamic movement is offset by light effects; **Veronese** (1528-88), whose sumptuous ornamentation and rich colours reflected the splendor of the Most Serene Republic; and **Tintoretto** (1518-94), a visionary whose dramatic technique reflects an inner anxiety.

The artists of the 18C captured Venice and its peculiar light, grey-blue, iridescent and slightly misty: **Canaletto** (1697-1768) whose works won favour with English Grand Tourists, and his pupil Bellotto (1720-80), were both inspired by townscapes; Francesco **Guardi** (1712-93) who painted in luminous touches; Pietro **Longhi** (1702-58), the author of intimate scenes; Giovanni Battista **Tiepolo** (1696-1770), a master decorator who painted frescoes with sacred and secular scenes full of light and movement. His son, Gian Domenico (1727-1804), adopted a similar style. Spontaneity and colour are also found in the musicians of Venice, of whom the best known is **Antonio Vivaldi** (1678-1743), who was master of violin and viola at a hospice, Ospedale della Pietà, for many years. (Hospices were charity institutions and orphanages but were also academies of music and drama.)

SIGHTSEEING

We recommend the Michelin Green Guide Venice for an extended visit.

Visitors spending one day in Venice should take in Piazza San Marco; those on a two- to three-day tour will have time to visit the Accademia and the Scuole (Schools) and churches which contain many treasures; those who spend a whole week will be captivated by the atmosphere of the alleyways and of the islands in the lagoon.

★★ PIAZZA SAN MARCO (ST MARK'S SQUARE) (EV) *1/2 day*

St Mark's Square is the heart of Venice. All around, the covered galleries of the procuratorships **(Procuratie)** shelter famous cafés (Florian, Quadri), and luxury shops.

The square opens on the Grand Canal through the delightful **Piazzetta** (EV **64**). The two granite columns crowned by "Marco" and "Todaro" were brought from the East in 1172.

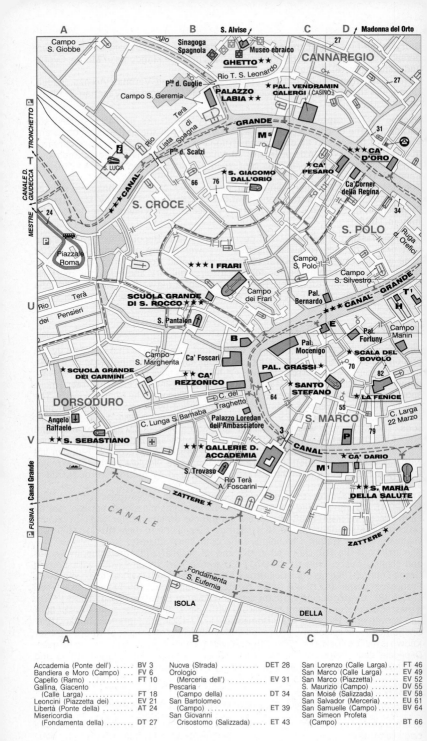

★★★ **Basilica di San Marco** – St Mark's combines the Byzantine and Western styles. Building was carried out throughout the 11C and when the basilica was consecrated in 1094, the body of St Mark had been recovered by a miracle. Visitors are overcome by a feeling of awe, perhaps owing to the rich decoration of marble and **mosaic**. Built on the plan of a Greek cross, the basilica is crowned by a bulbous dome flanked by four smaller domes of unequal height placed on the arms of the cross.

Façade – This is pierced by five large doorways adorned with variegated marbles and sculptures. The central doorway has three arches adorned with Romanesque-Byzantine low reliefs, and above are copies of the four famous **Bronze Horses** (the originals are in the gallery of the Basilica: see below).

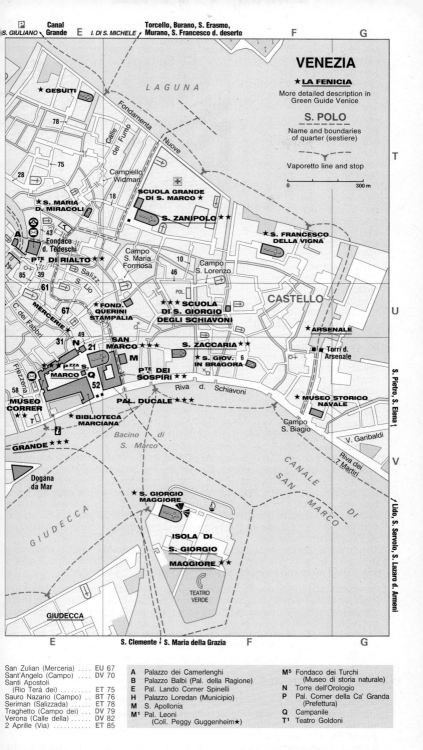

A	Palazzo dei Camerlenghi
B	Palazzo Balbi (Pal. della Ragione)
E	Pal. Lando Corner Spinelli
H	Palazzo Loredan (Municipio)
M	S. Apollonia
M¹	Pal. Leoni
	(Coll. Peggy Guggenheim★)

M⁵	Fondaco dei Turchi
	(Museo di storia naturale)
N	Torre dell'Orologio
P	Pal. Corner della Ca' Granda
	(Prefettura)
Q	Campanile
T¹	Teatro Goldoni

On the first arch on the left is depicted the Translation of the body of St Mark. On the south side near the Doges' Palace stands the porphyry group, known as the *Tetrarchs* (4C). At the corner is the proclamation stone *(pietra del bando)*, where laws were proclaimed. The pretty Piazzetta dei Leoncini (**EV 21**) lies to the north.

Atrium ⊘ – As an introduction to the narrative told in mosaic inside the basilica, the mosaics in the atrium depict scenes from the Old Testament.

The atrium gives access to the **Galleria e Museo marciano** ⊘ where are displayed the **gilded bronze horses**★★.

Interior – The dazzling decoration of St Mark's combines the luminous mosaics (1071) by artists from Constantinople and a 12C pavement decorated with animal and geometric motifs – its uneven surface has been caused by subsidence. An iconostasis separates the raised presbytery (sanctuary) from the nave. Beyond, a ciborium raised on **alabaster columns**★★ precedes the Golden Altarpiece **(Pala d'Oro★★★)** ⊘, a masterpiece of Gothic art dating from the early 10C. The relics of St Mark rest in the main altar.

Piazza San Marco

The mosaic decoration depicts the New Testament, starting with the dome of the apse with Christ as *Pantocrator* and ending with the *Last Judgement* in the area above the atrium. Near the entrance, the Arch of the Apocalypse illustrates the visions described in the gospel of St John. The dome nearest the doorway is dedicated to Pentecost. As one approaches the central dome, the west arch presents a synthesis of the Passion and Death of Christ. The south arch opening onto the south transept depicts the Temptation of Christ and His Entry into Jerusalem, the Last Supper and the Washing of the Feet. In the centre is the Dome of the Ascension depicting the Apostles, the Virgin, the Virtues and the Beatitudes. Christ in Benediction dominates the scene. The Presbytery Dome is dedicated to the Season of Advent. The mosaics on the North Arch giving onto the north transept, are after cartoons by Tintoretto (St Michael, Last Supper and Marriage at Cana) and Veronese (Healing of the Leper). The Dome of St John the Evangelist in the left transept illustrate the Sermon on the Mount and scenes from the Life of St John the Evangelist.

The south transept gives access to the treasury **(tesoro★)** ⊘ which contains a collection of religious objects and ornaments which came into Venice's possession after the conquest of Constantinople.

★★ **Campanile (Q)** ⊘ – The bell-tower (99m – 325ft high) which dominates the square is the symbol of Venice. It is a careful reconstruction of the 15C campanile which collapsed in 1902. The **panorama**★★ from the top extends from the Guidecca Canal to the Grand Canal across a sea of roofs and beyond, to the islands in the lagoon. At the base of the campanile is the **Loggetta Sansoviniana**; statues of Minerva, Apollo, Mercury and Peace adorn the niches. The terrace is enclosed by a balustrade punctuated by a 17C gate.

★★★ PALAZZO DUCALE (DOGES' PALACE) ⊘

The palace was a symbol of Venetian power and glory, and was the residence of the doges and the seat of government and the law courts as well as being a prison. It was built in the 12C but was completely transformed between the end of the 13C and the 16C.

A pretty, geometric pattern in white and pink marble lends great charm to the two façades. The groups at the corners of the palace represent, from left to right, the *Judgement of Solomon* (probably by Bartolomeo Bon), Adam and Eve, and *Noah's Drunkenness* (14C-15C Gothic sculptures). The small loggia on the first floor is a delicate structure with quatrefoil motifs.

The main entrance is the **Porta della Carta**★★, so called perhaps because of the scribes who worked there or the archives kept inside. It is in the Flamboyant-Gothic style (1442) and has on its tympanum a Lion of St Mark before which kneels Doge Foscari (19C copy). The gateway leads into the Porticato Foscari; directly opposite is the Giants' Staircase **(Scala dei Giganti)** dominated by statues of Mars and Neptune by Sansovino.

Interior – Start at the top of Sansovino's Golden Staircase **(Scala d'Oro★★★)** and pass through a suite of rooms as follows: the Room of the Four Doors **(Sala delle Quattro Porte)** where the ambassadors waited for their audience with the doge; an antechamber **(Sala dell'Antecollegio)** for diplomatic missions and delegations; the College Chamber **(Sala del Collegio)** where the doge presided over meetings; the Senate Chamber or Pregadi Chamber **(Sala del Senato o "dei Pregadi")** where the members of the Senate submitted their written request to participate in the meetings. The Chamber of the Council of Ten **(Sala del Consiglio dei Dieci)** is where met the powerful magistrates who used the secret police and spies to safeguard the institutions. Beyond the **Sala della Bussola**, the waiting-room for those awaiting interrogation and the armoury (Armeria) is the Grand Council Chamber **(Sala del Maggior Consiglio)**. In this vast room (1 300m² – 14 000sq ft) sat the legislative body which appointed all public officials; here also was conducted the constitutional election of the new doge. In the chamber hang paintings and portraits of 76 doges as well as Tintoretto's *Paradise*. Proceed to the Ballot Chamber **(Sala dello Scrutinio)** where the counting of the votes took place; the new prisons **(Prigione Nuove)**, the Bridge of Sighs (Ponte dei Sospiri). Further along are the Censors' Chamber **(Sala dei Censori)**, the seat of the judiciary body, and the Avogaria Chamber (Sala dell'Avogaria) – the *avogadori* were lawyers appointed by the state whose duty was to ensure that the law was obeyed.

★★ **Ponte dei Sospiri (Bridge of Sighs) (FV)** – The Bridge of Sighs connects the Doges' Palace with the prisons **(Prigioni Nuove)**. It was built in the 16C-17C and owes its name to romantic literary notions which held that the prisoners would suffer their final torment at the enchanting view of Venice from the window.

Torre dell'Orologio (N) ⊙ – At the top of the Clock Tower which dates from the late 15C are the famous Moors *(Mori)*, a pair of giant bronze jacks, which strike the hours.

★★ **Museo Correr (EV)** ⊙ – Next to the Ara Napoleonica which bounds the square to the west is a museum which traces the 1 000 year-old history of the city: paintings, sculpture and artefacts.

★ **Libreria Sansoviniana (EV)** – This noble and harmonious building was designed by Sansovino in 1553. At No 7 is a library (Biblioteca Nazionale Marciana) where it is possible to view manuscripts, maps and engravings.

★★ CANAL GRANDE (GRAND CANAL)

The Grand Canal (3km – 2miles long, between 30km and 70km – 18-44 miles wide and, on average, 5.5m – 18ft deep) takes the form of an inverted S and affords the best view of the palazzi.

Left Bank

★★ **Palazzo Labia (BT)** ⊙ – The elegant late-18C residence of the Labia family who were Spanish merchants.

★ **Palazzo Vendramin-Calergi (CT)** – An early-16C mansion, the residence of the Codussi, where Wagner lived and died.

★★ **Ca' d'Oro (DT)** ⊙ – Although it has lost the gilded decoration which gave it its name, the mansion retains an elegant façade in the ornate Gothic style. It houses the **Galleria Franchetti** which displays a fine *St Sebastian* by Mantegna.

★★ **Ponte di Rialto (ET)** – The Rialto Bridge was built by Antonio da Ponte and was opened in 1591. The present structure is the sixth version but the first one built of stone. It is the main crossing between the two banks. The original 12C bridge was built of wood.

★ **Palazzo Grassi (BV)** – It was built in the 18C by Giorgio Massari and was the last great Venetian palace to be constructed before the fall of the Republic. It is the venue for major exhibitions.

Right Bank

★ **Ca' Pesaro (DT)** – The palace built by Longhena has an unusual ground floor with diamond-pointed rustication. It is the home of the Museum of Oriental Art **(Museo d'arte orientale)** ⊙ and the International Gallery of Modern Art **(Galleria internazionale di arte moderna)** ⊙.

★★ **Ca' Rezzonico (BV)** – This was the last palace designed by Longhena which was completed by Massari. It houses the Museum of 18C Venice **(Museo del Settecento Veneziano)** ⊙.

★ **Ca' Dario (DV)** – The small late-15C palazzo is embellished with polychrome marble decoration. It has gained a sinister reputation owing to the death in suspicious circumstances of several of its owners.

Ca' d'Oro

★★★ GALLERIE DELL'ACCADEMIA (ACADEMY OF FINE ARTS) (BV) ⓥ

The Academy presents the most important collection of Venetian art from the 14C to the 18C. Masterpieces include a *Madonna enthroned* and the *Virgin and Child between St Catherine and Mary Magdalene* by Giovanni Bellini; the *Calling of the Sons of Zebedee* by Marco Basaiti; *St George* by Andrea Mantegna; *The Tempest* by Giorgione, the crystallisation of a state of mind rather than the representation of a specific moment; a *Portrait of a young gentleman* in his study by Lorenzo Lotto, which suggests that the sitter is distracted from his book by a thought or memory; an impressive but sinister *Pietà* by Titian; *Christ in the House of Levi* by Veronese; the cycle of luminous paintings of the *Miracles of the Relics of the True Cross* by Gentile Bellini and Carpaccio. The latter also painted the colourful and magical series of canvasses relating the *Story of St Ursula*.

CHURCHES

★★ **Santa Maria della Salute** (DV) – The church, dedicated to St Mary of Salvation, was built in the 17C to fulfil a vow by the Venetians and marking the end of a plague epidemic (1630). The white church designed by Longhena is a distinctive feature with its modillions and concentric volutes (*orrechioni* – big ears). In the sacristy hangs a *Wedding at Cana* by Tintoretto in which the artist has included himself as the first Apostle on the left.

★ **San Giorgio Maggiore** (FV) – The church on the Island of San Giorgio, was designed by Palladio. The top of the tall campanile affords the finest **vista★★★** of Venice. In the presbytery (sanctuary) hang two large paintings by Tintoretto, the *Last Supper* and the *Harvest of Manna*.

★★ **San Zanipolo** (FT) – The square in which stands an **equestrian statue★★** of the mercenary leader Bartolomeo **Colleoni** by Verrocchio is flanked by the deceptive perspective of St Mark's School **(Scuola Grande di San Marco★)** to one side, and is dominated by the Gothic church of Santi Giovanni e Paolo, dedicated to St John and St Paul (in the Venetian dialect Zanipolo is a contraction of the two names). The grandiose and solemn church is a fitting setting as the burial place for the doges and is lit by the brightly-coloured stained glass windows in the right transept.

★★ **I Frari** (BTU) ⊘ – This great Franciscan church – its name is derived from the abbreviation of Fra*(ti Mino)*ri – can be compared to San Zanipolo on account of its imposing appearance and its funerary monuments. The focal point of the perspective is an *Assumption of the Virgin* by Titian in the main chapel, Cappella Maggiore.

★★ **San Zaccaria** (FV) – The Renaissance-Gothic Church of St Zachary has a tall white façade with its three tiers of round-headed windows; it is visible from the windows of the Palazzo Ducale. The interior is covered with paintings; the most important is Giovanni Bellini's *Sacra Conversazione*, a work of great sensitivity.

The Venetian Scuole

Instituted during the Middle Ages, the Scuole (literally meaning schools) were lay guilds drawn from the middle classes which were active in all aspects of life, be it devotional, charitable and professional, until the fall of the Republic. Each school had its own patron saint and Mariegola, a rule book and constitution of the guild.

In the 15C the scuole were housed in magnificent palaces with their interiors decorated by famous artists.

To appreciate the rich artistic heritage of the guild, visit the **Scuola Grande di San Rocco**★★★ (BU) ⊘, decorated with scenes of the Old and New Testaments by Tintoretto, and the **Scuola di San Giorgio degli Schiavoni**★★★ (FU) ⊘, a perfect setting for the exquisite paintings in warm colours by Carpaccio relating the lives of St George, St Tryphon and St Jerome.

OTHER AREAS AND MUSEUMS OF VENICE

Arsenale (FGUV) – There was a dockyard in Venice as early as 1104 when the crusades stimulated shipbuilding activity. The Arsenal is enclosed by a medieval wall punctuated by towers and has two entrances: the land gateway surmounted by lions from Ancient Greece, and the water gate marked by two towers through which passes the *vaporetto*.

★★ **Ghetto** (BT) – The Jewish quarter (ghetto) is a hauntingly beautiful and secret corner of the Canneregio district close to the bustling Strada Nuova. It was the first Jewish quarter to be differentiated as such in Western Europe. In the Venetian dialect the term *geto* referred to a local mortar foundry. The g, normally pronounced soft (as in George) was hardened by the first Jews who came from Germany. The term ghetto now evokes the persecutions endured by the Jewish people. A museum (Museo ebraico) and synagogues (**sinagoghe**) ⊘ are open to visitors.

Giudecca (AV-FV) – Giudecca Island offers visitors a simple, quiet charm as well as a glorious view of Venice.

The Palladian Church of the Redeemer (**Il Redentore**★), *(Fondamenta S. Giacomo)*, was built like Santa Maria della Salute after the 1576 plague. On the third Sunday in July the church celebrates the Feast of the Redeemer which ends with a spectacular fireworks display.

★ **Collezione Peggy Guggenheim** (DV M¹) ⊘ – An 18C palazzo where the American Peggy Guggenheim lived from the end of the Second World War until her death, is the setting for an interesting collection of paintings and sculpture by the best 20C artists.

★ **Fondazione Querini-Stampalia** (FU) ⊘ – The museum is a must for those interested in the Venice of old. There is a charming series of **panels**★★ by Pietro Longhi dedicated to the sacraments and to the hunt.

LAGOON

See the plan of the lagoon in the current Michelin Green Guide Venice.

Lido – Venice's seaside resort on the Adriatic has a slightly decadent air. It has a casino, which is one of the few in Italy, and hosts a Film F.estival.

★★ **Murano** – By the end of the 13C, the threat of devastating fire was constant in Venice with its wooden buildings and the Grand Council decided to move the glassworks away from the city to Murano. It became known as the glassmaking island and a museum (**Museo di arte vetraria**★) ⊘ displays a unique collection of glassware. The furnaces, the shouts of the vendors coaxing visitors into the glassware shops, should not detract from the artistic atmosphere of the island. The apse of the fine basilica, **Santi Maria e Donato★★**, is a masterpiece of 12C Veneto-Byzantine art and the **mosaic floor★★** recalls that of St Mark's.

★★ **Burano** – This is the most colourful of the islands in the lagoon. At the doors and windows of the brightly painted houses the women are engaged in lace-making.

★★ **Torcello** – It is almost a ghost island where only the stones speak of its glorious past. In 639 The inhabitants of Altinum fleeing from the Lombards settled on the island and built a church. Torcello became a See. The 10C witnessed the glorious ascent of Venice whose power extended over the lagoon; an aura of gloom pervaded the island as malaria decimated the population.
The noble Churches of **Santa Maria Assunta** and **Santa Fosca** and ruined buildings stand in a square overgrown with grass. The deserted air of the island is offset by the bright **mosaics★★** in the cathedral: in the *Last Judgement* Torcello seems to be repopulated as the sound of the angels' trumpets summons the dead from the bowels of the sea monsters that devoured them.

★ **Brenta Riviera** – *See Riviera del BRENTA.*

VERONA★★★

Veneto – Population 255 313
Michelin map 988 fold 4 or 428, 429 F 14/15
Town plan in the current Michelin Red Guide Italia

Verona stands on the banks of the Adige in a hilly setting and is, after Venice, the finest art centre in Venetia. The fashionable **Piazza Bra (ABVX)** is linked by the Via Mazzini (**BV**) to the heart of the old town. The opera and theatre summer seasons *(see the Calendar of Events at the end of the guide)* both draw large crowds.
This Roman colony under the Empire was coveted by the Ostrogoths, Lombards and Franks. The town reached the peak of its glory under the **Scaliger**, Princes of the Scala, who governed for the emperor from 1260 to 1387. Then it passed to the Visconti of Milan before submitting to Venetian rule from 1405. Verona was occupied by the Austrians in 1814 and united as part of the Veneto with Italy in 1866.

Romeo and Juliet – These two young people, immortalised by Shakespeare, belonged to rival families: Romeo to the Montecchi (Montagues), who were Guelphs and supported the Pope, and Juliet to the Capuleti (Capulets), who were Ghibellines and supported the Emperor. Verona was the setting for this drama which took place in 1302 when conflicts between the two factions raged.

Pisanello and the Veronese School – Artists of this school were influenced by northern art from the Rhine Valley and they developed a Gothic art which combined flowing lines with a meticulous attention to detail.
Pisanello (c1395-c1450), a great traveller, active painter, prodigious medal-maker and enthusiastic draughtsman, was the greatest exponent of this school. His painting, with the soft colours, the meticulous details and flowing lines, was reminiscent of the rapidly-disappearing medieval world and heralded the realism typical of the Renaissance.

SIGHTS

★★ **Piazza delle Erbe (BV)** – The Square of Herbs was the former Roman forum and it is today attractive and lively, especially on market day.
In line, down the middle of the square, stand the market column; the *capitello* (a rostrum from which decrees and sentences were proclaimed) of the 16C governors *(podesti)*; the fountain known as the Verona Madonna, with a Roman statue symbolising the town; and a Venetian column surmounted by the winged Lion of St Mark (1523).
Palaces and old houses, some with pink marble columns and frescoes, make an attractive framework round the square: on the north side is the Baroque **Palazzo Maffei (B)**.
In the Via Cappello (No 23) is Juliet's House **(Casa di Giulietta)** ⊘; in fact it is a Gothic palace which belonged to the Capulet family; the famous balcony is in the inner courtyard.

★★ **Piazza dei Signori (BV)** – Take Via della Costa to reach this elegant square which resembles an open-air drawing-room. On the right is the 12C **Palazzo del Comune** (Town Hall) (**D**) ⊘, also known as the Palazzo della Ragione dominated by the

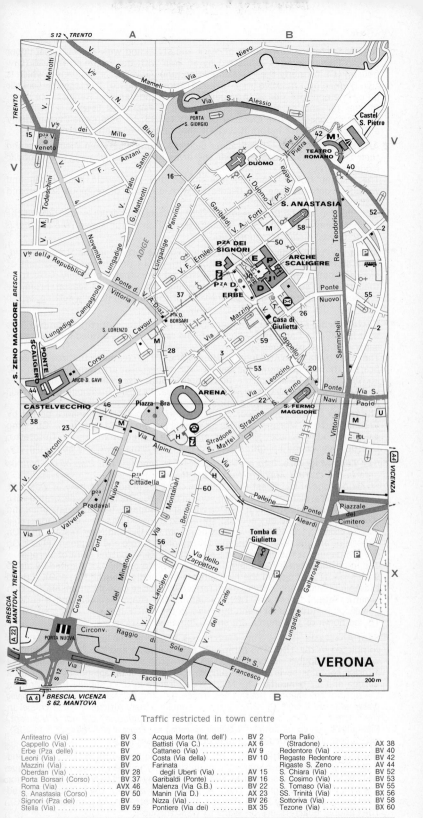

VERONA

Traffic restricted in town centre

B Palazzo Maffei	**E** Loggia del Consiglio	**M¹** Museo archeologico
D Palazzo del Comune	**J¹** Palazzo dei Tribunali	**P** Palazzo del Governo

Use the Map of Principal Sights to plan a special itinerary

Torre dei Lamberti, a tower built of brick and stone and with an octagonal upper storey. This building is connected by an arch with the **Palazzo dei Tribunali** (Law Courts) (**J'**), formerly the Palazzo del Capitano (Governor's Residence) which is also flanked by a massive brick tower, Torrione Scaligero. The **Loggia del Consiglio** (**E**) on the opposite side is an elegant edifice in the Venetian-Renaissance style. At the far end of the square the late-13C **Palazzo del Governo** (**P**) with its machicolations and fine Classical doorway (1533) by Sammicheli was initially a Scaliger residence before it became that of the Venetian Governors.

★★ **Arche Scaligere** (**BV**) – The Scaliger built their tombs between their palace and their church. The sarcophagi bear the arms of the family, with the symbolic ladder *(scala)*.

The elegant Gothic mausolea are surrounded by marble balustrades and wrought-iron rails, and are decorated with carvings of religious scenes and statues of saints in niches.

Over the door of the Romanesque Church of **Santa Maria Antica** is the tomb of the popular Cangrande I (d 1329) with his equestrian statue above *(the original is in the Castelvecchio Museum)*.

★★ **Arena** (**BVX**) ⊘ – This amphitheatre, among the largest in the Roman world, could accommodate 25 000 spectators with its 44 tiers of seats. It is built of blocks of pink marble, flint and brick; this indicates that it probably dates from the late 1C. In summer it is the venue for a prestigious opera season. From the topmost row there is a good **panorama**★★ of the town in its hilly setting, which on a clear day reaches as far as the Alps.

★★ **Castelvecchio** and **Ponte Scaligero** (**AV**) – This splendid fortified complex was built in 1354 by Cangrande II Scaliger. The castle itself is divided into two parts separated by a passageway guarded by a keep.

The castle contains an Art Museum **(Museo d'Arte★★)** ⊘ created by the architect Carlo Scarpa. The **collection** shows the development of Veronese art from the 12C to 16C and its links with Venice and the International Gothic *(see Index)*. There are frescoes by local artists and canvases by Stefano da Verona, Pisanello, Giambono, Carlo Crivelli (splendid *Madonna of the Passion*), Mantegna, Carpaccio as well as the Bellinis.

The rooms on the upper floor contain works from the Renaissance period by Veronese artists: Morone, Liberale da Verona *(Virgin with a Goldfinch)*, Girolamo dai Libri and Veronese. There are also some Venetian works by Tintoretto, Guardi, Tiepolo and Longhi. Also on display are arms, jewellery and sculpture.

★★ **San Zeno Maggiore** – *Access via Rigaste San Zeno* (**AV** 44). *Plan of the built-up area in the current Michelin Red Guide Italia.*

St Zeno is one of the finest Romanesque churches in northern Italy. It was built on the basilical plan in the Lombard style in the 12C. The façade is decorated with Lombard bands and arcading; the side walls and campanile have alternate brick and stone courses. In the entrance porch resting on two lions, there are admirable bronze **doors**★★★ (11C-12C) with scenes from the Old and New Testaments. On either side are low reliefs by the master sculptors Nicolò and Guglielmo (12C). On the tympanum of the doorway is a statue of St Zeno, patron saint of Verona.

The imposing interior has a lofty, bare nave with a cradle roof flanked by aisles with shallow roofing. On the high altar is a splendid **triptych**★★ (1459), a good example of Mantegna's style characterised by precise draughtsmanship and rich ornamentation. There are 14C statues on the chancel screen and a curious polychrome statue of St Zeno laughing in the north apse.

To the north of the church are small Romanesque cloisters.

★ **Sant'Anastasia** (**BV**) – This church was begun at the end of the 13C and completed in the 15C. The campanile is remarkable and the façade is pierced with a 14C double doorway adorned with frescoes and sculpture. The lofty interior contains several masterpieces: four **figures of the apostles** by Michele da Verona and 17 **terracottas**★ by Michele da Firenze in the Cappella Pellegrini, on the right of the chancel; the famous fresco showing *Knights of the Cavalli family being presented to the Virgin*★ (1380) by the Veronese artist, Altichero (first chapel in the south transept); and in the **Cappella Giusti** ⊘ *(opening off the north transept)* Pisanello's fresco depicting *St George delivering the Princess of Trebizond*★★ (1436), which combines meticulous details and Gothic fantasy.

★ **Duomo** (**BV**) – The cathedral has a 12C Romanesque chancel, a Gothic nave and a Classical tower. The remarkable main doorway in the Lombard-Romanesque style is adorned with sculptures and low reliefs by Maestro Nicolò. The interior has fine pink marble pillars. The altarpiece *(first altar on the left)* is decorated with an *Assumption* by Titian. The marble chancel screen is by Sammicheli (16C). The canons' quarters are pleasant to walk through.

★ **Teatro romano** (**BV**) ⊘ – The Roman theatre dates from the time of Augustus but has been heavily restored. Theatrical performances are still given here.

A former monastery, **Convento di San Girolamo** *(access by lift)* has a small museum **(Museo Archeologico)** (**M'**) ⊘ and there is a lovely **view** over the town.

Castel San Pietro (BV) ⊙ – *Take the stairway which leads off Regaste Redentore* (**BV 42**). St Peter's Castle dates back to the Visconti and the period of Venetian rule. The terraces afford splendid **views**★★ of Verona.

★ **San Fermo Maggiore** (BVX) – The church, dedicated to St Firmanus Major, was built in the 11C-12C and remodelled at a later date. The façade is in the Romanesque and Gothic styles. The aisleless church is covered by a stepped, keel-shaped roof. On the left by the west door the Brenzoni mausoleum (1430) is framed by a fresco of the *Annunciation*★ by Pisanello.

Tomba di Giulietta (BX) ⊙ – *Via del Pontiere.* Juliet's tomb is in the cloisters of the Church of San Francesco al Corso, where, it is said, Romeo and Juliet were married.

VICENZA★★

Veneto – Population 107 318
Michelin map 988 folds 4 and 5 or 429 F 16
Town plan in the current Michelin Red Guide Italia

The proud and noble city of Vicenza lies in a pretty setting at the foot of the Berici Mountains. This busy commercial and industrial centre now has, in addition to its traditional textile industry, mechanical and chemical industries and a reputation as a gold-working centre. Vicenza is strategically set at the crossroads of routes between the Veneto and Trentino.
The gastronomic speciality of Vicenza is *baccalà alla Vicentina*, cod with a sauce served with slices of *polenta* (maize semolina), which is best with wine from the Berici Mountains (Barbarano, Gambellara and Breganze).

HISTORICAL AND ARTISTIC NOTES

The ancient Roman town of Vicetia became an independent city state in the 12C. After several conflicts with the neighbouring cities of Padua and Verona, Vicenza sought Venetian protection at the beginning of the 15C. This was a period of great prosperity, when Vicenza counted many rich and generous art patrons among its citizens and it was embellished with an amazing number of palaces.

Palladio – Vicenza was given the nickname of "Venice on *terra firma*" due to an exceptionally gifted man, Andrea di Pietro, known as Palladio, who spent many years in Vicenza. The last great architect of the Renaissance, Palladio was born at Padua in 1508 and died at Vicenza in 1580. He succeeded in combining, in a supremely harmonious idiom, the precepts of ancient art with the contemporary preoccupations. Encouraged by the humanist Trissino, he made several visits to Rome to study her monuments and the work of Vitruvius, a Roman architect of the time of Augustus. He perfected the Palladian style and in 1570 published his *Treatise on Architecture*, in four volumes, which made his work famous throughout Europe.
The **Palladian style** is characterised by rigorous plans where simple and symmetrical forms predominate and by harmonious façades which combine pediments and porticoes, as at San Giorgio Maggiore in Venice *(see VENEZIA)*. Palladio was often commissioned by wealthy Venetians to build residences in the countryside around Venice. He combined architectural rhythm, noble design and, in the case of the country mansions, a great sense of situation and decoration with the utmost attention being paid to the base, so that the villas seemed to rise like a series of new temples on the banks of the Brenta *(see Riviera del BRENTA)* or the slopes of the Berici Mountains. His pupil, Vicenzo Scamozzi (1552-1616), completed several of his master's works and carried on his style.

★★THE PALLADIAN CITY *1/2 day*

★★ **Piazza dei Signori** – Like St Mark's Square in Venice, it is an open-air meeting-place recalling the forum of antiquity. As in the Piazzetta in Venice, there are two columns bearing effigies of the Lion of St Mark and the Redeemer. With the lofty **Torre Bissara**★, a 12C belfry, the **Basilica**★★ ⊙ (1549-1617) occupies one whole side of the square. The elevation is one of Palladio's masterpieces, with two superimposed galleries in the Doric and Ionic orders, admirable for their power, proportion and purity of line. The great keel-shaped roof, destroyed by bombing, has been rebuilt. The building was not a church but a meeting-place for the Vicenzan notables. The 15C **Monte di Pietà** (pawn shop) opposite, with buildings framing the Baroque façade of the Church of San Vincenzo, is adorned with frescoes. The **Loggia del Capitano**★, formerly the residence of the Venetian Governor, which stands to the left, at the corner of the Contrà del Monte, was begun to the plans of Palladio in 1571 and left unfinished. It is characterised by its colossal orders with composite capitals and its statues and stuccoes commemorating the naval victory of Lepanto *(see Index)*.

★★ **Teatro Olimpico** ⊙ – This splendid building in wood and stucco was designed by Palladio in 1580 on the model of the theatres of antiquity. The tiers of seats are laid out in a hemicycle and surmounted by a lovely **colonnade** with a balustrade crowned with statues. The **stage★★★** is one of the finest in existence with its superimposed niches, columns and statues and its amazing perspectives painted in *trompe-l'œil* by Scamozzi who completed the work.

★ **Corso Andrea Palladio** – This, the main street of Vicenza, and several neighbouring streets are embellished by many palaces designed by Palladio and his pupils. At the beginning is the **Palazzo Chiericati** *(see below)*, an imposing work by Palladio; at No 147 the 15C **Palazzo Da Schio** in the Venetian-Gothic style was formerly known as the Ca d'Oro (Golden House) because it was covered with frescoes with gilded backgrounds. The west front of **Palazzo Thiene** overlooking Contrà S. Gaetano Thiene was by Palladio, while the entrance front at No 12 Contrà Porti is Renaissance dating from the late 15C.
The **Palazzo Porto-Barbaran** opposite is also by Palladio. At No 98 the **Palazzo Trissino** (1592) is one of Scamozzi's most successful works. Next is the Corso Fogazzaro, where the **Palazzo Valamarana** (1566) at No 16 is another work by Palladio.

★ **Museo Civico** ⊙ – The municipal museum is housed on the first floor of Palazzo Chiericati. The collection of paintings includes Venetian Primitives (*The Dormition of the Virgin* by Paolo Veneziano); a *Crucifixion*★★ by Hans Memling; canvases by Bartolomeo Montagna (pupil of Giovanni Bellini), Mantegna and Carpaccio, one of the most active artists in Vicenza. There are Venetian works by Lorenzo Lotto, Veronese, Bassano, Piazzetta, Tiepolo and Tintoretto as well as Flemish works by Velvet Brueghel and Van Dyck.

ADDITIONAL SIGHTS

Santa Corona – *Contrà Santa Corona.* The church was built in the 13C in honour of a Holy Thorn presented by St Louis, King Louis IX of France, to the Bishop of Vicenza. The nave and two aisles have pointed vaulting while the chancel is Renaissance. Works of art include: a *Baptism of Christ*★★ by Giovanni Bellini *(fifth altar on the left)* and an *Adoration of the Magi*★★ (1573) by Veronese *(third chapel on the right)*. The fourth chapel on the right has a lovely coffered **ceiling★**, richly painted and adorned with gilded stucco, and a *Mary Magdalene and Saints* by Bartolomeo Montagna.

Duomo – The cathedral, built between the 14C and 16C, has an attractively-colourful Gothic façade and a Renaissance east end. Inside, the lovely **polyptych★** (1356) is by Lorenzo Veneziano *(fifth chapel on the right)*.

Giardino Salvi – This garden is attractively adorned with statues and fountains. Canals run along two sides of the garden and two lovely Palladian 16C and 17C loggias are reflected in the waters.

EXCURSIONS

★★ **Villa Valmarana "ai Nani"** ⊙ – *2km – 1 mile south by the Este road and then the first road to the right.* The villa dates from the 17C and was adorned in 1757 with splendid **frescoes★★★** by **Gian Domenico Tiepolo**, the son. He portrays with plenty of verve and vigour the different aspects of daily life in the province and in particular, carnival scenes.

★ **La Rotonda** ⊙ – *2km – 1 mile southeast by the Este road and then the second road to the right.* The Rotonda is one of Palladio's most famous creations and the plan of Chiswick House in London was inspired by it. The gracefully-proportioned square building is roofed with a dome and fronted on each side by a pedimented portico, making it look like an ancient temple.

★ **Monte Berico Basilica** and **Monti Berici** – *2km – 1 mile south by Viale Venezia and then Viale X Giugno.* As the Viale X Giugno climbs uphill, it is lined with an 18C portico and chapels. On the summit is the baroque basilica roofed with a dome. From the esplanade there is a wide **panorama★★** of Vicenza, the Venetian plain and the Alps. Inside, there is a *Pietà* (1500) by Bartolomeo Montagna. From here the road runs southwards to Arcugnano and Barbarano, where one can catch occasional glimpses of former patrician villas now used as farmhouses in this attractive countryside of volcanic hills.

Montecchio Maggiore – *13km – 8 miles southwest by the S 11.* The ruins of these two castles remind one of Romeo and Juliet. There are good **views★** of the Po Plain and Vicenza.
On the outskirts of Montecchio on the Tavernelle road the **Villa Cordellina-Lombardi** ⊙ has one room entirely covered with **frescoes★** by Tiepolo.

Villas and palaces by the 16C architect Palladio are to be found at Malcontenta, Maser and Vicenza.

VITERBO*

Lazio – Population 58 370
Michelin map 988 fold 25 or 430 O 18
Town plan in the current Michelin Red Guide Italia

Viterbo, still girdled by its walls, has kept its medieval aspect notably in the **San Pellegrino quarter★★**, a working-class area with many craftsmen. Here there are typical vaulted passageways, towers and external staircases.

★★ Piazza San Lorenzo – This square, which occupies the site of the former Etruscan acropolis, takes one back to the Middle Ages with a 13C house on Etruscan foundations (now a chemist's), its cathedral dating from 1192 and adorned with a fine Gothic campanile, and its 13C Papal Palace **(Palazzo dei Papi★★)** – one of the most interesting examples of medieval secular architecture in Lazio. From the Piazza Martiri d'Ungheria there is a lovely view of the piazza.

Museo Civico ⊘ – *Piazza F. Crispi.* The municipal museum is housed in the former Monastery of Santa Maria della Verità and contains collections of Etruscan and Roman objects discovered in the area: sarcophagi and grave artefacts from the tombs. The picture gallery, on the first floor, has a terracotta by the Della Robbias as well as works by Salvator Rosa, Sebastiano del Piombo and a local painter, Pastura (15C-16C).

EXCURSIONS

Madonna della Quercia – *3km – 2 miles northeast.* The church, dedicated to the Madonna of the Oak *(quercia)*, is in the Renaissance style with a rusticated façade and tympana by Andrea della Robbia. The cloisters are part Gothic, part Renaissance.

★★ Villa Lante in Bagnaia ⊘ – *5km – 3 miles northeast.* This elegant 16C villa was built to the designs of Vignola and became the residence of several popes. A lovely Italian terraced garden with geometric motifs and numerous fountains makes an ideal setting for the villa.

★ Teatro romano di Ferento ⊘ – *9km – 6 miles north.* The 1C BC Roman theatre is quite well preserved and is the most important vestige of the ancient Ferentium, the ruins of which lie scattered over a melancholy plateau. The theatre ruins stand between the road and the Decumanus and consist of a brick back wall as well as a portico of well-dressed blocks without any mortar, and 13 tiers of seats.

Bomarzo – *21km – 13 miles northeast by the S 204.* Extending below the town is the park **(Parco dei Mostri)** of the 16C **Villa Orsini** ⊘ which is a Mannerist creation adorned with a series of fantastically shaped **sculptures★**.

Montefiascone – *17km – 11 miles northwest.* Montefiascone stands in the vineyard country which produces the delicious white wine *Est, Est, Est.*
The imposing cathedral **(Duomo)** has a dome designed by Sammicheli, while a curious church, **San Flaviano★**, in the Lombard-Romanesque style is in reality two churches superimposed. In the lower church, frescoes illustrate the *Story of the Three Dead and the Three Living Men* symbolising the brevity and vanity of human life; opposite stands the tombstone of Johann Fugger, the German prelate who died on his way to Rome. As he was fond of good food and wine, he sent one of his servants ahead of him with orders to mark the inns where the wine was the best, with the word *est* ("is" short for *Vinum est bonum* in Latin). When he arrived at Montefiascone the faithful servant found the wine so good that he wrote, in his enthusiasm, "*Est, Est, Est*". And his master, becoming enthusiastic in his turn, drank so much, much, much of it that he died.

★ Lago di Vico – *18km – 11 miles southeast by the Via Santa Maria di Gradi.* This solitary but charming lake occupies a crater with forested slopes (beech, chestnut, oak and on the lake shores, hazel trees).

Civita Castellana – *36km – 22 miles southeast.* Civita Castellana occupies the site of the Etruscan city Falerii Veteres which was destroyed by the Romans in 241, but rebuilt in the 8C or 9C. The cathedral **(Duomo)** is fronted by an elegant **portico★** built in 1210 by the Cosmati *(see Index)*.
The late-15C castle **(Rocca)** was built by Sangallo the Elder and became the residence of Cesare Borgia.

MICHELIN GREEN GUIDES

Art and Architecture; Ancient monuments; History; Landscape; Scenic routes
Touring programmes; local maps; town plans; site plans

A selection of guides for holidays at home and abroad

VOLTERRA★★

Tuscany – Population 12 855
Michelin map 988 fold 14 or 430 L 14

The Tuscan hills, very different from those around Florence, a commanding position and well-preserved walls make a harmonious setting for the Etruscan, Roman and medieval town of Volterra. The town has numerous alabaster workshops. Large salt pans to the west are used in the manufacture of fine salt and soda. To the northwest of the town there is a view of the **Balze**★, impressive precipices, which are part of a highly-eroded landscape furrowed by gully erosion.

★★ **Piazza dei Priori** – The piazza is surrounded by austere palaces. The 13C Palazzo Pretorio has paired windows and is linked with the Torre del Podestà, also known as Torre del Porcellino because of the wild boar sculpted high up on a bracket. The early-13C Palazzo dei Priori, opposite, is decorated with terracotta, marble and stone shields of the Florentine governors.

★ **Duomo** and **Battistero** – The cathedral in the Pisan-Romanesque style, although it has been remodelled several times, stands in the picturesque Piazza San Giovanni. The interior comprises a nave and two aisles with monolithic columns and 16C capitals. On the second altar in the nave, on the left is a lovely late-15C *Annunciation*. The transept contains, in the north arm, a *Virgin* of the 15C Sienese school, and in the south arm, a 13C painted wooden sculpture, *Descent from the Cross*★★. The nave has a superb 17C pulpit with 12C low reliefs. The octagonal baptistery dates from 1283.
Take the Via Roma and then pass through the Arco Buomparenti.

Via dei Sarti – This street is lined with palaces: No 1, Palazzo Minucci-Solaini attributed to Antonio da Sangallo which now houses the art gallery *(see below)*, and No 37, the Palazzo Incontri (now Palazzo Viti) with its superb Renaissance façade designed by Ammanati.

Pinacoteca ⊙ – *1 Via dei Sarti.* The Art Gallery displays numerous works of art by 14C to 17C Tuscan artists, notably a lovely *Annunciation* by Luca Signorelli and a *Descent from the Cross*, a masterpiece of Florentine Mannerism by Rosso Fiorentino.

★ **Museo Etrusco Guarnacci** ⊙ – More than 600 Etruscan funerary urns, made of tufa, alabaster and terracotta, make up the exhibition.

★ **Porta all'Arco** – This Etruscan gateway is built of colossal blocks of stone.

Rovine romane – 1C BC Roman ruins lie to the west of the Porta Fiorentina.

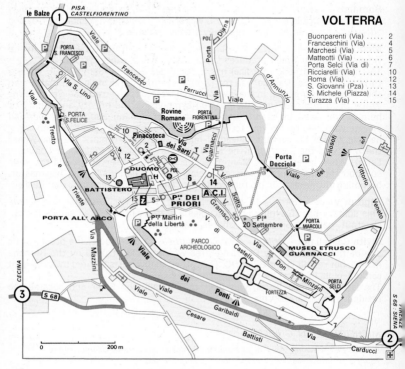

VOLTERRA

Buonparenti (Via)	2
Franceschini (Via)	4
Marchesi (Via)	5
Matteotti (Via)	6
Porta Selci (Via di)	7
Ricciarelli (Via)	10
Roma (Via)	12
S. Giovanni (Pza)	13
S. Michele (Piazza)	14
Turazza (Via)	15

Traffic restrictions in town centre

Porta Docciola – At the end of a very long flight of steps is a fortified gate near which there is a curious medieval washtub.

Viale dei Ponti – The Viale is a favourite walk with Volterrans. It affords splendid **views**★★ of the Colli Metalliferi *(see below)*. Above stands the Fortezza, now used as a prison, an impressive mass of military architecture formed by the 14C Rocca Vecchia and the Rocca Nuova, built in 1472 with a keep and four corner towers.

EXCURSION

Larderello – *33km – 21 miles south by* ③. Larderello is situated in the heart of the **Colli Metalliferi**★ or metal-bearing hills as the name suggests. In the past they were mined for iron ore, copper and pyrites. Larderello is one of Tuscany's more unusual places with its desolate landscapes, the hissing of its volcanic steam jets, belching smoke from the blast furnaces and the rumble of machinery.

The Balze

Sardinia

With an area of 24 089km² - 9 300sq miles, Sardinia (Sardegna) is the largest island in the Mediterranean after Sicily. It has a population of over 1 630 000. The Punta la Marmora in the Gennargentu Mountains is its highest peak with an altitude of 1 834m - 6 017ft. Sardinia lies 200km - 124 miles off mainland Italy from which it is separated by the Tyrrhenian Sea, and 12km - 8 miles south of Corsica which it resembles in many ways. Both islands were part of the Primary Era Tyrrhenian shield which was later submerged during the Quaternary Era. The Island is quite mountainous and its scrub vegetation consists mainly of holm oaks and aromatic plants and shrubs, all typical of the Mediterranean basin.

Since prehistoric times the island has had a mainly pastoral economy and more than half of Sardinia is suitable for grazing. Ewes' milk is used to make the famous Sardinian cheese *(pecorino)* with its pronounced flavour.

The Sardinians often cook their meat over hot embers or on a spit, and pecorino cheese is used to flavour numerous dishes. Specialities include the roussette *(burrida)*, smoked ham of wild boar *(prosciutto di cinghiale)*, a strong meat stock with semolina balls *(succutundu)*, and meat patties *(impanadas)*. As for pastries, try the flaky pastry with a cream cheese filling deep-fried and dipped in sour honey *(seadas)*. Taste one of the local wines, red or white: Nuragus and Vernaccia (dry white wine from the Oristano region, which is taken as an aperitif) are the best known.

Historical notes - Sardinia has traces of human settlement going back to prehistoric times. The **nuraghi** or fortified tower houses date from the 2nd millennium BC and are the island's earliest monuments. These strange structures in the form of a truncated cone were built of huge blocks of stone without any mortar. The only opening was a low door with a massive stone lintel. Inside, each storey was roofed by a corbelled dome. The basic design evolved and towers were added and linked by stout walls, which reinforced the primitive structure. The *nuraghi* have a family resemblance to the brochs of Scotland. It is assumed that these fortified tower houses served as refuges in times of danger. The island has over 7 000 nuraghi with a large concentration between Porto Torres and Barumini.

Other native monuments from this period are the Giants' Tombs **(Tomba dei Giganti)** or collective graves, no doubt intended for the ruling families. Five hundred of these remain today and they are usually to be found at some distance from the nuraghic settlements.

The funeral chambers lined and roofed with megalithic slabs (like a dolmen) were preceded by an arc of standing stones. In form they resemble a horned gallery grave. The dressed central stone has a small entrance at ground level.

The first settlers were the Phoenicians, followed by the Carthaginians but these seafaring traders settled mainly along the coasts, avoiding the mountains, but clearing the Campidano Plain for grain cultivation. The Romans, however, completely colonised the island for its agricultural land. From the 6C to the 8C BC the Byzantines ruled over Sardinia. Following a period of comparative independence, the country was ruled by the Pisans and Genoese before falling to the Spanish and later to the Austrian Empire in 1713. It was not long before the Emperor exchanged Sardinia for Sicily with the Dukes of Savoy. The latter took the title of Kings of Sardinia. The various settlers left few artistic traces with the exception of the Pisans, whose influence can be detected in the Romanesque and Gothic, as well as Aragon and Catalan churches.

Sardinia today - The economy of Sardinia was for a long time based on agriculture and was essentially pastoral. More recently tourism and industry have been developed. The intense industrialisation programme has accentuated the differences between the modern urban way of life and that of the many Sardinian shepherds, clinging to their traditional ways. The Sardinians have retained their keen sense of honour and hospitality. They still speak their own language and wear their magnificent costumes on feast days. Many cottage industries are still popular with the women (baskets, carpets, tapestry and fabrics).

Access - **By air:** *see the current Michelin Red Guide Italia.*

By sea: *see the Michelin map 988 and 433 as well as the current Michelin Red Guide Italia.*

Sightseeing - A quick tour of the island can be made in five days (petrol pumps are few and far between on the east coast). The map overleaf locates the towns and sites described in the guide, and also indicates other beauty spots in small black type.

Use Michelin Maps with Michelin Guides

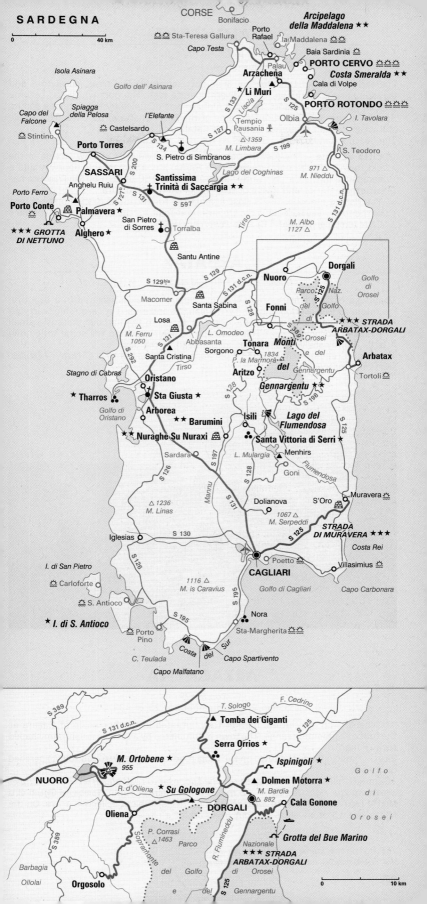

SARDEGNA

0   40 km

CORSE

Bonifacio

Arcipelago della Maddalena ★★

Sta-Teresa Gallura

Capo Testa

Porto Rafael
la Maddalena

Porto Rotondo

Arzachena ▲

Palau

Baia Sardinia

PORTO CERVO

Costa Smeralda ★★

Li Muri

Cala di Volpe

PORTO ROTONDO

Isola Asinara

Golfo dell' Asinara

l'Elefante

S 133

Liscia

S 125

Olbia

I. Tavolara

S. Teodoro

Capo del Falcone

Spiagga della Pelosa

Castelsardo

S 127

Tempio Pausania
△ 1359
M. Limbara

S 199

Stintino

S 134

S. Pietro di Simbranos †

Lago del Coghinas

971 △
M. Nieddu

S 131 d.c.n.

Porto Torres

S 200

SASSARI

Anghelu Ruiu

Santissima †
Trinità di Saccargia ★★

S 597

M. Albo
1127 △

Porto Ferro

S 727³

S 131

Porto Conte

Palmavera ★

San Pietro di Sorres †

Torralba

★★★ GROTTA DI NETTUNO

Alghero ★

Santu Antine

Tirso

S 129 bis

S 129

S 131 d.c.n.

Nuoro

Dorgali

Golfo di Orosei

Macomer

Santa Sabina

S 128

Fonni

Parco   Naz.
del   Golfo
di

Losa

△ M. Ferru
1050

S 131

Abbasanta

Sorgono

Tonara

Monti

Orosei

★★★ STRADA ARBATAX-DORGALI

Santa Cristina ▲

Tirso

P. la Marmora
△ 1834

del

Arbatax

Stagno di Cabras

S 292

Oristano

Aritzo

del

Gennargentu

Gennargentu

Tortoli

★ Tharros

Sta Giusta ★

S 128

S 198

Arborea

Golfo di Oristano

★★ Barumini

Isili

Lago del Flumendosa

S 125

★★ Nuraghe Su Nuraxi ⌂

Sardara

Santa Vittoria di Serri ★

S 126

L. Mulargia

Menhirs ▲

Goni

Flumendosa

△ 1236
M. Linas

S 197

S 128

S 131

Dolianova

S'Oro

Muravera

S 130

△ 1067
M. Serpeddi

S 125

STRADA DI MURAVERA ★★★

Iglesias

Costa Rei

I. di San Pietro

S 126

S 125

Villasimius

⌂ Carloforte

1116 △
M. is Caravius

CAGLIARI

Poetto

Capo Carbonara

⌂ S. Antioco

S 195

Golfo di Cagliari

★ I. di S. Antioco

Nora

S 195

Sta-Margherita

Porto Pino

C. Teulada

Costa del Sur

Capo Spartivento

Capo Malfatano

S 389

S 131 d.c.n.

T. Sologo

F. Cedrino

▲ Tomba dei Giganti

S 125

Serra Orrios ★

M. Ortobene ★
955

NUORO

★ Su Gologone

R. d'Oliena

Ispinigoli ★

▲ Dolmen Motorra ★

M. Bardia
△ 882

Cala Gonone

Golfo

di

Orosei

Oliena

▲ **DORGALI**

P. Corrasi
△ 1463

Parco

R. Flumineddu

Grotta del Bue Marino

Nazionale

★★★ STRADA ARBATAX-DORGALI

Barbagia

del

S 389

Sopramonte

Orgosolo

Ollolai

S 125

del
Gennargentu

Golfo

e

di   Orosei

0   10 km

ALGHERO ★

Population 39 056
Michelin map 988 fold 33 or 433 F 6

The early history of this pleasant little port set amid olive trees, eucalyptus and parasol pines is unknown. Coral divers operate from the port which has become popular as a seaside resort. In 1354 Alghero was occupied by the Catalans and its Spanish air has earned it the nickname of the Barcelonetta of Sardinia. The people still wear Catalan costumes and speak Catalan.
The beach extends 5km – 3 miles to the north of the village.

★ **Città Vecchia** – The fortifications encircle a network of narrow streets in the old town. The cathedral **(Duomo)** *(Via Roma)* has a remarkable doorway and a campanile in the Catalan-Gothic style. The 14C-15C Church of **San Francesco** has a Gothic interior and lovely **cloisters** in golden-coloured tufa.
The fishing harbour stands close against the fortifications in the northern part of the town. The harbour is the embarkation point for the boat trips to Neptune's Cave **(Grotta di Nettuno★★★)** *(see PORTO CONTE)*.

ARBATAX

Michelin map 988 fold 34 or 433 H 11

The name of this small port is Arab in origin. Arbatax is isolated in a beautiful mountain setting overlooking the Tyrrhenian Sea and is used by cargo ships carrying the island's exports of wood and cork. Not far from the harbour there is a small cliff face of porphyry rock. This outcrop has been exploited for some time now. A large, gently-shelving beach lies at the head of the bay.
The magnificent stretch of **road★★★** between Arbatax and Dorgali *(71km – 44 miles)* skirts impressive gorges.

East Coast, Arbatax

ARZACHENA

Pop 9 429
Michelin map 988 southeast of fold 23 or 433 O 10

Arzachena is an agricultural market town situated in the fine basin of Gallura at the foot of a mountain range. The town is dominated by a curious mushroom-shaped rock (Fungo).
2km – 1 mile outside the town on the Olbia road is a *nuraghe* (round tower) perched on a rock.
10km – 6 miles to the southwest *(by the Luogosanto road and after 7km – 4 miles a path to the right for 3km – 2 miles)* is the Giants' Tomb **(Tomba dei Giganti di Li Muri★)** *(see Introduction to SARDINIA)*, a particular type of collective grave. On the hilltop are 15 stone slabs laid out in an arc of a circle.

The key on the inside Front Cover explains
the abbreviations and symbols used in this guide

BARUMINI**

Pop 1 471
Michelin map 988 fold 33 or 433 H 9

The town of Barumini is surrounded by numerous traces of the earliest period of Sardinian history.

** **Nuraghe Su Nuraxi** – *2km – 1 mile west, on the left-hand side of the Tuili road.* This is an excellent example of a massive nuraghic fortress formed by several towers interconnected by galleries. To the east is a large nuraghic settlement.

* **Santa Vittoria di Serri** – *38km – 24 miles east by the Nuoro road and a road to the right in Nurallao.* There are remains of a prehistoric religious centre. On the way out pass through the village of **Isili** with two thriving craft industries (furniture-making and weaving).

S. Chirol

Nuraghic settlement

CAGLIARI

Pop 202 944
Michelin map 988 fold 33 or 433 J 9

Cagliari is the capital of the island. It is a modern-looking town with a busy harbour and an old nucleus surrounded by fortifications, built by the Pisans in the 13C. Before becoming Roman it was a flourishing Carthaginian city called Karalis.
The **Feast of St Efisio** (an officer in Diocletian's army who converted to Christianity and became the patron saint of Sardinia) is undoubtedly one of the most splendid in the whole of Italy *(see the Calendar of Events at the end of the guide).*
The **Terrazza Umberto** 1° (Z) affords a fine **view**★★ of the town, harbour and bay.

Cattedrale – Built in the 13C Pisan style, the cathedral was remodelled in the 17C. Inside are magnificent **pulpits**★★ (1162) by Guglielmo of Pisa with carved panels illustrating the Life of Christ. A little door on the right of the choir leads down to the Sanctuary or **Santuario**, a crypt with 17C decoration, which contains the remains of 292 Christian martyrs in urns placed along the walls.
A door opens on the right into a chapel containing the tomb of Marie-Louise of Savoy, the wife of the future King Louis XVIII of France and sister of the King of Sardinia.

* **Museo Archeologico Nazionale** ⊘ – The National Archeaological Museum has a large collection of arms, pottery and small **bronzes**★★★, grave artefacts from the earliest period of Sardinian history. Phoenician, Punic and Roman art are represented in the other rooms.

Torre dell'Elefante and **Torre San Pancrazio** – The early-14C Elephant and St Pancras towers were part of the Pisan fortifications.

Anfiteatro Romano – This amphitheatre is the most important Roman monument in Sardinia.

Orto Botanico ⊘ – The displays in the botanical garden are of both Mediterranean and tropical vegetation.

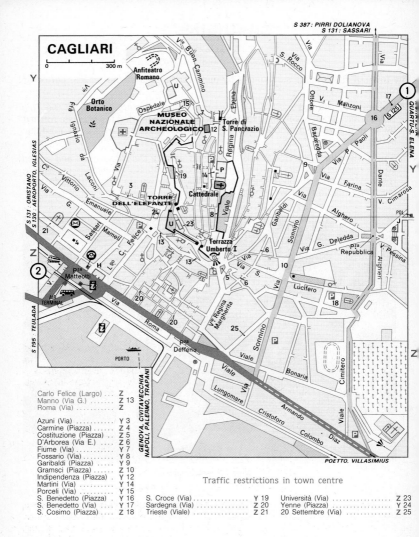

CAGLIARI

Traffic restrictions in town centre

Carlo Felice (Largo)	Z
Manno (Via G.)	Z 13
Roma (Via)	Z

Azuni (Via)	Z 3
Carmine (Piazza)	Z 4
Costituzione (Piazza)	Z 5
D'Arborea (Via E.)	Z 6
Fiume (Via)	Y 7
Fossario (Via)	Y 8
Garibaldi (Piazza)	Y 9
Gramsci (Piazza)	Z 10
Indipendenza (Piazza)	Y 12
Martini (Via)	Y 14
Porceli (Via)	Y 15
S. Benedetto (Piazza)	Y 16
S. Benedetto (Via)	Y 17
S. Cosimo (Piazza)	Z 18

S. Croce (Via)	Y 19	Università (Via)	Z 23
Sardegna (Via)	Z 20	Yenne (Piazza)	Y 24
Trieste (Viale)	Z 21	20 Settembre (Via)	Z 25

EXCURSION

★★★ **Strada di Muravera** – *Leave by ① on the town plan.* 30km – 19 miles from Cagliari, the road enters wild gorges with reddish-coloured walls of porphyritic granite.

COSTA SMERALDA★★

EMERALD COAST

Michelin map 988 folds 23 and 24 or 433 D 10

In the northeastern part of the island the wild and undulating region of **Gallura** has one of the most indented coastlines. It is a succession of pink granite headlands, forest-covered mountain ridges, sandy creeks and deeply-indented bays and has become a favourite area with holidaymakers.

The development of the **Emerald Coast**, started in 1961, was promoted by a consortium originally presided over by the Aga Khan. The coast was endowed with luxury facilities (palatial hotels, marinas and golf courses) to attract an upmarket clientele. The main resorts are **Porto Cervo**⌂⌂⌂, Cala di Volpe and **Baia Sardinia**⌂.

*Admission times and charges for the sights described
are listed at the end of the guide
Every sight for which there are times and charges is identified by
the clockface symbol ⊙ in the Sights section of the guide*

DORGALI

Population 8 045
Michelin map 988 fold 34 or 433 G 10

Monte Bardia stands between this important agricultural town and the sea. Dorgali makes an ideal excursion centre, especially for visiting the nearby megalithic sites.

Cala Gonone – *10km – 6 miles east.* A winding **road★★** leads to this resort with its small harbour. Boats leave from the port to visit the Sea Ox Cave **(Grotta del Bue Marino)** ⊘. The cave was occupied until recently by monk seals, survivors from the Ice Age. The galleried cave has some lovely concretions.

★ **Dolmen Motorra** and **Grotta di Ispingoli** ⊘ – *8km – 5 miles north by the Nuoro road and then the S125 or Orosei road to the right.*
The **dolmen** consists of an almost-circular slab of schist supported by eight uprights. The **Ispingoli Cave** *(continue along the Orosei road, then turn right and continue for a further 3km – 2 miles)* is an immense cavity at an altitude of 400m – 1 312ft. The roof is supported by an extraordinary **column★★** 38m – 125ft tall.

★ **Serra Orrios** and **Tomba dei Giganti** – *19km – 12 miles by the Nuoro road.* The important nuraghic village of **Serra Orrios** *(signposted to the right, 10km – 6 miles from Dorgali)* stands on a plateau strewn with asphodels.
Two temples remain. One immediately to the west of the village and the other, in the same direction but further out, is surrounded by a circular wall.
At the next crossroads go straight ahead towards Lula and almost 6km – 4 miles further, after a small pass, turn right at the signpost, "Tomba dei Giganti" 700m – 766yds.
Although overgrown by vegetation one can still make out the **Tomba Sa Ena e Tomes** which has the traditional layout of a Giants' Tomb. The funerary chamber, in the form of a passage roofed with large slabs like a dolmen, is preceded by a series of stones forming the arc of a circle. The larger central stone is carved with a moulding and pierced with a small passageway at ground level.

★★ **Dorgali to Arbatax Road** – *See ARBATAX.*

Monti di GENNARGENTU★★

GENNARGENTU MOUNTAINS
Michelin map 988 folds 33 and 34 or 433 G/H 9

The immense Gennargentu Massif in the centre of the island, culminates in Punta La Marmora (1 834m – 6 017ft). These bare, deserted and rounded peaks are to be found in the region of **Barbagia**, which was never completely conquered by the Romans. The relative isolation of the area has contributed to the shy and almost inhospitable manner of the people and to the preservation of local costumes and traditions.
The water which runs off the green slopes of the Gennargentu Mountains supplies the man-made reservoir of **Lago di Flumendosa** (good **view★★** of the lake from the road that climbs to Villanovatulo), which in turn is used to irrigate the plain of Campidano. **Aritzo** is the main holiday resort of the area. The town of **Tonara** standing at an altitude of 930m – 3 015ft in a green pass is known for its nougat *(torrone)* made with honey, almonds and hazel nuts. To the north **Fonni** is the island's highest village at an altitude of 1 000m – 3 281ft.

Arcipelago della MADDALENA★★

MADDELENA ARCHIPELAGO – Population 10 989
Michelin map 988 fold 23 or 90 fold 10 or 433 D 10

Access – See the maps given above as well as the current Michelin Red Guide Italia. The **Maddalena Archipelago** consists of 14 rocky islands and islets which are greatly appreciated by the tourists for their wild state. The two busiest islands, Maddalena and Caprera, are linked by a causeway.

★★ **Isola Maddalena** – Under 20km² – 8sq miles this, the largest island of the archipelago, has a magnificent coastline. A lovely scenic route *(20km – 12 miles)* follows the coast.

★ **Isola di Caprera** – This sparsely-inhabited island attracts many visitors to the one-time home, now a museum **(museo★)** ⊘, and tomb of Garibaldi, who died here in 1882.

NUORO

Population 37 519
Michelin map 988 fold 33 or 433 G 9/10

Nuoro lies at the foot of Monte Ortobene, on the borders of the Barbagia region to the north of the Gennargentu Mountains. In this large town of central Sardinia the customs, traditions and folklore have remained unchanged since ancient times. The **Sagra del Redentore** (Feast of the Redeemer) includes a procession through the town in local costumes and a folk festival *(see the Calendar of Events at the end of the guide)*.

★ **Museo della Vita e delle Tradizioni Popolari Sarde** ⊙ – *55 Via A Mereu*. The museum, evoking the popular traditions of the island, has a fine collection of Sardinian costumes. The author Grazia Deledda, a native of Nuoro, won the Nobel Prize for Literature in 1926 for her description of Sardinian life.

EXCURSIONS

★ **Monte Ortobene** – *9km – 6 miles east*. This is a popular excursion with local people. The summit affords several good viewpoints.

★ **Su Gologone** – *20km – 12 miles southeast by the Oliena-Dorgali road*. The large town of **Oliena** stands at the foot of a particularly steep slope of the Sopramonte. Locally the women still wear the traditional costume.
Just beyond Oliena take a local road to the left for about 6km – 4 miles. The lovely spring at Su Gologone gushes from a rocky face in a picturesque green setting.

Orgosolo – *20km – 12 miles south*. This large market town with its calm appearance is notorious for being the stronghold of bandits and outlaws. The Italian film producer Vittorio de Seta popularised them in his film *Banditi a Orgosolo* (1961).

ORISTANO

Population 31 048
Michelin map 988 fold 33 or 433 H 7

Oristano is the main town on the west coast. Founded in 1070 by the inhabitants of nearby Tharros *(see THARROS)*, Oristano put up a strong fight against the Aragonese in the 14C.

Piazza Roma – The crenellated tower, Torre di San Cristoforo, overlooking this vast esplanade, was originally part of the town wall built in 1291. Opening off Piazza Roma is **Corso Umberto**, the town's main shopping street.

San Francesco – The church, rebuilt in the 19C, has some interesting **works of art**★ including a wooden statue of Christ by the 14C Rhenish school, a fragment of a polyptych *(St Francis receiving the Stigmata)* by Pietro Cavaro, a 16C Sardinian artist, and a statue of *St Basil* by Nino Pisano (14C).

EXCURSIONS

★ **Basilica di Santa Giusta** – *3km – 2 miles south*. This 12C edifice stands in the town of the same name, on the banks of a lake.
The sober elegance of Santa Giusta is characteristic of all Sardinian churches where Pisan and Lombard influences mingle. The façade, divided into three sections in the Lombard manner, has an attractively-carved doorway typical of the Pisan style. Inside, the piers are either of marble or of granite. There is a crypt under the slightly-raised choir.

Arborea – *18km – 11 miles south*. This charming little town was planned and laid out in 1928 by the Fascist government, following the draining of the marshes and the extermination of the malaria mosquito.

PORTO CONTE

Michelin map 988 fold 33 – 13km or 433 F 6 – 8 miles northwest of Alghero

This, the ancient Portus Nympharum or Port of Nymphs, lies on the shores of a beautiful bay.

★★★ **Grotta di Nettuno** ⊙ – *9km – 6 miles southwest leaving from the head of the bay. Boats leave from Alghero*. The road out to the headland, **Capo Caccia**, offers splendid **views**★★ of the rocky coast. **Neptune's Cave** is on the point. A stairway (654 steps) leads down the cliff face. There are small inner lakes, a forest of columns, and concretions in the form of organ pipes.

★ **Nuraghe Palmavera** – *2km – 1 mile from the bay on the left-hand side of the Alghero road*. This nuraghe is surrounded by the remains of a prehistoric village. The individual dwellings were crowded closely together. The nuraghe is a particularly fine building in white limestone with two vaulted towers and two separate entrances.

PORTO TORRES

Population 21 231
Michelin map 988 folds 23 and 33 or 433 E 7

Situated at the head of a large bay, Porto Torres is the port for Sassari. Founded by Caesar it enjoyed considerable importance in the Roman period, as can be testified by the remains in the vicinity of the station.

★ **San Gavino** – The church was built at the end of the 11C by the Pisans (the long series of blind arcades on the north side are characteristic of the Pisan style) and enlarged shortly afterwards by the Lombard master builders. It is a fine example of medieval Sardinian art. A 15C doorway in the Catalan-Gothic style interrupts the arcades.
Inside, piers alternate with groups of four clustered columns giving a harmonious result. A large **crypt** enshrines the relics of St Gavin and a very fine Roman **sarcophagus**★, decorated with sculptures portraying the muses.

Isola di SANT'ANTIOCO★

SANT'ANTIOCO'S ISLAND – Population 12 290
Michelin map 988 fold 33 or 433 J/K 7

This volcanic island is the largest of the Sulcis Archipelago, lying off the southwest coast of Sardinia. It has a hilly terrain with high cliffs on the west coast.
The chief town, also called Sant'Antioco, is linked to the mainland by railway.

★ **Vestigia di Sulcis** ⊘ – The ancient town of Sulcis, founded by the Phoenicians, gave its name to this group of islands.
Before entering the necropolis, visit the **museum** which displays all the finds from the excavations and includes a fine collection of **steles**★.
The **tophet**★ *(500m – 1 640ft from the museum)* is where the Phoenicians gathered the remains of their first-born child, who was always sacrificed according to Phoenician custom. The **necropolis** was set apart and has 60 tombs cut in the rock.
The **catacombs**, under the parish church, were originally a Phoenician necropolis transformed by the Christians during the Roman period.

SASSARI

Population 122 131
Michelin map 988 fold 33 or 433 E 7
Town plan in the current Michelin Red Guide Italia

Sassari is the second largest town in Sardinia. Its spacious, airy modern quarters contrast with its medieval nucleus, nestling round the cathedral. The busiest arteries are the Piazza d'Italia and the Corso Vittorio Emanuele II.
Sassari is known for its festivals. The famous **Cavalcata Sarda** is a colourful procession of people from nearly all the provinces of Sardinia in their beautiful and varied local costumes. The procession ends with a frenetic horse race. The **Festa dei Candelieri** (Feast of Candles), dating from the late 16C, was the result of a vow to the Virgin, made during an epidemic of the Black Death. The different trade guilds each carry huge beribboned wooden candles, gilded or painted silver *(see the Calendar of Events at the end of the guide)*.

★ **Museo Nazionale Sanna** ⊘ – The museum contains rich archeological collections, including an interesting section devoted to Sardinian ethnography and a small picture gallery.

Duomo – The cathedral is built in many styles and has a 13C campanile with a 17C upper storey, a late-17C Spanish Baroque **façade**★ and a Gothic interior.

EXCURSION

★★ **Santissima Trinità di Saccargia** – *17km – 11 miles southeast by the Cagliari road, the S 131, and then the road to Olbia, the S 597.*
This former Camaldulian abbey church, dedicated to the Holy Trinity, was built in the 12C in decorative courses of black and white stone, typical of the Pisan style. The elegant façade includes a porch added in the 13C and is flanked by a slender campanile. Inside, the apse is adorned with fine 13C frescoes showing a strong Byzantine influence.

Avoid visiting a place of worship during a service

THARROS*

Michelin map 988 fold 33 or 433 H 7
1.5km – 1 mile south of San Giovanni di Sinis

The Phoenicians founded Tharros on the Sinis Peninsula north of the Gulf of Oristano. It was an important depot on the Marseilles-Carthage trading route, before it was conquered by the Romans in the 3C BC. The inhabitants left the site for Oristano in 1070 before it was buried under wind-blown sand.

Zona archeologica ⊘ – The excavation site lies near a hill crowned by a Spanish tower (Torre di San Giovanni). Below were houses, baths and a 5C Paleo-Christian baptistery. To the right of the hill road are the remains of a Punic temple and a Semitic temple. On the hilltop are the ruins of a Roman temple with further on a tophet *(see above)*. Beyond all this are the impressive basalt remains of the town's fortifications.

Necropoli ⊘ – Climb to the summit of the headland crowned by a lighthouse to see the Punic necropolis (6C-4C BC). Some of the rectangular tombs are cut in the rock while others are hypogea (underground chambers).

Sicily

Sicily (Sicilia), the largest of the Mediterranean islands, has an area of 25 709km^2 – 9 927sq miles. It is triangular in shape and was named Trinacria (Greek for "triangle") under Greek rule.

Nearly 5 million people live on the island, which is generally mountainous and reaches at its highest point, Mount Etna (an active volcano), an altitude of 3 340m – 10 958ft.

Throughout its history Sicily has suffered numerous earthquakes: the 1908 one almost entirely destroyed Messina and the 1968 one affected the western part of the island.

Access – *see PRACTICAL INFORMATION*

Sightseeing – The island can be visited in a quick tour of 6 to 7 days. The map overleaf locates the towns and sites described in the guide, and also indicates other beauty spots in small black type.

Look in the introduction at the Map of Touring Programmes for the suggested itinerary for Sicily.

HISTORICAL AND ARTISTIC NOTES

Sicily has been a constant pawn for marauding forces in the Mediterranean owing to its strategic location, lying near the peninsula and controlling the Mediterranean. Firstly there were the Greeks in the 8C who discovered an island divided between two ethnic groups: the **Sicani**, the oldest inhabitants, and the **Siculi** (Sicels) who came from the peninsula.

The Carthaginians were for several centuries the main rivals of the Greeks. Although they had colonised the coastal areas, they were finally pushed back to the western part of the island, where they remained until the siege of Mozia by Denys the Elder in 397 BC.

The 5C BC, excluding the rules of the tyrants of Gela and Syracuse *(see SIRACUSA)*, was the apogee of Greek rule in Sicily (Magna Graecia). After erecting some magnificent buildings, they neutralised their enemies and Syracuse grew to become the rival of Athens.

This fragile peace was broken by the arrival of the Romans who coveted the island for the richness of its soil.

By 241 BC, at the end of the First Punic War, the whole of Sicily had been conquered and it became a Roman province, governed by a praetor. The Romans exploited the island's resources to the full with the help of more or less dishonest officials. The island was also a victim of the numerous Barbarian invasions which unfurled on southern Italy.

In 535 the island passed to the Byzantines before experiencing a period of great prosperity under the Aghlabid dynasty (Tunisia), in the 9C. The Saracens were in turn expelled by the Normans (11C).

The son of the Great Count Roger I of Sicily, **Roger II** (1095-1154), created the Norman Kingdom of Sicily. He established his court at Palermo and during his reign the island was to enjoy a prosperous period of considerable political power and cultural influence.

The name of the Hohenstaufen Emperor, **Frederick II**, dominated the reign of this Swabian dynasty. The house of Anjou followed in 1266; however, Charles of Anjou was expelled following the Palermo revolt of 1282 known as the **Sicilian Vespers.** Power passed to the Aragon dynasty and it was Alfonso V the Magnanimous who reunited Naples and Sicily and took the title of King of the Two Sicilies (1442).

The island passed to the Bourbons of Naples by marriage until they were overthrown by the Expedition of Garibaldi and the Thousand (1860).

The Second World War left its mark on Sicily; the Anglo-American landings between Licata and Syracuse in 1943 ended in the abandonment of the island by the Germans after more than a month of heavy fighting.

Each period has left its mark on the island's heritage, be it in the field of art or customs and daily life. The Greeks built admirable Doric temples with the mellow local limestone, and also splendid theatres. During the brief period when the Normans dominated the island, Sicily knew an era of economic prosperity and artistic development.

This style was unique for its blending of a variety of different influences. The architectural style was still essentially Norman but the decoration (horseshoe-shaped arches, bulbous belltowers and intricately decorated ceilings) showed a strong Moorish influence, while the decoration of the walls with dazzling mosaics on golden backgrounds was Byzantine.

Known variously as the **Sicilian-Norman** or **Sicilian-Arab**, this style can be seen at Palermo, Monreale, Cefalu and Messina.

If the Renaissance has left few traces in the island – with some outstanding exceptions by **Antonello da Messina** *(see Index)* who usually worked on the mainland – the Sicilians adopted the Baroque style with great fervour in the late 18C. The main

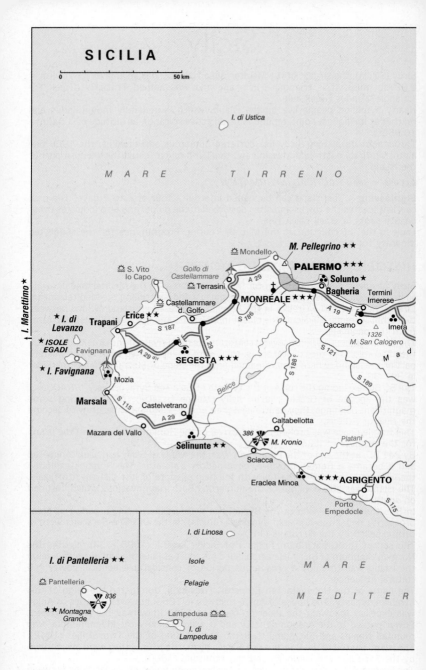

exponents were the architects **Rosario Gagliardi** in Noto and Ragusa, **Vaccarini** in Catania, and **Giacomo Serpotta** who embellished numerous oratories in Palermo with his sculpted fantasies.

Sicilian literature is particularly rich, especially in the 19C, with **Giovanni Verga** *(see Index)* who created a new form of Italian novel, and **Luigi Pirandello** *(see Index)*. Noteworthy among the 20C writers to describe contemporary life are **Elio Vittorini** (1908-66) and **Leonardo Sciascia** (born 1921).

SICILY TODAY

Owing to the mountainous nature of the land citrus fruit, vines and olive trees are grown mainly along the coast or on rare plains such as Catania and the Conca d'Oro inland from Palermo. In the rather desolate but grandiose interior, the main crops are cereals. Isolated dwellings are rare, as the Sicilian prefers to live in fairly large villages where the houses huddle closely together. The industries implanted on the outskirts of large towns have done little to stem the flow of emigration. Sicily has particularly suffered from the isolation which affected the whole of the Mezzogiorno.

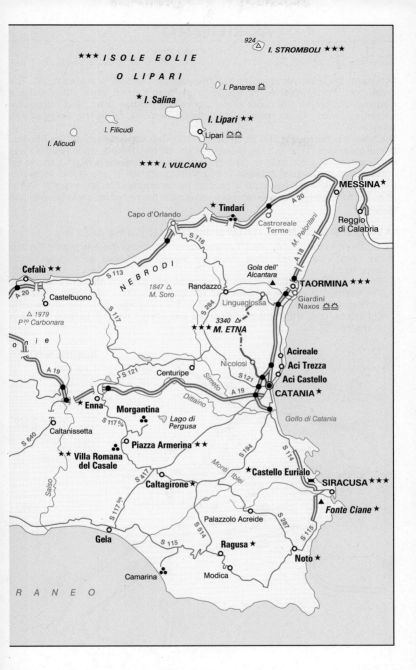

The island's difficulties have been exacerbated by the existence of the Mafia, a formidable secret society whose abiding rule is to defend its members to the extent of breaking the law if need be, and to impose a reign of silence *(omerta)* which creates an atmosphere of fear and mistrust. The Mafia first appeared in the 19C – although its true foundation goes much further back – and flourished initially in the countryside, where it tyrannised the peasant folk for the profit of the large landowners. Today it has become an urban phenomenon using definitely more violent methods.

The folk traditions and customs which once animated the streets have almost completely disappeared. It is only on feast days and in the museums that the visitor can now see the famous **Sicilian carts** which were gaily decorated. These colourful carts were masterpieces of craftsmanship and decorative ingenuity depicting, in four sections, stories of heroism. However, one can still see the popular puppet *(pupi)* theatres which are mentioned in the 12C *Song of Roland* or Ariosto's *Orlando Furioso (Roland the Mad) (See FERRARA).*

Consult the Index to find an individual town or sight

AGRIGENTO★★★

Population 56 273
Michelin map 988 fold 36 or 432 P 22 – Town plan in the Michelin Red Guide Italia

Agrigento, the Greek Akragas, is attractively set on a hillside facing out to sea. The Greek poet Pindar referred to Agrigento as "man's finest town". It includes a medieval quarter on the upper slopes above the modern town, and impressive ancient ruins strung out along a ridge below, wrongly called the Valley of the Temples.

The town was founded in 580 BC by people from Gela who originated from Rhodes. Of the governing "tyrants", the cruellest in the 6C was **Phalaris**, while **Tero** (7C) was renowned as a great builder. The 5C philosopher **Empedocles** was a native of Agrigento, as was **Luigi Pirandello** (1867-1936), winner of the Nobel Prize for Literature in 1934 and innovator in modern Italian drama *(Six Characters in Search of an Author)*, whose plays were woven around the themes of incomprehension and absurdity.

★★★ VALLE DEI TEMPLI (VALLEY OF THE TEMPLES) ⊙ *allow half a day*

Access from the west by the S 115 and then a left turn in the direction of Piazzale dei Templi (car park). Walk along the Sacred Way, lined with the principal temples.

Of the ten temples built in late 6C - late 5C BC, parts of nine are still visible. The destruction of the temples was for long thought to have been caused by earthquakes but is now also attributed to the anti-pagan activities of the early Christians. Only the Temple of Concord was spared when it became a church in the late 6C AD.

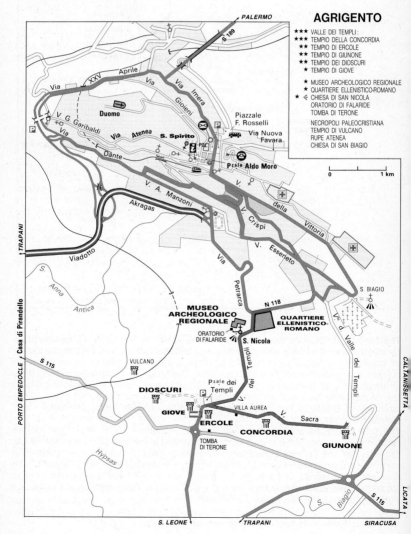

** **Tempio di Ercole** – Dating from the late 6C the Temple of Hercules is probably the oldest of the Agrigento temples and is built in the ancient Doric style. Eight of its columns have been raised and the others lie amid a jumble of ruins.
Further on to the left amid the vegetation can be seen the deeply-grooved ruts made by the wheeled vehicles used to transport the blocks of tufa used to build the temples.

** **Tempio della Concordia** – The Temple of Concord was built in the mid-5C BC; it is the most massive, majestic and best preserved of the Doric temples in Sicily. It has a peristyle of 34 tufa limestone columns, the original stucco facing having since disappeared.
It is not known to what deity it was dedicated and its present name (Concordia) is taken from a Roman inscription found nearby. The internal arrangement dates from the Christian period (mid-5C).

** **Tempio di Giunone** – Set on the edge of the ridge, this temple, dedicated to Juno, was built in 470 BC and conserves part of its colonnade and its architrave. On the east side there is a sacrificial altar and behind the temple an ancient cistern.
Return to Piazzale dei Templi.

* **Tempio di Giove** – Had this now-ruined temple been completed, its size (113m – 371ft long by 56m – 184ft wide) would have made it one of the largest in the ancient world.
The entablature of the Temple of Jupiter was supported by 20m – 66ft tall columns, between which stood **telamones** (columns in the form of male figures), colossal statues, one of which, standing 7.5m – 25ft high, has been reconstructed and is now on view in the Archeological Museum *(see below)*. A reproduction of the giant, lying on the ground in the centre of the ruins, gives some idea of the immense size of the building.

Tempio dei Dioscuri (Temple of Castor and Pollux) – This hexastyle temple lies lower down the slope than the previous temple. Only four of the columns supporting part of the entablature remain. The small rose at the corner of the entablature is the symbol of Rhodes.
Alongside is a **sacred area** dedicated to Demeter and Kore the Chthonic or underground gods: there are two sacrificial altars, one of which is circular, with a holy well in the middle, and the other square.

ADDITIONAL SIGHTS

* **Museo Archeologico Regionale** ⊘ – *Enter via the cloisters of the Church of St Nicholas (see below)*. The museum contains a fine collection of **Greek vases*** including the *Dionisius Cup* and the *Perseus and Andromeda Cup* on a white background. One room is devoted to the **telamones*** from the Temple of Jupiter. There are also the 5C BC marble statue of the youth **Ephebus of Agrigento** *(Room 10)* and the beautiful **Gela Cup**** *(Room 15)* which illustrates a centaur in the upper part and the battle between the Greeks and the Amazons in the lower part.

Oratorio di Falaride ⊘ – *Access via a passageway leading off the cloisters of the Church of San Nicola*. Legend has it that the palace of Phalaris, the first tyrant of Agrigento, was in the vicinity. The building is in fact a small Hellenistic temple which was transformed during the Christian period.

San Nicola ⊘ – This sober church, dedicated to St Nicholas, in the transitional Romanesque-Gothic style contains a magnificent **Roman sarcophagus*** on which the death of Phaedra is portrayed. From the terrace there is a fine **view*** of the temples.

* **Quartiere Ellenistico-Romano** ⊘ – In the Greco-Roman quarter, the layout of the main streets lined with houses is a good example of 4C BC town planning.

Tomba di Terone – *Visible from the Caltagirone road.*
The tomb (3m – 10ft high), said to be that of Tero, Tyrant of Agrigento, in fact dates from the Roman era.

Town centre – The shady **Piazzale Aldo Moro**, often thronged with birds at certain times of the day, is the centre of the town. The **Via Atenea** is a busy shopping street. Crowning the old town with its stepped streets is the cathedral (**cattedrale**) ⊘, a Norman building which was greatly altered in the following centuries. On the way back down to Piazzale A. Moro visit a small abbey church, **Abbaziale di Santo Spirito*** ⊘, which has four charming **high reliefs*** in stucco by Giacomo Serpotta.

Casa di Pirandello ⊘ – *6km – 4 miles west by the Porto Empedocle road, the S 115*. Shortly after the Morandi viaduct turn left. This small house surrounded by vineyards was the birthplace of the famous dramatist Luigi Pirandello (1867-1936), who is buried under a nearby pine tree.

313

CALTAGIRONE★

Michelin map 988 fold 36 or 432 P 25

Caltagirone is famous for its pottery which is not only displayed in profusion in the local shops (vases, plates, household goods) but also adorns bridges, balustrades, balconies (note the lovely balcony of the 18C **Casa Ventimiglia**), and the façades of palaces lining Via Roma in the town centre.

TOWN

★ **Villa Comunale** – This beautiful garden was designed in the mid-19C by Basile as an English garden. The side flanking Via Roma is bounded by a balustrade adorned with maiolica vases. On an esplanade stands the delightful Arab-style bandstand **(palco della musica)** decorated with ceramics.

  Museo della ceramica ⊙ – A curious little 18C theatre (Teatrino), decorated with ceramics houses an interesting museum which traces the history of local ceramics from prehistory to the early 20C. The importance of this craft is illustrated by a fine **cup**★ dating from 5C BC depicting a potter and a youth working at the wheel.

★ **Scala di Santa Maria del Monte** – The stairway built in the 17C to join the old and new town, has 142 steps in volcanic stone; the risers are decorated with polychrome ceramic tiles with geometric, floral and other decorative motifs. On the 24 and 25 July the stairway is covered in lights which form different patterns: the most frequent is the symbol of the town, an eagle with a shield on its breast.

CATANIA★

Population 333 485
Michelin map 988 fold 37 or 432 O 27
Plan of the built-up area in the current Michelin Red Guide Italia

Catania is a busy seaport and industrial town which has developed considerably in recent years, despite being destroyed several times by the eruptions of Mount Etna. This fine city has wide, regular streets overlooked by numerous Baroque buildings by the architect **Vaccarini**, who rebuilt Catania after the 1693 earthquake.
Natives of the town include the musician **Vicenzo Bellini** (1801-35), composer of the opera *Norma*, and the novelist, **Giovanni Verga** *(see Index)*.
Catania holds the heat record for the whole of Italy: over 40°C (104°F), and the less enviable one of the highest crime rate, which has earned it the nickname of "Sicilian Chicago".

★ **Via Etnea** (DXY) – The town's main shopping artery is over 3km – 2 miles long. All the way along it affords a view of Etna. It is bordered by numerous palaces, churches and gardens **(Villa Bellini**★**)**.

★ **Piazza del Duomo** (DZ) – This square is the centre of town and is surrounded by a Baroque ensemble designed by Vaccarini which includes the Elephant Fountain **(Fontana dell'Elefante – A)** dating from 1735, the **Palazzo del Municipio (H)** with its well-balanced façade, and the cathedral **(Duomo)** (EZ) ⊙ dedicated to St Agatha, the town's patron saint. The cathedral, built at the end of the 11C by the Norman, Roger I, was remodelled after the 1693 earthquake.

★ **Castello Ursino** (DZ) ⊙ – This bare, grim castle, fortified by four towers, was built in the 13C by the Emperor Frederick II of Hohenstaufen. It houses an interesting museum **(Museo Civico)**.

EXCURSION

Acireale – *17km – 11 miles north.* The itinerary passes through two fishing villages, both small resorts, **Aci Castello** and **Aci Trezza**. Offshore, the Cyclops' Reefs **(Faraglioni dei Ciclopi**★**)** emerge from the sea. These are supposed to be the rocks hurled by the Cyclops Polyphemus after Ulysses had blinded him by thrusting a blazing stake into his single eye.
The road leads to **Acireale**, a modern town with numerous baroque buildings which include those of the **Piazzo del Duomo**★ with the Basilica of Sts Peter and Paul and the Town Hall, as well as the Church of **San Sebastiano** with its harmonious **façade** embellished with columns, niches and friezes.

CATANIA

Etnea (Via) .... DXY
Umberto I (Via) .... DEX

Angelo Custode (Via) ..... DZ 3
Biondi (Via) .... EY 12
Bovio (Piazza G.) .... EY 15
Carlo Alberto (Piazza) ... EY 19
Castello Ursino (Via) .... DZ 21
Conte di Torino (Via) .... EY 25
Cutelli (Piazza) .... EZ 26
Dante (Piazza) .... DY 28

Giuffrida (Via Vincenzo) .... EX 39
Guardie (Piazza delle) ...... EY 42
Imbriani
  (Via Matteo Renato) .... DEX 43
Lupo (Piazza Pietro) .... EY 47
Orlando (V. Vitt. E.) ...... EX 60
Porticello (Via) .... EZ 68
Rabbordone (Via) .... EY 69
Rapisarda (Via Michele) .... EY 70
San Francesco (Piazza) .... DZ 78
San Gaetano
  alle Grotte (Via) ...... DEY 79
San Giuseppe
  al Duomo (Via) .... DZ 80

Spirito Santo (Piazza) ..... EY 87
Stesicoro (Piazza) .... DY 91
Teatro Massimo
  (Via) .... EYZ 92
Trento (Piazza) .... EX 95
Università (Piazza dell') .. DZ 96
Verga (Piazza) .... EX 98
Vittorio Emanuele III
  (Piazza) .... EY 100

A Fontana dell'Elefante
H Palazzo del Municipio

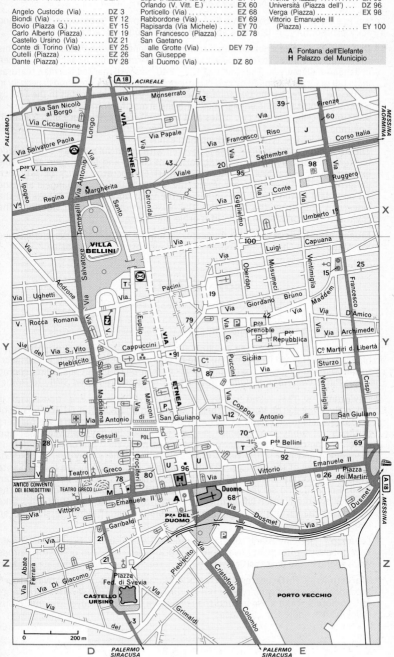

To plan a special itinerary:
- consult the Map of Touring Programmes which indicates the tourist regions,
  the recommended routes, the principal towns and main sights
- read the descriptions in the Sights section
  which include Excursions from the main tourist centres
Michelin Maps nos 428 to 433 indicate scenic routes, places of interest,
viewpoints, rivers, forests...

CEFALÙ★★

Population 13 873
Michelin map 988 fold 36 or 432 M 24

Cefalù is a small fishing town in a fine **setting**★★, hemmed in between the sea and a rocky promontory. It boasts a splendid Romanesque cathedral.

★★ **Duomo** ⊙ – Built of a golden-tinted stone which blends in with the cliff behind, this cathedral was erected to fulfil a vow made by the Norman King, Roger II (12C), when in danger of shipwreck. The church (1131-1240) has well-marked Norman features in its tall main apse flanked by two slightly-projecting smaller ones and especially in its façade, abutted by the two square towers. The portico was rebuilt in the 15C by a Lombard master and is emblazoned with the arms of a former bishop, Gatto.
The timber ceiling of the two aisles and the transept galleries are also Norman. Columns with splendid **capitals**★★ in the Sicilian-Norman style *(see INTRODUCTION)* support the typically-Moorish horseshoe arch.
The oven vault of the central apse is covered with beautiful **mosaics**★★ on a gilded background, displaying a surprising variety of colour and forming an admirable expression of Byzantine art. Above is Christ Pantocrator (Ruler of All) with underneath, on three different levels, the Virgin with four archangels and the 12 apostles. In the choir, the angels on the vaulting and the prophets on the side walls date from the 13C. Note the episcopal throne (south side) and the royal throne (north side), both in marble and mosaic.

Museo Mandralisca ⊙ – The museum, facing the cathedral in the picturesque Via Mandralisca, has a fine *Portrait of a Man* by Antonello da Messina.

Isole EGADI★

EGADI ISLANDS – Population 4 335
Michelin map 988 folds 34 and 35 or 432 M/N 18/19.
Access: see the Michelin map 988 and the current Michelin Red Guide Italia

The three islands ⊙ – Favignana, Levanzo and Marettimo – which make up this small archipelago lie offshore from Trapani. The islands are popular for their wild aspect, clear blue sea and beautiful coastlines. It was here in 241 BC that the treaty ending the First Punic War was concluded, in which Carthage surrendered Sicily to Rome.

★ **Favignana** – The island covers an area of 20km² – 8sq miles and is butterfly-shaped. The **Montagna Grossa** culminating at 310m – 1 017ft runs right across the island and ends as an indented coastline. The islanders are masters in the art of tunny fishing which they do for about 50 days between May and June. Having captured the tunny in a series of nets, they perform a dangerous manoeuvre and pull in the fish towards the shore where they are harpooned. The main town of the group of islands, **Favignana**, is guarded by the fort of Santa Caterina, a former Saracen lookout tower, which was rebuilt by the Norman King, Roger II, and served as a prison under the Bourbons. To the east of the harbour are the former **tufa quarries**★ now drowned by the sea. Boat trips take visitors to the various caves, including the **Grotta Azzurra**★ which is situated on the west coast.

★ **Levanzo** – This tiny island (6km² – 2sq miles) has no surfaced roads or springs. Few people therefore stay overnight. In 1950 traces of life in prehistoric times were found in the **Grotta del Genovese**, which is reached by boat from Cala Dogana.

★ **Marettimo** – Off the beaten tourist track, Marettimo with its attractive **harbour**★ *(no landing stage, rowing boats take visitors to the quay)* has several restaurants but no hotels. Take a **trip** around the island in a boat to discover the numerous caves which riddle the cliff faces.

ENNA★

Population 28 277
Michelin map 988 fold 36

Enna lies in an isolated, sun-scorched landscape at the centre of the island. Its panoramic **site**★★ at an altitude of 942m – 3 091ft has earned it the nickname of the Belvedere of Sicily.
According to legend it was on the shores of a lake, **Lago di Pergusa** *(10km – 6 miles to the south)*, that Pluto carried off the youthful Proserpine, future Queen of the Underworld.

★ **Castello di Lombardia** ⊙ – This medieval castle has six of its original 20 towers. From the top of the tallest there is an exceptional **panorama**★★★ of the hilltop village of Calascibetta, Etna and most of the Sicilian mountain peaks.

Belvedere – *Beyond the castle.* From the far side of the hillock, which was the site of a temple to Demeter, there is a fine **view**★ of Calascibetta and of Enna itself.

Duomo ⊙ – The cathedral was rebuilt in the Baroque style in the 16C and 17C but still has its 14C Gothic apses. The lovely Classical façade is 16C.

★ **Torre di Federico** – *At the far end of Via Roma facing the castle.* In the past Enna could have been described as the town of towers. The town's strategic, defensive function accounts for the large number of these. The octagonal tower built by Frederick II of Swabia is impressively located at the centre of a small public garden.

Isole EOLIE★★★

ÆOLIAN or LIPARI ISLANDS – Population 12 756

Michelin map 988 folds 36 and 37 –

Access: see the Michelin map 988 and the current Michelin Red Guide Italia

The **Æolian Islands**, also known as the **Lipari Islands**, are so called because the ancients thought Æolus, the God of the Winds, lived there. The archipelago comprises seven main islands, Lipari, Vulcano, Stromboli, Salina, Filicudi, Alicudi and Panarea ≙, all of exceptional interest for their volcanic nature, their beauty, their light and their climate.

A deep blue, warm, clear sea, ideal for underwater fishing, interesting marine creatures including flying-fish, swordfish, turtles, sea-horses and hammerfish, make the islands a refuge for those who like to live close to nature. The inhabitants fish, grow vines and quarry pumice-stone.

★★ **Lipari** – This, the largest island in the archipelago, is formed of volcanic rock dipping vertically into the sea. In ancient times Lipari was a source of obsidian, a glazed black volcanic rock. Today the islanders grow cereals and capers, fish and quarry pumice-stone on the east coast.

Two bays (Marina Lunga with its beach and Marina Corta) frame the town of **Lipari**★, dominated by its old quarter encircled by 13C-14C walls. Inside is the castle rebuilt by the Spaniards in the 16C on the site of a Norman building. The castle houses a museum **(museo**★**)** ⊙: re-creation of Bronze Age necropoli, lovely collection of painted **kraters** (two-handled vases) imported from Greece and terracotta **theatrical masks**.

There are **boat trips**★★ ⊙ leaving from Marina Corta which take the visitor round the very rugged southwest coast of the island. When making a **tour of the island by car**★★, stop at Canneto and Campo Bianco to visit the pumice-stone **quarries**. The splendid view from the **Puntazze** headland includes five of the islands: Alicudi, Filicudi, Salina, Panarea and Stromboli. However, it is the belvedere in **Quattrocchi** which affords one of the finest **panoramas**★★★ of the whole archipelago.

★★ **Vulcano** – This 21km² - 8sq mile island is in reality four volcanoes. According to mythology it is here that Vulcan, the God of Fire, had his forges – whence the term volcanism. Although there has been no eruption on the island since 1890 there are still important signs of activity: fumaroles (smoke-holes), spouting steam-jets often underwater, hot sulphurous mud-flows greatly appreciated for their therapeutic properties. The island has a wild but forbidding beauty, with its rugged rocky shores, desolate areas and strangely-coloured soils due to the presence of sulphur, iron oxides and alum. The island's main centre, **Porto Levante**, stands below the great crater. The beach is known for its particularly warm water due to the underwater spouting steam-jets.

Excursions to the **Great Crater**★★★ *(2 1/2 to 3 hours on foot Rtn)* are interesting for the impressive views they afford of the crater and of the archipelago. The headland, **Capo Grillo**, affords a view of several islands.

A tour of the island by boat *(starting from Porto Ponente)* offers the visitor many curious views, especially along the northwestern coast, which is fringed with impressive basalt reefs.

★★ **Stromboli** – The volcano of Stromboli, with its plume of smoke, has a sombre beauty, and is a wild island with steep slopes. There are very few roads and such soil as can be cultivated is covered with vines yielding a delicious golden-coloured Malvasia wine. The little square, white houses are markedly Moorish in style.

The **crater** ⊙, in the form of a 924m - 3 032ft cone, has frequent minor eruptions with noisy explosions and accompanying flows of lava. To see the spectacle climb up to the crater *(7 hours on foot Rtn, difficult climb)* or watch from a boat the famous flow of smoking and incandescent lava along the crevasse named Sciara del Fuoco towards the sea. At night the scene becomes both beautiful and awesome.

Strombolicchio, near Stromboli, is a picturesque rocky islet with a steep stairway leading to its summit which affords a splendid view of Stromboli, the Lipari Archipelago and the coasts of Calabria and Sicily.

★ **Salina** ⊙ – The island is formed by six extinct volcanoes of which two have retained their characteristic outline. The highest crater, **Monte Fossa delle Felci** (962m – 3 156ft) dominates the archipelago. There is a pleasant panoramic road round the island. Caper bushes and vines grow on the lower terraced slopes. The latter yield the delicious golden Malvasia wine.

ERICE★★

Population 29 426
Michelin map 988 fold 35 – 14km – 9 miles northeast of Trapani

This ancient Phoenician and Greek city occupies a unique and beautiful **setting★★★** almost vertically (750m – 2 461ft) above the sea. Erice is clustered within its town walls and is crisscrossed by a labyrinth of quiet alleyways lined with attractive dwellings. In antiquity Erice was a religious centre famous for its temple consecrated to Astarte, then to Aphrodite and finally Venus who was venerated by mariners of old.

Erice presents two faces: during the hot summers it is bright and sunny and the sun-drenched streets of this village, strategically located, offer splendid **views★★** over the valley, whilst in winter Erice is wreathed in mist and seems a place lost in time.

Castello di Venere – This castle, built by the Normans in the 12C-13C, crowns an isolated rock on Monte Eryx, on the site of the Temple of Venus (Venere). From here and the nearby gardens (Giardino del Balio) there are admirable **views★★**: in clear weather the Tunisian coast can be seen.

Chiesa Madre – This church was built in the 14C using stones quarried from the ancient temples. The porch was added in the 15C and flanked by the square battlemented bell-tower (13C) with its elegant openings.

ETNA★★★

Michelin map 988 fold 37 or 432 N 26/27 – Alt approx. 3 340m – 10 958ft

Etna is the highest point in the island and is snow-capped for most of the year. It is still active and it is the largest and one of the most famous volcanoes in Europe.

Etna was born of undersea eruptions which also formed the Plain of Catania, formerly covered by the sea. Its eruptions were frequent in ancient times: 135 are recorded. But the greatest disaster occurred in 1669, when the flow of lava reached the sea, largely devastating Catania as it passed.

The worst eruptions in recent times occurred in 1910, when 23 new craters appeared, 1917, when a jet of lava squirted up to 800m – 2 500ft above its base, and 1923, when the lava ejected remained hot 18 months after the eruption. Since then, stirrings of Etna have taken place in 1928, 1954, 1964, 1971, 1974, 1978, 1979, March 1981, March 1983 and 1985; the volcano still smokes and may erupt at any time.

The mountain has the appearance of a huge, black, distorted cone which can be seen from a distance of 250km – 155 miles. On its lower slopes, which are extremely fertile, orange, mandarin, lemon and olive trees flourish as well as vines which produce the delicious Etna wine. Chestnut trees grow above the 500m – 1 500ft level and give way higher up to oak, beech, birch and pine. Above 2 100m – 6 500ft is the barren zone, where only a few clumps of *Astralagus Aetnensis* (a kind of vetch) will be seen scattered on the slopes of secondary craters, among the clinker and volcanic rock.

★★★ **Ascent of Etna** ⊙ – By the south face from Catania via Nicolosi, or by the northeast face from Taormina via Linguaglossa. *Wear warm clothing and strong shoes*.

South face – From a point almost 3 000m – 9 843ft up on the central crater in the area of Torre del Filosofo (the refuge was destroyed in the 1971 eruption), the three craters can be distinguished: the one to the southeast which appeared in 1978, the immense **central crater**, and the highest one to the **northeast** which has been dormant since 1971.

On the way up go over towards the eastern face to see the grandiose valley, **Valle del Bove**, which is hemmed in by walls of lava (1 200m – 3 937ft high) pierced with pot-holes and crevasses belching smoke.

Night-time excursions are possible on request: tourists will enjoy a Dantesque spectacle of molten lava at the bottom of the crater and an impressive sunrise with a view of the Lipari Islands and the Valle del Bove.

Northeast face – The road goes through Linguaglossa, a lovely pinewood and the winter sports resort of Villaggio Mareneve. The surfaced road ends at Piano Provenzana (1 800m – 5 906ft). The area around the new observatory affords a magnificent view of the central and northeast craters. The climb ends amidst an extraordinary landscape of lava, which still smokes at times.

Night-time excursions are also organised on this slope. The intrepid are able to enjoy, from the edge of the crater, the grandiose sight of the sun setting and rising.

GELA

Population 72 532
Michelin map 988 fold 36 or 432 P 24

Gela was founded in 688 BC by islanders from Rhodes and Crete. The town was destroyed and restored several times and completely rebuilt in 1230 by the Emperor Frederick II of Hohenstaufen. It was in the very fertile plain of Gela that the US troops landed in 1943. The town prospered with the discovery of local oil. Gela is, however, also a resort and an interesting archeological centre.

Ancient remains – For those interested in archeology there are the ancient **Greek fortifications★★** *(at Caposoprano to the west of the town)* dating from the 4C BC, with their regular stonework of skilfully-dressed blocks below and brickwork above. The most interesting section is the part facing the sea. This type of construction is particularly fragile and is now protected by plexiglass. These walls owe their preservation to the fact that they were buried under the sand. A museum, **Museo archeologico regionale★** *(Corso Vittorio Emanuele, at the far-eastern end of the town)*, has a particularly attractive presentation of pottery and medals.

MARSALA

Population 80 235
Michelin map 988 fold 35 or 432 N 19

Marsala, the ancient Lilybaeum on Capo Lilibeo, the westernmost point of the island, is an African-looking town with its whitewashed buildings. The Saracens first destroyed and then rebuilt it and called it Marsah el Allah (Port of God). It is known for its wines which an English merchant, John Woodhouse, rediscovered in the 18C. It was at Marsala in 1860 that Garibaldi landed at the start of the **Expedition of the Thousand**, which freed southern Italy from the sway of the Bourbons.
The **Piazza della Vittoria**, near the public gardens (Villa Cavalotti) on the northern outskirts of the town, is a favourite meeting-place of the townsfolk.
A former wine cellar, near the sea, now houses a museum, the **Museo archeologico** ⊙ *(Via Boeo):* the exhibits include the wreck of a **warship★** which fought in the Punic War and was found off Capo San Teodoro. Only the prow has been rebuilt.

MESSINA

Population 231 819
Michelin map 988 fold 37 or 432 M 28
Town plan in the current Michelin Red Guide Italia

Despite having been destroyed numerous times throughout the centuries, Messina or the ancient Zancle of the Greeks, is today an active market town. Messina has suffered repeated earthquakes (especially the 1908 one which destroyed 90% of the town and killed 80 000 in the region), epidemics and bombings.

Antonello da Messina – The artist was born in 1430 and he studied in Naples where he was influenced by the then popular Flemish art. Later he was to be attracted by the innovations of Tuscan painting which with its increasing use of perspective emphasised volume and architectural details. His works show a complete mastery of his art: forms and colours, skilfully balanced, enhance an inner vision which greatly influenced the Venetian painters of the Renaissance, notably Carpaccio and Giovanni Bellini. Antonello died on his native island around 1479.

SIGHTS

★ **Museo Regionale** ⓥ - *North of the town at the end of the Viale della Libertà.*
The museum comprises an art gallery and a sculpture and decorative arts section.
In the sculpture section there is a fine wooden crucifix dating from the early
15C. The painting section displays a *polyptych of St Gregory* (1473) by Antonello
da Messina, a remarkable composition which combines the Tuscan idiom with
the earliest Flemish influences, a remarkable *Descent from the Cross* by the Flemish
artist, Colin van Coter (15C); two works by Polidoro da Caravaggio, one of
Raphael's pupils and two Caravaggios, *Adoration of the Shepherds* and *Resurrection
of Lazarus*, both painted towards the end of his life from 1608 to 1610.
The two sculptures representing *Neptune* and *Scylla* are attributed to the
Tuscan sculptor Montorsoli (16C) who was perhaps one of Michelangelo's
assistants.

Duomo ⓥ - The cathedral, almost entirely rebuilt after the 1908 earthquake
and the bombings of 1943, still displays the main features of its original Norman
style (12C). The finely-carved narrow central **doorway**★ dates from the 15C. To
the left stands the campanile (60m - 196ft tall) with its **astronomical clock**★ which
was made in Strasbourg in 1933 and is believed to be the world's largest.

Chiesa dell'Annunziata dei Catalani - *Take the Via Cesare Battisti from the
south side of the cathedral.* The church which was built in 1100 during the
Norman reign and altered in the 13C, takes its name from the Catalan merchants
who owned it. The **apse**★ is characteristic of the composite Norman style which
blends Romanesque (small columns supporting blind arcades), Moorish (geometric
motifs and polychrome stonework) and Byzantine (dome on a drum)
influences.

MONREALE★★★

Population 26 246
Michelin map 988 fold 35 or 432 M 21 - 8km - 5 miles southwest of Palermo

The town, dominating the green plain known as the Conca d'Oro (Golden Basin)
of Palermo, grew up around the famous Benedictine **abbey** founded in the 12C by
the Norman King, William II.

★★★ **Duomo** ⓥ - The finely-carved central doorway of the cathedral has beautiful **bronze
doors** (1186) embellished with stylised figures, which were carved by Bonanno
Pisano. The more Byzantine north door is the work of Barisano da Trani (12C).
The decoration of the **chevet** is remarkable for the blending of Moorish and
Norman styles.
The cathedral has a basilical plan. The interior is dazzling with multicoloured
marbles, paintings, and especially
the 12C and 13C **mosaics**★★★ adorning
the oven vaults and the walls.
They represent the complete cycle
of the Old and New Testaments.
A gigantic *Christ giving His Blessing* is
enthroned in the central apse.
Above the episcopal throne, in the
choir, a mosaic represents King
William II offering the cathedral to
the Virgin. Another mosaic opposite,
over the royal throne, shows
the same King William receiving his
crown from the hands of Christ.

Terraze - From the terraces there
are magnificent **views**★★ of the
cloisters and over the fertile plain
of the Conca d'Oro.

★★★ **Chiostro** ⓥ - The cloisters to the
right of the church are as famous
as the mosaics. They afford views
of the abbey church. On the south
side there is a curious fountain that
was used as a lavabo by the monks.
The galleries, with their sharply-
pointed arches, are supported by
twin columns with remarkably
carved capitals.

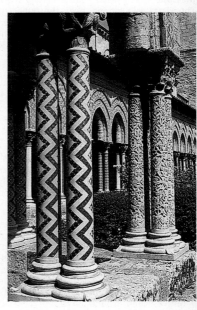

Cloisters, Monreale

NOTO*

Population 21 722
Michelin map 988 fold 37 or 432 Q 27
32km - 20 miles southwest of Syracuse

Noto, which dates from the time of the Siculi, was completely destroyed by the terrible earthquake of 1693. It was rebuilt on a new site 10km - 6 miles distant from the original town. Lining the streets, laid out on a grid plan, are handsome palaces, churches and other Baroque monuments in the local white limestone, which has mellowed with time to a golden hue. Several Sicilian architects worked together on this project. The most inventive was probably **Rosario Gagliardi.**

★★ **Corso Vittorio Emanuele** – This straight avenue is the town's most popular street. The street widens in three places which are overlooked by the monumental façades of churches designed in an imposing but flexible Baroque style. From east to west stand San Francesco all'Immacolata, the cathedral (the cupola collapsed recently) and San Domenico.

★ **Via Corrado Nicolaci** – This gently-sloping street offers an enchanting vista with the Church of Montevergine as focal point. It is lined with palaces sporting splendid balconies; the most notable is **Palazzo Nicolaci di Villadorata** with exuberantly-fanciful **balconies**★★.

PALERMO***

Population 698 141
Michelin map 988 folds 35 and 36 or 432 M 21/22
Plan of built-up area in the current Michelin Red Guide Italia

Palermo, the capital and the chief seaport of Sicily, is built at the head of a wide bay enclosed to the north by Monte Pellegrino and to the south by Capo Zafferano. It lies on the edge of a wonderfully fertile plain bounded by hills and nicknamed the **Conca d'Oro** (Golden Basin), where lemon and orange groves flourish.

HISTORICAL NOTES

Palermo was founded by the Phoenicians, conquered by the Romans and later came under Byzantine rule.
From 831 to 1072 it was under the sway of the Saracens, who gave it the peculiar atmosphere suggested today by the luxuriance of its gardens, the shape of the domes on some buildings and the physical type and mentality of the people.
Conquered by the Normans in 1072, Palermo became the capital under **Roger II**, who took the title of King of Sicily.
This great builder succeeded in blending Norman architectural styles with the decorative traditions of the Saracens and Byzantines: his reign was the golden age of art in Palermo. Later the Hohenstaufen and Angevin kings introduced the Gothic style (13C). After more than three centuries of Spanish rule, the Bourbons of Naples gave Palermo its splendid Baroque finery.

The Sicilian Vespers – Since 1266 the brother of Louis IX of France, Charles I of Anjou, supported by the pope, had held the town. But his rule was unpopular. The Sicilians had nicknamed the French, who spoke Italian badly, the *tartaglioni* or stammerers. On the Monday after Easter 1282, as the bells were ringing for vespers, some Frenchmen insulted a young woman of Palermo in the Church of Santo Spirito. Insurrection broke out, and all Frenchmen who could not pronounce the world *cicero* (chick-pea) correctly were massacred. The governor, Jean de St-Rémy, was besieged in his palace in Via Alloro.

FROM QUATTRO CANTI TO THE PALAZZO DEI NORMANNI *3 hours*

The route begins at two pretty squares which form the busy centre of Palermo and ends at the Palazzo dei Normanni, the focus of Sicilian politics, both past and present.

★ **Quattro Canti** (BY) – Two main streets, Corso Vittorio Emanuele and Via Maqueda, intersect to form this busy crossroads with four canted corners *(Quattro Canti)* decorated with statues and fountains. The crossroads form a fine early-17C ensemble in the Spanish Baroque style.
The Church of San Giuseppe has an astonishingly decorative interior.

★ **Piazza Pretoria** (BY) – The square has a spectacular **fountain**★★ surmounted by numerous marble statues, the work of a 16C Florentine artist. The town hall **(Palazzo Municipale - H)** occupied one side of this square.

It. ang. 9   321

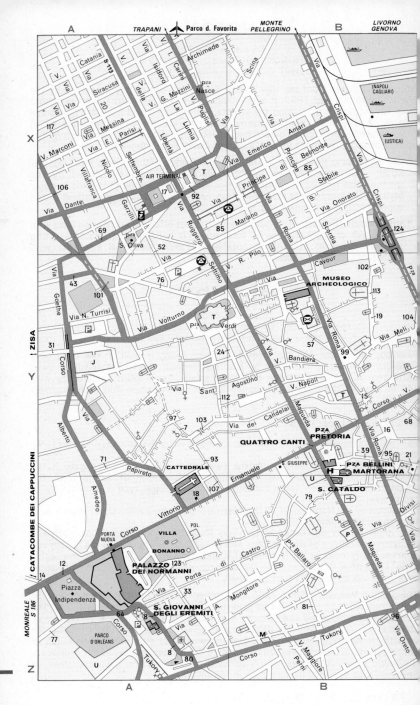

★★ **La Martorana** (BYZ) ⊙ – This church is also called Santa Maria dell'Ammiraglio (St Mary of the Admiral) because it was founded in 1143 by the Admiral of the Fleet to King Roger II. In the 16C and 17C it was altered by the addition of a baroque façade on the north side. Pass under the elegant 12C belfry-porch to enter the original church which is decorated with beautiful Byzantine **mosaics**★★ depicting scenes from the New Testament (*Annunciation, Nativity, Death of the Virgin*) and in the cupola, the imposing figure of *Christ Pantocrator* surrounded by angels, the Prophets and Evangelists. At the very end of the two side aisles note the two panels *depicting Roger II crowned by Christ (right)*, and *Admiral George of Antioch kneeling before the Virgin (left)*.

★★ **San Cataldo** (BZ) ⊙ – This splendid church, founded in the 12C, recalls Moorish architecture with its severe rectangular plan, its domes, its decorative crenellations and the traceried openings of the façade.

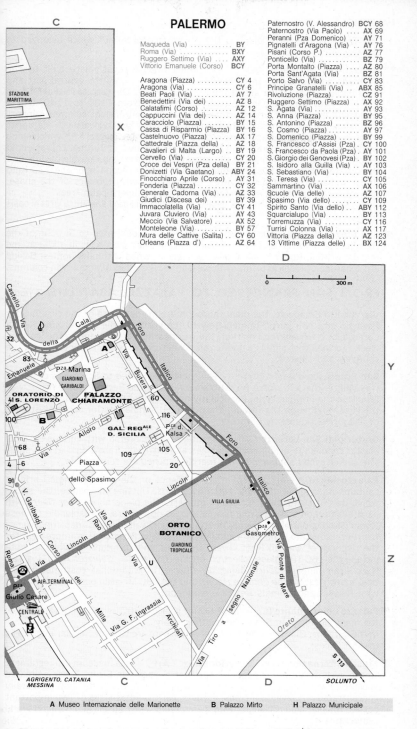

PALERMO

A Museo Internazionale delle Marionette   B Palazzo Mirto   H Palazzo Municipale

The two churches face each other on the small **Piazza Bellini★**. The Moorish and Norman features of the square are particularly evident in the three rose-coloured cupolas of San Cataldo.

★ **Cattedrale** (AYZ) ⊘ – Founded at the end of the 12C, the cathedral is built in the Sicilian-Norman style *(see Historical and Artistic Notes to Sicily)* but has often been modified and added to (15C south porch and the 18C dome). The **apses★** of the east end have retained their typically Sicilian-Norman decoration.
In the interior, which was modified in the 18C in the neo-Classical style, note on the right the tombs of the Emperor Frederick II and other members of the Hohenstaufen dynasty as well as other Angevin and Aragonese rulers.

323

The Treasury **(Tesoro)** ⊙ displays the ornate **imperial crown**★ which belonged to Constance of Aragon.

★★ **Palazzo dei Normanni** (AZ) ⊙ – Of the immense royal palace built by the Normans on the site of an earlier Moorish fortress, only the central part and the massive Pisan Tower are of the Norman period. The **Cappella Palatina**★★★ on the first floor was built in the reign of Roger II from 1130 to 1140. It is a wonderful example of Arab-Norman decoration. Ten ancient columns support horseshoe-shaped arches which separate the nave and two aisles. The upper walls, the dome and the apses are covered with dazzling **mosaics**★★★ which along with those of Constantinople and Ravenna are the finest in Europe. This splendid decoration is complemented by the carved stalactite ceiling, marble paving, and the ornate pulpit and paschal candelabrum. On the second floor the 12C King Roger's chamber, **Sala di re Ruggero**★★, is adorned with mosaics of the chase. The attractive gardens, **Villa Bonanno**★ (AZ), boast superb palm trees.

Only a stone's throw from the palace is **San Giovanni degli Eremiti**, a green oasis where even the noise of the traffic is dulled.

★ **San Giovanni degli Eremiti** (AZ) ⊙ – The church, dedicated to St John of the Hermits, which Arab architects helped to construct, was built in 1132 at the request of King Roger II and is picturesquely crowned with pink domes. Beside it is a garden of tropical plants with pleasant 13C **cloisters** of small twin columns.

FROM SAN FRANCESCO TO PALAZZO ABATELLIS *2 hours*

Via Vittorio Emanuele, the main thoroughfare in the centre of the city, divides Palermo into two parts. Immediately to the north, in the area around Piazza Caracciolo, is a lively food market, the **Vucciria** which is open during the working week. To the other side is a quieter area where visitors can enjoy exploring the churches and palaces.

★ **San Francesco d'Assisi** (CY) ⊙ – The church, dedicated to St Francis of Assisi, was built in the 13C. After its destruction during the Second World War it was rebuilt in the original style. Particularly noteworthy are the **portal** (original) and the rose window on the façade. The spacious, simple interior contains statues of allegorical figures by Serpotta.

★ **Oratorio di San Lorenzo** (CY) – The interior is decorated with curious Baroque plaster mouldings by Serpotta and has a *Nativity* by Caravaggio at the altar. The carved wood supports of the marble benches are remarkable.

★ **Palazzo Mirto** (CY B) ⊙ – The main residence of the Lanza-Filangieri princes contains its original 18C and 19C furnishings. Outside the palace, the **stables** which date back to the 19C, are of interest. The piano nobile *(1st floor)* with its drawing-rooms and formal rooms is open to visitors. The splendid Chinese Room **(Salottino cinese)** has leather flooring and silk wall coverings depicting scenes from everyday life. The Pompadour Room **(Salotto Pompadour)** is impressive for the richness of the silk that covers the walls and furniture. Exhibits of note include the 16C-18C glass collection *(in the Salotto del "Salvator Rosa")*, a 19C Neopolitan dinner service depicting figures in traditional costume *(in the passageway facing the Chinese Room)* and the 18C Meissen porcelain decorated with flowers and animals *(in the dining-room)*.

★ **Palazzo Chiaramonte** (CY) – A fine Gothic palace (1307) which served as a model for many buildings in Sicily and southern Italy.

In the gardens, Giardino Garibaldi, opposite there are two spectacular **magnolia-fig trees**★★ (ficus).

★ **Museo internazionale delle marionette** (CY A) ⊙ – This museum is a testament to the lively tradition of puppet (*marionette*) shows in Sicily. These animated spectacles were an even bigger part of Sicilian life in the past. Shows generally concentrated on chivalric themes, in particular the adventures of two important heros, Rinaldo and Orlando, who personified very different characters and temperaments.

The museum houses a splendid collection of Sicilian puppets. The delicate features of Gaspare Canino's puppets are admirable: these puppets are amongst the oldest in the collection (19C). The second part of the museum is dedicated to European and non-European craftsmanship and features puppets from all over Asia and Africa. The darkness of the room lends an air of mystery to the collection.

★★ **Galleria Regionale della Sicilia** (CY) ⊙ – This museum and gallery is housed in the attractive 15C **Palazzo Abatellis**. It includes a medieval art section and a picture gallery featuring works from the 11C to the 18C. The design of the gallery, which was built by Carlo Scarpa in the 1950s, is particularly interesting. The famous architect and designer concentrated on finding the best backdrop for the most important paintings, focusing on the frame and background, the materials and colours in order to maximise the impact of the natural light.

Outstanding works include the dramatic fresco of **Death Triumphant★★★** removed from Palazzo Sclafini, the *bust of a young woman* and a very fine *bust of Eleonora of Aragon* by Francesco Laurana. Paintings of note include the **Annunciation★★** by Antonello da Messina, with Mary's face exuding both a sense of peace and acceptance, and a triptych, the *Malvagna Altarolo,* by the Flemish artist, Mabuse.

ADDITIONAL SIGHTS

★ **Museo Archeologico** (BY) ⊙ – The archeological museum, which is housed in a 16C convent, contains the finds from excavations of the numerous ancient sites in Sicily. On the ground floor are displayed Phoenician sarcophagi, an Egyptian inscription known as the Palermo Stone, pieces from Selinunte including a fine series of twin stele and the reconstruction of a temple pediment *(Sala Gabrici)* and especially the remarkable **metopes★★** from temples (6C and 5C BC). On the first floor are displayed bronzes including the famous *ram★★*, a Hellenistic work from Syracuse, **Heracles with stag★★** and marble statues: *Satyr★*, a copy of an original from Praxiteles. On the second floor are two fine mosaics (2BC), *Orpheus with animals* and the *mosaic of the seasons*.

★★ **Catacombe dei cappuccini** ⊙ – *Access by Via dei Cappuccini* (AZ **14**). These Capuchin catacombs are an impressive sight. About 8 000 mummies were placed here from the 17C to 19C and have been preserved by the very dry air. They are decked in their finery and are placed in a line.

★ **La Zisa** ⊙ – *Access by Corso Finocchiaro Aprile* (AY **31**). This magnificent pleasure palace in the Arab-Norman style was built in the 12C and remodelled in the 17C. The palace (restored) now houses a collection of Egyptian works from the Mameluke and Ottoman periods, which probably complemented the decoration of the palace. The austere exterior is in contrast to the very ornate decoration inside.

★ **Orto Botanico** (CDZ) ⊙ – A quiet and secluded garden with a fine collection of exotic plants and trees. Nearby is the **Villa Giulia**, a fine example of an Italian garden.

Parco della Favorita – *3km – 2 miles north. Leave on the Via I Carini* (AX). This park was laid out for the Bourbons in the 18C. Beside the Chinese pavilion (Palazzina Cinese) is a museum, the **Museo Etnografico Pitrè** ⊙, which displays some fine **Sicilian carts★** *(see Sicily Today)*.

EXCURSIONS

★★ **Monreale** – *8km – 5 miles southwest. Leave by the Corso Calatafimi* (AZ **12**), *the S 186. See MONREALE.*

★★ **Monte Pellegrino** – *14km – 9 miles north. Leave by the Via Crispi* (BX). The road out affords splendid glimpses of Palermo and the Conca d'Oro. On the way up, the road passes a 17C sanctuary, Santuario di Santa Rosalia.

★ **Museo del carretto siciliano** – *Terrasini, 29km – 19 miles west of Palermo* – The museum houses a fine collection of Sicilian carts *(carretto):* the cart from Palermo (1953) which is decorated with scenes from the life of Roger the Norman, is particularly interesting.

★ **Rovine di Solunto** – *19km – 12 miles east. Leave on the S 113* (DZ). *See Rovine di SOLUNTO.*

Bagheria – *16km – 10 miles east by the A 19 motorway and then 4km – 2 miles southwest of Soluntum.* Bagheria is known for its baroque villas and especially for the **Villa Palagonia** ⊙, which is decorated with **sculptures★** of grotesques and monsters.

Isola di PANTELLERIA★★

PANTELLERIA ISLAND – Population 7 423
Michelin map 988 fold 35 or 432 Q 17/18

Situated in the Sicilian Channel, the Island of Pantelleria is only 84km – 52miles away from Cape Bon in Tunisia. It is the westernmost island of the Sicilian group and lies on the same latitude as Tunis. With an area of 83km² – 32sq miles it is also the largest island in the group.

Known as the "Black Pearl of the Mediterranean", the island is full of character with its indented coastline, steep slopes covered with terraces under cultivation, and its Moorish-looking cubic houses *(dammusi)*. The highest point of this volcanic island is **Montagna Grande** (836m - 2 743ft). The vineyards produce some pleasant wines such as the sparkling Solimano and the muscat Tanit. Capers are also grown on Pantelleria.

Isola di PANTELLERIA

Pantelleria has remains of prehistoric settlements and later suffered invasions like Sicily by the Phoenicians, Carthaginians, Greeks, Romans, Vandals, Byzantines, Moors and Normans who in 1123 united the island with Sicily.

Access: – **By air:** *see the current Michelin Red Guide Italia.* **By sea:** *see the Michelin maps 988 and 432 as well as the current Michelin Red Guide Italia.*

TOUR *3 hours*

★★ **Tour of the island by car** – *40km – 25 miles.* The very picturesque coastal road gives the visitor a good chance to discover the beauty of the indented coastline, cliffs, inlets, caves, thermal springs and lakes. On the west coast, 11.5km – 7 miles to the south of the town of Pantelleria, the village of **Scauri** boasts a lovely site. On the south coast towards **Dietro Isola** the corniche road affords beautiful plunging **views**★★ of this coastal area. The cape, **Punta dell'Arco**, is terminated by a splendid natural rock arch in grey volcanic stone known as the Elephant Arch (Arco dell'Elefante). On the northeast coast the inlet, **Cala dei Cinque Denti**, and the rest of the coastline further north make a lovely volcanic landscape.

★★ **Montagna Grande** – *13km – 8 miles southeast of Pantelleria.* From the summit of this peak there is a splendid **panorama** of the island. In clear weather the view extends as far as Sicily and Tunisia.

PIAZZA ARMERINA★★

Population 22 347
Michelin map 988 fold 36 or 432 O 25

The grey houses of Piazza Armerina huddle round the Baroque cathedral (**Duomo**) ⊙ on the pleasantly green slopes of a valley.

★★ **Villa Romana del Casale** ⊙ – *6km – 4 miles southwest.* This immense 3C or 4C Roman villa (3 500m^2 – 37 670sq ft) probably belonged to some dignitary and is important for its **mosaic pavements** which cover almost the entire floor-space. These picturesque mosaics, in a wide range of colours, are at times rather primitive and often show a certain North African influence.

The most famous pavements are: those showing **cupids** fishing or playing with dolphins, and the capturing and selling of **wild animals** for circus use (in the main corridor); those illustrating **sports** practised by young bikini-clad girls; and finally the mosaics of the **triclinium** portraying the *Labours of Hercules*, notably his struggle with the giants. Other scenes decorate the baths.

EXCURSION

Morgantina – *16km – 10 miles northeast by the Enna road, the S 117 bis, then the S 228 to the right. Continue for 6km – 4 miles beyond Aidone.*
Nor far from the village of Aidone excavations have uncovered an ancient site in an attractive setting. It has been identified as the early Siculi settlement of Morgantina which was later colonised by the Greeks. The city declined slowly from the 1C onwards. Amidst the extensive **ruins**, note on the valley floor the remains of an agora and a small theatre (rebuilt). The buildings on the hillside to the north house a number of **mosaics** which once adorned the 3C BC villas. The village of Aidone features a small museum (**museo**) displaying the finds from the nearby excavations.

RAGUSA★

Population 67 629
Michelin map 988 fold 37 or 432 Q 26

Ragusa, partly rebuilt following the 1693 earthquake, lies in a typical **setting**★ on a plateau between deep ravines. The modern town lies to the west while the old town, Ragusa Ibla, clusters on an outlier of the hills, Monti Iblei to the east. The Syracuse road offers magnificent **views**★★ of the old town.
Asphalt and oil are produced or refined locally in large industrial complexes.

★ **Ragusa Ibla** – The medieval area is a maze of streets, but much of the old town was rebuilt in the Baroque style. The lovely 18C Church of **San Giorgio**★ on Piazza del Duomo was designed by the architect Rosario Gagliardi who also worked in Noto. The pink stone façade has a slightly convex central section which is flanked by projecting columns.

Museo Archeologico Ibleo ⊙ – *Palazzo Mediterraneo, Via Natalelli.* In the modern town, below Ponte Nuovo, the viaduct which spans the Via Roma, this museum contains the finds from excavations undertaken locally, notably from the ancient Greek city of Camarina.

Rovine di SEGESTA★★★

SEGESTA (Ruins)

Michelin map 988 fold 35 or 432 N 20 – 35km – 22 miles southeast of Trapani

Splendidly situated against the hillside, its ochre colours in pleasant contrast to the vast expanse of green, the archeological park is dominated by a fine Doric temple standing in an isolated site. Probably founded, like Erice, by the Elimi it soon became one of the main cities in the Mediterranean basin under Greek influence, rivalling Selinunte in importance. It was probably destroyed by the Vandals.

★★ **Tempio** ⊙ – The temple of Segesta stands alone, on an eminence encircled by a deep ravine, in a landscape of receding horizons. The Doric building (430 BC), pure and graceful, is girt by a peristyle of 36 columns in golden-coloured limestone. The road leading up to the theatre *(2km – 1 mile)* affords a magnificent **view**★★ of the temple.

★ **Teatro** – This Hellenistic theatre (63m – 207ft in diameter) is built into the rocky hillside. The tiers of seats are orientated towards the hills, behind which, to the right, is the Gulf of Castellammare.

Rovine di SELINUNTE★★

SELINUS (Ruins)

Michelin map 988 fold 35 or 432 O 20

Selinus was founded in the mid-7C by people from the east coast city of Megara Hyblaea and was destroyed twice, in 409 and 250 BC, by the Carthaginians. The huge ruins of its temples with their enormous platforms, probably wrecked by earthquakes, are impressive. The admirable metopes which adorned these temples are in the National Museum at Palermo.

Zona archeologica ⊙ – Visitors to the site first reach an esplanade around which are grouped the remains of three **temples**. To the right of the road **Temple G**, probably dedicated to Apollo, was one of the largest in the ancient world. It was over 100m – 328ft long; its columns were built of blocks each weighing several tonnes. The rubble of the fallen stonework gives some indication of its great size. To the left of the road, behind the ruined Temple F, stands the **Temple E**★ (5C BC) which was rebuilt in 1958.

Cross the depression, Gorgo Cottone, to reach the **acropolis** with its perimeter wall. The site is dominated by the partially rebuilt (1926) columns of Temple C (6C BC), the oldest. There are four more ruined temples in the immediate vicinity.

Westwards, on the opposite bank of the Modione stand the remains of a sanctuary to Demeter Malophoros (the dispenser of fruits).

SIRACUSA★★★

SYRACUSE

Pop 125 972

Michelin map 988 fold 37 or 432 P 27

Syracuse, superbly situated at the head of a beautiful bay, enjoys a very mild climate. It was one of Sicily's, if not Magna Graecia's, most prestigious cities and at the height of its splendour rivalled Athens. Syracuse was colonised in the mid-8C BC by Greeks from Corinth who settled on the Island of Ortygia. It soon fell under the yoke of the tyrants, and it developed and prospered. In the 5C-4C BC the town had 300 000 inhabitants.

Captured by the Romans during the Second Punic War (212 BC), it was occupied successively by the Barbarians, Byzantines (6C), Arabs (9C) and Normans. The river Ciane *(see below)* with its papyrus beds was a centre of papyrus production. Since the 18C Syracuse has specialised in painting on papyrus, in the Egyptian manner.

Tyrants and intellectuals – In the Greek world, dictators called tyrants (from the Greek word *turannos*) exercised unlimited power over certain cities, especially Syracuse. Already in 485 BC **Gelon**, the tyrant of Gela, had become master of Syracuse. His brother **Hiero**, an altogether more unpleasant person, nonetheless patronised poets and welcomed to his court both **Pindar** and **Æschylus**, who died in Gela in 456.

Denis the Elder (405-367 BC) was the most famous but even he lived in constant fear. This was symbolised by the sword which he had suspended by a horsehair above the head of Damocles, a jealous courtier. He rarely left the safety of his castle on Ortygia. He wore a shirt of mail under his clothing and changed his room every night. He had Plato sold as a slave when the philosopher came to study the political habits of the people under his dictatorship.

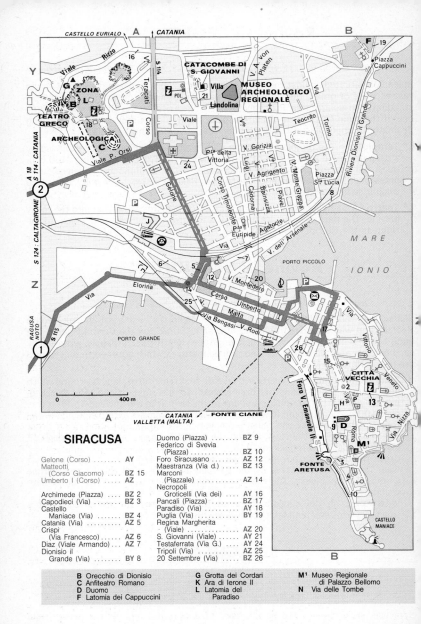

SIRACUSA

Archimedes, the famous geometrician born at Syracuse in 287 BC, was so absent-minded that he would forget to eat and drink. It was in his bath that he discovered his principle: any body immersed in water loses weight equivalent to that of the water it displaces. Delighted, he jumped out of the bath and ran naked through the streets shouting "Eureka" (I have found it !).

When defending Syracuse against the Romans, Archimedes set fire to the enemy fleet by focusing the sun's rays with a system of mirrors and lenses. But when the Romans succeeded in entering the town by surprise, Archimedes, deep in his calculations, did not hear them, and a Roman soldier ran him through with his sword.

★★★ ZONA ARCHEOLOGICA (AY) ⊘

2 hours on foot. Access by Via Paradiso (AY 18)

The archeological area extends over the ancient quarter of Neapolis (the new town) high above and overlooks the Ionian Sea.

From the **Viale Rizzo** which skirts the area, there is an excellent panorama of the ruins.

★★★ Teatro Greco

The Greek theatre dates from the 5C BC and is one of the largest of the ancient world. The tiers of seats are hewn out of the rock. The first performance of *The Persians* of Æschylus was held here.

A little further on stretches the **road to the tombs (N)**, which is hewn out of the rock.

★★ **Latomia del Paradiso (L)** – This former quarry, now an orange grove, dates from ancient times. Part of its roof fell in during the 1693 earthquake.
The Ear of Denis **(Orecchio di Dionisio★★★ – B)** is an artificial grotto in the form of an earlobe. The grotto was so named in 1608 by the painter Caravaggio as a reminder of the legend recounting how the exceptional echo enabled the tyrant Denis to overhear the talk of the prisoners he confined in a room below. The Cordmakers' Cave **(Grotta dei Cordari – G)** takes its name from the cordmakers who used to work there, as the humidity in the air and the fresh atmosphere enabled them to spin and plait the hemp.

Ara di Ierone II (K) – To the left of the Via Paradiso this altar (200m – 656ft long), partly hewn out of the rock, was used for public sacrifices.

★ **Anfiteatro Romano (C)** – This 3C or 4C BC Roman amphitheatre (140m by 119m – 459ft by 390ft) is hewn out of the rock. There are pines all around.

★★ **L'ORTIGIA** (BZ) *3/4 hour*

The Island of Ortygia boasts numerous medieval and Baroque palaces. The latter are found mainly in **Via della Maestranza (13)**. These narrow streets are shaded in summer and are ideal for a stroll.
The **Piazza Duomo★ (9)** is particularly attractive, lined by palaces adorned with wrought-iron balconies and the monumental façade of the cathedral **(Duomo★ – D)**. It was built in the 7C on the foundations of a Doric temple dedicated to Athena, some columns of which were reused in the Christian building (north and interior). Inside, there are several sculptures (including the *Madonna of the Snow*) which are attributed to the Gagini, a family of artists who settled in Sicily in the 16C.

★ **Fonte Aretusa** – This is the legendary cradle of the city. The nymph Arethusa, pursued by the river-god Alpheus, took refuge on the Island of Ortygia where she was changed into a spring (*fonte*) by Artemis. Though near the sea, the fountain, built into a wall, runs with fresh water.
From the nearby platform there is a view of the beautiful Bay of Syracuse. The **Passaggio Adorno**, a favourite walk for the Syracusans, starts below.

★ **Galleria Regionale di Palazzo Bellomo (M')** ⊙ – The museum is housed in the beautiful 13C palace which was remodelled in the Catalan style in the 15C. The art gallery has an admirable *Annunciation★* (damaged) by Antonello da Messina and *The Burial of St Lucy* by Caravaggio. There is also a collection of goldsmiths' work, Sicilian cribs, liturgical objects and furniture.

★★ **MUSEO ARCHEOLOGICO REGIONALE** (AY) ⊙ *1 hour*

In the charming grounds of the **Villa Landolina** stands the museum built in memory of the archeologist Paolo Orsi (1859-1935).
It presents the history of Sicily from prehistoric times up to the Greek colonies of Syracuse (7C BC).
The first section explains the local geology – skeletons of the two dwarf elephants – and prehistory, starting from the Upper Palaeolithic, when man made his first appearance in Sicily.
The second part features the Greek colonisation (from mid-8C BC onwards); many artefacts were salvaged in the Lentinoi excavations (marble kouros) but more importantly at Megara Hyblaea and at Syracuse: chalk statue of a **goddess-mother★**, ceramics, architectural fragments and small-scale replicas of the great sanctuaries of Ortygia, the oldest district in Syracuse.
The third part of the museum is devoted to the various Syracuse colonies. The town became very powerful and in 664 BC it founded Akrai (Palazzolo Acreide). Then followed Kasmenai (Monte Casale) in 644 BC and Camarina (598 BC); chalk statues, horsemen used in the ornamentation of temples etc. This part of the building also shows artefacts from the Greek colonies inland (large statue of Demeter or Koré enthroned) and the excavation sites at Gela and Agrigento, which were conducted by Paolo Orsi.
The exhibits concerning later periods of history are on display on the upper floor.

ADDITIONAL SIGHTS

★★ **Catacombe di San Giovanni** (AY) ⊙ – After the catacombs in Rome, these are the finest examples in Italy. In contrast to those in Rome that have been dug out of fragile tufa, the catacombs in Syracuse have been excavated from solid rock to create spacious chambers, big enough to hold up to seven tombs. They consist of a main gallery off which branch secondary galleries ending in circular chapels or rotundas; several of the tombs are in the form of arched niches.

★★ **Latomia dei Cappuccini** (BY F) – In 413 BC 7 000 Athenian prisoners were interned in these quarries by Denis of Syracuse. The quarries are now overgrown by luxuriant vegetation.

EXCURSIONS

★ **Fonte Ciane** ⊙ - *8km - 5 miles southwest. It is best to visit by boat.* The river, **Fiume Ciane**★★, is lined with papyrus beds, which are unique in Italy. It was here that the nymph Ciane was changed into a spring when she opposed the abduction of Proserpine by Pluto.

★ **Castello Eurialo** ⊙ - *9km - 6 miles northwest of the plan.* This was one of the greatest fortresses of the Greek period; it was built by Denis the Elder. Fine **panorama**★.

Rovine di SOLUNTO★

SOLUNTUM (Ruins)
Michelin map 988 fold 36 or 432 M 22
20km - 12 miles east of Palermo

Soluntum stands in an admirable **site**★★ on a rocky ledge on the promontory which overlooks a headland, Capo Zafferano. It was a Phoenician city before it fell under the sway of Rome in the 3C BC.

The site **(zona archeologica)** ⊙ *(access by a narrow road which branches off from the S 113 in Porticello, in the direction of a hill)* includes ruins of a forum, theatre, streets, houses, drainage system and numerous cisterns. Take the Via Ippodamo da Mileto to reach the summit. There is a splendid **view**★★ of the bay of Palermo and Monte Pellegrino.

TAORMINA★★★

Population 10 115
Michelin map 988 fold 37 or 432 N 27
Town plan in the current Michelin Red Guide Italia

Taormina stands in a wonderful **site**★★★ at an altitude of 250m - 820ft and forms a balcony overlooking the sea and facing Etna. It is renowned for its peaceful atmosphere and its beautiful monuments and gardens.

★★★ **Teatro Greco** ⊙ - The Greek theatre dates from the 3C BC but was remodelled by the Romans who used it as an arena for their contests.
Performances of Classical plays are given in summer. From the upper tiers there is an admirable **view**★★★ between the stage columns of the coastline and Etna.

★ **Giardino Pubblico** - From these terraced public gardens of flowers and exotic plants there are views of the coast and the sea.

★ **Corso Umberto** - The main street of Taormina has three gateways along its course: Porta Catania; the middle one, Porta di Mezzo, with the Torre dell'

Orologio (Clock Tower); and Porta Messina.
The Piazza del Duomo is overlooked by the Gothic façade of the cathedral and adorned by an attractive Baroque fountain. Almost halfway along, the **Piazza 9 Aprile**★ forms a terrace which affords a splendid **panorama**★★ of the gulf. The Piazza Vittorio Emanuele was laid out on the site of the forum and is overlooked by the 15C Palazzo Corvaja.

★ **Belvedere** - It affords a view of the Aspromonte Massif in Calabria, the Sicilian coast and Etna.

The theatre and Mount Etna, Taormina

EXCURSIONS

★ **Castello** - *4km - 2 miles northwest by the Castelmola road, and then a road to the right. It is also possible to walk up (1 hour Rtn).*
The castle was built in the medieval period on the summit of Monte Tauro (390m - 1 280ft), on the remains of the former acropolis. There are splendid **views**★ of Taormina.

★ **Castel Mola** ⊘ - *5km - 2 miles northwest.* This tiny village is strategically located near Taormina and enjoys a splendid **site**★ with panoramic views. The focus of the village is the attractive Piazzetta del Duomo with its fine, intricate paving. From various points there are fine **views**★ of Etna, the north coast and the beaches below Taormina.

Rovine di TINDARI★

TINDARI (Ruins)

Michelin map 988 fold 37 or 432 M 27 - 62km - 39 miles west of Messina

The ancient Greek Tyndaris, founded in 396 BC, is perched on the summit of the cape of the same name. At the very point stands a sanctuary **(santuario)** with a Black Virgin which is a place of pilgrimage. The ruins **(rovine)** ⊘ are essentially those of the city **ramparts**, the theatre on a site facing the sea, and a fine arcaded Roman building (access by the main street, the Decumanus) which preceded the forum.

TRAPANI

Population 69 562
Michelin map 988 fold 35 or 432 M 19
Town plan in the current Michelin Red Guide Italia

Trapani has a sheltered port within sight of the Egadi Islands. A pretty coastal road links the town centre with the beach at San Giuliano *(3km - 2 miles north).*

Santuario dell'Annunziata ⊘ - Built in the 14C, the church was remodelled and enlarged in the 17C. The campanile is Baroque. On the north side the attractive 16C Renaissance Sailors' Chapel **(Cappella dei Marinai)** is crowned with a dome.
Inside, the **Cappella della Madonna**★ contains a Renaissance arch carved in the 16C, a bronze railing dated 1591 and a graceful statue of the Virgin (14C) attributed to Nino Pisano.

★ **Museo Pepoli** ⊘ - The Pepoli Museum is located in the former Carmelite convent which adjoins the Annunziata. The works include sculpture (by the Gagini) and paintings (the 15C Trapani polyptych, a *Pietà* by Roberto di Oderisio, *St Bartholomew* by Ribera and *St Francis receiving the Stigmata* by Titian). There is also a display of local crafts: coral work and a very delicate crib.

Le saline - The coastal road which leads from Trapani to Marsala is lined with saltpans *(saline)* and fine open views; the water is divided into a multi-coloured grid by strips of land. In places there are windmills, a reminder of times gone by when they were the main way to pump water and grind the salt. The view is even more evocative in the summer, at harvest time, when the rose-coloured tint of the water in the basins is more intense (the colour changes as the saline content increases) and the shimmering pools of water inland are drying out in the sun. At Nubia there is a small, but interesting salt museum **(Museo del Sale)** ⊘ housed in a 17C saltworks where an exhibition illustrates this ancient craft: tools, display panels.

Practical
Information

Main tourist routes

This map gives the distances and journey times between some main towns in Italy. It does not aim to show all the fast routes throughout the country but to give an indication of the journey time to be allowed for on a trip.
The Italian road network ranks second in Europe; its bold design has produced some remarkable feats of engineering and brings the landscape into play to spectacular effect.

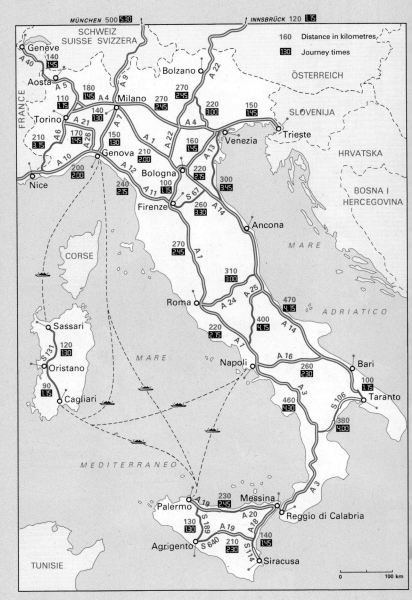

When planning a trip travellers should also consult:
● the map of Principal Sights
● the map of Touring Programmes
● the Calendar of Events at the end of the guide

A Map of Touring Programmes
is given at the beginning of the guide
To plan a special tour
use the preceding Map of Principal Sights

Travelling to Italy

Passport – Visitors entering Italy must be in possession of a valid national **passport**. Citizens of other European countries need only a national identity card. In case of loss or theft, report to the embassy or consulate and the local police.

Visa – Entry visas are required by Australian, New Zealand, Canadian and US citizens (if their intended stay exceeds three months). Apply to the Italian Consulate (visa issued same day; delay if submitted by mail). US citizens should obtain the booklet **Your Trip Abroad**, which provides useful information on visa requirements, customs regulations, medical care etc for international travellers, (US$1.25) from the Superintendent of Documents, PO Box 371954, Pittsburgh, PA 15250-7954, ☎ 202 512 1800.

Customs – A Guide to Travellers outlines British customs regulations and duty-free allowances; it is available from HM Customs and Excise. The US Customs Service, PO Box 7407, Washington, DC 20044, ☎ 202 927 5580, offers a free brochure **Know before you go** for US citizens.
There are no customs formalities for holidaymakers bringing their caravans into the Italy for a stay of less than six months. No customs document is necessary for pleasure boats and outboard motors for a stay of less than six months but the registration certificate should be kept on board.

By air – Many international and other independent airlines operate services to Rome and to the major provincial airports (Milan, Turin, Verona, Genoa, Bologna, Pisa, Naples; Florence often requires a change in Milan, although there are direct trains from Pisa airport to the centre of Florence – transport time about 1 hour). There are several flights per day from London (Heathrow) to Rome and Milan; 2 flights per day from London (Heathrow) to Turin, Verona, Genoa, Bologna, Pisa and Naples, from London (Gatwick) to Rome, Naples and Genoa, and from Manchester or Birmingham to Milan; and 3 flights per week from Dublin to Rome. There are package tour flights and Fly-Drive schemes available. Information, brochures and timetables are available from airlines and travel agents.
The domestic network operates frequent services covering the whole country. There are transfer buses to town terminals and railway stations.
It is advisable to book well in advance for the holiday season.

By sea – Details of passenger ferry and car ferry services from the UK and Eire to the Channel ports, linking up with the European rail and motorway network can be obtained from travel agents and from the main operators: P & O European ferries, Stena Sealink, Hoverspeed etc. For details of crossing via the **Channel Tunnel** (high-speed undersea rail shuttle link between Folkestone and Calais), telephone Le Shuttle Passenger enquiries: ☎ 01303 271100.
For the different shipping routes (passenger and car ferries) between the Italian peninsula and the various islands, consult the **Michelin map 988** and the **Michelin Red Guide Italia**.

By road – Roads from France into Italy, with the exception of the Menton/Ventimiglia (Riviera) coast road, are dependent on Alpine passes and tunnels. The main roads go through the Montgenèvre pass near Briançon, the Fréjus tunnel and Mont-Cenis pass near Saint-Jean-de-Maurienne, the Petit-Saint-Bernard pass near Bourg-Saint-Maurice and the Mont-Blanc tunnel near Chamonix.
Via Switzerland, three main routes are possible – through the tunnel or pass at Grand-Saint-Bernard, through the Simplon pass, and through the St Gottard pass which goes via Ticino and Lugano to the great lakes of Lombardy. Those planning to drive through Switzerland should remember to budget for the Swiss road tax *(vignette)*, which is levied on all motor vehicles and trailers with a maximum weight of 3.5 tonnes, instead of charging tolls on the motorways (the *vignette* costs 40 Swiss francs and can be bought at the border crossings, post offices, petrol stations, garages and cantonal motor registries, or in advance from the Swiss National Tourist Office).
For those driving down through Germany and Austria, there is the Brenner pass south of Innsbruck.
Remember that most of these tunnels or passes levy a **toll**.
Use **Michelin maps 987, 989 and 988** or the **Michelin Road Atlas Europe** to help you plan your route.
Regular **coach services** are operated from London to Rome and to large provincial Italian towns. Details and bookings from: Eurolines (subsidiary of National Express), Luton (Head Office), ☎ 0582 404511. Eurolines serves Rome, Turin, Milan, Bologna and Florence; the Rome service is on Mondays, Wednesdays and Fridays departing at 09.30 from London-Victoria coach station and arriving the following day at 18.15.
National Express, Victoria Coach Station, London SW1, ☎ 0171 730 0202.
Eurolines, 52 Grosvenor Gardens, London SW1W 0AU, ☎ 0171 730 8235.

By rail – From London and the Channel ports there are rail services to many Italian towns including many high-speed passenger trains and motorail services. For tourists residing outside Italy, there are rail passes offering unlimited travel, and group travel tickets offering savings for parties on the Italian Railways network. Tickets from Wasteels Travel, 121 Wilton Road, London SW1, ☎ 0171 834 7066 (fax 0171 630 7628); and from principal British and American Rail Travel Centres and travel agencies.

All trains for Italy from the UK go via Paris, daily.

Travelling by rail is a particularly good way of getting to Milan, Venice and Florence, as the rail stations here are within easy reach of the centre of town.

Motoring in Italy

Documents – Nationals of EU countries require a valid **national driving licence** with an Italian translation (except in the case of the UK pink licence); nationals of non-EU countries require an **international driving licence** (available in the US from the American Automobile Association for US$10).

For the vehicle, it is necessary to have the car **registration papers**, and a nationality plate of the approved size.

Insurance – Insurance cover is compulsory, and an International Insurance Certificate (Green Card), although no longer a legal requirement, is the most effective proof of insurance cover and is internationally recognised by the police and other authorities. Certain UK motoring organisations (AA; RAC; Routiers, 25 Vanston Place, London SW6, ☎ 0171 385 6644) run accident insurance and breakdown service schemes for their members. Europ-Assistance (252 High St, Croydon CR0 1NF) also has special policies for motorists. Members of the American Automobile Association should obtain the free brochure *Offices to Serve You Abroad*.

The **Italian Automobile Club (ACI)** has its head office at Via Marsala 8, 00185 Roma, ☎ (06) 4998. A car breakdown service (tax levied) is operated by the ACI for foreign motorists; dial 116 for assistance in case of breakdown. The ACI also offers a telephone information service in English (and other languages) for road and weather conditions as well as for tourist events: ☎ (06) 4477.

Highway Code – The minimum driving age is 18. Traffic drives on the right. It is compulsory for the driver and front-seat passengers to wear seat belts, and seat belts must be worn in the back where they are fitted. Children under 12 must travel in the back seats, unless the front seat is fitted with a child restraint system. Full or dipped headlights must be switched on in poor visibility and at night; use sidelights only when a stationary vehicle is not clearly visible.

In the event of a breakdown, a red warning triangle must be displayed in the road; these can be hired from the ACI offices at the frontier (deposit refunded).

Drivers should watch out for unfamiliar road signs and take great care on the road (it is not without some justification that people say Italian drivers prefer using their horn to their brakes!). At crossroads drivers coming from the right have priority.

Severe penalties are applicable for drink-driving offences.

Speed limits: in built-up areas, 50kph – 31mph
on country roads, 90kph – 55mph
on motorways, 90kph – 55mph for vehicles up to 1000cc and 130kph – 80mph for vehicles over 1100cc.

Parking – There are many car parks with attendants, particularly in the Naples area. Obviously, you should check the rates before parking, to avoid any unpleasant surprises as you leave, but it is advisable, particularly in the south, to use these car parks rather than leave vehicles unattended.

In many large towns, the historical town centre is subject to traffic restrictions (authorized vehicles only may enter), indicated by large rectangular signs saying "**Zona a traffico limitato riservata ai veicoli autorizzati**". In this case, park your vehicle outside the town before proceeding on foot, as the streets are often very narrow and have no pavements (sidewalks).

Petrol – Gazolio = diesel. Super = super leaded (98 octane).
Senza piombo = premium unleaded petrol (95 octane).
Super Plus or Euro Plus = super unleaded petrol (98 octane).
Petrol stations are usually open between 7am to 7pm. Many close at lunch-time (between 12.30pm and 3pm), Sundays and public holidays and many refuse payment by credit card.

Route planning – Michelin map 988 at a scale of 1:1 000 000 covers the whole country. At 1:400 000, **Michelin map 428** covers the northwest, **429** the northeast, **430** the centre, **431** the south, **432** Sicily and **433** Sardinia; at 1:200 000, **218** covers Bolzano and **219** covers from Aosta to Milan; at 1:100 000, **115** covers the very western stretch of the Italian Riviera.

The **Touring Club Italiano (TCI)**, Corso d'Italia 10, 20139 Milano, ☎ (02) 85 26 72, publishes a regional map series at 1:200 000.

The Italian road network is excellent, and there are many motorways *(autostrade)*, most of which are **toll-roads**. The toll is calculated according to the distance between the car axles and engine capacity. **Motorway tolls** can be paid with money or with the **Viacard**, a magnetic card with a value of L 90 000 or L 50 000 which is sold in Italy at the beginning of motorways, in Autogrill restaurants or in the offices of the ACI. See above for details of the ACI breakdown service.

Road signs – Motorways (autostrade – subject to tolls) and dual carriageways (superstrade) are indicated by green signs; ordinary roads by blue signs; tourist sights by yellow signs.

Car Rental – There are car rental agencies at airports, railway stations and in all large towns and resorts throughout Italy. European cars usually have manual transmission, but automatic cars are available on demand. An **international driving licence** is required for non-EU nationals.

Accommodation

Places to Stay – The maps on pp 8-11 indicate the recommended places for overnight stops. The **Michelin Red Guide Italia** which is revised each year, lists a selection of hotels, guest-houses and restaurants together with their type, location, price, amenities and level of comfort.

The provincial tourist boards and the local tourist offices of the various cities and resorts publish accommodation lists and leaflets available by writing direct to these offices (addresses from the Italian State Tourist Office and the Michelin Red Guide Italia). The TCI *(see previous page)* publishes a guide to tourist villages which are located in or near popular resorts.

Rural accommodation – Information is available from the **Associazione nazionale per l'Agriturismo, l'Ambiente e il Territorio**, Via degli Slavoia, 6 , 00196 Roma, ☎ (06) 36 11 051, or from provincial tourist offices.

Listings are also published in **Turismo Verde** (by Confedarazione Italiana Agricoltori, ☎ (06) 36 12 803) or **Vacanze Natura** (by Associazione Terranostra, ☎ (06) 46 821).

Youth Hostels – In Italy, these are called *Alberghi per la Gioventù*. Although some accept national cards, it is best to obtain an international youth hostel federation card. A list of youth hostels is available from the International Federation or the **AGI** (Italian Youth Hostels Association), Via Cavour 44, 00184 Roma, ☎ (06) 48 71 152.

Youth Hostels Association, Trevelyan House, 8 Stephen's Hill, St Albans, Herts AL1 2DY. American Youth Hostel Inc, National Offices, PO Box 37613, Washington DC 20013-7613.

Camping – Italy has over 16 000 officially-graded camp sites with varying ranges of facilities. There are very few possibilities for camping other than on an officially recognised site, and in the summer it is highly recommended that you **reserve a pitch in advance**, as camp sites get extremely crowded in high season.

An International Camping Carnet for caravans is useful, but not compulsory; it can be obtained from the motoring organisations or the Camping and Caravanning Club (Greenfields House, Westwood Way, Coventry CV4 8JH, ☎ 01203 694 995).

The Italian Camping Federation (Federcampeggio, Casella Postale 23, 50041 Calenzano (Firenze), ☎ (055) 88 23 91), Fax (055) 88 25 918, publishes a map of camp sites and a list of those which offer special rates to holders of the international camping card. It also publishes an annual guide *Campeggi e Villagi Turistici in Italia* in collaboration with the TCI. Local tourist boards also supply information on camp sites.

MICHELIN GREEN GUIDES

Art and Architecture; Ancient monuments; History; Landscape; Scenic routes Touring programmes; local maps; town plans; site plans

A selection of guides for holidays at home and abroad

General information

Electricity – The electric current is 220 volts AC (50 cycles). Circular 2-pin plugs are standard.

Time – In winter, standard time is Greenwich Mean Time + 1 hour. In summer the clocks go forward an hour to give Italian Summer Time (GMT + 2 hours) from the last weekend in March to the last weekend in September.

Medical treatment – British citizens should apply to the Department of Health and Social Security for **Form E111**, which entitles the holder to urgent treatment for accident or unexpected illness in EU countries.
Nationals of non-EU countries should check that their insurance policy covers them specifically for overseas travel, including doctor's visits, medication and hospitalization in Italy (in most cases you will probably have to take out supplementary medical insurance).
American Express offers its cardholders (only) a service called *Global Assist* to help in financial, legal, medical or personal emergencies. To request assistance, call collect ☎ 202 554 2639.
All prescription drugs should be clearly labelled, and it is recommended that you carry a copy of the prescription with you.
A list of chemists open at night or on Sundays may be obtained from chemists shops (*farmacia* – red cross sign). First Aid service (*pronto soccorso*) is available at airports, railway stations and in hospitals.

Currency – In Italy, the currency is the **lira** which is issued in notes (L 100 000, 50 000, 20 000, 10 000, 5 000, 2 000, 1 000) and in coins (L 500, 200, 100, 50). There are no restrictions on the amount of currency visitors are allowed to take into Italy. If exporting currency in foreign bank notes in excess of the given allocation, visitors are advised to complete a currency declaration form (V2) on arrival.

Banks – Banks are generally open from 8.30am to 1.30pm and from 3pm to 4pm and closed on Saturdays, Sundays and public holidays.
Money can also be changed at the Post Office (except travellers' cheques), in exchange offices and at railway stations and airports. A commission is always charged.
Most banks have cash dispensers which accept international credit cards.

Eurocard – Eurocheques are widely accepted, although the value guaranteed is restricted – it is advisable to check on the rules before departure. Money withdrawn from Bancomat machines with a PIN incurs a lesser commission than a withdrawal transacted over the counter at a bank.

Credit cards – American Express, Visa (Barclaycard), Diners Club and Eurocard (Mastercard/Access) are widely accepted in shops, hotels and restaurants, but not always at petrol stations. Call the Italian tourist board (ENIT) for details of special offers open to Visa card-holders ("Italy welcomes Visa – VIP pass").

Post – Italian post offices are open from 8.30pm to 2pm (12pm on Saturdays and the last day of the month). Stamps are also sold at tobacconists.

Telephone – The telephone service is organised by TELECOM ITALIA (formerly SIP). Each office has public booths where the customer pays for units used (*scatti*) at the counter after the call.

Public phones: Orange phones in the street or in bars may be operated by phone cards, coins or L 200 brass tokens. To make a call: lift the receiver, insert payment, await dialling signal, punch in the number.

Phone cards: These are sold in denominations of L 5 000, L 10 000, L 15 000 (shede da cinque, dieci, quindici mila lire) and are available from CIT offices, post offices, tobacconists and newsagents.
In Italy, phone calls are cheaper after 6.30pm. Lower rates apply from 10pm to 8am, at weekends (from 1.30pm on Saturdays) and public holidays.
The country code for Italy is 39. To make an international call from Italy, dial 00 + country code + area code (minus any preceding zeros) + correspondent's number.

Useful telephone numbers:
12 directory enquiries
15 Assisted operator service – reverse-charge (collect) call
112 *carabinieri* police (*in emergencies only*)
113 police, Red Cross, emergency first aid
115 fire brigade
116 ACI (Italian Automobile Club) vehicle breakdown service
176 information in foreign languages.

Tobacconists – Besides cigarettes and tobacco, *tabacchi* sell postcards and stamps, confectionery, phonecards, public transport tickets, lottery tickets etc.

Shopping

Opening hours – Most shops open from 8.30-9am to 12.30-1pm and 3.30-4pm to 7.30-8pm, although in the centre of large towns and cities, shops usually remain open at lunchtime. In northern Italy, shops often take a shorter midday break and close earlier. Late-night shopping is frequent in seaside resorts. Many tourist resorts have an open-air market once or twice a week.

Public holidays – The following are days when museums and other monuments may be closed or vary their hours of admission:
1 January
6 January (Epiphany)
Easter Day and Easter Monday
25 April (anniversary of the 1945 liberation)
1 May
15 August ("Ferragosto")
1 November (All Saints)
8 December
25 and 26 December
Each town also celebrates the feast day of its patron saint (details of local festivals can be obtained from the local tourist offices).

Beaches – In some of the extremely popular parts of Italy – Liguria, the Tuscan Coast, the Adriatic Coast, etc. – private beaches (often very clean and with excellent facilities), for which an entrance fee is charged, alternate with public beaches (free of charge), which are not as well maintained.

Tourist information

Italian State Tourist Office – ENIT (Ente Nazionale Italiano per il Turismo) – For information, brochures, maps and assistance in planning a trip to Italy, apply to the ENIT in your country:

Canada 1 Place Ville-Marie, Suite 1914, Montréal, Québec H3B 3M9, ☎ 514 866 7667/8/9

UK 1 Princes Street, London W1R 8AY, ☎ 0171 408 1254, Fax 0171 493 6695 ; 24-hour brochure request line : ☎ 0891 600280

USA 630 Fifth Avenue, Suite 1565, New York, NY 10111, ☎ 212 245 4822
12400 Wilshire Boulevard, Suite 550, Los Angeles, CA 90025, ☎ 310 820 0098

Regional and local tourist information centres – In each regional capital there is a regional tourist board **(Assessorato per il Turismo)**. The Michelin Red Guide Italia gives the addresses and telephone numbers of provincial tourist boards **(Ente Provinciale Turismo** or **Azienda di Promozione Turistica)** and local tourist boards **(Azienda Autonoma di Soggiorno, Cura e Turismo - AST)**, for information on particular towns or regions, and also the addresses of the offices of the Italian Automobile Club (ACI).

Tourism for the Disabled – A number of sights described in this guide are accessible to the disabled. They are indicated by the symbol ⟨ in the section entitled *Admission Times and Charges* at the end of the guide.
The Michelin Red Guide Italia (hotels and restaurants) indicates hotels with rooms which are easily accessible to the physically handicapped.

Embassies

Australia via Alessandria 215, 00198 Roma, ☎ (06) 83 27 21

Canada via G B de Rossi 27, 00161 Roma, ☎ (06) 44 59 81

Eire Largo Nazareno 3, 00187 Roma, ☎ (06) 67 82 541

UK via XX Settembre 80a, 10122 Roma, ☎ (06) 48 25 441/551

USA via Veneto 119a, 00187 Roma, ☎ (06) 46 741

Consulates

Australia via Borgogna 2, 20122 Milano, ☎ (02) 76 01 33 30

Canada via Vittor Pisani 19, 20124 Milano, ☎ (02) 66 97 451

UK Dorsoduro 1051, 30123 Venezia, ☎ (041) 52 27 207 or 52 27 408
Lungarno Corsini 2, 50123 Firenze ☎ (055) 28 41 33 or 21 25 94
via Crispi 122, 80122 Napoli, ☎ (081) 66 35 11
via S Paolo 7, 20121 Milano, ☎ (02) 72 30 01

USA Lungarno A Vespucci 38, 50123 Firenze, ☎ (055) 239 82 76
piazza Repubblica 2, 80122 Napoli, ☎ (081) 583 81 11
via Principe Amedeo 2/10, 20121 Milano, ☎ (02) 29 03 51

Recreation

Sport and Leisure

Useful addresses for outdoor enthusiasts include:

Canoeing – Federazione Italiana Canottaggio, viale Tiziano 70, 00196 Roma, ☎ (06) 36 851.

Cycling – Associazione Ciclista Italiana, settore cicloturismo, Stadio Olimpico, curva Nord, cancello L, porta 91, 00194 Foro Italico, Roma, ☎ (06) 36 851.

Fishing – Federazione Italiana Pesca Sportiva, Sezione Provinciale di Roma, piazza Emporio 16/a, 00153 Roma, ☎ (06) 57 55 253.

Hunting – Federazione Italiana della Caccia, viale Tiziano 70, 00196 Roma, ☎ (06) 36 851.

Mountaineering – Club Alpino Italiano, Via Ugo Foscolo 3, 20121 Milano, ☎ (02) 86 46 30 70.

Rambling – Federazione Italiana – Europea di Turismo Pedestre, via Salgari 1, 16156 Genova-Pegli, ☎ (010) 69 70 793.

Riding and Pony Trekking – Associazione Nazionale Turismo Equestre, via Borelli 5, 00161 Roma, ☎ (06) 44 41 179.

Sailing and Wind surfing – Federazione Italiana Vela, viale Brigata Bisagno 2, 16129 Genova, ☎ (010) 58 94 31.

Skiing – Federazione Italiana Sport Invernali, viale Olimpiadi, 00194 Roma, ☎ (06) 32 21 16 31.

Spas – For details, contact the National Italian Tourist Office (ENIT) in Rome, via Marghera 2, 00185 Roma, ☎ (06) 49 711 *(or see Tourist Information above for local ENIT addresses)*.

Speleology – Società Speleologica Italiana, via Zamboni 67, 40127 Bologna, ☎ (051) 35 45 47.

Exploring Italy

Travelling through Italy is quick and easy using the excellent motorway network. The extremely comprehensive national road network also offers the possibility of exploring localities which are more off the beaten track.

Roman roads

Many of Italy's modern roads follow the same routes as ancient Roman roads:
- the **Via Appia**, built in 312 BC, once went from Rome to Brindisi. Now, there is only a short section left in the immediate vicinity of the capital.
- the **Via Aurelia** (241 BC) went from Rome via Genoa to Arles in the south of France. It is now the SS1, known as the "Aurelia", and starts at Ventimiglia.
- the **Via Cassia**, paved in the 2C BC, crossed Etruria from Rome to Arezzo. It was later extended to Florence and Modena. The modern SS2, which bears the same name, goes from Rome to Florence.
- the **Via Emilia** (187 BC), which went from Rimini to Piacenza, gave its name to the region of Emilia. Under the Empire, it was extended to Aosta and Aquileia. The modern Via Emilia follows the exact route of the original road.
- the **Via Flaminia** (220 BC) led from Rome to Rimini. It is now one of the main roads of the Eternal City.

Nature parks

National nature parks are the ideal destination for holidaymakers more in search of contact with nature than regular tourist pursuits.

Gran Paradiso – Extends from the Valle d'Aosta to Piedmont *(see AOSTA)*.

Stelvio – This includes the Ortles-Cevedale massif and covers the provinces of Bolzano, Trento, Sondrio and Brescia. The park can be reached via Lombardy on the SS 38 to Bormio, or via Trentino by taking first the motorway, then the SS 43 to Rabbi.

Monti dell'Uccellina – Located in the heart of the Maremma. Take the A 12 motorway to Grosseto. After Grosseto, follow signs to Alberese or Talamone.

Abruzzi National Park – *See Appennino ABRUZZESE*.

Circeo National Park – *See TERRACINA*.

Calabria National Park – It covers the wooded massifs of Sila and Aspromonte. Leave the A 3 motorway at Cosenza or Reggio di Calabria. *See CALABRIA*.

Books to read

We list below only a selection of the many books on Italy. Some, which may be out of print, will be available only from libraries.

History and Art

A Concise Encyclopaedia of the Italian Renaissance by J R Hale *(Thames and Hudson)*
A History of Italian Renaissance Art by F Hartt *(Thames and Hudson)*
Architecture of the Italian Renaissance by Peter Murray *(Thames and Hudson)*
Leonardo da Vinci by Martin Kemp, Jane Roberts and Philip Steadman *(Yale University Press)*
Michelangelo by Howard Hibbard *(Penguin)*
Rise and Fall of the House of Medici by Christopher Hibbert *(Penguin)*
Roman Italy by T W Potter *(British Museum Publications Ltd)*
Siena: A City and its History by Judith Hook *(Hamish Hamilton)*
The Art of the Renaissance by Linda and Peter Murray *(Thames and Hudson)*
The Grandeur that was Rome by J C Stobart *(Sidgwick and Jackson)*
The Italian World by J J Norwich *(Thames and Hudson)*
Venetian Painting: A Concise History by John Steer *(Thames and Hudson)*
Villas of Tuscany by H Acton *(Thames and Hudson)*

Travel

Blue Guides: Northern Italy by A Macadam; **Southern Italy** by Paul Blanchard; **Sicily** by A Macadam; **Florence** by A Macadam; **Rome and Environs** by A Macadam; **Venice** by A Macadam.
D H Lawrence and Italy *(Penguin)*
Guide to Tuscany by Bently *(Penguin)*
Living in Italy by Y M Menzies *(Hale)*
Mediterranean Island Hopping by Dana Facaros and Michael Pauls *(Gentry Books Ltd)*
The Path to Rome by Hilaire Belloc *(Penguin)*
Stones of Florence and Venice by Mary McCarthy *(Penguin)*
Venetian Evenings by James Lees-Milne *(Collins)*
Venice by John Kent *(Viking)*

Food and Wine

Italy: The Beautiful Cookbook
Life beyond Lambrusco (Understanding Italian Fine Wine) by N Belfrage *(Sidgwick and Jackson)*
Traditional Italian Food by L B Birch *(Fontana)*

Fiction

Italian Short Stories by R Trevelyan *(Penguin Parallel Text)*
A Room with a View by E M Forster *(Penguin)*
Sicilian Carousel by Lawrence Durrell *(Faber)*
The Ant Colony by F King *(Flamingo)*
The Leopard by Giuseppe Tomasi di Lampedusa *(Flamingo)*
The Slow Train to Milan by Lisa St Aubin de Teran *(Penguin)*

The chapter on art and architecture in this guide gives
an outline of artistic achievement in the country
providing the context of the buildings and works of art
described in the Sights section
This chapter may also provide ideas for touring
It is advisable to read it at leisure

Films

See the chapter on CINEMA in the Introduction.

1935 **The Last Days of Pompeii** by Merian C Cooper
1945 **Roma, Città Aperta** (Rome Open City) by Roberto Rossellini
1948 **Ladri di biciclette** (Bicycle Thieves) by Vittorio de Sica
1950 **Domenica d'Agosto** (Sunday in August) by Luciano Emmer
1950 **Francesco, Giullare di Dio** (Francis, God's Jester) by Roberto Rossellini
1950 **September Affair** by William Dieterle (Capri)
1951 **Quo Vadis** by Mervyn Le Roy
1951 **The Little World of Don Camillo** by Julien Duvivier (in a village in the Po Plain).
     Followed by three sequels featuring Don Camillo and Peppone.
1953 **Roman Holiday** by William Wyler
1955 **Summertime** (Summer Madness) by David Lean
1957 **Le Notti di Cabiria** by Federico Fellini
1959 **Ben Hur** by William Wyler
1960 **Il Bell'Antonio** by Piero Piccioni (Sicily)
1960 **La Dolce Vita** by Federico Fellini
1960 **L'Avventura** by Michelangelo Antonioni (Lipari Islands and Sicily)
1960 **Spartacus** by Stanley Kubrick
1963 **Il Gattopardo** (The Leopard) by Luchino Visconti
1969 **Il Conformista** (The Conformist) by Bernardo Bertolucci
1971 **Death in Venice** by Luchino Visconti
1975 **Cadaveri eccellenti** (Illustrious corpses) by Francesco Rosi
1976 **Novecento** (1900) by Bernardo Bertolucci (Italy 1900-45)
1977 **Un giornata particolare** by Ettore Scola
1978 **L'albero degli zoccoli** (The Tree of Wooden Clogs) by E. Olmi (19C Lombardy)
1979 **Christ stopped at Eboli** by Francesco Rosi (Campania)
1985 **A Room with a View** by James Ivory (Florence and thereabouts)
1987 **Cronica Di Una Morta Annunciata** (Chronicle of a Death Foretold) by Francesco Rosi
1987 **Oci Ciornie** (Black Eyes) by Nikita Mikhalkov
1987 **The Belly of an Architect** by Peter Greenaway (Rome)
1989 **Cinema Paradiso** by Giuseppe Tornatore
1994 **Caro Diario** (Dear Diary) by Gianni Moretti
1994 **Il Postino** (The Postman) by Michael Radford

Art and architectural terms

Ambo: the pulpit of a primitive Christian basilica.
Ambulatory: an aisle curving round the chancel.
Apparatus: the arrangements of stones or bricks in a structure.
Apse: the end of a church behind the choir.
Apsidal Chapel: a chapel springing from the apse.
Archivolt: highest arch above a doorway.
Atrium: forecourt of a Roman house or Byzantine church.
Ciborium: a canopy over an altar.
Corbelling: a projection on a façade (balcony).
Foliage: ornamental foliated scroll stem.
Gable: a decorative, acute-angled structure over a window or doorway.
Intarsia or **tarsia:** inlaid wood, marble or metal.
Lintel: the horizontal traverse over an opening.
Machicolations: a corbelled balcony at the top of a wall, supported by consoles or brackets.
Maestà: Madonna and Child in Majesty.
Mascaron: carved medallion in form of human mask.
Matroneum: gallery reserved for women in early Christian churches.
Merlon: the solid part of parapet between two crenels (identations).
Misericord: the small tilting seat of a church stall.
Modillion: a small console supporting a cornice.
Narthex: the internal vestibule of a church.
Oculus: a round window.
Pietà: Virgin with the dead Christ.
Pilaster: a rectangular column often attached to a wall.
Polyptych: a painted or carved panel divided into several bays (triptych: three bays).
Predella: the base of an altarpiece often decorated with small scenes.
Recessed Orders: concentric receding arches surmounting a doorway.
Sinopia: sketch for a fresco.
Stucco: ornamental moulding made of lime, chalk and marble dust.
Triforium: a small gallery over the aisles of a church.
Tympanum: the part between the lintel and the arch of a doorway.

Vocabulary

ON THE ROAD AND IN TOWN

a destra	to the right	lavori in corso	men at work
a sinistra	to the left	neve	snow
aperto	open	passaggio a livello	level crossing
autostrada	motorway	passo	pass
banchina	pavement	pericolo	danger
binario	(railway) platform	piazza, largo	square, place
corso.	boulevard	piazzale	esplanade
discesa	descent	stazione	station
dogana	customs	stretto	narrow
fermata	(bus-) stop	uscita	exit, way out
fiume	river	viale	avenue
ingresso	entrance	vietato	prohibited

PLACES AND THINGS TO SEE

abbazia, convento	abbey, monastery	mercato	market
affreschi	frescoes	mura	walls
arazzi	tapestries	navata	nave
arca	monumental tomb	opere	works
biblioteca	library	pala	panel, altarpiece
cappella	chapel	palazzo	palace
casa	house	paliotto	altar frontal
cascata	waterfall	passeggiata	walks, promenade
castello	castle	piano	floor, storey
Cena	The Last Supper	pinacoteca	picture gallery
chiesa	church	pulpito	pulpit
chiostro	cloisters	quadro	picture
chiuso	closed	rivolgersi a	to apply to
città	town	rocca	feudal castle
cortile	courtyard	rovine, ruderi	ruins
dintorni	environs	sagrestia	sacristy
duomo	cathedral	scala	stairway
facciata	façade	scavi	excavations
funivia	cable-car	seggiovia	chair-lift
giardini	gardens	spiaggia	beach
gole	gorges	tesoro	treasure
lago	lake	torre, torazzo	tower
lungomare	seafront promenade	vista	view

COMMON WORDS

yes, no	si, no	goodbye	arrivederci
Sir	Signore	how much?	quanto?
Madam	Signora	where? when?	dove? quando?
Miss	Signorina	where is?	dov'è?
today	oggi	much, little	molto, poco
yesterday	ieri	more, less	più, meno
tomorrow		all	tutto, tutti
morning	domani mattina	large	grande
morning	mattina	small	piccolo
evening	sera	dear	caro
afternoon	pomeriggio	the road to...?	la strada per...?
please	per favore	may one visit?	si può visitare?
thank you so much	grazie tante	what time is it?	che ora è?
excuse me	mi scusi	I don't understand	non capisco
enough	basta	I would like	desidero
good morning	buon giorno		

NUMBERS

0 . . . . zero	8 . . . . otto	16 . . . . sedici	60 . . . . . . sessanta
1 . . . . uno	9 . . . . nove	17 . . . . . diciàsette	70 . . . . . . settanta
2 . . . . due	10 . . . . dieci	18 . . . . diciotto	80 . . . . ottanta
3 . . . . tre	11 . . . . undici	19 . . . . . diciannove	90 . . . . . novanta
4 . . . . quattro	12 . . . . dodici	20 . . . . venti	100 . . . . cento
5 . . . . cinque	13 . . . . tredici	30 . . . . trenta	1000 . . . . . . mille
6 . . . . sei	14 . . . . quattordici	40 . . . . quaranta	5 000 . . cinquemila
7 . . . . sette	15 . . . . . . quindicci	50 . . . . . cinquanta	10 000 . . diecimila

GASTRONOMIC GLOSSARY

Caffè corretto: *espresso* laced with brandy or *grappa*

Caffè decaffeinato (caffè "Hag"): decaffeinated coffee

Caffè latte: mainly hot milk, with a splash of coffee

Caffè lungo: coffee which is not quite as strong as *espresso*

Caffè macchiato: *espresso* with a splash of milk

Cannelloni: large pasta tubes filled with a meat or other sauce

Cappellini: very thin spaghetti

Cappuccino (or *cappuccio*): coffee topped with frothy milk and a dusting of cocoa

Cassata: ice cream containing chopped nuts and mixed dried fruit (similar to tutti-frutti)

Crema: vanilla (ice cream)

Farfalle: pasta bow-ties

Fettuccine: slightly narrower, Roman version of tagliatelle

Fior di latte: very creamy variety of ice cream

Fusilli: small pasta spirals

Gnocchi: tiny potato dumplings

Lasagne: sheets of pasta arranged in layers with tomato and meat sauce (or other) and cheese sauce, topped with Parmesan and baked

Maccheroni: small pasta tubes

Panino: type of sandwich (bread roll)

Panna: cream; similar to *fior di latte*

Prosciutto: cured ham

Ravioli: little pasta cushions, enclosing meat or spinach

Schiacciata: type of sandwich (on a pizza-type base)

Spaghetti: the great classic

Stracciatella: chocolate chip (ice cream)

Tagliatelle: long narrow pasta ribbons

Tiramisù: coffee-flavoured frozen gateau *(semifreddo)*

Tortellini: small crescent-shaped pasta rolls filled with a meat or cheese stuffing, often served in a clear meat broth

Tramezzino: type of sandwich (on slices of bread)

Zabaglione: dessert made from egg yolks and Marsala wine

Zuppa inglese: trifle

G. del Magro/SIPA PRESS

Calendar of Events

30 and 31 January
Aosta . . . . St Orso Fair: craft fair with sale of articles from the Valle d'Aosta.

Late January, February
Viareggio . . . . Carnival: masked processions; folklore events.

February
Venice . . . . Masked Carnival (period before Lent, finishing on Shrove Tuesday). *For information, apply to the Azienda di Promozione Turistica, San Marco 4089, 30100 Venezia; ☎ (041) 522 61 10.*

Last Friday of carnival
Verona . . . . Bacchanalian Carnival of the Gnocco; masked processions and competition for the best float; *gnocchi*, made under a canopy erected in front of St Zeno church, are given to town officials and passers-by.

1 April
San Marino . . . . Investiture of the town regents.

Holy Week (Maundy Thursday and Good Friday)
Taranto . . . . Processions.

Easter Day
Florence . . . . Scoppio del Carro; in the morning, in the Piazza del Duomo, fireworks display from a decorated float – the fireworks are set off by a dove sliding along a wire from the high altar of the Cathedral to the float.

Sulmona . . . . Feast of the "Madonna che scappa in Piazza".

Late April to early July
Florence . . . . Florentine May music festival; numerous cultural events (concerts, operas, ballets, etc.).

Around May
Taormina . . . . Festival of Sicilian costume and carts.

1 May
Cagliari . . . . Feast of Sant'Efisio.

Early May
Naples . . . . Feast of the Miracle of St Januarius inside the cathedral.

First week in May
Assisi . . . . Calendimaggio

7 to 10 May
Bari . . . . Feast of St Nicholas; 7 May – procession, 8 May – Mass and procession along the shore; the statue of the saint is taken out to sea and worshipped.

15 May
Gubbio . . . . Ceri race.

Penultimate Sunday in May
Sassari . . . . Cavalcata Sarda.

Last Sunday in May
Gubbio . . . . Palio della Balestra; archery competition in the Piazza della Signoria.

Corpus Christi
Spello . . . . "Le Infiorate;" festival of flowers and herbs decorating the streets of the town (decorative and liturgical pictures and patterns).

1st fortnight in June, even years

Venice .... Biennial Arts Festival. *Information from the Biennial Festival Committee in Venice. APT* ☎ *(041) 521 87 11.*

16 and 17 June

Pisa .... Luminaria di San Ranieri; 16 June in the evening – illumination of the Arno and river banks, 17 June – Feast of St Ranieri.

24 June

Florence .... Calcio Storico Fiorentino: ball game in the Piazza della Signoria, accompanied by magnificent procession in 16C costumes; fireworks in the Piazzale Michelangiolo.

Last Sunday in June

Pisa .... Games on the Ponte di Messo. ☎ (050) 56 04 64.

Last week in June – 1st fortnight in July

Spoleto .... Festival dei Due Mondi; international drama, music and dance festival.

Early July to late August

Verona .... Summer drama festival; opera season in the Roman amphitheatre. *Information from the Azienda di Promozione turistica, 6b via Dietro Anfiteatro, 37100 Verona,* ☎ *(045) 59 28 28.*

2 July

Siena .... Palio delle Contrade.

16 July

Naples .... Feast of Santa Maria del Carmine (illumination of the campanile).

3rd Saturday in July

Venice .... Feast of the Redeemer, on Saturday night, at the Giudecca.

1st Sunday in August

Ascoli Piceno .... Festa della Quintana; procession of representatives of the various districts, in 15C costumes; horsemen attack a dummy.

14 August

Sassari .... Feast of the Candles.

16 August

Siena .... Palio delle Contrade.

29 August and previous Sunday

Nuoro .... Feast of the Redeemer.

Late August-early September

Venice .... International Film Festival at the Lido.

Last Sunday in August and 1st Sunday in September

Arezzo .... Giostra del Saracine – Saracen's Joust.

1st Sunday in September

Venice .... Historical Regatta on the Grand Canal.

7 September

Florence .... Feast of the Rificolone (coloured paper lanterns); musical and folklore events in the different districts.

7 and 8 September

Loreto .... Feast of the Nativity of the Virgin.

8 to 12 September

Naples .... Feast of the Madonna di Piedigrotta.

2nd Friday, Saturday and Sunday of September in even years

Marostica .... Partita a Scacchi.

From mid-September for 10 days

Asti . . . . Wine Festival ("Douja d'Or"); Palio horse race.

2nd Sunday in September

Asti . . . . Festival of the Sagre *(Festival delle Sagre)*; wide variety of food served to visitors in the open air.

Sansepolcro . . . . Palio della Balestra; crossbow competition, in medieval costumes.

13 September

Lucca . . . . Luminara di Santa Croce, from 8pm onwards.

2nd and 3rd Sundays in September

Foligno . . . . Quintana Games; the day before, procession in 17C costumes.

From mid-September to mid-October, odd years

Florence . . . . Biennial Antique Fair at the Palazzo Strozzi.

19 September

Naples . . . . Feast of the Miracle of St Januarius, in the cathedral.

1 October

San Marino . . . . Investiture of the town's regents.

10 December

Loreto . . . . Feast of the Translation of the Santa Casa.

Christmas-Epiphany

Naples . . . . Typical nativity scenes in the city's churches.

S. Chirol

Saracen's Joust, Arezzo

Admission Times and Charges

As admission times and charges are liable to alteration, the information printed below - valid for 1998 - is for guidance only.

⊙: Every sight for which times and charges are listed below is indicated by the symbol ⊙ after the title in the Sights Section.

If up-to-date infomation was not available on time, the times and charges of the previous edition have been reprinted and appear in italics.

It is advisable to make an early start as many museums are closed in the afternoon (siesta time) and most churches close at lunch time. Some museums may be closed in part or in full for restoration or owing to lack of staff. Visitors are not admitted to churches during services.

As monuments are often undergoing restoration work which may last for long periods, it is preferable to telephone in advance before setting off on visits.

***Dress**: At the entrance to churches there are often notices stipulating correct dress - no shorts and sleeveless T-shirts.*

***Order**: The information is listed in alphabetical order of the name of the locality.*

***Dates**: Dates given are inclusive.*

***Charge**: The prices quoted apply to individual adults with no reduction. Special conditions for both times and charges are generally granted to groups if arranged beforehand.*

Charges for admission are given in Lire: L.

During heritage week(Settimana dei Beni Culturali - Dec) admission to many monuments is free.

***Telephone**: The local dialling code (prefisso) is indicated in brackets; do not dial the zero if phoning from abroad.*

See the Practical Information section for a list of national holidays.

&/(&): symbol indicating facilities (partial facilities) for the disabled when available in the entry for the sight.

A

Parco Nazionale d'ABRUZZO

Access: By car the main access points are Bisegna (north), Villetta Barrea and Barrea (east) and Forca d'Acero (west). For information about the Park's activities contact the headquarters (Centro Parchi) in Rome or local offices in Pescasseroli, Barrea, Villetta Barrea, Civitella Alfedena, Villavallelonga and Forca d'Acero: open 9am-noon and 3-7pm. The Ufficio Operativo del Parco (park office) is in viale S. Lucia, ☎ (086) 91 07 15; the Sede Centrale (Central Office) is in viale Tito Livio 12, ☎ (06) 35 40 33 15.

ALBA FUCENS

Scavi - Open all year, 9am until an hour before sunset. Apply to Signor Di Mattia. ☎ (0863) 23 561.

ALBISOLA MARINA

Villa Faraggiana - Guided tours (45min) daily (except Mon), mid June-mid Sept, 3-6.30pm and 8.30-11pm; mid Sept-Oct and Mar-mid June, 3-7pm. Closed Easter, Nov-Feb. 8 000 L. ☎ (019) 48 06 22.
www.Savonaonline.it/albissolamarina/index.htm

ALTILIA SAEPINUM

Ruins - Open all year, 9am-7pm. ☎ (0874) 79 02 07.

ALTOMONTE

Museo civico - (&) Open daily, Apr-Sept, 9am-1pm and 3-8pm; Oct-Mar, 10am-1pm and 4-7pm. Guided tours in English, German. 3 000 L, child 1 000 L. ☎ (0981) 94 80 41.
www.diemme.it/altomonte

AMALFI

 corso delle Repubbliche 27 ☎ (089) 87 11 07

Duomo di Sant'Andrea: Chiostro del Paradiso - Open June-Oct, 9am-9pm, Nov-Mar, 9am-1pm and 2.30-5.30pm, 11 Mar-May, 9am-7pm. Closed 21 Dec-9 Jan. 3 000 L. ☎ (089) 87 22 03.

ANAGNI

Cattedrale: crypt and treasury - Guided tours (15min, also in English and French by appointment), Apr-Oct, daily, 9am-1pm and 4-7pm; Oct-Mar, daily, 9am-2pm and 3-6pm. 3 000 L, child no charge. ☎ (0775) 72 78 52.
www.axa.it/anagni

ANCONA

Santa Maria della Piazza - Open Apr-Oct, daily, 7.30am (9am Sun)-7pm (7.30pm Sun); Oct-Mar, daily, 7.30am (9am Sun)-5.30pm (6pm Sun).

Museo Nazionale delle Mare - (♿) Open all year, daily, 8.30am-1.30pm (Sat also 2.40-7.30pm). Longer opening hours in summer. Closed public holidays. 4 000 L. Audio-visual presentation. ☎ (071) 20 75 390, 20 26 02.

Galleria Comunale Francesco Podesti - Open daily (except Mon afternoons), 9am (3pm Sun)-7pm. Closed public holidays. 5 000 L, no charge Sun. ☎ (071) 22 25 041.
www.comune.ancona.it

ANDALO

Monte Paganella - Access by cable-car or chairlift July-mid Sept and Dec-Apr. Prices are revised every year.
Access also by chairlift from Fai della Paganella. Same conditions.

ANGERA

Rocca Borromeo - Open daily, late Mar-Sept, 9.30am-12.30pm and 2-6pm (5pm in Oct). Closed the rest of the year. 10 000 L (ticket also valid for Museo della Bambola). Guided tours (1hr 30min) in English, French, German. Bar-restaurant. ☎ (0331) 93 13 00.

ANSEDONIA

Cosa: Ruins - Open daily, May-Sept, 8am-8pm; Oct-Apr, 9am-7pm. No charge. ☎ (0564) 88 14 21.

AOSTA

Collegiata di Sant'Orso - Open June-Sept, 9am-7pm; Oct-May, 10am-5pm.

Cattedrale - (♿) **Tesoro:** Open Apr-Sept, daily (except Mon), 9.30am-noon and 3-6pm; Oct-Mar, Sat, 9.30am-noon and 3-6pm, Sun 3-6pm; otherwise by appointment. Guided tours in English, French, German, Italian. 4 000 L, child 1 500 L). ☎ (0165) 31 361.

AQUILEIA

Basilica: Cripta degli affreschi - Open Apr-Sept, 8.30am-7pm; Oct-Mar, 8.30am-12.30pm and 2.30-5.30pm. No visits during services. 3 000 L, child under 10 years old 2 000 L. ☎ (0431) 91 067. e-mail: grmarin@tin.it
www.grmarini Basilica di Aquileia

Basilica: Cripta degli Scavi - (♿) Open Apr-Sept, 8.30am-7pm; Oct-Mar, 8.30am-12.30pm and 2.30-5.30pm. 3 000 L, child under 10 years old 2 000 L. ☎ (0431) 91 067.
www.grmarini Basilica di Aquileia

Roman ruins - (♿) Open all year, 9am-1hr before sunset. Closed 1 Jan, 1 May and 25 Dec. ☎ (0431) 91 016, 91 035.

Museo Archeologico - Open all year, 9am-2pm. Closed 1 Jan, 1 May and 25 Dec. 8 000 L; no charge for visitors from EU countries, under 18 years old or over 60, and during heritage week. ☎ (0431) 91 016, 91 035.

Museo Paleocristiano - Open all year, 9am-2pm. Closed 1 Jan, 1 May and 25 Dec. No charge. ☎ (0431) 91 131.

AREZZO

Casa del Vasari - Open all year, daily, 9am-7pm (1pm Sun and holidays). Closed 1 May. No charge. ☎ (0575) 30 03 01.

Museo d'arte medievale e moderna - Open all year, daily, 9am-7pm (1pm Sun and holidays. Closed 1 Jan and 1 May. 8 000 L. Interactive audio-visual/multimedia programme available. ☎ (0575) 30 03 01.

Museo archeologico - (♿) Open Apr-Dec, 9am-1pm; Jan-Apr, 9am-2pm. Closed public holidays. 8 000 L, no charge during heritage week. ☎ (0575) 20 882.

ARQUÀ PETRARCA

Casa del Petrarca - Open daily (except Mon), Mar-Sept, 9am-noon and 2-5pm; Oct-Feb, 9am-noon and 3-6.30pm. Closed 1 Jan, 1 May, 15 Aug, 25 Dec. 6 000 L, 4 000 L child.

ARONA

Colosso di San Carlone - Open late Mar-early Oct, daily, 8.30am-12.30pm and 2-6.30pm; early Oct-early Nov, daily, 9am-12.30pm and 2-5pm; early Nov-late Mar, Sat, Sun and public holidays, 9am-12.30pm and 2-5pm. Closed 25 Dec. Guided tours in English, French, German, Italian. 4 000 L, 2 500 L child 8-12 years old. ☎ (0322) 24 96 69.

ASCOLI PICENO
🛈 piazza del Popolo 1 ☎ (0736) 25 30 45

Sant'Agostino - Open daily, 7am-12.30pm and 3.30-8pm.

Santi Vincenzo ed Anastasio - Apply in advance at the tourist information centre. ☎ (0736) 25 52 50, 25 30 45.

Ponte romano di Solestà - To visit the interior, apply at the tourist information centre at least two days in advance. ☎ (0736) 25 30 45, 25 52 50.

Duomo - Open daily, 7am-12.30pm and 4-8pm. ☎ (0736) 25 52 50.

Pinacoteca - ♿ Open 15 June-15 Sept, Mon-Fri 9am-1pm and 3-7.30pm, Sat 9am-1pm, Sun 4-8pm; 16 Sept-14 June, daily 9am-1pm (12.30pm Sun). Closed 1 Jan, Easter Day, 25 Apr, 1 May, 15 Aug, 1 Nov and 25 Dec. 6 000 L, 4 000 L under 25 years old and over 60; 2 000 L 7-14 years old, no charge child. ☎ (0736) 29 82 82.

ASSISI
🛈 piazza del Comune 12 ☎ (075) 81 25 34

Basilica inferiore: tesoro, Collezione Perkins - Temporarily closed.

Rocca maggiore - Closed for restoration.

Oratorio dei Pellegrini - Closed for restoration.

Excursions

Eremo delle Carceri - ♿ Open daily, sunrise to sunset.

Convento di San Damiano - Open all year, daily, 10am-12.30pm and 2-4pm (4.30pm Nov-late Mar).

Basilica di Santa Maria degli Angeli - Open in summer, 7am-sunset; in winter, 7am-noon and 2pm-sunset. ☎ (075) 80 511.

ATRI

Cattedrale - Open June-Sept, weekdays, 9am-noon and 5-8pm, Sun, 8am-1pm and 6-8pm; Oct-May, weekdays, 9am-noon and 3-6pm, Sun, 8am-1pm and 4-7pm. ☎ (085) 87 300.

B

BACOLI

Cento Camerelle - Open 9am-1hr before sunset. Apply to the custodian in via Cento Camerelle. For information contact the Tourist Office in Bacoli. ☎ (081) 86 87 541.

Piscina Mirabile - Open 9am-1hr before sunset. Apply to the custodian in via Piscina Mirabile. For information contact the Tourist Office in Bacoli. ☎ (081) 86 87 541.

BAGNAIA

Villa Lante - Guided tours (30min), daily (except Mon), mid Apr-mid Sept, 9am-7.30pm; 1 Apr-mid Apr and mid Sept-end Oct, 9am-6.30pm; Mar, 9am-5.30pm; Nov-Feb, 9am-4.30pm. Closed 1 Jan, 1 May and 25 Dec. 4 000 L. ☎ (0761) 28 80 08.

BAIA

Terme - Open all year, 9am-1hr before sunset. 4 000 L. ☎ (081) 86 87 592.

BARI
🛈 piazza Aldo Moro 33/A ☎ (080) 52 42 244

Castello - (♿) Open all year, daily (except Mon), 9am-1pm and 3.30-7pm; Sun, 8.30am-1pm. Closed 1 Jan, 1 May and 25 Dec. Guided tours (1hr). 4 000 L, no charge for visitors under 18 years old or over 60. ☎ (080) 52 14 361.

Pinacoteca - (&) Open all year, daily (except Mon), 9am-1pm and 4-7pm; Sun, 9.30am-1pm. Closed Mon and weekday public holidays. 5 000 L. Guided tours (about 1hr 30min). ☎ (080) 54 12 423.

Museo archeologico - Closed for reorganisation.

BARLETTA

Basilica di San Sepolcro - Open daily, 9.30am-11.15am, 5.30-6pm and 7-8pm.

Pinacoteca Comunale - Open May-Sept, Tues-Sun, 9am-1pm and 4-7pm; Oct-Apr, Tues-Sun, 9am-1pm and 3-7pm. 5 000 L, 2 000 L for visitors 12-18 years old and university students, no charge for visitors under 12 years old and over 60. Guided tours (1hr, also in English, French). ☎ (0883) 57 86 12.

BASSANO DEL GRAPPA

Museo civico - Open daily (except Mon), 9am-6pm; Sun and holidays, 3.30-6.30pm. Closed 1 Jan, Easter Sunday and Mon, 25 Apr, 1 May, 15 Aug, 1 Nov, 25 and 26 Dec. 7 000 L, no charge child under 6 years old and during heritage week. Guided tours available on Sun afternoons (1hr 30min). ☎ (0424) 52 22 35, 52 33 36. e-mail: Museobas@x-land.it
www.x-land.it/museobassano

BELLAGIO

Villa Serbelloni: Giardini - Guided tours (1hr 30min) in English, French, German, Italian, Apr-Oct, daily (except Mon), 11am-4pm. Closed Nov-Mar. 6 000 L. ☎ (031) 95 02 04; e-mail: prombell@tin.it
www.fromitaly.it/bellagio

Villa Melzi: Giardini - Open Apr-Sept, daily, 9am-6.30pm; Mar, Oct, daily, 9am-12.30pm and 2.30-5.30pm. Closed Nov-Feb. 5 000 L.

BELLUNO

Museo civico - Open Apr-Sept, Tues-Fri 10am-noon and 4-7pm; Sunday afternoons and public holidays, 10.30am-12.30pm; Oct-Mar, Tues-Fri, 10am-noon and 3-6pm, Mon and Sat, 10am-noon; closed Sun. Closed 1 May, 15 Aug and 11 Nov all day. 4 000 L, 2 000 L visitors over 6 years old, no charge for child under 6 years old and during heritage week. Guided tours (1hr 30min). ☎ (0437) 99 48 36.

BENEVENTO

Teatro Romano - Open 9am-1hr before sunset. 4 000 L.

Museo del Sannio - Closed for restoration. ☎ (0824) 21 818.

BERGAMO   🛈 viale Aquila Nera 2 ☎ (035) 24 22 26

Cappella Colleoni - Open Apr-Oct, daily (except Mon), 9am-12.30pm and 2-6pm; Nov-Feb, daily (except Mon), 9.30am-12.30pm and 2-4pm. Closed 1 Jan, Easter and 25 Dec. Guided tours apply to the tourist information centre.

Basilica di Santa Maria Maggiore - Open daily, 9am-noon (11am Sun) and 3-6pm. ☎ (035) 22 33 27.

Palazzo della Ragione: Bell Tower - Open by appointment. Apply in advance to the Council for Culture (Assessorato alla Cultura). Guided tours available in English, French, German, Spanish. For information contact the tourist information office. ☎ (035) 24 22 26.
www.apt.bergamo.it

Via Bartolomeo Colleoni Nos 9 and 11 - Open by appointment only. Apply a few days in advance by phone to Ing. Berizzi. ☎ (035) 25 24 16. Guided tours (about 30min) in English, French, German, Spanish. For information contact the tourist information office. ☎ (035) 24 22 26.
www.apt.bergamo.it

Accademia Carrara - & Open all year, Wed-Mon, 9.30am-12.30pm and 2.30-5.30pm. Closed Tues and public holidays. 5 000 L, no charge on Sun and for visitors under 18 years old and over 60. Guided tours (1hr 30min). ☎ (035) 39 96 43.

BISUSCHIO

Villa Mazzoni Cicogna - Open last Sun in Mar-last Sun in Oct, Sun and public holidays only, 9.30am-noon and 2.30-7pm. In Aug, open afternoons daily. ☎ (0322) 47 11 34.

BOLOGNA

Palazzo Comunale – ♿ Open 10am–6pm. For information ☎ (051) 20 31 11, 20 30 41.

Collezioni comunali d'arte – (♿) Open all year, Tues–Sun, 10am–6pm. Closed 1 Jan and 25 Dec. 8 000 L, no charge for child under 14 years old. ☎ (051) 20 31 53.

Museo Morandi – ♿ Open all year, Tues–Sun, 10am–6pm. 8 000 L, 4 000 L visitors under 18 years old and over 60, no charge for child under 14 years old. Guided tours in English, French; audio guide English, Italian. ☎ (051) 20 36 46. www.comune.bologna.it/bologna1/Cultura/Museicomun/Morandi/MorandiItaliano.html

Palazzo del Podestà, Palazzo di Re Enzo – The interior is open only during exhibitions. ☎ (051) 23 96 60 (tourist information centre).

Museo Civico Archeologico – ♿ Open Tues–Fri, 9am–2pm, Sat, Sun, 9am–1pm and 3.30–7pm. Closed Mon except holidays and public holidays. 8 000 L, 4 000 L visitors under 18 years old and over 60, no charge for child under 14 years old. Guided tours (1hr 30min) in English, Italian. ☎ (051) 23 38 49. www.comune.bologna.it/bologna/Musei/Archeologico

Palazzo dell'Archiginnasio (Teatro Anatomico) – (♿) Open all year, Mon–Sat, 9.30am–1pm. Closed Sun, public holidays and 4 Oct. No charge. Audiovisual presentation. ☎ (051) 27 68 11. www.comune.bologna.it/bologna.archigin

Torre degli Asinelli – Open daily, 9am–6pm (5pm in winter). 3 000 L.

Basilica di Santo Stefano: museo – Open 9am–12.30pm (1pm Sun) and 3.30–6pm. ☎ (051) 22 32 56.

Pinacoteca Nazionale – Open Tues–Sun, 9am–2pm (1pm Sun). Closed Mon and public holidays. 8 000 L, no charge visitors under 18 years old and over 60. ☎ (051) 24 32 22.

San Giacomo Maggiore: frescoes – Open daily, 7am–noon and 3.30–6pm. ☎ (051) 22 59 70.

Museo d'Arte industriale – (♿) Open Tues–Sun, 9am–2pm (1pm Sun). Closed public holidays and weekday holidays. No charge. ☎ (051) 23 67 08.

Galleria Davia Bargellini – Same admission times and charges as the Museo d'Arte Industriale.

BOLSENA

Santa Cristina – Open daily, Apr–Oct, 7.30am–1pm and 4–7.30pm, Nov–Mar, 7.30am–12.30pm and 3–5.30pm in winter. 5 000 L. Guided tours of the Grotto only, every 30min from 9.30am–3pm. Book a week ahead. ☎ (0761) 79 90 67.

BOLZANO

Chiesa e Chiostro dei Dominicani – Open daily, 9.30am–5.30pm. Guided tour Fri at 10am, Mar–Dec. Donation. ☎ (0471) 30 70 00. www.SUDTIROL.COM/BOLZANO

Chiesa dei Francescani – Open daily, 10am–noon and 2.30–6pm. Guided tour Mon at 11am, Mar–Dec. Donation. ☎ (0471) 97 72 93. www.SUDTIROL.COM/BOLZANO

BOMARZO

Villa Orsini: Parco dei Mostri – Open all year, 8.30am–sunset. 15 000 L. ☎ (0761) 92 40 29.

BOMINACO

Churches – Visit accompanied by the custodian, Signor Cassiani. Allow a few days' advance notice. Donation. ☎ (0862) 93 604.

Isole BORROMEE

Pass for visiting the three islands: from Sesto Calende, Arona, Stresa, Baveno, Intra, Pallanza, Laveno, Luino, Cannobbio; 10 000-26 300 L, 5 000-13 000 L child. ☎ (0323) 30 416 (Stresa tourist information centre).

Isola Bella – Palace and Gardens: Open late Mar–late Oct, 9am–noon and 1.30–5.30pm (5pm in Oct). 13 000 L.

Isola Madre – Palace and Gardens: Open late Mar–late Oct, 9am–noon and 1.30–5.30pm (5pm in Oct). 12 000 L.

BREMBO DI DALMINE

Museo del Presepio - ♿ Open Dec, Jan, Mon–Sat, 2–5pm, Sun and public holidays, 9am–noon and 2–7pm; Feb–Nov, Sun and public holidays, 2–6pm;. 5 000 L. ☎ (035) 56 33 83.

Riviera del BRENTA

Villa boat trip - The "Burchiello" excursion runs from late Mar–early Nov: departure from Padua (Piazzale Boschetti) on Wed, Fri and Sun in the morning and arriving in Venice (Piazza San Marco) in the afternoon including visits to Villa Pisani, Villa Widmann (also known as Barchessa Valmerana) and Villa Foscari (known as *La Malcontenta*); departure from Venice on Tues, Thur and Sat; same programme but visits in reverse order.
return by coach. Price: 114 000 L, 60 000 L for 6–17 years old; no charge for children under 6.
For information, apply to:
- in **Padua**: *New Siamic Express S.r.l.* ☎ (049) 66 09 44.
- in **Venice**: *Azienda di Promozione Turistica della riviera del Brenta* (tourist information centre), Via don Minzoni 26, Mira Ponte. ☎ (041) 42 49 73.
For visiting times, see separate villa entries under the name of the locality.
Along the Riviera, yellow signs with a cyclist mark themed cycling trails (with a number indicated). For information contact the Brenta tourist information centre.

BRESCELLO

Museo - Open May–Sept, Mon–Sat, 9am–noon and 3–6pm (6.30pm July–Sept); Sun, 10am–12.30pm and 2.30–6pm (7pm July–Sept); Oct–Apr, Mon–Sat, 9am–noon and 2.30–5.30pm, Sun, 10am–12.30pm and 2.30–5.30pm. For weekday morning visits, apply at the town hall, Piazza Matteotti. Guided tours (1hr) in English, French, German; advance booking. Donation. ☎ (0522) 68 75 26.

BRESCIA
🖪 corso Zanardelli 34 ☎ (030) 43 418

Pinacoteca Tosio Martinengo - Open daily (except Mon), June–Sept, 10am–5pm; Oct–May, 9.30am–1pm and 2.30–5pm. Closed 1 Jan and 25 Dec. 5 000 L, no charge visitors under 16 years old and over 65. ☎ (030) 37 74 999.

Museo delle armi Luigi Marzoli - Open daily (except Mon), June–Sept, 10am–5pm; Oct–May, 9.30am–1pm and 2.30–5pm. Closed 1 Jan and 25 Dec. 5 000 L.

BRESSANONE

Museo diocesano - ♿ Open mid Mar–Oct, daily (except Mon), 10am–5pm. Closed Nov–mid Mar, 24, 25 Dec. Open Dec–10 Feb, daily, 2–5pm only for the Crib Collection. 8 000 L, 4 000 L child. ☎ (0472) 83 05 05.

BREUIL CERVINIA

Cable-car trip - The cable-car for Rosa Plateau operates daily except in May, June, Sept and Oct. The cable-cars leave every 15min.

BRINDISI

Museo archeologico F. Ribezzo - Open all year, daily except Sat and Sun, 9.30am–1.30pm; on Tues, also 3.30–6.30pm. No charge. When temporary exhibitions are held, only part of the museum's permanent collections is on view. ☎ (0831) 22 14 12.

BRUNICO

Museo Etnografico - Open daily (except Mon), 9.30am–5.30pm, Sun and holidays, 2–6pm. Closed Nov–mid Apr. 5 000 L. Guided tour by appointment. ☎ (0474) 55 20 87.

C

Val CAMONICA

Parco nazionale delle incisioni rupestri di Naquane - Open daily (except Mon), 9am–5.30pm. Closed public holidays. 10 000 L. Guided tours (3hr) by appointment (at least 7 days in advance). Fax (0364) 42 572.
www.globalnet.it/ccsp/ccsp.htm

Riserva naturale delle incisioni rupestri di Ceto, Cimbergo e Paspardo - Open daily, 9am–noon and 2–5pm. 3 000 L, no charge for child under 8 years old. Guided tours (about 3–6hr). ☎ (0364) 43 34 465.
www.globalnet.it/visite.htm

Museo di Nadro - Same admission times and charges as the Riserva naturale delle incisioni rupestri.

CAMPO CARLO MAGNO

Passo del Grosté - The cable-car operates from the 1st weekend in July-the 3rd weekend in Sept. ☎ (0465) 44 77 44.

CAMPO IMPERATORE

Access - By cable-car (7min) Oct-Mar, departure every 30min between 8.30am and 4.45pm (except at 1.30pm); in summer, every hour between 8.30am-5pm (20 July-25 Aug, every 30min between 8.30am-6pm). Rtn fare 22 000 L Sat and holidays, 18 000 L weekdays. ☎ (0862) 60 61 43, 40 00 07. Access also by cable-car from Fonte Cerreto by S 16 bis (closed Dec-Apr).

CANOSA DI PUGLIA

Ipogei Lagrasta - Open May-Sept, Tues-Sat, 9am-1pm and 5-7pm, Sun 8am-2pm; Mar, Apr, Tues-Sat, 9am-1pm and 4-6pm, Sun, 8am-2pm; Oct-Feb, Tues-Sun, 8am-2pm. No charge. ☎ (0883) 66 21 83.

CAPRAROLA

Palazzo Farnese - Open Tues-Sun, 16 Apr-15 Sept, 9am-7.30pm; Mar-15 Apr, 16 Sept-Oct, 9am-3.30pm; Nov-Feb, 9am-4.30pm. Last admission 1hr before closing time. Closed Mon except Easter Mon, 1 Jan, 1 May and 25 Dec. 4 000 L, no charge for visitors under 18 years old and over 60 and during heritage week. ☎ (0761) 64 60 52.

CAPRI   🄸 piazza Umberto 1, 19 ☎ (081) 83 70 686

Grotta Azzurra - Boat trip and visit to the cave all year, daily (except at high tide and when the sea is rough), 9am-one hour before sunset. Time: 1hr. Price: 7 000 L (small boat), 8 000 L (grotto) Excursion from Marina Grande: 23 000 L including trip by fast boat, small boat and grotto). Prices may be increased by 700 L (small boat) and 1 000 L (fast boat) on public holidays.

Tour of the Isle - Boat trip all year, daily (except when the sea is rough). Departure from Marina Grande at 9.30am. Time: about 2hr. Price: Mon-Sat, 19 000 L (plus 14 600 L to visit the Blue Grotto); Sun and public holidays, 17 900 L (plus 15 200 L to visit the Blue Grotto).

Villa Jovis - Open all year, 9am to one hour before sunset. 4 000 L, no charge during heritage week. ☎ (081) 83 70 381.

Certosa di San Giacomo - (&.) Open all year, Tues-Sun, 9am-2pm. Closed Mon and public holidays. ☎ (081) 83 76 218.

Villa San Michele (Anacapri) - Open May-Sept, 9am-6pm; Mar, 9.30am-4.30pm; Apr, Oct, 9.30am-5pm; Nov-Feb, 10.30am-3.30pm. 6 000 L, no charge for child under 12 years old. ☎ (081) 83 71 401.
www.caprionline.com/axelmunthe

Monte Solaro (Anacapri) - Closed for maintenance. The cable-car usually operates daily (except Tues, Nov-Feb), 9am-1hr before sunset. Bar. 7 000 L. ☎ (081) 83 71 428.

CAPUA

Museo Campano - Open daily (except Mon), 9am-1.30pm (1pm on Sun). Closed public holidays. 8 000 L, no charge for visitors under 18 years old and over 60,. Guided tours (1hr 30min). ☎ (0823) 96 14 02.

CARPI

Castello dei Pio - Open Thur, Sat and Sun, Jun-Aug, 10am-1pm and 4-7pm; Apr, May, Sept, Oct, 9.30am-12.30pm and 3.30-6.30pm. Closed Nov-Mar. 2 000 L, no charge for child under 6 years old. Guided tours (1hr 30min) in English, French, German, Italian. ☎ (059) 64 92 98.

CASAMARI

Abbazia - Guided tours daily, 9am-noon and 3-6pm. ☎ (0775) 28 23 71.

CASERTA

La Reggia - Open daily, 9am-2pm. Closed public holidays. 8 000 L, no charge for visitors under 18 years old and over 60. ☎ (0823) 32 14 00.

Park - Open daily (except Mon), 9am-1hr before sunset. Closed public holidays. 4 000 L, no charge for visitors under 18 years old and over 60. ☎ (0823) 32 14 00.

English Garden - Guided tours 10.30am, 11.30am and 12.30pm.

CASTEL DEL MONTE

Castello – Open Apr–Sept, 9am–7pm; Oct–Mar, 9am–1pm. Closed 1 Jan, 1 May and 25 Dec. 4 000 L, no charge for visitors under 18 years old and over 60, and during heritage week. Guided tours (1hr 30min). ☎ (080) 52 14 361.

CASTELFRANCO VENETO

Casa natale di Giorgione – Open Tues–Sun, 9am–noon and 3–6pm. Closed 1 Jan, Easter, 15 Aug, 25 Dec and Feast of San Stefano. 2 500 L, 1 500 L child. Guided tours (30min) in French, Italian, German. Audio-visual presentation. ☎ (0423) 49 12 40.

CASTELLAMMARE DI STABIA

Antiquarium – The collection is moving-new premises. Information ☎ (081) 14 541.

Villa di Arianna – Open all year, daily, 9am–1hr before sunset. Closed 1 Jan, 1 May and 25 Dec. No charge. ☎ (081) 87 14 541.

Villa di San Marco – Open all year, daily, 9am–1hr before sunset. Closed 1 Jan, 1 May and 25 Dec. No charge. ☎ (081) 87 14 541.

CASTELLANA

Grotte di Castellana – Guided tours (1km/0.5mi, about 1hr) daily: in summer, every hour 8.30am–1pm and 2.30–7pm; the rest of the year, every hour 8.30am–12.30pm. 15 000 L, 12 000 L child 6–14 years old. Longer tour ending at Grotta Bianca (3km/2mi, about 2hr) by appointment, 9am–6pm. 25 000 L, 20 000 L child 6–14 years old. ☎ (080) 49 65 511.

CERRO

Museo della Ceramica – Open July and Aug, Tues–Sun, 10am–noon and 3.30–6.30pm; Sept–June, Tues–Sun, 10am–noon and 2.30–5.30pm. Closed 1 Jan, Easter, 15 Aug and 25 Dec. Guided tours (1hr). 4 000 L. ☎ (0332) 66 65 30.

CERTALDO

Casa di Boccaccio – Open all year, daily, 10.30am–12.30pm and 3.30–6.30pm. No charge. Guided tours (20min). Audio-visual presentation (15min). ☎ (0571) 66 42 08.

Palazzo Pretorio – Open daily (except Mon), Apr–late Oct, 10am–1pm and 2.30–7.30pm; late Oct–Mar, 10am–12.30pm and 3–6pm. 5 000 L, 2 500 L child. Guided tours in English, French, German, Italain. ☎ (0571) 66 12 19.

CERVETERI

Necropoli della Banditaccia – Open daily (except Mon), Mar–Sept, 9am–7pm (last admission 6pm); Oct–Feb, 9am–4pm. Closed 1 Jan, 1 May, 15 Dec. 8 000 L, no charge for visitors under 18 years old and over 60 and during heritage week. ☎ (06) 99 40 001.

CESENA

Biblioteca Malatestiana – Guided tour (45min) mid June–mid Sept, Mon–Sat, 9am–12.30pm and 5–7pm, Sun, 9am–1pm; mid Sept–mid June, daily, 9am–12.30pm and 3–6pm. Closed 1 Jan. Audio-visual presentation. 5 000 L, 3 000 L child. ☎ (0547) 61 08 92.

CHIARAVALLE

Abbazia – Open Mon–Sat, 9–11.30am and 3–5.30pm, Sun, 11am–noon and 3–6pm. Guided tours Sun afternoons. ☎ (02) 57 40 34 04.

CHIAVENNA

Collegiata di San Lorenzo – Baptistery and Treasury: Open in summer, Mon–Sat, 10am–noon and 3–6pm, Sun, 2–6pm; in winter, Mon–Fri, 2–5pm, Sat, 10am–noon and 2–5pm, Sun, 2–6pm. 6 000 L, 3 000 L for visitors under 18 years old and over 60.

Giardino botanico e archeologico – Open in summer, daily (except Mon), 2–6pm, Sat, Sun, also 10am–noon; in winter, daily (except Mon), 2–5pm, Sun, also 10am–noon. 3 000 L, no charge during last two weeks in Sept. ☎ (0343) 33 795, e-mail: cmarch@clavis.it. Guided tours in English, French, Italian, German by appointment with the tourist information centre in Chiavenna, ☎ (0343) 33 442.

CHIETI

Museo archeologico Nazionale d'Abruzzo - (&) Open all year, daily, 9am-7pm. Closed 1 Jan and 25 Dec. 8 000 L, no charge for visitors under 18 years old. Guided tours (1hr) in English, Italian. ☎ (0871) 33 16 68, 33 09 55. http://mars.unich.it/museo.chieti.htm

CHIUSI

Museo archeologico e tombe etrusche - Open July-Sept, daily, 9am-8pm; Oct-June, daily, 9am-2pm (1pm Sun and public holidays). Closed 1 Jan, 1 May and 25 Dec. 4 000 L, no charge for visitors under 18 years old and over 60 and during heritage week. Audio-visual presentation (15min). ☎ (0578) 20 177.

Museo della cattedrale - Open all year, daily, 9.30am-12.45pm and 4.30-7.30pm (4-7pm Sun and public holidays, mid Oct-May). Closed Easter and 25 Dec. 3 000 L (museum), 4 000 L (Etruscan tombs, guided tour only), no charge for children under 10 years old. Guided tours (about 30min) of the museum in Italian, also in English, French, German by appointment. ☎ (0578) 22 64 90.

CIVIDALE DEL FRIULI

Museo cristiano - & Open all year, daily, 9.30am-noon and 3-7pm (6pm Nov-Mar), public holidays 3-6pm only. No charge. ☎ (0432) 73 13 98.

Museo archeologico nazionale - & Open in summer, daily, 9am-7pm (2pm Mon); in winter, daily, 8.30am-2pm. Closed Jan. 4 000 L, no charge for visitors under 18 years old and over 60, and during heritage week. Guided tours (30min). ☎ (432) 70 07 00.

Tempietto - & Open daily, Apr-Oct, 9am-1pm and 3-6.30pm; Nov-Mar, 10am-1pm and 3.30-5.30pm. 4 000 L, 2 000 L child. Guided tours. ☎ (0432) 70 08 67.

CIVITAVECCHIA

Museo nazionale archeologico - Open all year, daily (except Mon), 9am-2pm. Closed 1 Jan, 1 May and 25 Dec. No charge. ☎ (0766) 23 604.

Terme di Traiano - Open by appointment only. Apply at least a week in advance-Signor Edmondo Boni, ☎ (0766) 23 604.

CLITUNNO (Fonti)

Tempio - Open daily (except Mon), Apr-Oct, 8am-7pm; Nov-Mar, 8am-2pm. No charge. ☎ (0743) 27 50 85.

COLLODI

Parco di Pinocchio - (&) Open all year, 8.30am-sunset. 11 000 L, 6 000 L child. Bar. ☎ (0572) 42 93 42. www.pinocchio.it

Villa Garzoni - Closed for restoration until end of 1999. **Gardens**: Open mid Mar-early Nov, daily, 9am-sunset; early Nov-mid Mar, daily, 10am-late afternoon when a bell is rung (to sunset on public holidays and the preceding day); last admission 1hr before closing time. 10 000 L, 5 000 L child. Guided tours in English, German, Italian. Bar. ☎ (0572) 42 95 90, 42 91 43.

COMO

Villa Olmo: (&) Open all year, Mon-Sat, 8am-6pm. Closed Sun and public holidays. ☎ (031) 25 24 43.

Lago di COMO

Boat services from Como to Colico, Lecco, Tremezzo, Bellagio, Menaggio; from Tremezzo to Dongo, Domaso to Colico. By hydrofoil from Como to Tremezzo, Bellagio and Menaggio.
Car ferry via Bellagio, Varenna, Menaggio and Cadenabbia.
Day pass available for unlimited travel. Night services on Sat in summer.

Villa Carlotta, Lago di Como

CONEGLIANO

Duomo – Open by appointment only (at least 15 days in advance), daily except Wed and on days when religious functions are held, 9am–noon. Apply to Monsignor Romano Nardin, Parrocchia del Duomo, via XX Settembre, Conegliano. ☎ (0438) 22 606.

Castello – Open Tues–Sun, 10am–12.30pm and 3.30–7pm (3–6.30pm in winter). Closed Mon (except public holidays) and in Nov (except public holidays) and the next day after a public holiday. 3 000 L, 2 000 L child from 6–14 years old. Bar-restaurant. ☎ (0438) 22 871 (Museo Civico del castello).

CORFINO

Basilica di San Pelino – Open daily, May–Sept, 9am–7pm; Jan–Apr,9am–5pm; the rest of the year, on request. ☎ (0864) 72 81 20.

CORTINA D'AMPEZZO

Tondi di Faloria – Cable-car service from Via Ria di Zeto to Faloria. From Faloria to Tondi di Faloria: in winter, "Tondi" ski-lift and "Girilada" chairlift; in summer, a jeep service operates.

Tofana di Mezzo – "Freccia nel Cielo" cable-car 40 000 L there and back.

Pocol Belvedere – Hourly bus service from Piazza Roma from Dec–Mar and mid July–mid Sept.

CORTONA   🛈 via Nazionale 42 ☎ (0575) 63 03 52

Museo diocesano – Open daily (except Mon), Apr–Sept, 9.30am–1pm and 3.30–7pm; Oct–Mar, 10am–1pm and 3–5pm. 8 000 L, 1 000 L child. ☎ (0575) 62 830.

Museo dell'Accademia Etrusca – Open daily (except Mon), Apr–Sept, 10am–1pm and 4–7pm; Oct–Mar, 9am–1pm and 3–5pm. Closed 1 Jan and 25 Dec. 8 000 L. ☎ (0575) 63 72 35, 63 04 15.

CREMONA   🛈 piazza del Comune 5 ☎ (0372) 23 233

Torrazzo – Open Easter–Oct, Mon–Sat, 10.30am–noon and 3–6pm, Sun and public holidays, 10.30am–12.30pm and 3–7pm; Nov–Easter, Mon–Sat by appointment, Sun and public holidays, 10.30am–12.30pm and 3–6pm. Apply at least two days in advance to Signor Giordano, Archeoclub for appointment. 5 000 L. ☎ (0330) 71 59 35.

Palazzo comunale – Open all year, Tues–Sat, 8.30am–6pm; Sun, 10am–6pm. Closed 25 Dec. 6 000 L. ☎ (0372) 40 71.

Museo civico – Open all year, Tues–Sat, 9am–7pm; Sun and public holidays, 10am–7pm. Closed 25 Dec. 6 000 L. ☎ (0372) 40 71.

CROTONE

Museo archeologico – Open all year, daily, 9am–7pm. Closed when preparations for exhibitions are in progress. No charge. ☎ (0962) 20 179.

CUMA

Acropoli – Open 9am–1hr before sunset (last admission 1hr earlier). Closed 1 Jan, 1 May and 25 Dec. 4 000 L, no charge for visitors under 18 years old or over 60. ☎ (081) 85 43 060.

D – E

DESENZANO DEL GARDA

Villa Romana – ♿ Open Mar–mid Oct, Tues–Sat, 8.30am–7pm, Sun and public holidays, 9am–6pm; mid Oct–Feb, Tues–Sat, 8.30am–4.30pm, Sun and public holidays, 9am–4.30pm. Closed Mon except holiday Mon (in this case, closed Tues), 1 Jan, 1 May and 25 Dec. 4 000 L, no charge for visitors under 18 years old and over 60. ☎ (030) 91 43 547.

Isola d'ELBA   🛈 Calata d'Italia 26, 57037 Portoferraio ☎ (0565) 91 46 71

Portoferraio: Museo Napoleonico – Open daily, Apr–Sept, 9am–7pm (1.30pm Sun and public holidays); Oct, 9am–5.30pm (1pm Sun and public holidays); Nov–March, 9am–4.30pm (1pm Sun and public holidays). Closed 1 Jan, 1 May and 25 Dec. 8 000 L, no charge for visitors from EU countries and for visitors under 18 years old and over 60 (ticket also valid for Villa Napoleone di San Martino, same admission times and charges). ☎ (0565) 91 58 46.

Isola d'ELBA

Monte Capanne - Cable-car **(cabinovia)** operates from Easter-Oct. 10am-12.15pm and 2.45-5.30pm (later in July, Aug). 20 000 L, 12 500 L child there and back, 12 000 L one way. ☎ (0565) 90 10 20.

Marciana: Museo archeologico - Open Easter-Sept, Mon-Sat (except Thur), 9am-1pm and 4-7pm; Sun and public holidays, 8am-1pm. 3 000 L, no charge child under 6 years old. ☎ (0565) 90 12 15.

San Martino: Villa Napoleone - Same admission times and charges as Museo Napoleonico. ☎ (0565) 91 46 88.

ERCOLANO

Ruins - Open 9am-1hr before sunset. Closed 1 Jan, 1 May and 25 Dec. 12 000 L. ☎ (081) 90 963.

ESTE

Museo Nazionale Atestino - ♿ Open all year, daily, 9am-7pm. Closed 1 Jan, 1 May and 25 Dec. 4 000 L, no charge for visitors from EU countries, for visitors under 18 years old and over 60, and during heritage week. Guided tours (1hr 30min-2hr). ☎ (0429) 20 85.

F

FAENZA

Museo internazionale delle Ceramiche - Open Apr-Oct, daily (except Mon), 9am-7pm, Sun and holidays, 9.30am-1pm and 3-7pm; Nov-Mar, Tues-Fri, 9am-1.30pm, Sat, 9am-1.30pm and 3-6pm, Sun, 9.30am-1pm and 3-6pm. Closed public holidays. 10 000 L, no charge for child under 11 years old, 5 000 L student. Guided tours in English, French, Italian, German by appointment with Pro Loco - ☎ (0546) 21 231, or Agenzia Guidarelle di Ravenna - ☎ (0544) 33 690. ☎ (0546) 21 240.
www.RACINE.RA.IT

Pinacoteca comunale - Closed for restoration. ☎ (0546) 66 07 99.

FANO

Museo civico - (♿) Open mid June-mid Sept, Tues-Sat, 8.30am-12.30pm and 5-7pm, Sun, 8am-1pm; Oct-mid June, Tues-Sun, 8am-1pm. Closed 10 Jul and public holidays. 4 000 L, no charge child. Guided tours (1hr 30min). ☎ (0721) 82 83 62.

FELTRE

Museo civico - Open daily (except Mon), Apr-Sept, 10am-1pm and 4-7pm; Oct-March, 10am-11pm and 3-6pm. Closed public holidays and August holiday. 8 000 L, 3 000 L child 8-14 years old, no charge child under 8 years old. ☎ (0439) 88 52 42.

FENIS

Castello - Guided tours (30min) in English, French, Italian, German, daily, Apr-Sept, 9am-7pm; Oct-Mar, 10am-5pm. Closed 1 Jan and 25 Dec. 4 000 L, 2 000 L child under 6 years old. ☎ (0165) 76 42 63 or (0165) 312 464 (Servizio museografico).

FERENTILLO

Abbazia di San Pietro in Valle - Open all year, daily, 10am-12.30pm and 2pm-sunset. Donation. ☎ (0744) 78 03 16.

FERENTO

Teatro romano - Open daily (except Mon), in summer, 9am-5pm; in winter 9am-1pm (5pm Tues, Sat). No charge. ☎ (0761) 32 59 29.

FERMO

Duomo - Open by appointment June-Aug, Mon-Sat (except Wed afternoons), 10am-noon and 3.15-7pm, Sun 11am-1pm and 4.30-7pm. Closed Sept-May. Apply one week in advance. ☎ (0734) 22 86 31 or (0734) 22 87 29.

FERRARA

Museo del Duomo – Open Mar-Dec, Tues-Sat, 10am-noon and 3-5pm; Sun, 10am-noon and 4-6pm. Donation. ☎ (0532) 20 74 49.

Castello Estense – Open all year, Tues-Sun and holiday Mon, 9.30am-12.40pm and 1.30-6.30pm. 8 000 L, no charge child under 10 years old. Audio-visual presentation. ☎ (0532) 29 92 33.

Palazzo Schifanoia – Open all year, daily, 9am-7pm. Closed public holidays. 6 000 L, no charge for visitors under 18 years old and on 2nd Sun of each month, 8 000 L combined ticket for the Palazzo and Palazzina di Marfisa d'Este. ☎ (0532) 64 178.
www.comune.fe.it/musei-aa/schifanoia.hmtl

Palazzina di Marfisa d'Este – &. Open all year, daily, 9.30am-1pm and 3-6pm. 3 000 L, no charge for visitors under 18 years old and on 2nd Sun of each month. ☎ (0532) 20 74 50.

Casa Romei – (&.) Open all year, daily, 8.30am-9pm (2pm Mon, Sun). Closed public holidays. 4 000 L, no charge for visitors under 18 years old and over 60. ☎ (0532) 24 03 41.

Palazzo di Ludovico il Moro – Open all year, daily (except Mon)days, 9am-2pm. Closed 1 Jan, 1 May and 25 Dec. 8 000 L, no charge child. Guided tours in English, Italian. Audio-visual presentation. ☎ (0532) 66 299.

Sant'Antonio in Polesine – Open all year, Mon-Fri, 9.30-11.30am and 3-5pm. Guided tours. Donation. ☎ (0532) 64 068.

Palazzo dei Diamanti: Pinacoteca Nazionale – Open all year, daily (except Mon), 9am-2pm (1pm Sun). Closed public holidays. 8 000 L. ☎ (0532) 20 58 44.

Palazzo Massari: Museo Boldini – &. Open all year, daily, 9am-1pm and 3-6pm. 6 000 L, 3 000 L child, no charge on 1st Mon of each month. Guided tours in English, French, German, Italian, Spanish. Audio-visual presentation. ☎ (0532) 20 99 88.

Casa dell'Ariosto – Closed for restoration. ☎ (0532) 23 92 81.

FIESOLE

Convento di San Francesco – Open Apr-Sept, Mon-Sat, 9.30am-12.30pm and 3-7pm, Sun, 9-11am and 3-7pm; Oct-Mar, Mon-Sat, 9.30am-12.30pm and 3-6pm, Sun, 9-11am and 3-6pm. Donation.

Zona archeologica – Open daily, late March-Sept, 9am-7pm; late Oct-Feb, 9.30am-5pm; March and 1-late Oct, 9.30am-6pm. Closed first Tues of each month, 1 Jan and 25 Dec. 10 000 L, 5 000 L for students and visitors over 65 years old, 2 000 L child and shool children, 20 000 L for family (4 persons). Guided tours (1hr 30min) in English, French. Bar-restaurant. ☎ (055) 59 118 , 59 477.

Museo archeologico – Open daily, late March-Sept, 9am-7pm; Jan-Feb, late Oct-Dec, 9.30am-5pm; March and 1-late Oct, 9am-6pm. Closed first Tues of each month, 1 Jan and 25 Dec. 10 000 L, 5 000 L child. Bar-restaurant. ☎ (055) 59 118.

Antiquarium Costantini – Same admission times and charges as for zona archeologica.

Museo Bandini – Open daily, late March-Sept, 9am-7pm; Jan-Feb, 9.30am-5pm; March and 1-late Oct, 9am-6pm; late Oct-Dec, 9.30am-5pm;. Closed first Tuesday of each month, 1 Jan and 25 Dec. 10 000 L, 5 000 L child (combined ticket with zona archeolgico and Museo archeologico). Bar-restaurant. ☎ (055) 59 118.

FIRENZE

Duomo – Open all year, daily, 10am (1pm Sun and public holidays)-6pm. ☎ (055) 29 08 32.

Top of the dome – 464 steps. Access all year, Mon-Sat, 8.30am-7pm (5pm Sat), last admission 6.20pm. Closed 1 and 6 Jan, Holy Week, 24 June, 15 Aug, 1 Nov, 8 Dec, 25 and 26 Dec. 10 000 L. ☎ (055) 23 02 885.

Campanile – Open daily, Apr-Oct, 9am-7.30pm (last admission 6.50pm), Nov-Mar, 9am-5pm (last admission 4.20pm). Closed 1 Jan, Easter, 8 Sept, 25 Dec. 10 000 L. ☎ (055) 23 02 885.

Battistero – Open all year, Mon-Sat, 1.30-6.30pm, Sun and public holidays, 8.30am-1.30pm. 5 000 L. ☎ (055) 23 02 885.

Museo dell'Opera del Duomo – Open Apr-Oct, Mon-Sat, 9am-7.30pm (last admission 6.50pm); Nov-Mar, Mon-Sat, 9am-7pm (last admission 6.20pm). Closed Sun, 1 Jan, Easter, 25 Dec. 10 000 L. ☎ (055) 23 02 885.

Palazzo Vecchio – &. Open all year, Mon-Wed, Fri and Sat, 9am-7pm, Sun and public holidays, 8am-1pm. Closed Thur, 1 Jan, Easter, 1 May, 15 Aug and 25 Dec. 10 000 L, 7 500 L for visitors 12-18 years old and over 60 and during heritage week, no charge child up to 12 years old. ☎ (055) 26 25 961.

Closed Mon. ?

Galleria degli Uffizi - Open all year, Tues-Sun, 8.30am-6.50pm (1.50pm Sun and public holidays, 10pm in summer), last admission 45min before closing time. Closed 1 Jan, 1 May and 25 Dec. 12 000 L, no charge for Italian visitors under 18 years old and over 60 and during heritage week. Bar-restaurant. ☎ (055) 23 88 651/2. www.uffizi.firenze.it

Palazzo Pitti: *closed Mon ?*

Galleria Palatina - Open all year, Tues-Sun, 8.30am-10pm (8pm Sun and public holidays). 12 000 L. ☎ (055) 23 88 614.

Appartmenti reali - By appointment only. Closed Mon. Apply-the Galleria Palatina. ☎ (055) 23 88 611/614. 12 000 L, no charge child.
www.sbas.firenze.it

Galleria d'Arte Moderna - ♿ Open all year, daily (except 1st, 3rd and 5th Sun and 2nd and 4th Mon in the month, 8.30am-1.50pm - last admission 1.15pm). Closed 1 Jan, 1 May, 25 Dec. 8 000 L, no charge for visitors under 18 years old and over 60. ☎ (055) 23 88 601/616.
www.sbas.fi.it

Museo degli Argenti - (♿) Open all year, daily (except 1st, 3rd and 5th Mon and 2nd and 4th Sun in the month), 8.30am-1.50pm. Closed 1 Jan, 1 May and 25 Dec. 4 000 L, no charge for visitors under 18 years old and over 60, on the European Day of Culture and during museum week. ☎ (055) 23 88 709/710.

Giardino di Boboli - Open daily (except 1st and last Mon in the month) 15 June-Aug, 9am-7.30pm; Apr-15 June, Sept, Oct, 9am-6.30pm; Mar, 9am-5.30pm; Nov-Feb, 9am-4.30pm. Closed 1 Jan, 1 May and 25 Dec. 4 000 L, no charge for visitors under 18 years old and over 60 and during heritage week. Bar. ☎ (055) 26 51 71.

Museo della Porcellane - Open all year, daily (except 1st and last Mon and 2nd and 4th Sun in the month), 9am-1.50pm. Closed 1 Jan, 1 May and 25 Dec. 4 000 L (same ticket as Giardino di Boboli), no charge for visitors under 18 years old and over 60, on the European Day of Culture and during museum week. ☎ (055) 23 88 605.

Palazzo e Museo Nazionale del Bargello - (♿) Open all year, daily (except 1st and last Sun and 2nd and 4th Mon in the month), 9am-1.50pm. Closed 1 Jan, 1 May and 25 Dec. 8 000 L, no charge for visitors under 18 years old and over 60. ☎ (055) 23 88 606.
www.sbas.firenze.it

Biblioteca Medicea Laurenziana - (♿) Open all year, Tues-Sat, 9am-1pm (last admission 12.40pm). Closed Sun and 1 and 6 Jan, Easter Sun and Mon, 24 Apr, 1 May, 15 Aug, 1 Nov, 8 Dec. No charge. ☎ (055) 21 07 60.

Cappelle Medicee - Open Apr-Sept, Tues-Sat, 8.30am-5pm (1.50pm, Mon, Sun - except 1st, 3rd, 5th Mon and 2nd and 4th Sun in the month - and public holidays); Oct-Dec, Jan-Mar, daily (except 1st, 3rd, 5th Mon and 2nd and 4th Sun in the month), 8.30am-1.50pm. 10 000 L. ☎ (055) 23 88 602.

Palazzo Medici Riccardi - Open all year, Mon, Tues, Thur-Sat, 9am-1pm and 3-6pm, Sun and public holidays, 9am-1pm, Closed Wed, 1 May, 25 Dec. 6 000 L, 4 000 L child. ☎ (055) 27 60 340.

San Marco: museum and monastery - (♿) Open all year, daily (except 1st, 3rd, 5th Mon and 2nd and 4th Sun in the month), 8.30am-1.50pm. Closed 1 Jan, 1 May and 25 Dec. 8 000 L, no charge for children and visitors under 18 years old and over 60 from EU countries. ☎ (055) 23 88 608/704.
www.sbas.firenze.it

Galleria dell'Accademia - *closed Mon?* Open all year, Tues-Sat, 8.30am-6.50pm; Sun and holidays, 8.30am-1.50pm. Closed 1 Jan, 1 May and 25 Dec. 12 000 L, no charge for visitors under 18 years old. ☎ (055) 23 88 612/609.

Santa Maria Novella - Open all year, Mon-Fri, 7am-noon and 3-6pm, Sat, 7am-noon and 3-5pm, Sun and public holidays, 3-5pm. ☎ (055) 21 59 18.

Chiostro Verde - (♿) Open all year, Mon-Sat (except Fri), 9am-2pm; Sun and public holidays, 8am-1pm (last admission 12.30pm). Closed 1 Jan, Easter, 1 May, 15 Aug, 25 Dec. 5 000 L, 25% discount for visitors 12-20 years old, no charge under 12. ☎ (055) 21 59 87.

Santa Croce:

Church and Sacristy - Open all year, Mon-Sat, 8am-12.30pm and 3-6.30pm, Sun and public holidays, 3-5.30pm. ☎ (055) 24 46 19.

Cappella dei Pazzi and Museo dell'Opera di Santa Croce - Open Mon, Tues, Thur-Sun, Mar-Sept, 10am-12.30pm and 2.30-6.30pm; Oct-Feb, 10am-12.30pm and 3-5pm. Closed 1 Jan and 25 Dec. 4 000 L, 2 000 L child. ☎ (055) 24 46 19, 23 42 289.

Santa Maria del Carmine: Cappella Brancacci. - Open Mon, Wed-Sat, 10am-5pm. Sun and holidays 1-5pm. 5 000 L, 2 500 L child 10-14 years old. ☎ (055) 23 82 195.

Casa Buonarroti - Open all year, Wed-Mon, 9.30am-1.30pm. Closed Tues, 1 Jan, Easter, 25 Apr, 1 May, 15 Aug, 25 Dec. 10 000 L, student 8 000 L. Guided tours (about 2hr) in English, French, Italian: fee. ☎ (055) 24 17 52; e-mail: casabuonarroti@theta.it.
www.casabuonarroti.it

Cenacolo di Sant'Apollonia - Open all year, daily (except 2nd and 4th Mon and 1st, 3rd, 5th Sun in the month), 8.30am-1.50pm. Closed 1 Jan, Easter, 25 Apr, 1 May, 15 Aug, 25 Dec. No charge. ☎ (055) 23 88 607.

Cenacolo di San Salvi - Open all year, daily (except Mon), 8.30am-1.50pm. 4 000 L. ☎ (055) 23 88 603.

Ognissanti - Open all year, Mon-Sat, 8am-noon and 4-7pm; Sun and public holidays, 4-6pm. ☎ (055) 23 98 700.

Museo archeologico - Open all year, Tues-Sat, Mon following Sun closing, 9am-2pm; 2nd and 4th Sun in the month, 9am-1pm. Closed 1st, 3rd, 5th Sun in the month, 1 Jan, 1 May and 25 Dec. 8 000 L, no charge for visitors under 18 years old and over 60 and during heritage week. ☎ (055) 23 575.

Museo della Casa Fiorentina Antica (Palazzo Davanzati) - Closed for restoration. ☎ (055) 23 885.

Museo Marino Marini - Open June, July, Sept, Wed-Mon, 10am-5pm (11pm Thur, 1pm Sun and public holidays); Jan-May, Oct-Dec, Wed-Mon, 10am-5pm (1pm Sun and public holidays). Closed Tues, 1 May and 25 Dec. Guided tours in English, Italian. 8 000 L, 4 000 L for child 6-12 years old and over 60, no charge for child under 6 years old and during heritage week. ☎ (055) 21 94 32.

Museo di Storia della Scienza - Open all year, weekdays, 9.30am-1pm, and also 2-5pm on Mon, Wed and Fri. Closed Sun and public holidays. 10 000 L, 7 500 L for visitors 15-25 years old, 5 000 L for 4-15 years old; no charge during science week. ☎ (055) 29 34 93.
www.imss.fi.it

Opificio delle Pietre dure - ♿ Open all year, Mon-Sat, 9am-2pm. Closed Sun and public holidays. 4 000 L, no charge for visitors under 18 years old and over 60 and during heritage week. ☎ (055) 26 511. e-mail: opd@dada.it.
www.dada.it/propart/opd.htm

Ospedale degli Innocenti: Pinacoteca - Open daily (except Wed), 8.30am-2pm. Closed 1 Jan, Easter, 1 May, 15 Aug, 25 Dec. 5 000 L, no charge child. ☎ (055) 24 91 708.

Villa della Petraia - Same admission times and charges as for Villa di Castello.

Villa di Castello - Open (park only) daily (except Sat, and Sun afternoons) June-Aug, 9am-7.30pm; Apr, May, Sept, 9am-6.30pm; Mar, Oct, 9am-5.30pm; Jan, Feb, Nov, Dec, 9am-4.30pm (last admission 1hr before closing time). Closed 2nd and 3rd Mon in the month. 4 000 L (ticket also valid for Villa della Petraia). ☎ (055) 45 47 91.

Villa di Poggio a Caiano - ♿ Open June-Aug, 9am-6.30pm; Apr, May, Sept, 9am-5.30pm; Mar, Oct, 9am-4.30pm; Jan, Feb, Nov, Dec, 9am-3.30pm. Closed 2nd and 3rd Mon in the month, 1 Jan, 1 May and 25 Dec. 4 000 L, no charge for visitors under 18 years old and over 60. ☎ (055) 87 70 12.

Villa La Ferdinanda di Artimino: Etruscan museum - Open all year, daily (except Wed), 9am-1pm (12.30pm Sun and public holidays). Guided tours (1hr), audio-tours. Audio-visual presentation (20min). 5 000 L, 2 000 L child. ☎ (055) 87 18 124.

Certosa del Galluzzo - Open, all year, daily (except Mon), 9am-noon and 3-6pm (5pm in winter). No charge. ☎ (055) 20 49 226.

FOLIGNO

Palazzo Trinci - Open all year, daily (except Mon) 10am-6pm. Closed 1 Jan and 25 Dec. 5 000 L.

FONTANELLATO

Rocca San Vitale - ♿ Guided tours (1hr) Apr-Sept, Mon-Sat, 9.30-11.30am and 3-6pm, Sun, 9am-noon and 2.30-6pm; Oct-Mar, Tues (also Mon in Oct)-Sat, 9.30-11.30am and 3-5pm, Sun, 9am-noon and 2.30-5pm. Closed 1 Jan, 25 Dec. 7 000 L, 4 000 L child. ☎ (0521) 82 23 46.

FONTE COLOMBO

Convento - Open all year, daily, 8am-7pm (5pm Oct-Mar). Guided tours on request. ☎ (0746) 21 01 25.

La FORESTA

Convento - Guided tours all year, daily, 8.30am-noon and 2.30-7pm. ☎ (0746) 20 00 85.

FORLI

Pinacoteca - () Open Tues-Sun, 9am-1.30pm (1pm Sun; also 2.30-5pm Tues, Thur). Closed public holidays and 4 Feb. No charge. Guided tours (1hr) by appointment. ☎ (0543) 71 26 06.

Abbazia di FOSSANOVA

Guided tours by appointment at least two weeks in advance, Apr-Oct, Mon-Sat, 7am-noon and 4-7.30pm, Sun and public holidays, 9-11am and 4-7.30pm; Nov-March, Mon-Sat, 7am-noon and 3-5.30pm, Sun and public holidays, 9-11am and 3-5.30pm. ☎ (0773) 93 061.

FRASCATI

Villa Aldobrandini: parco - Open all year, Mon-Fri, 9am-1pm and 3-6pm (5pm in winter). Closed holidays. ☎ (06) 94 20 331 (I.A.T., Piazza Marconi, 1) for appointment on the day or in advance.

G

GAETA

Monte Orlando: tomb - To visit, apply to the park office. ☎ (0771) 46 92 20 or (0336) 66 53 86.

Lago di GARDA

Boat trip on the lake - From Desenzano to Riva del Garda, via Sirmoione and Salo; also by hydrofoil.

GARDONE RIVIERA

Il Vittoriale - Open daily, Apr-Sept, 8.30am-8pm; Oct-Mar, 9am-12.30pm and 2-5.30pm (6pm Sat, Sun). 8 000 L. ☎ (0365) 20 130.

La Priora - Guided tours in English, French, German, Italian, Apr-Sept, 10am-1.30pm and 2.30-6pm; Oct-Mar, 9am-12.30pm and 2-5.30pm (6pm Sat, Sun). 16 000 L. ☎ (0365) 20 130
http://vittoriale.gsnet.it

GENOVA
🚊 Stazione Principe ☎ (010) 24 62 633

Port: Boat trip - Departing from the aquarium and main harbour station "Ponte dei Mille", daily, all day, frequency according to demand. Time: 45min. 10 000 L; it is advisable to telephone in advance. ☎ (010) 26 57 12.
Mini-cruises are also organised from Mar-Sept for San Fruttuoso, Portofino, the Cinque Terre and Porto Venere. Departure 8.30-10.45am , return to Genoa at 7pm. 20 000-40 000 L. Book several days ahead. ☎ (010) 26 57 12.

Cattedrale di San Lorenzo: Treasury - Guided tours daily, 9am-noon and 3pm (4pm Sun)-6pm. 8 000 L. ☎ (010) 31 12 69; e-mail: tesoro@publinet.it

Palazzo Carrega-Cataldi - Open by appointment only (apply in advance to the Ufficio Presidenza Camera di Commercio di Genova), daily (except Sat, Sun and public holidays), mid June-mid Sept, 9am-1pm; mid Sept-mid Mar, 9am-6pm. No charge. ☎ (010) 27 041.
www.lig.camcom.it/cciaa-ge

Palazzo Municipale Doria Tursi - Open Mon-Thur, 8am-noon amd 1-5pm; Fri, 8am-3pm; Sat, 8am-noon. Closed Sun and public holidays. Guided tours. ☎ (010) 55 71 11.

Palazzo Bianco - Open Tues, Thur, Fri, 9am-1pm; Wed, Sat, 9am-7pm; Sun, 10am-6pm. Closed Mon and public holidays. 6 000 L, no charge Sun and for visitors under 18 years old and over 60. ☎ (010) 27 58 098.

Palazzo Rosso - Open Tues, Thur, Fri, 9am-1pm; Wed, Sat, 9am-7pm; Sun and holidays, 10am-6pm. Closed Mon and public holidays. 6 000 L, no charge Sun. ☎ (010) 55 74 741.

Palazzo Reale - (&) Open Sun-Tues, 9am-1.45pm; Wed-Sat, 9am-7pm. Closed 1 Jan, 1 May and 25 Dec. 8 000 L, no charge during heritage week. Guided tours (about 1hr) in English, French, Italian. ☎ (010) 24 70 640.

Galleria nazionale di Palazzo Spinola - Open all year, Tues-Sat, 9am-7pm; Sun and public holidays, 9am-10pm. Closed 1 Jan, 1 May and 25 Dec. 8 000 L. ☎ (010) 24 77 061.

Acquario - Open all year, Tues-Fri, 9.30am-7pm; Sat, Sun and public holidays, 9.30am-8.30pm (last admission 1hr 30min before closing time). Closed mid Sept-Mar. 19 000 L, no charge for child under 3 years old. ☎ (010) 24 81 205.

Villetta di Negro: Museo Chiossone - Open all year, Tues, Thur, Sat, Sun, 9am-1pm. Closed public holidays. 6 000 L, no charge Sun. Guided tours (1hr-1hr 30min) in English, French, Italian. ☎ (010) 54 22 85.

Grotta del GIGANTE

Cave and museum - Guided tours (45min), daily (except Mon unless holiday Mon) Apr-Sept, every 30min from 9am-noon and 2-6.30pm (daily, mid July and Aug); Mar, Oct, every 30min from 9am-noon and 2-5pm; Nov-Feb, 10am, 11am, noon, 2.30pm, 3.30pm and 4.30pm. Closed 1 Jan and 25 Dec. 8 000 L (in summer the charge also includes the return trip by train from Opicina and bus no 45. ☎ (040) 32 73 12.

GIGNESE

Museo dell'ombrello e del parasole - Open daily (except Mon unless holiday Mon), Apr-Sept, 10am-noon and 3-6pm. Closed Oct-Mar. 2 500 L, 1 000 L child. ☎ (0323)20 80 64.

GRADARA

La Rocca - Open daily, in summer, 9am-7pm (2pm in winter). Closed 1 Jan, 1 May and 25 Dec. 8 000 L, no charge for visitors under 18 years old and over 60. Guided tours in English, French, German, Spanish; apply a few days in advance. ☎ (0541) 96 41 81 or 96 41 15 (Pro Loco, mornings only).

Parco Nazionale del GRAN PARADISO

Guided tours - The Ente Parco Nazionale Gran Paradiso (PNGP) organizes guided tours. Apply to Centro Visitatori di Noasca. ☎ (0124) 90 10 70.
Guides and support organisations: Cooperativa Habitat, via E. Aubert 48, Aosta ☎ (0165) 36 38 51; Cooperativa Il Roc, via Umberto I 1, Noasca ☎ (0124) 90 11 01; Associazione Opuntia, via V. Monti 11, Torino ☎ (011) 66 90 891.

PNGP Information Centres - Accessible from the Val d'Aosta road:

Rhêmes-Notre Dame Valley (Chanavey refuge) - Open daily in summer; weekends, in winter, Easter and Christmas.

Val Savaranche (Degioz refuge), via the Val Savaranche road: Open daily, July and Aug; weekends, June-Sept, Easter and Christmas.

Cogne Valley (Valnontey refuge): at Cogne, turn right: "Paradisia" Alpine Botanical Gardens: Open in summer.

Accessible from Locana Valley:

Ronco Canavese (Piazza Municipio), Valle Soana: Open daily, July, Aug; weekends, June-Sept, Easter and Christmas.

Locana, former Church of San Francesco, Valle Orco: Open daily, July, Aug; weekends, June-Sept, Easter and Christmas.

Ceresole Reale (Pian della Balma), Valle Orco: Open daily, July, Aug; weekends, June-Sept, Easter and Christmas.

GRECCIO

Convento - Open all year, daily, 9am (9.30am Sun)-12.30pm and 3-6.30pm (6pm in winter).

GUBBIO

Palazzo dei Consoli - Open all year, daily, 10am-1pm and 3-6pm (5pm, Oct-Mar). Closed 14, 15 May and 25 Dec. 7 000 L, 4 000 L visitors 7-25 years old and over 60.

Palazzo ducale - Open all year, Mon-Sat, 9am-1.30pm and 2.30-7pm; Sun and public holidays, 9am-1pm. Closed 1 Jan, 1 May and 25 Dec. 4 000 L, no charge for visitors under 18 years old and over 60,. ☎ (075) 92 75 872.

Duomo: Episcopal Chapel - Open all year, daily, 9am-7pm. ☎ (075) 92 75 138.

I-J-L

Lago d'ISEO

Boat trips - In spring and summer: Tour of lake, with morning departure (from Sarnico, Iseo or Lovere) and evening return; time: about 7 hours; stop at Monte Isola; lunch on board optional.
Tour of lake with afternoon departure (from Sarnico, Iseo, Lovere or Monte Isola) and evening return.
Trip to the 3 islands in the afternoon, departing from Iseo; time: 1hrs 30min. Apply to I.A.T. in Iseo, Lungolago Marconi, 2. ☎ (030) 98 02 09.

JESI

Pinacoteca - Open July, Aug, daily (except Mon), 10am-1pm and 5-midnight; the rest of the year, Tues-Sat, 10am-1pm and 4-7pm; Sun, 10am-1pm and 5-8pm. 4 000 L, no charge for visitors under 12 years old. Guided tours (1hr). ☎ (0731) 53 83 42/43.

Regione dei LAGHI

Numerous boat and hydrofoil (aliscafo) trips can be combined for each of the lakes (see listing in alphabetical order). Look under the name of each lake, where some of the trips will be mentioned. For further details concerning times, rates, etc. apply to the local tourist office.

L'AQUILA
🛈 piazza Santa Maria di Paganica 5 ☎ (0862) 41 08 08

Basilica di San Bernardino - Open daily, 9.30am-noon (9.45-10.30am Sun) and 4-6pm (5pm in winter). ☎ (0862) 22 255.

Castello: Museo nazionale d'Abruzzo - (&) Open early Apr-late Oct, daily (except Mon), 9am-7pm (10pm Sun); the rest of the year, daily, 9am-1.30pm (1pm Sun). Closed public holidays. 8 000 L, no charge for visitors under 18 years old and over 60. ☎ (0862) 63 31.

Basilica di Santa Maria di Collemaggio - Open 8am-12.30pm and 3-7pm (6pm in winter). For information or key (when closed) ☎ (0862) 26 744, 28 073.

LAVENO MOMBELLO

Sasso del Ferro: cable-car - Operates from Apr-Sept, Mon-Fri, 10am-5.30pm; Sat, 9.30am-6pm; Sun,and public holidays, 9.30am-7pm; Oct-Mar, Sat, Sun and public holidays only, 9.30am-5pm. ☎ (0332) 66 80 12.

LECCE
🛈 corso Vittorio Emanuele 24 ☎ (0832) 24 80 92

Museo Provinciale S. Castromediano - & Open all year, Mon-Fri, 9am-1.30pm and 2.30-7.30pm; Sun, 9am-1.30pm. Closed 1 and 6 Jan, 25 Apr, 1 May and 25 Dec. No charge. ☎ (0832) 24 70 25.

LIGNANO

Beach - Developed along its entire length, but no charge. May-Sept, beach umbrellas and deck chairs can be easily hired, by the half-day, full day or on a longer term basis. Rates differ according to the season - low, medium and high.

Parco zoo Punta Verde - & Open 9am-sunset, Mar-Oct, daily; in Feb, Sun and public holidays only. Closed Jan, Nov, Dec. 12 000 L, 8 000 L child over 3 years old. ☎ (0431) 42 87 75.

LORETO

Santuario della Santa Casa:
Basilica - Open all year, daily, 6am-8pm (7pm in winter). ☎ (071) 97 01 08.
Santa Casa - Open all year, daily, 6am-12.30pm and 2.30-8pm (7pm in winter). ☎ (071) 97 01 08.

Pinacoteca - Open daily (except Mon), Apr-Oct, 9am-1pm and 4-7pm; Nov-Mar, by appointment. 5 000 L. ☎ (071) 97 77 59, (071) 97 01 02

LOVERE

Galleria Tadini - Open 3 Apr-late Oct, daily, 3-6pm (also Sun 10am-noon). Closed late Oct-2 Apr. 7 000 L. Guided tours (about 1hr) in English, French. ☎ (035) 96 27 80.

LUCCA
🛈 Vecchia Porta San Donato, piazzale Verdi ☎ (0583) 41 96 89

Casa dei Guinigi: Torre - Open daily, Mar-Sept, 9am-7.30pm; Oct, 10am-6pm; Nov-Feb, 10am-4.30pm. 4 500 L, 3 000 L child. ☎ (0583) 48 524.

Museo Nazionale di Palazzo Mansi: Pinacoteca – Open all year, daily (except Mon), 9am-7pm (2pm Sun and public holidays). Closed 1 Jan, 1 May and at Christmas. 8 000 L, no charge for visitors under 18 years old and over 60, and for EU visitors. ☎ (0583) 55 570.

Museo Nazionale di Villa Guinigi – Open all year, daily (except Mon), 9am-7pm, (2pm Sun and public holidays). Closed 1 Jan, 1 May and at Christmas. 4 000 L, no charge for visitors under 18 years old and over 60, and for EU visitors. ☎ (0583) 46 033.

LUCERA

Museo civico G. Fiorelli – Open all year, Tues-Sun, 8am-1pm; also Tues and Fri, July-Sept, 4-7pm, Oct-June, 3-6pm. Closed Mon and weekday public holidays. 1 500 L. Guided tours. ☎ (0881) 54 70 41.

Lago di LUGANO

Boat trip on lake – The "Gran Giro del Lago" tour takes place daily, early Apr-mid Oct, departing from Lugano at 2.40pm, returning at 5.15pm. 28 Swiss francs. Commentaries in 4 languages; restaurant. Other boat trips, of variable length and price are available: contact the Società Navigazione del Lago di Lugano. ☎ (00 41 91) 97 15 223.

M

Lago MAGGIORE

Boat trip on lake – Main trips: from Stresa, Baveno, Pallanza to the Isole Borromee every 30min in spring and summer. Arona-Stresa-Locarno, every 20min only on public holidays and the day before in spring, daily (except Wed) in summer. Car-ferry between Intra and Laveno. Lake passes for unlimited travel are also available for one, three or seven days. ☎ (0322) 23 32 00.

MALCESINE

Monte Baldo – The cable-car operates daily, 8am-7pm; departure every 30min. Closed Mar, Nov-mid Dec. 13 000 L (one way); 18 000 L (return). ☎ (045) 74 00 206 or (045) 74 00 044.

MALCONTENTA

Villa Foscari – Open Apr-mid Nov, Tues and Sat, 9am-noon. Closed Mon. 10 000 L. Out of season, by prior appointment only, 15 000 L. ☎ (041) 52 03 966.

MANTOVA   🛈 piazza Mantegna 6 ☎ (0376) 32 82 53

Palazzo Ducale – Guided tours (1hr 30min), daily (except Mon afternoons), 9am-2pm and 2.30-7pm. Also Sun, 4-10pm, early Apr-early Oct; and Thur, Fri, Sat, 8.30-11pm, mid June-mid Sept. Last admission 1hr before closing time. Closed 1 Jan, 1 May and 25 Dec. 12 000 L, no charge for visitors under 18 years old and over 60 and during heritage week. Bar. ☎ (0376) 32 02 83.

Rotonda di San Lorenzo – Open daily, in summer, 10.30am-12.30pm and 2.30-4.30pm; in winter, 11am-noon and 3-4pm. Closed 1 Jan, 1 May and 25 Dec. Donation. ☎ (0376) 32 82 53.

Teatro Bibiena – Open all year, daily, 9.30am-12.30pm and 3-6pm. 2 000 L. Closed 1 May and 25 Dec. Guided tours. ☎ (0376) 32 76 53.

Palazzo d'Arco – Guided tours (about 1hr), Mar-Oct, Tues-Fri, 9am-12.30pm, Sat, Sun, 10am-6pm; Nov-Feb, Sat, 10am-12.30pm and 2-5pm, Sun, 10am-5pm. Closed 1 Jan and 25 Dec. 5 000 L. ☎ (0376) 32 22 42.

Palazzo del Te – (&) Open all year, daily, 9am (1pm Mon)-6pm. Closed 1 Jan, 1 May and 25 Dec. 12 000 L. ☎ (0376) 32 58 86.

MARLIA

Villa Reale – (&) Guided tours (1hr), Mar-Nov, daily (except Mon), 10am, 11am, 3pm, 4pm, 5pm and 6pm. Closed Dec-Feb. 9 000 L. ☎ (0583) 30 108.

La MARMOLADA

Malga Ciapela cable-car – Operates daily, all year. Times vary every year. For information ☎ (0437) 72 13 19.

Cascate delle MARMORE

Mon-Fri: 16 Mar-31 May, noon-12.30pm and 3.30-4pm. June and Sept, 3-4.30pm. July and Aug, 11am-12.30pm and 5-6.30pm.

Sat: May-31 Aug, 11am-12.30pm and 5-10pm; 16 Mar-Apr, Sept, Oct, 11am-12.30pm and 4-9pm.

Sun, public holidays: 22 May and 16 Aug, 10am-1pm and 3-9.30pm; 16 Mar-Apr, Sept, Oct, 10.30am-12.30pm and 3-8pm; Nov-15 Mar, 3-4pm.

MASER

Villa - Open Mar-Oct, Tues, Sat, Sun and public holidays, 3-6pm; Nov-Feb, Sat, Sun and public holidays, 2.30-5pm. Closed Easter and 24 Dec-6 Jan. 9 000 L. ☎ (0423) 92 30 04.

MASSA MARITTIMA

Museo archeologico - Open daily (except Mon), Apr-Oct, 10am-12.30pm and 3.30-7pm; Nov-Mar, 10am-12.30pm and 3.30-5pm. 5 000 L, 2 500 L child. Guided tours. ☎ (0566) 90 22 89.

Fortezza dei Senesi and **Torre Candeliere** - Open daily (except Mon), Apr-Sept, 11am-1pm and 3-6pm; Oct-Dec, 10m-1pm and 2.30-8pm. 3 000 L, 1 500 L child. ☎ (0566) 90 22 89.

Museo di Storia e Arte delle Miniere - Closed for maintenance. ☎ (0566) 90 22 89.

MATERA   🛈 via De Viti de Marco 9 ☎ (0835) 33 19 83

San Pietro Caveoso - Open all year, Mon-Sat, 9am-noon and 3.30-7pm; Sun, 9.30am-12.30pm and 4-7pm. No charge. ☎ (0835) 31 15 10.

Museo Nazionale Ridola - Open all year, daily, 9am-7pm. Closed 1 Jan, 1 May and 25 Dec. 4 000 L. ☎ (0835) 31 00 58.

MERANO

Castello Principesco - ♿ Open, Jul, Aug, Tues-Sat, 10am-5pm, Sun and public holidays, 4-7pm; Jan,-Jun, Sept-Dec, Tues-Sat, 10am-5pm, Sun and public holidays, 10am-1pm. Guided tours in German late May-mid Oct, Thur, 3.30pm. ☎ (0473) 23 60 15.

MERANO 2000

Cable-car - Operates 1 June-7 Nov and 18 Dec-10 Apr approx., daily, 9am-5pm. ☎ (0473) 23 48 21.

MILANO   🛈 via Marconi, 1(piazza Duomo) ☎ (02) 72 52 43 00

Duomo - **Cripta, Tesoro:** Open daily, 9am-noon and 2-6pm. 2 000 L.

Visita ai Terrazzi - Open daily, 9am-5.30pm (4.30pm in winter). On foot: 5 000 L; by lift: 8 000 L. ☎ (02) 86 46 34 56.

Galleria Victorio Emanuele, Milano

Museo del Duomo - Open daily (except Mon), 9.30am-12.30pm and 3-7pm. Closed Easter, 25 Apr and 25 Dec. 10 000 L. ☎ (02) 72 02 26 56.

Museo del Teatro della Scala - Open Mon-Sat all year, and Sun (except Nov-Apr), 9am-12.30pm and 2-5.30pm. Closed public holidays. 6 000 L. Guided tours (about 1hr) in English, French, German, Spanish. ☎ (02) 80 53 418; e-mail: scala@energu.it
www.evecom.com

Pinacoteca di Brera - Open Tues-Sat, 9am-10pm; Sun and public holidays, 9am-12.45pm and 2.30-8pm. Closed 1 Jan, 1 May and 25 Dec. 8 000 L, no charge for visitors under 18 years old and over 60. ☎ (02) 72 26 32 29.

Castello Sforzesco - Open daily (except Mon), 9am-5.45pm. Closed 1 Jan, Easter, 1 May and 25 Dec. No charge. ☎ (02) 86 46 30 54. Guided tours ☎ (02) 65 99 914.

Biblioteca Ambrosiana - Open daily (except Mon), 10am-5.30pm (last admission 4.30pm). Closed Easter, 1 May, 15 Aug and 25 Dec. 12 000 L, 6 000 L for visitors under 18 years old and over 60, no charge child under 6. ☎ (02) 80 69 21.

Museo Poldi-Pezzoli - Open daily (except Mon), 9.30am-12.30pm and 2.30-6pm (7.30pm Sat). Closed Sun afternoons Apr-Sept, and public holidays. 10 000 L, no charge for child under 10 years old. ☎ (02) 79 48 89.

Galleria d'Arte Moderna - (&) Open daily (except Mon), 9am-5.45pm. Closed 1 Jan, Easter, 1 May, 15 Aug and 25 Dec. No charge. ☎ (02) 76 00 28 19.

Casa di Manzoni - Open Mon-Fri, 9am-noon and 2-4pm. Closed Sat, Sun, also during Aug and from 25 Dec-7 Jan. No charge. ☎ (02) 86 46 04 03.

Museo civico di Storia Naturale - Open Mon-Fri, 9.30am-5.30pm (6.30pm Sat, Sun). Closed 1 Jan, 1 May, 15 Aug and 25 Dec. Guided tours in English. ☎ (02) 78 13 12.

Palazzo Bagatti Valsecchi - Open daily (except Mon), 1-5pm. Closed public holidays. 10 000 L (5 000 L Wed). ☎ (02) 76 00 61 32.

Museo della Scienza e della Tecnica Leonardo da Vinci - (&) Open Tues-Fri, 9.30am-5pm; Sat, Sun and public holidays, 9.30am-6.30pm. Closed Mon except holiday Mon, 1 Jan and 25 Dec. 10 000 L. Guided tours (1-2hr) in English, French, German, Russian, Spanish. Bar, restaurant. ☎ (02) 48 55 51.
www.museoscienza.org

Santa Maria delle Grazie: Cenacolo - Open all year, daily (except Mon), 8am-1.45pm and 7-10pm (5-8pm Sun). Closed 1 May. 12 000 L. ☎ (02) 49 87 588.

Museo Civico di Archeologia - Open daily (except Mon), 9.30am-5.30pm. No charge. Audio-visual presentation. ☎ (02) 80 53 972.

Basilica di San Lorenzo Maggiore: Cappella di Sant'Aquilino - Open all year, daily, 8.30am-noon and 3-5.30pm. ☎ (02) 83 22 940.

MIRA

Villa Widmann-Foscari-Rezzonico - Closed for restoration.

MIRAMARE

Castello di Miramare: Museo storico - (&) Open daily, Apr-Sept, 9am-6pm; 5pm, Mar and Oct; 4pm, Nov-Feb. 8 000 L, no charge for visitors under 18 years old and over 60, for EU visitors and during heritage week. Guided tours (1hr) in English, French, German, Italian, Russian. Bar. ☎ (040) 22 41 43.
www.lloydadriatico.it/miramare

Parco di Miramare - & Open daily, Apr-Sept, 8am-7pm; 6pm, Mar and Oct; 5pm, Nov-Feb. No charge. Guided tours (1hr) in Italian, and on request in English. Bar. ☎ (040) 22 41 43.
www.lloydadriatico.it/miramare

Lago di MISURINA

Toll-road - 30 000 L Rtn. per car.

MODENA

🛈 piazza Grande 17 ☎ (059) 20 66 60

Museo del Duomo - Closed for restoration.

Biblioteca Estense - Open Mon-Thur, 9am-7.15pm; Fri, Sat, 9am-1.45pm. Closed Sun and public holidays. No charge. Guided tours (1hr). ☎ (059) 22 22 48; e-mail: estense@kril.cedoc.unimo.it

Galleria Estense - Open Tues, Fri, Sat, 9am-7pm; Wed, Thur, 9am-2pm; Sun, 9am-1pm.. Closed public holidays. 8 000 L, no charge for visitors under 18 years old and over 60. Audio tours; audio-visual presentation. ☎ (059) 22 21 45, (059) 23 50 04.

MONTECASSINO

Abbazia – Open all year, daily, 8.30am-noon and 3.30-5pm (6pm July, Aug). ☏ (0776) 31 15 29.

Museo abbaziale – Open Apr-Oct, daily, 9am-noon and 3.30-5pm (6pm in summer); Nov-Mar, Sat, Sun, 9am-noon and 3.30-5pm. 2 000 L. ☏ (0776) 31 15 29.

Museo archeologico nazionale – Open all year, daily, 9am-sunset. Closed 1 Jan, 1 May and 25 Dec. 4 000 L, no charge for visitors under 18 years old and over 60 and during heritage week. ☏ (0776) 30 11 68.

MONTECATINI TERME   ⎀ viale Verdi 66/a ☏ (0572) 77 22 44

Museo dell'Accademia d'Arte – Open daily (except Sun), Apr-Oct, 9am-12.30pm and 4-7.30pm; Nov-Mar, 9am-noon and 4-7pm (closed Sat afternoons). Closed public holidays. No charge. ☏ (0572) 78 952.

MONTECCHIO MAGGIORE

Villa Cordellina-Lombardi – Open Apr-Oct: Tues-Fri, 9am-1pm; Sat, Sun and public holidays, 9am-noon and 3-6pm. Closed Nov-Mar. 4 000 L, 2 500 L students and pensioners.

MONTEFALCO

Torre Comunale – Closed for restoration.

San Francesco – Open daily, Aug, 10.30am-1pm and 3-7.30pm; June, July, 10.30am-1pm and 3-7pm; Mar-May, Sept, Oct, 10.30am-1pm and 2-6pm; Nov-Feb, daily (except Mon), 10.30am-1pm and 2.30-4pm. 7 000 L, 4 000 L for visitors 15-25 years old, 2 000 L for 7-14 years old. ☏ (0742) 37 95 98. www.krenet.it/regione/MUSEI/MONTEFALCO

MONTEFIORE DELL'ASO

Church – Usually open in the morning. ☏ (0734) 93 81 03.

MONTE ISOLA

Access by boat – daily departures from Iseo: in summer and on public holidays in spring, every 30min, the rest of the year, every hour. From **Sulzano** : all year, every 15min; 4 100 L return. The island can also be reached from other lakeside towns (Sale Marasino). For further information contact I.A.T. Iseo, Lungolago Marconi 2c. ☏ (030) 98 02 09.

MONTE OLIVETO MAGGIORE

Abbazia – Open all year, daily, 9.15am-noon and 3.15-6pm (5pm Nov-Mar). No charge. ☏ (0577) 70 70 17/61.

MONTEPULCIANO

Torre del Palazzo Comunale – Open, all year, Mon-Sat, 9am-1pm. Closed Sun and public holidays. No charge. ☏ (0578) 71 69 35.

Museo civico – Closed for restoration. ☏ (0578) 71 69 43.

MONTE SANT'ANGELO

Tomba di Rotari – Open Apr-Sept, 9am-7.30pm; Oct-Mar, by appointment. 1 000 L. Guided tours (15min). ☏ (0884) 56 18 09.

MONZA

Duomo: Tesoro – Open daily (except Mon), 9-11.30am and 3-5.30pm; Sun and public holidays, 9am-12.30pm and 3-5.30pm. 5 000 L. Guided tours (30min) by appointment: contact Pro Monza. ☏ (039) 32 32 22.

MORTOLA INFERIORE

Giardini Hanbury – (&) Open mid June-Oct, daily, 9am-7pm; Apr-mid June, daily, 10am-6pm; Nov-Mar, daily (except Wed), 10am-5pm. Last admission 1hr before closing time. 8 500 L. ☏ (0184) 22 95 07.

MURANO

Museo di arte vetraria – Open daily (except Wed), in summer, 10am-5pm; in winter, 10am-4pm. Closed 1 Jan, 1 May and 25 Dec. 8 000 L, 5 000 L students and foreign visitors over 60 years old, no charge child. ☏ (041) 73 95 86.

N

       ▉ piazza dei Martiri 58 ☎ (081) 40 53 11

Castel Nuovo - (♿) Open all year, Mon-Sat, 9am-7pm. Closed Sun (except at Easter, in May and summer),1 Jan and 1 May. 10 000 L, no charge for child under 12 years old. ☎ (081) 79 52 003.

Teatro San Carlo - Open by appointment. ☎ (081) 79 72 111.

Palazzo Reale - Open Apr-Oct, Mon-Sat (except Wed), 9.30am-10pm, Sun and public holidays, 9.30am-8pm; Jan-Mar, Mon-Sat (except Wed), 9am-6.30pm, Sun and public holidays, 9am-2pm; Nov, Dec, daily (except Wed), 9am-6.30pm. Closed 1 Jan, 1 May and 25 Dec. 8 000 L, no charge for child, on Euroepan Day of Culture and during heritage week. Bar, restaurant. ☎ (081) 58 08 326.

Chiesa del Gesù Nuovo - Open all year, daily, 4-7pm. ☎ (081) 55 18 613.

Santa Chiara: cloisters - Open all year, daily, 9am-1pm and 4-7pm. ☎ (081) 55 26 209.

Cappella Sansevero - Open all year, daily (except Tues), 10am-5pm (1.30pm, Sun and public holidays). 8 000 L. ☎ (081) 55 18 470.

San Gregorio Armeno: church and cloisters - Open all year, daily, 9.30am-noon. ☎ (081) 55 20 186.

San Lorenzo Maggiore - Open all year, Mon-Sat, 9am-1.30pm and 4-7pm, Sun 9am-1.30pm. ☎ (081) 45 49 48.
Tour of the archeological excavations, Mon-Fri (except Tues), 9am-1.30pm and 3.30-5.30pm (4-6pm in summer), Sat, Sun, 9am-1.30pm. 5 000 L, 2 500 L child. ☎ (081) 29 00 34.

Decumanus Maximus - Visit of all monuments all year, Mon-Fri, 9am-1.30pm
Pio Monte della Misericordia ☎ (081) 44 69 73.
Chiesa dei Girolami ☎ (081) 44 91 39.
San Paolo Maggiore: also open Sun mornings ☎ (081) 45 40 48.
Purgatorio ad Arco: also open Sun mornings ☎ (081) 45 93 12.
Santa Maria Maggiore ☎ (081) 45 81 01.
Croce di Lucca: closed for restoration. ☎ (081) 56 65 285.

Museo archeologico nazionale - ♿ Open all year, Mon-Sat (except Tues), 10am-10pm; Sun, 9am-8pm (the time is likely tochange, it is advisable to telephone for information). Closed 1 Jan, 1 May and 25 Dec. 12 000 L, no charge for visitors under 18 years old and over 60. ☎ (081) 29 28 23.

Certosa di San Martino - Open all year, daily (except Mon), 9am-2pm. Closed public holidays. 8 000 L. ☎ (081) 57 81 769.

Palazzo e Galleria Nazionale di Capodimonte - ♿ Open all year, Tues-Sat, 10am-7pm; Sun and public holidays, 9am-2pm. Closed public holidays. 12 000 L. Guided tours. Bar, restaurant. ☎ (081) 74 41 307.

Museo Nazionale di Ceramica Duca di Martina - Open all year, daily (except Mon), 9am-2pm. Closed public holidays. 4 000 L. ☎ (081) 57 88 418.

Catacombe di San Gennaro - Guided tours (40min, at least two persons) daily, 9.30am, 10.15am, 11am and 11.45am. 5 000 L, 3 000 L child. ☎ (081) 74 11 071.

Duomo

Capella di San Gennaro - Open Mon-Sat, 8am-noon and 4.30-6.30pm; Sun, 8am-1.30. Guided tours from 10am. 5 000 L. ☎ (081) 29 47 64.

Basilica di Santa Restituta - Open Mon-Sat, 9am-noon and 4.30-7pm; Sun and public holidays, 9am-noon. 5 000 L. ☎ (081) 44 90 97.

Palazzo Como: Museo civico Filangieri - Open all year, Tues-Sat, 9am-2pm and 3.30-7pm, Sun, 9am-1.30pm. Closed 1 Jan, 1 May and 25 Dec. 5 000 L, 1 000 L child. Guided tours (1hr) in English, French, German, Polish. ☎ (081) 20 31 75.

Sant'Anna dei Lombardi - Open daily (except Sun), 8am-noon. Closed public holidays.

Acquario - ♿ Open Mar-Oct, Tues-Sat, 9am-6pm, Sun, 9.30am-7pm; Nov-Feb, Tues-Sat, 9am-5pm, Sun, 9am-2pm). 3 000 L, 1 500 L child 5-12 years old. Guided tours (45min) in English, French on request. ☎ (081) 58 33 263.

Museo Principe di Aragona Pignatelli Cortes - (♿) Open all year, daily (except Mon), 9am-2pm. Closed public holidays. 4 000 L. ☎ (081) 66 96 75.

NONANTOLA

Abbazia - Open all year, daily, 9.30am-12.30pm and 3-6pm. ☎ (059) 54 90 25.

NOVACELLA / NEUSTIFT

Abbazia - Guided tours daily (except Sun and public holidays), 10am, 11am, 2pm, 3pm and 4pm (Nov-Easter, in the morning only). 7 500 L. Apply in advance to the abbey, via Abbazia 1, 39040 Varna ☎ (0472) 83 61 89.

ORVIETO
🛈 piazza Duomo 26 ☎ (0763) 34 24 77

Palazzo dei Papi: Museo dell'Opera del Duomo - Closed for restoration. ☎ (0763) 34 24 77.

Pozzo di San Patrizio - Open daily, Mar-Sept, 9.30am-7pm; Oct-Feb, 10am-6pm. 6 000 L, 4 000 L child and visitors over 65. ☎ (0763) 34 46 64.

Museo archeologico Faina - ♿ Open daily (except Mon), late Mar-late Sept, 10am-1pm and 3-7pm; late Sept-late Mar, 10am-1pm and 2.30-5pm. 7 000 L, 4 000 L child 7-12 years old and visitors over 65, no chrage child under 7. ☎ (0763) 34 15 11.

OSTIA ANTICA

Excavation site - Open late Mar-late Sept, 9am-7pm; Mar and Oct 9am-6pm; the rest of the year, 9am-5pm. Last admission 1hr before closing time. Closed 1 Jan, 1 May and 25 Dec. 8 000 L, no charge for visitors under 18 years old and over 60. ☎ (06) 56 35 80 99
itnw.roma.it/ostia/scavi

Museo - Closed for restoration. Re-opening mid 1999. ☎ (06) 56 35 80 99.

OTRANTO

Grotta Zinzulusa - Near Castro Marina. Visit daily, mid June-mid Sept, 9.30am-7pm; the rest of the year, 10am-4pm. No tours when the sea is rough. 4 000-5 000 L. Bar, restaurant. ☎ (0836) 94 38 12.
www.anet.it/Castro

P

PADOVA
🛈 Stazione ☎ (049) 87 52 077

Cappella degli Scrovegni - Open daily, Feb-Oct, 9am-7pm; Nov-Feb, 9am-6pm. 10 000 L, 7 000 L visitors 6-17 years old, students under 26, no charge child and on 25 Mar. Combined ticket for the Battistero, Museo agli Eremitani and Palazzo della Ragione: 15 000 L, 10 000 L reductions. ☎ (049) 82 04 550.

Museo Civico agli Eremitani - Open daily (except Mon), Feb-Oct, 9am-7pm; Nov-Feb, 9am-6pm. Closed 1 Jan, 1 May, 15 Aug, 25 and 26 Dec. 10 000 L, 7 000 L visitors 6-17 years old, students under 26, no charge child. Combined ticket for the Battistero, Cappella degli Scrovegni and Palazzo della Ragione: 15 000 L, 10 000 L reductions. ☎ (049) 82 04 550.

Basilica del Santo - Open all year, daily (except Sun and public holidays), 6.30am-7.30pm (7pm late Oct-late Mar). Guided tours by appointment (book at least 10-15 days in advance), noon-4pm. Donation. ☎ (049) 66 39 44, Fax (049) 66 31 79.

Oratorio di San Giorgio and **Scuola di Sant'Antonio** - Open daily, Mar-Sept, 9am-12.30pm and 2.30-7pm; Oct-Mar, 9am-12.30pm and 2-5pm. Closed 1 Jan and 25 Dec. 3 000 L, 2 000 L child. Guided tours. ☎ (049) 87 55 235.

Palazzo della Ragione - Open daily (except Mon), Feb-Oct, 9am-7pm; Nov-Feb, 9am-6pm. Closed 1 Jan, 1 May, 15 Aug, 25 and 26 Dec. 10 000 L, 7 000 L for visitors 6-17 years old, students under 26, no charge child. Combined ticket for the Battistero, Cappella degli Scrovegni and Museo agli Eremitani: 15 000 L, 10 000 L reductions. ☎ (049) 82 05 006.

Università: Teatro Anatomico - No visits until further notice.

Caffè Pedrocchi: sale - Open daily (except Mon unless hol Mon), 9am-12.30pm and 3.30-6pm (7.30pm Sat, Sun and public holidays). Closed 1 Jan, 1 May, 15 Aug, 25 Dec. 5 000 L, 3 000 L child. ☎ (049) 82 05 007.
www.padova.net.it

Orto Botanico - (♿) Open Apr-Oct, daily, 9am-1pm and 3-6pm; Nov-Mar, Mon-Sat, 9am-1pm. Closed public holidays Nov-Mar. 5 000 L. ☎ (049) 65 66 14.

PAESTUM

Museo - ♿ Open all year, daily, 9am-6.30pm. Closed 1st and 3rd Mon in the month. 8 000 L, no charge for visitors under 18 years old and over 60. ☎ (0828) 81 10 16.

Ruins - Open all year, daily, 9am-2hr before sunset. Closed 1 Jan, 1 May, 25 Dec. 8 000 L, no charge for visitors under 18 years old and over 60. Guided tours (2hr): apply in advance to the tourist information centre. ☎ (0828) 81 10 16.

PALLANZA

Villa Taranto - Open Apr-Sept, daily, 8.30am-7.30pm (5.30pm Oct); last admission 1hr before closing time. Closed Nov-Mar. Bar, restaurant. 11 000 L, 10 000 L child. ☎ (0323) 40 45 55 or 55 66 67.

PALMI

Museo comunale - Open Mon-Fri, 8.30am-1.30pm and 3.30-5.30pm. Closed Sat, Sun and public holidays. Guided tours (3hr): apply in advance to the museum office, via F. Battaglia. 3 000 L. ☎ (0966) 26 22 50.

PAOLA

Convento - Open all year, daily, 6am-12.30pm and 2-8pm (6pm in winter). Guided tours: apply in advance to Santuario San Francesco, via Santuario 1, 87027 Paola. No charge. ☎ (0982) 58 25 18.

PARMA

San Giovanni Evangelista: convent cloisters - Open all year, Mon-Sat, 8.30am-noon and 3.30-6pm; Sun, 10am-noon and 3.30-6pm. Donation. Apply one week in advance. ☎ (0521) 23 55 92.

Antica Spezieria di San Giovanni Evangelista - Open all year, daily, 9am-2pm. Closed public holidays. 4 000 L, no charge for visitors under 18 years old and over 60. ☎ (0521) 23 36 17, 23 33 09.

Museo nazionale di Antichità - Open all year, daily (except Mon), 9am-7pm (last admission 1hr before closing time). Closed 1 Jan, 1 May and 25 Dec. 4 000 L, no charge for visitors under 18 years old and over 60. ☎ (0521) 23 37 18.

Galleria nazionale - Open all year, daily, 9am-2pm. Closed public holidays. 12 000 L, no charge for visitors under 18 years old and over 60. ☎ (0521) 23 33 09, 23 36 17.

Teatro Farnese - Open all year, daily, 9am-1.45pm. Closed public holidays. 4 000 L, no charge for visitors under 18 years old and over 60. ☎ (0521) 23 33 09, 23 36 17.

Camera del Correggio - Open all year, daily, 9am-1.45pm. Closed public holidays. 4 000 L, no charge for visitors under 18 years old and over 60. ☎ (0521) 23 33 09, 23 36 17.

Museo Glauco-Lombardi - Closed for restoration. ☎ (0521) 23 37 27.

Madonna della Steccata - Open 9am-noon and 3-6pm. ☎ (0521) 23 49 37.

Casa Toscanini - Guided tours (30min) in English, French, Tues-Sat, 10am-1pm and 3-6pm; Sun, 10am-1pm. Audio-visual presentation. 3 000 L, 1 000 L child. ☎ (0521) 28 54 99.

PASSARIANO

Villa Manin - Open all year, daily (except Mon), 9am-12.30pm and 3-6pm. No charge. Guided tours (2hr) in English, French, German. Bar, restaurant. ☎ (0432) 90 66 57.

PAVIA

Castello Visconteo - Open all year, daily (except Mon), 9am-1.30pm (1pm Sun). In Apr-June, Sept, Oct, afternoon opening on Sat, Sun. Closed 1 and 6 Jan, 13 and 25 Apr, 1 May, 15 Aug, 8; 9, 25 and 26 Dec, 5 000 L. ☎ (0382) 33 853.

Certosa di PAVIA

Guided tours (about 1hr), daily (except Mon unless holiday Mon), Apr-Sept, 9-11.30am and 2.30-6pm (5.30pm in April); Oct-Mar, 9-11.30am and 2.30-4.30pm (5pm Sun and public holidays). Donation. ☎ (0382) 92 56 13.

PERUGIA

Galleria Nazionale dell'Umbria - ♿ Open all year, Mon-Sat, 9am-7pm; Sun and public holidays, 9am-10pm. Closed 1st Mon in the month, 1 Jan, 1 May and 25 Dec. 8 000 L, no charge for visitors under 18 years old and over 60, and during heritage week. ☎ (075) 57 41 257.
www.sbaas.umbria.it

Museo Archeologico Nazionale dell'Umbria - (&) Open all year, Mon-Sat, 9am-1.30pm and 2.30-7pm; Sun and public holidays, 9am-1pm (last admission 1hr before closing time). Closed 1 Jan, 1 May and 25 Dec. 4 000 L, no charge for visitors under 18 years old and over 60, and during heritage week. ☎ (075) 57 27 141.

Collegio del Cambio - Open Mar-Oct (and 20 Dec-6 Jan), daily, 9am-12.30pm and 2.30-5.30pm (closed afternoon on Sun and public holidays); Nov-Feb (except 20 Dec-6 Jan), daily (except Mon), 8am-2pm (12.30pm Sun and public holidays). Closed 1 Jan, 1 May and 25 Dec. 5 000 L, 3 000 L child. ☎ (075) 57 28 599.

Rocca Paolina - Open all year, daily, 8am-7pm. No charge.

Ipogeo dei Volumni - Open July, Aug, Mon-Sat, 9.30am-12.30pm and 4.30-6.30pm; Sept-June, Mon-Sat, 9.30am-12.30pm and 3-5pm; Sun and public holidays all year, 9.30am-12.30pm. Closed 1 Jan, 1 May and 25 Dec. 4 000 L, no charge for visitors under 18 years old and over 60, ☎ (075) 39 33 29.

PESARO

Casa natale di Rossini - Open daily (except Mon), May-Sept, 9am-7pm (1pm Sun); Oct-Apr, 10am-1.30pm (1pm Sun). 8 000 L, 4 000 L for visitors over 60 years old, no charge child. Bar. ☎ (0721) 38 73 57.

Museo civici - Open daily (except Mon), May-Sept, 9am-7pm (1pm Sun); Oct-Apr, 10am-1.30pm (1pm Sun). 8 000 L, 4 000 L for visitors over 60 years old, no charge child. Guided tours available (1hr). ☎ (0721) 67 815.

Museo Oliveriano - & Open July-Aug, Mon-Sat, 4-7pm; Sept-June, visit by appointment, Mon-Sat, 9am-noon. Closed Sun and public holdiays. No charge. ☎ (0721) 33 344.

PESCOCOSTANZO

Santa Maria del Colle - For information ☎ (0864) 64 14 40.

PIACENZA
🛈 piazzetta dei Mercanti 10 ☎ (0523) 32 07 42

Duomo - Open all year, daily, 7am-noon and 4-7pm. Information from Ianua. ☎ (0523) 32 20 74.

San Savino - Open all year, daily, 6.45am-noon and 3-4pm (noon Sun). Information from Ianua. ☎ (0523) 32 20 74.

San Sisto - Open all year, daily, 7-10am and 4.30-6.30pm (3-6pm Sat, 3-5.30pm Sun). Information from Ianua. ☎ (0523) 32 20 74.

Madonna di Campagna - Open all year, daily, 8.30am-noon and 3.30-6.30pm. Information from Ianua. ☎ (0523) 32 20 74.

Palazzo Farnese: Musei civici - Guided tours (1hr 30min) July-Dec, Tues-Fri, 8.30am-1pm, Sun 10am-6pm; Jan-June, Tues-Sat, 8.30am-1pm and 2.30-6pm; Sun, 10am-6pm. Closed 4 July and public holidays, 10 000 L, 8 000 L for visitors 6-18 years old. Audio-visual presentation. ☎ (0523) 32 82 70, 32 69 81.
www.Farnese.net

Galleria d'Arte Moderna Ricci Oddi - Closed for restoration. ☎ (0523) 32 07 42.

Galleria Alberoni - Guided tours (1hr 10min) in English, French German, Italian, Spanish by appointment, Apr-June and Sept, Oct, Sun, 3pm and 4.30pm. 7 000 L. Apply a few days in advance to Ianua ☎ (0523) 61 31 98.

PIENZA

Museo della Cattedrale - Open mid Mar-Oct, daily (except Tues). 10am-1pm and 3-7pm; Nov-mid Mar, Sat, Sun only, 10am-1pm and 3-6pm (except 20Dec-7 Jan, daily - except Tues). Guided tours by appointment; apply one week in advance to Pienza tourist information centre, corso Rossellino 59, ☎ (0578) 74 90 71. 8 000 L. ☎ (0578) 74 90 71.
www.NAUTILUS MP.COM/INFOTUR.PIEN

Palazzo Piccolomini - Guided tour (30 min) in English, daily (except Mon), Italian, July, Aug, 10am-12.30pm and 3-7pm; Sept-June, 10am-12.30pm and 3-6pm. 5 000 L. ☎ (0578) 74 85 03.

PIEVE DI CADORE

Museo Tiziano - Open 20 June-19 Sept, daily (except Mon), 9.30am-12.30pm and 4-7pm; August, daily; 1-15 Sept, daily (except Mon); the rest of the year, apply to Magnifica Comunità del Cadore, ☎ (0435) 32 262. 2 500 L. ☎ (0435) 31 644.

PISA

Ⓘ piazza del Duomo ☎ (050) 56 04 64

Duomo – Open in summer, spring and autumn, daily, 10am (1pm Sun and public holidays)–7.40pm; in winter, Mon–Sat, 10am–12.45pm, Sun and public holidays, 3–4.45pm. 2 000 L, no charge from late Oct–Feb.

Battistero – Open daily, in summer, 8am–7.40pm; in spring and autumn, 9am–5.40pm; in winter, 9am–4.40pm. 2 000 L.

Camposanto – Same admission times and charges as for the Battistero.

Museo dell'Opera del Duomo – Open daily, in summer, 8am–7.20pm; in spring and autumn, 9am–5.20pm; in winter, 9am–4.20pm. 2 000 L.

Museo delle Sinopie – Same admission times and charges as for the Battistero.

Museo Nazionale di San Matteo – (♿) Open daily (except Mon), 9am–7pm (2pm Sun). Closed 1 Jan, 1 May and 25 Dec. 8 000 L, no charge for EU visitors under 18 years old and over 60. ☎ (050) 54 18 65.

PISTOIA

Ⓘ piazza Duomo 4 ☎ (0573) 21 622

Duomo: Altar of St James – Open all year, daily (except during services), 7.30am–noon and 4–7pm. 3 000 L, 1 000 L child. ☎ (0573) 25 095.

Battistero – Open all year, daily (except Mon), 9.30am–12.30pm and 3–6pm, (12.30pm Sun and public holidays). ☎ (0573) 25 095.

Palazzo Comunale: Museo Civico – Open all year,Tues–Sat, 10am–7pm; Sun, 9am–12.30pm. Closed all day: 1 Jan, 1 May and 25 Dec; afternoons: other public holidays. 5 000 L, no charge for visitors under 18 years old and over 60. Combined ticket for Musei Rospigliosi e Diocesano and Marino Marini Information Centre: 10 000 L. ☎ (0573) 37 12 96/214/278.

Palazzo del Tau: Marino Marini Information Centre – (♿) Open all year, Tues–Sat, 9am–1pm and 3–7pm, Sun and public holidays, 9am–12.30pm. Closed 1 Jan, 1 May and 25 Dec. 5 000 L, 2 500 L child, no charge Sat afternoons. Guided tours (1hr) in English, French, Italian. Audio-visual presentation (40min). ☎ (0573) 30 285, 31 055.

PLOSE

Access – From the village of Sant'Andrea southeast of Bressanone, a cable-car takes visitors to Valcroce (operates in winter and from July–mid Sept), then by chairlift to Plose (in winter only). For further information, apply to the Bressanone Tourist Information Centre. ☎ (0472) 83 64 01.

POGGIO BUSTONE

Convento – Open all year, daily. ☎ (0746) 68 89 16.

POMPEI

La città morta – Open all year, daily, 9am–1hr before sunset. Closed 1 Jan, 1 May and 25 Dec. 12 000 L. ☎ (081) 86 11 744.

Abbazia di POMPOSA

(♿) Open daily, Apr–Oct, 8.30am–7pm; Nov–Mar, 9.30am–4pm. Closed 1 Jan, 1 May and 25 Dec. 4 000 L. ☎ (0533) 71 91 10.

PORTOFINO

Castello – Open all year, daily (except Tuesday), 10am–6pm (5pm Apr–Sept). Closed 10 Jan–10 Feb. 3 000 L, no charge child under 12 years old). ☎ (0185) 26 90 46.

PORTOFINO VETTA

Access – Private toll-road: 5 000 L for vehicle including passengers. No charge for pedestrians and cyclists. ☎ (0185) 77 01 60.

PORTOGRUARO

Museo nazionale Concordiese – Open all year, daily, 9am–7pm. Closed 1 Jan, 1 May and 25 Dec. 4 000 L, no charge for visitors under 18 years old and over 60, and during heritage week. ☎ (0421) 72 674.

PORTONOVO

Santa Maria – Guided tours by appointment in summer, daily, 6.30–7.30pm; the rest of the year, Sat and Sun only. Book at least 2 weeks in advance. For information ☎ (071) 80 14 50. Advance booking (0338) 72 73 936.

POSSAGNO

House and gipsoteca – (&) Open May-Sept, Tues-Sat, 9am-noon and 3-6pm; Sun and public holidays, 9am-noon and 3-7pm; Oct-Apr, daily, 9am-noon and 2-5pm. Closed Mon except public holidays, 1 Jan, Easter and 25 Dec. 5 000 L, 4 000 L child. ☎ (0423) 54 43 23.

Temple of Canova – Open May-Sept, Tues-Sat, 9am-noon and 3-6pm; Sun, 9am-noon and 3-7pm; Oct-Apr, Tues-Sun, 9am-noon and 2-5pm. Closed Mon except holiday Mon, and during religious services. 3 000 L for tour of the dome. ☎ (0423) 54 40 21.

POZZUOLI

Anfiteatro – Open all year, daily, 9am-1hr before sunset. 4 000 L.

Solfatara – & Open daily, May-Oct, 8.30am-7pm; Apr, May, 8.30am-6pm; Nov-mid Mar, 8.30am-4pm. 8 000 L, 4 000 L child. Guided tours (45min) in Czech, English, French, German, Italian. Bar, restaurant. ☎ (081) 52 62 341. www.kenno.com/solfatara

PRATO   🄱 via Cairoli 48 ☎ (0574) 24 112

Museo dell'Opera del Duomo – (&) Open all year, Mon, Wed-Sat, 9.30am-12.30pm and 3-6.30pm; Sun and public holidays, 9am-12.30pm. Closed 1 Jan, Easter, 1 May, 15 Aug and 25 Dec. 8 000 L (combined tickets for all diocesan and local museums), 5 000 L concessions, no charge child and on St Stephen's Day. ☎ (0574) 29 339.

R

RAVELLO

Villa Rufolo – (&) Open all year, daily, 9am-8pm (5pm Oct-Mar). Closed public holidays. 5 000 L, 3 000 L child. Guided tours (about 1hr). ☎ (089) 85 76 57.

Villa Cimbrone – Open all year, daily, 9am-1hr before sunset. 6 000 L. ☎ (089) 85 71 38.

Museo del Duomo – Open all year, daily, 9am-1pm and 3-7pm. 2 000 L. ☎ (089) 85 72 12.

San Giovanni del Toro – Open 10am-1pm and 3-6pm.

RAVENNA

Combined ticket for the Mausoleo di Galla Placidia, Basilica di San Vitale, Battistero Neoniano, Basilica di Sant'Apollinare Nuovo and Museo Arcivescovile and other monuments in the town: 10 000 L.

Mausoleo di Galla Placidia – Open daily, Apr-Aug, 9am-7pm; Sept-Mar, 9am-4.30pm. Closed 1 Jan and 25 Dec. 6 000 L, ticket also valid for Basilica di San Vitale, no charge child under 11 years old. ☎ (0554) 21 81 58. ☎ (0544) 34 266.

Basilica di San Vitale – Open daily, Apr-Aug, 9am-7pm; Sept-Mar, 9am-4.30pm. Closed 1 Jan and 25 Dec. 6 000 L, ticket also valid for Mausoleo di Galla Placidia, no charge child under 11 years old. ☎ (0554) 21 81 58. ☎ (0544) 34 266.

Museo Nazionale – Open all year, daily (except Mon), 8.30am-7pm (possible additional opening Fri, Sat, Sun in summer, 8.30-11.30pm - phone to check). Closed public holidays. 8 000 L. ☎ (0544) 34 424.

Battistero Neoniano – Open daily, Apr-Aug, 9.30am-6.30pm; Sept-Mar, 9.30am-4.30pm. Closed 1 Jan and 25 Dec. 5 000 L, ticket also valid for Museo Arcivescovile. ☎ (0544) 21 81 58.

Basilica di St Apollinare Nuovo – Open all year, daily, 9am-6.30pm (4.30pm in winter). Closed 1 Jan and 25 Dec. 5 000 L. ☎ (0544) 21 62 92.

Battistero degli Ariani – Open all year, daily, 8.30am-7pm (1.30pm in winter). No charge. ☎ (0544) 34 424.

Basilica di Sant'Apollinare in Classe – Open all year, daily, 8.30am-noon and 2.30-7.30pm (4.30pm in winter). ☎ (0544) 34 424.

Mausoleo di Teodorico – Open daily, Apr-Oct, 8.30am-7pm (1pm Nov, Feb, 6pm the rest of the year). Closed public holidays. 4 000 L. ☎ (0544) 34 424.

Museo Arcivescovile – Open all year, daily, 9.30am-6.30pm (4.30pm in winter). Closed 1 Jan and 25 Dec. 5 000 L, ticket also valid for Battistero Neoniano. ☎ (0554) 21 81 58.

Pinacoteca Comunale – Open Mon, Wed and Thur, 9am-1pm; Tues and Fri, 9am-1pm and 2.30-5.30pm; Sun, 2.30-5.30pm. 6 000 L, 3 000 L for visitors under 18 years old and over 60. Guided tours (1hr 30min). ☎ (0544) 48 28 74. WWW.RACINE.RA.IT

RECANATI

Palazzo Leopardi – Guided tours (20min), daily, July-Sept, 10am-10pm; Oct-June, 9am-12.30pm and 3-6.30pm. Closed 1 Jan and 25 Dec. 5 000 L, 2 500 L for 6-15 years old, no charge for visitors over 65 and on 1st Mon in the month (except holiday Mon). ☎ ((071) 75 73 380.

Pinacoteca civica – Guided tours (30min), daily (except Mon), Apr-Sept, 10am-1pm and 4-7pm; Oct-Mar, 10am-1pm and 3-6pm. Closed public holidays. 5 000 L, 1 000 L students, no charge for visitors over 65 years old. ☎ (071) 75 87 291.

REGGIO DI CALABRIA

Museo Nazionale – ♿ Open all year, daily, 9am-1.30pm and 2.30-6.30pm. Closed 1st and 3rd Mon in the month, 1 Jan, 1 May and 25 Dec. 8 000 L, no charge for visitors under 18 years old and over 60. Audio-visual presentation (20min). ☎ (0965) 81 22 55/56.

REGGIO NELL'EMILIA

Galleria Parmeggiani – Open Tues-Fri, 9am-noon; Sat, Sun also 3-6pm; July-15 Aug, only 9-midnight. Closed 1 Jan, 15-31 Aug and 25 Dec. No charge. ☎ (0522) 45 10 54.

Madonna della Ghiara – Open all year, Mon-Sat, 10am-noon and 4-5.30pm, Sun, 10,25-10.50am and 3.30-5.30pm. ☎ (0522) 43 97 07.

RIMINI

Italia in Miniatura – ♿ Open Mon-Sat, 3 July-5 Sept, 9am-midnight; 6 Sept-1 Nov, 9am-sunset; 28 Mar-2 July, 9am-8pm; Sun and public holidays, open at 8.30am. The attractions are open 1hr after the park opens and close 1hr earlier and do not operate from 1 Nov-15 Mar. 22-24 000 L, 17-18 000 concessions, no charge for disabled visitors and small children (less than 1m tall). Bar, restaurant. ☎ (0541) 73 20 04.
www.italiainminiatura.com

RIVA DEL GARDA

Museo civico La Rocca – (♿) Open July, Aug, Tues-Fri, 4-11.30pm; Sat, Sun, 4.30-10.30pm; Sept-June, daily (except Mon), 9.30am-12.30pm and 2.30-5.30pm, Sun, 10am-noon and 2.30-5.30pm. Closed Mon. 4 000 L.

RIVOLI

Castello: Museo d'Arte Contemporanea – ♿ Open Tues-Sun, 10am-5pm (7pm Sat, Sun, 10pm 1st and 3rd Wed in the month). Closed public holidays. 10 000 L, 7 000 L child 11-14 years old; no charge child under 10. Guided tours (1hr) in English, French, Italian. Audio-visual presentation. ☎ (011) 95 81 547.
www.regione.piemonte.it/cultura/rivoli/rivoli.html

ROMA

Capitol:

Palazzo dei Conservatori: Museo – Major reorganisation in progress. The atrium, some rooms and the picture gallery are open. Open daily (except Mon), 9am-7pm (6.45pm Sun, 1.45pm public holidays). Closed 1 Jan, 1 May and 25 Dec. 10 000 L, no charge for visitors under 18 years old and over 60, on last Sun in the month, 21 Apr, 15 Dec and during heritage week. ☎ (06) 67 10 20 71.

Musei Capitolini – Reorganisation in progress. ☎ (06) 67 10 20 71.

Palazzo Senatorio – It is not possible to visit the interior which houses the offices of the Palazzo Comunale.

Terme di Caracalla – Open all year, daily, 9am-1hr before sunset (2pm Mon, Sun and public holidays). Last admission 1hr before closing time. Closed 1 Jan, 1 May and 25 Dec. 8 000 L, no charge for visitors under 18 years old and over 60, and during heritage week. ☎ (06) 57 58 626.

Catacombe di San Callisto – Guided tour (1hr) daily (except Wed), 8.30am-noon and 2.30-5.30pm (5pm in winter). Closed Feb. Bar. ☎ (06) 51 36 725.

Catacombe de San Sebastiano – Open daily (except Sun), 8.30am-noon and 2.30-5.30pm (5pm in winter). Closed mid Nov-mid Dec. ☎ (06) 78 50 350.

Catacombe di Domitilla – Guided tour (1hr) daily (except Tues), 8.30am-noon and 2.30-5.30pm (5pm in winter). Closed Jan. 8 000 L. ☎ (06) 51 10 342.

Castel Sant'Angelo – Open all year, daily, 9am-2pm (last admission 1hr before closing time). Closed 1 Jan, 1 May and 25 Dec. 8 000 L. ☎ (06) 68 75 036.

Colosseo - Open all year, daily, 9am-1hr before sunset (2pm Sun and public holidays). Closed 1 Jan, 1 May and 25 Dec. 10 000 L, no charge for visitors under 18 years old and over 60, and during heritage week. ☎ (06) 70 04 261.

Mercati Traianei - (&) Open daily (except Mon), 9am-6.30pm (4pm in winter). Closed public holidays. 3 750 L, no charge last Sun in the month and during heritage week. ☎ (06) 67 90 048.

Foro Romano and Palatino - Open all year, daily, 9am-1hr before sunset (2pm Sun and public holidays). Closed 1 Jan, 1 May and 25 Dec. Foro Romano: no charge. Palatino: 12 000 L, no charge for visitors under 18 years old and over 60, during heritage week and on 21 Apr. ☎ (06) 69 90 110.

Pantheon - Open all year, daily, 9am-6.30pm (1pm Sun). Closed 1 Jan, 1 May and 25 Dec. No charge. ☎ (06) 68 30 02 30.

Palazzo Venezia: Museo - & Open daily (except Mon), 9am-2pm (1pm Sun and public holidays). Closed 1 Jan, 1 May and 25 Dec. 8 000 L, no charge for visitors under 18 years old and over 60, and during heritage week. The great halls house temporary exhibitions. ☎ (06) 69 99 43 19.

Basilica di San Giovanni in Laterano - Open all year, daily, 7am-7pm (6pm Oct-Mar). ☎ (06) 69 88 64 33.

Basilica di Santa Maria Maggiore - Open all year, daily, 7am-6.45pm (except during religious services). ☎ (06) 48 81 094. **Loggia:** open 9.30am-5.30pm. 5 000 L. ☎ (06) 48 81 094.

Basilica di San Paolo Fuori le Mura - Open all year, daily, 7am-6.30pm.

Vaticano

Città e giardini - Guided tour (about 2hr), daily (except Wed and Sun) only at 10am (Sat only in Jan, Feb, Nov, Dec). Closed same public holidays as for Musei Vaticani). Apply in advance to the Ufficio Informazioni: ☎ (06) 69 88 44 66. 18 000 L.

Papal Audiences - When the Pope is in residence, these are held on Wed. Apply in advance to the Prefettura della Casa Pontificia, 9am-1pm.

Basilica di San Pietro - Open all year, daily, 7am-7pm (6pm in winter) depending on religious services. ☎ (06) 69 88 33 33.

Ascent of the Dome - Access all year, daily (except Wed), 8am-6pm (5pm in winter). Closed during religious services. Lift: 6 000 L; on foot, 5 000 L.

Museo Storico - & Open all year, daily, 9am-7pm (6pm Oct-Mar). Closed Easter and 25 Dec. 8 000 L. ☎ (06) 69 88 18 40.

Musei Vaticani - & Open mid Mar-Sept, Mon-Fri, 8.45am-4.45pm (1.45pm Sat and last Sun in the month and Oct-mid Mar). Last admission 1hr before closing time. Closed 1 and 6 Jan, 11 Feb, 19 Mar, Easter Monday, 1 May, Ascension Day, Corpus Domini, 29 June, 15 Aug, 1 Nov, 8, 25, 26 Dec. Guided tours (4 itineraries, 1hr 30min-5hr). Audio-tours in English, French, German, Japanese, Spanish. 4 itineraries for disabled visitors, wheelchairs. Bar, cafeteria, self-service restaurant. 18 000 L, 10 000 child under 14 and students under 26 with a student card. No charge last Sun in the month. ☎ (06) 69 88 33 33.

Santa Cecilia in Trastevere - Open daily, 10-11.45am and 4-5pm. Crypt: same admission times. 2 000 L. **Cavallini's Last Judgement:** Open Tues and Thur, 10-11.30am. Donation.

Galleria Nazionale d'Arte Moderna - & Open daily (except Mon), 9am-10pm (8pm Sun and public holidays). Closed 1 Jan, 1 May and 25 Dec. 8 000 L, no charge during heritage week. Guided tours. Bar, restaurant. ☎ (06) 32 29 82 25.

Museo Borghese - & Open by appointment daily (except Mon), 9am-10pm (8pm Sun). Admission times may vary: 9am-7pm (1pm Sun). ☎ (06) 85 48 577. For advance booking ☎ (06) 85 48 577 (office open Mon-Fri, 9.30am-6pm). 10 000 L plus 2 000 L booking fee.

Museo Nazionale Romano - (&) Open Tues-Sat, 9am-2pm (1pm Sun and public holidays). Closed 1 Jan, 1 May and 25 Dec. 12 000 L. ☎ (06) 48 90 53 00.

Museo Nazionale Villa Guilia - Open Tues-Sat, 9am-7pm (2pm Sun and public holidays). Closed 1 Jan, 1 May and 25 Dec. 8 000 L, no charge during heritage week. ☎ (06) 33 26 571.

Palazzo Barberini: Galleria di Pittura - (&) Open daily (except Mon), 9am-7pm (1pm Sun and public holidays). Closed 1 Jan, 1 May and 25 Dec. 8 000 L. ☎ (06) 48 14 591.

Palazzo Braschi: Museo di Roma - Closed for restoration.

Palazzo Corsini: Picture Gallery - Open in August, daily (except Mon), 9am-2pm (1pm Sun); the rest of the year, Mon-Sat, 9am-7pm (2pm Sat). Closed 1 Jan, 1 May, and 25 Dec. 8 000 L, no charge during heritage week. Guided tours (1hr 30min). ☎ (06) 68 80 23 23.

Palazzo Doria Pamphili: Galleria – ♿ Open daily (except Thur), 10am–5pm. Closed 1 Jan, 1 May and 25 Dec. 13 000 L. Guided tours in English, French, Italian. Audio-visual presentation (about 1hr). ☏ (06) 67 97 323.

Palazzo Farnese – Not open to the public.

Palazzo Spada: Galleria di Pittura – Open daily (except Mon), 9am–7pm (1pm Sun). Closed 1 Jan, 1 May and 25 Dec. 10 000 L, no charge for visitors under 18 years old. Guided tours (about 1hr). ☏ (06) 68 61 158.

Villa Farnesina – Open Mon–Sat, 9am–1pm (last admission 12.40pm). 8 000 L. ☏ (06) 68 80 17 67.
www.lincei.it

Museo della Civiltà Romana – Open daily (except Mon), 9am–7pm (1.30pm Sun). Closed 1 Jan, 1 May and 25 Dec. 5 000 L, no charge on last Sun in the month and for visitors under 18 years old and over 60. ☏ (06) 59 26 135.

ROSELLE

Ruins – Open daily, May–Aug, 9am–8.30pm; 7.30pm, Sept, Oct; 6.30pm, Mar, Apr; 5.30pm, Nov–Feb. Guided tours available (1hr 30min). 4 000 L, no charge for visitors under 18 years old and over 60. ☏ (0564) 40 24 03.

ROSSANO

Museo Diocesano – ♿ Open all year, daily, 9am (10am Sun)–noon. 2 000 L. ☏ (0983) 52 02 82.
www.cs.cnr.it/biblio/rossano

RUVO DI PUGLIA

Museo Archeologico Jatta – ♿ Open all year, daily, 8.30am–1.30pm (also Fri, Sat, 2.30–7.30pm). Closed 1 Jan, Easter and 25 Dec. Guided tours (about 1hr). ☏ (080) 81 28 48.

S

SABBIONETA

Guided tours – Organized by the Ufficio del Turismo, Piazza d'Armi 1, 9am–noon and 2.30–6pm (7pm Sun and public holidays). Tickets available until 30min before closing time. The Tourist Office is closed Mon except public holidays. 10 000 L.

SACRA DI SAN MICHELE

Benedictine Abbey – Open daily (except Mon unless holiday Mon), mid Mar–mid Oct, 9.30am–12.30pm (noon Sun) and 3pm (2.40pm Sun)–6pm (5pm the rest of the year). Guided tours (20min) on Sun. 4 000 L, 2 000 L for visitors under 14 years old and over 65, no charge child under 6. ☏ (011) 93 91 30; e-mail: SMICHELE@LAKESNET.IT

SALERNO

Duomo – Open all year, daily, 8am–noon and 4–8pm. ☏ (089) 23 13 87.

SAN FRUTTUOSO

Access by boat – From Rapallo, Santa Margherita and Portofino, 13 000 L–21 000 L there and back, Servizio Marittimo del Tigullio, ☏ (0185) 28 46 70. From Camogli, 13 000 L there and back, Servizio Motobarche "Golfo Paradiso". ☏ (0185) 77 20 91.

SAN CLEMENTE A CASAURIA

Church – Open all year, daily, 8am–7pm (5pm in winter). ☏ (085) 88 85 828.

SAN GIMIGNANO   🛈 piazza Duomo 1 ☏ (0577) 94 00 08

Collegiata – Open all year, daily, 9am–12.30pm and 3–6pm (except during mass at 11am and 6pm on Sun). 3 000 L. Guided tours.

Palazzo del Popolo – Open daily (except Mon), Mar–Oct, 9.30am–7.20pm; Nov–Feb, 9.30am–12.50pm and 2.30–4.50pm (last admission 20min before closing time).7 000 L, 5 000 L students under 18 years old and family with child 6–18 years old, no charge child under 6. Ufficio Informazione Turistiche, Associazione Pro Loco, ☏ (0577) 94 00 08. e-mail: prolocsg@mbox.vol.it. web.tin.it/san gimignano

Isola di SAN GIULIO

Access by boat - Boat services from Orta San Giulio: Easter-Oct, every 30min; the rest of the year, Sun and public holidays only, every 45min (also Sat in Mar, Oct, Nov). Time: 5min. 3 000 L return. ☎ (0322) 84 48 62. For information about a fast boat service (3 500 L return) apply to Signor Urani ☎ (0338) 30 34 904 or Signor Fabris ☎ (0330) 87 98 39.

Basilica di San Giulio - Open daily, 9.30am (11am Mon)-12.15pm (10.45am Sun) and 2-6.45pm (5.45pm in winter). For guided tour apply to the Orta tourist information centre ☎ (0322) 91 19 37.

SAN LEO

Museo-Pinacoteca - (&) Open daily, 9am-7pm (11pm mid July and Aug). 10 000 L, 5 000 L child. Guided tours (1hr) in English, French, German. ☎ (0541) 91 63 06 or 167 55 38 00.

Repubblica di SAN MARINO   🛈 contrada Omagnano 20 ☎ (0549) 88 24 10

Palazzo del Governo - & Open daily, Apr-mid Sept, 8am-8pm; in winter, 8.45am-4pm; the rest of the year, 8.30am-12.30pm and 2-6pm. Closed 1 Jan, 2 Nov (afternoon) and 25 Dec. 4 000 L. Guided tours (1hr) in English, French, German, Italian. ☎ (0549) 88 27 08.

Museo delle Armi Antiche - Open daily, Apr-mid Sept, 8am-8pm; in winter, 8.45am-4pm; the rest of the year, 8.30am-12.30pm and 2-6pm. Closed 1 Jan, 2 Nov (afternoon) and 25 Dec. 4 000 L, no charge for child under 10 years old. Audio tours in English, French, German, Italian, Spanish. ☎ (0549) 88 26 70.

Museo di San Francesco - Same admission times and charges as for Museo delle Armi Antiche. ☎ (0549) 88 26 70.

Museo Filatelico e Numismatico - Closed for restoration. ☎ (0549) 88 24 00.

SAN MARTINO DELLA BATTAGLIA

Ossuary-chapel, Museum, tall tower - Open daily, Apr-Sept, 9am-noon and 2-6.30pm, Oct-Mar, 9am-noon and 2-5.30pm. 6 000 L. ☎ (030) 99 10 370.

SANSEPOLCRO

Museo Civico - (&) Open daily, June-Sept, 9am-1.30pm and 2.30-7.30pm; Jan-Mar, 9.30am-1pm and 2.30-6pm; Oct-Dec, 9.30am-1pm and 2.30-6pm. 10 000 L, 5 000 L for visitors 11-16 years old and no charge for child under 10, and on 12 Oct. ☎ (0575) 73 22 18.
www.sansepolcro.net

SANTA CATERINA DEL SASSO

Eremo - Open in summer, daily, 8am-noon and 2.30-6pm (2-5pm, Mar-Nov); the rest of the year, Sat, Sun, 8.30am-noon and 2-5pm. ☎ (0332) 64 71 72.

SANT'ANTIMO

Abbazia - Open all year, Mon-Sat, 10.30am-12.30pm and 3-6.30pm; Sun and public holidays, 9.15-10.40am and 3-6pm. ☎ (0577) 83 56 59. Liturgy in Gregorian chant: 9am weekdays, 11am Sun.

SAN VIVALDO

Sacro Monte: Chapels - Guided tours, daily, 9-11.30am and 3pm until sunset. Book three days in advance at Convento di San Vivaldo. Unaccompanied visit on Sunday afternoons. ☎ /Fax (0571) 68 01 14.

SARZANA

Fortezza di Sarzanello - Visits suspended temporarily. ☎ (0187) 61 42 48.

SEGROMIGNO

Villa Mansi - Open daily (except Mon), May-Sept, 10am-1pm and 3-7pm; Oct-Apr, 10am-1pm and 2.30-6pm. Closed 25 Dec. 9 000 L (park and villa). ☎ (0583) 92 00 96.

SIBARI

Museo Archeologico - & Open all year, daily (except 1st and last Mon in the month), 9am-7pm. Closed 1 Jan, 1 May, and 25 Dec. 4 000 L, no charge child and during heritage week. Audio-visual presentation (30min). ☎ (981) 79 391/2.

Scavi - Open all year, daily, 9am-7pm. Closed 1 Jan, 1 May and 25 Dec. No charge. ☎ (0981) 79 166.

SIENA

Palazzo Pubblico - Open Mar-Oct, Mon-Sat, 9.30am-6.30pm; Sun and public holidays, 9.30am-1.30pm; Nov-Feb, Mon-Sat, 10am-1.30pm; Sun and public holidays, 9.30am-1.30pm. Closed 1 Jan, 1 May, 1 and 25 Dec. 8 000 L, 4 000 L student, no charge child under 11 years old. ☎ (0577) 29 22 26.

Torre - Open daily, Mar-Oct, 10am-6pm (1.30pm Nov-Feb). 7 000 L.

Duomo - Open daily, mid Mar-Oct, 7.30am-7.30pm (last admission 7.10pm); Nov-mid Mar, 7.30am-1.30pm and 2.30-6.30pm. ☎ (0577) 28 30 48. Libreria Piccolomini:open daily, mid Mar-Oct, 9am-7.30pm; Nov-mid Mar, 10am-1pm and 2.30-5pm; closed 1 Jan and 25 Dec. 2 000 L, no charge child under 10.

Museo dell'Opera Metropolitana - Open daily, 9am-7.30pm mid Mar-Sept, 6pm Oct, 1.30pm Nov-mid Mar. Closed 1 Jan and 25 Dec. 6 000 L, no charge child under 10. ☎ (0577) 28 30 48.

Battistero di San Giovanni - Open daily, mid Mar-Sept, 9am-7.30pm; Oct, 9am-6pm; Nov-mid Mar, 10am-1pm and 2.30-5pm. Closed 1 Jan and 25 Dec. 3 000 L, no charge child under 10. ☎ (0577) 28 30 48.

Pinacoteca - (&) Open all year, Mon, 8.30am-1.30pm; Tues-Sat, 9am-7pm; Sun and public holidays, 8am-1pm. Closed 1 Jan, 1 May and 25 Dec. 8 000 L, no charge for EU visitors under 18 years old and over 60. ☎ (0577) 28 11 61, 41 246.

SIRMIONE

Rocca Scaligera - Open daily (except Mon), Apr-Sept, 9am-6pm (except for lack of staff); Oct-Mar, 9am-1pm. Closed 1 Jan, 1 May and 25 Dec. 8 000 L, no charge for visitors under 18 years old and over 60, and during heritage week. ☎ (030) 91 64 68.

Grotte di Catullo - (&) Open Mar-Oct, Tues-Sat, 8.30am-7pm, Sun 9am-6pm; Oct-Feb, Tues-Sat, 8.30am-4.30pm, Sun 9am-4.30pm. Closed Mon (except holiday Mon, then closed the next day), 1 Jan, 1 May and 25 Dec. 8 000 L, no charge for visitors under 18 years old. ☎ (030) 91 61 57.

Grotta dello SMERALDO

Access and tour - Access by lift from the road, Apr-Sept, 9am-5pm; Oct-Mar, 10am-4pm. 5 000 L (including the lift and tour of the cave). Access possible by boat from Amalfi Harbour in spring and summer. 10 000 L.

SOLFERINO

Museo - Open Tues-Sun, Mar-Oct, 9am-12.30pm and 2.30-6.30pm; Nov-Feb, 9am-noon and 2-5pm. Closed Jan, Dec and Mon (except holiday Mon). Guided tours (1hr) in English, French, German. 3 000 L. ☎ (0376) 85 40 19; e-mail: proloco@intesys.it
www.intesys.it/solferino

Ossario - Same admission times as Museo. No charge.

SORRENTO

Museo Correale di Terranova - Open daily (except Tues), Apr-Sept, 9am-12.30pm and 5-7pm (closed Sun afternoons); Oct-Mar, 9am-12.30pm and 3-5pm (Jan, Feb 9am-1.30pm only). Closed 15 days in Jan, 14 Feb and public holidays. 8 000 L. ☎ (081) 87 81 846.

SPERLONGA

Museo Archeologico - Open daily, 9am-8pm, May, June, July; 7.30pm, Aug; 7pm, Apr; 6.30pm, Mar, Sept; 6pm, Feb-Oct; 5pm, Jan, Nov, Dec (last admission 1hr before closing time). Closed 1 Jan, 1 May, 25 Dec. 4 000 L, no charge for visitors under 18 years old and over 60. ☎ (0771) 54 028. No access to the cave.

La SPEZIA

Museo navale - Open all year, Mon, Fri, 2-6pm; Tues, Wed, Thur, Sat, 9am-noon and 2-6pm; Sun, 8.30am-1.15pm. Closed weekday public holidays. 2 000 L, no charge on San Giuseppe's Day and on Armed Forces Day. ☎ (0187) 77 07 50.

STILO

La Cattolica - Open all year, daily, 8am-8pm. No charge. Guided tours (30min) in English, French, German, Greek, Spanish. Audio tours. Bar. ☎ (0964) 77 50 31/34.

STRA

Villa Nazionale - Open daily (except Mon), Apr-Nov, 9am-6pm; Dec-Mar, 9am-4pm. Closed 1 Jan, 1 May and 25 Dec. 8 000 L, no charge for visitors under 18 years old and over 60, and during heritage week. ☎ (049) 50 20 74.

STRESA

Mottarone – Access by toll-road (Strada Borromea) from Alpino, 6 000 L there and back; by cable-car from Stresa. ☎ (0323) 30 399 or (0323) 92 24 03.

Villa Pallavicino – Open daily, Mar–early Nov, 9am-6pm. Bar, restaurant. 11 000 L, 8 000 L child. ☎ (0323) 32 407.

STUPINIGI

Palazzino di caccia – Guided tours (45min; in English, French on request), all year, daily (except Mon), 9.30-11.50am and 2-5.20pm (4.20pm in winter). Closed public holidays. 10 000 L, 8 000 L child. ☎ (011) 35 81 220.

SUBIACO

Monastero di Santa Scolastica – Guided tours all year, daily, 9am-12.30pm and 4-7pm. ☎ (0774) 85 525.
www.osb-subiaco-it.org

Monastero di San Benedetto – Open 9am-12.30pm and 3-6pm. Book 10-15 days in advance. Donation. ☎ (0774) 85 039.
www.osb-subiaco-it.org

SUPERGA

Basilica: royal tombs – Guided tours all year, daily (except Fri), 9.30am-noon and 3-6pm (5pm in winter). Donation. ☎ (011) 89 80 083.

T

TARANTO

Museo Nazionale – Open all year, daily, 9am-1.30pm and 2.30-7.30pm (10pm Sat, Sun). Closed public holidays. 4 000 L. ☎ (099) 45 90 411.

TARQUINIA   🛈 piazza Cavour 1 ☎ (0766) 85 63 84

Necropoli Etrusca – Open all year, daily (except Mon), 9am-sunset (7pm in summer). Closed 1 Jan, 1 May and 25 Dec. 8 000 L.

Museo Nazionale Tarquiniese – Open all year, daily (except Mon), 9am-7pm. Closed public holidays. 8 000 L, no charge for visitors under 18 years old and over 60.

Santa Maria in Castello – To visit, apply at the house behind the tower. Leave a gratuity.

TIROLO

Castel Tirolo – Open early Apr–early Nov, daily (except Mon), 10am-5pm. Closed Nov–Easter. 7 000 L, 14 000 L family, 3 000 L student. Guided tours 45min) in German, Italian; fee: 3 000 L, 1 000 L student ☎ (0473) 22 02 21.

TIVOLI

Villa d'Este – Open all year, daily (except Mon), 9am-1hr before sunset. Closed 1 Jan, 1 May and 25 Dec. 8 000 L, no charge for visitors under 18 years old, and during heritage week. Bar. ☎ (0774) 31 20 70.

Villa Adriana – Open all year, daily, 9am-1hr before sunset (last admission 1hr before closing time). 8 000 L, no charge for visitors under 18 years old and over 60. Closed 1 Jan, 1 May and 25 Dec. ☎ (0774) 53 02 03.

Villa Gregoriana – Open all year, daily, 10am-1hr before sunset. Closed on rainy days, and 1 Jan, 1 May, 15 Aug and 25 Dec. 3 500 L. Guided tours (1hr) in English. ☎ (0774) 31 12 49.

TODI

Palazzo del Popolo and **Palazzo del Capitano** – ♿ Open, daily (except Mon), Apr (daily)–Aug, 10.30am-1pm and 2.30-6pm; Sept, Mar, 10.30am-1pm and 2-5pm; Oct-Feb, 10.30am-1pm and 2-4.30pm. Closed 1 Jan and 25 Dec. 6 000 L, 4 500 L for visitors 15-25 years old and over 60, 3 000 L child 6-14, no charge child under 5. Guided tours (1hr) in English,Italian. ☎ (075) 89 56 216, 89 44 148.
www.umbrars.com/sistemamuseo

TOIRANO

Grotte – Guided tours all year, daily, 9am-noon and 2-5.30pm (5pm in winter). ☎ (0182) 98 062.

TOLENTINO

Basilica di San Nicola and museums - Open all year, daily, 9.30am-noon and 4-7pm. ☎ (0733) 96 99 96.
www.meti.it/s.nicola

TORGIANO

Museo del Vino - Open all year, daily, 9am-1pm and 3-7pm (6pm in winter). 5 000 L, 4 000 L child. Guided tours (1hr) in English, German, Italian. ☎ (075) 98 80 200, 98 33 444.

TORINO
🄸 piazza Castello 161 ☎ (011) 53 51 81

Museo Egizio - Open all year, daily (except Mon), 8.30am-10pm (8pm Sun). 12 000 L, no charge for visitors under 18 years old and over 60. ☎ (011) 56 17 776.

Galleria Sabauda - (&) Open all year, Tues-Sat, 9am-2pm (Thur in summer 1.30-7pm, in winter 10am-7pm); Sun, 10am-10pm. Closed public holidays. 8 000 L, no charge for visitors under 18 years old and over 60. Guided tours (1hr 45min) in English, French. ☎ (011) 54 74 40.

Palazzo Madama: Museo d'Arte Antica - Closed for restoration. ☎ (011) 44 29 911.

Museo Nazionale del Cinema - Closed; the musuem is moving to Mole Antonelliana (see below).

Palazzo Reale:

Appartamenti - (&) Guided tours (45min) all year, daily (except Mon), 9am-7pm (last tour 6.15pm). Closed 1 Jan, 1 May and 25 Dec. 8 000 L, no charge for visitors under 18 years old and over 60. ☎ (011) 43 61 455.

Armeria Reale - Open Tues and Thur, 1.30-7pm; Wed, Fri and Sat, 9am-2pm; alternating Mon and Sun, telephone for opening times. 8 000 L, no charge for visitors under 18 years old and over 60. ☎ (011) 51 84 358.

Museo del Risorgimento - & Open all year, daily (except Mon), 9am-6.30pm (12.30pm Sun). Closed 1 Jan, Easter, 1 May and 25 Dec. 8 000 L, 5 000 L students and visitors over 60, 3 000 L for visitors under 18 years old. Audo-visual presentation. ☎ (011) 56 21 147, 56 23 719.

Duomo - Closed for restoration. ☎ (011) 43 60 790.

Mole Antonelliana - Closed for restoration to house a new Cinema Museum (opening late 1998).

Museo dell'Automobile Carlo Biscaretti di Ruffia - (&) Open all year, daily (except Mon), 10am-6.30pm. Closed 1 Jan and 25 Dec. 10 000 L, 7 000 L child. Guided tours (1hr 30min). Bar. ☎ (011) 67 76 66.

Borgo e Castello Medievale - Open all year, daily, 9am-9pm (8pm in summer). Castello: daily (except Mon), 9am-7pm. Closed public holidays. 5 000 L, 3 000 L for visitors under 18 years old and over 60, no charge child under 10. Audio guides (30min). Bar ☎ (011) 66 99 372.

TORRE ANNUNZIATA

Villa di Oplontis - Open all year, daily, 9am-1hr before sunset. Closed public holidays. 4 000 L. ☎ (081) 86 21 755, 86 24 081.

TORRECHIARA

Castello - Open in summer, Tues-Fri, 9am-2.30pm; Sat, Sun, 9am-7pm; in winter, daily, 8.30am-2pm, afternoons on request. Closed public holidays. 4 000 L, no charge child under 12 years old. Guided tours (45min) in English, French, German, Italian. ☎ (0521) 35 52 55.

TORRE DEL LAGO PUCCINI

Villa Puccini - Guided tours (30min) in English, French, German, Italian, all year, daily (except Mon), 10am (9.30am Sat, Sun and public holidays)-12.30pm and 3-7.30pm (6pm in winter). Closed on some weekdays in winter. 5 000 L, 3 000 L child. ☎ (0584) 34 14 45.

TORRIGIANI

Villa - Guided tours (20min) in English, French, Mar-Oct, daily (except Tues), 10am-12.30pm and 3-6.30pm. Closed Nov-Feb. 12 000 L, no charge for child under 14 years old. ☎ (0583) 92 80 41, (0368) 32 09 614.
www.telemaco.it/adsi

TREMEZZO

Villa Carlotta - Open daily, Apr-Sept, 9am-6pm; Mar, Oct, 9-11.30am and 2-4.30pm. Closed Nov-Feb. 11 000 L. Guided tours. ☎ (0344) 40 405. www.unicel.it/uni/villacarlotta/97

Isole TREMITI

San Nicola: Abbazia di Santa Maria al Mare - Open all year, daily, 10am-8pm. Donation. ☎ (0882) 46 31 16.

San Domino: boat trips - To go around the island of San Domino, San Nicola or the archipelago, apply to the operators near the pier. ☎ (0882) 66 30 32 (Società cooperativa AMA).

TRENTO   🛈 via Alfieri 4 ☎ (0461) 98 38 80

Basilica paleocristiana - Open daily (except Sun), 10am-noon and 2.30-6pm. Closed public holidays. 2 000 L; combined ticket with Museo Diocesano 5 000 L, 1 000 L for visitors 12-18 years old. Guided tours by appointment. Apply 10 days in advance to Museo Diocesano Tridentino, piazza Duomo 18 ☎ (0461) 23 44 19. www.eclipse.it/asteria/museo.htm

Museo Diocesano - ♿ Open daily (except Sun), 9.30am-12.30pm and 2.30-6pm. Closed public holidays except 6 Jan, Easter Monday, 25 April, 1 May and 26 Dec. 5 000 L, 1 000 L for visitors 12-18 years old, no charge child under 12. Ticket also valid for Basilica paleocristiana. Guided tours (1hr 30min) in Italian by appointment. Audio-visual presentation (30min). ☎ (0461) 23 44 19. www.eclipse.it/asteria/museo.htm

Castel del Buon Consiglio - Open daily (except Mon unless hol Mon), late June-early Nov, 10am-6pm; Apr-late Jun, 9am-noon and 2-5.30pm; early Nov-Mar, 9am-noon and 2-5pm. Closed 1 Jan, 1 Nov and 25 Dec. 9 000 L, 5 000 L visitors under 18 years old and over 60 and students, no charge child under 12 and during heritage week. Guided tours (1hr 30min) in summer. ☎ (0461) 23 37 70.

TREVISO

Monte di Pietà - Guided tours daily (except Sat, Sun), 9am-1pm and 3-5pm. Closed public holidays. No charge. Apply for appointment to Segreteria Generale della Cassmarca. ☎ (0422) 65 43 20/1.

Museo Civico Bailo - (♿) Open all year, Tues-Sat, 9am-12.30pm and 2.30-5pm; Sun, 9am-noon. Closed 1 Jan, Easter, 25 Apr, 1 May, 15 Aug, 25 and 26 Dec. 3 000 L, no charge on opening day of exhibitions and during museum season (Musei d'estate). ☎ (0422) 51 337.

TRIESTE

Castello di San Giusto - Open all year, daily, 8am-9pm (5pm Oct-Mar). Closed 1 and 6 Jan, 25 and 26 Dec. 3 000 L, 2 000 L for visitors 5-14 years old and over 60, no charge for child under 5 and during museum week. ☎ (040) 30 93 62.

Museo di Storia e d'Arte - Open all year, daily (except Mon), 9am-1pm (7pm Wed). Closed 1 Jan, Easter, 25 April, 1 May, 15 Aug and 26 Dec. 3 000 L, 2 000 L for visitors 5-14 years old and over 60, no charge for child under 5 and during museum week. ☎ (040) 31 05 00, 30 86 86.

Museo del Mare - Open all year, daily (except Mon), 8.30am-1.30pm. Closed public holidays. 5 000 L, 3 000 L for child over 5 years old, students and for visitors over 60. ☎ (040) 30 49 87.

TUSCANIA

San Pietro: cripta - Open daily, in summer, 9am-1pm and 2-7pm; in winter, 9am-noon and 2-5pm. No charge. ☎ (0761) 43 63 71.

U

UDINE

Castello - Open daily (except Mon), 9.30am-12.30pm and 3-6pm; Sun, 9.30am-12.30pm. Closed 1 and 6 Jan, Easter, 25 Apr, 1 May, 15 Aug, 1 Nov and 25 Dec. 4 000 L, 1 000 L child, no charge on Sun. ☎ (0432) 50 28 72.

Duomo - Open all year, Mon-Sat, 7am-noon and 3.30-7pm; Sun and public holidays, 7am-1pm and 4-7pm. ☎ (0432) 50 68 30.

Palazzo Arcivescovile - Open all year, daily (except Mon, Tues), 10am-noon and 3.30-6.30pm. Closed 1 Jan, Easter and 25 Dec. 7 000 L. ☎ (0432) 25 003.

URBINO

Galleria Nazionale delle Marche – Open all year, daily, 9am–7pm (2pm Mon, 10pm Sun). Closed 1 Jan, 1 May and 25 Dec. 8 000 L, no charge for visitors under 18 years old and over 60. ☎ (0722) 32 90 57, 27 60.

Casa di Raffaello – Open all year, daily, 9am (10am Sun)–1pm and 3–7pm. 5 000 L, no charge for visitors under 14 years old. ☎ (0722) 32 01 05.

Chiesa Oratorio di San Giovanni Battista e San Giuseppe – Open all year, Mon–Sat, 10am–12.30pm and 3–5.30pm (Nov–Jan, Mon–Fri, mornings only); Sun and public holidays, 10am–12.30pm (also 3–5.30pm on Easter Sun and Mon, 25 Apr, 1 May and 15 Aug). To visit outside regular opening times, contact Signor Antonelli, ☎ (0722) 32 09 36, 67 11 161 (mobile).

V

VALEGGIO SUL MINCIO

Parco Giardino Sigurtà – ♿ Open Mar–early Nov, daily, 9am–sunset. 30 000 L car (up to 5 persons), 20 000 L motorcycle, 10 000 L bicycle or scooter. ☎ (045) 63 71 033; e-mail: sigurta@gardanet.it. www.sigurta.it

VARENNA

Villa Monastero – Open Mar–Oct, daily, 9.30am–noon and 2.30–7pm. Closed Nov–Apr. 3 000 L, 2 000 L child. ☎ (0431) 81 52 18.

VENEZIA

Paying garages and car parks:

Piazzale Roma: Municipal Garage – 20 000 L–30 000 L per day, depending on the engine capacity. ☎ (041) 522 23 08.

Piazzale Roma – San Marco Garage – For the first 12hr: 22 000 L–33 000 L, or for 24hr 34 000 L–46 000 L depending on the engine capacity; 2 000 L extra if leaving during the night or on public holidays. ☎ (041) 52 22 13.

Tronchetto Car Park – Cars: 25 000 L (24hr). Caravans and camping-cars: 30 000 L (12 hrs); subsequently, 25 000 L every 12 hours. Information: ☎ (041) 520 75 55.

Vaporetto – One way ticket: 4 000 L. 24hr-pass valid from first journey: 15 000 L; 72hr-pass: 30 000 L; weekly pass: 55 000 L.

Basilica di San Marco:

Atrium: mosaics – Guided tours (meeting point on the right), Apr–Sept: in Italian, Mon–Sat 11am (Wed 3pm).

Pala d'Oro and Tesoro – Open mid May–late Sept, 10am (1pm Sun)–5pm; late Sept–mid May, 10am (1pm Sun)–4pm. 4 000 L, 2 000 L. ☎ (041) 52 25 205.

Galleria e Museo Marciano – Open daily, mid May–late Sept, 10am–5pm; late Sept–mid May, 10am–4pm. 3 000 L, 1 500 L child.

Campanile – By lift: mid Mar–mid Sept, 9.45am–7.30pm (5.30pm Apr–mid March; 4pm late Jan–Mar; 4.30pm Oct–early Jan). Closed 7–25 Jan. 8 000 L, 4 000 L child. ☎ (041) 52 25 205.

Palazzo Ducale – Open daily, Apr–Oct, 8.30am–7pm (last admission 5.30pm); Nov–Mar, daily, 8.30am–5pm (last admission 3.30pm). Closed 1 Jan, 25 Dec. 14 000 L, 8 000 L (student 14-29 years old), 4 000 L (student, 6-14), no charge (children under 6 and disabled visitors). Audio-guided tours available. Ticket also entitles holder to entry to the Museo Correr. ☎ (041) 52 24 951, 52 09 219.

S. Chirol

VENEZIA

Torre dell'Orologio - Scheduled to re-open in 1999 following restoration work (no date specified).

Museo Correr - Open daily, Apr-Oct, 8.30am-7pm (last admission 5.30pm); Nov-Mar, 8.30am-5pm (last admission 3.30pm). Closed 1 Jan and 25 Dec. 14 000 L, 8 000 L (student 14-29 years old), 4 000 L (student 6-14 years old), no charge children under 6 and disabled visitors). Audio-guided tours. Ticket also gives access to Palazzo Ducale. ☎ (041) 52 24 951, 52 09 219.

Palazzo Labia - Salone del Tiepolo: open by prior appointment only, Wed, Thur, Fri, 3-4pm. Closed Aug and Christmas. ☎ (041) 42 42 812.

Ca'd'Oro: Galleria Franchetti - Open all year, daily, 9am-2pm (last admission 1.30pm). Closed 1 Jan, 1 May and 25 Dec. Guided tours (1hr). Audio-visual presentation. 4 000 L, no charge for EU visitors under 18 years old or over 60 and during heritage week. ☎ (041) 52 22 349.

Ca' Pesaro: Museo d'arte orientale - Open daily (except Mon), 9am-2pm. Closed 1 Jan, 1 May and 25 Dec. 4 000 L. ☎ (041) 52 41 173.

Ca' Pesaro: Galleria internazionale d'Arte moderna - Closed for restoration. For latest information on admission times and charges: ☎ (041) 72 11 27.

Ca' Rezzonico: Museo del Settecento Veneziano - Open daily (except Fri) in summer, 10am-5pm; in winter, 10am-4pm. Closed 1 Jan, 1 May and 25 Dec. 12 000 L, 8 000 L students 15-30 years old. no charge child under 14. ☎ (041) 24 10 100.

Gallerie dell'Accademia - Open all year, daily, 9am-10pm (2pm Mon). Closed 1 Jan, 1 May and 25 Dec. 12 000 L, no charge for EU citizens under 18 years old or over 60, and all children under 12. ☎ (041) 52 22 47.

I Frari - Open all year, daily, 9am (3pm Sun and public holidays)-6pm. 3 000 L. ☎ (041) 27 70 233.

Scuola Grande di San Rocco - Open late Mar-early Nov, daily, 9am-5.30pm; Nov, New Year's week and Mar, 10am-4pm; Dec-Feb, Mon-Fri, 10am-1pm, Sat-Sun and public holidays, 10am-4pm (last admission 30min before closing time). Closed 1 Jan, Easter and 25 Dec. 8 000 L, no charge visitors under 18 years old accompanied by parents; free admission to all on 16 Aug. Audio tours. ☎ (041) 52 34 864.

Scuola di San Giorgio degli Schiavoni - Open Apr-Oct, Tues-Sat, 9.30am-12.30pm and 3.30-6.30pm, Sun, 9.30am-12.30pm; Nov-Mar, Tues-Sat, 10am-12.30pm and 3-6pm, Sun, 10am-12.30pm. Last admission 20min before closing time. Closed 1-6 Jan (except Sun), festival days during the week, 1 May, 15 Aug and 25 Dec. 5 000 L, 3 000 L visitors under 18 years old). ☎ (041) 52 28 828.

Museo ebraico - Open daily (except Sat), 10am-7pm (4.30pm Oct-May). Longer opening hours during festivals. Closed 1 Jan, 1 May, 25 Dec and Jewish festivals. Possible early Fri closing for religious services. Bar. 5 000 L, 3 000 L child. ☎ (041) 71 53 59.

Ghetto: sinagoghe - Guided tours (45-60min) daily (except Sat and Jewish festivals), 10am-7pm (4.30pm Oct-May). Closed 1 Jan, 1 May, 25 Dec and Jewish festivals. Possible early Fri closing for religious services. Bar. 12 000 L, 9 000 L child. ☎ (041) 71 53 59.

Collezione Peggy Guggenheim - Open all year, Wed-Mon, 11am-6pm. Closed Tues and 25 Dec. 12 000 L, 8 000 L student, no charge child under 10. Audio tours available. Bar. Restaurant. ☎ (041) 52 06 288.

Fondazione Querini-Stampalia - Open Tues-Sat, 10am-1pm and 3-6pm (10pm Fri and Sat, concerts from 5-8.30pm); open Sun and public holidays, 10am-1pm and 3-6pm. Closed 1 Jan, 1 May, 15 Aug and 25 Dec. 10 000 L, no charge child under 14. ☎ (041) 27 11 411.

VERONA ▪ piazza delle Erbe 38 ☎ (045) 80 00 065

Casa di Giulietta - Open all year, daily (except Mon), 9am-7pm. 6 000 L, 2 000 L child/student. ☎ (045) 80 34 303.

Palazzo del comune: Torre dei Lamberti - Open all year, daily (except Mon), 9-6pm. 4 000 L by lift, 3 000 L on foot, 2 000 L child/student. ☎ (045) 80 32 726.

Arena - Open daily (except Mon), 9am-6pm; 8am-3.30pm during opera season. 6 000 L, 2 000 L child/student. ☎ (045) 80 03 204.

Castelvecchio: Museo d'Arte - Open all year, daily (except Mon), 9am-7pm. Audioguide. Guided tours (1hr, English and Italian). 6 000 L, 2 000 L child/student. ☎ (045) 59 47 34.

Chiesa di Sant'Anastasia: Cappella Giusti – Open Mar–Oct, daily, 9.30am–6pm. 3 000 L. For further information, contact the Associazione Chiese Vive, via Garibaldi 16/B, 37 121 Verona. ☎ (045) 59 28 13.

Teatro Romano – Open all year, daily (except Mon), 9am–7pm. 5 000 L, 2 000 L child/student. ☎ (045) 80 00 360.

Museo Archeologico – Same admission times and charges as for Teatro Romano.

Tomba di Giulietta – Open all year, daily (except Mon), 9am–7pm. 5 000 L, 2 000 L child/student. ☎ (045) 80 00 361.

VESUVIO

Ascent – Paying car park at the end of the road or at Herculaneum; there is a bus service from the railway station – the "Circumvesuviana" line. At the top, visitors wishing to go to the crater edge must be accompanied by a guide (fee). Head guide: Signor Pompilio. ☎ (081) 73 22 726, 77 75 720.

VICENZA
🛈 piazza Matteotti 12 ☎ (0444) 32 08 54

Basilica – Open all year, Tues–Sat, 9.30am–noon and 2.15–5pm; Oct–Mar, Sun and public holidays, 9.30am–12.30pm; Apr–Sept, Sun and public holidays, 9am–12.30pm and 2–7pm (last admission 15min before closing time).

Teatro Olimpico – Open all year, Tues–Sat, 9am–12.30pm and 2.15–5pm; Apr–Sept, Sun and public holidays, 9.30am–12.30pm and 2–7pm; Oct–Mar, Sun and public holidays, 9.30am–12.30pm. 5 000 L. ☎ (0444) 32 37 81.

Museo Civico di Palazzo Chiericati – ♿ Open Apr–Sept, Tues–Sat, 9am–12.30pm and 2.15–5pm, Sun and public holidays, 9.30am–12.30pm and 2–7pm; Oct–Mar, Mon–Sat, 9am–12.30pm and 2.15–5pm, Sun and public holidays, 9am–12.30pm; open 1 Jan, 25 Apr, 1 May, 15 Aug and 25–26 Dec, 9.30am–12.30pm and 2–7pm; 6 Jan, 8 Sept, 1 Nov and 8 Dec, 9am–12.30pm. 5 000 L, no charge child under 14. Audiovisual presentation. ☎ (0444) 32 13 48.

Villa Valmarana "ai Nani" – Open Wed, Thur, Sat and Sun, 10am–noon; also every afternoon in Mar and Apr, 2.30–5.30pm, May–Sept, 3–6pm, Oct–Nov, 2–5pm. Closed Mon and early Nov–mid Mar. 8 000 L.

La Rotonda – Open mid Mar–early Nov, Tues–Thur, 10am–noon and 3–6pm (complete visit Wed only); Fri–Sun and public holidays, opening times depend on availability of staff. Closed early Nov–mid Mar. 10 000 L, 5 000 L (garden only).

VIESTE

Museo Malacologico – Open daily, 9am–1pm and 4–9pm, mid Mar–May and 1–15 Oct; 11pm, June; midnight, July, Aug; 10pm, Sept. Closed mid Oct–mid Mar. No charge. ☎ (0884) 70 76 88.

VIGO DI FASSA

Catinaccio Massif – The cable-car operates from early Dec–mid Apr and mid June–mid Oct. ☎ (0462) 76 32 42.

VILLA OPICINA

Access by funicular – The funicular operates daily, every 20min; from 7am–8pm (departure from Opicina); from 7.11am–8.11pm (departure from Piazza Oberdan). ☎ (1670) 16675 (Mon–Thur, 8.30am–3.30pm, Fri–Sat, 8.30am–1pm).

VINCI

Museo Leonardiano – Open daily, Mar–Oct, 9.30am–7pm (6pm Nov–Jan). Guided tours (1-2hr) in English, French, German, Italian. Audio-visual presentation (30min). 5 000 L, 3 000 L child. ☎ (0571) 56 80 12, (0571) 56 055.

Casa di Leonardo – (♿) Same adimssion times as for Museo Leonardiano. No charge. ☎ (0571) 56 80 12.

VITERBO

Museo Civico – ♿ Open all year, daily (except Mon), 9am–7pm (6pm in winter). Closed 1 Jan, 1 May, 25 Dec. Guided tour (2hr) English, French, German. 6 000 L, no charge visitors under 18 years old and during heritage week. ☎ (0761) 34 82 75.

VITTORIO VENETO

Museo della Battaglia – Open daily (except Mon), May–Sept, 10am–noon and 4–6.30pm; Oct–Apr, 10am–noon and 2–5pm. Closed Mon, 1 Jan, 1 May, Easter and 25 Dec. Guided tours (30-40min) in Italian. Audio-visual presentation. 5 000 L, no charge for visitors under 18 years old or over 60). ☎ (0438) 57 695; email museobattaglia@emmenet.it
www.bibliotecaw.it

VOLTERRA

Pinacoteca – Same admission times and charges as for Museo Guarnacci.

Museo Etrusco Guarnacci – Open daily, mid Mar–early Nov, 9am–7pm; the rest of the year, 9am–2pm. Closed 1 Jan and 25 Dec. All-inclusive pass for museums and archeological sites (can be used over a period). 12 000 L, 8 000 L student/senior citizen, 25 000 L (family, max 4 persons).

SARDINIA

CAGLIARI

Museo Archeologico Nazionale – & Open daily (except Mon), Apr–Sept, 9am–2pm and 3–8pm; Oct–Mar, 9am–7pm. Closed 1 Jan, 1 May and 25 Dec. Audio-visual presentation. 4 000 L, no charge for visitors under 18 years old or over 60. ☎ (070) 65 59 11.

Orto Botanico – (&) Open daily, Apr–Sept, 8am–1.30pm and 3–6.30pm; Oct–Mar, 8am–1.30pm. Closed Easter, Easter Monday, 15 Aug and 25 Dec. Guided tour in Italian, 2nd and 4th Sun in the month, 11am; advance booking at the ingresso dell'Orto Botanico, viale Fra Ignazio 11, on the morning of the tour. 1 000 L, no charge for visitors under 6 years old or over 60. ☎ (070) 67 53 501/3523/3522.

CALA GONONE

Grotta del Bue Marino – Guided tours (about 1hr) in English, French, Italian, daily, July and Sept, 10am, 11am and noon; Aug, 9am, 10am, 11am and noon; Mar–June and Oct–Nov, 11am and 3pm. Closed 11 Nov–23 Dec and 7 Jan–4 Mar. 9 000 L, 4 000-6 000 L child. ☎ (0784) 96 243, 93 696, 93 305.

DORGALI

Grotta di Ispinigòli – Guided tours only, every hour, Jul, Aug, 9am–1pm and 3–6pm; Mar–May, 9am–noon and 3–7pm; June and Sept, 9am–noon and 3–6pm; Oct , 10am–noon and 3–5pm. Closed Nov–Feb (at Christmas, Oct opening times apply). 9 000 L, 4 000 L child/student. ☎ (0784) 96 243.

Arcipelago della MADDALENA

Isola di Caprera: Museo – Guided tours (20min), all year, daily, 9am–1.30pm. Closed 1 Jan, 1 May and 25 Dec. 4 000 L, no charge for visitors under 18 years old and over 60 and during heritage week. ☎ (0789) 72 71 62.

NUORO

Museo della Vita e delle Tradizioni popolari Sarde – Open daily, mid June–Sept, 9am–7pm; Oct–mid June, 9am–1pm and 3–7pm. 3 000 L, no charge for visitors under 18 years old or over 60). ☎ (0784) 24 29 00, 31 426.

PORTO CONTE

Grotta di Nettuno – Guided tours daily, Apr–Sept, every hour from 9am–7pm; Jan–Mar and Nov–Dec, 9am–2pm; Oct, 10am–5pm. 13 000 L, 6 000 L child 3-12 years old. ☎ (079) 97 90 54.

Isola di SANT'ANTIOCO

Vestigia di Sulcis – Open mid Apr–mid Sept, daily, 9am–1pm and 3.30–7pm. Closed 1 Jan, Easter, 8 Dec and 25 Dec. 8 000 L, 5 000 L (child). Guided tours (about 2hr 30min for 4 sites) in English, French. Bar, restaurant. ☎ (0781) 83 590, 84 10 89.

SASSARI

Museo Nazionale Sanna – Open all year, daily (except Mon), 9am–7pm (1pm Sun and public holidays). Closed 1 Jan, 1 May and 25 Dec. 4 000 L, no charge child and during heritage week. ☎ (079) 27 22 03.

THARROS

Zona archeologica and **necropoli** – Open daily, Mar–June, 9am–7pm; July–Sept, 9am–8pm; Oct–Feb, 9am–5.30pm. 7 000 L, 4 000 L for visitors under 14 years old and over 60

SICILY

AGRIGENTO

Valle dei Templi - Open all year, daily, 8.30am-1hr before sunset. No charge.
☎ (0922) 49 72 26. The archeological area (Tempio di Zeus e dei Dioscuri) is open daily, in summer, 8.30am-7pm; in winter, 8.30am-6pm. 4 000 L, no charge for visitors under 18 years old and over 60. ☎ (0922) 49 72 21.

Museo Archeologico Regionale - (&) Open all year, daily, 9am-1pm; also Wed-Sat, 3-7.30pm. Opening hours subject to change, telephone in advance. 8 000 L, no charge child. ☎ (0922) 49 72 10.

Oratorio di Falaride - Open all year, daily, 9am-1pm; also Wed-Sat, 2.30-5pm. No charge.

San Nicola - Open all year, daily, 9am-1pm and 3-6pm (closed Sun afternoons).

Quartiere Ellenistico-Romano - Open all year, daily, 9am-7.30pm. No charge. ☎ (0922) 40 15 65.

Cattedrale - Open all year, daily, 9am-1pm and 3-6pm.

Abbazia di Santo Spirito - Visit: apply at the adjacent monastery. Information: contact the Curia Vescovile, ☎ (0922) 24 181.

Casa di Pirandello - Open all year, daily, 8am-8pm. Audio-visual presentation. 4 000 L. ☎ (0922) 44 41 11, (091) 51 11 02.

BAGHERIA

Villa Palagonia - Open all year, daily, 9am-12.30pm and 4.30-7.30pm. 4 000 L. ☎ (091) 90 39 38.

CALTAGIRONE

Museo della Ceramica - Open all year, daily, 9am-6.30pm. No charge. ☎ (0933) 21 680.

Market, Catania

S. Chirol

CATANIA

Duomo - Open daily, 8am-noon and 4 (4.40 Sun)-7pm. ☎ (095) 32 00 44.

Castello Ursino - Interior currently undergoing restoration. After re-opening Museo Civico (only Pinacoteca open at present) will open Mon-Fri, 9am-1pm and 3-10pm (midnight Fri); Sat, 9am-1pm; Sun, 9am-12.30pm and 6-10pm. No charge. ☎ (095) 34 58 30.

CEFALU

Duomo - Open all year, daily, 7.30am-12.30pm and 3.30-6.30pm. ☎ (0921) 92 20 21.

Museo Mandralisca - Open daily, Apr-Sept, 9am-12.30pm and 3.30-7pm; Oct-Mar, 9.30am-12.30pm and 3.30-6pm. 5 000 L, no charge child. ☎ (0921) 42 15 47.

Isole EGADI

Access – Ferries and hydrofoils leave from Trapani for Favignana, Levanzo and Marettimo Islands: see details in the Michelin Red Guide Italia.

Levanzo: Boat trip to the Grotta del Genovese. Apply to Signor Natale Castiglione, via Calvario 27, Levanzo. ☎ (0360) 63 92 61 (mobile).

ENNA

Castello di Lombardia – Open daily, Apr–Oct, 9am–1pm and 4–6pm; Nov–Mar, 9am–1pm and 3–5pm. Guided tours. No charge. ☎ (0935) 53 11 23.

Duomo – Open all year, daily, 9am–1pm and 4–7pm. ☎ (0935) 50 31 65.

ETNA

Ascent of Etna – As the volcano may erupt at any time, tourist facilities (roads, paths, cable-cars and refuge huts) may be closed, moved or withdrawn. Excursions may be cancelled in the case of bad weather (fog) or volcano activity. The best time for the ascent is early morning. Wear warm clothing even in summer (anorak, thick pullover) and walking shoes (no heels – the stony terrain of the paths through the lava can cause injuries particularly to ankles). Wind-cheaters and walking shoes for hire. Wear sunglasses because of the glare.

South face – From mid Apr–Oct. Time: 3 hours there and back. Price: 58 000 L (including insurance and guide).
For additional information and details regarding nightime excursions, apply to Gruppo Guide Alpine Etna Sud, via Etna 49, Nicolosi, ☎ (095) 79 14 755 or Funavie S.I.T.A.S., piazza Vittorio Emanuele 45, Nocolosi, ☎ (095) 91 11 58, 91 41 41.

Northeast face – From mid May–mid Oct departing from Piano Provenza. Time: about 2hr 30min there and back. Price: 50 000 L (including guide). For additional information and details regarding nightime excursions, apply to S.T.A.R., via G. Marconi 28, Linguaglossa, ☎ (095) 64 31 80 or Piano Provenzana, ☎ (095) 64 34 30 or Pro Loco (Tourist Office) in Linguaglossa, piazza Annunziata 5, ☎ (095) 64 30 94.

Isola di LIPARI

Museo – Open all year, daily, 9am–2pm (1pm Sun) and 3–7pm (6pm Oct–May). Last admission 1hr before closing time. Guided tours. 8 000 L. ☎ (090) 98 80 174.

Boat Trips – Trips to all the islands mid Mar–mid Oct (from July, 3–4 departures per day). For information, apply to Società VIKING, vico Himera 3, 98055 Lipari, ☎ (090) 98 12 584; Compagnia di Navigazione G. LA CAVA, via Vittorio Emanuele 124, ☎ (090) 98 11 242; PIGNATARO SHIPPING, via Prof. Carnevale 29, ☎ (090) 98 11 417, (0368) 67 59 75.

MARSALA

Museo Archeologico di Baglio Anselmi – Open all year, daily, 9am–1pm; also Mon, Wed, Sat and Sun, 4–7pm. No charge. Audio-visual presentation. ☎ (0923) 95 25 35, 0923 80 81 11.

MESSINA

Museo Regionale – Open all year, Mon–Sat, 9am–2pm; Sun, 9am–1pm; also Tues, Thur and Sat, 4–7pm (3–6pm winter). Last admission 30min before closing. Guided tours available (1hr). 8 000 L, no charge (under 18). ☎ (090) 36 12 92.

Duomo – Open 9.30am–noon and 4.30–6.30pm. Guided tours: apply 1 day in advance. ☎ (090) 77 48 95.

MONREALE

Duomo – Open all year, daily, 8am–noon and 3.30–6pm. 2 000 L. ☎ (091) 64 04 413.

Chiostro – Open in summer, daily, 9am–1pm and 3–7pm; in winter, weekdays, 9am–1pm; also Mon, Tues and Thur, 3–6pm; Sun, 9am–12.30pm. 4 000 L. ☎ (091) 64 04 403, 091 69 61 427.

PALERMO

La Martorana – Open all year, daily (except Sun afternoons), 9.30am–1pm and 3.30–7pm (5pm in winter). ☎ (091) 61 61 692.

San Cataldo – Guided tours all year, weekdays, 9am–1pm and 3.30–7pm (5pm in winter). For information apply to Chiesa della Martorana.

Cattedrale – Open daily, July–Sept, 9am–5.30pm; Oct–June, 9.30am–noon and 4–5.30pm. ☎ (091) 33 43 73. **Tesoro:** Same opening times as for Cattedrale; also Sun, 4–5.30pm. 1 000 L. ☎ (091) 33 43 76.

Palazzo dei Normanni – Guided tours (15min) by prior authorisation.
☎ (091) 70 54 317.

Cappella Palatina - Open all year, Mon-Fri, 9am-noon and 3-5pm; Sat, 9am-noon;
Sun and public holidays, 9-10am and noon-1pm. Advance booking advised.
☎ (091) 70 54 878.

San Giovanni degli Eremiti - Open all year, daily, 9am-1pm, also Mon and Thur,
3-6pm; Sun and public holidays, 9am-12.30pm. ☎ (091) 69 61 427.

San Francesco d'Assisi - Guided tours all year, daily (except Sun), 10.30am, 11am,
11.30am, noon, 4pm and 4.30pm. Book three days in advance.
☎ (091) 61 62 819.

Palazzo Mirto - Open all year, daily, 9am-1.30pm; also Tues and Thur, 3-5.30pm;
Sun and public holidays, 9am-12.30pm. 4 000 L, no charge (under 18 or over 60).
☎ (091) 61 64 317.

Museo internazionale delle Marionette – Open all year, daily (except Sat afternoon
and Sun), 9am-1pm and 4-7pm. Closed public holidays. 5 000 L, 3 000 L
child/senior citizen. Audio-visual presentation. ☎ (091) 32 80 60.

Galleria Regionale della Sicilia - Open all year, Mon-Sat, 9am-1.30pm, also Tues
and Thur, 3-5.30pm; Sun, 9am-12.30pm. 2 000 L, no charge for visitors under
18 years old and over 60. ☎ (091) 61 64 317.

Museo Archeologico - Open all year, Mon-Sat, 9am-2pm; also Tues and Fri,
3-7pm; Sun, and public holidays, 9am-1pm (last admission 30min before closing).
2 000 L, no charge (under 18 or over 60). ☎ (091) 61 16 805.

Catacombe dei Cappucini – Open all year, daily, 9am-noon and 3-5pm. Donation.
☎ (091) 21 21 17.

La Zisa - Open all year, Mon-Sat, 9am-1.30pm and 4-7pm (3-6pm winter); Sun,
9am-12.30pm. 4 000 L, no charge for visitors under 18 years old and over 60.
☎ (091) 65 20 269.

Orto Botanico - Open all year, daily, 9am-6pm (1pm Sun and public holidays).
No charge. ☎ (091) 61 62 472.

Parco della Favorita: Museo Etnografico Pitrè - (&) Open all year, daily (except Fri),
8.30am-1pm and 3.30-6.30pm. Closed public holidays. 5 000 L, no charge for
visitors under 18 years old and over 60. ☎ (091) 74 04 893.

PIAZZA ARMERINA

Duomo - Open all year, daily, 7am-12.30pm and 3-7pm.

Villa Romana del Casale - Open all year, daily, 9am-1pm and 3-2hr before sunset.
4 000 L, no charge for visitors under 18 years old and over 60. ☎ (0935) 68 00 36.

RAGUSA

Museo Archeologico Ibleo - Open all year, daily, 9am-1.30pm and 4-7.30pm.
4 000 L, no charge for visitors under 18 years old and over 60; no charge for all
on 1st and 3rd Sat, and 2nd and 4th Sun in the month. ☎ (0932) 62 29 63.

SALINA

Tour of Island - See Lipari.

SEGESTA

Tempio - Open all year, daily, 9am-1hr before sunset. No charge. Shuttle bus to
the theatre (teatro): 2 000 L. Bar, restaurant. ☎ (0924) 95 23 56.

SELINUNTE

Zona Archeologica - Open all year, daily, 9am-two hours before sunset. 2 000 L,
no charge (under 18 or over 65). ☎ (0924) 46 277, 0923 80 81 11.

SIRACUSA

Zona Archeologica - Open daily, Mar-Oct, 9am-8pm and Nov-Feb, 9am-4pm.
☎ (0931) 71 17 73.

Museo Archeologico Regionale P. Orsi - (&) Open Tues-Sun, 9am-1pm. Closed
Mon and some Sun. Telephone in advance to confirm opening times. Audio-visual
presentation. 8 000 L, no charge for visitors under 18 years old.
☎ (0931) 46 40 22.

Galleria Regionale di Palazzo Bellomo - Open all year, daily, 9am-1.30pm
(12.30pm Sun and public holidays). 8 000 L, no charge for visitors under 18 years
old. ☎ (0931) 69 511.

SIRACUSA

Catacombe di San Giovanni - (♿) Guided tours (30min), daily (except Tues) 9am-noon and 2-5pm. 4 000 L, 2 000 L (child). ☎ (0931) 67 955.

Fonte Ciane - Visit: telephone Sigg. Vella. ☎ (0931) 69 076, 0931 39 889, 0368 31 68 199 (mobile).

Castello Eurialo - Open all year, daily, 9am-1hr before sunset. No charge. ☎ (0931) 71 17 73.

SOLUNTO

Zona Archeologica - Open daily, Apr-Sept, 9am-6pm (12.30pm Sun); Nov-Mar, 9am-4pm (12.30pm Sun). 4 000 L. ☎ (091) 90 45 57.

Isola di STROMBOLI

Ascent to the crater - Guided tours: apply to the Information Office of the Alpine Guides, Piazzale San Vincenzo, Stromboli. ☎ (090) 98 62 63, 98 62 11.

TAORMINA

Teatro Greco - (♿) Open all year, daily, 9am-2hr before sunset. 4 000 L, no charge (under 18 or over 60). ☎ (0942) 23 220.

TINDARI

Rovine - Open all year, daily, 9am until 2hr before sunset. 4 000 L, no charge for visitors under 18 years old and over 60. ☎ (0941) 36 90 23.

TRAPANI

Santuario dell'Annunziata - Open all year daily, 9am-noon and 4-6pm. Guided tours: apply 1 day in advance. ☎ (0923) 53 91 84.

Museo Pepoli - Open all year, daily, 9am-2pm (1pm Sun and public holidays). Audio-visual presentation. 2 000 L, no charge for visitors under 18 years old and over 60. ☎ (0923) 55 32 69.

Museo del Sale di Nubia - Open daily, in summer, 9am-8pm; in winter, 9.30am-12.30pm and 4-6pm. ☎ (0923) 86 71 42.

Isola di VULCANO

Tour of the Island by boat - See Lipari.

Index

Amalfi *Campania* . . . . . . Towns, sights and tourist regions followed by the name of the region.

Dante Alighieri . . . . People, historical events and subjects.

Baptistery . . . . Important sight in a large town.

Isolated sights (castles, abbeys, sanctuaries, villas, baths. belvederes, mountains, lakes, islands, gorges, caves, dolmens, nuraghi) are listed under their proper name.

S